Behind Ghetto Walls

465
370

Behind Ghetto Walls

Black Families in a Federal Slum

Lee
Rainwater

Harvard
University

Aldine
Publishing
Company

Chicago

First published 1970 by
Aldine Publishing Company
529 South Wabash Avenue
Chicago, Illinois 60605

First paperbound edition 1974
Third printing 1974

Library of Congress Catalog Card Number 77-113083
ISBN 0-202-30113-3 (clothbound edition)
       0-202-30114-1 (paperbound edition)
Designed by Willis Proudfoot
Printed in the United States of America

To Carol

Preface

The research on which this book is based began as a study of problems in a public housing project, Pruitt-Igoe in St. Louis, and ended as a study of the dynamics of socioeconomic inequality. The original principal investigators were concerned with what could be learned about the people in the project to assist the government agencies involved in developing more effective social welfare programs. As the study developed, the principal policy concerns shifted toward questions involving the changes in the socioeconomic system that would be necessary to eliminate the kinds of inequality from which the residents of Pruitt-Igoe suffer. These shifts in concern, and the consequent shifts in the kinds of data seen as important, mirror the basic change during the 1960's in the focus of social diagnosis. In the research process itself, this meant that instead of addressing the subjects of our research primarily as tenants in a public housing project, we came to be interested in them as lower-class black people, and even more generally as representative members of the American underclass, a group of many hues.

Throughout the book the people whose patterns of family life are discussed are referred to as *Negro* rather than by the recently fashionable terms *black* or *Afro-American*. The term *black* as the appropriate appellation for people who have traditionally been called Negroes represents a healthy infusion of directness and down-to-earthness in American race relations. However, the sociologist must face the fact that the great majority of black people still refer to themselves as Negroes and prefer that name to the more militant *black* or *Afro-American* as well as to the old fashioned *colored*. Certainly during the period in which the bulk of the field work for this study was done—roughly the summer of 1963 through 1966—few of the people in the Pruitt-Igoe housing project or the larger St. Louis black community ever used *black* as a racial label in other than a negative way. This general situation was reflected in our data, where *black* was very rarely used as it is now used among militants and the "informed" black and white public.

Unfortunately, while the sophistication of social diagnoses of racial subjugation and socioeconomic inequality was increasing during the 1960's, the political prospects for change in line with these diagnoses worsened. This worsening followed upon the buildup of the war in Southeast Asia, then the development of a dead-end militant radicalism that seems now to serve principally the expressive goals of the young white elite and young aspirants to elite status, and finally the setting in of reaction and a repressive governmental stance as the nation's war mentality provided new opportunity to the right wing.

In this context, the policy implications of the research developed in the last chapter of this book may strike the reader as naively optimistic in tone. My optimism is based on the conviction that the problems of inequality are solvable, that the often repeated notion that the poor will always be with us is an unnecessary indulgence in metaphysical pathos. To say that the problems of poverty and those aspects of the race problem closely connected with poverty are solvable by unremarkable governmental action does not of course mean that the problems *will* be solved. Here the issue is one of political will, courage, and commitment to the goal of equality. In these respects the beginning of the decade of the 1970's provides little room for optimism.

In writing this book I relied most heavily on the work of four of the field researchers and research associates who were involved in the Pruitt-Igoe research: Boone Hammond, Joyce Ladner, David Schulz, and Jerome Stromberg. As the reader will gather from the footnotes throughout the book, each of these persons has prepared his own analysis of one or another aspect of family behavior in the Pruitt-Igoe project. Their analyses have appeared in the form of dissertations, articles, and books, and additional reports of their research will appear in the future. In a very real sense these four were direct collaborators in the enterprise recorded here. However, the particular formulation of the data presented in this book, the theoretical perspectives brought to bear, and the policy implications drawn are my responsibility, each of the four persons on whose work I have relied would disagree with some of my conclusions, and each has developed his own views in detail elsewhere.

Sociologists and anthropologists who rely on participant observation and conversational interviewing for their data on human life necessarily rely also on the interest, good will, and trust of the people they study. No group of people could have been more helpful, more open, and more frank about difficult reality than the residents of Pruitt-Igoe. They were as aware as anyone else that theirs is a story the world should not be allowed to forget, and many of them spent countless hours helping the university field workers learn enough to be able to tell that story like it is.

The personnel of the St. Louis Housing Authority were understandably

ambivalent about cooperating with the research team, but they coopera-
tively met our requests for data and information and facilitated our work
where their help was needed. I particularly appreciate the assistance and
the frankness and openness that I consistently found in my contacts with
Irving Dagen, former executive director of the Authority.

Many persons worked as research assistants, field workers, and data
analysts on the Pruitt-Igoe research. In addition to the four whose role
was most central, I wish to thank William Fiegelman, Gwendelyn Jones,
Martin Liebowitz, Coleman Romalis, Ethyl Sawyer, Robert Simpson,
Muriel Sterne, Lyle J. Woodyatt, and Martha and William Yancey. I thank
all of them for giving me the opportuinty to work with a remarkably
stimulating and dedicated group of people.

The Pruitt-Igoe research was originally planned by Alvin W. Gouldner,
David J. Pittman, and Gilbert Shapiro; had they not had the foresight to
conceive it as something more than narrow "evaluation research," this
investigation of family life and its implications would not have been
possible. In the early period of the research, frequent staff conferences
and more informal exchanges among the project staff provided stimula-
tion, encouragement, and useful critical examination of the ideas reported
here as they developed. For this I am especially grateful to Drs. Gouldner
and Pittman, and to Jules Henry, who joined us as senior research associate on the project until his untimely death. Other colleagues at Washington University provided an atmosphere uniquely conducive to serious
policy-oriented research, and over the years I have profited in particular
from the advice and critical views of Joseph Kahl, Irving Louis Horowitz,
and Norman Whitten.

In addition, I have had the benefit over the past few years of discussions
and critical readings of the material in this book with Robert Blauner,
Robert Coles, Leonard Duhl, Herbert J. Gans, Hylan Lewis, S. M. Miller,
Hymen P. Minsky, Roger Montgomery, Daniel Patrick Moynihan, Hyman
Rodman, Marc J. Swartz, Alvin Schorr, Harold Watts, and David Wellman.

Mrs. Patricia Rutherford served during the entire period of the Pruitt-
Igoe research as its administrative assistant; her efforts kept the field work,
transcribing, manuscript preparation, and all the entailed tasks of a project of this size moving. She organized the production of the manuscript
for this book and saw it through its several revisions. In addition, under
her supervision Alfreda Fletcher, Rita Hammond, Betty Higgins, Irma
Morose, Diane Sattley, and Margaret Wedel handled the demanding
chore of coding, indexing, and transcribing thousands of pages of interviews and observations, and of preparing the numerous memoranda and
manuscripts related to their analysis. Finally, I want to thank Ann Aubrey
Brown for typing the last version of the manuscript and Cathy Minicucci
for her careful proofreading.

The Pruitt-Igoe research was supported by the National Institute of
Mental Health, U.S. Public Health Service, Grant No. MH09189. Addi-

tional analysis was supported by Grant No. MH-15567. Some of the data analysis was carried out by the Computer Center of Washington University with the support of a grant from the National Science Foundation, No. G-22296.

I am grateful to Alexander J. Morin for his careful and thorough-going editing of the book; only an author who is stubborn about revising and shortening can fully appreciate his skills and tenacity.

Cambridge, Massachusetts
June, 1970

Contents

Introduction:
Houses Divided

This book is about the family lives of some 10,000 children and adults who live in an all-Negro public housing project in St. Louis. The Pruitt-Igoe project is only one of the many environments in which urban Negro Americans lived in the 1960's, but the character of the family life there shares much with the family life of lower-class Negroes as it has been described by other investigators in other cities and at other times, in Harlem, Chicago, New Orleans, or Washington, D.C.[1]

We will be primarily concerned in this book with private life as it is lived from day to day in a federally built and supported slum. The questions which are treated here have to do with the kinds of interpersonal relationships that develop in nuclear families, the socialization processes that operate in families as children grow up in a slum environment, the informal relationships of children and adolescents and adults with each other, and, finally, the world views (the existential framework) arising from the life experiences of the Pruitt-Igoeans and the ways they make use of this framework to order their experiences and make sense out of them.

The lives of these persons are examined in terms of life cycles. Each child there is born into a constricted world, the world of lower-class Negro existence, and as he grows he is shaped and directed by that existence through the day-to-day experiences and relationships available to him. The crucial transition from child of a family to progenitor of a new family begins in adolescence, and for this reason we pay particular attention to how each new generation of parents expresses the cultural and social structural forces that formed it and continue to constrain its behavior.

This book, in short, is about intimate personal life in a particular ghetto setting. It does not analyze the larger institutional, social structural, and

1. See Clark (1965), Brown (1966), Clayton and Drake (1962), Honnerz (1969), Jeffers (1967), Liebow (1967), Rohrer and Edmundson (1960).

1

ideological forces that provide the social, economic, and political context in which lower-class Negro life is lived. These larger macrosociological forces are treated in another volume based on research in the Pruitt-Igoe community. However, this book does draw on the large body of literature on the structural position of Negroes in American society as background for its analysis of Pruitt-Igoe private life.[2]

The contemporary efflorescence of writings about the Negro in America takes its place in the long history of scholarly and popular concern with interpreting race in American society. There has never been much that was detached about this intellectual activity. Until the twentieth century the polemical quality of race study was its foremost characteristic. During this century more conscientious efforts at detachment have been made as the fledgling skills of social scientists were applied to questions of race, but that detachment has not, nor should it, obscure commitments to the overriding questions of equity and justice that constitute the American race dilemma.

Most of the scholarly writing and research concerning Negro Americans has been directed toward the questions of relations between the races and of the position of Negroes in the American social, political, and economic structure which, as noted above, are not taken as problematic in this study. But a constant minor theme of scholarly and popular writing in this area has been concerned with Negro private and family life. For as long as Negroes have been in America, their marital and family patterns have been the subject of curiosity and amusement, moral indignation and self-congratulation, puzzlement and frustration, concern and guilt on the part of white Americans.[3] As some Negroes have moved into middle class status or acquired common standards of American respectability, they too have shared these attitudes toward the private behavior of their fellows, sometimes with a moral punitiveness to rival that of whites, at other times with a hard-headed interest in causes and remedies rather than moral evaluation. Moralism permeated the subject of Negro sexual, marital, and family behavior in the polemics of slavery apologists and abolitionists as much as in the civil rights controversies of today.

The social reality in which Negroes have had to make their lives during the 450 years of their existence in the western hemisphere has been one of victimization "in the sense that a system of social relations operates in such a way as to deprive them of a chance to share in the more desirable material and non-material products of a society which is dependent, in

2. See Batchelder (1964), Becker (1957), Blau and Duncan (1967), Coleman (1966), Davis and Dollard (1940), Davis (1966), Drake (1965), Ferman, Kornbluh and Miller (1968), Franklin and Starr (1967), Glazer and Moynihan (1963), Harrington (1962), Johnson (1934), Lefcowitz (1965), H. Lewis (1967), Myerson, Terrett and Wheaton (1962), H. Miller (1966), Morgan et. al. (1962), Moynihan (1965[b]), Myrdal (1944), Schorr (1963), Sheppard and Striner (1966), Spear (1967), Tobin (1965), Udry (1966), Valentine (1968), Wilson (1960).

3. See, for example, the various works written in justification of slavery and southern Jim Crow tactics: Fitzhugh (1965), Bledsoe (1856), Elliott (1860), Shannon (1907), Bailey (1914).

part, upon their labor and loyalty." In making this observation, St. Clair Drake goes on to note that Negroes are victimized also because "they do not have the same degree of access which others have to the attributes needed for rising in the general class system—money, education, 'contacts,' and 'know-how.'"[4] The victimization process started with slavery; for 350 years Negroes worked out their adaptations to slave status as best they could. After emancipation, the cultural mechanisms which Negroes had developed for living the life of victim continued to be serviceable as the victimization process was maintained first under the ideology of white supremacy and black inferiority, later by the doctrines of gradualism which concealed a lack of improvement in the Negro's position and finally by the modern northern system of ghettoization and indifference.

When Pruitt-Igoeans use the expression, "Tell it like it is," they intend to strip away pretense, to describe a situation or its participants as they really are, rather than in a polite or euphemistic way. "Telling it like it is" can be used as a harsh, aggressive device, or it can be no more than an attempt to face reality rather than retreat into fantasy.[5] In any case, As he goes about his field work the participant observer studying a ghetto community, learns to listen carefully to any exchange preceded by such an announcement because he knows the speaker is about to express his personal understanding of how his world operates, of what motivates its members, of how they actually behave.

The first responsibility of the social scientist can be phrased in much the same way: "tell it like it is." His second responsibility is to try to understand why "it" is that way and to explore the implications of what and why for more constructive solutions to human problems.

Social research on the Negro American has been based on four main goals: to describe the disadvantaged position of Negroes; to disprove the racist ideology which sustains the caste system; to demonstrate that responsibility for the disadvantages Negroes suffer lies squarely upon the white caste which derives economic and psychic benefits from the operation of the system; and to suggest that in reality whites would be better off if the whole caste structure were dismantled. The successful accomplishment of these intellectual goals has been a towering achievement, in which the social scientists of the 1920's, '30's, and '40's can take great pride. That white society has proved so recalcitrant in utilizing this intellectual accomplishment is one of the great tragedies of our time and provides the stimulus for further research on "the white problem."

The implicit paradigm of much of the research on Negro Americans has been overly simplistic, concentrating on two terms of an argument.

White cupidity
creates
Negro suffering.

4. Drake (1965).
5. For a less sanguine view of "telling it like it is," see Hippler (1969).

As an intellectual shorthand, and even more as a civil rights slogan, this simple model is both justified and essential. But the paradigm is inadequate as a guide to greater understanding of the Negro situation as human adaptation to human situations because it fails to specify fully enough the *process* by which Negroes adapt to their situations as they do, and the limitations any one kind of adaptation places on possibilities for subsequent adaptations. A reassessment of previous social research, combined with examination of current research on Negro ghetto communities, suggests a more complex, but more truthful model:

White cupidity
creates
structural conditions highly inimical to basic social adaptation (low income availability, poor education, poor services, stigmatization)
to which Negroes adapt
by
social and personal responses which serve to sustain the individual in his punishing world but also generate aggressiveness toward the self and others
which results in
suffering directly inflicted by Negroes on themselves and on others.

In short, whites, by their greater power have created situations in which Negroes do the dirty work of caste victimization for them.

The white caste maintains a cadre of whites who function in brutal or refined ways to preserve the system (the Klan, the rural sheriff, the metropolitan police, the businessman who specializes in a Negro clientele, boards of education). Increasingly, whites recruit to this cadre middle class Negroes who can soften awareness of victimization by their protective coloration. These special cadres, white and Negro, enforce caste standards by whatever means are required, at the same time concealing from an increasingly "unprejudiced" public the unpleasant facts they would prefer to ignore.

For their part, Negroes creatively adapt to the system in ways that keep them alive and permit them to extract what gratification they can find, but in the process of adaptation they are constrained to behave in ways that inflict a great deal of suffering on themselves and on those with whom they make their lives. The ghetto Negro is constantly confronted by the immediate necessity to suffer to get what he wants of those few things he can have, or to make others suffer, or both. For example, he suffers as exploited student and employee, as tenant, as loser in the competitive games of his peer group. He may inflict suffering as disloyal spouse, bad neighbor, petty thief, or gun-wielder.

The caste-facilitated infliction of suffering by Negroes on other Negroes appears most poignantly within the confines of the family, and the victimization process as it operates in families prepares and toughens its members to function in the ghetto world at the same time that it seriously interferes with their ability to operate in any other currently available world. The presentation of this situation, however, is very different from arguing that "the family is to blame" for the deprived situation of ghetto Negroes, for their lack of ability to move out of the ghetto. We are looking, rather, at the constrained outcome of a widely ramified and interconnecting caste system. Only palliative results can be expected from attempts to treat directly the disordered family or the personality patterns to be described. Only a change affecting the caste system itself can change behavior in the ghetto and thereby change family forms.

Almost 30 years ago, E. Franklin Frazier foresaw destruction of the Negro family in the city. His readers would have little reason to be surprised at what we know of slum ghetto life today:

> As long as the bankrupt system of southern agriculture exists, Negro families will continue to seek a living in the towns and cities . . . They will crowd the slum areas of southern cities or make their way to northern cities where their families will become disrupted and their poverty will force them to depend upon charity.[6]

The Autonomy of the Slum Ghetto

Just as the deprivations and depreciations practiced by white society have had their effect on the personalities and social life of Negroes, so also has the separation from the ongoing social life of the white community had its effect. In a curious way, Negroes have had a measure of freedom within the separate world in which the whites have obliged them to live. The larger society provides them with few resources but also with minimal interference in matters which do not seem to affect white interests. Because Negroes learned early that there were many things they could not depend upon the larger society to provide they developed in their own communities their own solutions to recurrent human issues. These solutions can often be seen to combine a predominance of elements from the larger culture with many elements that are distinctive to the Negro group.

It is in this sense that we may speak of a Negro subculture, a distinctive patterning of existential perspectives, techniques for coping with the problems of social life, views about what is desirable and undesirable in particular situations. This subculture, and particularly that of the lower-class Negro—the slum Negro—can be seen as his own creation from the elements available to him, in response to the conditions of life set by white society and the selective freedom which that society allows (or which he must bear given the pattern of separateness on which it insists).

Out of this kind of "freedom" slum Negroes have built a culture which has some elements of intrinsic value and many more elements that are

6. Frazier (1966), p. 487.

destructive to the people who must live in it. Whites constantly borrow the elements that they value. Negro arts and language have proved so popular that many commentators (such as Norman Mailer and Leslie Fiedler) have noted the Negroization of whites as a minor theme of American culture the past thirty years.[7] A large proportion of Negroes with national reputations are engaged in diffusing to the larger culture these valued elements.

For our purposes, however, the most important thing about the freedom which whites have allowed Negroes within their own world is that it has required them to work out their own ways of making it from day to day, from birth to death. The lower-class subculture that Negroes have created has been viable for centuries; it behooves white and Negro leaders and intellectual to seek to understand it even as they hope to see it change.[8]

Negroes have created, again particularly within the lower-class slums, a range of institutions to give structure to the tasks of living a victimized life and to minimize the pain it inevitably produces. Prominent among these institutions are those of the social network—the extended kinship system and the "street system" of buddies and girls which tie the members to each other though tenuously and unpredictably—and those of entertainment (music, dance, and folk tales) by which they instruct, explain, and accept themselves. Other institutions provide escape from the society of the victimized: the church (*Hereafter!*) and the black freedom movement (*Now!*)

At the center of Negro institutional life lies the family. It is in the family that individuals are trained for participation in the culture and find their personal and group identity and continuity. Whites have interfered less in the relations between the sexes and between parents and children than in other areas of the Negro's existence, although even here interference has been great at each stage of the Negro's experience of American life—slavery, segregation, *de facto* ghettoization. Still, Negro adaptations in this area have been much less constrained by whites than in many other areas, and this freedom has been used to create an institutional variant more distinctive perhaps to the Negro subculture than any other. Much of the content of Negro art and entertainment derives exactly from the distinctive characteristics of Negro family life.

Now that the larger society is becoming committed to integrating Negroes into the mainstream of American life, increasing constraint (be-

7. Mailer (1957), Fiedler (1964).
8. See Gouldner's discussion of autonomy in functional theory (Gouldner, 1959). We are suggesting here that lower class groups have a relatively high degree of functional autonomy vis à vis the total social system because that system does little to meet their needs. In general, the fewer the rewards a society offers members of a particular group, the more autonomous will that group be with reference to the norms of the society. Only by constructing an elaborate repressive machinery, like concentration camps, can the effect be otherwise. This point will be discussed in considerable detail in Chapter 13.

nevolent as it may be) will be placed on the autonomy of the lower class Negro family system. This constraint will be designed to oblige, or persuade Negroes to give up ways that are inimical to successful performance in the larger society and to adopt new ways that are functional in that society. The strategic policy question has to do with how one provides functional equivalents for the existing subculture before the capacity to make a life within its confines is destroyed.[9]

1.
The Pruitt-Igoe Community

The particular housing project in which the families we studied lived has a unique history. The Pruitt-Igoe projects were planned in the early 1950's and first occupied in 1954. Originally the city's plan was to build two segregated projects, Pruitt for Negroes and Igoe, across the street, for whites. This plan was ruled unconstitutional by the Supreme Court, however, and after a short period of integration the project became occupied by Negroes only. Early in our study there were 2,762 apartments in 33 eleven-story slab-shaped buildings near downtown St. Louis. The project had the highest vacancy rate of any public housing complex in the country; at one point 27 per cent of the available units were vacant.

By 1959 the project had become a community scandal, both because of certain unattractive design features (for example, the elevators stop only on the fourth, seventh, and tenth floors) and because of the wide publicity given to crimes and accidents in the project. In response to steadily unfavorable publicity and a grand jury investigation, former Mayor Tucker appointed a Committee on Public Housing and Social Services in 1960. This Committee included representatives of business, labor, the general public, and various private and public agencies whose services and facilities were available to public housing residents. The Committee directed its primary attention to Pruitt-Igoe "because it had been much in the public eye and because the tangle of needs and services present and potential could be grappled with in the smaller area first."[1] By February, 1961, the Committee had presented its findings of fact and its recommendations.

At about the same time, the Federal Government's concern with urban problems was quickening. The President's Committee on Juvenile Delinquency and Youth Crime, which had been the main instrumentality of Federal interest, had been supplemented by a Joint Task Force of the

1. Demerath (1962).

8

Public Housing Administration and the Department of Health, Education, and Welfare, which came to be most centrally concerned with "community planning for concerted services in public housing." "Concerted services" meant that special efforts would be made in selected demonstration areas to maximize the input and coordination of social services. St. Louis was selected as the first city for a demonstration of the concerted services program because considerable interest in problems of public housing and welfare services had been evidenced at the local level. The program was planned to be accompanied by a research project to study the community and to evaluate the effectiveness of the services. To fund this research the Joint Task Force in Washington drew on the Special Projects Branch of the National Institute of Mental Health, and negotiations were begun with the Social Science Institute of Washington University.

During these negotiations the original principal investigators (Alvin Gouldner, David Pittman and Gilbert Shapiro) expressed considerable doubt about the possibility of systematically evaluating the proposed concerted services program because no one knew exactly what the program would involve, or indeed whether it would involve anything more than a slight increase of activity by social welfare professionals. In the end, therefore, the research was designed as basic social science research and, the research proposal stated, was "not conceived primarily as an engineering task to measure the effectiveness of such actual programs as might be instituted by federal or local agencies." Instead, the primary objective was "diagnostic." The research would seek to result in a "basic analysis of the conditions underlying the pathological behavior currently found in urban public housing, and hopefully, in new proposals for social remedies for these pathologies." In other words, the research was not to be tied to the activities of the concerted services program but would be independent of them. The basic charter of the research project was, then, that of a broad community study in the social anthropological tradition.

The description of Pruitt-Igoe which follows is not offered as typical of the lower class world; no other public housing project in the country approaches it in terms of vacancies, tenant concerns and anxieties, or physical deterioration. Rather, Pruitt-Igoe condenses into one 57-acre tract all of the problems and difficulties that arise from race and poverty and all of the impotence, indifference and hostility with which our society has so far dealt with these problems. Processes that are sometimes beneath the surface in less virulent lower-class slums are readily apparent in Pruitt-Igoe. Because Pruitt-Igoe exists as one kind of Federal response to problems of poverty, the failure of that response is of particular importance.

The Dumping Ground

Pruitt-Igoe houses families for which our society seems to have no other place. The original tenants were drawn very heavily from several land clearance areas in the inner city. Although there were originally some white tenants, all of the whites have moved out and the population is now all Negro. Only those Negroes who are desperate for housing are willing to live in Pruitt-Igoe—over half the households are headed by women; over half derive their principal income from public assistance of one kind or another; and many families are so large they cannot find housing elsewhere. The project has proved particularly unappealing to "average" families, that is, families in which there is both a mother and father and a small number of children. Thus, while the overall vacancy rate ran between 20 and 25 per cent for several years, the vacancy rate in two-bedroom apartments was in the 35 to 40 per cent range.[2]

In the slum people are continually confronted with dangers from human and non-human sources. Public housing removes some of the latter (like rats and faulty electrical wiring) but may leave others (like high windows and exposed elevator shafts in Pruitt-Igoe's tall buildings, exposed steam pipes and broken glass outside). After two years of intensive field observation, a questionnaire was administered to a representative sample of Pruitt-Igoe tenants to discover how extensive were the problems of this nature that were revealed in the field work. Some of the troubles that were characterized as "very big problems" by over half the respondents in this sample are listed below. A few of these had to do with the design and maintenance of the project:

> There's too much broken glass and trash around outside.
>
> The elevators are dangerous.
>
> The elevators don't stop on every floor, so many people have to walk up or down to get to their apartments.
>
> There are mice and cockroaches in the buildings.
>
> People use the elevators and halls to go to the bathroom.

However, by far the greater number of complaints had as much to do with human as with non-human sources of danger and difficulty:

> Bottles and other dangerous things are thrown out of windows and hurt people.
>
> People who don't live in the project come in and make a lot of trouble by fights, stealing, drinking, and the like.
>
> People don't keep the area around the incinerator clean.
>
> Little children hear bad language all the time so they don't realize how bad it is.

2. These data and the Housing Authority and questionnaire data discussed in this and the following section come from reports periodically issued by the Housing Authority and from more detailed reports of the Pruitt-Igoe Research Project. The questionnaire data are summarized in several reports prepared by Jerome Stromberg (1966a, 1966b, 1967, 1968).

The laundry rooms aren't safe: clothes get stolen and people get attacked.

The children run wild and cause all kinds of damage.

People use the stairwells and laundry rooms for drinking and things like that.

A woman isn't safe in the halls, stairways, or elevators.

Given these experiences, it is hardly surprising that only a minority of the tenants demonstrate any real attachment to the project community. The great majority feel that their present apartments are better than their previous dwellings, but most would very much like to move out, to a nicer and safer neighborhood.

Most Pruitt-Igoe residents liked their apartments very much. Seventy-eight per cent said that they were satisfied with their apartments; 62 per cent indicated that their present apartments met their needs "much better" than their previous dwellings and an additional 18 per cent found their needs met "a little better" in Pruitt-Igoe. But they did not like the project community to anything like the same extent: 51 per cent said they were dissatisfied with living in the project. In contrast, those living in private housing were more often dissatisfied with their apartments or houses (45 per cent), but more satisfied with the neighborhood in which they lived (only 26 per cent were dissatisfied).

Given their limited resources and the special burdens of their large families, it is not surprising that in Pruitt-Igoe 69 per cent of the household heads said either that they planned to stay in public housing indefinitely or that they had no idea when they would be able to leave, although 86 per cent indicated a preference to live elsewhere.

Only 38 per cent of the households had a male household head, most of the female heads had been married but were now separated, divorced, or widowed: 56 per cent of the female heads of households said that they were separated, 10 per cent said they were divorced, and 17 per cent said they were widowed. Twelve per cent indicated that they were still married but that their husbands were elsewhere, often in the armed services, and five percent had never married.

It is also understandable that many tenants develop a rather jaundiced view of the public housing program. Thus, when we asked tenants what the government was trying to accomplish by building public housing and how well this had in fact been accomplished, we got answers like these:

They were trying to put a whole bunch of people in a little bitty space. They did a pretty good job—there's a lot of people here.

They were trying to better poor people (but) they tore down one slum and built another; put all kinds of people together; made a filthy place.

> They were trying to get rid of the slum, but they didn't accomplish too much. Inside the apartment they did, but not outside.

Other troubles make life difficult for the project tenants. For example, we asked our respondents to indicate how serious and how frequent they felt various kinds of aggressive and deviant behaviors to be. The following items were judged by most of the tenants to be very serious and very frequent:

> Holding somebody up and robbing them.
>
> Being a wino or an alcoholic.
>
> Stealing from somebody.
>
> Teenagers yelling curse words at adults.
>
> Breaking windows.
>
> Drinking a lot and fooling around on the streets.
>
> Teenagers getting in fights.
>
> Boys or girls having sexual relations with a lot of different boys or girls.

In short, though some social scientists have quarreled with Kenneth Clark's emphasis on the "tangle of pathology" in the ghetto, it would seem that at least this sample from one federally-supported ghetto shared his views.

Ordinary Lives

Despite the world of troubles that Pruitt-Igoe and the ghetto generally present to their inhabitants, systematic observation of family life in the community impresses the observer also with its ordinariness. The basic pattern of life is simply the ordinary American way of family living. The Pruitt-Igoeans get up in the morning like everyone else, the men put their pants on one leg at a time, the women cook meals, someone shops for groceries, brothers and sisters bicker with each other, children go off to school and straggle home at the end of the day, mothers worry about their children's behavior as they try to live up to their responsibilities for socializing them—all like everyone else. There are variations sometimes slight, sometimes major, on the basic themes of American life that are distinctive to this place and time and to these people, and these variations will be treated problematically in the analysis that follows because we must understand them if we are to understand the particular suffering that ghetto life represents and thereby help to eliminate this special suffering. But we cannot appreciate daily life, family life, child-growing-up life in Pruitt-Igoe without realizing that it mixes in complex and ineffable ways the ordinariness of all American life (indeed of all human life) with the special qualities of the ghetto, and the even more special qualities of the Pruitt-Igoe community.

Indeed, the very ordinariness of it all contributes to the suffering of the Pruitt-Igoeans, because while they regard themselves as "people like everyone else" they must also and continually confront the way they are disadvantaged by and deviant in the larger society. The following analysis highlights that which is special about life in Pruitt-Igoe, but from a perspective that seeks to take into account also its ordinary, taken-for-granted qualities. The case studies which are interspersed among the analytic chapters, will help to make the contrapuntal qualities of ordinariness and special suffering as clear to the reader as they are to the observers working with all of the data from Pruitt-Igoe tenants.

The Family Demography of Pruitt-Igoe

Pruitt-Igoe has a rather unusual demographic structure. In September 1965, toward the end of our field work, some 9,952 people lived in the project; 3,067 were adults and 6,895 were minors. The adult sex ratio was heavily weighted in favor of women; there were two-and-a-half times as many women as men living in the project. The minors were heavily weighted toward the lower ages, 25 per cent were under six and 70 per cent under twelve.

At that time there were 2760 apartments available but only 74 per cent of them were occupied. During its 12-year history the project had proved particularly unattractive to small families, the vacancy rate in the one or two bedroom apartments was much higher than in the three bedroom apartments. Over the years the Housing Authority had converted a number of one bedroom apartments into four and five bedroom apartments, and these were always heavily in demand, seldom vacant for long. Thus the average number of minors in households with any minors at all was 4.28, and forty per cent of the households included five or more minors.

Once in the project, families tended to stay for a fairly long time; in 1965 the average family had lived there for six years, compared to an average tenancy of only three years for families in the private housing neighborhood just to the west. Women headed 62 per cent of the families, compared to only 50 per cent in the private housing to the west. The households were heavily dependent on public assistance; 38 per cent included no employed person, and many of those who were employed produced income only intended to supplement assistance payments. In only 45 per cent of the households was employment the sole source of income.

In 1966 the median income for households in Pruitt-Igoe was $2,454, the second highest among the seven St. Louis public housing projects. However, because of the large numbers of minors, average per capita income in Pruitt-Igoe was the lowest of all the projects, only $498 per year, $78 below the next lowest, and $234 below the per capita figure for the project with the highest income.

Only 30 per cent of the households with children included all the members of our society's typical grouping: husband, wife, and children.

Fifty-seven per cent included only mother and children. Six per cent were three-generational female-headed households.

The median education of household heads was nine years. Of those who worked, over half held unskilled jobs, about one-third had semi-skilled jobs, and fewer than ten per cent worked at skilled or white collar occupations.

Characteristically, the majority of household heads (62 per cent) were born in a southern or border state; only one-third were born in the St. Louis metropolitan area.

The apartments in Pruitt-Igoe were larger (2.9 bedrooms) than the private housing to the west (1.9 bedrooms). The residents of the private housing area were slightly older, more of them were southern-born, and they were less educated. Their family incomes were slightly higher than those in Pruitt-Igoe, though they had the same occupational distribution. In part this resulted from the presence of more adults in the households, and money stretched further because there were fewer children.

Methods

The principal methods of research in Pruitt-Igoe were participant observation and intensive, repetitive, open-ended interviewing. The bulk of the data was collected from the summer of 1963 through the summer of 1966. During that time, on the average, about eight field workers were collecting data in the project, working half-time during the academic year and full-time during the summers. The observational and interview data occupy much more than 30,000 doubled-spaced pages of field notes and dictated or tape recorded interviews. Each field worker developed rapport with a small number of families and individuals and tried to follow them over a period of time. In some cases observations and interviews with families or individuals extend over a period of up to three years, but in most cases observations and interviews continued for a much shorter period of time.

Making use of this amount of data is, of course, a difficult task, and we cannot pretend that we have systematically analyzed all the data contained on each of more than 30,000 pages. However, we tried to organize the data so that it could more readily be analyzed first by indexing approximately the first 20,000 pages of observations and interviews into a set of some 50 categories and then abstracting the information in these categories in such a way that an IBM card could be prepared, sorted by category, and printed out. This allowed the analyst to determine where in all of the data he could find information about a particular subject (e.g., relations with the Housing Authority). Using the index, the interviews were analyzed into categories so that it was possible to read all the excerpts that deal with a particular subject. This allowed for "horizontal" analysis of the data and was particularly useful in comparing the way different individuals dealt with the same subjects.

A companion method involved the intensive analysis of the information about particular families and individuals for whom a great deal of data are available. This "vertical" analysis was especially useful in identifying themes that cut across content areas such as family relations, attitudes toward police, relations with friends, and the like. The case studies that alternate with the analytical chapters of this book present interview and observation records on a number of individuals and families so that the reader may get some feeling for the raw data from which the analysis was made.[3]

In addition to participant observation and interviewing, two surveys were carried out, each involving approximately ten per cent of the households in the project.[4] The first took place in the summer of 1965, the second in the summer and fall of 1966. To facilitate comparisons between the people in public and in private slum housing, a survey of some 69 households in which minors were present was carried out in a 17-block private rental housing area just west of Pruitt-Igoe. This area was selected as one in which the population was similar to that of Pruitt-Igoe in terms of race, average rental value, and average number of persons per room. The two Pruitt-Igoe surveys covered various socioeconomic characteristics of the households as well as a wide range of information about the attitudes of our respondents.

The two surveys produced interviews with four hundred adults in the project. In the participant observation field work, the observers had intensive, repetitive contact with well over three hundred people, and observed and spoke more fleetingly with over one thousand others. The surveys were based on random samples of project households; the participant observation field work and the intensive conversational interviewed that was a part of it involved more purposive sampling, designed to tap different population segments of the community, and to sample the variety of activities pursued by the tenants.

Finally, we also abstracted information from the Housing Authority records about most of the families that were studied intensively. These provided data about the history of occupancy of the family, rent delinquencies, contacts with the project police and Housing Authority social workers. No systematic use was made of these data, because they reflect not only the behavior of the families and individuals involved but also the

foibles and biases of the Housing Authority personnel. However, the

3. In these narrative case study chapters, and elsewhere in this book, all identifying information dealing with the personal characteristics and idiosyncratic experience of particular individuals has been either changed or eliminated. Our effort has been to prepare case studies that might be recognizable to the individual involved but not to others. At the same time, we have tried to make the necessary changes in such a way that the validity of the data as a reflection of the particular life experiences of the individuals involved is not markedly reduced.

4. The questionnaires are reproduced in Appendix A of a forthcoming volume devoted to community life in Pruitt-Igoe by Yancey and Rainwater.

Housing Authority record data provided another perspective to compare with that acquired by the field workers from the intensive case studies.

The case studies that are presented in alternate chapters below are intended not merely as illustrations or citations of data to support the generalizations made in the analytic chapters. We hope rather that they will allow the reader an opportunity to become acquainted with the complexity and multi-faceted quality of the information from which we draw conclusions, and to confront more directly the continuing nature of an individual experience in the Pruitt-Igoe community. Each case is based on a particular individual—the cases are not composites—and presents simply the edited and condensed transcripts of the field data as reported by the field worker. The case chapters have been located in the book so that each illuminates the dominant theme of the succeeding chapter, to help the reader to focus both on analysis and on ethnographic description. But each case illuminates much more than any single theme; each of them reflects the complex stuff of life and concentrates in varying degree all of the themes with which we are here concerned.

2.
Thomas Coolidge

In the fall of 1963 Boone Hammond climbed to the fifth floor
of one of the Pruitt buildings to knock on the door of a two-bedroom
apartment which opened to the tiny stairwell landing. Mrs. Coolidge invited him into the living room after he explained that he was a student
from Washington University interested in knowing how she felt about
living in Pruitt-Igoe. As they sat down at the kitchen table in the combined living-dining room, he observed that the apartment was clean but
bare, without any other furniture, floor covering, or curtains on the
windows. Hammond learned later from the Housing Authority records
that the Coolidges had been married about a year and a half and that
they had a 15-month-old son. Mr. Coolidge was 21 years old, and Mrs.
Coolidge, 19. Mrs. Coolidge explained that they had lived in their apartment for only three months, having lived in the West End of St. Louis for
the first few months of their marriage. Both, however, had grown up in
Pruitt-Igoe, and he learned later that both their parents still lived in the
project.

Hammond asked Mrs. Coolidge why they moved to the project.

> Cause we could save on rent. When we lived on Waterman,
> the rent was $13 a week, which was $52 a month. But we just
> had a kitchenette—one room with an icebox, stove, and bed
> all combined. So we thought we could save money here be-
> cause it's only $43 a month for the apartment.

Is there anything else you like here?

> We have enough heat and we have a private bath. It's more
> convenient. We don't have to run out and catch the trash man;
> all we have to do is just take the garbage downstairs and dump
> it into the incinerator. When you move in here, there aren't
> any insects, rats, and so on, like the other place. In these apart-

17

ments, after every tenant moves they clean up the apartment and repaint it.

Do you have some other likes and dislikes about the project?

What I dislike is when people mess up the hallways, when they don't cooperate, and when the elevator is broken I have to carry the baby upstairs. What I do like is that I have the type of kitchen and bath that I can keep clean. It's easier to keep these apartments clean except the dust that comes in from having so many windows. They also just put these new locks on which are sturdier than the old ones, and you can't lock yourself out as easy as you could with the others. You know when I lived over on Waterman Street, the apartments used to get so cold in the winter time that you had to put the baby's blankets into the oven to warm them up so he wouldn't be too cold. You could talk to the landlady all of the time and complain about there not being enough heat, but she never turned it up. That is one thing you don't have to worry about here in the project, because in winter time it's always warm in these apartments.

Our People Aren't Ready

At this point Mr. Coolidge came into the living room from one of the bedrooms. Hammond, after explaining his interests, asked how he felt about the project.

As far as I'm concerned, if the rent wasn't as reasonable as it is I'm sure that many of the people wouldn't be here. The environment is definitely bad. The conditions here are fair. *This is a city within a city, and the people make their own laws.*[1] To a person who cannot afford the luxuries that a person can have, Pruitt-Igoe is what you might say was forced upon them. This is the last resort. It could be better than what it is. But then again the people help destroy it.

Having established what he thought was good initial rapport, Hammond left, intrigued with the family and impressed with the intelligence and willingness to talk of both husband and wife. A week later he returned and reminded Mr. Coolidge of their previous discussion of the project as "a city within a city." Mr. Coolidge's views on the subject were apparently well formulated because he immediately took up where he left off.

Yes, the environment here is very bad. If a person could get on the outside I'm sure that he wouldn't be here. If I could get on the outside and still get the conveniences that I have here I wouldn't be here either. By the conveniences I mean water, gas, and electric all being included in one bill. This place is very well heated in the winter time. Another thing bad here

1. Emphasis here and elsewhere mine.

is that there are mice and bugs. The Authority doesn't come around to spray like they said they would, and if you don't go and tell them then they will not come at all. They are supposed to spray the apartments when one family moves out so that it will be clean for the new family moving in. Now I'm not saying that they didn't do that, but no matter how clean you keep your apartment, bugs and mice will come in because the other people don't keep their apartments clean, and the bugs and mice come in from their apartments. The Housing Authority by spraying these apartments periodically keep down the threat of bugs and mice.

Earlier you were talking about "environment." What did you mean by that?

Well, a child cannot be properly raised here because of the environment. Each person here has a different way of teaching and learning their children. This means that some of the children will be committed to the teachings of others, I mean it will rub off on them. This in turn may be hard on the parent, because this is the time that a child is learning. Just like now, you can go down below and hear a five or six-year-old child calling another a "mother fucker." *This place is just like a jungle but you can't get away from it, so you must submit yourself and submitting is the worst thing that you can do.* Submitting is like letting yourself do what other people want you to do. It's like tilting the scale, if you have the bad on one side and the good on the other and the bad outweighs the good then bad comes out best in the end. Now if you're one of the good and you're constantly coming in contact with one of the bad and there are a whole lot of bad and very few good, then you don't have any other choice but to go along with the bad whether you want to or not. You can call it the good old days if you want to but I can remember a time if you stepped on someone's foot you could tell them "excuse me ma'am, I'm very sorry." But if you go downstairs now and step on someone's foot then the first thing you would hear is the popping of the case (knife being opened). People don't act the way they used to and I'm not saying that the way they used to act was the best, but at least they showed respect for others. Down here there's no respect shown for anyone. The rule of the game is go for yourself.

From this time on it was obvious that the field worker "belonged" to Mr. Coolidge; Mrs. Coolidge began to take a back seat. Had the relationship with both of them lasted longer, Hammond might have been able to rectify this situation. Two weeks later Hammond found them home again early in the afternoon. He learned that both Mr. and Mrs. Coolidge worked from late in the afternoon until about midnight. Hammond and Mr. Coolidge continued their discussion.

Well, we were talking about what we can do to make the project a better place to live. I would like to start out by saying that I don't think the administration is responsible for the project being in the state that it is in. As I told you before, the environment seems to be the big problem here in the project, and I explained to you what I meant by environment. You know there is every type of person that lives in St. Louis here who have the chance to do right. *I guess they feel that because they are members (Negroes) that the world owes them something, so they are going to take their part.* When they come in here they have the chance to do right and there is no excuse for them not to, but it looks like every one of them who moves in here seems to mess up in some kind of way. Our people have always had the feeling that the world owes them something. The world don't owe them a damn thing and the sooner they realize that the better off they'll be. People move in here with a chip on their shoulder against the white man and against anybody who has any kind of authority, so they try to take it out on everybody and everything. That's the reason why the project is all torn up and in the bad shape it's in. If they would turn around and try to do something with themselves and try to make something out of themselves, both the project and the world would be a better place to live in. Our people have got to realize nobody owes them a thing. The sooner they realize that, the better off they'll all be.

People talk about how bad these projects are but yet they keep moving in here. *They like this life here, it's adventurous and exciting, something is always going on. But still this is a hell of a place to live; you can't keep any kind of order here. The Housing Authority can't keep order, the project police can't keep order—it's got to a point now where even the city police are afraid to come in.* I can remember last year when the city police tried to come in to get a man here, so many people gathered around that the thing turned into a riot.

The people here have got all kinds of ways of protecting themselves from the police. For instance, if I do something on the outside of the project and then run into the project here, I'll bet you that I can come in here and knock on any of these doors and find somebody who will let me hide. Somebody is always robbing a store or a filling station around here and then running to the project for protection. The police never find them and they're hiding right in these apartments all the time. Now the police know that, but the people act like they don't know what's going on when the police come around. So what kind of chance do the police have of finding a person here? The way to straighten this project out is to clear the whole thing out and make everybody get out of the apartments and start all over again and abide by the rules and regulations.

That won't work, Thomas, that's not the way to do it. You can't get all the bad people out.

It's true that there are bad apples in every batch, but there are so many bad ones here that you couldn't straighten it out if you wanted to. Of course that's not only here but everywhere. You can't trust anybody here because everybody is always trying to beat you up, so you have to be on guard. A person is naturally skeptical of a stranger, but you usually try to trust your friends. *But down here it's not the stranger that you want to be afraid of, because you're going to be ready for him. That's just by the fact that he's a stranger. Your friends are the ones that'll put you in the trick.* **They are the ones that you really have to watch. You don't know what he's going to do. He might even try to work some game on you so you're always ready for him so that he won't be able to put you in the trick.**

Hammond thought he would test his rapport with Mr. Coolidge by commenting on his own role *vis-a-vis* the respondent.

It's just like me coming down here—I tell you that I'm from Washington University but you don't actually know who I am or where I'm from. So you say to yourself, "I wonder who this guy really is and I wonder what he really wants. He says that he's from Washington University and that he's not connected with the project but he might be telling me anything—trying to put me into a trick bag."

That's true, but I really do think that you're from the University. I mean I just have a feeling, especially since I've got to know you better, but if it were someone else then I would have my doubts.

But you really have your doubts about me, you don't know exactly what I want and what I'm doing. When you see me coming you say to yourself, "Here comes that guy again, I really wonder what he wants."

That's true, you see, but I keep myself ready so that you won't be able to put me in a trick. *You know yourself, man, when you walk out in the streets you have got to be ready. Everybody walking out there is game on everybody else. If you don't watch what you're doing, before you know it you're going to be put in a trick bag.*

Is that only true for Pruitt-Igoe?

No, it's true anywhere where the members are found. Our people are always plotting and scheming. **I was talking to a cat yesterday who said this to me, "I can send you a letter without putting a stamp on it." So I asked him how he could send me a letter without putting a stamp on it and the cat** told me this, and this goes to show how these guys are always plotting and scheming. He said that he would put my name where you put the return address and then he would put his name where you put the name of the person that you're going to send the letter to, then you drop it in the mailbox. Now when the postman gets the letter and sees that it doesn't have a stamp on it he will return it to the sender. That way he sent me a letter without putting any postage on it.

You see, man, these cats have got a scheme going all the time. We call it trick-ace—in other words they're always trying to put somebody in a trick. Now you know it's hard to put the U. S. Government in a trick, but this cat has got a scheme all worked out where he can send letters all over town without putting any postage on it and that's just one scheme—this cat's got a whole bag full of tricks. Now it's not the stranger that's going to do this to you, it's your friend that works this kind of game on you and that's what I mean when I say *it's not the stranger you have to look out for but rather your friend.* Man, it's like a game in the streets, like I said, somebody always trying to put you in a trick so you have always got to be ready. Now the way that you stay ready is to have the attitude that you do unto others before they do unto you.

There used to be a time when you could go to church and kinda forget your troubles but you can't even do that any more. Half of the preachers are jack-leg preachers that have never been to any type of school and found out that they could play on somebody's emotions and make a fortune. The other half are running around in the streets stealing more trim (having illicit sex relations) with all the good sisters of the church. Now I shouldn't say the other half because some of them mean what they say, but a whole lot of them are just trying to con the people out of their bread (money). The people in church are really not digging what a preacher has to say. They really come there to see what kind of clothes everybody is wearing and to see who's doing wrong. You know, man, making eyes at somebody else's husband and all that kind of stuff. You can go to church every Sunday and watch some of them sitting up there making a play. People just won't do right for nothing in the world, especially our people. Then they get mad because the white man is down on them. You know a friend of mine who was a Black Muslim says that the Negro should be given a country all of his own to live in. Now you know I'm not ready for all this, I like this country just fine and I don't want to be moved to a separate country just for us. This cat is out of his mind and all the people who believe like him. I will say that our people are not ready for integration in many cases, because they really don't know how to act. You figure if our people don't want to be bothered with them then why in the hell should the white man want to be bothered with them.

I'm a Good Worker

A month later Hammond again visited the Coolidges. This time the living room area contained new furniture; there were two large couches and a matching chair, two end tables, two lamps, a tear-shaped coffee table, and a rather good phonograph. There were also new curtains on the windows. When he arrived Mr. Coolidge was attaching legs to the coffee table.

Hammond asked Mr. Coolidge about his income and his rent. Mr. Coolidge indicated that his $43 per month rent was based on the income of $30 per week he had been receiving the previous summer when they moved into the apartment. At that time he worked for an auto supply company, but since then had gotten a job at a drive-in diner and was now earning $70 per week on the afternoon-to-midnight shift, although these hours were not regular.

Sometimes I go to work at 11:00 and don't get off until 12:00 the next day. These people try to work you to death. They want you to be a porter and also do some of the cooking. When I go to work I'm supposed to mop the floors four hours and then cook four hours, but I never get out of there with just working eight hours because they always have something they want me to do when I get ready to leave. Now they know that the buses run every other hour, so they work you right up till the time the bus comes in order to make me miss it and then they say since you missed the bus why don't you do this or that.

I told the cat that slavery days were over. I told him that I wasn't going to keep working the way that I had been, missing buses and getting home late from work, and if he had anything that he wanted me to do extra he should tell me to do it when I first come in. Yesterday when I finished work he told me that he wanted me to mop an extra floor. I gave the mop back to him and told him to mop it himself, that I wasn't going to do it because he hadn't told me when I came in to work.

They are pretty good people to work for, you know, but they try to work a man too hard. There are two brothers and a sister who own the shop, and they are all pretty young people—the oldest brother is about 28 and he is the boss and he is always getting into it with the younger brother because he tries to work him just as hard as he does me. His younger brother who is larger than him tells him to come out into the alley so that they can settle their differences. The older brother has never taken him to task yet but I think that if he keeps pushing him, one of these days the older brother is going to go out into the alley and show the younger brother what he can do for him. The girl that works there is only about 18 years old. She keeps making eyes at me but I won't give her a hustle.

Why?

Well, I don't know what she's up to but if she's trying to make a play for me, I'm not going to respond. When she looks at me I always just look the other way so that I won't get into any trouble on the job.

They Put Me in a Trick-Bag

It was the middle of January before Hammond visited the Coolidges again, and several changes had taken place. Mr. Coolidge lost his job around Christmas time and he and his wife were increasingly in conflict. It had been a depressing holiday, though the baby had new toys and they had managed to buy a small used television set.

Hammond met Mr. Coolidge as he entered the building and they went up to the apartment to talk. When they entered the apartment Mr. and Mrs. Coolidge exchanged dirty looks and she went to the bedroom to dress for work. Mr. Coolidge followed her and they argued for ten minutes before he returned to talk. While Hammond waited he played with the Coolidge son and observed that he now had quite a few toys, most of them on a shelf outside his reach so that he was only able to play with the few toys at a time that his parents gave him. Hammond noted that this was the first of his visits when the apartment was messy, with freshly laundered clothes spread on furniture in the living room, kitchen dishes on the table, and floor not yet swept.

While they waited for Mrs. Coolidge to leave for her job as an attendant at a home for the aged, Mr. Coolidge asked Hammond if he had finished a paper he was writing on "The Contest System." On learning that he was still working on the paper, Mr. Coolidge went on to give some of his views about the contest system and life in Pruitt-Igoe.

When I grew up the big boys were always picking on the little boys.

Why?

Because the little boys didn't know any better. When you grow up it's always the same. It becomes an everyday thing. You just have to do it. *They don't have anything to give so they must take. In the middle class it's different—you keep what you've got and I keep what I have or else we can share.* In here the environment makes you this way. It just keeps going back to the environment. *What we need is time and understanding and we can get together and have more than the white man ever had. We need love. If a person doesn't have any money and someone else says that they love him, then you can believe it. But if you do have money, then you have to doubt it.* Without money, I mean if a person doesn't have money and someone else says that they love him, then they really have to love him.

There is a lot of tension down here because one man doesn't know what another man is thinking, so it's hard to get along with each other. You see, a man tries to outslip another and pretty soon he outslips himself. It's like a boxer, he keeps his guard up so long and then he lets it down and when he lets it down, he is in trouble. It's awful bad when someone outslips you.

As Mrs. Coolidge left for work, her husband talked with her for a while in the hallway and then returned to the room. After pausing for a short time, he began to talk again, but very hesitantly.

I went to work the other day and the man told me that I would have to work until 1:00. I asked him why and he said that I would just have to. I asked him if there would be an increase in pay and he said no. I asked him why and he said if you don't like it you can kiss my ass. He said this to me. I said, "why do I have to do all that?" He said, "Because I said so." I told him that I wouldn't do all that. I wanted to jam him (fight him) but I said that I don't want to be that ignorant, I don't want to be as ignorant as he is, so I just cut out and left. Then he told me to kiss his ass. I wanted to jack him off (hit him) but I told myself that it's not worth it, don't be as ignorant as that man is and I just left the place. Later, the father of the man that told me to kiss his ass called me and wanted to know if I was coming back to work. The father really owns the place but the two young boys run it for him. I told him that I didn't know if I was coming back to work or not. He asked me why I walked out and I told him the same thing that I just told you. I told him that I thought his son was wrong. The father asked me why I thought his son was wrong. I asked him how he would like it if I told him to kiss my ass. He said it would be a different thing. I asked him why. He just said that it would. I told him to go to hell, that it would be the same. He said I should have done what his son told me to do. I told him to go to hell. Then I said, "I apologize. I should not have told you to go to hell." He said if you don't want to go along with my son then you are fired. I said okay. They had another Negro man come in to help me part time before they fired me. I think they were trying to have him work full time because he worked for them before and quit. He has seven kids and he takes their shit. *I think they put me into a trick with that "kiss my ass" game rather than say you are laid off or that you have been fired for no reason at all.* I would rather they had said, "Tom, we will have to lay you off for a couple of weeks," and then not have called me back at all.

When were you fired?

Right at Christmas time. I haven't had a job since. Christmas was mighty poor around here. I go out in the morning and look for a job and in the afternoon I come back home and baby sit.

Did you work long enough to draw Unemployment Compensation?

No, I didn't work long enough there.

The only income that you have is that of your wife?

Yes. She works at the old people's home. She works full time on the afternoon shift. If the project knew that she was working they would raise our rent.

You mean that no one has told yet?

I don't know. I don't think so. *Our people are unpredictable. You would think that they would be glad to see someone try to make it, but it just don't work out like that. They are jealous of anyone who looks like they are getting ahead and the first thing that they can get on you they will run over to the project and tell the man over there.* I have just got to find a job or else I don't know what I'm going to do.

Well, things aren't as hard as they could be, after all your wife does have a job and that does help out.

Yes, I know. That's just where the trouble is. My wife has become independent since she began working. If I don't get a job pretty soon I'll go crazy. We have had a lot of little arguments about nothing since she started to work and got independent.

Hammond had noticed that as Mr. Coolidge's wife left for work he kept running from window to window as if he were trying to see what she was doing. After coming back from looking out of the windows, he began to clean up the house while he was talking. He continued to talk, but so rapidly that Hammond was unable to reconstruct the rest of the interview verbatim.

Mr. Coolidge observed that his wife's independence was not only economical but emotional, and was becoming a wedge to drive the marriage apart. His wife had become a completely different person. She was hard to talk to because she felt that now that she was working and he wasn't there was nothing he could tell her; she was now the breadwinner and in a sense the new head of the household. Mr. Coolidge, an independent person himself, could not take this situation. He felt that if he were to get a job, he would be able to ask his wife to stop working and reverse the roles which now existed.

Mr. Coolidge said that when his wife received her last pay check ($137), she did not return home for three days, and when she got back she had only 7¢ left. He said that he did not know where his wife went or what she did. He said that he loved his wife very much, that he would do anything to make a go of his marriage, that he had begged his wife to quit fooling around and try to do right. He asked Hammond to please try to do something to help him.

Mr. Coolidge said that it was impossible for a woman to work and take care of her children, to "run the streets" and still be a true and a good wife. He was afraid that if Mrs. Coolidge stayed out in the streets too long something might happen to her, that she might no longer love him when she came back. He felt that much of her running around was because she had lived a sheltered life and had not been exposed to all the things the street has to offer. They were engaged for four years before they were married and during that time she had not gone out with any other fellow.

Now that she was working at the home she was able to ride with many different men and women, and they were influencing her behavior. When she left work at 11:00 she did not come home immediately; sometimes it was 3:00 or 4:00 in the morning when she came home. Thomas thought she was having an affair with the fellow she rode to work with. On two occasions he had to go into the street and take her out of his car. Her sister, with whom she stayed when she did not come home, told her she did not have to go back to Thomas if she didn't want to, and that she certainly did not have to give him any of her money.

His fear of loosing his wife to someone in the street was the core of his concern.

> *It is like a disease—you have to catch it when it starts or it will spread, and if you don't catch it before it spreads too far, then it is too late.*

He said that he didn't know where to turn, that his problems seemed to be mounting. During the several years that he and his wife had been together his wife had "put a sign on his mind," that is, he had become very attached to her. He tried to do everything to make his wife happy; he babysat during the day, cleaned the house, washed the dishes, washed the clothes and had hot food ready for her when she came home from work; he would rush around the kitchen before she came home so that when she came in she would not have to spend time fixing something for herself. When she came in and he had hot food ready, she often would say that she didn't want to eat, claiming she was not hungry. He felt that his wife was now working game on him to find out just how strong she was with him and how far she could carry her affairs without his taking drastic measures.

It was clear that Mr. Coolidge's world had fallen in on him. The white man, The Man, had screwed him, put him in a trick bag so that he had quit his job and then his tenuous hold on his wife had been loosened. As he said, "we need love," and he was forced into a test of his wife's "real love" for him because he no longer had any money. She had failed that test, and now he was trying desperately to hold on to her and to his status as head of the household. But he had little hope that he would succeed, because there were too many competing attractions outside. As he said, "They just take what they can from the small boys because they know that the small boys can't do anything about it." Without money he could no longer keep his guard up, so he was in trouble, someone was outslipping him. When Hammond asked, "Do you think it is a bad feeling to be put in a trick?" he replied, "It's the worst." Then, as he talked, he revealed how his white employer, his wife, her lover and her relatives had put him in a trick-bag from which he could not escape.

But I Still Love Her

In the months that followed, Hammond returned to the apartment at different times on different days, but no one was ever home. Finally he saw that the curtains had been removed from the windows and guessed that the Coolidges no longer lived there. In June, however, he managed to establish contact with Mr. Coolidge's parents and learned that he had moved in with them when his wife left him. He learned that Mrs. Coolidge had moved out of the apartment, taking their son and some of the furniture and breaking up a few of the pieces that were left. He learned from Mr. Coolidge's mother that he had not gotten another job, but had broken his arm in a bus accident and was now trying to collect money from the driver who was responsible. His younger brother told Hammond that when Mrs. Coolidge moved out of the apartment, her husband had threated to get his gun and kill her, but though he kept threatening he had not really done anything. Instead, arm-in-cast, he played ball with the boys and bought a lot of candy which he ate himself, without sharing any. In the middle of June, Hammond managed to find him at his parents' home and they renewed their acquaintanceship. Mr. Coolidge began by telling Hammond of his accident.

> I was in a bus accident. I was riding and this guy ran into the bus. It wasn't the bus driver's fault but I been trying to get some bread out of the deal. I'm suing for $50,000. I had an attorney representing me but I just dropped him and got a new one. I might not get the whole amount but I expect I'll get about $20,000 out of it.

He gave Hammond a letter that was lying on top of the television set; it was from an attorney who said he was sorry that the Coolidges (Thomas' parents) had dropped him as their legal counsel. He said he had made an investigation of the accident and his findings would be made available without obligation to whomever they were going to retain as their attorney. The letter further stated that all fees accrued up to this point would be dropped.

> Why are you dropping this attorney?

> Because we found out that it was the same man that represented the bus company. You know I wouldn't get any bread

if I let things go like this. I'm trying to get some bread so I can go into some kind of business. I want to go in the liquor store business but I don't have the education for it, but I have a friend who owns one and I have been learning from him. I believe I could make it if I got started. By getting this large sum I could also have enough money to get my family back together again. I could tell my wife to quit work and I would be the man of the house again; then we could make it, if it ain't too late. You know I haven't see my wife or my son for six months. I didn't even hear from her until I got this (pointing to his broken arm). After I got this she called three times. My parents say that the only reason that she called is because she thinks that I'm going to get some money but I'll tell you the truth, I don't care. I love her and I want her back. I miss her and I think that we can make it if we can get back together again and sit down long enough and talk to each other about what's happening to us. With the money I can start a business and still have plenty in the bank to run us when things aren't going too well. You know when I saw you the last time my wife and I weren't going too well. Well, I had to go somewhere one day and when I came back my wife had packed everything that she was able to carry with her and didn't leave anything but the larger pieces like the couch and the table. She didn't say anything about leaving me but as I told you before she had stayed away several times for three or four days. But I didn't expect this, she just packed up and sorta slipped away.

I have heard reports from other guys that my wife is running around. One of them told me that he has seen her in East St. Louis nightclubbing it up. I mean, when they bring back reports like this it really does hurt me because I wonder how she could have time to be a mother and a player (promiscuous) at the same time. This is one of the things that I had talked to her about earlier. It is impossible for a woman to take care of her child and be out in the streets at the same time. I don't know what she is doing with him when she is out. I heard that she is not getting along too well moneywise and I just wonder if she is out in the streets trying to get a little extra money. I hope this is not the case. I *would much rather have us be fighting and fussing all the time and have her with me than to have her get a bad name by being out in the streets.* I just don't know what to do about it. Sometimes I think I should go talk to her and see if I can't get her to settle down if she won't come back to me. It makes a bad name both for her and for my son to think that his mother is out playing around.

I was doing a little playing around myself but I never did let my wife find out about it. But the things that she is doing now all comes back to me and I think partially she is doing it just to try to hurt me. In spite of this I still love her and I am willing to try to make a go of it.

Mr. Coolidge went to the telephone and tried several times to call his wife, without success. He said that he was calling her because he was in the mood to talk to her and maybe they could get something worked out.

Someone Out There Is Going to Die

Several months later, while walking through the project Hammond met Mr. Coolidge on the sidewalk. After a few minutes of casual conversation, he asked Hammond if he knew anything "about that Fun Boat out there." The Fun Boat was a trailer that had been decorated and equipped for recreational activities for children. It was driven into the project for several hours every afternoon and again in the evening, and was staffed by about a dozen recreational workers, mostly young white college students under the supervision of a nearby settlement house. They organized games for the smaller children in the project, and whenever they arrived, from 50 to 150 children would take part in their activities.

Mr. Coolidge cautiously questioned Hammond about whether he had any friends who worked on the Fun Boat, whether any of the workers were from his university. Finally, Hammond asked why he was asking these questions and he replied,

> Well, I thought that I might be able to do something about helping to save somebody's life. As soon as the "corruptors" get their program together, one of those kids out there is going to die.

> What have they done?

> They haven't done anything specifically, but just their presence here is a threat and if you know anyone there you had better warn them not to come into the project any more.

> Well, what have they done that this group feels it is necessary to kill one of the workers?

> They aren't doing anything, that's just the point. What good are they doing? The only thing that they are doing is coming here and making us look ignorant, silly, and stupid with those silly games. They make us look like we don't know anything and that they, the great white people, are coming in here and treating us like kids and showing us to play Ring Around the Rosy and learning nursery rhymes. What we need is for somebody to come in here and teach us a vocation so that we can go out and get a job in order to make some money for ourselves. In other words, they are coming in here and making a fool out of the Negro, making him look small and making him appear not to know anything at all. We would be much better off if they didn't come into the project any more. And if you have any influence with anyone out there at the school, I wish that you would please tell them to keep all of the whites out of the project because within the next two or three weeks one of these people is going to die.

The people, let's say, between the ages of 16 and 20 who have quit school or who have dropped out or been put out don't have a chance when they try to find work. *Now we don't need anybody down here to teach us how to play games, we already know how to do that. We need somebody to teach us how to learn a trade, how to fix a car, how to fix shoes, how to run a printing press. We need somebody to train us for some occupations so that we can get some money to help support our parents and if somebody is married to help support his family. These games don't teach. These games don't teach us how to do a damn thing.* They are useless and a waste of time.

Hammond demurred and Mr. Coolidge became angry.

Look, man, I am only telling you what I know. As soon as these guys get their program together and get things organized the way that they want them, one of these Paddys is going to die. They are going to carry him out on a slab. Now what I am trying to do is to tell you before it happens so that if you know anybody at all that can pull these white people out of here, you can go talk to them and get them out before it happens. Because just as sure as we are standing here, before long one of them is going to die.

Tell me about this group.

It is a group that is trying to get freedom and equality for the Negro. They feel it is time to get the Negro together so that he can show that he too deserves what there is to be had in this country. We have given the white man, that is, they have given him—because I'm not really a member of the group, I just go to the meetings—but the white man has been given 400 years to prove what he can do and try to give the Negro an equal chance. All that he has done so far is to show that he is the ruler and that the Negroes must take orders that he hands down. We feel that it is time for this thing to come to an end. It is time for the Negroes to start fighting back and showing that they are human beings just like everybody else. And that they deserve what is coming to them. The white man has killed our people and keeps on killing them so it is time for us to start fighting back in the same way. The organization has regular meetings where we work out plans to go about doing these things. We intend to get what's coming to us in time, but we don't feel like waiting forever, we want what is coming to us now. If we have to use these means to show the white man that we want it now, that is what we are going to have to do.

Is this just a small group of people, or an organization?

This is a large organization and we are trying to get things together now. This organization covers all of St. Louis.

I see, and do they have regular meetings?

Yes, in fact there will be a meeting tomorrow to decide what's going to happen. That's the reason I'm telling you what I'm telling you to try to get the whites out of here, because I don't know whether it is going to be after this meeting or the next meeting; but I know that in two or three weeks one of them is going to get killed and I am begging you to try to get all of the whites out of here that you can before then or else I'm going to have to sit back and say "I told you so" and I would rather not do that.

We are together, man. We have got leaders and we have got followers. The followers listen to what the leader has to say, we plan our action and then we carry it out. This is not something that just got together overnight, this is a large organization. Part of it is here, part of it is in Chicago, part of it is in New York. It is scattered all over the country and when we begin our program here in St. Louis it will continue simultaneously in the cities that I just mentioned. This is only the beginning of what is going to happen because we are getting things together now, and when it happens we are going to try to pull all the Negroes in so that they can be ready for what is going to come. We want freedom and equality like everybody else has, and we want to become part of the power structure of this country. We don't want to be sitting below, we want to be sitting right even with white power structure of this country so that we can have an equal voice into what's going to happen, as to how things are going to be shared in this country. We are sick and tired of being the underdog and not having any voice. We say that we have given them enough time to show what they are going to do and all that has come out of it is talk. It is now time for some action. We intend to use examples as the whites have used. We intend to have the same type of examples as the whites had down south when they killed Medgar Evers, when they drug the Negro behind the car, when they killed the Muslim members in California.

Mr. Coolidge mentioned more than a dozen incidents for which this group intended to take revenge.

What do you expect to gain by your violent means? I mean what do you expect to gain by killing off whites?

We have in mind, I mean *they* have in mind, a program of complete extermination of the white race. We are going to start with the reproducers. That is, we are going to start with the young people that are able to reproduce the race. We intend to exterminate all of them. That will leave only the older whites who are unable to reproduce and eventually the race will die out. That way we won't have to worry about them anymore. We intend to use the same type of program that Hitler used. We intend to exterminate all those who might be harmful to us.

If you intend to use the same type of program that Hitler used, you probably will end up in the same state that he did.

We don't intend to make the same mistakes that Hitler did; we have gone to school on his mistakes and we don't intend to kill the whites all off at once. We don't intend to have a mass extermination. We are going to attack them a little bit at a time in a lot of different places. That way they will not think that it is an organized group that is doing the attacking.

We haven't actually started to initiate the program that I am telling you about now. It will not start until two or three weeks from now. It will be somewhat like the program that is being carried on in New York at this time (subway killings), but that is another group. That thing that is being done in New York is not together. Our program is together, man, and it is going to be even more together before long. We intend to get this thing situated so that when we strike here in Pruitt another group will strike out on the West Side and another group will strike out on the South Side and then we'll hit for awhile and then lighten up and at the same time that we're striking here the group will be striking in New York, Chicago, Philadelphia, Los Angeles, and all over the country. That thing that happened up on Grand Avenue where those teen-age boys killed that white boy, that was an accident. But as soon as our program is together it will be happening like that all over the country and it won't be an accident, it will be something that has been planned and organized and then you know that the group is together and then you know that either you are a part of it or you're not. *And those that are not a part of it will fall just like the enemy. My own parents who think that there are some good whites will have to go just like those good whites that they are talking about.* We can't have anybody against us. *We got to get together and either you're on our side or you're not.* If something should happen, my parents would have to go too, because they're still thinking that there are good whites left.

Certainly you can't be serious, man. You don't think that all of these people are down here because they hate you and because they are trying to do you harm? You can't be serious when you say that all whites are wrong and none of them are for real.

They have had 400 years to show what is it they feel, and they still have us under their foot trying to smash us at every turn. Now, if they are going to prove themselves, in 400 years they should have done it. We can't be bothered with those few who are trying to do right. We look at the group as a whole and as a whole they have made a damn poor showing, so we are down on all whites; we don't make any exceptions. And we don't make any exceptions for any Negroes who try to get in our way and stop us. All you can do, man, is thank God that you're black because while you are down here they won't bother you. But shame on all of the whites because they have got to go. We want the same kind of equality that Marx wrote about. The kind of communal life that they have in Russia where everybody shares the same in whatever there is to be had.

Is it a Black Nationalist group? Is it going under the name of Black Nationalist, or is it a group like the Muslims?

It is the Muslims, man. It is the Black Muslims. It's the group that meets in the Temple on Grand Avenue, and the way the program is designed now is this: there are to be 13 meetings and at the end of the 13th meeting we will start the action that I told you about before on the whites. But before it starts, the head of our group here is going to go to New York where there will be a meeting of the heads from all over the country. Then the leader will go to Washington to try to talk to the President and see if we can't get our demands met. If that doesn't work, then we will put our program into action.

But first they are going to use two or three people as an example of what is to come, and one of the first ones will be here in the project. That is the reason why I keep urging you to try to get the whites pulled out before it happens. I just hate to see anyone being killed. Like I told you before, I am not a member of this group and when they go into the planning stages of these meetings I have to leave. But I have friends that are in the group and they have told me what is going to come . . . . When the program starts here it will start all over the country and there will be no stopping it. Pretty soon you will hear about a shipload of guns being stolen along with a lot of ammunition. That is so we can get our arms ready. Of course, they intend to sacrifice two or three people. I mean, they are going to let somebody take the rap. It has all been planned out. What is the life of two or three men when the whole race is at stake? So we intend to have two or three fellows go to jail for having stolen the guns, but they will never find out where the guns are. This will happen very shortly. This whole thing has all been planned out and I am urging you again, if there is anybody that you know at the university that has any influence—if you can talk to one of your directors or somebody that can do something— please have them take the whites out of this project before it is too late.

I am going to show you just how together we are in the project. When someone gets in trouble they can come to the project and the police will never find out who they are or where they are. The white city police don't even come into the project at night. We started getting together about two years ago. I don't know if you remember, or not but there was a big fight between two fellows here in the project. When the police came in to get them we all just swarmed around and cut the police off so that they couldn't get to the fellows who were fighing. There were about 150 people who just closed the police off by forming a circle around them and the men fighting got away. When the police come into the project looking for someone here no one knows anything about it. They have even gone so far as to show the pictures of the people that they are looking for and all they get is the door slammed in their face. We are getting together down here and the program is getting tighter all the time and is spreading through the project. What we eventually intend to do is to keep all whites away from here. This thing is really something, it's not just something that I am dreaming up. I am telling you what I really know.

Hammond did not know what to make of Mr. Coolidge's story; it sounded farfetched, yet he had never had any reason to regard his informant as other than a sane and intelligent observer of the world around him. Certainly he had never seemed to be lying in any important way, and though he had a rather dramatic view of project life, it was no more so than that of many of the young men who live in Pruitt-Igoe and who were alternatively attracted and disgusted by the life there. Hammond and I discussed the matter in considerable detail and decided that, although in all likelihood Mr. Coolidge believed what he was saying, the plan did not seem like one that would actually be carried out. It certainly seemed unlikely that the local Muslims were involved. Therefore we decided not to take any action other than to go back for more information.

No One Should Play with No One Else's Life

Hammond arranged to meet with Mr. Coolidge the following week for further discussion of the plot. Mr. Coolidge knew that he was now talking through Hammond to the white director of the university research project (the "you" he keeps referring to). Instead of giving more details about the plot, however, he seemed more interested in spelling out the reasons for it, perhaps because with the passage of time he had decided that the plot was more a desperate hope than a likely event.

These discussions took place before any of the major ghetto riots of the mid-1960's. The first of these, the Harlem riot, occurred several weeks later, and the Watts riot was over a year in the future. Therefore, Mr. Coolidge was not reacting to the widespread attention the mass media later gave to ghetto violence, but was reflecting directly and innocently the deep frustration and hatred that was beginning to be ideologically formulated within the black community. Much of his rhetoric obviously came from the Black Muslims, but its sources were much broader. Though the Fourth of July was still a week away, firecrackers were constantly being set off outside the apartment where they talked, adding a sur-realistic validity to the tape of their conversation.

The thing of it is this: *the colored people are tired of being third class citizens, they're tired of being pushed to the edge.* They want to come and be human beings instead of animals, or third, second choice. No one wants to be better than no one else—not really. All we want is equal rights. We want to be equal, we want to say what we want to say when we want to say it. For many years, for many years, we've been dominated by the whites. *The time has come now to be equal or to have it all. To share with the whites or to take from the whites. To make them respond or make them extinct.*

We're going to start to move; we're not going to wait. We're not going to wait, we're not going to wait at all. We're not going to wait till the meeting of the 13th. Your boss, whoever he is, is real ignorant. I hate to say it, but he is, because any time he rather put someone else where he should be here to see it himself. I'm tired of giving the warning and won't give any more.

You feel like he should take heed of your warning and pull their people out of here?

Pull them out of here and quick. I don't mean like a week from tomorrow or today, I mean out of here quick, in a hurry, because they'll take those white people in here now. Next they're going to come and get him. They're gonna have him. *It's just like any disease, once it start to eat and get a good hold, it completely corrodes the body.* And if you don't get them out of here, then it's gonna be on his hands, it ain't gonna be mine.

Well, now, since no Negro here in the project has been killed by any of the whites associated with the project, then why does this group feel that they should take someone's life that is working among them?

Just that he's white. You might think that this is selfish, to me it is. But the way they were explaining it to me, when two countries fight each other they fight for what they believe in and hope that the outcome will come in one of them's favor. When two nationalities fight, the strong will win, the weak will perish. There's a whole great deal that the white man doesn't know about—dirty fighting. He learned to fight with money and power, when it actually comes down to physical fighting he doesn't know anything. *It all boils down to this—take his money and you take his power. You take his power and he becomes equal.*

If you look around here you'll find that there's more black than there is white. Not only will we stomp out white, we'll stomp out the colored that will go along with the white—not only the white but the white sympathizers too who are happy to be in the white race.

Why have they specified or narrowed down one of their victims to come from this project?

Because the project is a jungle. I can hide in the project, but I can't hide outside the project; too wide open. I can go and select a victim, assassinate that victim, and go to anybody's house in the project that I want to and will be shielded as long as it's been a white man. It will be all the projects over St. Louis, take the Peabody, take Carr Square, anywhere there's colored folk. Project, like I said, is just a big old mess of colored. Where else is there a great body of black men? In this project. But the white man seen to that; threw us all together. Oh, he teased us, he say, "Well, now, pay one bill and do it all." Like the black man supposedly not having any sense or ignorant to the fact, he goes along with this. Because at the time we moved here, because you tear down where we just come from. They're tearing down to reconstruct new ones. If they want to make a city beautiful, this is all right with us. But don't take two pennies from me when you only supposed to take one to satisfy your needs.

I think the white man crazy, I do. *He studies keep on skinning that cat. He don't give up. When he skin him one way, he turn around and skin him another. But he's just gone too far now. He's become the cat, he's gonna get skinned this trip.* And he ain't gonna like it at all, he's not gonna like it one bit. There's no stopping now, you or no one else can not stop it now. With the incidents happened down south, that boy that came up missing, they've been killing colored people down there ever since there was a south and getting away with it. The man that killed him and went to court and got out—got away with it. If that would have been another white man and a colored man had killed him they would have sent him to the gas chamber quicker than you can blink your eye. They're both human beings—they're made of flesh and bone. Because I'm black and you're white, you are superior over me? No, I don't think that way. I'm not my grandmother or my grandfather. I wasn't brought up that way at all. Cause if one of them get me, I'm gonna try to hit him twice as hard. We'd do just like the white man do—shake your hand and stab you in the back at the same time.

White people puts on a front. Like now, they're here playing with the children here, winning their confidence. Like I said before, the white people have brilliant minds, they know that the children today will be the leaders of tomorrow. They

Inconsistent

started washing their brains now cause later on it wouldn't be so easy to get what you want from them. We don't want that. Brainwash them while they're young and orient them to white man thinking and then when they get to be adults and get into positions of leadership, they think the white man's thoughts and really take away from what you're trying to do in promoting a program that is for the full benefit of the Negro.

There is a mind in every person and you are supposed to think for yourself. If we're supposed to, and I do mean supposed to be free, then let us be free. *Don't hold us with strings attached, let us be free completely. If you want to set us aside from the rest, this is good, too, because among ourselves I believe we can reach an understanding.*

You mean separate the whole race, the whole group together?

Whole group together. Of course, it's going to have some ironing out because that's the way it started. You don't want us to go to your schools. When we apply for a job we got to have a first-rate education. No, we don't want this, we don't want this at all. Think of all the people that the white man treated wrong to get what they want. They've held the Indians on the reservation all their lives, all their lives. When they can seek a chance to be free again they're gonna be free, they gonna stomp down anything that stands in their way. You can't hold anything caged too long because somewhere along the line you gonna learn how to get out of that cage. If you say we're wild animals, then that's what we intend on being. But instead of being victims, the white people will be—and believe me, we'll eat you up.

You're trying to get to the moon now. There's people in the United States suffering, I mean suffering. Not only white and colored, everybody here is suffering. Yet they say, "Send money to CARE, for the needy across the sea." What about the needy here? What about the people here that need help? You're spending millions of dollars missing the moon. You're not gonna hit it that way, Buddy. Spend a million dollars right in your own states.

They consider this Fun Boat as a form of help right here in this country. Now, what do you think about this?

Do you have a Fun Boat out in Ladue?

I doubt it.

Do you have a Fun Boat out in Clayton or out where the surroundings are very, very high?

I doubt it.

No, I can tell you that they don't, because they don't need it. Why is it that they don't need it? Do their children do what we do? No, they don't do that. Then why put something up that you don't want to sell? They won't have any use for it at all. I say they have everything they want. *Out there they don't need any outsiders.* But they feel that us not having what they have to offer, then we'll just do that, then we'll go all out for it. I do, too. We go for it. The parents go for it even. The children being outside, they go for it. *But don't shake our hands and spit at us after you walk away. When you get in your car after you're through with this Fun Boat, don't say, "Well, I was proud I met with them nigger dawsys," because we didn't ask you to come here.*

You're willing to take other people's lives to prove that you're not wrong, but you're not willing to give your own. *No one should play with no one else's life because that's something that you cannot give back to them. You can't say, "Well, he's dead and I'm going to get him back," because you can't do that.* If you think that there must be a sacrifice, then let it be your own life, don't take no one else's. No one is God, but a great number of them try to be.

Anyone Can Be a Nigger

And if we're willing to be with you, why aren't you willing to be with us? *Do our color make us look dirty and low down and cheap? Or do you know the real meaning of "nigger?" Anyone can be a "nigger," white, colored, orange, any other color. Anyone can be a "nigger."* But just like another Herod it's something that you labeled us with. You put us away like you put a can away on the shelf with a label on it. The can is marked "poison, stay away from it." You want us to help build your country but you don't want us to live in it. We can build the places that you're eating in but we can't eat the same food. We can prepare it, oh yes, we can prepare it, we can even serve it to you but we can't sit at that same table and eat it with you.

There are going to be a lot of changes in this world and just like prehistoric animals became extinct, you don't watch how you play this game you're going to become extinct—you're going to become eliminated. Don't say it can't be done, that you are so skillful that nothing of this sort can happen. You did it. You came to America and took everything in reach; took it and make it seem right, made it seem justifiable. Why can't we?

This was the end of the plot. In fact the Fun Boat was never troubled, and Hammond and Mr. Coolidge never again discussed the assassination program. Rifle shooting in the project did occur; on several occasions people were shot at from high in the buildings; the culprits were sometimes discovered, sometimes not. But there was no evidence of the kind of organized terrorist campaign that had been described.

The People Are Up Tight

It was several weeks before Hammond found Mr. Coolidge again, and this time they talked about his adolescence, but as before this quickly led to a general discussion of the plight of the people in the project and of the responsibility for that plight borne by the people themselves and by white society.

> Once I was in the project shooting dice on the 10th floor of a building and was caught by the project police. Me and another fellow and the two policemen stopped to talk about it and we was told the seriousness of the crime, what could happen if we were reported. But with a little conversation, a pint of whiskey, and two dollars, I walked away. Just goes to show that not only is the people in the project helping to corrupt it but (also) the people who are potentially supposed to be protectors, the enforcers. This is bad, because who knows if stronger crimes, bigger crimes aren't happening but not being reported. It's not just that the policemen here are what you would call poor colored people, because just like every other job they get paid. But if every time a crime is committed you can put something in your pocket, you can gain from the crime, then what kind of help are you giving people—not any at all. All you doing is living off the wealth of the people. No one wants to feel that his money is being spent unwisely. The taxes paid help the policemen make their living regardless of what type of policemen they are.
>
> *It's gonna continue to be the same thing until something is done about it. Because when I, when you, come home and feel, "Well, this is just a jungle where everybody is out to beat somebody up," what kind of home is that? When you come on home, you want to feel secure. You want to have something to offer your family to be proud of, and you don't have that here in the project. Because you're wondering at night when you come in from work if you're gonna get jumped on or not or something will be taken from you.*
>
>
> *And it's not really the people's fault to a certain extent, cause as I heard a man say "You give me a job where I can support my family and give my family a decent way of living and the crime and corruption I'm doing will stop."* It is no place to raise your family in the projects any more because the environment is just too bad and you look at all the trouble of the people—and the project police too—and they're all taking more than they're giving. People are not willing to help each other or to get along with each other like human beings, and you find out it's just like the jungle.

One beast of the family becomes the king, takes the crown from somebody else. It's constantly a fight, or it's something going wrong. This is no place to live or to consider it a home because it is not. I mean if something isn't done to help the people see the mistakes they are making, then something is going to happen. These projects are going to be empty, because the people in the projects that are trying will eventually get fed up with it. All night long people singing in front of your windows, hollering, and hooting, and carrying on. They're going to get tired of it and one by one they'll start to leave and then the people who are left are the people who will not pay the rent. No one wants to be around no one that is scared to come in the house, in his own house, or to get on the elevator afraid that he's going to get jumped on, knocked in the head.

No one wants to have that kind of security for their families, or that when his child gets to be six or seven years old he'll be out stealing something. Because the environment down here is just that way. They're (older children) taking the younger people and taking them with them to steal. They know that they don't know any better and they're going to follow them because they're bigger than they are and they think more of them than they think of themselves. The people that are misleading the younger people are the ones that should be really locked up. And the parents should even be locked up, because you don't really blame the kids or the young people because if they have the correct training at home then none of this would be. If the parent says that he doesn't know what the child is doing he's a liar. It's a lie because they know. Each parent knows approximately what their child is capable of doing and what he's not capable of doing. And then too there's what you call nosey people in this project. But they'll tell the parent what their child is doing and the parent doesn't take heed. Well then, the child will say, "Well, if she doesn't care I'm going to continue doing it."

Let the Moon Take Care of Itself

Not talking just about the project, but talking about the United States as a whole, I feel this way. When I was approximately 17 years old, they were trying to hit the moon and so forth. They advertised on television to send money to CARE to help the needy—and the needy is right here! The people that really needs help is right up under their nose. They pretend they don't see them. *They trying to keep up with another country, but who cares who gets to the moon first? I want to be full when I go to bed. I want my family to be full.* Let the moon take care of itself. It's been there all the time taking care of itself. They spend more money trying to get a president than after they get him.

Don't tell me that cause I'm colored I don't have a concept of the way the world is going. I don't have to be or went to college to see what's right in front of my eyes. They try to correct themselves by getting rid of the slums but it's not the slums, it's the people—people that want the same thing that the next man wants but are unable to have it. That's why they live in the slums, because they're unable to live in any other place. But yet and still, they say help CARE.

Survival is what we're trying to do. Survive. Each country should take care of its own country before it tries to help another one. It's just like home. You find many husbands going out in the street and doing something wrong, but when he comes home he takes care of home. He knows when the street cuts him loose home will still be there.

There's nothing I can say for this country because it's done me no favors. Not that I'm looking for a favor or the world owes me something, it doesn't owe me anything. *But I'm looking for the same thing that that paleface is looking for. And when you have to damn near fight for that! They don't believe in that give a little, take a little; they believe in taking it all and forget about giving.* All they looking for is to help themselves and see that they are well taken care of, to see that they have something to eat every day.

Hammond asked him what he thought about the recent riots in New York and the police brutality issue which set off the riots.

I really believe that the white man is getting scared, because they feel that the police are their protection. But when the protection starts to get jumped on or shot at, it's just like an empire; when the empire falls, the people fall with it. Now they feel that they're jumping on the police and they're supposed to be the protectors—what's going to stop them from jumping on him next? You see, you can't bottle up no one; you can't give them a certain place to be and say, "Well, stay there, because when you cross the tracks, you're out of your area, or you're not supposed to be here." That happened in slavery and it's not going to happen any more. No one is going to be caged up in one particular place. Do I think it's going to make any changes? Yes, I do. For the simple reason it's best to have a little than not to have none. *Not only the white but all will see that we can't live without each other. In order to survive, we got to have unity. And it's just like a game of baseball. One person can't call the whole game, you've got to work as a team.*

3.
The Potentialities
of People

One Man's Search For Meaning

As an observer of the world and an informant, Thomas Coolidge told us much about Pruitt-Igoe, about the patterns and processes of social life in that particular community. To be sure, he had his own particular perspective on the project, but that perspective is not uncommon, and comparison of his observations with those of our field staff impresses us with his perceptiveness about the world in which he grew up and now lives. But what of Thomas Coolidge as a person? As an individual, as a person who is at once participant, expression, and product of the Pruitt-Igoe community, he tells us as much about that world by what he is and is becoming as by the observations he reported to us.

In the year during which Hammond came to know him, Thomas Coolidge covered a very wide range of observations. But an examination of the record of their conversations suggests that Thomas returned again and again to a small number of themes which represent his sense of himself in the world in which he exists.

One of the formal characteristics of his world view is a certainty about the world which at the same time contains many contradictions. Every observation he makes is stated with a high degree of confidence, but over and over again he contradicts himself on a later occasion and says very much the opposite of what he said earlier. Thus, at one point he observes that Negroes are not ready for equality, but at a later time argues even more persuasively that Negroes are ready and that it is only the whites who stand in their way. He argues that Pruitt-Igoe is a jungle in which each man's hand is turned against the other, later says that it is a solidary community which can bring itself together against the whites, and still later, he returns to his earlier image of a fragmented community. These seemingly contradictory statements about his world mirror the different feelings it engenders in him, and the different wishes, hopes and strategies

43

that he entertains from time to time. Taken together, these dualities de-limit the possibilities he sees in his environment.

Thomas Coolidge's world seems most centrally defined by his wish to *find a home, to be a man, and to search out valid ways of expressing him-self*. The problems of achieving all this, the hopes and aspirations he has in these regards and his equally great fears of failure, run like taut threads through his conversations.

As a young adult, he tried to make a home for himself in the conven-tional way, through marriage, parenthood, and work. But over and over again he expresses the ways in which *family* eluded him, in which, instead, he confronts the world as a *jungle*. He wants to be and feel *at home* but instead finds himself *isolated* and *alone*. He seeks to be *accepted* by those who are significant to him but instead meets only *rejection*. He seeks *un-derstanding* but instead, meets with *hostility* and *arbitrariness*. In all these respects, his wife, his parents, his white bosses behave in ways that frus-trate his efforts to escape the jungle. That white bosses, The Man, should do so was expected, although he hoped against hope that he could escape their exploitation and rejection. He gave up on his parents, seeking instead through his love for his wife and his pride in being a father a sense of home that was more meaningful than the prison-like environment he found in his parents' house. But in the end his wife failed him too. She did not love him enough, and she was too weak to resist the seductions of the streets to which she had to go because he could not earn enough money to support his family.

Like every human being, he sought nurturance from the significant others around him and instead he found emotional starvation and inse-curity in his relations with them. It is little wonder, then, that in place of the love he wanted to give and receive he found a world of hate, and that, when in the end he could not sustain his love for his wife against her re-jection, he moved increasingly to define the world as a hateful and hating place, and to express his own hatred in return.

Equally as important is striving to be a man. His experiences continually force him to ask himself whether he is a child or an adult. When he is working, even at a menial job, he experiences a sense of manly competence; when his boss puts him in a trick, he must see himself as a child confront-ing an exploitative white adult. He seeks strength, but he continually finds himself in situations in which he is made to appear impotent. Thus to the rage stimulated in him by his inability to find nurturance and understand-ing is added rage at the frustration of his manly efforts. He wants to feel pride in his ability to make out in the world but instead he is forced to feel shamed and ashamed because he cannot stabilize his manly assertive-ness by maintaining a steady flow of provisions into his household or by maintaining control over his wife. In recent years he sought a sense of pride successively as a man of the streets, as a husband-father-worker with a family of his own, as part of the vanguard of a victorious black national-ism. But in each case he had to confront the shame that comes from fail-

ure; he was arrested and put on probation; he was deserted and humiliated by his wife; his conspiracy fizzled, although his increasingly sharp
ideological awareness of the immorality of white power and the increased
tempo of black attacks on it give him some consolation.

With pride comes an augmented effort to achieve something for himself;
with failure, the seduction of giving up is hard to avoid. His willingness to
try was perhaps above average. About each of his jobs he felt optimistic
and hopeful, but when his last chance to work was ended by his accident,
he was forced to return to live with his parents like a child; like a child he
hoards and eats candy by himself, plays ball. The events of his life seemed
to tell him over and over again to give up, to quit trying, to settle for the
third-rate life to which whites have consigned Negroes.

The frustration of his desire to be an autonomous person in a rewarding
world seems to have stimulated Mr. Coolidge to become a folk philosopher-
sociologist-political scientist. Perhaps this thoughtfulness made him more
attentive than others to the Black Muslim influences that were available in
his neighborhood. He has absorbed their view, working it over to develop
his own personalized and often eloquent understanding of the situation of
the black man in American society. Here again one is struck by the dualities between which he tends to alternate, as he tries to come to grips with
himself as a black man, with whites as an ever-present influence. At times
he sees his own and his people's solution in constructive effort, but the
blows of his fate make destructiveness seem a more real and valid response.

He wants togetherness—of the family, of the gang, of all black people
if not of whites and Negroes. He combines the image of black solidarity
with that of juvenile gangs and produces the fantasy of a paramilitary
group that is going to be "really together," that will punish its white enemies and stimulate the solidarity of the black community at the same time
that it discards the old-fashioned Negroes who won't go along. But against
the goal of togetherness, he must confront the reality of white colonialism
and separation, just as at the more personal level he is confronted with
marital separation and alienation from his parents. The togetherness of
the community which he desires seems a direct extension of the image of
a loving home for which he has strived and lost.

Just as the duality of love and hate has dominated his personal relations,
the social counterpart to togetherness appears as killing. He wished to kill
his wife when she deserted and humiliated him; he harbors similarly mur-
derous impulses toward his parents who behave hatefully toward him, suggesting that they too will have to be killed if they stand in the way of
black togetherness. Finally, whites must be killed until those who remain
come to their senses, recognize the potency of blacks, and give them their
fair share of what the society has to offer.

Yet for all his rage and with all his wish for a racial Armageddon,
Thomas Coolidge has little interest in black consciousness and negritude
as opposed to black militancy and self-defense. Although at one point he

does say that "black is beautiful," it is an unelaborated passing remark. Instead, his image of an ideal world seems to be one that is colorless, not one of white-black pluralism and equality. He seems to have no basic attachment to an idea of black culture. His interest in jazz and urban blues proves to be superficial; he is too serious and determined a man to find black expressiveness appealing. His goals are primarily those of conventional respectability, in which the question of black or white culture is irrelevant. In opposition to his ideal of color irrelevance, he perceives the hard reality of despised blackness—whites despise Negroes, exploit them, and look down on them—but he, too, has these feelings, and he criticizes those around him for their moral laxness toward their children and their fellow men.

Thomas' black nationalism seems largely reactive. If whites drive him to it, he will take up the flag of black nationalism, but only because there is no hope for a colorless togetherness, or a world in which a man is simply a man, in which he can build a home, in which he can be free of racist exploitation. For Mr. Coolidge black nationalism means having to use the worst of himself to combat whites doing their worst to spoil life for Negroes. He longs for a world in which there are no "niggers"—and as he says, anyone can be a nigger regardless of color—but in that world he wants to live a private life, a life that is neither ideologically color-bound nor personally crippled by the impotence, alienation, and hate that black poverty produces.

Pruitt-Igoe Meaning Systems

As an introduction to a more detailed consideration of the social patterns that characterize family relations in Pruitt-Igoe, it is necessary to examine the system of understandings and meanings that serves to order and make rational one's relations with those significant in life—mates, children, kin, friends, and relatives. Such a system is reflected in Thomas Coolidge's observations on his community.

People in social groups acquire complex sets of conceptions that express their sense of what their own lives and the life around them are all about. These "typifications" incorporate ideas about how lives should develop, how they are most likely to develop, how one should, may and can act in various situations, and what attitudes one should take toward these situations and one's own and other people's behavior in them.[1] These complex sets of conceptions are "meaning systems" that embrace what are variously described in sociological studies as norms, values, beliefs, world views, ways of life, prescriptive and proscriptive and permissive guides to action.

Such meaning systems incorporate many disparate, often contradictory elements. Outlining them does not suggest that everyone in Pruitt-Igoe

1. See the discussion by Peter Berger and Thomas Luckmann (1966). We will return in Chapter 13 to the discussion of lower class subculture. By far the most carefully reasoned analysis of lower class subculture as a heuristic concept is that of Ulf Hannerz (1969).

holds tightly to each view at all times, but rather that all Pruitt-Igoeans are familiar with these ways of looking at the world and of thinking about social actions in it. All understand that anyone may hold such views, and that under certain circumstances they themselves may uphold their validity. The salience of any particular view varies from person to person, and, more important, may change for any one person from time to time. But the views constitute an important part of the Pruitt-Igoeans' culture in the sense that they are familiar, taken for granted, readily drawn upon when the occasion requires, and that the individual has no sense of surprise at being confronted by such views when offered by others, implicitly or explicitly, in the course of their actions.

The meaning systems outlined represent the considered judgment of people in Pruitt-Igoe, derived from their own experience of life. This experience includes not only the results of all the various interactions in which they have participated as they have grown up, but also the cultural learning that comes from listening to other people comment upon, explain, and philosophize about life. Some observers of lower class life, or social life in general, emphasize values as relatively autonomous factors in accounting for the particular actions characteristic of a group, but this is not the view offered here. The meaning systems are rather to be seen as mediating between past experience and present and future experience, not autonomous influences. The meaning systems described here are themselves the result of the basic socio-economic situation in which lower-class Negroes find themselves, and of the particular kinds of interpersonal relations encouraged by that situation. Immediately, however, the established, taken-for-granted character of these systems has direct influence on behavior, because it is from such understandings that men and women in Pruitt-Igoe calculate the rewards and dangers of their possible lines of action.[2]

The Battle of the Sexes

The meaning systems that define heterosexual relationships from first mating through marriage and post-marital experience can usefully be seen as embodying two major perspectives: one called the *good life*—ideas about what life ought to be, and the other called *our life*—ideas about the way life really is for the men and women of Pruitt-Igoe, or more generally of the lower-class Negro ghetto. For each of these major perspectives one can discern meaning complexes which *define* the situations which typify for the individual an image of how things ought to be in a good, satisfactory life, or how things really are in life as it is most likely to be lived. Another meaning system surrounds and defines *strategies for behavior* in the defined situation, conventional ways to achieve the good and satisfactory life and existential or "survival" strategies for life as it is. Each of these two major images of life, then, has two principal aspects: one a

2. These ideal types are roughly comparable to those offered by S. M. Miller and Ian Harrison in their concepts of the "now world" and the "if world" (Miller and Harrison, 1964).

definitional aspect in the form of statements about what "ought" to be or what "is," and the other in the form of what is entailed by the definition, what one does given the definition of the situation. In the latter case, statements about strategies for the good life implicitly have the form of "if only . . . then . . ." For the world as it is, strategy statements implicitly have the form of "because . . ."

These meaning systems are abstractions, derived for Pruitt-Igoe from the many different kinds of data available, ranging from questionnaire results to open-ended and autobiographical interviews to participant observation of social activity in the project. For any one individual at any one time, both systems are possibly alive for him at once; much of his thinking will be devoted to determining which way things are going for him—toward the good life or toward an ordinary ghetto life—and which way they are likely to go in the future. Both conceptions are present for him as he grows up. Though individuals and families vary in the salience to them of one or the other attitude, no resident of Pruitt-Igoe finds his life so totally depriving that he cannot formulate a minimal sense of a possible good life, and no child growing up there is so protected from the destructive and depriving qualities of ghetto life that he does not absorb the elements that make up the meaning of our life.

However, for the people in many communities like Pruitt-Igoe the accumulating experiences of growing up progressively attenuate their belief in the possibility of the good life; the individual is left with only a hope against hope. But ideas about the good life remain alive, and the individual is always ready for experiences that suggest the possibility of a kind of "rebirth" which can lead to it. Such themes of rebirth are, of course, particularly apparent in the church, in the idea of a better life after death, but there are also more worldly versions in the revitalization movements that from time to time attract followers within the ghetto, a possibility most recently illustrated by the growth of the Muslims.

The Good Life Is a Stable, Conventionally Contracted Marriage

The conventionality and ordinariness of Pruitt-Igoeans' conception of good family life is striking. Neither in our questionnaires nor in open-ended interviews or observational contexts did we find any consistent elaboration of an unconventional ideal. In the working class, a good family life is seen to have at its core a stable marriage between two people who love and respect each other and who rear their children in an adequate home, preferably one that has its own yard. If only things went right, according to most Pruitt-Igoeans, their family life would not differ from that of most Americans.

Thus Pruitt-Igoeans are "cottagers" in their ideals, just as other Americans at the bottom of the social ladder have been before them. Stephan Thernstrom tells how mid-nineteenth century lower-class Irish and Yankee workers in Newburyport, Massachusetts saved their money over the years until they could buy a small cottage that would become their home:

> While many (poor workers') families had a total combined income
> which hovered around the minimum subsistence budget carefully
> calculated by contemporary middle-class investigators, they still
> managed to save. Their conception of subsistence was far more spar-
> tan—it was potatoes! and their subculture had given them a goal
> which was clear, which was within reach—a piece of property, a
> piece of respectability which made all those potatoes tolerable.[3]

Thernstrom notes that most workers who stayed in Newburyport long
enough bought their own homes and most built up small savings accounts.
Their economic situation was much the same as that of lower-class Negroes today in that their employment opportunities were highly unstable
and their wages were very low. However, there was one important difference: children were an economic asset in the mid-nineteenth century.
Typically they went to work in the mills when they were 10 or 12, and
often one-third to half the family's income came from child labor. This,
plus the manifest availability of a home of one's own if one saved for it,
encouraged these immigrant and migrant families to strive for the eventual
achievement of the good cottage life. Neither the modern economic system, nor the other aspects of ghetto life facilitate the achievement of this
dream, but it is clear from our data that the ideal did not die.

To have the good family life there must be a good man and a good
woman at the head of the family. A good man must have a steady income
and he must be faithful. A good woman must above all be faithful; she
must want to be respected and must seek that respect both from her husband and from the community around her. She must be willing to maintain
a conventional home in which the children are supervised and the husband's needs are catered to.

Whether a good woman should work and contribute to the family income is a more troublesome issue, especially for the men. The income a
woman may bring into the house makes it much easier to achieve security
and an economic level that can sustain the good life. But a wife who earns
money can also be dangerous. The work takes her out of the home and into
an area of temptations to be disloyal to her family. Her own income may
make her too proud to accept her husband's authority and she may compete with him, derogate his earning ability and insist that the money she
earns is *her* money. Despite these dangers, economic necessity often requires lower-class Negro women to work, and husband and wife together
must develop ways of handling the dangers if they are to realize their ideal
of a good family life.

For both partners, such a life involves "settling down." A couple is considered to have the best chance at a good life if the wife was either a virgin
at marriage or had only had sexual relations with the man she subsequently married, and if the husband, perhaps not virginal, was at least
discreet in his premarital sexual activities (though it is understood that

3. Thernstrom (1969).

adolescents are likely to have been irresponsible before marriage). But married, the partners and those to whom they are significant expect the initial marital period to be one of settling down, of giving up some of the attractive, self-indulgent possibilities of being "foot loose and fancy free." Settling down means working together to develop a home and family life and foregoing some of the pleasures of the outside world.

The marriage should have been contracted out of love, not forced by the pregnancy of the wife; even so, if the husband is the father that, too, can be worked out. With love and marriage should come the development of mutual understanding. Though working-class family ideals do not involve the heavy emphasis on togetherness and shared interests and activities that is more typical of the middle class, the husband and wife are expected to show mutual consideration for each other and over time to develop an understanding of each other's needs and hopes.

Part of love and understanding is companionship, and good married life means that one is not lonely or isolated. This is probably more important to women than to men, because men continue to enjoy their relationships with other men while women do not regard their relations with other women as a substitute for companionship with their husbands. Because women maintain the home and must stay close to it because of their children, their image of married life involves a stronger emphasis on companionship. Indeed, the most common lament of Pruitt-Igoe women whose marriages have broken is that they miss their husbands, that they are lonely, that they need someone around the house.

If these conditions of the good life exist or seem possible to achieve, then, Pruitt-Igoeans feel, each partner can afford to live up to his responsibilities, to give love and understanding and companionship, to be faithful, to work and to maintain the home, to perform all the hundreds of entailed small tasks that fit together to make up the approximate realization of the ideal. To themselves, to each other, to those who know them, the marital partners are seen as realizing individually the status of a good person and together the status of the founders of a good family. Under these circumstances, they can responsibly meet what is universally seen as the most immediate danger to a good family life: they can pass up the temptations of the streets—extramarital relations, excessive drinking, and (for men) gambling and other competitive involvements with male peers. A good family will have children who will become good children, and success in rearing them will be the final test.

The realization of these Pruitt-Igoe ideals would produce a style of life hardly distinguishable from other working-class life, white or black. And it seems likely that the resources necessary to maintain such a family life would require the stability and level of income characteristic of the upper working class, a level of income anywhere from 50 to more than 100 per cent higher than is available to most families in Pruitt-Igoe.

But many of our informants maintained that it should be possible to live in this way regardless of poverty. And, further, it was often said that stable, conventional family life of this kind was maintained in the rural south despite great poverty there. Very few people held themselves responsible for not realizing these ideals in the face of their limited resources, but it is often maintained that other people should do so no matter how poor they are. The ideal of the good family life is a two-edged tool. It provides a goal toward which people can strive; it can be used in conflict situations as a way of derogating those around you who fall short of the goal. The tenuousness of a family's hold on a conventional family life is often itself a source of considerable tension. Husbands, for example, may want to enforce very strict standards for their wives (and children), demanding that they not visit with neighbors, that they spend all of their time at home, as a way of protecting them from the dangers of the streets. Wives may be oversensitive to their husbands' time spent away from home and work, or to how much they drink or to whether they seem to be turning over all of their money for the family. Thus the desperate hope of realizing the ideal may itself contribute to tensions which interfere with that realization.

Many of these themes are seen in the following statements of a 14-year-old girl. She had recently begun to go steady with a boy friend, and for her the issues of mating relations, marriage, and family were becoming salient. She told the interviewer that she had not yet had intercourse with her boy friend, but that she expected to do so within a couple of months because she felt such activity was "natural" after going with a boy for four or five months. Her 16-year-old sister and an older cousin had both advised her that she should choose a "decent" boy and that:

> **If I have a baby just make sure he'll take care of it instead of getting around here with these boys that will get you pregnant and leave you.**

What's a decent boy?

> **Like if you're pregnant he'll come see you and if you have a baby by him he'll buy clothes and baby food and stuff like that, be clean and decent I guess. Have a decent mouth—not talk bad language, talk a whole lot of nasty off-the-wall stuff.**

Do you think you can tell a decent boy from a boy that's not decent?

> **Yeah. It's a lot of decent boys around here and some not decent that don't have respect for grown people. If you know him for a long time and know some of the girls he went with they'll tell you about him. They'll tell you how he act and if he's nasty and how he dress and everything.**

How else can you tell?

> **Some boys they won't wait until you've been going together for about two months and they'll start asking if you'll have an intercourse with them and I think that's not decent.**

Do they ask you too soon?

Yes, sir.

As you think about marriage what do you think would make a good one?

Be a good wife and have a good husband—he don't drink or go out all the time and stay out and get drunk when he come home.

Have you ever given it any thought as to whether you'd rather have a husband . . . or maybe you'd rather not get married?

I think I'd rather have a husband. I don't want to stay around my mother all my life and worrying her and having her question this and this.

Well how do you feel about having a boy friend after you have a husband?

It would be all right, but I want to get married and try to stay with my husband until I get old and gray. I don't want to get no divorce from the man I marry.

How do you feel about your mother having a boy friend?

Well it's all right, but I'd rather be close to my father.

Do you remember living with your father when he was in the house with you? How different do you think things are now than the way they were?

It was different. We had strict rules in the house and we had certain jobs to do around the house and we couldn't hardly go play like we do now.

What rules?

Well, the only thing we had to do in the house was dust and my mother cleaned up the house. That's because we were small. He didn't like us to stay all night with nobody. And my mother's sister would babysit and if we didn't mind he would ship us when he came back. We was minding our mother gooder then that we is now.

You were younger too, though, weren't you?

I think if we were staying with our father now we would mind better too.

How would you feel if your mother decided to marry?

I don't know. But he all right sometimes but he drinks, that's the reason I don't like him. He tries to boss people. Like if my boy friend come over here he be saying I can't have no com-

pany and sometimes he tries to start a argument with my mother.

In a home what do you think is most important?

Having a mother and father and a good family.

What's a good family?

When your father don't drink and your mother don't drink and they stay home all the time and if they go places they go together and don't have no arguments.

What kinds of things do you need to have besides having a good husband and a good wife?

If you don't have a good father you've got to have a good mother. They've got to have a good job—the mother or whoever you stay with.

What else?

Good hospitality. I don't know what to say, just got to have good hospitality. If you don't have no job I don't see how you can live.

Does it make any difference which one has a job?

Mostly the husband if you stay with him but like if you don't have but like one child you can stay with your mother and work and help her out. But if your husband don't stay with you they'll have to put you on welfare.

How do fellows go about getting jobs today?

Good education. Some of them want to be a drop-out, they ain't no good. They want to be bums all their life. Some boys don't like school.

When you think about your friends whom you know real well, who of them has the best family that you can think of—not thinking of your own family—but just your friends?

Miss Jones live downstairs I think they got a good family. Well, first her and her husband broke up and they managed to get back together. He takes care of all his children. Now he's in the hospital now. I think he got low blood pressure. Most of the kids are grown. I think she got eight or nine and he got one graduating from high school and one is a sophomore. He got three of them grown. And one of them fixing to graduate from grade school.

Well, do you know any other families that you think are good families?

The Smiths who live upstairs. They got a good mother in this case. Their father kind of mess them up cause he drinks and

sometimes I think he do construction work. He make good money but he laid off now and he got another job until he get back on his job. He drinks and spends up the rent money and grocery money. But the mother is nice. She work every night and sometimes on Sundays too. She works from one until ten or ten-thirty at night.

Do you know any families whom you know fairly well that you would consider to be bad families?

A lady names Miss Mathews stay upstairs. She haven't got no husband and she's on ADC and she don't work. She don't keep her house clean. She have a lot of men up at her house, all different men. And mostly all her children got different fathers. I know her daughter very well and she talks to me about her mother. She said she's big enough to take care of the house but her brothers bad and everytime she clean up they mess it back up so she said if she's big enough to clean up, her mother should be cleaning too. But sometimes her mother be gone and they don't eat.

How do you feel about your own family?

I think we're getting along fine.

Would you say you have a good family?

It's good enough for me. Like if my father was here it would be excellent but mama try to do what she can with her little money and she buy enough food to last a whole month.

The good life is, of course, capable of many variations in the way particular individuals seek to live it. Some people think of the good life in conservative terms, emphasizing ultra-respectability and perhaps a close relationship between family and church. Others see the good life more as a "pursuit of happiness" that includes an active social life, going out dancing and to parties and to bars and so one. This differentiation parallels what has been observed in the stable working class, variations that can be symbolized by the images of "lace curtain" versus "tavern" life styles. What is common to both is an insistence on the solidarity of the family unit, and the resistance of husband and wife to whatever attraction solo participation in the world of the streets might have for them.

Our Life the Way It Is

No matter how clear the image of the good life, few of the Pruitt-Igoe adults have been able to achieve it, and most of the children growing up in Pruitt-Igoe come to learn that their luck won't stretch far enough to allow them to approximate it.

When one falls short of the stable, conventionally contracted and continuing marriage that is the one standard of the good life, there are many ways of living life as it is. These reflect the various points at which the ideal trajectory from discreet or virginal premarital status to a stable first marriage can be broken. Premarital sexual relations are the first danger point along the non-ideal trajectory. Premarital pregnancy is next, then becoming a mother to an illegitimate child, then an unsuccessful marriage, then divorce or separated status, and so on. At each point along the way, Pruitt-Igoeans believe the distance to the goal of the good family life and the difficulties and unlikelihood of achieving it increases.

Basic to the conception of our life is the belief that respectability, conventional life, is a tenuous and unstable achievement, and that in the lower class ghetto world, the individual who is conforming to conventional expectations may fail at any time. Closely entwined with this generalized judgment about respectability is a basic distrust of other persons, no matter how close they may be by blood or affection. This distrust has two focuses: others may seek to exploit a person and, more subtle but equally important, even without trying to exploit him, others may simply fail one if he depends on them. Relationships may just not work out, whether between lovers, spouses, relatives, or friends. One knows that the other person is as short as he is on the resources necessary for survival, and therefore he knows that he may not be able to be a resource even though he may want to. And because he is short on resources for himself, he may seek to gain them from the other person without giving comparable return.

Pruitt-Igoeans attach specific meanings to what happens at each of the various points at which things can go wrong for the formation of an ideal family, and they draw conclusions from what happens for the moral status of the individuals involved, themselves and others.

Premarital Sexual Relations

The formation of a family begins with adolescent courtship. In the white middle class there have developed elaborate and complex institutions centering around dating as a mechanism for guiding individual boys and girls toward marriage. These courtship institutions have as a central feature the management of the possibilities and dangers inherent in sexual relations between youngsters before marriage.[4] In the lower-class Negro ghetto there are comparable institutions, which will be described in detail in Chapter 11; here is presented an examination of the meanings which both adults and children come to attach to the various outcomes of premarital heterosexual relations. The issue here is sharply focused for the Pruitt-Igoeans. All but a small minority feel that sexual relations between girls and boys before marriage is a serious problem in the project, and about half of them believe that having sexual relations with many partners occurs frequently.

Some observers of lower-class Negro behavior have suggested that extensive premarital sexual experience is regarded as normative in that

4. See the discussion of peer-run courtship institutions in Reiss (1967).

group. However, our data suggest that this is not at all the case, although the frequency with which such behavior is thought to take place certainly attenuates the strength of conventional double-standard norms. Pruitt-Igoeans believe that premarital sexual relations are extremely common and begin quite early. When we asked (in the 1965 survey) at what age respondents thought boys and girls were most likely to have sexual intercourse for the first time, the average age given for both was 14, with a standard deviation from 12 to 16. (It is interesting that men in the project averaged about half a year earlier in their guesses than did the women.)

Over and over again there are indications in the field data that parents and young girls are concerned about the implications of premarital sex relations for a girl's reputation and for her marriage chances. In the 1965 questionnaire, a random subsample of 50 adults was asked open-ended questions concerning premarital sex relations, one of which tapped quite directly the conventional standard of virginity at marriage and the other a somewhat more flexible standard. The first of these questions was "How important is it that a girl be a virgin when she gets married? Why?" Overall, 50 per cent of both the men and the women indicated that it was very important for a girl to be a virgin when she got married, although many of these people, and even more of those who said it was not important, also indicated that this standard was honored more in the breach than in the observance.

The general tenor of the responses of those who said that virginity is important clearly indicates the pragmatic grounds on which their judgment is based, as well as the traditional and more abstract, religious or moralistic justifications:

> It's very important. It would be better for her future.
>
> It's very important. It's right. It's the teaching of the church.
>
> It's very important. She wants to be married in white and she can only wear white if she's a virgin. Her husband would think more of her.
>
> It's very important, because it means she took care of herself. Men will take her better. It gives the husband something he hasn't had.
>
> Yes, it's important to her husband. He will trust and respect her more. In marriage trust is an important thing.
>
> It's very important. Boys leave girls that they've had sex with.
>
> It's real important. A husband won't trust his wife if she isn't a virgin and that is embarrassing to the women.
>
> It's very important. Reputations is what you have to rely on. No man wants to marry a girl who stoops under every boy she sees.
>
> Very important, because no one knows anything about her. There's nothing they can say about her. I think her husband would appreciate her better.

About half of those who said that virginity was not important gave as their rather tenuous reason that they believed it to be very infrequent: "It's not important. You're not going to find any, so it doesn't make no difference to the fellow" or, "It's not very important, but the husband would be glad." Or, "Oh, it's not important. There are very few virgins nowadays."

The only clear-cut reason given by these respondents has to do with the necessity of testing a relationship to see if it is gratifying to both parties. This is phrased sometimes in the form of, "You have to try the shoe on before you buy it."

Our question did not specify whether the only person with whom the girl might have sexual relations was the man she would later marry, and in this case a smaller proportion of the respondents might have considered virginity important. However, our second question was meant to secure evaluations of more extensive sexual relations. We asked, "Do you think it matters much if a girl has sexual relations with boys but does not get pregnant?" Here the implication was clear that she might have more than one partner. Although men and women responded similarly on the question of virginity, here there was a substantial difference. Only 50 per cent of the men indicated that it matters much if a girl has sexual relations with boys, while 80 per cent of the women indicated concern. The combination of pragmatic and moralistic responses was even more clear, and there was much talk of a girl getting a bad reputation and of the loss of self respect and the respect of others that would come from this kind of activity.

> **News gets around and nobody will respect her.**
>
> **Her reputation is as stake; all kinds of men will be talking about her.**
>
> **It makes them fast and hard to hold down.**
>
> **Makes her common, people won't respect her.**
>
> **Takes away from her morals, and lowers her chance of marriage.**

From all of this, the conclusion can be drawn that, just as in more conventional society, sexual relations for a girl before marriage are regarded in Pruitt-Igoe as dangerous and fraught with problems. The most direct danger, of course, is pregnancy, but even if a girl were not to get pregnant Pruitt-Igoeans feel she lowers her chances of being treated as a respectable person, and sharply increases the suspicion and distrust with which she is likely to be regarded by potential mates and the community generally.

Premarital Pregnancy

As with premarital relations, all but a small minority of our respondents believed that premarital pregnancy was both very frequent and a very serious problem in the project. The respondents believed that boys impregnated a girl for the first time at the age of about 15.5 years with a

standard deviation range from 14 to 17, and that girls became first pregnant at about the age of 14, with a standard deviation range of 12.5 to
15.5. Women saw very little time lapse between a girl's first intercourse
and first pregnancy, only two-tenths of one year on the average. The
women consider premarital sexual relations to be very serious, because
they believe that relations lead almost inevitably and at once to pregnancies.

Some commentators on lower-class ghetto life have suggested that premarital pregnancy is not thought to be a particularly great problem, but
our data suggest that this is certainly not the case. Illegitimacy is seen as a
frequent occurrence and people have developed customary ways of dealing with it, but this does not mean that it is not also considered to represent a real difficulty for the girl and her family, or that it is approved. To
appreciate this fact, one must differentiate between how people in the
project may talk about illegitimacy when it actually occurs and to how
they speak abstractly about the issue. Illegitimacy departs far from what
is considered desirable and moral. While only a minority of our respondents would agree with the flat statement that it is disgraceful to have an
illegitimate baby (about 40 per cent), the majority express their understanding of premarital pregnancy as a problem and danger even greater
than that of premarital sexual relations. Thus, after asking about how important it was for a girl to be a virgin when she gets married we asked the
open-ended question, "How about if she gets pregnant but isn't married,
does that matter much? Why?" Ninety per cent of the women and 60 per
cent of the men said that it matters much, and most were able to give
compelling reasons why it mattered.

If marriage takes place subsequent to pregnancy, it is often felt that the
marriage is unfortunate because it is more likely to break up as the couple
discovers that they are not really compatible. If marriage does not take
place, the child represents a burden to the girl and to her family and is
believed to weaken her chances for marriage to another man.

> Lots of times it matters. She'd have to spend a lot of time alone
> until she finds someone who don't care.
>
> People lose respect for her and it isn't fair to the child.
>
> It matters because of the child. The child is coming up, no
> name and might have to go hungry.
>
> (Even if she married him) the husband would always wonder
> what she did before, and he'll put it up to her.
>
> Her equals don't want her for a wife; they just want her for a
> handout girl.
>
> It matters because she's got to explain.

The last quotation wraps up the whole issue in a nutshell: illegitimacy
is much too frequent for Pruitt-Igoeans to express horror or great condem-

nation of it; nevertheless, getting pregnant before marriage significantly exposes the girl and the child to potential stigmatization—"she's got to explain."

Despite the threat that illegitimacy represents, it is taken for granted within the Pruitt-Igoe community. It is not something to be pleased about and it may precipitate unhappiness and conflict within the girl's family and between her and the boy and his family, but it is such a familiar occurrence that people know how to think about the problems it presents and how to work toward the best solutions, given the limited alternatives that are available to them. In general, marriage is considered the most attractive solution, but it is not automatic; shotgun weddings are to be carefully considered, because if the couple is not compatible they are not likely to stay married. Even if the boy is willing to marry, he is usually considered not a very promising provider for the family. When (in the 1966 survey) we asked people whether they thought a 17 year old girl who is pregnant by a boy she has been going with should marry him, only slightly more than half our respondents (men and women alike) gave an unqualified affirmative response. Very few (15 per cent) said categorically that she should marry him, but almost one third addressed themselves to the other conditions that would have to exist for such a marriage to be good: commonly it was believed that both should be willing to marry and be fond of each other, and given this willingness, it was thought important that the husband be old enough to have some chance of supporting a family.

A Mother Needs To Be Mrs.; A Baby Needs a Name

One of the strongest pressures for marriage has to do with legitimating the status of both the mother and the child. For the mother this legitimation may be less important, because even if she does not marry before the birth of her first child she may subsequently do so (although her chances of a successful marriage are lowered). For the baby, however, this is his only chance to have the name that "belongs" to him. Thus, in family arguments in Pruitt-Igoe it is not at all uncommon for a child who has not been legitimated by a father to be taunted with the accusation, "You don't have a name." Some respondents, in arguing that a young girl with an illegitimate child should marry, mentioned this problem in particular.

> She should marry him for the child's sake, so that the child will have a name and a good future life. They should get married if they love each other.
>
> Because it would give the baby a father, because it's an honor for a baby to have a father.
>
> I've got no sympathy for a girl of that age going around having babies. What name is she going to give the child and who is going to be its daddy if they don't marry?

> The baby needs a name. However, if they don't want to, then they shouldn't.
>
> He is the father of the child and he should marry her before the child is born in order to give the child a name.
>
> Anybody having children should get married to give the child a name.

A responsible father will want to give his child his name if he possibly can, although it is understood that other aspects of his situation may prevent him from doing so. The fact that a child does not "have a name" subtly affects his status within his family, and perhaps his self conception. It can point him on the road away from the good life at birth, although again the frequency of illegitimacy serves to attenuate the impact of these negative implications.

The masculine counterpart of the reputational elements in a girl's evolving biography has not been dealt with extensively. It is apparent that a boy's involvement in premarital sexual relations is not considered so fateful as that of a girl. However, "pimping"—a form of premarital sexual relationship involving elaborate exploitative activities on the part of the boy —is taken as evidence of his greater commitment to "street life" than to more conventional life. If the boy has constructed for himself a social identity that involves the exploitation of many women for money and other favors, he is suspect as a potentially disloyal husband and one who is likely to be a poor provider.

When asked how they thought boys who impregnate girls premaritally felt about their own behavior, Pruitt-Igoeans—all adults—responded with the belief that men are primarily responsible for sustaining the high degree of nonmarital sexual activity that takes place in the community. Most respondents indicated that boys are either indifferent to the fact that their girlfriends are pregnant or, with surprising frequency, that they are proud because making a girl pregnant shows that they are men. The men in our sample were even more inclined to say this than the women.

> How do boys feel when they get a girl pregnant?
> They feel fancy.
>
> (Feel like a) big brave boy; they did something their friends haven't.
>
> Some of them be proud. They think they are a man when this happens.
>
> Feel like they are a man, that they accomplished something. Something to sit around and talk about.

The first real test of a boy's conceptions of family life is likely to appear in his reaction to the impregnation of his girlfriend if that happens. A boy who is going to become a good husband should at this point evidence great concern for his girlfriend, express his desire to marry her, to legitimate the child, to support it, and if he pulls back from any of these responsibilities he becomes suspect. This suspicion is not conclusive because he may have "lost respect" for the girl and be seeking a more respectable girl with whom to settle down, but in the community view, he is more likely demonstrating that he is "no good." If he continues to maintain some relationship with his child, he will be looked at as a less than perfect potential partner by other girls because he has competitive affections and responsibilities which may divert his resources from a future marriage and may erupt in disloyalty to his future wife and family. Because the mother of his child has shown herself to be less than respectable by her behavior, other girls will be concerned that she may try to win him back as a way of insuring his contribution to her family.

The performance in school of both boys and girls can be used by the community as a way of judging their future development toward stable or unstable marital life. Young people who complete high school have shown themselves to be in some sense successful at conventional strategies. A boy who drops out of school is less attractive as a mate for reasons in addition to his presumed lower earning power. Similarly, a girl who drops out of school, because of pregnancy or for other reasons, is thought to have admitted her failure to pursue her life along conventional lines. For this reason, people often emphasize the importance of a girl going back to school even though she has had an illegitimate child.

Another major clue to a boy's future trajectory is provided by his work experience. If he is able to maintain a job or gives strong evidence of wanting very much to work, he is considered to be pointed toward more conventional strategies; if he shows disinterest in work or has an irregular work history, preferring perhaps to pimp off his mother and girlfriend, he is a much higher risk. However, because of the very poor work opportunities available to teenage Negroes, whether a young man is working is not regarded as a good predictor of his potential, provided he gives evidence of wanting to work. This is not the case for older men, who are given very little credit for good intentions if they are not actually working. It is often felt that they simply do not want to work.

Extramarital Relations

Pruitt-Igoeans apparently perceive a tremendous disjunction between actual behavior in their world and their norms about what that behavior should be. Their typical experiences up to the point of marriage seem to demonstrate the tenuousness and instability of respectable desires on the part of young men and women and validate the basic distrust marital partners have of each other and of the potential seducers around them. Most Pruitt-Igoe marriages start out with some desire on the part of each partner to try to achieve a conventional marital relationship. From the beginning, however, contending beliefs about our life as it is tend to interfere with such an achievement.

Within marriage a number of contending beliefs about the way it is as opposed to the way it should be sustain a sense of pessimism. One of the most striking is the opposition between conventional norms and the view advanced to participant observers by many men and women that "it's all right if a husband or wife each step out by themselves sometimes and have a girlfriend or boyfriend on the side, as long as the other one doesn't know about it." In our 1965 survey, more than 85 per cent of the respondents thought that this happens very often and 70 per cent believed that "many people" share these views. (On both of these counts there were no differences in the distribution of responses between men and women or between women who were currently married and women whose marriages had been disrupted.) However, the majority believed that infidelity inevitably causes trouble. Many believed that even if the infidelity were not discovered it would affect the couple's relationship in other ways; an even larger number asserted that sooner or later the infidelity would be discovered and that when this happened it would inevitably make trouble between husband and wife.

> I don't think it works out. Eventually they'll butt into each other.
>
> As time goes by the man and woman can begin to suspect what's going on and each will begin to wait until they can catch someone with the other.
>
> Everyone has a conscience. A person will bear the burden of loss of self-respect.
>
> (Won't work) because somebody is missing something somewhere. You can't take care of two women or two men. They'll come across each other sooner or later.

In the 1966 questionnaire in a series of closed-end questions it was again clear that the counter-norm approving infidelity was not upheld. Fewer than 10 per cent, men and women alike, agreed with the statement, "It's okay for people to step out on their husband or wife as long as the other doesn't know about it." Similarly, 87 per cent of the women and 78 per cent of the men disagreed with the statement, "It's quite natural for married persons to have sexual relations with persons they're not married to." And finally there was almost no disagreement (less than five per cent) from either men or women that a man or woman who expects his spouse to be faithful should be faithful in return. Everyone is aware that many couples do not live up to these norms, and they can understand why a partner might be tempted to step out discreetly, hoping that it will not disrupt the marriage. But no one seems really to take seriously a belief that this is the workable norm. Thus, the rejection of conventionality that is apparent in the assertion of this counternorm appears more a rationalization or a wish than a viable alternative; it is not really supported even by those who assert it.

Pruitt-Igoeans believe that marriages in the community are highly unstable. We asked the 1965 survey respondents, "Out of every ten couples around here who get married, how many do you suppose break up, separate, or divorce sooner or later?" The mean estimate was that 5.8 marriages out of ten eventually break up. Considerably more than a third of the respondents believed that 70 per cent or more of the marriages eventually break up. (There were no differences between men and women or between women who were currently married or widowed and those who were separated or divorced.)

Sex was the most common reason given why these marriages broke up. More than 40 per cent of the respondents, both men and women, gave as at least one of the reasons, often as the only reason, a complex of sexual references that included "running in the streets," "jealousy," and more directly, "having another lover."

> It's (the cause of breakup) on both sides . . . When they run out, you know they're going to run into something out there, and they neglect what's at home.
>
> If they would be satisfied with each other and not see what's in the streets and try to get that too (there wouldn't be so many breakups). Don't cheat on each other.
>
> (They should) stay out of the streets and stop cheating. It's better to enjoy your family than the streets; they have more to offer.
>
> Must be the woman (who causes the breakup). She figures he's going out with another girl and wants him home all the time.

It should not be supposed that these responses mean the respondents believe that the spouses in fact are unfaithful, because they also believe that unfounded jealousy breaks up marriages or itself encourages infidelity. (The actual facts concerning infidelity in marriage are unclear. In the sexual histories of the women in our 1965 sample, only eight per cent of those who were currently married admitted having extra-marital affairs, but 31 per cent of those who were no longer married made such admissions.)

For mature men and women, nonsexual loyalty becomes increasingly salient in determining the direction of marital and courting relations. Among older women (and to some extent men) there exists a concern with heavy drinking as a threat to the possibility of achieving the good life. A man or woman who has a reputation as a heavy drinker is thereby seen as less likely to achieve a stable marital relationship, partly because of the effect of drinking on instrumental responsibilities like work or homemaking, but also because drinking is thought to make him or her more susceptible to seduction. Gambling is a similarly poor indicator in the meaning system of the Pruitt-Igoeans. Gambling takes assets away from the family, exposes a man to the possibility of stigmatization by the law, and signifies his unwillingness to "settle down." The woman who has a husband who drinks heavily or gambles frequently is regarded with sympathy, unless he is also a good provider. In that case, the threat of his behavior to a conventional stable marriage is regarded as more likely to be contained.

Taking all of these negative indicators together, it is little wonder that 83 per cent of the women and 65 per cent of the men in our 1966 sample agreed with the following statement: "The thing that really drags people down is a lot of sex and drinking."

The Potentialities of Children

Just as the polarity between the way life ought to be and the way it is, between the good life and our life, permeates Pruitt-Igoeans' meaning systems for heterosexual and marital relations, it also permeates the meaning systems they apply in their understandings of children, their own and those of others. Indeed, some of the themes that characterize their most highly generalized conceptions of human beings are expressed most sharply in the ways the people of Pruitt-Igoe talk about children and teenagers. As they attempt to make sense of their experiences in life, they show the same sensitivity to clues which indicate whether their children are pointed toward a good life or our life as they do in their assessment of adult relationships. For parents this sensitivity is heightened by the anxious knowledge that as a parent one is held responsible for whether children turn out respectably. In mating and marital relations one can to some extent disavow responsibility for the moral behavior of one's partner, but a parent does not have this luxury, although he is often tempted to claim it.

Before children start school they are regarded as morally neutral; there is not much concern about the moral implications of their behavior or one's relations with them. There is also a relative lack of the typical middle class concerns about children talking early, walking early, and so on. Instead, babies and young children are generally enjoyed or ignored, and there is a great deal of tolerance for childish behavior of all kinds. In our 1966 survey, 74 per cent of the respondents agreed that children are more trouble the older they get. When the respondents were asked at what age children are most likely to become problems, fewer than five per cent specified an age before nine years. It was the teenage period that was regarded as the time of trouble; 70 per cent said boys become problems between the ages of 13 and 16, and 77 per cent said girls become problems between the ages of 13 and 15.

As the child matures, as he becomes more and more involved in the outside world (starting roughly with his entry into school), Pruitt-Igoe mothers become increasingly concerned about whether he is pointed toward a good life or toward a life more characteristic of their community as it is. Parents often take strong measures to insulate their children from the outside world which they regard as morally dangerous to them. They seek to keep them in their apartments as much as possible, and they worry whenever they are outside but not in school. They seem to assume that if the child can be insulated from the outside world he will manage to grow up without its unrespectable and dangerous potentialities rubbing off on him. But they also know that they are fighting a losing battle, because the child pulls away from this isolation. The outside world is too interesting; the company of his peers becomes increasingly important. Given their deeply engrained belief that human nature is innately bad, Pruitt-Igoe parents think that only they and their influence stand between the child's potentialities for respectability and the outside world's genius for destroying these potentialities.

The early age at which parents feel that it is no longer possible to keep their children out of trouble is suggested by the responses to a question in the 1966 survey, "At what age do you think it is impossible for parents to keep their kids out of trouble if the kids want to get in trouble?" The median age chosen was 13 years, with 33 per cent choosing 12, 13, or 14. A significant minority (26 per cent) chose ages under 11.

The conception of the good child is simple enough. A good child is primarily obedient. He does what his parents tell him to do and does not do what they tell him not to do. He does not cause trouble. He is helpful around the house, doing those chores he is asked to do and holding himself ready to help out whenever necessary. He does not insist on indulging himself in play and outside activities when his parents want something of him. A good child performs adequately in school, and does not get into trouble there. While parents would very much like their children to do well in school, they are generally not attentive to the finer gradations of scholastic achievement; it is enough if the child seems to be progressing in an average way and if the family receives no complaints from the school.

As the child grows and his potentialities for elaborate peer group involvement multiply, the measure of a good child becomes more and more sharply focused on whether he stays out of trouble with other children, with neighbors, with the police. In general, then, a good child, somewhat unlike a good spouse, is defined in negative terms by what does not happen, by what he does not do, more than by what he does.

A good child is sharply marked off from the others in his world, perhaps even more sharply than the good man or woman. People in Pruitt-Igoe have very negative impressions of children, especially of teenagers. They believe that the project community, even more than the ghetto in general, is a very bad place to raise children because of the many opportunities for getting into trouble. The parent knows that he will have to be very lucky indeed to interpose his authority effectively between the troublesome world and the growing child. Seventy per cent of those in our 1965 Pruitt-Igoe sample believed that "many children in the project get into trouble," compared to only 36 per cent of those in the sample from the ghetto neighborhood nearby. Fifty-one per cent of those in the neighborhood believed that "nearly all children try to do well in school," compared to only 28 per cent of those from Pruitt-Igoe.

Our field observations contain many comments on children as pervasive sources of trouble:

> **The devil is in these children.**
>
> **The children are lazy today, and their parents are too lax.**
>
> **These kids are sophisticated, so when they're sharp they take advantage of anyone.**
>
> **The kids in Pruitt are very destructive.**
>
> **The small kids are as tough as the large ones around here.**
>
> **Pruitt-Igoe is good for adults, but it's bad for children.**
>
> **These older kids take advantage of the young ones in sex and things.**
>
> **The kids around here are so noisy you don't know whether there's play or foul play going on.**
>
> **The teenagers nowadays just want to hurry and grow up.**
>
> **Kids used to steal to eat, now they steal for kicks.**
>
> **The older children get, the lazier they are around the house.**
>
> **These teenage girls are just as bad as the boys.**
>
> **The younger people don't respect the older ones around here.**
>
> **The children nowadays know everything.**

Parents are very anxious about their children's behavior and potential involvement in an outside world defined as negatively their world, but their self-respect requires them to believe that their own children are better behaved than are most children in Pruitt-Igoe. When we asked in the 1966 survey how they compared their own children to the other children in Pruitt-Igoe, 66 per cent of the mothers said that their children were better behaved, and none that their children were less well behaved. In general, they maintained that they were satisfied with the way their children had grown up (only 13 per cent said they are dissatisfied). Even so, their anxiety was reflected in the fact that a majority of mothers felt they were not able to keep their children confined to the home long enough to perfect their resistance to the destructive outside world. Most of those whose children had reached the age at which the parents felt they might play outside unwatched said that they began to do so at too young an age. Similarly, most of those whose children were at the age at which the mother felt they might appropriately stay out late at night said that they began to do this too young.

The most important effect of the interaction between the exceedingly dim views that most Pruitt-Igoe parents take of children generally and their feelings of gradual loss of control over their own children is that they begin to distrust their children; they sense that the youngsters may be involved in activities they hoped would be avoided. As time goes on, the parents tend more and more to accept the idea that their children will not behave in the ways most likely to assure progress towards the good life, whether by this they mean acceptable accomplishment in school, avoiding extensive heterosexual relations, avoiding the troubles that come from stealing or aggressive "gang" behavior. Most parents hold back from any firm conclusion that their children are inevitably confined to a future in the lower class ghetto, but their expectations become less optimistic than before, less than the expectations of the stable working class.

Parents in Pruitt-Igoe want their children to finish school because they believe that high school graduation is necessary for a chance at the good life, but they are less likely to have strong expectations that this will occur than are higher-status parents. As a way of assessing this issue, in our 1966 survey we asked how surprised the parent would be if their boy were to quit school after the eighth or tenth grade, or just before finishing the twelfth grade, or if he were to graduate from high school or go on to college. It is clear that parents would be much more surprised if the child quit school after the eighth grade or went to college than by any of the other possibilities, but the striking fact is that there is very little difference in how surprised they would be if the child quit after the tenth grade or during the twelfth grade or graduated from high school; all of these seemed equally possible. Given these perceptions of what is likely, it is understandable that Pruitt-Igoe parents find it difficult to do anything other than accept what their children achieve despite their aspirations for them.

The situation is much the same for the issue of pregnancy among female children. Our field observations suggest that although parents hope their daughters will not become pregnant before marriage, and that they will neither marry nor become pregnant until they finish high school, they are not very sanguine. If a girl does become pregnant, it comes as no great shock, although there is sadness because of it.

For a small but not inconsequential proportion of parents there is a further stage of scaling down expectations. For these people their children's (most commonly, teenager's) behavior is such that they feel they must disavow all responsibility for the child, at least for the time being. The parents felt in a number of situations that the best thing to do when the child made trouble was to turn him over to the authorities, because he was too troublesome to be controlled or because he caused too much difficulty for the family (as when his behavior led to threats of eviction). But we never encountered the traditional Victorian stance, "Never darken my door again." No matter how badly behaved a child had been, no matter what crime or difficulty he was involved in, whenever he seemed to have settled down his family was ready to give him a chance again. Thus youngsters come out of juvenile homes or prisons and return to live at home with relatively little recrimination. Once the emergency which his behavior precipitates is over, the child is accepted, though perhaps not fully trusted.

The understanding of children in general and (in modified form) of one's own children that is common in the Pruitt-Igoe world makes it difficult for parents to take pleasure in their children once the preteen period begins. Parents may enjoy the company of their children, but when they have to confront how they are developing, what has become of them, they tend to feel defensive, pessimistic, and depressed. The parents' adaptation to this situation is often to treat their children as peers at an early age. Of course this is much easier with female than with male children; an almost sister-like relationship often appears even between early teenage girls and their mothers, but boys can come to feel very much like strangers in their own homes.

The peer bias of parent-child relations is important for preserving the solidarity of the family because it makes it possible to avoid and under-emphasize issues of parental control. Parents may then concentrate their efforts simply on the children's demeanor in the household, and implicitly allow the children great freedom outside. Finally, as time goes on and as the children become increasingly aware of their parents' behavior and sophisticated about its "respectability," they learn to use their parents' failures as a way of denying any efforts to control their own behavior. These maneuvers simply reinforce the tendencies already within the family either toward everyone going his own way or toward strained relations between parents and children.

The Potentialities of Friends and Relations

The conceptions of informal social relations which in Pruitt-Igoe are seen as the good life are clear enough. In a good world the "golden rule" would work. People would be helpful, considerate, understanding, fair, mutually supportive. Our respondents expressed over and over again their very strong wishes that such relationships would exist within families, among relatives, between friends and neighbors. In the abstract, relatives and friends were exempt from the generalized sense of mistrust which characterizes the ghetto world-view. Beliefs about how relatives should relate to each other were quite conventional: blood is thicker than water, and one ought to be able to depend on one's relatives for help and understanding when needed. The same general norms applied to friends and neighbors, but with less force.

The importance of relatives was apparent in response to a question in the 1966 survey asking about "the best thing that anyone ever did for you." As might be expected in the depriving world in which the respondents live, most of their responses can be characterized as "rescues," in that they dealt with help they had been given in connection with a pressing need or crisis—being broke, having a serious illness in the family, not having a home, losing a job. In half the cases the person who proved helpful was a relative. From the examples people gave of "the worst thing that happened to you" as well as from observational data, it is obvious that kinship ties are normatively defined as involving heavy reciprocal obligations. The sense of deep gratefulness which the respondents expressed as they described the help they received reinforces this interpretation. Similar feelings were expressed about friends and neighbors who proved helpful, but these friends "didn't really have to" help, there was not the same kind of obligation that exists among kinsmen. All of this has to do with how things ought to be and only occasionally are. There is a contrary set of typifications of the way things usually are in our life. Instead of the golden rule these beliefs emphasize, one must constantly be on guard against being taken advantage of by other people; one must be distrustful of others, no matter how close.

Such attitudes were strikingly illustrated by responses to two statements in the 1965 survey. The first was, "It's not good to let your friends know everything about your life because they might take advantage of you." Ninety-one per cent of the respondents agreed with this statement; 80 per cent of them agreed "very much." The second said, "It's not good to let your relatives know everything about your life because they might take advantage of you." Here 69 per cent of the respondents agreed with the statement, half of them "very much."

Ambivalence about closeness with others also was reflected in responses to a series of questions probing beliefs about visiting patterns in the project. We asked respondents to estimate "how often people in the project visited in someone else's apartment to stay for a while and talk." Then we asked how often they themselves visited. Respondents perceived the project norm as higher than their own. Fifty-five per cent of the respondents who made an estimate (42 per cent said they didn't know) thought that visiting was a daily occurrence among project residents while only 17 per cent said that they themselves visited that often. Indeed, the majority said that they made visits less often than once a week, while 90 per cent guessed that the normal pattern involved visits of at least this frequency. People believe that it is not a good idea to visit either often or seldom. Thus half of those who thought the Pruitt-Igoe norm was daily visiting said they thought this was bad; at the same time, sixty per cent of those who thought that people visited less than once a week thought such infrequent visiting was bad. When people were asked why infrequent visiting was bad, they emphasized loneliness, isolation, and lack of friends to help you out when you have trouble; the reasons for disapproval of more frequent visiting patterns consisted again of warnings against letting relatives and friends know too much about your affairs.

The answers to these two sets of questions illustrate the basic distrust of others which people in the project share. The responses also echo observations made during the field work which together suggest a set of core concerns about the dangers of close relationships with others, whether relatives, friends, or neighbors. Basically, these concerns are with being used. In close relationships there is greater risk of exploitation; relatives are a greater danger than friends, and friends greater than neighbors and acquaintances, because the closer the person, the less likely you are to be on guard, even though you should know better.

The kinds of dangers that people fear in this context can be grouped into three major areas, all aspects of being used by others in ways that are detrimental to one's own goals. Most simply, people whom you permit to become close may take advantage of you by borrowing your money or taking other material resources. When asked why they thought relatives or friends "shouldn't know too much about your life because they might take advantage," people said:

> My husband and I had a savings and told relatives about it, a couple of weeks later they borrowed the money and never paid it back.

> Certain things are confidential and you are supposed to keep them in your house. We came into a large amount of money once because one of the children got hurt. We saw all of the relatives then who were expecting to have a big time off of it.

> They (relatives) find out if you've got anything and they always need it. Friends also try to borrow things just like relatives.

> A friend is the only one that gets close enough to you to do you some harm. A lady I met, we went out drinking together and she borrowed money from me. She was a friend so she knew I needed the money, but she never paid it back.

> Friends are not always friends, I've had them steal money from me.

This concern reflects a realistic awareness of the poverty of the group and their constant struggle to make ends meet, a struggle which can lead people to be insensitive to the needs and rights of those close to them. This reflects the obverse of the Pruitt-Igoeans' responses to our question about "the best thing that anyone ever did for you." The receiver can feel grateful and pleased that someone has been helpful. The giver can feel that he has been taken advantage of by his relatives or his friends.

Just as money and other material resources may be lost through a rash openness in one's relationships with relatives and friends, so may the interpersonal resources represented by a spouse or a boyfriend or girlfriend. One of the concerns expressed about frequent visiting and about letting relatives and friends know too much about your life is that such openness may cause significant others to be attracted from you. This can come about particularly when relatives are let in on arguments about family or love life and counsel behavior which leads to separation, but it can also come about when exposure of the private life of a couple leads directly to a new partner for one of the spouses. Thus our respondents spoke along the following lines:

> There was a time when we were getting along bad and I think that they (relatives) tried to influence me in the wrong way. Sometimes when you are mad at your husband you will say something. Then a little while later you might forget it, but they will still be mad about it. If they don't know everything about you and your life, relations between in-laws are better.

> If you tell them (friends) everything that goes along with you and your husband and if you're doing pretty good, they'll try to show him that he shouldn't do all that for you.

> It just isn't good to let people know all of your business. Friends have taken advantage of me by going out with my husband.

> Relatives can sway you the wrong way and break up your home.

> (Too much visiting is bad because) people drink and get together and start talking about going with people's husbands.

> You have a lot of girls who don't have a man and they try to break up homes (so you shouldn't visit too much).

> If you have a good boyfriend and tell too many ladies about him, they'll try to get him.

The threat from friends of the same sex is simple and direct: they may become competitive for the affections of a spouse or friend. With relatives this is less of a problem, but family possessiveness or bossiness may lead them to seek to attenuate the marital or lover relationship for their own reasons. In short, just as openness in interpersonal relations can lead to the loss of money and material resources, it can lead to the loss of some of the significant people in your life.

Perhaps the most commonly perceived danger is the less specific fear of losing one's identity resources. Pruitt-Igoeans fear that losing control over information about oneself and one's life will interfere with or even destroy one's chances of doing and being what he wants. This loss seems to be very threatening.[5] It is summed up by one respondent who said, "If you don't want to let your personal life get out into the street, then you shouldn't tell your friends." Another woman commented about too frequent visiting, "People meddle in each other's business. They start up a lot of old humbug—she said . . . he said . . ."

The detrimental effect of openness can come about directly through a change in one's image in the eyes of a friend or relative, or indirectly as a result of gossip about you that is spread to others. In both cases the

5. See Goffman's (1963) discussion of information control and personal identity.

identity the individual wishes to maintain in his social world is undermined by exposing himself to friends or relatives. This negative effect may take the form of envy on the part of others when they learn that you are doing well, or of a loss of status in their eyes when they discover discreditable things about you. Finally, openness can result in creating a new kind of relationship with friends or relatives such that the individual is seduced into behavior which heightens his discreditability and thus further exposes him to the danger of gossip. Respondents suggest their fear of envy, shaming, or seduction by the following comments:

> They visit other people and talk about you; always talking about people—gossiping. They should go to church. People sometimes go to the welfare telling stories about people, about when they are drunk and so on.

> I have told several that I have had a nervous breakdown and they think I'm odd because of this. They know their friends' situations and they try to take advantage of them. Sometimes they (relatives or friends) use what you tell them as a threat.

> If there are problems in the home, sometimes relatives take advantage by keeping the fight going. They might entice you to do things that you normally wouldn't do because you have having problems—like drink or go out on the town to forget your problems.

> (It's not good if they know too much about your business) because some relatives are jealous of other relatives when they try to get ahead.

> I have seen so many times where you have a friend who learns things about you and she can take this and use it against you in so many ways.

> Your friends are the closest to you and know how to hurt you the most.

> Some members of your family really hate to see you get ahead.

> When people give out all their business, they are really just asking for trouble.

> (Visiting too much is not good) because talking can lead to drinking and this can lead to conflict.

Given these dangerous potentialities in their relationships with relatives and friends, Pruitt-Igoeans draw a number of conclusions as guides to survival in their milieu. In addition to being on guard when one communicates with others, no matter how close, he tries not to count on others for much, not to expect others to live up to their putative responsibilities as relatives or friends. Instead, one expects to manipulate others to get what he wants—and this manipulation, of course, reinforces the generalized mistrust each has of the other.

In addition, one learns to avoid responsibility to others not only because they may take advantage but also as a way of protecting relationships. If one's resources are so limited that he cannot live up to putative responsibilities, it is better for all parties to try to avoid a clear statement of these responsibilities. From the responsible person's point of view, if he can avoid claims made on him he thereby protects his relationship with another because neither partner will have to face the fact that they cannot live up to their responsibilities and they will not have to accept blame from each other.

In short, in Pruitt-Igoe people learn that relationships are brittle; therefore the reasonable person takes care not to place too much strain on them lest they shatter. It is, of course, difficult always to act in terms of this understanding because people are needful, and their needs can be satisfied through relationships. One resolution is to reconcile oneself to moving through life treating relationships as readily replaceable and interchangeable, rather than making heavy investments in a few relationships.

People in Pruitt-Igoe are continually confronting isolation as an alternative to the risk of trouble that comes from full participation in relationships with relatives and friends. People often find themselves more involved than they feel is optimal. They know that they must run the risk of trouble to satisfy their instrumental needs, their needs for affiliation, for avoiding loneliness. The problem is particularly exacerbated in a community like Pruitt-Igoe where so few of the adults have stable marital relationships and therefore must turn to outsiders for many of the needs ordinarily fulfilled by spouses. Women separated from their husbands in particular feel a strong need to relate to others—be they relatives, neighbors, or boyfriends—to alleviate their loneliness. But these women embark on such a course with great ambivalence, because they know they run the risk of being taken advantage of, of having their business bruited about in the streets. If such a woman does embark on the dangerous course, she may do so in a guarded way that itself contributes to the brittleness of her relationships, because it enhances mutual suspicion. In the end she must be ready to fall back on the philosophical understanding that relationships can be costly, and that they often must be given up to minimize costs, hoping only that they can be replaced.

Managing Oneself in a Distrusted World

The family experiences men and women have are not the only ones that encourage a pessimistic view of life, but they are central because they tend to involve a person's most intimate relationships, or at least his efforts to form intimate relationships. From these experiences and others, people in the lower class ghetto develop a set of strategies for surviving in a world defined in these ways. These strategies are not offered in the folk philosophy of the group as intrinsically desirable, or as the best way in the abstract to manage one's life, but rather in the form of "because" statements—because other people are the way they are, because I have so few resources available to me, because everything is unpredictable.

One central view is that one must learn to "go for yourself." To operate in the kind of world in which he lives, the rational individual is one who takes what he can get even though it won't be very much. He is expected to be concerned only for himself even though that is not the way a person ideally should be. "Going for yourself" involves two aspects, one more dramatic than the other. The more dramatic is the development of a highly exploitative attitude toward other people, in which the individual seeks to manipulate them to achieve strictly personal ends. This strategy is apparent at all stages in the development of mating relationships, whether in premarital relations, in response to pregnancy, in marriage, or in the post-marital state. Exploitative relations with others are the dynamic aspect of the basic distrust pervasive within the ghetto community.

The other way in which the individual "goes for himself" is less obvious. When opportunities for exploitating others are not available or are considered too dangerous, the individual resigns himself to what comes his way and is preoccupied with the mechanics of getting the little bit for which he has a chance—an ADC check or a low-wage job, or the tentative companionship of a girlfriend or wife. The unpredictable and depriving world in which lower-class Negroes live encourages them to develop strategies limited to making it from one day to the next. Their experience tells them not to try too hard to achieve something they don't have, whether it be the longed-for companionship of a stable marital partner or the love of a girl or boyfriend. Elaborate projects are unreasonable not only because the individual does not have the resources to feel secure about achieving them but also because anything he may build up with the few resources he can pull together may be readily torn down, particularly if it requires continuing inputs or the cooperation of other people. Therefore, the investment the individual makes in building relationships with others—most clearly apparent in family relations—tends to be confined to immediately expected pay-offs—the seduction of a girl, enjoyment of the immediate pleasures of marriage. With the vulnerability of meaningful relationships it hardly seems worthwhile to make heavily investments and sacrifices to develop them, and this applies also to more instrumental activities such as school or work.

The Pruitt-Igoean builds his life on the assumption of unstable and replaceable relationships, whether with friends, mating or marital partners, or others. To the extent that he begins to entertain ideas of achieving some part of the good life, he may hope for more stable and more permanent relationships, but the typical difficulties of our life encourage him to shift his perspective toward more temporary liaisons.

In such a world, the individual is constrained to cleave to his kin as much as possible because these relationships are regarded as having greater permanency. Even so, one cannot really count on kin because they are all in much the same boat, and the sensible individual knows that the extent to which he can turn the implicit claims of kinship into meaningful and satisfying relationships is variable. Only mothers are to some extent

exempted from this doubt. Fathers, brothers, sisters, sons and daughters—
and most of all, spouses—may not acknowledge claims on them in a
meaningful way.

Because one must "go for yourself" and because he doesn't have enough
to feel secure, strategies for survival encourage the individual to minimize
or avoid the responsibilities he ought to assume according to the standards
of the good life—to spouses, to children, to relatives, to others. This
avoidance of responsibility is not just "selfishness" although it is often so
regarded within his personal community when claims that should be
acknowledged are not met. Rather, the individual knows that he cannot
make good on many of the claims that others have the abstract right to
make on him—the claim of a wife that he should provide well for his
family, that he should be faithful, that he should not spend his time in
the streets. One must be careful in the way he conducts himself with
others so that he does not promise more than he can deliver. Unless, of
course, he is embarking on a clear-cut exploitative strategy; then he may
make promises to extract gains before the emptiness of the promise is
revealed.

Implicit in all these strategies is the belief that one is better off if he
does not care too much for himself, if he is not too proud in his relationships with other people. This applies both to relationships with those who
have power (bureaucrats and bosses) and to peers. One should not hold
oneself out as capable of functioning wholly in terms of good life respectability because the claims that result would be a burden to meet.
The word "uppity" may originally have referred to caste relations between
Negroes and whites, but now in Pruitt-Igoe the word is used to refer to
any presentation of self that implies more self-control and respectability
than the individual can make good.

Low self-esteem, in short, is not only a result of living in a ghetto world
but also a technique for modulating interpersonal demands and expectations. Part of this technique is learning to accept exploitation by others.
The individual can afford to accept exploitation by his peers and in heterosexual relations because he has little to lose, and because relationships are
unstable and replaceable, he can cut his losses by moving on to other
friends or spouses. Because everyone is vulnerable, all have an interest
in not dwelling for long on the loss of pride and self-respect that comes
from being exploited.

In these ways the individual draws on the existential folk philosophy
of his group to school himself in accommodating to patterns of mating
and marital relations which fall short of his ideal. He tries to become
expert in deriving whatever gratifications are present in the kinds of relationships that are available to him. He applies constructive efforts to
prolong satisfying relationships, but if he can keep his feelings and
hopes and wishes under control, he does not bank too strongly on them.
Because he lives in a world of people who confront the same problems
he can to some extent count on them to validate his ways of operating in

our life even though he may have to suffer the enmity of particular individuals whom he has failed.

There is considerable variation in how individuals and couples put together their particular version of our life out of the specific events of their lives and out of the particular strategies that are available to them. The same continuum of adaptation from constrictive to a more expressive style that was discussed for the good life is apparent here, although its manifestations are perhaps more dramatic at the extremes.

The expressive, high-life ways of surviving involve an attachment to life in the streets. At the other extreme is a strategy that limits one's demands on the world and the demands that the world is allowed to make. This is particularly apparent among older women who tend to retreat from the attractions of street life, who may refuse to have a boyfriend because they prefer to avoid the trouble that may come from such relationships even though in the process they have to bear loneliness. They may seek companionship in the church, becoming active there as a way of finding meaningful involvement, particularly as they find that their children give them less gratification and more trouble as they grow up and become involved in the outside world. In this way they may seek some semblance of the respectability of the good life, the respectability that comes from minding one's own business and having as little as possible to do with the dangerous world outside.

Existential statements and strategies that revolve around the dichotomy of the *good life* versus *our life* do not represent choices that individuals make once and for all. Many individuals alternate between these possibilities. Women seem more often to seek the good life, perhaps because to them it seems more achievable even within the limited available resources. However, they are often brought back to less desired ways by the unavailability of men to cooperate with them and by the involvement of their children in street life. In such situations the mother is herself strongly pushed toward "going for herself" in an effort to find some gratification to compensate for her failure to put on a "respectable" front.

When married or considering marriage, women also tend to be very tough in testing whether a man can be of real help in pursuing strategies for the good life. They have very little tolerance for any deviation from the model of a "good man," given their pessimistic assumptions about the trustworthiness of men in general and the very real problem of a man around the house who can't make good on his responsibilities. All of these forces often result in a way of life that provides some of the gratifications of the good life without risking too much. For example, careful calculations go into the arrangements whereby a separated or divorced woman accepts a steady boyfriend without relying on him to fill the role of husband-father-provider so strongly that the security of the whole family unit is endangered.

4.

The Madison Family

In the early fall of 1963 Robert Simpson knocked on the door of a second-floor apartment in the Pruitt part of the project, near the commercial area on Jefferson Avenue. He was greeted by a very large 51-year-old woman, Mrs. Annette Madison. It was during school hours, so only two of the seven children who lived in the apartment were at home. Seven-year-old Mark was not feeling well that day, and five-year-old Timmy seemed to be rather severely retarded. Simpson later learned that the five other children were Bill, 15; George, 13; Harry, 11; Nat, 9; Ophelia, 8. In addition, there was an older son, Paul, 25, who, though still single, lived on his own. Mrs. Madison had moved from a nearby area to the project when it opened. The last three children had been born in the project. When she moved into the project, she was separated from her husband, but the family kept in contact with him and when he was able to find work he made contributions to their maintenance. The last child had been fathered by a Mr. Vardaman who initially made a contribution of about $41 a month, but this ceased after two or three years. The two next youngest children had been fathered by a Mr. Caine, who seems never to have made any contribution to their support.

Simpson observed that the furniture and facilities of the apartment gave evidence of long and hard use. The furniture was old, covered by slipcovers that had not been washed in a long time, and the kitchen gave a general impression of disarray. The grim appearance of the sparsely furnished living room was relieved by several pictures. Hanging on one wall were two Utrillo-like reproductions along with a picture of the crucifixion and a plaster head of the Virgin Mary. On another wall was a colored picture of the head of Christ which changed expressions as you moved from one part of the room to another, and a calendar picture showing a ball, glove, bat, and baseball with a glass of beer.

77

Just Give It All to God

Simpson explained to Mrs. Madison that he was a student from Washington University doing a study of the Pruitt-Igoe Project and that he was interested in talking to people about what it was like to live there. He also explained that he did not have anything to do with the housing administration or with the social workers in the project. He began the conversation by asking how many people lived in the apartment.

> Well, there's me and my seven kids. That's all there is here. You saw two of them when you came in. The oldest one is staying home today, he's got stomach trouble of some sort. The other one is my baby. Maybe you noticed that he is handicapped, he has convulsions and fits and things like that. He's been like that ever since he was born. He can't talk and for a long time we didn't even think he was going to be able to walk either. They're going to take him away sometime soon. They say when he gets to be five they will take him away to a hospital. I just put it all in God's hands. He makes things come out all right. He could have been a lot worse. It could have been one of the other kids or it could have been me or it could have been a lot worse on him. It could have been that he would be down in bed and couldn't run around and play like he does.

> When he goes to the hospital, will he live there all the time?

> Oh yes. God knows what's best. Why, God could put me right down on that couch there and somebody could come in here and steal all of my money and I couldn't even move. That's how much God is around. He'd end things. You get my point.

> You mean that God is present in everything and is around all the time.

> Yes, that's it. He makes things happen. I just put things in the hands of the Lord and then God's going to make them come out all right.

> I imagine your littlest boy has been a big burden on you . . .

> Oh, honey, I tell you it's the truth! He's bad all the time. He'd just as well throw over that stove right now and pull all of that hot scalding water down on him if we didn't watch him. He did scald himself once. I have to watch him all the time or somebody does. He's always happy to have someone play with him but you gotta watch him. He'll hit you with his shoe or get to fighting and someone has to be watching him all the time. My children, they understand. When other children come in, they play with them right here in the apartment. Outdoors the kids just don't understand.

You say the rest of your children are in school?

All but this one. He's got stomach trouble today. Someone told me that everybody is having it. He's helping out by playing with the little one though. Oh, I say the Lord will help things come out all right though. The children they help. We all go to church. I go and leave the little one with some of the children and the rest of them go to church. The next time the other ones go to church and the others stay home with the little boy. I think that's the way that God intended it to be. The devil, I know, is always tempting us. He tempts me by saying you ought to stay home with your son instead of going to church. But we take care of the young 'un and all of us get to go to church just as well.

What church do you go to?

The one over on Franklin. We got one mighty fine preacher. He's just the finest man there is. You oughta come to our church sometimes.

Well, I would like that very much. I really would. Do you think I could?

Sure, you come right ahead now. We'd be glad to have you. That's the Lord's work. You know it don't make no difference about white and black. He wants me to love everybody and not to hate anybody. Even people that come around here and break things up, I supposed to love them and pray for them— that's what God wants. You know some people come around and messes things up down here. They're not the people from inside, they're the people from outside. You know when I moved here years ago, this was the nicest and prettiest place I just ever did see. I just never seen a place that was prettier than this one. I still think that it's the finest place I've ever been to live and I just think it's fine. There's some people who have been making it worse in the last eight years. They aren't the people from in here, they are the people from outside. The Lord just wants me to love 'em and to pray for 'em and to help them see that they get to know Him. That's what God wants, isn't it?

Yes, it is. Sometimes it's pretty hard though when somebody kicks us in the face, to do that . . .

Oh, I know it is. We just give it all to God and pray for them that they get to know Him and to love Him and to get right in their hearts. You know that's what He's concerned about, how my heart is, do I love people or do I hate 'em. When you get next to God you can do it because He's going to make it happen. There's just nothing that He can't do—even against the devil. That's why I always try to get my children to go to church.

Did you ever live anywhere else in St. Louis before coming here?

Oh, yes. Before I came here years ago, I lived over on Alcott for a while, before that somewhere else and I've just lived all around in St. Louis. But I just like it here better than any place. I just think this is the finest place there is for me to live in. I'm gonna get the house painted one of these days. The painter was suppose to come last week but I got sick. He's gonna paint things up. (Pause.)

You have one girl and seven boys then?

That's right . . . Oh, it's hard bringing up a bunch of kids. I tried to bring my children up right. I tell them not to do something because others do it or just because they think it's right. It's not really easy to raise kids around here. They're all fine children but you know that 15 year old of mine he got a bad idea. He wants to get up and quit school and get a job. I don't like that at all. I didn't have much schooling and I keep telling my children they ought to get all that they can get. I didn't start until I was 12 and I only went through four grades.

Do you think there's any difference between raising children here and anywhere else?

It's a lot better for raising kids down South. I found that you don't get all that shouting back and forth. Kids don't see so much, you don't have any of that stuff of kids doing murder. There just ain't any. It was easier raising kids down there.

Are there more problems raising kids here in Pruitt than in other places in St. Louis?

Yes, there is. If I was back where I was before, we'd have a back yard and there wouldn't be so many people and the kids wouldn't be seeing so much. It would be easier to raise up the kids over there.

On Simpson's next visit to the home a few weeks later, he found Mrs. Madison as talkative as before but in a more excited state. He thought perhaps she was disturbed by a recent Housing Authority decision to evict a number of families who were said to be troublemakers. Despite her general uneasiness (which was perhaps related to the fact that Simpson began to take notes during the interview), he was made to feel welcome. When he had to leave after two and a half hours, he was pressed to stay and have a beer before he went.

As the interview started, Simpson greeted Timmy, who came over to him, ran his hand over Simpson's face, arms and back, and then grabbed his shirt and began pulling it. His mother told him not to bother the visitor and Timmy moved away. Simpson asked her how Timmy was getting on.

> Well, he was wanting you to get up and go with him somewhere, Lord knows where. He was sleeping there (nodding to the divan) and I guess all my loud talking woke him up. (To the boy) You go on now and play in the back room and let us talk now. (The boy then left the room for a short while.)

> Well, how is he getting on now? I think you said something last time I was here about his going away.

> Yeah, to that place where they take all them bad boys. Doctor said they were going to take him one of these days and try to train him but they haven't done it yet.

At this point Mrs. Madison sat down on the end of her sofa so that she could alternately look at Simpson and out of the window.

> Oh, I worry about him and I am concerned about what is good for him, but I know that God, He will make it come out all right. It could have been worse, he could have been worse —it could have been one of us who was sick—it could have been me—it could have been one of the other kids. He could have been like another boy I saw a while back who was just like him only he couldn't walk—he was in bed all the time. At least we know that Timmy can get up and walk. For a long time we didn't know whether he could do that or not. Still I want to do what is good for him. We ain't doing him no good here, we're not giving him what he really needs.

> Perhaps at the hospital they will be able to do things for him that they couldn't begin to do here.

> Well, that's what I say, they can help him, I don't think I can and yet I want to help him, but I just put it all in the Lord's hands and He will make it come out right.

> Well, how have things been with you?

> Oh, they're about the same. We had two funerals. We had a funeral at the church last Sunday, just a young woman, a mother 29 years old—she died of cancer. One of my boy's teachers died and Harry he tell me last night he said he wants to go to the funeral. We been to the funeral place last night to see the body.

> He must have thought quite a bit of her.

> Oh, he thought she was just fine, he liked her a lot. He come up to me and said he wanted to go to the funeral and I didn't want to go but he did. She been teaching right along. She died only about two or three days ago and she was still teaching up to about a week and a half ago. My boy has another teacher

now, though, to take her place. He say that this new teacher is going to be rough on him. New teacher say, "we're going to buckle down—going to do some work." I say, yeah, I know, I know, that's what they all say at first.

Is the new teacher a man?

No, she is a woman. It would sure be a good thing if he could have a man teacher, that's what he needs, that's what a lot of these boys need is a man teacher but they don't have them.

I've got to go on a diet, I guess. Those diets are hard. The pounds don't come off very easy, but the doctor he tell me I gotta lose some weight. He say I got a bad heart and high blood pressure. He tell me that I'm just gonna have to lose some weight. He sure been after me on that.

The doctor tell me that I was so nervous I was just going to have to lose some weight. I guess I am nervous, I'm getting more nervous all the time. But I tell you the things I see here from my windows, it ain't no wonder I'm nervous. I see some of these children do things that I just never thought I'd see children do. You know I can watch over at that store over there, I see these boys and these children out there just waiting for somebody to come out so they can rob them. Two of them get right out in the middle of the street and lay down, cars have to stop when they are going down the street—just like they want to get themselves killed. I seen 'em take bricks and bang up the side of the cars, break the windows and folks stop and get out and they just go runnin' clear across (the project). Then the police come and they try to chase them and then one of the boys that was doing it point out and say, "They went that way, officer; they went that way." One of the boys that actually did it was tellin' that.

Oh, I tell you it is bad! It's no wonder that I'm nervous. Here, just a week or two ago my 15-year-old boy had some roller skates taken from him by a boy about 17. I done taught my boys that if they ever get in trouble with anyone to get out of it, and if they can't get out of it, then the first thing they do is go to the nearest police box and they calls them, and that's what my boy does. The police come, my boy just happened to recognize this fellow by face, he didn't know him by name, but he knew where he live so the police went up there. My youngest son called me down and I said to Bill, "Bill, what happened?" and he tells me that he knew where he lived but he didn't know his name.

So we went up there and here the boy had already gone home and he changed his clothes and was sitting there watching TV when we got there. He said he hadn't done it, he didn't have any skates anywhere. You know, some of these parents will stick up for their kids whether they are right or wrong, and you know we kinda have a tendency to do that when we are parents. That's what I think happened. Here was this boy, his parents stood by him even though he done somethin' wrong. Well, we went to court with it and they asked my boy a bunch of questions—he couldn't answer them. They got my boy up there and asked him some questions, but he didn't understand and I don't know if they were legal questions or somethin' and my boy didn't understand 'em, he didn't know how to answer 'em. They just threw the case out of court. And the other lady, she had a lawyer. I didn't have a lawyer, I have all I can do to get enough food and clothes for us here. I just didn't have no money for a lawyer.

Did you say Bill didn't get his skates back at all?

No, no, that boy went just free, they threw it out of court.

Well, that's a poor deal, that really is, that's too bad.

Oh, I tell you honey, it's a mean world, it's a mean world, it's a mean world we're living in. Do you know what I heard on the radio just the other day? Did you hear it? They're throwing 88 families out of here. They're given them a notice and told them they gotta move. They don't know where they are going to go or anything, but they gotta move, and it is all because of their kids.

Do you happen to know any of the folks who received one of these notices?

No, I ain't talked to nobody, I just heard it on the radio. . . . If they done them things, I don't care if it is me then I ought to be out of here, and they oughtn't to be in here.

Well, you know I feel a little bit sorry for them myself.

Yeh, well I feel sorry for 'em too, but still if that's what they did they ought to be gone.

Simpson told a story about his son's fighting and said that although parents should try to discipline their kids, he didn't feel that such childish trouble making justifies eviction.

Oh no, honey, I don't think that that is the way it is at all. If peoples was gonna get evicted for what your boy was doing why they would have to clean out almost the whole project here. This is more than that and if these folks' kids were doing what they say then they ought to get out, I don't care if it is even me and my family. That double payment stuff just don't go. I see it down here and I tells my kids that it ain't right. But there are some parents down here that actually tells their kids to beat up on other kids and that double payment is all right, and if they don't beat up on somebody else, somebody else will beat up on them.

Is that right? You mean the parents actually tell their kids to be bullies? Have you ever actually heard a parent tell their kids this?

Well, no, I ain't hear them talking to their kids but they tells me that that is what they tell the kids. I talked to some parents and they say that that is what they tell the kids. They tells the kids to carry a knife or tells them to carry an ice-pick cause if they don't then somebody gonna get them with a knife or an ice-pick so they better have one. I had the parents tell me that that is what they done told the children. But I tell mine that that stuff just ain't right, that don't go. If they get in any trouble, if anybody comes up trying to make trouble with them just back away, they just don't fight. Ain't that right, or do you think that's the way it ought to be? What do you think?

Oh, this is a tough place down here. Like I told you last time, this is a tough place to raise kids. This is no place to raise kids. I'd sure like to get out of here. I like the conveniences, though, and I like the location and these apartments they're just so much better than those slums there across the street. It's just not good for kids. Why, when I moved in here nine years ago these were just the prettiest places I ever did see. They were just fine, they were wonderful and I still think it is a fine place to live, but it's just no place to raise kids. I wish it was possible to get them out of here somehow.

Simpson later learned from the Housing Authority records that this family had been close to model tenants. There had been no rent delinquencies and the yearly household inspection generally specified the condition of the apartment as good. There was a record of contact with the project police on only three occasions, and in two of these the family member was the victim of difficulty rather than the cause. Three years earlier, when Bill was 13 years old, one of the project police officers had lodged a complaint against him for fighting, but apparently the matter was considered too minor to follow up. Later that year Harry, who was then eight, had been returning from the grocery store when he was struck on the head by rocks thrown by two other boys. The boys were identified and the parents agreed to pay Harry's hospital bills; Mrs. Madison agreed not to prosecute because the parents had been cooperative. Later in the same year, Bill complained to the project police that when he was leaving a Boy Scout meeting a group of boys had attacked him for no apparent reason, but he had not been seriously injured and the matter had been dropped. Nevertheless, the idea that the Housing Authority was searching out trouble-makers was disturbing Mrs. Madison, and she must have been even more disturbed when a month later she received a form letter from the Housing Authority, as did all the other tenants. This letter stated in a very sharp way that an effort was being made to clean up some of the difficulties in the project, that over 50 families had been asked to move, and that her building and its occupants were under careful observation to see if there were any tenants who were failing to live up to their responsibilities for continued occupancy. The threat of this letter, that tenants must "shape up" or move out, was missed by few of them.

As this part of the conversation came to a close, Timmy began to interrupt the conversation by pestering the two adults and making a good deal of noise. After some conversations about whether the hospital would be able to help him, Mrs. Madison said:

> Yeh, I suppose, but he is awfully small. Yet he is bigger than that other little boy I saw who can't run or walk at all. For a long time the doctor didn't think this one was going to be able to. It's all because he's got conversation and he's retarded and he has these conversions. (She probably meant convulsions)

> Well, you know, I think they might well be able to do some fine things with him at that Training School.

> Yeh, I think he's a pretty smart boy, he's learning more things all the time. I never did think he would go this far . . . What is this here that you're doing now? Would it be possible for you to help him in some way? Could you get him in there at the hospital?

> Oh, I really wish I could help, but really I can't, I'm a student, just a student from Washington University and like I say we're just going around and talking to people like we're talking here. Me and some others just been doing this. I sure do wish I could help, but I don't know how.

I'm the Old Faithful

> Well, you're doing a fine work, you really are. You are like a missionary, aren't you? I think you're doin' a good thing and God loves what you're doing. It's like me being a missionary in my church. Like I was tellin' you, I go and take people's names, write them down and give them to the Pastor, and when this boy here (Tim) goes into the hospital I just plan to go around assisting people, whoever's sick here in the project. I don't care what church they're from, if they're sick I just want to go and visit with them as a missionary from my church just to show that God loves people. You know God loves you, He loves me, He loves everybody. He loves you just as much as He loves me and He loves me just as much as He loves you, it don't make any difference whether it's white or black or what.

> The preacher calls me the "old faithful." Last Sunday it was "Men and Women's Day" and the women they outdid the men. The women they got $433 and the men they only raised $387.

> Oh, how did you raise all that money?

Well, we just everybody on each side was asked to give $10 and the women made more than the men did. Pastor, he calls me "old faithful." I always try to help out whenever there was a call with one, two or three dollars—whatever I can give. There's been times when I've given the last dollar I had to the church. It makes me feel good to help myself, help my family, and to help other people, and to help God's work. Sometimes I don't have much money but I say, "Lord, this money is going to you, it's yours to use." After all, He give me everything I got. It just makes me feel good to give something back to Him so He can work with it in His church. I'm doing it for Him when I give it to the church. You know, I give 'em the last dollar one day and in a couple of days later it comes back in another way.

You mean every time you give something to God He rewards you in return?

That's right. It comes back to you in another way. If it ain't in dollars it's in some other way real good.
(Pause.)
You know we try to raise money that way because we got 800 people in our church but some of them they're just members, they don't really help out like they should. Like the Pastor said, you may be a church member but that don't make you obedient to God. They're lots of people in church who aren't doing what they should, if they did we wouldn't have to be raising money all the time.
You know for a while there I didn't go to any church at all. I was a member of the church but I didn't go. You know that just ain't right, you get the feelin' that the devil makes you free. When you don't go to church you get the feelin' that you're right and what you're doin' is right but you're all wrong cause it ain't right. That's what I keep tellin' my kids. They ought to go to church. They need to go to church all the time but it is hard to get it through to them. They gotta learn for themselves just like I did, I guess. You know they's lots of people livin' around here they never go to church at all. They just a few people in our church over there and an awful lot of people livin' around here. They don't go on Sundays so they razz me and my kids cause we go to church and that makes them feel bad and they don't want to go, cause they just don't want to be teased. I tell you it's a hard thing to do today.
What a parent should do is to tell their kids what they should do, to be obedient to God. They oughta, like I do, read the Bible with them, get them to read the Bible, go to church all the time. But it's hard to get them to do it. That's what I don't like about it. I wish I could get out. You know what I would like to do? I would like to get down south and look around. Like to take a vacation and go down for a week or a month and just be down south and see how it is there. I feel so

bound up here. That's it, I'm just bound up here all the time. About five years ago I took a vacation and went to Detroit for about a month, but that's no place to go—there's people all bound up there too. I don't want to go to no city. I got folks in Detroit and I got 'em in Chicago.

Mrs. Madison had been looking out of the window. The children were beginning to come home from school, filling up the streets and other people were beginning to drive into the project. After a few minutes, Harry and Nat came into the apartment. They looked at Simpson with curious smiles and walked over to their mother. Mrs. Madison addressed them in a teasing manner. "You better watch yourself now, this here is a policeman —see that pad he got there in his hand, he come down to take you to jail."

In the process of getting acquainted with the boys, Simpson made them paper airplanes to play with and gave Harry some paper because he wanted to draw. Nat asked his mother for money for a Halloween celebration but she refused him, saying that she hardly had enough money for food until the next check came. Nat showed Simpson his collection of trading cards; the vogue at that time was for horror pictures of Frankenstein monsters and the like, each with a caption such as, "My baby sitter" or "You should see me when I'm mad." The discussion of drawing brought George into the conversation. George showed his school notebook, which contained many pictures of animals and a strong man called Hercules. Each of the animals was named for one of George's friends; for example, the shark was named David because, George said, David was "a strong one." Simpson was impressed by the talent the pictures showed, and thought at first that George had traced them, but George explained that he drew them free hand.

The last to arrive was the oldest son, Paul, who had stopped by for a visit after work. The three adults began to talk among themselves while the children played. Finally, Nat asked, "Are you really a policeman?" Simpson laughed and said, "No, aw no, I'm no policeman; I was just joshing you. What do you call it when somebody is putting you on?"

Bill said, "Pulling your leg."

"That's what I was doing, I was pulling your leg."

I Can't See That Marriage Nohow

> *Paul:* Well, what is your job?
>
> *Simpson:* Well, I'm just a student going to school, not a social worker or nothin' like that. There are just a bunch of us, about ten of us, who are students who are just interested in knowing more about family life so we're just going around talking to people, just about anything, just like I've been talking with you all today.
>
> *Paul:* (Smiling) Well, it sounds like a good job to me. The thing that gets me about this place is that it's so rough around here. It just ain't this way out there where I live.
>
> *Simpson:* Where's that?

Paul: Oh, it's out on Washington.

Simpson: Oh, what direction is that? I'm just new in town.

Paul: It's out west aways. We just don't have this kind of stuff out there. You know there's lots of men around that don't have no work. There's lots of unemployment, and I'm all for this not having any overtime—that way they got more jobs for people.

Simpson: Oh, is that right? You mean you can't work an overtime now?

Paul: You get a 40 hour week and nobody can work overtime in these big building jobs, in that way you gotta' give more jobs to more people. I'm all for that.

Mrs. Madison: Another thing they ought to do is to take all these machines and throw them away. These machines are doing the work of men.

Paul: Yeah, but they gotta have those machines, they can't do the work; they gotta have those machines.

Mrs. Madison: Aw, they'd put more men to work if they would do away with all that machinery. They could put more men to work and there'd be more jobs.

Paul: Yeah, this employment is a pretty bad thing. There's lots of men around here that don't have a job but they got big families. How's a man going to feed his family if he can't get any work? I just can't see this marriage stuff. I can see livin' with a woman, but I don't go for this marryin'. If she wants to be with ya, that's all right, but you get that name down there on the paper, boy, that's bad. She can leave you and you gotta pay her a bunch of money and you don't make enough. I like to keep all mine, I can do with it what I want.

Mrs. Madison: Well, that's right, but you know some people can save more money when they're married than when they're single. When they're single it just all seems to go somewhere.

Simpson: You know, I seem to be saving more money now than before I was married.

Mrs. Madison: You speaks the truth there, honey. Yeah, I've been separated from my husband about twelve years. All he did was just to sit around and drink whiskey and beer. He just never was no count.

Paul: Well, when you get married there just isn't any more love. Love goes when you get married. She's got you hooked down there on a piece of paper and you can't go out or nothing. She's really got ya when you got that marriage paper. But if you don't have that why she gotta stay on her toes cause she knows if she don't you are going to go out and get someone else, and that's what keeps love goin'. That married thing, it takes away the love. I sure don't want none of that for me.

Mrs. Madison: Well, I tell you one thing. When a woman gets married she ought to be in the home. She shouldn't be out there workin', she should be with her children at home and the husband he oughta be out makin' a livin', bringing the money home. That's what makes a family work, now don't it? Now is that right?

Simpson: Well I just don't know if I can answer that, really I just don't know. You see in my family my wife works half the time and she's home half the time, so we just don't have an answer to that one.

Mrs. Madison: Well that's a good deal, you say she's home half the time with the kids and the other half time she works?

Simpson: That's right.

Mrs. Madison: Well, O.K., that's fine. I would like to have somethin' like that myself if I could, if it weren't for young Tim. You'd be home half the time and you'd be working half the time.

Paul: I can't see that marriage no how.

Nigger Is Just A Word

Simpson returned for a visit after a few months' absence, and on this occasion he tried to explain more carefully to Mrs. Madison his purpose, since she insisted on treating him as a kind of "visiting missionary." He explained that the field workers in the project were interested in getting to know the people and to understand their lives. He emphasized again that they were in no way connected with the agencies that operated in the area and that they were not church people. This still sounded like a missionary to Mrs. Madison. "Well, I know, you're kinda like missionaries. You know there are a lot of people down here that are real lonely and they need people to go around and talk to them and when people talk to them, it makes them feel better. It makes them feel not so lonely." Simpson gave up trying to dissuade her from this notion, because each time he tried to explain further she replied by saying, "Yes, I know, it's like a missionary." In any case, she said, she was happy to have him visit as often as he wanted, but she would appreciate it if he would call before he came, because once Timmy was admitted to the training school she might be there visiting him. Simpson felt that she wanted him to call because she wanted to clean the apartment and dress up for his visits.

Mrs. Madison explained that Timmy was getting her down, that she couldn't work or do anything because of him. Simpson asked if she planned to work once Timmy was in the hospital and she replied,

Well, I like work. I used to work, but I can't do it now even though Timmy would be in the hospital. You see, I got all my kids and I got to be with them. I don't want them running around and getting in trouble. I want to be around taking care of them. I think I ought to watch after my children. That's the main thing. I like to work, but even if it weren't for the chil-

> dren, I couldn't because I got these nerves. I'm so nervous and then also I got a bad heart and the doctor says I couldn't work.

The interview was interrupted by the arrival of the children from school. They were much intrigued with Simpson's tape recorder and organized first an impromptu interview of their own and then a show.

> *Nat:* Harry, what is your school teacher's name?
> *Harry:* You know, Miss Mathews.
> *Nat:* Is she mean?
> *Harry:* No.
> *Nat:* Is she nice?
> *Harry:* Yeah.
> *Nat:* Do your teachers fuss at you all the time?
> *Harry:* Uh, uh.
> *Bill:* (In the background) Miss Smith does.
> *Nat:* Tell us about Miss Smith, is she good or mean?
> *Bill:* A little in-between. (All laugh.)
> *Nat:* Now, Bill, Miss Smith ain't that bad, is she? (All laugh.)
> *Bill:* Just about!

After Simpson replayed their interview session for them, they decided to sing. Harry sang, "Oh, How I love Jesus," but Nat and Bill managed to drown him out with their rendition of "I Wanna Hold Your Hand." Finally Harry was allowed to sing, "Oh, How I Love Jesus," first in a very somber way and then jazzing it up a bit. By the time he finished almost all the children had joined in. Ophelia sang, "Jesus Loves Me This I know," starting off as Harry did in a rather somber way and then beginning to jazz up the hymn. Toward the end Bill joined in, but then he and Nat drowned her out by singing, "I Wanna Hold Your Hand" again.

As she finished, Nat and Bill started to sing a blues song, but Mrs. Madison interrupted, saying, "You ain't gonna sing no blues, are you? That's bad stuff. Blues aren't for church people to sing." A neighbor woman who had come into the apartment just as the singing started chimed in, "Yeah, you don't wanna sing them blues, they're no good." Bill encouraged Nat to sing some blues but finally Nat refused, repeating several times, "I ain't gonna sing no blues." Instead he concluded the performance by telling a long and rather involved story about a little boy who had two dogs and got treed by a bear while his mother and father were away. He called his two dogs to chase the bear away long enough for him to escape into the house, lock all the doors and go to sleep.

Simpson's contacts with the family so far suggested that the Madison children were not greatly involved in the usual activities of the project peer group which so often led pre-adolescent children into trouble of one kind or another. The churchiness which their mother emphasized again and again seemed to have some effect on them, although the older children resented having to go to church. Bill would not sing blues when his mother told him not to, and in his story the little boy who was the hero got into trouble when he went out, had to be rescued, and then retreated rapidly to his house.

This aloofness from the peer group did not seem to be maintained only when their mother was around to admonish them. The boys seemed to be more interested in "respectable" activities (as at school) than in the usual project activities. For example, about a week later, the boys talked about what they wanted to be when they grew up. Nat and Harry wanted to be firemen. They had taken the trouble to talk to some firemen in the neighborhood to find out how they might realize their ambition, and they had learned that one needed to finish high school and perhaps college, although there was some doubt on that score. Nat observed that he had once wanted to be a policeman but had changed his mind. The problem with being a policeman was that it was dangerous and "the boys be against the police more than the fireman." He thought it wouldn't be bad to be a detective, but you had to be a "uniformed" policeman before you could become a detective. Also, he thought he would like to be active in the church when he grew up, "be a secretary, or play the piano, or sing." He had thought of being a doctor, but that "scared" him because you had to operate on people and see them die.

A couple of weeks later, Simpson met Paul standing in the building breezeway looking out on the project grounds. It was a very windy spring day and as they stood watching, an especially heavy gust of wind came through the project grounds in which they could see several hundred pieces of paper blowing around. Paul observed, "Look at that. I just can't understand it. I can't see why people can't keep things up down here. Look at all them papers blowing around. It don't have to be that way. I work out at the west end and out there today the wind was blowing but all the paper was picked up and there wasn't any stuff like that blowing around."

Simpson said that there were many more people living in a small area here and perhaps that made the difference, but Paul replied,

> Naw, people just don't care down here. They do care out west, though. And the people are friendlier out there, too. I get invited into white people's homes to sit down and drink beer with them and they are all friendly. Down here, somebody's always getting mad. Somebody calls them a nigger and they get mad. I don't know why they get mad, it's just a word. A man will call his buddy a nigger and he don't do nothing, but then some white fellow comes along and calls some of these guys a nigger and they get mad. It's the same word, it don't make sense.

Simpson said that he could understand why it would make a guy mad, Paul stuck to his point:

> It's just a word. One man uses it and it doesn't make you mad, and it shouldn't make you mad when another guy uses it. It's

just a word like any other word. You know I work at this store
out west and every once in a while some white man who's had
a lot to drink will call some of us nigger and it will sure make
some of the boys mad, and we can use the same word between
each other and it don't make no difference.

The Devil's Got Them

When Simpson went to visit the Madisons a couple of months later, he
met eight-year-old Mark walking toward Jefferson Avenue. Mark asked
Simpson to help him get a cab for Mr. Sawyer, a man in his late twenties
who was in charge of a youth organization sponsored by a local newspaper
and a church group. The Madison household, Simpson learned, had become one of the main centers for this youth group and all of the sons were
active in it.

When Simpson entered he was struck by how much more orderly the
apartment was than on his previous visits. In addition, he found Mrs.
Madison better dressed. It seemed to him that not having to cope with
Timmy's disorganizing behavior made it possible for Mrs. Madison to
present herself and her apartment more consistently with her insistent
respectability.

Simpson discovered the boys busily involved in making preparations
for a coming hike and overnight campout at a nearby park. The Madison
boys and several others were in the apartment checking over their equipment and preparing to buy food to put in their knapsacks. They were
going to start their hike to the park (a distance of four or five miles) at
10:00 that night. Mrs. Madison was pleased that the boys were involved in
organized and supervised youth activities, although she still worried about
them. She told Simpson that George, who was by then 14 years old, had
been beaten up by a group of boys the day before. This led to a discussion
of fighting in which Mrs. Madison's strong desire to avoid conflict was
made explicit.

> *Mrs. Madison:* I don't know about these boys, I worry about
> them. George there got beat up yesterday when he was with
> this group.
> *Simpson:* (to George) What does she mean?
> *George:* Well we were comin' out of these big high weeds, see,
> and a bunch of these boys started chasin' us and they got me
> (he laughed). There was this bunch of guys that threw a
> rock at us. The rest of our guys didn't say anything but I
> told them, "Don't you hit me with that rock." Well, they
> started chasin' us and one of the little guys was fallin' be-
> hind and he dropped the canteen so I want back to get it and
> I got it and they came up on me. I started runnin' and I got
> to the street and these cars came along and I couldn't get
> across. I had to wait for the cars or I'd a made it but they
> caught up with me (he laughed.)

Mrs. Madison: I sure do worry about them.

Simpson: (Noting a friend of Harry's listening raptly to George's story) Are you going on the trip tonight?

Friend: (With sad face.) No sir, I'm not.

Mrs. Madison: His parents won't let him go. I don't like to let mine go but there's nothing I can do about it. I give 'em up to God and know that he will take care of them all right. If they'll just trust in God, well they'll be all right. George here, he should have been like the rest of 'em; when those boys threw the rock he shouldn't have said anything. He should have just walked away.

Simpson: George, I've got a question I'd like to ask you about fighting. A fella told me the other day something about fighting that I hadn't heard before and I want you to tell me if it's right. He says if one fella is out with a bunch of his buddies and he gets mad at some other guy and then he goes and tries to start a fight with this other guy and the other guy won't fight, he just kind of backs away and says, O.K., brother, I don't want to cause any trouble and he won't fight. Well, this fella was telling me that the guy that says he'll start the fight and wasn't able to start it was the loser. Is that right?

George: (Smiling.) Naw, I don't think so. I think the guy that turned away was the loser.

Mrs. Madison: No, that boy was right. He was right. The one who was the winner was the one that could turn away. It takes a lot of courage to turn away from a fight but if you trust in God and then you turn away, why He'll take care of you. Why if that boy that was startin' a fight had raised his hand and he was gonna hit the other one, if the other one would have put his trust in God and just turned around and walked away then God would have protected him. Course I know that there are some people who turn away and they get hit in the back or they been cut down from behind. I don't know what happened there, but I do know if they had put their trust in God and had faith in Him and turned away, why He would take care of them and would protect them.

George: Naw, I think the guy that walked away was the loser.

Mrs. Madison: You see, Mr. Simpson, they go to Sunday School every week but they got the wrong idea.

Bill: But I don't think that's right, Ann. I don't believe that. You make me go to church but I don't want to. I'm not gonna confess myself and if I don't believe it I don't think you ought to make me go. I don't think it's right.

Mrs. Madison: You hear the way he talks?

Simpson: You know Pastor Jones told me that if a person didn't feel like he needed something that it was a waste of time for him to come to church.

> *Mrs. Madison:* Well, you've got to feel that you need God. If you don't then the devil's got you for sure.
>
> *Bill:* You see, Ann, you shouldn't make me go to church. You just make me go because you had to go when you were a kid.

Bill retreated to the stove in the kitchen saying rather sullenly that he still didn't think it was right. George had been laughing uproariously over this exchange, and he let Mrs. Madison know that he felt the same way that Bill did. Mrs. Madison had become quite nervous during the exchange and snapped at the children with greater severity than was customary. She seemed to recognize this by saying at one point, "You see how nervous they make me. I just can't do anything with them, the devil's got them."

As the boys continued their preparations, Harry told his mother that he would need money for food. His mother replied, "If you want some money you'd better be calling your father. In fact, I could use some money, too." While Harry called his father she explained to Simpson that their father had been giving the children the money they needed for dues and equipment for the youth organization. Bill asked his mother if she needed money and began moving toward the door as if to go to get some. She replied, "Yes, I need some money, but don't you go get me any stolen money now. I don't want none of that." Bill was gone for two or three minutes and returned with a dollar bill. George explained that Bill had friends in the building who had given it to him, but Mrs. Madison continued to be concerned: "I'll take some if it isn't stolen." Then turning to Simpson she commented again, "These boys sure do make me nervous."

Then God Gave Me Timmy

In a subsequent conversation, Mrs. Madison reverted to the problem of church-going.

> You know, Bill Jr. the other day said that I was makin' him go to church because I had to go to church, but I'm just trying to see to it that they respects God, they have faith. And you know we can go on thinkin' that we don't have any need for God and lots of people don't think that they have a need for God, things are goin' all right for 'em so they're just not gonna go to church. They wants things the way they want them and not the way God wants them.
>
> When I moved to St. Louis I stopped going to church. You know some people can just fall away from the church, not think it's important to them and just quit comin'. They can't see any need of God. They don't have faith and they don't think that they need grace and they just, they can be good people but they just live their lives not doin' what God wants 'em to but doin' what they want to. You know I had a woman who was a friend of mine once and I was visiting her in the hospital. She was a nice woman but she liked the night life like some people do and she was always havin' parties on the

weekend and she'd get sick and off she'd go. She'd be sent away and then God would bring her back again and then when He brought her back why then on the weekend she would have some more parties and pretty soon she'd get sick and off they'd take her away again. Then God would bring her back, take her away up to the hospital and then God would bring her back. That's just the way she lived her life. She was doin' what she wanted to and she'd get sick and they'd take her away and God would make her well and bring her back and then she'd go her own way instead of doin' what God wanted her to do.

I remember one night I was up visiting her in the hospital and she was real sick. I was rubbing her feet for her and then she asked me for some water and I propped her head up and gave her some water. Lord, I was actin' just like a nurse. I don't know what they'd done to me if they'd seen me (grins). I remember her telling me this: She said, 'Ann, if I ever get back again, if God brings me out of this I'm gonna do what he wants. I'm gonna go to church.' But God didn't bring her back that time. She never did leave the hospital. You know she had a sickness just like mine. She had heart trouble, high blood pressure. She had kidney trouble and she was too fat.

That must have been a difficult experience for you.

Yes, it sure was. She didn't have faith and she had all those chances and she never took them. You got to live by faith, do what God wants you to do.

Well, what was it that finally convinced you that you had to get back in the church again?

Well, like I said, it was this friend of mine that died. She was just like me and here she ran out of chances and I thought some day I was gonna run out of chances too, so I wanted to do something about it. And another thing, there's Timmy. God gave me Timmy, and God doesn't give you things like this without some kind of a reason. God gave him to me and I was to take care of him and I took care of him and then I let him go to the hospital and I gave him back to God. God gave him to me and now I give him back to God and I hope and pray that some day Timmy will get well and he'll come back. I know there was a woman I knew that lived here. She went to the hospital out there, I didn't even know she was gone. She got well, she came back. I hope some day that God will do that for Timmy.

Does God want you to do anything now in relation to Timmy?

Yes, He wants me to visit him like I do, to go out and visit him. You know one woman was tellin' me out there that there are lots of people that bring their children out there and never come back to see them and it's true on both sides. That's true on both sides, both colored and white.

You did all you possibly could for him, Annette.

That's right, and now I've given him up to God and I hope that I've left him with Him. You know I love Timmy, I loved Timmy and done more for him than I've done for these other children. I think maybe I've loved him more than them because he was the way he was, he couldn't help it.

Everything's Going Too Fast

The next evening Mrs. Madison, sounding quite distraught, called Simpson at his home. She had learned from a friend who worked at the home where Timmy was staying that he had been transferred to a general hospital. Mrs. Madison was very concerned and frightened about Timmy, for apparently he had been in the hospital eight days and no one had informed her. Simpson picked her up early the next afternoon and took her to the hospital, where, after a frustrating series of encounters with the hospital personnel, they finally found their way to Timmy's room. There they found him tied in bed in such a way that he could move around but could not crawl out. Timmy was ecstatic at their arrival and soon he was laughing with delight as his mother played with him. Although he was in the hospital, he looked very healthy, and they learned that he had gained almost five pounds in the eight days he had been there. His mother commented, "He's really somethin' else today, isn't he? He is one happy child!"

Reassured that Timmy wasn't seriously ill, Mrs. Madison then asked the nurse why he had been brought there. The nurse did not know and sent Mrs. Madison off to find the doctor. Simpson and Bill were sent outside, because only parents and grandparents were allowed to visit. Mrs. Madison tried unsuccessfully to have Simpson granted permission to visit since Timmy had no grandparents; she was also unsuccessful in finding the doctor on that visit, so she did not learn the reason for Timmy's hospitalization. But she was much reassured, commenting as they drove back to the project, "Oh, he looked fine to me. He is a happy baby. He even gained four pounds." She was still concerned that there was something they were not telling her, although perhaps she was just as happy not to know the details. She observed, "Well, I don't know why they didn't tell me about it. I know sometimes they won't tell people what's wrong with a loved one if they're sick themselves. You know I've got high blood pressure and I've got this heart condition and maybe they don't want to tell me, thinking that it might not be good for me, but I sure wish they would."

The next time Simpson visited the Madisons, about a month later, he found the apartment in the same state of disorder that he had been used to earlier. Now it became apparent that the neatness of the apartment and Mrs. Madison's dress on the previous occasions were due to Mr. Sawyer's presence. Simpson also noticed that Mrs. Madison had added a good deal to her already substantial weight since Timmy had gone into the hospital.

After apologizing for the state of the apartment, Mrs. Madison said, I just can't seem to get things done like I used to when I had to take care of Timmy. I just sort of sit around and think about things and don't do nothing'. I've got this high blood pressure and the doctor tells me to take it easy but then when I take it easy I just start worrying.

What do you worry about?

Well, I can't seem to handle my children, my older boys. Bill, he's getting too big, I can't take care of him. My children know that I'm not well and they help out and try to think of me but it just seems that there are times when they've just got to have their way. You know when my children go out they stay out so late at night, the older ones, and when I tell them that I want them to be in say by 10:30 or 11:00 I want them to come in then but Bill, he wants to stay out later. He comes in at 1:00 or 2:00 and I don't particularly like the friends he's keeping that causes him to stay out that late. I don't know what he's doing or who his friends are but I'm afraid he's going to get into some trouble and I can't handle him. He won't listen to me. He thinks he's grown up already. He thinks he knows as much as anybody else.

How about Bill's father? Can he talk to him?

Yeah, he's talked to him, tried to tell him these things but (here she laughed despairingly) he won't listen to him. I've just got to have faith in God that He'll take care of him. If I didn't have faith I don't know what I would do. I don't think I could handle it. You've just got to trust in Him.

Does Mr. Sawyer have any influence over Bill?

Oh, Mr. Sawyer has tried but Bill won't listen to him either. He said he wanted to quit Mr. Sawyer's group and I asked him why and he said well, Mr. Sawyer had made him some promises, made the rest of the boys some promises, and he didn't keep them, and I told him that Mr. Sawyer was doing the best that he could and sometimes it takes longer to make your promises good than you think, but he's gone ahead and quit and I think George is not wanting to continue with the group either.

Has George been giving you any worry?

No, George, he behaves pretty good. Sometimes he doesn't do what he's told but most of the time he's good. . . . You know, Mr. Simpson, I sit up here thinking about things—how easy it would be for me to die, I could have been dead long ago. I think God is keeping me alive for some kind of a purpose. I don't know what it is. I trust in Him. I think we're getting near the end. We're getting to the last days, they're coming on us. Don't you think so?

Well, I don't know. What do you mean by the last days, Annette?

Well, it's just everything's going too fast. Things change so much. Our lives are so complex and difficult and they're so out of control. I think that judgment is coming. That's what I mean."

Well, I'm sure there are many people, Annette, that have the feeling that things aren't just right with them. I know there are a lot of things about my life that I would like to be better and I worry about my children too.

"Yes, but you see I can't control my children. I'm sick and they're getting old where I can't handle them and it seems so hopeless at times. Oh, I don't think that you could understand . . .

5.
Daily Life in Pruitt-Igoe

The Madison family provides a clear focus on the mundane aspects of daily family life in Pruitt-Igoe—the round of daily routine, relationships with relatives, friends and neighbors, keeping house, and the style of life which these activities express. Within the context of the ordinariness of these activities exists also the extraordinariness of striving to make a life in the context of deprivation and social danger which characterizes this environment.

The interviews with Mrs. Madison centered on the ordinary because of her adeptness at impression management which proved a constant frustration to Simpson. He was unable to get biographical information to learn about the three men who fathered her children, or about how she coped with the pressures of her life before religion became its central non-family focus a few years earlier. However, the Housing Authority records and the implicit testimony of her children suggest that whatever may have been her involvement in less "respectable" activities during those years, it was quite discreet. The Housing Authority records reveal not a single complaint against her, and only a single complaint against one of the eight children who had lived with her in the apartment. Similarly, her children never seemed to reproach her for unrespectable behavior. They accepted her as she presented herself to the world, as a godly churchwoman. Even when they felt restive about her insistence that they go to church and her anxiety that they would get into trouble outside, they did not reproach her or try to unmask the way she presented herself to the world.

For all the apparent calmness of her days, she seemed to feel that her family was continually on the edge of a precipice and that the children were always in danger of falling into bad behavior. Considering the range of seductions that are available to a child growing up in the project, it is remarkable that her children seemed by-and-large content to devote themselves to the respectable activities of school, family-centered play, and the definitely "square" youth group which Mr. Sawyer organized over the summer. Because the oldest son, Paul, was an adult and had a steady job, Mrs. Madison could tolerate the fact that he drank in moderation and that he had a girl friend with whom he spent time in the project, but sixteen-year-old Bill concerned her greatly. She had the pervasive anxiety of mothers in the project that Bill was getting involved with bad company and that his friends would lead him astray. She knew that as the children got older her ability to influence them lessened.

She longed deeply for a life of peace and quiet, but it constantly eluded her. When she attended to her older children and their growing up she was forced to examine anxiously the very real possibility that she couldn't "handle" them and that they might get into trouble. When she turned for solace to religion and the church she also seemed to become anxious. Exactly why is not clear, but she may have regarded as dangerous the emotions which full participation in the expressive life of the church ("getting happy") aroused in her. Thus she was left hanging somewhere in between, displaying a kind of obsessive elaboration of the necessity of placing her trust in God. She hoped against hope that He would neither fail her nor try her faith any more demandingly than He already had.

The bind in which she found herself pushed her inevitably to thoughts of death—"I sit up here thinking about how easy it would be for me to die; I could have been dead long ago . . . I think we're getting near to the end. We're getting to the last days; they're coming on us." She feared that "the judgment is coming" to her for the way she had lived her life and the way she had raised her children. But with judgment comes death, and she would then no longer have to worry as she did—about her own moral status, about Timmy, about how Bill and the others would turn out.

Keeping to Home

As we have seen, Pruitt-Igoeans are ambivalent about their fellow tenants. They give them credit for trying to make a decent life even as they themselves are doing; yet they have a low opinion of others' ability to accomplish this, or to avoid making trouble even with the best of intentions. This sense of alienation from others in the community was apparent in even the most casual conversations about the project. It also stood out in the responses to survey questions which asked how much the respondents thought they had in common with the other people living in Pruitt-Igoe: only one-fourth of the respondents felt they had "quite a bit" or "a lot" in common with their neighbors. Further, when they were asked to contrast the people in Pruitt-Igoe with those in the neighborhoods in which they lived before, fewer than one-fourth felt that they had more in common with people in the project than with their former neighbors; 40 per cent indicated they had more in common with their former neighbors, and the rest saw no difference. Similarly, almost half the respondents said that their previous neighbors were friendlier than people in Pruitt-Igoe, and only 11 per cent saw their Pruitt-Igoe neighbors as friendlier. These views are striking, given the fact that Pruitt-Igoe residents typically came from the worst slums in the St. Louis area and not from neighborhoods that had any traditions of stable community life.

These dim views of the project community encourage people to keep to themselves, and relations with others there always have a tentative and ambivalent quality. Women particularly find themselves confined to their apartments, by their responsibilities for numerous children and for keeping the house operating, and because of their suspicion of those outside. In this respect Pruitt-Igoe women are much like other lower class housewives—white and Negro—who generally lead rather isolated lives.[1] In Pruitt-Igoe half the women say they get away from their apartments for an hour or more no more often than twice a week. Similarly, half say that they do not leave the apartment for an evening out even as often as once a week. On the average, Pruitt-Igoe women estimate that they spend no more than ten hours a week outside the apartment, including all shopping activities, visiting and, for some, work. Men, however, spend a good deal of time away from the apartment, whether they work or not; they average over 60 hours a week away from home. Seventy per cent go out for an evening at least once a week and half of them have an evening out at least twice a week. When the men do not work, they still manage to organize other projects that take them into the larger world. They seldom have the sense of confinement that the women continually express. Also, the men range more widely into the larger community than the women; when the women leave their apartments, they stay fairly close to the project area, whereas the men venture farther for work and entertainment.

Keeping House in Pruitt-Igoe

However much their situations depart from those of ordinary, conventional American families, the women of Pruitt-Igoe are bound up in the quite ordinary role of housewife. Their daily routines have much in common with those of more fortunately situated stable working class and lower-middle class housewives across the country.[2] Despite the fact that their milieu is strikingly different, the women see themselves as carrying out all the quite ordinary responsibilities that go with the housewife role —seeing to the maintenance of the household, the preparation of food, caring for the children. Once they settle down as wives and mothers, they consider their *raison d'être* to be the maintenance of a home for whomever at any given time is defined as of their family. As the composition of that family changes through time with the arrival and departure of husbands, children, and perhaps grandchildren, the woman knows and takes for granted, and finds that others know and take for granted, that she is the

1. See Rainwater, Coleman and Handel (1959) and Rainwater (1960).
2. See Komarovsky (1964) and Rainwater, Coleman and Handel (1959).

head of the family. Her worth as a person will be evaluated on the basis of her persistence in housing and caring for that family. She will do this at least until all of her children are grown, until all of her daughters become homemakers and all of her sons leave home.

As in the lower and working class everywhere, these responsibilities are highly confining for the women of Pruitt-Igoe. The confining nature of their role is exacerbated for most Pruitt-Igoe women because they have large families or no husbands or both, so they must carry the responsibilities for maintaining the household alone. Even when the woman who heads a household is able to train her children to do part of the work, her burden of responsibility is not appreciably lightened, because she must still supervise the children at their household tasks. Eighty per cent of the households in our survey included children who were given the responsibility on occasion of cleaning up the apartment, usually when the children were between seven and eight years of age. Similarly, two-thirds of the households had children who could be delegated to get the mail from the mail boxes downstairs, or to go to the store to buy groceries; these responsibilities could be assigned to children when they got to be nine or ten years old.

Most stable working and lower middle class housewives share many of these structural difficulties of the homemaker role, but Pruitt-Igoe women find less gratification in that role because they have fewer resources with which to create a comfortable home and to express their own identities. There is an instrumental discrepancy between the demands of their role and their resources for meeting those demands.[3] It should be obvious, but often it is ignored, that it is very difficult to be a good homemaker with little money, particularly when one's relatives are equally poor. Typically, almost all the monthly income of an ADC mother will go to pay for rent and food, and it is a struggle to meet the needs of the children for clothes, particularly shoes. What is left over provides almost nothing with which to perfect the home as the comfortable, cozy place that is the standard for the working class. These women must be energetic and imaginative in seeking charity or conning boyfriends or in other ways putting together the bare necessities of furniture—beds, a few chairs, a table. Once that is done, furnishing is likely to be regarded as finished because one cannot count on improvement.

The other major interference with possible gratifications in the homemaker role comes from the competition of the more exciting street life. For both the children and the husband there are always interesting things to do and see outside. With her meager financial resources and her own uncertainties about her ability to provide more than bare shelter and subsistence, the homemaker is in a poor situation to compete with that outside world for their loyalty. Though a woman may be the *de facto* leader

---

3. See Spiegel (1960) for a discussion of "instrumental discrepancy" as a factor in role conflict within the family. The following section is condensed from a somewhat more extended discussion in Rainwater (1966).

of her home, she is often a leader without much honor from her own family. She is depended upon for all the forms of subsistence, but often ignored by her children and husband. She has only her persistence in adversity to offer, her ability to keep the family's head barely above water. These are virtues suitable for sentimental, retrospective admiration, but they seem to earn these women relatively little in their day-to-day struggle for recognition as competent and authoritative homemakers, mothers, and wives.

Some unsympathetic observers of the ghetto have pointed with derision at the conspicuous presence of a few expensive objects amid the barren decor which the skimpy resources of ghetto residence permits. When television was still new enough not to be taken completely for granted, the presence of television sets in the homes of mothers on welfare often was taken as a token of irresponsible and spendthrift attitudes. In fact, over 95 per cent of the households sampled in our 1965 survey had television sets, almost all of them operable. It is even more striking that 68 per cent of the households had telephones, and of these, 62 per cent had either color telephones or princess telephones despite the fact that such phones cost more money. But they are colorful and "nice" and enliven what is often otherwise a rather barren decor. Other objects that serve to deny the pervasive sense of bare existence are expensive hi-fi sets. These are found only in a small proportion of the households, but a majority of the homes in Pruitt-Igoe have at least one such special object. Some few families, by virtue of greater resources or strategic gifts from relatives or boyfriends, do manage to put together dwellings that are sumptuous by lower class standards, but these are striking exceptions to the general rule.

Most homemakers manage to maintain reasonable orderliness and neatness in their apartments. At the beginning of our study, the field workers were struck by the dirtiness and disorganization of some of the households, but as time went on, it became apparent these, too, were exceptions, involving families that were extraordinarily disorganized. As the field workers became accustomed to the poverty characterizing almost all the homes in the project, they came to see that within the limits of what was available to them, all but a minority of the homemakers kept reasonably orderly and clean households. Thus, for example, the field workers, all of whom had been in the project for at least a year, in the 1965 survey rated only 18 per cent of the apartments as messy or poorly kept and only 11 per cent as dirty. For the homemaker to maintain her home at this level requires a great deal of effort, particularly because she cannot afford many cleaning aids and labor-saving devices. Intensive observation of some families suggests that the degree of order and cleanliness is related to the degree to which the female head feels pressed by interpersonal tensions and psychic conflicts. Some homes were observed to be highly disorganized for several months while the homemaker was going through some particularly difficult situation; when these difficulties were resolved, the household was maintained better.

In addition to the pressures that stem from her marginal economic position and from the internal difficulties that may be experienced within the family, the Pruitt-Igoe homemaker also must contend with the fact that she lives in a milieu that she and everyone else perceives as dangerous and threatening. The threats are both physical—the ever-present possibility of physical attack or of theft or destruction of property—and moral, in the sense that her "respectability" and that of her family are constantly threatened by the possibilities of the seduction of her spouse, herself, or her children into the "immorality" of the streets.

By their own report in the 1965 survey, a significant minority of families had been involved in these kinds of threatening experiences. For example, 41 per cent of the households reported that something had been stolen from them since they moved into the project; 35 per cent said someone in the family had been hurt by bottles or other objects dropped out of windows onto the walkways outside; 39 per cent said some adult in the family had been "insulted" by teenagers cursing them outdoors; and 51 per cent said their windows had been broken from outside. In addition, 16 per cent of the women reported rapes or attempted rapes of a female in the family; 10 per cent reported that someone in the family had been held up; and 20 per cent reported cutting, shooting, or other kinds of physical assaults. These were all situations in which the family members affected were defined as victims, but in addition, other threatening situations involved family members as initiators or equal participants. One-fifth of the families reported adult quarrels and arguments with neighbors and one-fifth reported teenage fights involving family members. These are the environmental potentialities which each homemaker in Pruitt-Igoe must take into account as she goes about the daily tasks of maintaining a household and rearing her children.

It is little wonder, then, that for most of the mature, settled women in the project, daily life is both tense and depressing. A depressive tone runs through their days, relieved only on occasion by an especially enjoyable or gratifying event. As the women (and to some extent the men) mature and settle into roles as parents and householders, they may give up enthusiastic participation in the more expressive street activities, partly because the young have a competitive advantage there and partly because accumulated experience warns them of danger. Instead, they sharply confine their activities to their homes and often give the observer the feeling that they simply live from day to day. This is most clearly manifest in our survey results in a set of responses which suggests the widespread prevalence of a complex of subjective experiences that blend feelings of sadness, nervousness, and purposelessness. Table 5-1 presents the proportion of men and women who agreed or disagreed with a series of questions designed to tap these feelings.

Along with these subjective feelings often go complaints about physical illness and disability. Obviously the interaction between psychic and or-

Table 5–1

Perceived Depressive Feelings

	Men (N = 45)			Women (N = 115)		
	Very Much	A Little	Total Agree	Very Much	A Little	Total Agree
			per cent			
Many mornings I wake up so tired I don't feel like doing much of anything (agree)	54	24	78	68	19	87
I often have days when I feel nervous and jumpy (agree)	38	32	70	62	25	87
Sometimes it's hard to keep my mind on the things I need to do (agree)	38	36	74	48	33	81
I often feel down in the dumps and blue about life (agree)	22	40	62	38	30	68
When I wake up in the morning, I feel full of pep, ready and raring to go (disagree)	16	20	36	35	27	62

ganic causes for these complaints is extremely complex. The fact that when men and women mention their physical complaints it is often coupled with the idea of nervousness ("nervous stomach," "nerves and high blood pressure") suggests a strong tendency to somaticize psychic tensions. In any case, there were few families observed for any length of time in which one or another member did not complain of a physically debilitating illness, and when asked in our 1965 survey whether they had any illnesses, or injuries, or chronic long-lasting conditions that bother them, 37 per cent of the men and 50 per cent of the women said they did. Two-thirds of these responded affirmatively when asked whether their condition interfered much with their lives. These results are consistent with responses to another survey question which asked for agreement or disagreement with the statement: "I get sick fairly often and can't do my work." To this, 34 per cent of the men and 45 per cent of the women agreed.

The interfering conditions listed by the respondents cover a wide range, the most common being muscle and bone disabilities (crippled, rheumatism), heart and circulatory problems, and afflictions of the stomach and lower intestinal tract. All of these were mentioned by more than a quarter of those who have conditions that bother them. It is of particular interest that nervous disorders of one kind or another, whether coupled with somatic complaints or not, were mentioned by a quarter of the women who were troubled by illness but by only 14 per cent of the men. Because a significant proportion of the adult men living in Pruitt-Igoe are receiving physical disability pensions, it is perhaps not surprising that as many as 37 per cent have complaints. They are probably not as representative of lower-class Negro men generally as are the women, few of whom receive disability pensions.

The Lower Class and the Body

These findings, and the many references to bodily concerns in our interview data, suggest that Pruitt-Igoe people are preoccupied with their bodies. As other researchers have documented, concerns with the body and folk beliefs are generally common among the lower class; they are heavy consumers of patent medicines and they frequently ingest various substances (alcohol, drugs) and indulge in activities (dancing, fighting) that have as one goal a heightened state of awareness of physical existence. It has frequently been noted that lower-class people tend to express their psychic difficulties somatically, but it might be more correct to say that lower-class people do not differentiate between psychic and somatic symptoms of stress. It is usually apparent that their references to "nervous stomach" or other "nervous" conditions signify an undifferentiated state of unease which manifests itself both psychically (in anxiety, confused feelings, and disturbed cognition) and somatically (in various physical symptoms or discomforts).[4]

Lower-class people perceive the world as dangerous and chaotic. This perception carries with it a tendency also to see the body as immediately or potentially dangerous. Many lower-class people seem to think of their bodies as in some way likely to injure or incapacitate them, and they relate to their bodies in magical rather than instrumental ways. When they talk about illness, they communicate a sense of distance from the processes going on in their bodies. Unlike middle-class people, they do not identify themselves with their bodies and work toward cure of physical difficulties the same way they work toward appropriate solutions to other kinds of problems.

This tendency to see the body as mysterious and potentially dangerous carries with it a rather poor differentiation of bodily parts and functions. For example, in a study of how lower-class men and women think about the process of reproduction, there appeared a low differentiation of the female sexual parts among both men and women, and the majority of respondents had poor notions of the process of conception. This was

4. A 1968 survey by the Louis Harris organization reports that nearly two-thirds of blacks (and Appalachian whites) reported that feeling sick was their usual condition and more than half of both groups said that their health was worse than their parents' and grandparents' (Wiener, 1969).

closely related to their inability to understand or trust chemical methods of contraception or feminine methods such as the diaphragm.[5]

The low self-evaluation that is generally characteristic of lower-class people means that they do not uphold the sacredness of their persons in the same way as middle-class people, and their tendency to think of themselves as of little account is, of course, readily generalized to their bodies. For the middle-class person lowered body functioning is readily taken as an insult to both the body and the self, an insult which is intolerable and must be remedied as quickly as possible. For lower-class people a body which does not function as it should simply resonates with a self with the same characteristics. These attitudes are particularly prevalent among older people in the lower class, who must face themselves as failures as the psychosocial adaptive techniques they have used to ward off a negative self-image begin to play out.

Related to these interactions between self-concept and body image is Bernice Neugarten's finding that lower-class people believe they become "middle-aged" at a much earlier chronological time than working- or middle-class people.[6] Rosenblatt and Suchman's characterization of blue-collar attitudes toward the body takes on special significance when related to these differential notions of aging held by social classes:

> The body can be seen as simply another class of objects to be worked out but not repaired. Thus, teeth are left without dental care, and later there is often small interest in dentures, whether free or not. In any event, false teeth may be little used. Corrective eye examinations, even for those people who wear glasses, is often neglected, regardless of clinic facilities. It is as though the white-collar class thinks of the body as a machine to be preserved and kept in perfect functioning condition, whether through prosthetic devices, rehabilitation, cosmetic surgery, or perpetual treatment, whereas blue-collar groups think of the body as having a limited span of utility: to be enjoyed in youth and then to suffer with and to endure stoically with age and decrepitude. It may be that a more damaged self-image makes more acceptable a more damaged physical adjustment.[7]

The low body esteem applies by extension to the persons under their care, including their children. The low esteem in which others are held as social beings easily extends to a minimal exercise of protectiveness and solicitude toward their physical needs and states. In Pruitt-Igoe parents often seemed indifferent to all kinds of obvious physical illnesses their children had—particularly infections, sores, colds, and the like. This greater tolerance for physical disability or malfunctioning means that medical professionals cannot count on parents to exercise careful observation or

5. See Rainwater (1960).
6. Neugarten (1964).
7. Rosenblatt and Suchman (1964).

supervision when their children are ill, and any program of treatment in which these attitudes are ignored is likely to fail. The acceptance of something short of good health has implications both in the care of people who are already ill and in preventive medicine, because it means that parents are not likely to carry out a consistent preventive regimen. The much higher accident rate among lower-class individuals, particularly children, while partly a result of the greater dangers of their environment (more broken bottles, dangerous housing), in part also results from the lack of consistent circumspection on the part of parents.

Low body esteem is associated with an important secondary gain. If one's body is not working right, then one has a legitimate excuse for failing to live up to one's own standards and those expressed by others. The people in Pruitt-Igoe had a great number of health complaints, and to understand them, it is useful to distinguish between the "sick role," the "patient role," and the "disabled role." The notion of the "sick role," as used by Parsons and others, involves basically a withdrawal from all normal responsibilities because of physical incapacity; the "patient role" is superimposed on this when the individual brings himself within the purview of healing agents.[8] It may be true, as some researchers have suggested, that higher-status persons find it easy to accommodate themselves to these two roles whereas lower-status persons are more likely to disavow them. However, it is also clear that lower-class people more commonly see themselves in the "disabled role," in that their physical condition does not allow them to function properly as fully active adults.

The difficulties of coping with their world in such a way that their self-esteem can be maintained tempts lower-class people to assume the role of the partially disabled. This assumption of the disabled role was described in dramatic form by Halliday,[9] in his description of the psychosomatic diseases of English workers during the depression, but it also exists in more moderated but chronic form in lower-class individuals, particularly women, where the connection with unemployment and the possibility of compensation is absent. Once impaired functioning is defined as the "normal" state of the body and self, expectations of what one can and cannot do are greatly modified. It is possible for the individual to counter the claims of others by pointing to his own physical condition. To the extent that the disabling condition is defined as "normal," the individual's motivation to seek treatment is considerably lowered, and self-medication then becomes a ritual which symbolizes the disabled state.

The Depressive Adaptation

All these observations taken together characterize the depressive style of adaptation that is common in the project.[10] As women move into the

8. Parsons (1951), pp. 285 ff.
9. Halliday (1948).
10. See also Wiltse (1963).

adult role of homemakers, as their youthfulness wanes, and as they experience repetitive self-defeat in their wishes for a more stable and
secure family life, they adapt by increasingly constricting their self-
expressiveness, by learning not to ask too much of life, and by not putting
themselves out too much in the hope of garnering more meaningful interpersonal rewards. They come to see themselves as struggling just to meet
minimum standards of being a homemaker, mother, and (perhaps) spouse.
Though their daily routine would be demanding if they lived up to their
own aspirations for maintaining a nice home and supervising their children closely so that they may grow up to be "respectable" and successful,
they find themselves spending a great deal of time doing nothing—sleeping, napping, or quietly drinking. As they come increasingly to see themselves as slightly disabled by nervousness or excessive tiredness or some
more specific physical illness, they seek to compensate by training their
children to do their chores and by restricting their aspirations. They come
to hope simply that each day will bring nothing worse than the previous
day, and that when there is trouble, they will be able to cope with it at
least to maintain the integrity of the family unit. This depressive style
may be quiet, in which case the woman seeks mainly to mind her own
business and to keep her children out of trouble. Or it may take a more
agitated form, in which there remains still a quality of dramatic acting
out and a more hostile orientation to those around her.

The depressive adaptation, with its constriction and limiting interpersonal relations, poses a problem of pervasive loneliness for the homemaker. As she isolates herself to try to bring under control the pressures
on her, she finds herself increasingly lonely, and therefore tempted to
reach out for meaningful human contacts and rewards. But as we have
seen, this reaching out is perceived as involving a great deal of danger,
particularly for one who has come to regard herself as defeated and
vulnerable. Despite these dangers, despite a profound distrust of others,
loneliness can be so punishing that from time to time efforts must be made
to establish contact with some other person on whom one can depend
for meaningful interpersonal response and reward. Women who are
separated from their husbands seem to alternate between trying to live
within their constricted life space and reaching out for boyfriends to
lessen the subjective discomfort of their isolation. Similarly, as their
children enter adolescence they may come to depend on the children and
their friends for entertainment and sociability, becoming less vigilant
about the dangers of their children's relationships.

It is possible for a woman over a period of years to experience ups and
downs, alternations between the depressive adaptation of isolation and
more involved and expressive adaptations, either directly, participating
again in the high life with a new boyfriend, or vicariously through the
involvement of her children in their peer group. In between there may be
periods of relative psychosocial comfort when, for example, she establishes a stable relationship with a boyfriend who neither exploits her nor

demands too much in the way of commitment to him and faith in him as a permanent member of the household.

Kin and Friend

About half of the people living in Pruitt-Igoe did not move there as total strangers; they already knew someone there when they moved in. Twenty-eight per cent had relatives living in Pruitt-Igoe, and 27 per cent had friends. At the time of our 1965 survey most respondents claimed two or three persons in the project with whom they visited most often, and these represented nearly half of all the persons whom they considered to be close visiting associates. However, about one-fourth of the respondents did not count anyone in Pruitt-Igoe as among their close associates; so there is a significant minority who did not include fellow tenants in their social network.

In the 1965 survey, respondents were asked to name up to ten people who were those "you see most often to visit or have visit you or go out with, etc." Questions were asked that allowed each person named to be classified as a friend or relative and the type of relative, his place of residence, the frequency of visiting, and the duration of the relationship. Two-thirds of those named by both men and women were non-relatives (Table 5-2). Although women in Pruitt-Igoe named close associates comparable in number to those of their white lower-class counterparts, their associations were apparently less permanent in nature, in that relatives and long-time friends made up a smaller proportion. For Pruitt-Igoe women, friendship is more likely to involve comparatively recent associations based primarily on physical proximity.[11]

In part this may be attributed to the high physical mobility of Pruitt-Igoe residents, of whom almost two-thirds were born in the south. However, there is no lack of available kindred for Pruitt-Igoeans and perhaps the pattern illustrates better the characteristic Negro lower-class concern with the immediate environment. Because a broad social network constitutes a personal and family resource on which people can draw when they are in need, the comparative paucity of durable relationships within the social networks identified by Pruitt-Igoeans underscores their lack of strong mediating and supporting associations. The prevalence of impermanent relationships and those based only on physical proximity illustrates the adaptive necessities of Negro lower-class life. Weak as these relationships may be, they represent efforts by Pruitt-Igoeans to cope with their most pressing needs.

To further test the limits of the social networks of Pruitt-Igoeans, our interviewing approach was altered slightly in the 1966 survey, in which respondents were asked to name persons "you are close to—that is, people you think the most of or have the most to do with." After the respondent

11. This discussion is adapted from Stromberg (1967).

Table 5–2

Comparative Patterns of Informal Social Relations

Item	Pruitt-Igoe Males (43)	Pruitt-Igoe Females (110)	SRI* Lower Class Females (80)	SRI* Working Class Females (258)	SRI* Lower Middle Class Females (141)	SRI* Upper Middle Class Females (24)
Average number of persons listed as close visiting associates (up to 10 persons could have been listed)	5.0	5.3	5.3	5.8	6.2	6.2
Per cent of associates who are relatives	32	32	55	40	28	17
Per cent of respondents with at least two close visiting associates who are friends rather than relatives	77	84	55	79	92	87
Per cent of respondents with friends they have known "since their school years" (SRI) or "since they were children under 18" (Pruitt-Igoe)	14	12	65	59	46	33

*Source: *The Working Class World: Identity, World View, Social Relations and Family Behavior Magazine,* by Lee Rainwater and Marc J. Swartz, Social Research, Inc., 1965, Table VIII-1, p. 120.

named as many persons as he wished, he was prompted to mention any other relatives, neighbors, or friends to whom he was close. This further probing increased the number of persons mentioned by about 25 per cent. However, this increase was confined to relatives, whose names rose from an average of 1.7 to 3.1 while the number of non-relatives named stayed at 3.5. These results suggest that our questions tapped fairly completely the networks of close neighbors and friends, but that the kinship network is relatively expandable, depending on how much probing is done.

Almost half of the close visiting associates who were named spontaneously lived in the project, an average of 2.7 for women and 3.2 for men. The majority of the neighbors named by women lived in their own building, whereas for men the majority lived outside, suggesting again the wider range of male sociability. Overall, 59 per cent of the women had at least one close visiting associate within their own building compared to 45 per cent of the men. Few of these associates—only about 10 per cent—were relatives, although in the 1965 survey 48 per cent of the respondents indicated that they had at least one relative living in Pruitt-Igoe and 17 per cent indicated that there was more than one other household in which they had relatives. But only about 30 per cent of these relatives were identified as close visiting associates, a proportion not particularly higher than that of relatives outside the project. Apparently propinquity within the project does not strongly influence visiting associations so far as relatives are concerned.

Despite ambivalence and uncertainty about relationships with others. most people in the project maintain fairly regular ties with at least a few other tenants. On the average, women have at least two neighbors whom they see more than twice a week, and the men average even more, 3.6. Indeed, 57 per cent of the women in the project have at least one friend whom they see every day and the same is true of 78 per cent of the men. But it should be stressed that Pruitt-Igoe social networks are limited in that they are dominated by neighbors and relatives. The average tenant has at least one non-relative whom he visits outside the project, but that is all.

It is clear from the field data that most tenants know a fair amount about their immediate neighbors, and that their socializing within the project is not confined to close relatives and friends. In addition to more regularized relationships there is a fair amount of casual visiting and passing the time of day on the grounds or in the halls or laundry rooms. This is particularly true of the men, who spend more time away from the apartment even if they do not work. When the weather is warm enough, many Pruitt-Igoeans congregate outside their buildings, in the breezeways under the buildings or on the broad sidewalks nearby. These gatherings tend to be heterogeneous in age, with children and adults mixing comfortably together, and casual conversation is the rule. Such sociability involves little commitment by the participants; it is understood that co-presence and conversation do not obligate one more deeply. As might be expected, the general ambivalence about social relationships applies also to these situations; they are enjoyed, but the staple of conversation is often gossip, and personalized gossip is very much feared.

Borrowing small things from neighbors is also part of casual social interaction. Borrowing and lending are considered appropriate even among those whose relationships are incidental, so long as it is kept within bounds. These bounds require that the items be small—using a telephone, borrowing small amounts of food or money—and that there be a real effort to pay back or reciprocate. Indeed, it is as if two methods of relating to others are available, one based on manipulation and exploitation (as described in Chapter 3) and one based on a fairly rigorous adherence to standards of reciprocity and mutual aid. Part of the prevalent uncertainty about relationships with one's neighbors is based on unsureness about which of the two standards will be operative in any given relationship. Neighbors keep careful track of reciprocal obligations, and so long as these are met it is possible to develop relationships of mutual support at the level of minor resources. When a neighbor does not keep up his share of the relationship, either by not paying back or by refusing to be helpful when help is needed, he ceases to enjoy the privileges of casual reciprocity. In general, people who want to participate in this system try to keep their borrowing to a minimum so as not to run the risk of developing a reputation as a person who tries to take advantage.

In their effort to use relationships with others to adapt to their situation, Pruitt-Igoeans build alliances with some tenants and display avoidance or hostility toward others. In several respects, the administrative structure of public housing tends to exacerbate tension among the residents. For example, tenants are responsible for cleaning the stairwells outside their apartments; each tenant is expected to sweep the area in front of her door and the stairs down to the next floor. Theoretically, if every tenant does this, starting at the top floor and working down, the stairwell would be cleaned once a day. Tenants who fail to sweep the dirt on their floor can be fined, and many tenants express concern over this possibility, although in fact the Housing Authority has not tried to enforce the rule. If the tenant on a lower floor does her sweeping before the tenant living above, she ends up with a pile of refuse in front of her door after she has done her job, and this leads to conflicts with her neighbor. Tenants told of such occasions in which they were unjustly put in a bad light because of the failure of the common stairwell cleaning system to work.

An even greater concern is that tenants may and do inform on each other, and the Housing Authority may be responsive to information provided in this manner. Tenants are constantly expressing their concern that if neighbors learn too much about them, and if what they know involves something that is or seems to be in violation of any of the numerous Housing Authority regulations, they may inform the Housing Authority out of anger or malice and cause trouble. One of our respondents told of such an event:

> A family lived on the 10th floor. They were on ADC and APTD and had lots of children, perhaps ten or eleven. The boys would run down the stairs—I don't think they ever walked—and they had a way to stop the elevator while you were on it, and you would have to pay to get off. They did things like this—I put seven wreaths on that door for Christmas, and they took down every single one of them. They didn't do anything with them or take them anywhere, they just tore them up and destroyed them. We put up with that family because the mother was a very lovely person. Then an older son moved in who lived somewhere else before (an unauthorized person, which is cause for eviction). So, we saw our chance and reported them.

Because of the number, complexity, and unworkability of Housing Authority regulations and the problems of Pruitt-Igoe families, a large proportion of the tenants are from time to time subject to eviction or fines or milder sanctions for one reason or another. Given the willingness of other tenants to act as informers when they feel provoked, it is little wonder that neighbor relationships are guarded, that they are often short lived, and that within any given building there are usually structured relationships of hostility and suspicion among particular tenants, just as there are positive networks.

In a few buildings there were relatively organized structures of neighboring relationships, in one case involving two mutually hostile cliques. More commonly, the networks were looser and more chain-like, often involving alliances among two or three families who had neutral relations with other tenants. Sometimes such relationships between families persist over a long time, and may indeed change through marriage from neighboring to familial.

Kinship Relationships

Relatives loom large in the social networks of Pruitt-Igoeans, and few respondents in our surveys did not have kin available to them in the St. Louis area. In the 1966 survey we asked about particular categories of consanguinial kin, and the respondents (men and women alike) named an average of more than ten kinsmen in the area. Comparing this average with the average number of kinsmen mentioned as persons the respondents feel close to indicates that respondents were naming as close about a quarter of their available kin pool, with men naming a somewhat higher proportion (about a third of their recognized kin) because they responded more fully to our prompting.

The most frequently named kinsmen were mothers, brothers, sisters, and cousins. Table 5-3 lists those close kinsmen mentioned by at least ten per cent of men or women respondents. Relatives in almost every other category are mentioned by at least a few respondents.

Table 5–3
Kinsmen Named as Close Visiting Associates (1966)

	Men	Women
	per cent	
Mothers	39	31
Brothers	51	20
Brothers-in-Law	29	6
Sisters	23	39
Cousins	29	20
Aunts	10	16

The inclusion of a relative in one's intimate network depends, of course, on whether there is a relative who is recognized in that category for close and frequent relating in addition to being available because he lives in the city. Table 5-4 indicates the proportion of respondents who have each of several relatives available to them and the proportion of those who include those relatives in their social networks.

Table 5–4

Recognition of Relatives (1966 Survey)

	Proportion Who Have a Relative in this Category	Proportion Who Have a Relative in St. Louis	Proportion of those with Relatives in St. Louis Area who Identify Relative as Member of Their Social Network	
	per cent		*Males*	*Females*
Mother	64	45	63	69
Father	48	23	25	21
Grandparent	30	15	40	5
Brother	86	61	67	35
Sister	79	63	32	56
Cousin	75	57	36	26

Another way of examining the selection of kinsmen for one's intimate social network is to ask whether they come from the mother's or father's side of the family. Table 5-5 gives these data.

These data strongly suggest the matricentral emphasis of kinship relations in Pruitt-Igoe. Whether we look specifically at the inclusion of mothers and fathers or at whose side of the family is chosen for inclusion

Table 5–5

Direction of Referent's Relationship to Respondent

Direction of Referent's Relationship to respondent	Male Respondents	Female Respondents	Total
	per cent	*per cent*	*per cent*
Mother's Side	88	68	75
Father's Side	9	24	19
Both Sides	3	8	6
Total	100	100	100

in the intimate networks, we find that mothers and mother's relatives stand out. Even when fathers are available in St. Louis, only one third as many name them as name mothers as members of their intimate social network. Men even more than women select relatives from their mother's side of the family. Perhaps women are less exclusively maternally oriented because they assume the pivotal responsibilities of maintaining kinship relations with the whole family including relatives on the father's side.

The matricentral pattern described here is characteristic of lower class groups. Firth, commenting on data from a lower class neighborhood in London, summarizes them as follows:

> The question of kinship grouping has especial reference to the critical role of wife/mother in the system. It is clear that this woman is a key figure in South Borough kinship. In terms of emotional relationship, communication, and services . . . the tie between a mother and her children is normally very strong, and tends to remain so throughout her life. Mother and married daughter are commonly in frequent, often daily, contact, and a married son also tends to visit his mother at least weekly, if possible. Continuity between households forming a kinship network is usually provided largely by the mother. This is epitomised by the remark of one informant that 'in England, at Christmas all the children and in-laws go to Mother's', and by that of another, 'Since my mother died, we've all drifted away.' We might speak then of South Borough kinship as being *matri-centred* or *matral* in action, and in sentiment.

> But how far does this emerge in more crystallised form, perpetuated from one generation to another, in such manner as to constitute a system of matrilineal descent groups? The answer from the South Borough material is clear—it does not do so. Analysis of the genealogical material shows that on the whole there tends to be somewhat more knowledge of maternal kin than of paternal kin, and some tendency to greater intimacy with them. It could be suggested that while South Borough kinship is patrinominal, the emotional ties tend to be more matrilateral.

> The strong matral orientation is then primarily one of everyday behavior, not one of systematic unit recognition, and it is not reflected in any clear-cut genealogical differentiation.[12]

This last point relates to Firth's observation that the kinship system of this group of Londoners was of shallow genealogical depth, that the kinship system had relatively full lateral extension to cousins several times removed, but little vertical extension. Though kinship relationships may be very important to lower-class people ,their importance should not lead one to confuse the kinship system of such groups with the more highly organized corporate kinship groups of other societies.

12. Firth (1956), pp. 41-42.

A strong *matrifocal* emphasis characterizes Pruitt-Igoe families. The matricentric characteristic of the kinship relation is, of course, a logical extension of the centering of authority and resource provision in the wife-mother, and each characteristic reinforces the other.

The following data illustrate both tendencies. Respondents were asked with whom they would be most likely to engage in a number of different activities, ranging from discussing a family problem to lending and borrowing small things to sitting outside and talking. For those with a mother or father available, the mother overshadowed the father by far in exchanges of sociability and services, whether the activity was talking over family or personal problems, or lending and borrowing cigarettes, or as a source of advice for buying something or looking for a job, or as a source from whom to borrow money when it is needed in a hurry. Much the same pattern of behavior was observed in our field work. Older women living alone in the project had active relationships with their children and grandchildren, sometimes with nieces and nephews; they were still treated not as old people who had "retired" but rather as mothers on whom one could depend for resources of various kinds. To the outside observer, the relationships of younger persons with these older mothers often seem downright exploitative, given the very small income that is available to these women. However, the women themselves seem, despite some complaints, to value the dependence their younger kinsmen have on them, and to see the apparently one-sided relationships that they maintain with them as a way of combating loneliness and a sense of uselessness. The older men in the project, however, do not seem to maintain such relationships with their relatives and live more isolated lives.

6.

The Patterson Family

David Schulz came to know the Pattersons through another family with whom he was doing field work. When he began to interview members of the family intensively in the summer of 1966, he learned that there were, in addition to Mr. and Mrs. Patterson, eight children in the household, ranging in age from 9 to 19. In addition, there were four grown children—two were hers by previous relationships and two his—and Mr. Patterson had several other children by other women living in St. Louis. At the time the data were collected Mr. Patterson was 46 years old and Mrs. Patterson was 42. They had been living in St. Louis for about 16 years and in Pruitt-Igoe for about ten years.

The Patterson apartment was quite clean; the floor was covered with a dark green flower-print linoleum and the walls had also been decorated in a pattern of dark and light green. All in all, the apartment was more pleasant than most of those in the project. Schulz learned that Mr. Patterson was steadily employed and that he prided himself on the fact that he was able to work steadily and earn good money without having to do heavy manual work.

Mrs. Patterson was a short, rather heavy woman who expressed considerable concern about her health and energy level. She had a tendency to make the most of her illnesses. For example, early in the interviewing she developed a nosebleed that proved difficult to stop and required her to go to the hospital for care. For several weeks afterward she complained of her hemorrhage to anyone who would listen.

Mr. Patterson was a trim, muscular man who gave the impression of being very much a gentleman. In ordinary interaction he was self-controlled and apparently straightforward. However, his behavior over the years had caused him to lose considerable respect from other members of the family. Schulz observed that he ate alone almost every evening and that in general his children were tentative and guarded in their relationship with him.

118

He's Going to Make You Cry for Many Days

Mrs. Patterson had grown up in rural Arkansas. In one of her interviews she described how she had come to marry Edward Patterson.

I was mostly a sickly child from the time I was 15 until I was around 18. I would have sick spells. My mother carried me from doctor to doctor until they finally got me over that. I never was able to work in the fields. I always did the house cleaning, the cooking, the washing, and the ironing. I always was the delicate one of the family because I didn't weigh but 90 pounds. I weighed 90 pounds from the time I was 15 until I was 22. That's when I first started to gain weight. I started gaining weight when I was 22 and I gained from the time I was 22 until now which brought me up to 215½.

My mother let me have my way at most everything. I've never been a problem child. I never was a spoiled child. I never give my mother and father no kind of trouble. I was a very good child. They were the kind of parents, they would sit down and talk with us and talk problems over with us. If we had a problem we could always feel free to carry it to them and they would always work it out for us. I think that's about the most wonderful thing that a parent could do. Nowadays I wish I was able to show my husband the same way with our children so we could talk over the problems with the children instead of one trying to go one way and the other one trying to go the other. Which when the kids go to my husband with a problem he gives them a short answer. I think that's about the worst thing that a father could do to the children. For instance, yesterday my daughter said, "Daddy, I've got to go to school today." He said, "So what?" I don't think that was the right answer. So he said, "What do you want me to do about it?" She really didn't say anything. He said, "Well, you hear me talking to you?" She said she didn't think he cared. So I think it's better for the parents to try to appreciate their children instead of trying to get them to set in one spot. And now my children seem to think that their father don't care if they get their education or not, which I'm trying to browbeat them and get out of their head. As long as he continue the way he is it's nothing I can do about it.

How did you decide to get married?

Well, I don't know. I really don't know how that come about.

How did you meet Edward?

I met Edward at a store. They had a store up from where we lived and we would go up to get soda and ice cream so I'd go up there to get soda and ice cream. I knew his sister but I didn't know him so I was standing up talking with her and so he came up and started talking. So we got to talking and so he asked me about walking me home. I let him walk me home. So the next time I went up there I seen him again and so that's how we got started.

How long had you known him before you decided to get married?

A year. He had real nice manners around my mother and he always carried himself in a nice way. Well, he just had nice manners and I always respected a boy with nice manners and the way they carry theirself and so I think that's really what made me want to get married. But otherwise I don't think I would have.

My father, he didn't have too much to say. But my mother told me this—she said, "You can marry him if you want to." She said, "I can't stop love. You can marry him if you want to, but he's going to make you cry many days. Because," she said, "he's not the man for you." She always said she can always look at a man and tell what he was and what he wasn't. She said, "He's going to make you cry for many days." She said, "You're going to have a lots of children and you're going to always be crying. He's not going to treat you like you should be treated by a man and as kind as you is." My mother always said I was real kind. "And, she said, "he's not going to treat you the way you should be treated. You're kind and you should be treated the way you're going to treat them." I said, "I don't know mama, maybe he ain't like that." She said, "Mark my word. If I live long enough you will get a chance to tell me."

How do you feel about that now?

Well, I feel that my mother was right. But as I said I have stuck with it and I will try to remain. Otherwise, if I didn't have all these children I wouldn't because just as my mother said, that's the way it is. Because I feel that if you ain't living a happy life it's not the life for you, but if you're stuck with it the best thing is to try to remain and make the best of it if you can.

What do you feel is the basis of your unhappiness?

Well, Mr. Schulz, I'm going to tell you like it is. My husband have walked off and left me two or three times. Each time my husband have walked off and left me it has been another woman. My husband have three extra kids excusing mine. The children know about it. He have never tried to keep it hid from them. And my husband is a man like this. He wants everything to go his way regardless whether it's right or wrong. He can know he's wrong but he never admits he's wrong. And I can try to show him where he's wrong—no, he's not wrong, I'm the one wrong and he's right. Like something can come up about the children. I can go to him. I don't care what will happen to them for whatever they do, it don't make him no difference. Well I don't feel that way. I feel that we have the children and it's our business.

And he's very close with money with his family but he's not with other people. He's not close with other people, and with me he's very tight. The only way I know when he makes a pay day is I just know when his pay day is. He never gives me an allowance—not at all. He will say we are going to the grocery store. Whatever I get at the grocery store he will pay for it and if we go buy food stamps he ain't going to buy no more than $25 worth of groceries unless I go get the food stamps. And when it don't last two weeks, he'll say, You waste it. You don't take care of nothing. I just don't understand how you do this and that and the other. When the boys give you money what do you do with it? I say, Well, that's the only allowance I do have is what the boys do give me because you don't give me anything. I say, I have to pay the telephone bill with what the boys do give me and I do have to have a little spending change for the house and for myself. He said, "It don't take no $10 for that. You waste money." Just like this past week I asked him. I said, "Buy me a watermelon. I don't have no appetite. I believe I want a watermelon." He said, "You got fever. You don't need no watermelon." I said "O.K." I tries not to argue. So he got up this morning, he said, "You're taking your money and you buy watermelon with it and now the children need shoes and they ain't got no shoes." I said, "Well the dollar I bought the watermelon with I couldn't buy no shoes."

See my husband is the type, he likes to play cards. He goes over to his friends and plays cards. They makes a fool out of him which I know they do. They're supposed to be boy friends but some of everybody hangs out at this house where he goes. And try to tell him that. He said "Well, I makes my money and I can spend it the way I want to. As long as I make it, it's mine and you don't tell me how to spend it." I said, "Well I'm not telling you how to spend it, I'm only telling you because it's making bad management for the house." So he tries to start an argument and I gets hurt and turns around and walks away. I don't like to argue. When I know I'm right I don't argue about nothing.

Well, why haven't you turned the tables on him and played his own game? That is why don't you check out on him?

I just, I don't believe in it. My mother always talked against such things and I've never been that type. I have had people to tell me that, why don't I do that. I just can't do it. I know I have made up my mind and even dressed to do it, but I'd go back and pull my clothes off and set right here with the kids. I just have never been the type to do it. And I have set up many days and wished I could do it, but I just can't do it. I can't seem to do a person like they do me. I always feels like that. I don't know.

What do you do with the money that you get when you've been working?

Well the money that I earn I takes it and if the kids need any clothes, underclothing, winter clothing, winter socks, or something like that I buy it. And I try to get me clothing because that's the only way I get my clothes is when I go out to work. I don't get nary piece unless I go to work. I haven't had a new coat in five years. I've been begging for me a coat. I haven't been able to get it. I told him the other day, I said the doctor said I'm going to have to have glasses. He said, "So you ain't the only one that ever needed glasses." So I said, "Well, maybe I'll get them when I start to work." And I have to mostly get what I need when I work. Otherwise I don't get it. That's the reason why I say my life is real unhappy. It's very difficult to live.

What do you live off? That is, what does your husband earn and what do you earn?

My husband earns every two weeks about two hundred and three or four dollars.

Is that take home pay?

Yeah, take home pay. He only has $58 rent to pay out once a month. He pays the rent and he will buy maybe $20 worth of food, and the rest of it he spends with his women. And he never gives me one cent. Not one cent. Because I have had Mrs. Jones tell me a couple of times she don't see how I do it, how I put up with it. She said I just take too much and why should you take it? I said, 'Well, with the kids I'm going to try to keep going until they get old enough, because with the kids just with me by myself, which he never do anything. He never tells them what to do or what not to do. They can get out there and climb up on the bricks and he never says get down or nothing. If I never holler he never says a word. When they come in in the evening, I have to be the one to send for them to come up.

Well, the older children, I appreciate the way they helps me. They helps me very much with the kids. Andrew (a son in his twenties who does not live at home) is very nice. They pays him more attention than they do their father because he, he speak, that's it. Otherwise if it wasn't for Andrew, I don't know what I'd do. He gives me $10 a week. Now Mark (also in his twenties and living away from home), he works. He gets paid every two weeks and he give me $20 every two weeks. And if I need something else I can go back to them and they will always give me something. So I never bothers Edward. I never bothers him about anything because any time I ask him for any money he says, "What do you think of me to be? You must think I'm a bank or something." I said, "Well, I feel that it's worth something for some of my time," you know. Just like I tell him I think if I'm . . . I'm going to be here at the house, I'm going to take care of home and I'm going to try to keep him clean, I'm going to fix his meals, his breakfast, lunch and dinner, and do everything that's supposed to be did for him, it's worth something. But he don't seem to see it that way. I don't know just what's got into him. But I don't know whether I can keep going along with it. I'm going to try but I don't know if I can keep up. But truly speaking that's what keeps me upset and keeps my blood pressure up.

How were your earlier years with Edward? How do you re-member the first few years of your married life?

Well, the first year of my married life was very happy. The second year of my marriage my husband started to running with other women. I don't know why. His sister said the only thing she could see was he was just that type. After Joe was born, he was about four months, I got pregnant with my other one, Patsy. Well, after Patsy was born I got stuck with two babies. I never could go any place unless he helped me go, you know, would carry me. So we moved out from his sister, moved out to ourself.

So when you got married you were living originally with his sister? That was in Arkansas?

Then we moved to ourselves. He bought him a car and he got so he would just go, go, go, all the time. I was there all the time with just me and the kids by ourselves. So then some other old lady taken up with me. She started coming over there with me. I never went to town but twice a year. And every year I would have a baby, I never missed a year and that would set me that much closer to the house. He never would worry with the babies, he never did help me with the babies at all. My mother who would come up and help and she would tell me, "Josie, I told you." She would always remind me of what she told me. And I kept having babies and kept having babies.

Finally he came to St. Louis in '50. So when in December in 1950 he came back and got me and the family, he brought all of us up here to live in one big storefront about as big as this whole thing here. We stayed there five years. And well, I would see him like this morning and I wouldn't see him no more until the next day. So he had a grocery account opened up down the street for me. I would go down there and buy groceries, but I never would see no money. I never would get nothing but the groceries.

Finally he came in one night, me and the girl in the back had walked up to White Mill. We walked up there to get some hamburgers. She was going to buy me and her some so I went up there with her. So my oldest son was there at the house, he was going to watch the children. So he came in and asked where I was and he told him. So when I came back in he jumped on me. He said I was out with a man. Me and this girl came back together. Andrew said, "Daddy, mama didn't leave with no man. Mama left with Miss Jane." He blackened my whole face. He bruised my whole face so I called the police. They taken him down and he came back home. He didn't jump on me no more until two years later.

We moved from there down about three blocks. I worked around the corner there. So I got paid that week. I didn't tell him anything about I was working because he went to work in the morning and I went to work after he went to work and I got off before he got back so I had some money. After I got paid I had some money in the drawer. So he found the money in the drawer. He went to rambling and he found the money and he said I got it from a man and he jumped on me and he taken the money. So I called the police and they made him give my money back.

When I was pregnant again he left me when I was six months pregnant. I went to work and worked until I had the baby. I went to work that day and she was born that night. She was about four months old before he came back. He had been in Detroit. He came back home. And every time he came back he do worser and worser, he always says he's going to do better, but he do worser. Just like this time. He walked off and left me. He left me with nary bite to eat in this house, not nary bite to eat. We didn't have a bite to eat and I didn't have a penny to buy nothing with. I was sitting there in that chair. The man come to the door and said, "We are going to set you out tomorrow at 9:00." I couldn't do nothing but sit up and cry.

I goes up to Miss Jones crying. This was three years ago. I went up to Miss Jones crying. So Miss Jones said, "What's the matter?" So I told her. So Edward had came in from work that morning, he came in about 9:00. He worked at night and he was supposed to have got in around 8:00. I said, "The man said he's going to set us out in the morning." He said, "So? That's your business cause I'm fixing to leave." So he got up and went on in there and went to packing his clothes. He got the children to help him take them out and put them in his car. He went up there and lived with this Mary Lou and stayed with her for two year. So then he got tired of living with her and decided to come back home. He was going to do better and he wasn't going to mistreat us no more and he was going to be nice to his family and he could see where he made his mistake and he wasn't going to do that no more. He was going to treat his family right. He come home and he did right for about four months and he'd start right out on the same road again.

If I had this life to go over again I don't think I'd marry nobody. I'd never marry no more. As I told him the other night, before I let him keep me upset, I'd have to leave. I'd go over to my brother's and stay for a while and I will because it ain't doing me no good. It seems like he just try to start a argument over nothing, just nothing.

I asked him the other night about some barbecue. Steven (19 years old) came in and got me some barbecue. I was sleepy. I was tired and I decided to go to bed. I took my clothes off and went to bed. I put some of the barbecue in the refrigerator and I put the rest in the deep freeze so they could have it for the next day. And so Steven came in and got a piece. Edward came in there. I was asleep, and he said, "Josie, I don't see what makes you do no kind of mess like that!" I said, 'What are you talking about?" He had scared me, I was real nervous. He said, "That boy's got the barbecue and got the roast pan and gone." I said, "Aw naw, he ain't." He said, "Yes he is, cause the whole roast pan is gone." I said, "I know he ain't." He kept on so I got up and looked and the roast pan was still in the deep freeze with the barbecue in it. I said, "What is you trying to do to me? Is you trying to kill me or what?" I said, "You just waking me up and scaring me. I just got over a hemorrhage and the doctor said for me to get rest. I said how do you expect for me to get any rest when you doing some kind of mess like that." I said, "Your making me nervous and everything and suppose I start back to hemorrhaging?" He said, "Well, maybe I'm wrong. I'm wrong about every thing and you're right about everything." I said, "Forget it, and I'll try to go back to sleep."

What does he say is the reason for what he does?

He will not give you no kind of reason because I have set down and tried to talk with him and ask him why he be the way he bes and why he act like he do and why he talk to the kids the way he do. He says, "I ain't got nothing to say." That's what he says, he don't have nothing to say. Well, when he's with this other woman over there he used to come over and get the kids. I'd let them go and they come back and you should hear how they say, "Mother, daddy is helping Miss Mary Lou clean up the house and help her cook and he cleans up the kids," and some of our kids would see them out and see him with the baby and leading the little boy by the hand, something he ain't never did for all twelve I have. And I feel that if he could be nice to her, he could be nice to me. I haven't never give him no kind of trouble. I mean everybody knows me and knows him, they know what kind of person he is and they knows what kind of person I am. I have had so many people tell me that they don't see how I can put up with him. Which Miss Jones tells me that time after time. She says, "Josie, you is too good to be treated like you treated." That makes me so mad I feel like killing him myself.

Does he have children by Mary Lou?

Yeah, he has two.

Does he have children by another woman then also?

Uh huh. He used to get letters from a girl that used to be up here. She moved back down south. He's been getting letters from her. He went down there in June before school was out. He found her and he was going to send this kid a typewriter, a camera, and money for school clothes because she wrote letter after letter back in return. So the first letter I got I showed it to him. I said, "Well she's not giving me no kind of respect. Why did you have to give her this address?" He raised his hand and the rest of the week he wouldn't buy groceries. I'd never say nothing. So the next letter come in and I showed him that one. He says, "I can't keep people from writing." I said, "Well, you had to give them the address and tell her. If you promise people something they look for what you promise them." And this little Pearl, she just kept writing. I got a letter she wrote last month out of the mail box. I have the letter, I'm not going to destroy it, I'm going to keep them. As I told him, I'm going to keep them for evidence. He said, "Well, if they're mine why should you keep them?" He said he didn't get a chance to answer the first one because I've got the address off of it. I said, "Not only the letters, anything else that you do I'm going to keep for evidence. Anything that you mistreat me out of the clear blue sky for nothing, I think if anything that you do that I can get my hands on, I'm going to hold it for evidence."

Does he support the other children he has?

He claims to me that he does. But if he didn't the welfare would. He got a letter from the welfare, they wanted to talk to him. I have the letter. I said, "Well, why don't me and you both go over there to the welfare office and talk to the people. After all you is married. When that woman accept you she knew you was married. She knew you had walked off and left your family. After all, men with a family, I don't see how they can make you support those outside children." He said, "That's my responsibility and it's my problem. You ain't got nothing to do with it and I ain't asking you to do nothing. I ain't asking you to go over there with me and I ain't looking for you to go."

So he got another letter about a month ago. I haven't heard nothing else from them so he's got to be giving some support because if he didn't welfare would constantly be on him .

About a month later Schulz continued Mrs. Patterson's autobiographical interview. She started by talking about her current state of health.

I'm doing pretty good, but I have a cold. I haven't gotten quite rid of it. I don't know, I think this cold is partly from me using so much ice at the time I had the hemorrhage. It seems like it's in my chest now, I cough so bad at night. And otherwise I feels fine. Every once in a while I feel nervous, at least when somebody gets on my nerves.

How do you like your job now?

Well, I'm not so pleased with it. It's not a matter of working, I don't have too much to do but it's just the pay, $1.10 an hour, and I don't feel that I'm accomplishing anything working just two hours and a half for a dollar and a dime an hour and with the walk down there and the walk back because I think the walk harms me more than anything in the world. So I'm going to put an application in at the youth center and as soon as it comes through I'm going to let them have this (job) and go to this training school. In the meanwhile I haven't got nothing too heavy . . . something that I have to rush in because I can't stand to rush. If I rush it makes me nervous.

I get off from work on Friday at 2:30 and by the time I get home it's quarter to three or 3:00. If I walk slow it's 3:00 when I get here because I never rush. So last Friday I came on in and I felt so bad, I laid down. When the kids come in I was still laying down. I was taking all those nerve pills which I'm going to have to get the doctor to get me off of because those things are drugging me, cause at night I can get up and walk through the house and be so sleepy I don't even know where I'm going. So I'm going to have to leave them alone.

I was laying down and my little girl kept waking me up but as fast as she'd wake me up I'd doze on back to sleep. She said, "Mother, what are we going to eat?" I said, "When daddy come he can go and get fish." Then I'd go back to sleep. She said, "Daddy in there now." I said, "Well, go in there and ask daddy to go and get fish." He said, "Tell her to come ask me herself." Well I dozed right on back to sleep. So finally I woke up and it was about quarter to six. So I woke up and I said, "Did daddy get the fish?" She said, "No, mother, he said to tell you come ask him yourself." I don't know, it seemed like it just got on my nerves real bad. So later I said, "Well, why didn't you go and get the fish?" He said, "Well you come and ask me yourself." I said, "Well, when you came in I was there asleep." He said, "You can't be that tired. You just walked down there and worked and just walked back." I said, "Well, my goodness, don't you realize that I have lost a lot of blood and strength and then two weeks later I go to work down there. Don't you know I haven't gained that blood I lost back and my strength. And then, too, I have to diet. Dieting you lose strength anyway. I wasn't feeling good and I did lay down, but you could have went and got the fish." He said, "Well, I didn't."

So that just got on my nerves. So he was hollering about he had to support the family and he had to buy all the food and he got to do this. I said, "Well, any man that has a family don't want to support them, then he don't need to be with the family." He said, "Well, you'd just better go on and leave here." I said, "I'm not going any place. I have these children and I'm going to stay with them and see after them." But the problem is that I've never said anything about what I have to do. He's all the time grumbling about what he has got to do for the family and what's on him. I never helps and I never buys nothing. I have proof, what money I get I put into the house. If we're low in food I take and put it in food. Which I do, if I know our food is low if I make any money I go to the store and buy what I know I need.

How do the kids feel about this situation?

Well, the kids don't feel good at all. I mean the larger kids. They are constantly saying, "Mother, you shouldn't have let daddy come back, we told you that. You shouldn't have let him come back. You had it made better before he come back. Now that he's home you're just having trouble." And they said, "We was living better before Daddy come back. You wasn't all nervous, you wasn't upset." My son Steven always says, "Why don't you just go on and tell him to leave?" I said, "Well, it's not as simple as that. I mean I can just tell him to leave, that don't make him leave because I tell him to. I would prefer that he would just go on his own because if I tell him to leave then I've got troubles. If he don't give me no support, it's hard for me to get support."

So if you tell him to leave you figure he won't give you any support and you can't get it from him.

Well, I could get support from him but the support from him wouldn't be enough to support the family. He wouldn't be made to give me no more than $70 every two weeks, but $70 every two weeks would not support the family and pay rent and bills. I know it wouldn't be enough to keep the kids in school clothes. And if I tell him to leave it's hard for me to get support from welfare. But if he leave on his own it wouldn't be as hard. But it is a possibility now as I've told him. He have threatened sometimes when we argue, "If you don't hush I'm going to hit you." As I told him, "Don't do that because that I can't stand, no lick." I said, "I don't want to have to hurt you and I don't want you to hurt me" because I'm not going to stand for him to hit me because I don't feel I'm able to be beaten up. If he has to feel that he's got to hit me then he goes. Because that way I will get rid of him because I'll call the police. I will definitely give them orders that they had better get him out. Because if they don't then somebody's going to get hurt.

Monday night a fellow came to the door and one of the kids went to the door and said, "Come in." He said, "Naw, I want to talk to your daddy out in front of the door." So I said, "Tell him to come in." I was sitting here and my husband was sitting over there. He said, "Tell your daddy I said come out in front of the door. I want to talk to him out in front of the door." So he goes out and talks to this fellow, then he comes and sits down a few minutes. He say, "I'm going out here for a few minutes. I'll be back after a while." I said, "I don't think you should go because . . . Where are you going? You've got to talk to the fellow in front of the door?" He said, "Yeah." I said, "Well, I don't think you should go because I don't like this situation. If there was something he had to tell you he could have come in here and told you before me as well as in front of the door." "Well, I'm going. I'll be back after a while."

So he goes and stays about an hour and comes back. He changed coats and takes off again. I said, "Where are you going?" I had some things in my lap and I got them out of my lap and went to the door. By the time I got to the door he didn't have time to wait and had got half way down the steps. I said, "What did you want?" He said, "That's all right now. It taken you too long to come to the door. You've got to talk to the kids before me." I figured if he was fixing to go somewhere else he could have told me to step there a minute when he went in the room to change coats. I said, "Forget it." He went and grumbled all night. I said, "Well, I'll tell you what, we ain't got to argue. I'll get up and sleep with the girls." Because now everything—I don't care what it is—everything I say he's going to call me a lie. Regardless of whether it's true or not. I'm a lie and he's telling the truth. I could be done told him something. I'll say, "No, I didn't tell you that way. I said it was this way." "You're a lie." And I'm knowing the way I said it. I said, "Now it's a possibility that you could be lying." He said, "I know I'm not lying, but you is lying." I said, "Well, you're one every time you open your mouth. I'm not going to be called too many of them." I said, "I still say you're one every time you open your mouth." Because every word he says he just makes me angrier and angrier and see that I go to getting nervous.

Have you ever had a boyfriend since you've been married?

I never have, I never had a boyfriend since I've been married. My mother fought against that so I never did do it. When me and my husband separated my husband have his first time just seeing me and a man walk out together. He have never seen me. If he ever seen me in a car with another man I didn't know it. I never have walked out in front of him. But this lady he used to live with he have had her right out in front of my door. Because the first time he brought her down there I didn't say anything so I asked him not to do it again, because it seemed like he was boasting about it. And the next time he did it, which I would have killed them both if I had got downstairs. I got a gun and started down the steps and he ran down there by the car. By the time I got down under the building he had done pulled off. Because I was looking at them both right out there in the car. As I told him, whatever he do is his business, but don't boast on me because I wouldn't do him like that. Then after that I guess I was glad I didn't. The kids was all hollering.

Why did you invite him back this last time?

I didn't invite him back, he came back to me himself. He asked to come back. He promised me he would do better, I mean he was just almost on his knees. He promised me he would do better, he wouldn't do this and he wouldn't do that, he would bring his money back and he would be better than he have did. But I don't know, I guess I have always felt this way. I felt that these was his kids and rather than to marry some other man I guess I'll just as soon go ahead on and put up with him if he wants to do right. I mean he promised me that he would do right but for about two months he did. After that he started out again. So now I don't feel that I could ever let him come again.

Why did he want to come back, did he say?

No, he didn't, but I found out later. You know you can find out quite a bit from other people. Now I never did go too much even though we were separated. I just never did go too much, every once in a while. But I understood that this woman what he was living with he caught her in the house with another man. He beat her and she left. He had bought all new furniture and she taken the biggest of it. She left a bedroom suite and an old refrigerator that they had and an extra bed. She left a gas stove and a cooking stove, and a table, all the rest she taken it.

Did the children go visit him while they were together?

I let them go visit him about five times. They'd go out there and the first and second time was fine. The third time they went they come back, "Mother, the children tells me things that hurt me." The children said, "Anything we do Mr. Patterson pays us to do it. He pays us to sweep the steps, he pays us to take the trash out. I bet he didn't do you all that way." I said, "Oh, forget it." I didn't pay it too much attention because sometimes I feel the children can exaggerate. So the next time they go they come back with the same mess, so I sat down and thought. I said maybe these children are telling the truth, I didn't feel that each time they'd go they're going to come back lying about the same thing. So the next time he came and got them and asked me could they go, when he brought them back I noticed all of them sat and just looked me right in the face. As long as he was here they didn't have a word to say. I said, "Did you all have a nice time?" Nobody would say nothing. He'd say, "You hear your mama talking to you." Nobody still wouldn't say nothing, so I didn't say more. He sat here a few minutes and he got up and left.

Before he got out the door good they started, "Mother, daddy gives these children all a quarter and give us a nickel." They said, "He give all of them a quarter and give us a nickel and they was laughing at us." They was talking about, "You-all's daddy give us more money than he give you-all." I said, "Well, do you all ever want to go with him again?" "No, ma'am. We don't ever want to go with them no more." So when he came back I told him. I said, "I don't intend for you to take none of these children to your house or either in the car riding with her and those kids ever no more. If I ever hear talk of you doing it I'm going downtown. I'm going to have something did about it. I mean it. I don't want none in your house." So that stopped it right there. Because see at first I wasn't believing what they was saying but I was paying attention and sometimes it pays to pay attention to what kids say. When a child first comes to me with something I always figure they exaggerate. The next time they come then I don't get that feeling.

Have the children been involved in your squabbles in any way other than just witnessing them? They don't tend to take sides?

When we argue they never say anything. About two weeks ago him and I went to the packing house and bought some stuff. So we came back and it was dark. Well they was already down so instead of him sending up and telling the kids to tell the boys to come down and get the groceries, he gets the box and we come up on the elevator. He came in and says, "Mark, how come you didn't come down and help get the groceries?" He said, "Daddy I didn't know you all was down there. If I had known it, I didn't have on no shoes but I would have got some and put on." "You don't have to have on no shoes. You could have come down there barefooted and what did you say anyhow." He said, "I said I didn't know you all was down there

and I didn't have on no shoes." So by that time he balled up
his fist and come around that corner with his fist balled up just
as though he was going to hit him. Mark said, "No, daddy,
don't do that. You did that once before and hit me upside my
head. I'm not supposed to be hit upside my head."

And he just kept walking so we had a stool over there and I
just grabbed the stool. I said, "You all ought to be ashamed of
yourself. Don't be doing that. You get me all upset and I
haven't been long having a hemorrhage and if I get upset it
ain't no telling what might happen." They just had me screaming. And so he said, "I'm not going to let daddy hit me. I
haven't said nothing to him or did nothing to him." And so he
was running from room to room just like he was looking for
something, you know. And Mark ran and grabbed a knife, and
somebody said, "Mark got a knife, Mama." I said, "Give me
the knife, Mark," so he handed it to me. I was standing about
right there. So when daddy came in he reached in his pocket
and pulled a knife out of his pocket. Charles (age 13) grabbed
his hand just like that. He said, "All right, fellow, it ain't no
use in that." He said, "You get on out of the way, Charles, because I don't want to have to hit you." So he just kept arguing.
I said, "Mark, you hush, don't say a word." He said, "Mama, I
ain't going to say nothing, but I'm not going to let daddy hit
me." See Mark had epileptic spells. I don't know what they
come from. The doctor said he had to have a lick in his head,
so that way he's not supposed to get licks upside his head.
That's what makes him very conscious about somebody hitting
him upside the head. He said, "You did that once before and
I ain't going to let you do it no more. If you want me to leave
I'll leave." So he had invited this other fellow over and he told
this other fellow, "You can go too." He was trying to talk to
him, you know. He was just as ornery, he didn't say it in a nice
way. He jumped up and grabbed his coat and things and ran
on out of the house.

So I told Mark, "Mark, if there is ever misunderstanding between you and your father, you leave because it seems like it's
going to be something. I don't want you to hurt your daddy
and I don't want your daddy to hurt you." He said, "Okay,
Mama, I'll leave." So he got his clothes and went over to his
sister's where he's staying now. He haven't had his feet inside
the door since. I was just screaming I was so nervous, I couldn't
sleep that night. The next morning when I got up I couldn't eat
I was so nervous. I said, "You're making me nervous." He said,
"If you're nervous get out." So Steven said, "Daddy, you ought
to be ashamed of yourself. You know mother ain't been long
having a hemorrhage and it looks like you're trying to get her
upset." He said, "Get your mammie and get out of here."

So Alice (age 17) said, "Lord have mercy, what kind of family is this? We're supposed to be a family and everybody's

arguing. This ain't no way for a family to do." He said, "It's too damn many in the family." She said, "Lord have mercy, I ain't got nothing else to say," and she got her a chair and sat down. Alice is a very easy child, she never has nothing to say about nothing. After he spoke that way to her it really hurt her. She just went on and sat down and just laid her head down in her hands. He said, "It's too damn many in the family." That just hurt her to her heart. Later she said, "Mother, what did daddy mean when he said it's too damn many in the family?" I said, "I don't know. I don't think he knows what he meant hisself." I said, "Maybe some day when you're talking with your daddy you can ask him yourself." She said, "No, Ma'am, I'd rather not ask him anything."

It's hard for me to understand what kinds of benefit he derives from staying in the family with so many people who are either afraid of him or don't get along with him very well.

Well, Mr. Schulz, I think truly my husband's reasons to come back home was my husband moved here when he owed me back money from child support. He knew that he was either going to have to pay that back money in two or three payments or go to the work house. And rather than do that I think he would rather beg his way back in here. So I think that was really his problem.

I Had Great Dreams

Schulz was not able to develop rapport as fully with Mr. Patterson as with Mrs. Patterson, partly because Mr. Patterson worked and therefore was not available so often, and partly because he had more to conceal. He, too, had grown up in the rural south. His version of the family's history did not sharply contradict his wife's but of course his perspective on it was rather different.

What do you remember as you think back on your life?

Well, definitely speaking I think that I could have improved my life in a better way than what I have if I had known what to do like I do now. Referring to owning my own home probably with a nice bank account, I'll just say better living *period* than what I have although when I started out I started completely at the bottom. Definitely speaking I would be going along today and tomorrow wondering if it would be as comfortable as it was the day before. Such as working, for instance. There have been times when I didn't have a job and didn't have no assurance of being able to work the next day.

When was this?

Well, I'll say from about 1945 up until '53. I came here in '48 so I was here from '48 until now. I was farming up to '45. I was doing farm work and it just got to the place where it was so rough and you couldn't make anything out of farming so I just completely give it up and didn't know where I was going or what I was going to do or anything. Definitely speaking I was just from one place to another and I'd catch odd jobs and work when I could be trying to find something that was suitable with some meaning to it.

Before I married (in 1942) I always had great dreams that if I'd get married I wanted a nice car, a trailer house. What I believed in was that I could go and work as work was available. If the work transported to another place I would be able to follow with it and I would have my own living apartment and everything along with it. That was my desire, a couple of kids—maybe not any. I mean those wasn't in the plans at all. I did have in mind to be married.

How did you meet Josie?

Well, where my little baby sister was living it was what you might say as a dance more or less. Well I knew her brothers long before I knew her. In fact we used to go around together but they never went home with me and I had never went to their house. We would just see each other out so I don't know, I think I happened to be dancing one day or something, but anyway finally I asked her for a dance and I found out she was the sister to my friend and we started to going back and forth. We went out and made different dates and things and got married. It was all did real quick.

How did you come to decide that she was the one you wanted to marry?

I guess you would call it confidence that I had in her. Well, after we started seeing each other we'd break off and stay away from each other for a while and then when we'd see each other again, I guess everything was normal where we could afford to forgive each other and forget so I don't know. I guess it's more or less like the phrases they use today. Love is a wonderful thing but you have so much fun trying to win I guess.

Where did you live when you got married?

Well, I lived with my sister for six or eight months until I was able to find a place. I had already bought my own furniture and everything. Definitely speaking I did that before we married, but I didn't have no dream of marrying as quick as I did. I just happened to be walking along one day, me and my brother-in-law. So I told him, I said, 'I believe I'm going to get married.' I and Josie had talked about it beforehand but as far as I was concerned it wasn't anything serious about it. So when I mentioned it to her she agreed so within two weeks of the time I made this statement to him well more or less he gave me a little bet. He said I wouldn't, I said I would so . . .

How would you describe the household when you lived in the country and had three children? Was that a happy home?

I would think so. Definitely speaking I think that a city life is more or less the life that has ruined so many children simply because a child is just like anything else that's small and don't have a stabilized mind. He wants to be always going, he likes excitement and anything to laugh about. It's more or less what has caused the children to be as rough as they are today. They don't realize what bodily harm they can be doing to something but I think a child thinks that, well one child don't want the other one to be no better than he is in nothing. If it's riding an automobile or riding a bicycle or what and a person that comes along that's not going to take sides . . . say four or five kids . . . if he's not going to let all four or five of these kids ride his bike and he's got a bike and they don't have one. If they ask him for a ride maybe he don't have the time to let all of them ride and he lets one of them ride or don't let any of them ride then the first thing they'll say is let's ride it anyway. We can pull him off of there and we'll ride it ourselves. They'll probably take it away from him, see, because they don't have anything to do. If he isn't in my back yard he's in yours and if he's not there he's in this other man's and they just don't have room enough to get around so that they can play to themselves without interfering with somebody else.

How did you decide to come to St. Louis?

Well as I said in the little town in which I was staying and also around in that area I had practically worked for everybody that there was around there close even if I wasn't working for myself to say the man I worked for had a lots of equipment and a lots of land and a lot of time people would get them to come over and do some work for them and also he had a lots of people to do the work. So if I didn't work for, you know, just live with him to work for myself, well I'd work for them through this fellow. I didn't know anything about any factory work and most of the time when you're around some place like that and everyone knows you and probably knows who you work for, if you can't get along with the big man then ain't none of the rest of them going to hire you. I started off working down there for International Harvesting Company. I worked there three weeks and a half and I don't know today why those people laid me off. I mean they would compliment me on everything I did. The fact is I was installing all those different appliances and I was doing some driving too but I worked three weeks and a half and the guy told me, "Patterson, we hate it but we're going to have to lay you off for a couple of days. Maybe your old boss will have something for you to do before we call you back." So I figured then that that meant I didn't have no more job, I mean he didn't offer anything. As I say it wasn't no reason. He didn't say that I wasn't doing my job. I would have understood that.

How would you say your marriage has been?

I would say that if I had to do it all over again I don't think I would select this route that I have gone. It hasn't been too pleasant at all times. It has been fair but there is room for improvement to it. I'll say it that way. But by both of us not knowing it made it quite difficult.

What would you say have been your problems?

Well, I would say lack of understanding between the two of us. I'd say that's mostly it, referring to things that should be did. I mean there's a ruling to everything. You can't run in the house and what's on the outside of the house both at the same time, you've got to take care of one of them at a time. If you're in the house, you take care of what's in the house. If you're outside, you take care of what is out there. So I don't know whether I came in the house too much or whether I just stayed on the outside too long. It's a problem there somewhere. So I'd say that's the way it just ended up.

How do you feel about your marriage today?

Well, I mean due to the things that have passed I would say that they would be improved referring to a separation for one. I mean now I don't think it would get serious enough where it would cause another separation.

How did the separation come about?

Well as I said, lack of understanding as I said before. Simply because there's somebody right and there's somebody wrong. Well everyone thinks he's right to a certain extent so it's two sides to everything. My side is make the best out of what you have, that's the way I understand it. So I just feel that, I don't know, I take whatever it is and go along with it as long as it's nothing that's hurting me. I don't want to bother anyone and if they start to bother me I figure I can walk, shun them a lot easier than the other person could shun me.

It's the Air in Which You Were Brought Up

Steven, 19, was the oldest child still living at home. He had graduated from high school the previous spring and had married the 16-year-old daughter of a neighbor family when she got pregnant. Because Schulz knew something about the other family's view of the marriage, he was particularly eager to have Steven's version.

Steven, what I want to get is your perspective on your wedding. How did it come about? How did you decide to get married?

It was through her mother. She threatened to, well, after all, Agnes was under age, you know. And her mother decided to start coming to my mother and me and saying that if I didn't marry her she was going to try to prosecute me. And I was going to graduate that following June. I decided that that was the best way out. But sometimes we have something to say to each other and sometimes we don't have anything to say. That is under the circumstances. You know, she young and she haven't realized life yet.

How do you feel about being married now?

I just still can't understand the circumstances with her mother.

You kind of hold that against her?

True.

What do you plan to do about the situation?

I've given it a great deal of thought. It's my feeling that me and her mother never could get along. We might talk one minute and the next minute she'd be behind my back talking about me so we never could get along. Because as I said, she's a young child, you know, I mean in age. I seen her last night. Last night I was walking over in Pruitt and the young lady told me that she saw her and a fellow sitting up in the kitchen kissing and all like that. So I went up there and asked her about it. She ran to her mother and then she went in the back and closed the bedroom door. I didn't go back there, you know, cause I didn't want to start no conflict in their house. I wasn't going to do nothing to her anyway.

Have you been dating anyone else since you've been married?

No. It's just that I study a great deal and then most of the time when I get off from work I might go over to my cousin's house or my friend's house and we might play baseball or some sports like that, or we might just go out.

How come you've taken the idea of being faithful to her and still have trouble with marriage?

Well, so that way if I ever decide that I actually want a divorce it wouldn't be no static on my part.

How much do you and Agnes see each other now?

For the last couple of weeks we have been seeing each other regularly. I was trying to work and staying in the house studying. She didn't seem to realize that when I'm not at home I don't have to be with a young lady, I might be in some night

club or some social affair that I might see someone I know and
I might stop and talk but she figures I have to take this young
lady, I can't go alone. That's what she says. I think it was
drilled into her mind by her mother.

If you had your preference, would you like to see something
come out of your marriage?

Well, in a couple . . . say in 1969, when I was able, I mean I'm
able now but under the circumstances of the time when we
was married I was in school and we needed a great deal of
money to graduate and such things like that, and she was expecting at the time . . . I mean I couldn't give too much toward
her hospital bill that was coming up because I wasn't working.
Her mother started a lot of static and such things as that. She
commenced in calling the school about three times a week
cussing the principal out and such things like that. It made it
look bad on my behalf because I was playing sports. Me and
the principal we was really close. By her calling the assistant
and putting my business in the school, cause a lot of kids at
school didn't know I was married, and such things like that,
by her calling word just got around. So I mean if we were
under different circumstances we just might end up with
something.

But under present circumstances you find it difficult to see how
it could work out?

Right. I think it would have been best if we didn't get married
because during the whole nine months in which she was pregnant I didn't see her but a total of about 10 or 15 times. Because I mean I wouldn't go up to her house and she might
come down here but I usually wouldn't be here because like
I said I was playing sports and stayed late at school for practice and such things as that. Then most of the time when I'd
leave there we might . . . sometimes I might come home and
change clothes and sometimes I might go up to some center
and finish playing.

Do you think things would have been different if you could
have lived together?

No. Because I've seen the way in which her mother abuse her
brother, and she tries to run his household. He's supposed to
be the man of his house and I couldn't stand her trying to run
mine.

In general, what are the problems of teenagers here in the
project?

No, it's not the problems, I mean it's not the parents, it's them.
I mean look at a young girl . . . Well take me for example—
O.K., when she was 14 I was 17 and her mother didn't object
to us going together, so when she was 15 I got 18. Then she

became pregnant. Well her mother knew the circumstances which we were under at the present time. I mean, she couldn't wait, she wanted now and she knew she had the law behind her so she wanted to show everybody that she tried to get everything that she wants, so she forced the issue. She forced us into marriage but that's all she got out of it.

So I mean it's not just the area in which you live in. It's the air in which you were brought up and how you were taught during your life span to become or to achieve things that makes you, because a person makes himself, no one else makes a person. That's my general idea about this. I have the thought that when she's 14 and she's going with a fellow 17 and when she's 15 he's 18, I mean I'd sit down and I'd talk to both of them. I'd say you know he's older and you're younger than him. I'd say now do you all want each other? You all think a little bit cause don't no one know actually what it is. I might be up one day and the next day it might be down. And I'd just sit down and analyze to both of them. And so if she happen to become pregnant, I mean, I'd just have to sit and ask her, I'd say, even before I thought I'd be onto her head about marriage or something. You understand? The only thing I could do is just bear with her and understand her problems instead of putting her out on some fellow. That's just showing that I don't want her myself. So I feel that if they start undersanding the teenage problems more thoroughly than what they are doing nowdays we'd have a better world.

At what age in life do you think it is best to get married?

For a young man I would say 23 to 25. For a young lady I would say between 21 and 23 because they should have all the childhood behind them and understand what is toward them in the future. They should have made their plans by then if they have been going together for three or four years. They should know what they want in life, do each one of them have the same idea, do she have the same ideas which he has and do he have the same ideas which she have. I mean that's really what makes things stick. Because some women today when they get married they are not going to work. I mean you have to work a part of the time according to the predicament. I mean if you marry a rich man you ain't got no business working, why sit up there and be lazy and then there's no fun in life. I mean when your husband come home from work you tell him that the maid wash the dishes or you washed them, that's all that you could tell him. So if I marry again I want a woman that's willing to work, I mean to a certain age or until she has some kids or something and then I would like for her to retire and I'll take over the responsibility.

How would you feel about your wife at the age of 23 having relations with other men?

Well, 23, by that time I should have my divorce or me and her should be able to make it good, you know. But I mean if I had a divorce it wouldn't bother me in the least. I mean things about her don't bother me, I just would like to know why she did this and why she did that. And see, this is a large part of doing anything, that's why.

Would you marry a woman now with a child, that had a child before you got to her?

I think I would if she would understand life and she would try to help me. If she's working and I'm working and we come to an agreement about the money, the way it should be spent and which way she's go. I mean I would marry her. I give everyone the benefit of a doubt. I mean you can make a mistake.

How do you feel about your own daughter?

I'm crazy about her.

What kind of plans do you have for her?

A great deal of them for one thing. I mean I would like for her to go through high school and college, you know. At least I should say I'll try to give her the best out of life.

Do you think it's your responsibility or Agnes' to take care of the baby?

I think it's both of us. She had it and I helped make it in the process, so I feel it's both of us. I'll buy her certain pieces of clothing and extra milk and so forth like that. I'm doing what I can at the present time until things get better. I have been doing it regularly but I let my mother give it to her like she's been doing it. I didn't want her to know that I was doing it, you know.

I Want the Better Things in Life

The next oldest child still at home was Alice, 17, whose main concern seemed to be finishing high school and going on to further training for a good job so that her future would be fairly secure, even should her husband turn out to be a failure.

What can you remember about your childhood, say when you were about five years old?

I don't hardly remember too much. I just remember when I first went to grade school but that was when I was six because my birthday came around at the wrong time. I don't hardly remember too much else. I had judged life in a different way when I was about five. You know, I thought all it was was ice cream and cake and stuff like that. Then I was just like every other little young girl trying to hurry up and grow up so I could enjoy the better things in life. On my birthday they give birthday presents and getting dolls and things like that for Christmas and on special occasions. And on special occasions I like to get my little hair in a pony tail, you know, instead of wearing my hair in pigtails.

I didn't have to do anything at home because I had two big sisters and big brothers. I was considered as the baby so therefore I didn't have to do anything. I'd play and get out of their way or something like that. My big brother was really nice. He would carry me places with him and buy me nice things, you know, since I was the baby. Patsy was nice too. She would be . . . you know how big sisters are, they'd be trying to teach their little sister what's right and what's wrong, and trying to show them how to dress and stuff like that. She would teach me how to be a young lady.

What kinds of things stick out in your mind in your early schooling?

During my elementary grades in school I was mostly thinking about graduating, you know, trying to reach the top so I could come on out and get to high school. You know, trying to do my best to succeed and try to help myself to better my education and help me when I'd get much older. You know because we understood that when you do bad in school and make bad grades when you go out to find a job they will rely on your records and things. So you know I . . . tried to stay in school as often as I could and be on time because I know they look back to that too. If you didn't hardly go to school, they'd gather you wouldn't want to come to work and be late. There isn't too many employers that like for people to be late on the job. That's all I tried to do. I tried to get to the eighth grade so I could graduate and get to high school.

What about friends?

I had several friends, mostly girls. All of us was really tight. Three of them was older than I, you know, they graduated before I did and graduated out of high school before I did too. We do things together and have fun, you know, mostly after school, you know. After you do your chores at home, you know, and finish your homework and stuff like that, well we mostly get together and go down to the center. We go down there for recreation—volley ball and modern dancing and stuff like that or else we go skating and to basketball games. We have a singing group also, we rehearse singing.

What do you expect of your tight friends, the ones you're really close to?

I really expect a lot from them just like I expect them to expect a lots out of me, you know. They're my friends, if I'm in need . . . if I really need something and they have it I expect to be able to go to them and get it. And if they're my friends they wouldn't lie or nothing like that to me. If you're my close friend I wouldn't expect for you to go with my boyfriend either. You know, I wouldn't expect that because we're friends and I wouldn't expect for you to be going with him because if a friend of mine was going with this boy and they quit and he'll try to go with me I wouldn't go with him because me and the girl are good friends and the persons might start thinking that I was liking him at first and trying to go with him at first. So therefore I wouldn't like that.

Do you have a boyfriend?

Yes, I have one now. I just have one boyfriend, the rest of them are just my friends. I met him at the skating rink.

When did you have your first boyfriend?

I had my first boyfriend when I started in high school. That was in 1964. He was really a boyfriend, the others weren't really boyfriends.

When you really become girlfriend and boyfriend, what does that mean to you?

I don't know, things change so much in years. It seems like sometimes if a boy asks you to be his woman, well, you say yeah so you all go together. I guess because you all like each other. Then again some boys, like if they be talking to you— you know just keep talking to you—well, you all just take it for granted that you all go together instead of him asking you and he'll treat you like you're his girlfriend or somebody he likes. But then again some people just go with people for to be doing something. You know, they might not really like them and they just go with them. Like, you know, the pimps. The boy pimps be calling girls their girlfriends and they don't really like them, they just be going with them to get some money. So people take it in different ways.

When I call someone my boyfriend it would be someone that I like. I might not like them a great deal but I do care for them. I don't call it love because I don't know what that is right now, but, you know, I like them.

Have you ever done it with a boy?

No, I haven't, because I really haven't liked anybody enough to really go through those changes and when I do I want it to be with someone I really like and who really likes me. And furthermore that's my pride. When I give that away I haven't got anything else to offer a boy.

I imagine you have boys ask you, though.

Yes, they ask me, but when I first start going with a boy I get that plainly understood that I'm not ready for that type of thing, and if they can understand they'll stay on and if they can't it doesn't make me any different. My boyfriend understands that I'm trying to get out of school and I guess he knows I want the better things in life and I guess he wants to see that I try to get it, so I guess he can understand it. We've been going together two years and nothing has happened. He asks me because if he wouldn't I believe he would have went ahead on or something like that.

What about your girlfriends?

You know how girls are, you know they be sitting around talking and saying what's best for themselves. I don't think that's right for you to be going through those changes at this early age and you don't even know if the boy care about you or nothing like that, because they might pretend they do and say they love you but love is an everyday word, you know. So some of the girls might take it into consideration. Most of them do. We talk about those things often. And plus it's so many examples. You can see how boys are doing these girls today—getting them pregnant and going on to somebody else.

How would you describe your famliy?

Well, now I really don't know because every family has its ups and downs. You know, like sometimes the financial situation is good and they can buy a couple of things for the house and buy everybody in the house something and then again the financial problems are down. One day we get this and then you have to sacrifice one thing for something else that's really needed. As a whole I think we're going pretty well in the house. My father, I think he budgets his money and that's a nice thing for a family as large as ours, therefore I think it's pretty nice. Of course, Steven works now and he contributes to the family. I guess he knows how it is with all of us in school and we need this and that—clothing and things for school so as a whole it's going pretty nice right now. But then it will probably get better but then again it might get worse.

What sort of person is your father?

He's about like any other father—I don't know how any other father is, but he's okay. Like if he be mad, he's not okay. I guess it's just like when I be mad—I be angry at everybody or something like that. But he will give, like if we need something and come to him, if he have it to spare he'll give it to us and if he haven't got it to spare he won't. Sometimes we can't understand that, you know. At one time I didn't but now I seem to understand those things. The older I get the more I consider the person. You know, you learn those different things in school about financial problems.

What sort of person is your mother?

My mother, she's really nice. I guess all kids feel that way about their mother because the mother be with them mostly all the time when the father is at work and when you're sick she's always there or something like that. Mother is really nice. She goes out of her way to do things for us and whatever she can do to help us we can always depend on her.

How would you say your mother and father get along?

I think they get along fine. Some parents they be arguing and fighting all the time, all parents quarrel sometimes, but they don't hardly quarrel. Like if they be angry at each other they might say a couple of words and let it go at that, one of them will walk away from it. I guess because they have us and don't want to be setting a bad example in front of us.

What sort of things are you looking forward to when you think about your future?

The first thing I want to do is graduate. Then when I get out . . . I wanted to go to college, but I don't know if I'll have the money. If I don't have the money I'm going to try to get a government loan so I can go on and further my education. If I do be able to get the loan I'm thinking about going to IBM school so I can maybe get me a job for so long and then save the money and go on my own or else be working with the IBM key punching and still go into college working my way through.

Well, when do you plan to get married?

I think about it but I was thinking about getting married after I have gotten out of school, going to some kind of business school or some kind of college, having my own good job. In case, you know, if you don't have an education or anything like that and your husband walks out on you, you're just left there with nothing to rely on. So in case it happens to me in my future I'll be able to make my own way in life.

I Don't Want to Marry Just Anybody That Asks Me

Patsy, 23, no longer lived at home but had her own apartment in the project. She had four children, although she had never been married. Because she lived nearby, she and her children were very much part of the Patterson family. At the same time Patsy took considerable pleasure in maintaining her own apartment, which was very clean and neat, sparsely furnished with furniture that was by and large in good condition.

What do you remember your father being like when you were young?

Well, to me he was a lot better then than he is now because at that time he used to smile more and everything, and you could say something to him, no matter what it was, he always had a smile. But now whether you say anything to him or not he seems like he's withdrawn into himself, he acts like he's mad at the world. That's the impression I get. He seems like he don't appreciate things now as he did then. I mean he never had no compliments to make about anything. He criticizes more now.

Who does he criticize?

Well, my mother mostly. I mean it seems like she can't do anything to satisfy him. I mean if she fixes dinner he don't want it or either he'll walk in the house and he'll look at it and walk out the door. Just like this past Mother's Day my sister, my oldest sister, Mae, we usually every year get together and buy her something for Mother's Day. We bought her a suit and so she tried it on and she asked him how did he like it. He said, "You need to take it off and send it back wherever you got it from." So she didn't say anything, she went in the bedroom and changed back into what she had on. So she asked him after that why did he say what he said and he just looked at her and got up and went in the bedroom and closed the door. He's been like this for the past year. To me it seemed like he just changed overnight. He just sits there. If he's not in the living room he's in the bedroom. Just like you go in and you say, "Good evening." If he doesn't hear you he'll say "Oh, you're not speaking this afternoon." You'll say, "Well, I spoke." Then he'll say, "Oh well, that's all right then. I'm sorry I didn't hear you." But it's just the way he says it. And then just like if you go in and he be sitting in the chair in the living room you walk in and he'll glance at you and say good evening or how are you doing, but that's it. He'll turn back around. He just don't care about anything. But yet and still he just seems like he's mad about everything.

Did you like the project when you moved here?

Yes. When we moved in it wasn't very many people living in the project, in the building my mother lived in it was only about three families then. Before we moved in the project lots of the kids I went to school with moved here first. My brother and I used to come to visit them. On weekends some of them was always having a party and dances and we'd come. We knew quite a few of the people when we moved in. I didn't have any trouble. Some of my friends gave me a reputation. I used to fight all the time. When we moved here the kids that we knew from the other school had told everybody that I like to fight and didn't nobody bother me, they all was real friendly. My brother and I didn't have no trouble. A couple of the other girls that moved in after we did, well, we used to run around together at school but after school I didn't want to be with them because they would go downtown and steal and play hookey from school and I was afraid. I never did try. My brother did it once and I told on him. I told him I was going to tell. I told my mother and the principal and he got a whipping. He didn't bother me though.

Is Jackie your oldest child?

No, Ann is oldest, she's eight and then Bob is seven and Jackie is four and Joe is three.

You had your first child when you were . . . ?

Fourteen. While I was going to school. Ann's father, Bill, wasn't going to school when I met him. Him and some more fellows used to be down by the school when school let out. Every afternoon he would chase me home and then he started coming over to the school during recess when we would be outside taking exercises. One night a boy gave a dance. He lived two flights over us on the sixth floor. Bill was there. He introduced me to Bill. Bill would come down to see me. Sometimes I would be downstairs with one of my sisters and he would come and sit on the bench with me. We'd talk and everything. After that we started going together, he gave me his ring and everything. I didn't know anything about sex or where babies come from because didn't nobody tell me. We had been going together for about nine months and this lady I used to babysit for she didn't mind me having company or nothing like that as long as they leave at a reasonable time if she wasn't home. Bill would come down there and sometimes my sister or my brother would come down. This particular night he asked me and I refused and one thing led to another. He wanted to know why; I told him I was scared. He said it wasn't going to hurt. I told him I didn't know and I didn't want to find out. We got to wrestling and . . . this is sort of embarrassing . . . he just kept on pestering me. He told me I didn't care anything for him and things like that. He said he wouldn't let anything happen to me or something similar to that. This went on for about an hour and a half. I said okay and that was that. I told him to leave and he asked me if I was going to see him again, and I told him I didn't know, I told him to just leave me alone. He left. I saw him about two or three days later. He had called my mother's house, but I wouldn't talk to him on the phone. He came up there looking for me and I just didn't want to have anything else to do with him.

How did you feel about having done it with him?

I felt bad because I always have been shy to a certain extent. I didn't know I was pregnant. I was still going to school but I just kept getting bigger and I had to leave my skirt unfastened and I slept a lot. One day the principal sent for me and said he wanted to see me. I went down there and a girl that stayed in the building where mother lived had gotten in some trouble and she told the principal that I was pregnant. He asked me if I was and I told him I didn't know. He said he was going to have the nurse examine me and explained to me that if I was that he would have to send me home. So the nurse told me to turn around so she could look at me from the side and said something to him. So he told me to go on home and he would call my mother and I guess he called because when I got home she asked me why I didn't tell her. But I didn't know anything about nothing like that. She was hurt and everything, but I just told her I was sorry it had happened so she called Bill's mother and talked to her and talked to Bill.

The juvenile officer came and talked to me, he wanted to find out what had happened and he explained to me that I could have Bill locked up for statutory rape, but he said if I pressed charges against him that I had to go to jail too or something for overnight. I told him no. He asked if he had forced me or anything and I told him no and I didn't want to have him locked up. He asked me if we was planning on getting married. At the time we were. We had talked about it but at the time Bill was running around with a rowdy crowd and they was forever into fights and things. If they weren't doing that they were stealing and he stayed in jail more than he did out at that time. So I just told Mother that I didn't want to marry him. She asked me why and I told her, so she said it was left up to me. But my father felt different about it, he felt we would get married. My mother said if I didn't want to get married it didn't make sense to force me.

Before I had my baby I couldn't stand Bill. I didn't know why at the time but I know now, I guess because he was the cause of my being pregnant. I could see him walking down the street and I'd get angry and want to cry. I'd go in my room and lie down; my mother asked me what was wrong and I told her nothing. We had to go down to the children's building down on Clark and we talked to a lady down there. She was trying to find out if I helped around the house and everything and if I cause a lot of trouble. It was left up to her and my mother but it depended on what my mother told her. Besides that she would have sent me to a home, I guess. My father felt that my mother should have let me went to the home. After this lady questioned me I have to leave the room and she talked to my mother. She didn't say what sort of a home it was.

My mother said my father wanted to let me go. I know they had quite a big spout about it when we was on our way back home. I believe he was more hurt and disappointed than she was by me being his favorite. But he did everything he could for me, he was forever bringing me fruit and stuff. My older sister was pregnant at the time also, but he always bought me fruit and ice cream and things like that. I never sit down and eat a meal, I always eat lots of junk, I guess that's why.

How did you feel after you had your child?

I don't know exactly how I . . . well I don't know how to explain how I felt. Gee, I really don't know how I felt. I mean I didn't feel any different but . . . well, I knew that things were a little different than they was before. But I didn't let it bother me because the girls that I used to go to school with came around and everything. They'd come and get the baby and take her out to their house or something. So I didn't feel too much different, in a way I felt the same as I did before only I just had the baby.

Did your boyfriend treat you any different?

No, I actually treated him different. In other words as I said before, before I had the baby I couldn't stand the sight of him and as I had the baby I still felt the same way, but it wasn't as strong as it was before I had the baby. He'd call me and come by to see me but I just didn't have anything to do with him because at that time I thought I hated him. I don't know, maybe I didn't, I just didn't have anything to say to him.

How long did you wait before you started dating again?

That's hard to say. I don't know how long but I know it was quite some time after that. No, it wasn't a year, it was maybe five or six months, but we didn't go out any place, usually we'd stay around the house or something like that. We might go to the show but outside of that we didn't go out.

How did you meet Bob's father?

To tell you the truth, I don't remember. Bob's father, him and another boyfriend and some of the other fellows, they used to all play ball together I believe. And Bob's father, his name is Sam, his cousin and I used to go to school together. I met him through her. He used to come by and see me and everything. We'd sit and talk or either go to his mother's house and sit around and talk with his sisters and brothers and his mother and father. But we never went out or anything. We went to the show a couple of times—the drive-in. We never go out to dances or anything.

What got you started dating again?

Well, for one thing I was just tired of staying around the house and everybody else they was going places and doing things and I was just there. It wasn't as if the baby was holding me down or anything because if I wanted to go any place my mother she would usually watch the baby for me. But at that time before I started back to dating I didn't want to go any place. When I did I went to a couple of dances and things with the girls that I used to go to school with but I felt out of place because . . . Well the kids that was at the dance seemed more like my little sisters and brothers.

How did you come to have Bob?

I'm going to tell you the truth, I don't know. I don't remember just what happened.

Well, what was the occasion?

I don't remember. To tell you the truth I actually don't remember. I think maybe the reason I can't remember is because when I found out I was pregnant I was so hurt and disappointed and everything else and I didn't know just what to do and I thought about giving the baby away when I had it. But my mother she talked me out of that. And I just tried to forget everything about Bob's father and Bob and how it happened, because Sam and I, we were going to get married, but I found out that he was already married and I didn't know this and he hadn't never gotten a divorce from his first wife, and I just tried to forget things concerning him and Bob and myself, so actually I don't know just what happened or nothing. I don't know how to explain this but Sam he was a very nice person. He was good to me and everything but after I found out that he was married and everything, well it hurt me and I was shocked because he hadn't told me. He hadn't even mentioned anything about ever being married, not that I didn't ask him or anything. Because as a matter of fact I asked him and so had my mother and he said he wasn't married.

So when you had Bob you were 16?

No I was 15 going on 16.

You must have gotten pregnant very quickly then the second time?

Yeah, well Bob and Ann are 11 months apart.

How did you come to have Jackie? Was the next boyfriend you had after Sam the father?

No. After Sam I went with Nat.

How long was it before you met your next boyfriend?

About two or three years. It was a very long time. I went out occasionally. I stayed around the house mostly.

Jackie is four, so that must have been about two years or so. Is Jackie's father your next boyfriend? How did you meet him?

He was a friend of the family. As a matter of fact he knew me but I didn't know him. He came up to the house to see my mother and father. Harry and my cousin got together and went out and Harry started coming up to the house regular. And if he wasn't coming up to mother's house he was down at my cousin's. We went out different places.

We had fun. I did as I wanted to do and he did the same. He was forever buying me something. I don't know about other women he dated but he would always buy me candy or something and bring it to me and when I realized I was pregnant he was forever buying me things. He would come and get me after he got off from work but lots of times he would be out of the city but he wouldn't call me or anything and tell me he was tired. He's just come on by the house and tell me to put on some clothes and take me out for a while or take me out to dinner, and things like that. He was very affectionate.

Did you know Harry very long before you were pregnant?

Yes, I met him about a year and some months after Nat left, but at that time I had seen him outside but I didn't know his name or anything. But he knew my mother and my father and he knew me, but I didn't know him. He'd come up to the house. During the time he would come up to see them I would be in my room or downstairs some place, maybe I would be down at my cousin's house. So I knew him for a year and some months. My cousin said at that time him and some lady was living together. It was a couple of months.

Where did you and Harry do it ordinarily?

At his house . . . We would go out there. When we went out we would go to his house and sometimes we'd just go and get dinner and go sit for a while. He would come by and let me keep the car and when he got off from work I would go get him, or if he had the car he would come pick me up after he got off from work.

How did you feel about this pregnancy?

I don't know, I didn't feel quite so bad about it, I didn't really feel anything. Mother just asked me. She watches me, which she always says I guess because I stayed sick so much. She asked me and I told her. She asked me what were we planning on doing. Harry and I were planning on getting married and we had even went so far as having blood tests and applying for a license, but I changed my mind. I think it was more or less the idea of getting married. I was thinking about the types of marriages they had on the television and in the books. I know it's not like that. I always said I would never get married because lots of men do their wives so bad. I wanted to but when the time come I just didn't want to.

Did this have anything to do with your feelings about your mother and father's marriage?

I suppose so in a way. I don't know just why. It was other people that I knew that was married too.

When you had Jackie how did Harry take this?

He was pretty good. Jackie is his first child, at least that's what he says. He seemed to be proud of the baby and everything. He came to see me at the hospital. Sometimes he would work overtime and the people would still let him come up to see me and the baby because he explained to them that he had to work late and couldn't make it up there at visiting hours. After I went home with her he bought her clothes to wear home. He's bought her clothes since she's been home. He was always doing something for her. When Jackie was about four or five months old the girl that my brother has a baby by, she was his girlfriend, they were talking about getting married but something happened and they broke up, she was forever throwing this up about Harry and everything and at that time I was still carrying Jackie. She was living with her aunt and she had her baby before I had Jackie. She would come over to my mother's house and she'd want Harry to help her home if he wasn't there. That was all right but it became a habit. She couldn't do anything unless somebody helped her, so he started going over there or either she would call and things like that. I asked Harry what was going on between him and her. He said nothing. He finally told me that she had been calling and everything and she was expecting another child. Anyway I told him to go on if that's what he wanted. I think they got married about two or three months later. But before he ever became involved with her she had told me that this child was by some fellow who went to school with me, so I don't know.

Did you feel that you were in love with Harry?

No, I don't think so.

How did you come to meet Joe's father?

We met at a bowling alley. He lived across the street from mother. I met him at this bowling alley the night I found out his name and everything. After that night when my friends and I would go to the bowling alley he would usually be there and he would buy all of us something to drink or whatever we wanted. When we got ready to leave, he would tell me he would see me the next night we would be there. The last time we all was there together he asked me if he could take me out and I told him yes, so we went out together quite a few times, we went bowling and things like that. We didn't go to the show because he didn't care to go to shows. We would usually get something to drink and then go bowling or either we would bowl first and then go in the lounge and have something to drink or go to his mother's house and listen to records or something. That was about all.

Were you looking for a boyfriend at the time when you met him? Are you still going with him?

No, I haven't seen him in I don't know how long, since Joe was a year and some months. No, I wasn't looking for a boyfriend.

What sort of relationship did you have with him?

To tell you the truth, not any, really, not hardly any. I'll put it that way. Because after he and I had been going together for —I don't know how long we had been going together, anyway I think it was about two and a half months—he told me he was leaving, he was going to Memphis because the place he worked was sending him there to open up a restaurant or something, I forgot exactly why. Anyway he was due to leave that Friday or that Saturday after he got off from work. Anyway we went out together and afterwards we went back to his house over here and we sat there and played records and the man that stayed next door came over and they sent and got something to drink and we sat there talking and listening to some records. Then that fellow left. He and I had an intercourse and after that he walked me home and he left that next morning. Well, during the time he was gone I found out I had gotten pregnant.

He had written me and I knew where he was, the address and everything, even the phone number, but I didn't call to tell him and I didn't write him. I was about three or four months pregnant when he came back and he called me. He told me to meet him because he was on his way down to my mother's house and he told me to meet him. So I walked down there and when he saw me he said, "What wrong with you?" I said, "I'm going to have a baby." He said, "Well why didn't you write and tell me?" I told him I didn't want to. He said, "Why, you thought maybe I'd say it's not mine or something?" I said, "I don't know. I just didn't want to do it." He asked me how far along was I and I told him. Then he kept asking why I didn't call and why I didn't write. I told him I didn't know. Which I didn't know. It was just something I didn't want to do.

How old was he?

He was 24.

You were . . . ?

Nineteen. We talked about getting married and everything which I said, we even went down to the courthouse and had our blood tests taken. We applied for a license and he paid for it but when the day came for us to get married, I got sick. I guess it was from being afraid. I went down there. He called me from work and told me to meet him in front of City Hall. I caught a cab and went down there and he wasn't there and he wasn't there when I got there so I waited for him. When I saw him coming I met him. He said, "Come on and let's go in and get married." I said, "Wait a minute. Something is wrong with my shoe." Which it *was* something wrong with my shoe. He said, "What's wrong with your shoe?" I said, "I don't know." So I took it off and he looked and something was wrong with the heel. He said, "Well, come on, it won't take but a minute. It won't take but a minute and it will all be over." He said it's just a couple of steps to the door, all you have to do is walk those few steps and go on inside. I said, "Okay." We started walking and I said, "I don't know. Take me home." He told me to come on since we were down there we could go on and get it over with. I said, "Naw, I want to go home. I told you I'm sick." So he stopped a cab and we got the cab and went up to mother's house. He told my mama, "Do you know what she did to me?" My mother said "What?" He said, "She got down there and started talking about she was sick." My mother said, "Patsy, what's the matter?" I said, "Nothing, I just didn't want to get married." She said, "Why?"

I didn't know why at that time, but afterwards I was glad I didn't marry him because we wouldn't have really been married no way. Because he hadn't never got a divorce from his first wife. She doesn't live in St. Louis, she lives in Chicago, but he's never gotten a divorce from her. I'm kind of glad I didn't go ahead and marry him. Afterwards I guess my mother understood why. I just felt funny. It's not that I didn't want to get married, I wanted to get married, but it was this one thing there and I didn't know what it was, so I just didn't go through with it. After that he kept coming around and everything trying to get me to go on and marry him. He would come down and bring the money for Joe to get his milk and things with and for his medicine. At that time Joe was real sickly and at that time I was running back and forth to the hospital and then his milk cost me $1.50 a can. He bought him and Jackie's clothes most of the time. As a matter of fact he bought more things for Jackie than he did for Joe.

Are you afraid of getting pregnant again?

No. I don't know why but I'm not because I would like to have another little boy, but to tell you the truth I don't believe I can have any more kids. I need building up because I have a very weak stomach and even if I did get pregnant I wouldn't be able to hold the baby. I had such a hard time with the last two I really don't believe I'll be able to hold a baby. I'm taking vitamin pills and iron pills and about four or five other different kinds of pills. The doctor says I'm anemic and I need building up.

But you don't use any contraceptive?

No, I don't believe in that.

How do you feel now about marriage?

I want to get married, but I don't want to marry just anybody that asks me. I don't know what type of man I'm looking for, not exactly, but my present boyfriend seems to meet standards. Lots of women marry a man and they've got kids by someone else and don't have any by this man, he mistreats her kids and if she has a child by him he treats his like a queen. And then if they don't have any by him he still might mistreat the kids, but yet and still he's supposed to be so much in love with the mother and care so much for her. I don't want anything like this. If necessary I'll wait until my kids are big enough to take care of themselves before I get married.

Do you think Ralph would do this?

No, he wouldn't do it. Out of all this time we have been together he haven't done it so far. Now if we did get married he might change but I doubt it seriously.

What would your idea of a good marriage or the most perfect kind of marriage be?

It don't necessarily have to be perfect because I don't think there is a marriage today that is perfect. The only thing I'm looking for and the only thing I ask is that they respect my kids and me and do whatever they can for us. I'll try and I'm sure they would also do whatever they can and whatever is in their power for the other person. If a person loves you and if you love a person and have some sort of feeling toward them, you're not going to hurt them.

7.

Marital Roles
and Marital Disruption

The Patterson children, Steven and Patsy, suggest the variety of marital and mating relations that exist in the Pruitt-Igoe community, and the personal histories that result in unwed ADC mothers, marriages forced by pregnancy, marital instability, and the like. The relationship of the elder Pattersons shows something of the struggle to maintain marriage against the competing attractions of the streets, although Mr. Patterson's penchant for maintaining more than one family is relatively uncommon, and Mrs. Patterson is notably forebearing in her willingness to accept his departure each time he leaves. Perhaps she behaves as she does because the rural value of monogamy is very strong in her, and perhaps because she knows Mr. Patterson can be an above-average provider if he ever settles down.

In Alice we see how fragile is the hope for significant improvement on the instability and insecurity that characterized the conjugal experiences of her parents and her older siblings. She hopes to acquire the training that will allow her to be economically independent so that she will not be at the mercy of a man like her father. From her observation of her father, her older sister, and her brother, it is all too apparent that a woman needs to be able to make her own way in life should her man walk out on her. Yet her desire for the conventional good life, and the tenuousness of her hope for it, make her turn away from what goes on at home; she puts a normalized face on it when she says of her parents, "I think they get along fine . . . I guess it's because they have us and don't want to be setting a bad example in front of us." Her sister, having long ago accepted the hopelessness of her own situation, can afford to be honest with herself about her father and to accept the anger she feels toward him for his treatment of the family.

Conjugal Separateness and Conjugal Discretion

Marital relations in the white and Negro lower class are generally characterized by a high degree of conjugal role segregation.[1] The partners tend to organize their married life on the basis of separate kinds of functioning, both in carrying out the instrumental tasks of family life and in pursuing recreational and outside interests. The husband's role as provider dominates his wife's conception of what he must do, and husbands tend to resist taking responsibility around the home, feeling that while they are bringing home a pay check little else can be asked of them. Husbands expect the right to spend time away from the family pursuing their individual interests. When they do stay around the house they expect to be free to watch television or pursue their hobbies. Wives are responsible for home and children and are expected to depend little on their husbands for assistance or advice in carrying out these responsibilities. Wives expect to pursue independently of their husbands whatever legitimate interests they have outside the home; these consist primarily of maintaining relations with kin or, particularly in the Negro lower class, participating in church activities.

This pattern of conjugal role segregation accurately characterizes the marital relations of Pruitt-Igoe husbands and wives. It highlights as particularly problematic the issues of loyalty, intimacy, and stability. These issues can be seen as a particular version of the general marital problem of establishing a satisfactory pattern of separateness and connectedness. In discussing this basic process in the family Hess and Handel observed:

> Two conditions characterize the nuclear family. Its members are connected to one another, and they are also separate from one another. Every family gives shape to these conditions in its own way. Its life may show greater emphasis on the one or the other: yet both are constitutive of family life. . . This fundamental duality of family life is of considerable significance, for the individual's efforts to take his own kind of interest in the world, to become his own kind of person, proceed apace with his efforts to find gratifying connection to the other members. At the same time the other members are engaged in taking their kinds of interest in him, and in themselves. This is the matrix of interaction in which a family develops its life. The family tries to cast itself in a form that satisfies the ways in which its members want to be together and apart. The pattern it reaches is a resultant of these diverse contributions.[2]

1. For discussions of white lower-class families see Rainwater, Coleman, and Handel (1959), Rainwater (1964), Gans (1962), Cohen and Hodges (1963), Miller (1964), Komarovsky (1964). Discussions of lower class Negro family life can be found in Frazier (1966), Bernard (1966), Cayton and Drake (1962), Clark (1965), Davis, Gardner and Gardner (1941), Jeffers (1967), Liebow (1967), Lewis (1955), Rohrer and Edmonson (1960).

2. Hess and Handel (1959).

These issues are expressed in the continuing interaction of husband and wife most directly in the extent to which they pursue individual interests separate from (irrelevant to or competitive with) those of the couple as joint heads of a family. Either partner can define his role so that he devotes the major portion of his time, energy, and emotional commitment to activities intrinsic to the family's well-being, or so that he can invest some significant portion of his energies in activities thought to be purely for his own benefit and gratification. Very schematically, then, either partner can be committed or relatively uncommitted. Either partner can carry out his marital role to characterize himself as a "free" man or woman in the sense that non-family interests and activities loom large enough in the way he spends his time and the commitments he makes for his behavior to be regarded as inimicable to family interests. Or he may subordinate these outside interests sufficiently to be characterized as a home-committed man or woman in the sense that family interests are assumed to take precedence over non-family interests. For the home-committed husband, activities aside from those related to his job (which always implicitly involve central family interests) are subordinated to any conflicting claims of family need. For the home-committed wife, no interests aside from those directly related to the care and maintenance of the family are allowed precedence.

It should be understood that these types represent adaptive orientations to the situations in which people find themselves, and are not to be conceived as character types or orientations that are immune to the changing situations of the persons involved. When Pruitt-Igoe families are observed over a period of time it is possible to see shifts in the orientation of both husbands and wives to their outside and home commitments. Indeed, far more important than the simple existence of these different kinds of role commitments or their representation and justification in the subcultural meanings of the group is the ebb and flow of commitment as the spouses' marital careers develop.

The four marital types that result from the combination of these two different kinds of commitments by the two marital partners can be characterized in the Pruitt-Igoe community as follows.

When both husband and wife forsake competing outside commitments they jointly define as in the family's interest, they follow a pattern to which the common sense term *togetherness* might be applied. Togetherness is the ideal conception of marriage-in-a-good-world held by the men and women in Pruitt-Igoe, and it is in fact the typical stable working-class and lower-middle-class marital pattern. In this kind of relationship the bond between husband and wife is consciously strengthened in every possible way and the outside interests of either partner are seen as threats to marital solidarity. Both husband and wife define the primary locus of self-expressiveness as in the family. They regard the family and its well-being as their principal source of self expression, recognition, love, and a general sense of being gratifyingly engaged in life. But the achievement of this kind of marital relationship for any period of time is difficult in the lower-class Negro situation. In those few cases in our data where this characterization can be applied its achievement is tenuous. Those couples who begin their marriage with one or both partners employed often move in this direction as they "settle down," but as time goes on they tend to meet frustrations that discourage their efforts to build a home together. In response, one or both may become increasingly attracted to the possibilities for self-expression and self-esteem on the outside.

The "free-man" and "home-committed woman" pattern is characteristic of lower-class family life generally and quite characteristic of marital relations in the Pruitt-Igoe sample. This is the most common way in which a segregated conjugal role organization is expressed. Here the man defines himself as justified in pursuing his own outside commitments to friends and activities that subtract from family resources; the extent to which such behavior is accepted by the wife varies depending on other characteristics of their situation. The home-committed woman can be characterized as "long-suffering." She devotes her energies to maintaining the household and caring for the children. She seeks emotional gratification principally in these activities and in her relations with her children and perhaps one or two close kinsmen. She is dissatisfied with her relationship with her husband, but tolerates it as the best that is available to her.

The other two patterns do not usually support stable marital relationships. Although they occur with some frequency, they are harbingers of disruption. For example, the pattern of "home-committed man" and "free-woman" is unlikely to persist for long because the cultural values of the group define this situation as intolerably insulting to the man. The wife's pursuit of outside interests is more visible than comparable pursuit by the man and therefore more troubling because her responsibilities are defined so that she is expected to be around the home almost all of the time. The transitory nature of this pattern is, however, much more characteristic of lower-class Negro than lower-class white groups.

The "free-man" and "free-woman" pattern is similarly unstable. However, it can occur for a time, either when marriages are entered with a relatively weak commitment by both partners or when the partners, frustrated in their efforts to maintain a family consistent with their ideal conceptions, react by seeking outside avenues of self-expression and self-esteem. Again this kind of relationship, even on a temporary basis, is more likely to occur in the Negro lower class than in the white lower class. Both white and Negro lower-class men strive to prevent their wives from developing outside interests, whether they themselves cultivate such interests, but white men seem to be more successful and can draw more on peer-group resources in support of their efforts, whereas the Negro lower-class woman can draw on important subcultural resources to support her decision to de-emphasize marital ties. To the extent that the Negro woman can develop meaningful outside interests that provide her with a sense of social stability, she will be less inclined to put up with her husband when she finds the relationship frustrating than will her white counterpart.

In Chapter 3 we discussed the argument common in the project that "stepping out" on one's spouse is not destructive so long as the partner does not learn about it. Often this argument is not selfish, in that (in the abstract) the same right is accorded to one's spouse. However, very few respondents maintained that infidelity can be practiced without high risk.

The existence of this counternorm of discreet "stepping out" suggests that the principal concern of spouses is with loyalty and affection more than with exclusive sexual rights. That is, the focus of concern seems to be that sexual infidelity will become part of a pattern of disloyalty in which resources devoted to a competing relationship are withdrawn from the family. For instance, a man may spend time, money, and affection in an extramarital relationship that his spouse would prefer to have available to maintain the family and for herself. The counternorm may represent an effort to say that sexual infidelity is no great issue, but what is really feared is a competing social relationship that makes it even more difficult to maintain the family as a going enterprise.

In fact, most Pruitt-Igoe spouses are quite vigilant about their partner's behavior, by their actions denying the counternorm they assert. For example, one woman in her forties said:

> My husband and I, we go out alone and sometimes stay all night. But when I get back my husband doesn't ask me a thing and I don't ask him anything . . .
> A couple of years ago I suspected he was going out on me. One day I came home and my daughter was here. I told her to tell me when he left the house. I went into the bedroom and got into bed and then I heard him come in. He left in about ten minutes and my daughter came in and told me he was gone. I got out of bed and put on my clothes and started following him. Soon I saw him walking with a young girl and I began walking after them. They were just laughing and joking right out loud right on the sidewalk. He was carrying a large package of hers. I walked up behind them until I was about a yard from them. I had a large dirk which I opened and had decided to take one long slash across the both of them. Just when I decided to swing at them I lost my balance—I have a bad hip. Anyway, I didn't cut them because I lost my balance. Then I called his name and he turned around and stared at me. He didn't move at all. He was shaking all over. The girl just ran away from us. He still had her package so the next day she called on the telephone and said she wanted to come pick it up. My husband washed his face, brushed his teeth, took out

his false tooth and started scrubbing it and put on a clean
shirt and everything, just for her. We went downstairs together
and gave her the package and she left.

So you see my husband does run around on me and it seems
like he does it a lot. The thing about it is he's just getting too
old to be pulling that kind of stuff. If a young man does it then
that's not so bad—but an old man, he just looks foolish. One
of these days he'll catch me but I'll just tell him, "Buddy you
owe me one," and that'll be all there is to it. He hasn't caught
me yet though.

Discretion is important in determining the effect of extensive outside
involvements on the marital tie. Thus, it is possible to find stable family
relationships in which the husband engages in discreet affairs, from time
to time, but in these situations the husband limits his outside involvements
and exercises care to keep them from intruding on his marriage. In turn,
a certain amount of discretion is required of the wife, who may have sus-
picions but who makes an implicit bargain with her husband by not being
vigilant or enterprising in testing them. The woman quoted above precipitated a family crisis, apparently because she felt her husband had
violated their implicit bargain by not being discreet enough. The indiscreet man (or more rarely, woman) threatens his role within the family
and tends to disrupt the relationship by the obviousness of his infidelities
or disloyalties.

On occasion men seem to use disloyalty almost consciously as a way of
breaking up a relationship they find oppressive for one reason or another.
Wives tell stories over and over about husbands' flaunting their girlfriends
by sitting in a car outside the family's apartment or by walking where
their wives are likely to see them, or generally by having a relationship so
public that gossip is inevitable and the wife must take cognizance of the
outside relationship. Sometimes a husband may go so far as to bring the
other woman into the home by one ruse or another. In the cases we have
observed, the wife seldom tolerates this behavior; she either reacts violently and attacks her husband or the other woman, or ends the relationship, temporarily or permanently. The husband's behavior in many of
these situations is so blatant that it is difficult to believe the family crisis is
precipitated by "accident"; flaunting another woman may be seen better
as an institutionalized way of ending a relationship. Later, of course, the
man may change his mind and try to persuade his wife to take him back,
as in the case of Mr. and Mrs. Patterson.

Women whose husbands have been indiscreet freemen often seem more
angered and hurt by the indiscretion than by the infidelity itself. The
indiscretion results in intolerable insults to their pride and lowers their
status before their peers whereas the discretely managed infidelity, even
though suspected by the wife, allows her some autonomy in determining
her response to it. If the relationship is important enough, she can by her

own discretion limit the impact of infidelity, or she can decide to precipitate a crisis by bringing the outside relationship into the open.

The combination of the variable of outside involvement which withdraws resources from the family and the variable of circumspection in the
obviousness of this withdrawal, then, yields four categories of spouses for
which we can find representatives in our data.[3] These four types are
identified as follows:

1. Those who do not have competing outside involvements and
   who are circumspect about attending to family matters we call
   home-committed.

2. Those who do have outside involvements but are circumspect
   about appearing to attend to the family's interests we call *discreet free men or women.*

3. Those who have outside involvements and do not prevent them
   from becoming central in the social identity they assume within
   the family we call *indiscreet free men or women.*

4. Finally, those self-absorbed persons who have no strong outside involvements but who at the same time fail to manifest circumspect attention to family interest and family matters we
   call *withdrawn.*

This latter pattern seems frequently to characterize somewhat older
working- and lower-class white husbands, but was not commonly observed
among the men in Pruitt-Igoe. Perhaps the allure of ghetto street life at-
tracts men whose relations with their families are weak, so that they do not
retreat into themselves at home. Perhaps because of the forces which tend
to disrupt ghetto marriages early in their history, men never reach this
later point in married life when they turn increasingly inward. The pattern
of withdrawal, however, does characterize some women in Pruitt-Igoe,
particularly some older female heads of household who become increasingly remote from their family without at the same time taking up outside
interests. The pattern then takes on the characteristics of the depressive
style of adaptation described in Chapter 5.

Highly segregated conjugal role relationships receive strong support
from others in the social network of a husband and wife. In the lower
class, men know they must begin to settle down when they get married,
but one of the marks of masculinity is not to become too quickly or too
thoroughly domesticated.[4] The young husband, Negro and white, expects
to continue to enjoy some of the pleasures of his peer group, and his attachment to that group is often a source of tension during the early period
of lower-class marriages. In the lower-class Negro ghetto these tendencies
are stronger because of the elaborately developed street culture; a young
man often finds it easier to achieve self-respect from the response of his

3. Schulz (1969) discusses three of these types with extensive case examples.
4. W. Miller (1963).

peers in the streets than from playing the role of good provider to his new family. In the streets no one is greatly concerned about whether the players are married or single, and in fact part of the game can be to cause husbands to be disloyal to their spouses. If (as is often the case) the wife was pregnant before marriage, has already had illegitimate children, or had developed a street reputation, others can suggest to the husband that he need not be too concerned about remaining loyal to her.

Female relatives and girlfriends support the wife's definition of her role as completely in charge of the household. In advising her of her rights *vis-a-vis* her husband and of her duties as the central person of the family, they will systematically reinforce a highly segregated role relationship. Although if they see the husband as a "good man," a stable provider, they will advise her of ways to solidify her relationship with him. They will share with the wife a basic conception of the marital relationship as one in which the joint involvement of the spouses in family activities and decisions is minimal.[5] If the husband is particularly difficult or irresponsible, the wife can generally count on at least the tolerance, if not the active assistance and encouragement, of her female relatives and friends if she becomes involved with boyfriends. They will share the common view that a woman has as much right as a man to sexual and affectional activities, and that she is justified in engaging in such behavior if her husband proves himself to be so indiscreetly disloyal as to threaten the integrity of the marriage.

Conjugal role relationships characterized by a high degree of segregation can become routinized ways of organizing marital life, but as with other styles, stability can only exist in situations where the relationship is not subject to heavy external pressures. The lower class Negro world is one in which such pressures abound. They come from the economic marginality which affects the husband's ability to fulfill his role as provider, from the seductions and depredations of the surrounding social world, and from the deep suspicion of others which the partners themselves feel as a result of growing up in that world. In the marriages of Pruitt-Igoeans a competitive struggle develops over time in which each spouse seeks to control the other's behavior to ensure commitment to the home. This struggle can be to maintain highly solidary relations in which both partners are heavily committed even though their role relationship is on a segregated basis, or it can be to maintain an asymmetrical relationship in which one partner remains home-committed while the other is free to cultivate outside involvement. Husbands often try to enforce a home-committed and self-effacing role for the wife, while reserving for themselves the right to step out when they want to. Wives are liable to respond to this first by asserting themselves through threats, insults, and withdrawal of the hus-

5. Compare Komarovsky's (1964) discussion of "Barriers to Marital Communication" and "Confidants Outside of Marriage" for the white working class.

band's rewards and privileges around the home in an effort to force him to devote himself wholeheartedly to his family. Failing this, wives may then embark on a punitive relationship in which the husband is merely tolerated around the home for the little he contributes to it but is not accorded the full status of head of the household, even within the relatively restricted meaning that status has in the highly segregated relationship.

This situation puts heavy pressure on a husband who seeks to live up to the role of loyal breadwinner. Basically, his status within the home rests narrowly on his ability to bring money into the household. Because of their culturally-supported low estimation of men as providers, wives have low tolerance for any departures by the husband from this role. Indeed, they are often ready to blame an unemployed husband for his unemployment, accusing him of not wanting to work rather than not being able to find work unless he has a good work history that distinguishes him from other men.

Even if he does provide well, the husband is subject to a good deal of suspicion about what he does with his time away from home. He will often feel that he must spend time with other men in the streets if he is to retain his self-respect as a man and not be regarded as a henpecked husband; but his wife will be doubtful about what he does there, and will be especially sensitive to evidence that he is diverting money outside, either for free spending or for self-indulgent items such as automobiles. His wife will generally be unreluctant to criticize him before their children and close adults for such behavior. If the husband can control his situation so that he is both a good provider and an assertive but not irresponsible masculine person both at home and outside, the stability of the relationship is reinforced. If however, he slips in either of these respects, he is subject to increasing pressure from his wife and often from his older children.

A husband responds to these pressures with prickly self-defensiveness. He is inclined to counter-attack, perhaps most strongly when he is most aware of his role failures—when he is unemployed or deeply involved in outside relationships. Then he seeks to enforce respect by beating up the wife or the children, or by aggressive outbursts that stop short of physical attack but threaten it in the future. Beatings and arguments precipitated by a husband seem to occur particularly when there is a disjunction between the demands on him as provider and his ability to meet those demands—when he becomes unemployed and cannot or does not find another job. They also seem to occur when the wife becomes pregnant with an unwanted child. Such behavior is regarded as inexplicable by both the wife and the husband; no clearcut reason for these outbursts or attacks can be pointed to by the wife, and the husband himself may claim that he does not know why he acted as he did. The lack of explanation for such behavior of course enhances such basic beliefs as "men are no damn good," or in a slightly more flattering masculine version, those beliefs Elliot Liebow has called the "theory of manly flaws."[6]

Matrifocality

The high degree of conjugal role segregation in lower-class Negro families combined with a conception of men as unstable providers and inherently disloyal husbands results in a pervasive matrifocal emphasis in marital and family life. By matrifocal we mean simply that the continuing existence of the family is focused around the mother, that the father is regarded (to a greater or lesser degree) as marginal to the continuing family unit composed of mother and children. In such families the wife makes most of the decisions that keep the family going and has a sense of ultimate responsibility for maintaining the family as a solidary unit and the family is oriented for support when necessary to the mother's female relatives. The many female-headed households are of course, matrifocal by default, but observation of households in which the husband/father is present suggests that even there the male tends to take a back seat, regarding his role as met in substantial part simply by the provision of income. Because wives are socialized to expect this kind of relationship, they can even be quite resistant to husbands who assert themselves in an effort to become more central to the family's functioning.

The matrifocality of these families has several aspects, one of which is *feminine authority*. Wives readily assume that theirs is the basic responsibility for the family. They look to a husband to make it easier for them to meet this responsibility, but they do not regard the husband as equally responsible. Their full authority over the family is almost automatically asserted at any point at which the husband seems to fail as provider and father. Wives will defer to husbands who are fulfilling the provider role in a satisfactory way but their acceptance is almost transparently provisional.

Matrifocality involves a strong assertion of *feminine equality* in the marital relationship. Women are deemed to have equal rights to find in marriage personal gratification equal to that of the man, or to ignore their marriage with equal irresponsibility. There is a taken-for-grantedness about wifely infidelity in Pruitt-Igoe that is quite uncharacteristic of the white lower class (which is not to say that it is not strongly disapproved by husbands and others). This equal right to conjugal irresponsibility is in striking contrast to the strong responsibility a woman accepts in her parental role; she may have the right to step out on her husband if she has sufficient justification, but she has no right to abandon or ignore her children. For fathers, however, there is an almost equally taken-for-granted quality about their potential irresponsibility in both conjugal and parental roles.

6. Liebow (1967), p. 116 ff.

A further characteristic of the matrifocal pattern is recognition of the reality of *male marginality*. It is assumed that men will often be unable to fulfill their provider role, that additionally and at the same time they may prove to be irresponsible with what little they earn, and that they will not seek to compensate for their failure as providers by being especially helpful around the house. "Men are just like that;" they are "naturally" irresponsible are two common arguments; in other circumstances it may be argued that men cannot help themselves because they do not get a chance to behave responsibly (as in the case of John Martin in Chapter 12). But whatever folk explanations are offered, the reality of male marginality is taken for granted; the matrifocal pattern provides a way of conducting necessary family business despite the fact that "men are no help."

When wives have jobs, this matrifocal emphasis is exacerbated, because working wives show an even greater tendency to resist male assertions of authority. The husbands, for their part, are even more inclined to withhold some of the money they earn from the family coffers, and contention is common over how the money each partner earns is to be used. It is especially in this situation that the basic assumptions about feminine responsibility and authority appear most clearly. The field workers observed several situations in which the husband felt that when the wife worked it was her responsibility to spend all of her earnings on the family and it remained his option to withhold more of his earnings for his own indulgence.

Men are very sensitive to the exercise of feminine authority. They find themselves frequently at a disadvantage *vis-a-vis* their wives within the family and in their intimate social network. When they cannot provide for the family properly or when they allow themselves to be seduced by the attractions of the street world , they have great difficulty maintaining status in the eyes of their wives and in the eyes of their children as they grow up and come to appreciate what is going on. Because of their marginality, they are locked in an asymmetrical power relationship in which it is much easier for wives to earn respect and status than it is for husbands. Wives are often attracted by the possibilities of earning status with other women by attacking and demeaning their husbands, contrasting their own strength as family heads. The husband often reacts punitively in a desperate effort to regain status and respect, at least for his power to disrupt things. He may do this by flaunting his disloyalty or by physical efforts to assert his authority over his family, but in both cases the very methods by which he seeks to impress the family lower further his legitimacy in their eyes.

It is important to understand how deeply taken for granted these matrifocal patterns are. For the woman, taken for grantedness involves most centrally the knowledge that she can head a household if she must, that this is not a remarkable event in her world, and that her culture provides techniques and support for doing this. The man takes for granted that he can ignore paternal responsibilities without serious penalty and in fact without great loss of status for his wife and children. He knows that his wife (by herself or with the aid of her female relatives) can take over the family with a minimum of strain, because the family has been economically marginal all along and because female-headed households, while not considered desirable, are expected in their world.

Finally, all this affects the meaning of marriage. Given this matrifocal pattern, and given the events of courtship and mating, getting married can be regarded not so much as the contracting of a long-term relationship but as a *rite de passage*, which everyone should go through to signify his coming of age, his maturity as an adult. One may marry only to give a baby a name, to confer the title of Mrs., or (in a less clear-cut way) to denote arrival at the status of adult man or woman.

Marital Instability

Our examination of marital relationships in Pruitt-Igoe suggests that these relationships characteristically involve a heightened and constant concern with problematic aspects of conjugal roles—particularly with issues of subsistence and of conjugal solidarity and intimacy. The last of these is the first goal of marriage liable to be sacrificed. In response to the many pressures upon them, marital partners scale down their expectations for a sense of intimacy in marriage. However, the desperate interpersonal needs and anxieties of the partners, needs and anxieties heightened by their depriving existence, lead them to make heavy demands on each other. These demands are often expressed as conflicts over resources, over roles, or over loyalty, but often they reflect a hunger for intimacy and security of companionship. Each partner is wary of trying to meet this hunger lest the exigencies of their situation cause him to promise more than he can deliver and thus further erode the fragile marital tie. In response to the frustrations thus introduced into the relationship, partners are often incited by their own feelings and by the hostile responses of their spouses to action which by small or large steps lead to disruption of the marriage and to the very high proportion of "female-headed households" so often noted by commentators on the Negro family.

The destructive chain of influences leading to marital instability and dissolution is schematized in the following diagram. Figure 7-1 indicates the major paths of causality indicated by our analysis of the Pruitt-Igoe community, and of the lower class Negro ghetto more generally. (The relationships are, of course, mutual, in the sense that there is a feedback from each of the factors phrased here as dependent variables, the single arrows indicate priority of causality both in time and in larger sustaining social forces.)

At the root of these marital problems, as of all other problems peculiar to the lower-class Negro ghetto, is the pattern of racial oppression which produced the ghetto and operates to sustain it. These ghettoes are sustained by two principal effects of racial oppression. The first is the eco-

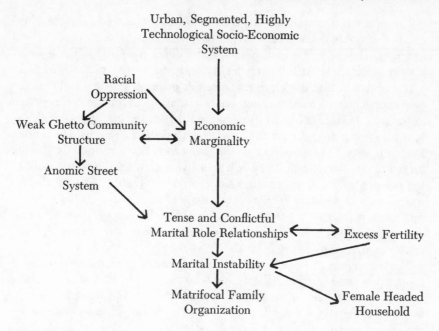

Figure 7–1

nomic marginality of lower-class Negro men, a product of the interaction of race victimization with the urban, segmented, high-technology socio-economic system that produces few jobs for unskilled persons at adequate wages, and that tends to substitute education for work experience as an avenue for progression from one skill and income level to another. The second is the weak ghetto community structure, which has not developed the same kinds of local control and surveillance that appeared in the white lower-class areas in the course of the odyssey of white immigrants to the city.[7] This weak community structure sustains an anomic street system within the ghetto community in which the possibilities for manipulation and exploitation of the members by each other are almost unlimited.

The joint effect of the anomic street system and economic marginality is to create a situation in which marital role relationships are highly conflictful and in which great doubt is introduced into the relationship, because neither partner can ever be sure of the extent to which he can depend upon his spouse. Added to this system of troubled marital role relationships are the pressures of excess fertility, stemming from poor access to contraceptive methods and poor marital communication about family planning. As the couple has more and more children the pressure on the wife to be increasingly demanding of her husband increases and her resentment of him grows apace. From his perspective, the impossibility of meeting these growing demands becomes more and more apparent.

7. See Glazer and Moynihan (1963), Suttles (1969).

The result is a pattern of unstable marriages. This instability is adaptively resolved in one of two ways: either by breaking the conjugal tie and forming a female-headed household, or by developing a family role organization characterized by matrifocality and marginality of the husband.[8]

It is apparent that the generalized beliefs of Pruitt-Igoeans and the specific experiences of husbands and wives establish conceptions of marriage as highly unstable. It is taken for granted that many marriages break up. It is also taken for granted that one's own marriage may be vulnerable. Estimates among respondents of the proportion of marriages that break up ran to well above half; the mean estimate was that 5.8 marriages out of ten eventually break up; and considerably more than a third of the respondents believed that 70 per cent or more of marriages eventually break up. These views did not seem to be affected by the sex of the respondent or even by whether the respondent was currently married, widowed, separated, or divorced.

The awareness of the stresses on marriage is clear in our respondents' replies to a series of questions asking why they believed marriages break up, whether the man or the woman is most at fault, and what might help to prevent marriages from breaking up. The principal categories of response were as follows:

Running Around and Jealousy

> The man is more likely to leave because the woman can't do too much if she has a lot of children to take care of. It could be prevented by being a good wife to your husband, by staying at home and taking care of children and not running the streets so much. The biggest majority of men don't want no wife who runs the streets. They want them to stay at home to take care of the children.
>
> The women go around with other men. The woman most often causes the break-up. If the woman would stay home and care for the family, the marriage wouldn't break up. She has to show that she's doing her obligations to the children.
>
> They get married too young. Most often it's the woman who causes the separation. She figures he's going out by another girl and wants him home all the time. A man should be prepared for marriage, have his job situated so they won't have to suffer.
>
> Mainly it's misunderstandings. More likely the man breaks it up. If both would do right and treat each other right and not have no boyfriends, they could stay together. They don't treat him right if they have a boyfriend.
>
> Marriages break up because they know too much about each other beforehand. I think it's mostly the man's fault. If they

8. For discussion of the impact of social structural factors on rates of marital disruption see Bernard (1966), Udry (1966), and Rainwater (1966).

would stay home and try to stop drinking and running around both of them, then the marriage wouldn't break up. They care more for one another and get interested in their homes and take care of their children.

They break up because the husband doesn't bring money home or the wife takes up with other men or the husband be messing around with other women. If they take care of each other and their children instead of all that, the marriage would work.

It's caused by a woman lying to her husband, stepping out on him. If they get together and seek things out as they should, work out their differences, they can pick up from there.

I guess the fault's on both sides. If the family would do things together, when the husband come from work, it would probably work out better. When they run out you know they're going to run into something out there, then they neglect what's at home.

Money and Jobs

The men don't have jobs. The woman, she starts nagging. He don't have the money so he leaves. She ADC's it. If he had a job the family unit could come back together. Going to church could bring the family together.

Marriages break up because boys lose jobs, and some won't bring their money home. If they could get a house right off to themselves, this helps them. Sometimes they have to start off in the home with the parents. But if they live by themselves, they wouldn't have anyone there to take care of them so he would have to work.

The main cause is finance. The man leaves his job. Man don't have responsibility so they break up. Like the Black Muslims say, if men take responsibility and take care of their families, they'll stay together.

Settling Down and Compatibility

It's the man's fault because he doesn't want to settle down. He's not willing to accept responsibility. He doesn't know how to be a husband.

It's because they didn't care for one another in the first place. I ain't going to tell no lie, it's the fault of both sides. If I had a good husband, I would be with him now.

It's not a strong marriage to begin with. They're either too young or there's a lack of income. Usually it's the man, sometimes the woman, who causes it. Steady income is the main problem. If the husband is working she would not have to seek aid, and you can't get aid with a man around the house.

It is important to note that distrust of spouses is reciprocal. Many people comment that both the husband or wife can be disloyal or irresponsible; women say that men run in the streets too much and men say that women cannot be trusted to remain faithful. Both sexes are also likely to accuse the other of jealousy and of needlessly restricting the other's freedom of action.

What is common to all these perspectives is the belief that a marriage has a chance to survive only if both partners stay within the family circle in their free hours. Yet we have seen that (in common with other lower-class groups) conjugal role relationships in the Negro lower class tend to be highly segregated. Such relationships, in which husband and wife pursue separate leisure-time activities, can nevertheless prove stable so long as each spouse can be trusted to participate in outside activities while holding himself aloof from sexual involvement. Indeed, white lower-class communities are often highly structured to maintain sexual segregation and prevent the development of competitive heterosexual attachments.[9] In such a situation, even the husband's patronizing a prostitute may not be a threat to marital stability because such commercial arrangements do not compete with the marriage tie. However, in the Negro lower-class community neither the high degree of sexual segregation nor a limitation of sexual relationships to commercial prostitution exists. Instead, "the streets" are an arena in which sexual liaisons are expected, are understood to be potentially equal in meaning with marital ties, and therefore are expected to cause great trouble.

All of this could, of course, represent an exaggerated set of fantasied dangers which in fact play a small role in actual marriages. However, our field observations as well as the responses of separated women in our survey suggest that this is not the case, and the generalized conceptions of how marriages break up that are quoted above seem to be realistic. In the 1965 survey, women were asked to list all of their marriages, and for those which had dissolved, they were asked why the marriage had broken up. Of the 60 marriages among the women in our sample that had been disrupted by divorce or separation, the distribution of reasons given by the wife was as follows:

Husband's sexual infidelity	40 per cent
Husband wouldn't support her, wouldn't work	27 per cent
Husband lost job and couldn't find another	3 per cent
One of the partners was immature (too attached to parents, too young)	17 per cent
Husband drank excessively	15 per cent
Husband cruel, beat her	15 per cent
Husband gambled too much	7 per cent

9. See Suttles (1968) for a discussion of sharp sex segregation in a white lower-class neighborhood.

Husband in jail	3 per cent
Unspecified incompatibility	22 per cent
Husband deserted, no reason given	8 per cent

This is, of course, a feminine view. If we had asked the ex-husbands of these women why their marriages broke up, we would probably have obtained a similar set of reasons but related to the sexual infidelity or the exaggerated and unreasonable jealously of their wives.

Three main patterns of dissatisfaction are apparent in the reasons given by these women for the termination of their marriages. One pattern, not the most common but nevertheless significant, might be called that of the marriage that is not a marriage. This generally involves a young couple who, although they go through the marriage ceremony, never really establish a continuing marital relationship, as when each partner continues to live with his own parents, or when the man goes into the armed services and returns to find that a conjugal relationship does not exist.

> When he came back from service I was working and was living with my mother and father and there was just nothing there any more.

> He liked to stay around his mother. He didn't want to work and support the family. I had to stay with my mother.

> We couldn't get along living together after he got out of the army. It was impossible. He didn't care about work. He was jealous.

> I married him after he raped me, but I never wanted him and never lived with him.

> Our families couldn't get along, so he moved out. He still comes back once a week to give me support money and have sex.

> He went to the army, and when he came home he said he didn't want to be married any more.

These marital disruptions are the end result of ill-conceived marriages, very often contracted only to legitimate a pregnancy or to satisfy a feeling on the part of the partners that it is "about time to get married." Where such marriages are forced by pregnancy, the boy is often resentful and refuses to take his status seriously; the wife may also have been unenthusiastic. Women who speak in this way about their disrupted marriages often seem detached and not particularly disappointed or unhappy.

Women who give other reasons, however, are not nearly this casual. They portray the period in which the break-up took place as stressful, and often they still display considerable resentment at what they perceive to be their husbands' disloyalty. The most common precipitating cause for separation as seen through women's eyes in Pruitt-Igoe is the husbands' sexual infidelity. As suggested earlier, the blatant quality of much of this infidelity suggests that the husbands were motivated to communicate their outside activities to their wives in a very forceful way (as in the case of the woman who said, "He moved another woman into the house so I left him"). In other cases the actions are not quite so blatant but more cumulative over time so that involvements the woman might be willing to ignore if they occurred only once begin by their repetition to make her feel more and more foolish for persisting in the marriage. This infidelity is for the most part simply the most insulting aspect of a generalized pattern of masculine involvement in outside peer group activities, which the wife comes to view as intolerable disloyalty to the family. In essence, although the husband continues to call the household home, the wife feels that he has broken the relationship by putting so much of his energy and interest elsewhere. Her pride often requires that she either "put him out" or herself leave before he runs off with another woman. If she does not do this, she feels she is likely to find herself in the position of Mrs. Patterson, whose husband left her from time to time only to come back always promising to do better. Mrs. Patterson is unusual in her tolerance for this kind of behavior; most women seem to be willing to run the risk of a clear separation rather than tolerate the uncertainty of a husband whose stepping out may at any time be translated into desertion.

He was an alcoholic so I had to put him out of the house.

He moved another woman into the house, so I left him. He ran around with too many women.

We didn't get along, didn't agree. He got wild, ran around with women, threw money around, got mean and would fight me.

I put him out because he spent more time in the streets than at home.

We separated because he had three children by another woman. The bills kept coming to our house. Then he left us for her.

He was too jealous and wanted to fight all the time.

He used to beat me. I put the police on him a lot, and then he left St. Louis.

He started going with my best girlfriend. He's living with her now, common law.

Whether men work or not, they spend a good deal of time away from home. It is apparent that in these activities they are under strong pressure to engage in activities that put strain on their marriages and may eventually lead their wives to terminate the relationship. Whether the particular behavior that she finds most intolerable be sexual infidelity or excessive drinking (which may in turn lead the man to come home and beat her—a classical lower-class pattern not infrequent in this group), or gambling, the outside involvement which might otherwise be unobjectionable or even desired, given the pattern of conjugal role segregation, becomes intolerable. The beliefs of the group permit a woman to be disloyal by becoming sexually involved with other men. This involvement is very often reactive, and follows upon a situation in which the wife feels that her husband has already been disloyal to her and to the children. Her sexual infidelity occurs only after the marriage tie has to all intents and purposes been broken, though the husband may seize upon her actions as an excuse for leaving her. However, her sexual infidelity may predate his. This may occur when she has a job that takes her out of the home and into the company of men as well as women, or (particularly in the case of younger women with mothers to take care of their children) she may continue to participate in her peer group and through this participation become sexually involved. More rarely, a mature woman with older children may, because of dissatisfaction with her husband, begin to go out with a girlfriend or relative and in this way become involved with a man. Such involvement may not be so much reactive to an awareness of current sexual involvement by the husband as to a long-term sense of generalized indifference on his part.

Disloyal activities of this kind in the white lower class seem to be particularly characteristic of the early years of marriage, as the man continues his involvement with his masculine peer group. Wives in the white lower class often tell stories of family problems that revolve around their husbands' disloyalty, and of their threats to separate because of such disloyalty. There, however, it seems that tension is often resolved by the husband's agreement that it is time for him to "settle down," and older husbands often speak with some pride of weathering this crisis and coming to understand that they had to live up to their responsibilities by giving up some of their freedom. What is distinctive in the Negro lower class is the highly sexualized way in which disloyalty is expressed, thus striking at the core of the marital relationship, and the fact that Negro wives are much less likely than white wives to persist in their attempts to persuade their husbands to settle down.

Seldom do the wives speak of trying to persuade or reason with their husbands or to argue out the issues of disloyalty that impel them toward separation. One's first impression is that the husband is regarded so much as a free agent that the wife can only accept what he does or leave him. On closer examination it also becomes apparent that part of the woman's passivity has to do with her perception of the husband as not particularly valuable even if he were to end his disloyal activities. She does not perceive herself to be as dependent on her husband as does the white lower-class wife. She does not generally regard her husband as a good provider and she knows that she can probably scrape by with work or with family and welfare support even if the marriage is terminated.

Here, then, the economic marginality of the lower-class Negro husband means that the wife's incentive to "rescue" him from his disloyal activity is minimal. Compared to the white lower-class husband, his earnings are generally less and come less regularly. In addition, he confronts his wife's reasonable expectation that eventually he will prove to be a less stable provider. Her husband, in short, represents less economic capital to her. He also represents less social capital. Because of the institutionalization of matrifocality and the prevalence of the female-headed household, the Negro wife is confronted with less in the way of social loss when she loses her husband than is the white lower-class wife (though that is not to say that the social loss is inconsequential). The relatively higher rate of marital disruption can be seen as a result both of the greater stress placed on the marriage by the highly developed subversion of the family by the street system and the less cohesion within the marriage resulting from the wife's lower incentive to retain her husband.

It is in this respect that the second most commonly given reason for marital breakup, *unwillingness to provide support,* achieves significance. We were surprised that few women said their marriages broke up because their husbands could not support them. Indeed, in all our field observations we found hardly any instances where respondents said marriages broke up in sadness because of the husband's inability to earn enough money for the family.

> He couldn't support me so he decided to leave.

> He wouldn't work and support his family. He got drunk. When he didn't work, he wouldn't support his family.

> He said he didn't want to be married because it took all the money he could make and he never had any for himself, so I divorced him. He gambled and fooled around in the streets.

> He messed up the money. He wouldn't support the family.

> He wouldn't support or feed us, so I left him.

The economic marginality of husbands seemed generally to be converted into a moral issue; the wives maintain not that their husbands cannot but that they will not support them. This may seem an insignificant distinction because the effect is the same: lack of sufficient income to support a family. Within the family, however, it is not a minor issue at all because the moral opprobrium encourages the wife, the children, and the husband himself to locate the nature of their problem in the husband's character rather than in his socioeconomic situation.

The conversion of the socioeconomic problem into a problem of character tends to foreclose any hope for improvement. If the husband were seen as wanting to work but not able to find a job, there would always be the possibility that later he would support them better and family circumstances would improve. If instead the problem is one of his character, the social logic of this community (in which character is seen as unlikely to change) suggests that the situation cannot get better.

The wife contributes to this pattern by her understandable anxiety when the husband is bringing home no income or very inadequate income. Because it is his responsibility to support the family, she is inclined to become critical and demanding of him. Because he finds close involvement within the family punishing under these circumstances, he is encouraged to be among people to whom he does not have such responsibilities. His inability to support the family, then, is compounded by reactive behavior that can then be interpreted as disloyalty to the family. In the end the wife decides that he is "no good" and she has a range of evidence to choose from in supporting that view—that he will not support the family, that he spends too much of what little income he does receive outside, that he is running around in the streets. The husband, for his part, receives support for his inclination to abandon the relationship—his wife is jealous, unreasonable, without understanding. The husbands are accused of being uncommitted to the relationship; the wives of expecting too much.

In the early years of marriage or during courtship, men and women may both believe that their love for each other will somehow enable them to maintain commitment to their relationship without expecting too much of it, but such selflessness proves difficult to maintain. Each partner is then on his own to salvage his self-esteem, but the manner in which this is done may contribute to the disruption of the relationship. The husband seeks his self-esteem in the streets or by trying to enforce his authority physically within the house; the wife seeks hers by demeaning him and taking over more and more exclusive responsibility for the maintenance of the family, treating him as either irrelevant or disloyal or both.

The problems the man has in maintaining a credible stance as provider are compounded by the fact that given the realities of employment for lower-class Negroes, he seldom has a steady work history. If a man earns a reasonably adequate income for several years and then becomes unemployed, he can command respect from his wife on the basis of his past performance and can expect her to be understanding of his difficulties in finding a new job.[10] If he has an irregular work history with frequent periods of unemployment, it is much more difficult for him to maintain the status of good provider in her eyes and to deny her accusations that his inability to support his family is his own fault rather than the fault of the labor market. Because stable work opportunities are least available to late teenagers and young adults, early marriage means that the husband has few credits in the provider role and a high degree of uncertainty surrounds his motivation to work. If his work experience in fact proves to be marginal during the early years, he has little to fall back on during times of unemployment to sustain his status in his wife's eyes. His situation is quite different from that of steady workers in a time of depression, whose families tend to react to unemployment with tolerance and understanding.

10. Studies of unemployment during the depression highlight the importance of the man's previous work history in his family's response to his unemployment. See Bakke (1940), Komarovsky (1940), and Koos (1946).

In our 1965 survey we sought to tap attitudes toward unemployed men by asking for responses to a statement reflecting the negative attitudes field observers had observed among women in the project. This statement asserted that "Men who are out of work are that way because they simply don't want to work. That is, anyone can get a job if he really wants one. The problem with unemployed men is that they would rather hang around with their friends gambling, drinking, and running with women." Respondents were asked whether this observation was "generally true." Less than one third of the men in the sample, and the same proportion of the married women, expressed flat agreement with the statement, but half of the separated or divorced women agreed without qualification. While there is not a solid consensus supporting the negative evaluation of men's motivations to be providers, it is clear that there is widespread sentiment to the effect that some men do not work because they don't want to rather than because they cannot get jobs. The sharp terms in which agreement was expressed shows the negative definition to which men out of work are subject:

> *A married woman:* Some of these mothers take food out of their children's mouths and feed these men, but I wouldn't do it. The women making their men like that. Man find a woman going to take care of him, naturally he going to take advantage of her. If she would like the man to get out on his own, he'd have more respect for her.

> *Separated woman:* Some of them would rather have a different kind of job, but this is an excuse. I think they're lazy and no good and just want to sponge off other people. Laziness, just plain laziness. People who just don't have anybody who they really care for, feel responsible to.

> *Married woman:* They would work if the job paid more, but any job is better than no job. They should do anything. They don't like porter work, would rather dress up. Thirty dollars for shoes and $100 for clothes. The wife's home worrying about the groceries. These men have been down-graded for so long they don't care. They want to be hep. Been doing low jobs for so long that they don't care.

> *Separated woman:* They really don't want to work. Many have women who support them. Some of the women are the cause of the problem.

> *Man:* Lots of them don't want to work. They want women to support them for their needs. They get lazy. In a way once a man start that way he gets a habit, he just want to continue. They should be put away.

> *Married woman:* A man like that is really not a family man and shouldn't be married. He should divorce his wife so she can get on welfare, get a job, or find another man. They may have problems at home with a wife who doesn't appreciate them. Their working conditions can cause it too—a lot of

> times a family man takes a lot of stuff to hold his job and
> then when he gets laid off. This is what happens.
>
> *Separated woman:* Some don't want to work. There are some
> who can get jobs. He don't want nothing out of life or any-
> thing for the woman he lives with. He is a dead beat. The
> older women folk, they get young men and take the money
> and buy them cars. Then the men think they'll be taken care
> of.

The responses of both those who generally agree and disagree with the statement make clear that all agree that there are some men who simply do not want to work and other men who do—the variation within the sample is as to whether the majority do or do not want to work. In a community like Pruitt-Igoe very few people believe that there are not some "dead-beats," and similarly that there are not some men who try very hard to work. Similarly, in the abstract, most people are able under certain circumstances to be quite understanding of the problems of the unemployed or of the marginally employed man who after a while simply can not face the insult of working on a low-paying, degrading job. However, in the concrete, in the person of a wife who needs money to feed and clothe and house herself and her children, this understanding is hard to maintain. The wife finds herself inexorably drawn to the conclusion that her husband has proved himself to be a "bum," a "no-good," and that the fault lies in him and not in the labor market.

It is in these attitudes toward one's fellows that we see with particular poignancy the tragedy of race victimization. From the macrosociological perspective, nothing could be clearer than that lower-class Negro men are deprived and exploited by the economic system, and by the educational system which fails to prepare them for adequate economic functioning. At the level of day-to-day man-woman relationships, these forces are converted by cultural learning and personal desperation into faults of individual character and thereby add to the suffering of an economically marginal life.

A Household Head Alone

Whatever the dissatisfactions that lead to the break-up of marriages, wives know that heading a household alone confronts them with many problems. They generally have mixed feelings about remarriage, and given their increasingly dim evaluation of men as husbands and providers they are uncertain whether they would be better off if they made a second try. They are often doubtful that they will even have a chance for a second marriage, particularly if they have children, because they believe that men are reluctant to take on the responsibility of an existing family. In addition, they are concerned that if they become involved with boyfriends they may lower their reputations and make it still more difficult to make a good second marriage.

In any case, women are often inclined to argue that the separated woman is better off trying to make it on her own, rather than trying to reinstate a marital situation that is likely to involve more trouble than bliss. But women know that the postmarital state is fraught with difficulty, and that they may be worse off than they were in marriage, with all its problems.

When a group of separated women were asked specifically whether a woman is better or worse off if she remarries after her marital breakup, a slight preponderance said she was worse off if she did not remarry, but the contrary view was vigorously expressed. These respondents were also asked what a woman misses most after her marriage breaks up and what a woman can do about what she missed. Representative views are given below:

Worse off:

> She'll be worse off because she do need companionship. Everyone needs a husband. She'll miss the companionship. You can only share your troubles with your husband. There's nothing you can do about it. You can't tell these things to other people.

> She'll be worse off. A husband can help with the kids, discipline them, especially boys. She'll miss the companionship and financial help, security, because she's alone. It's not sex.

> She'll be worse off. Kids need someone to help raise them. She'll miss the affection, that's the way I feel. There's nothing she can do. A boyfriend can't provide the same kind of affection.

> I think she is worse off if she doesn't get married again. I think married life is better if she can find someone who is nice. She misses being in a home and love for one husband is better than not being loved. A woman is just better off if she has a husband. I don't know what she can do about it; just stay home and treat her home right. Good things come to those who wait. She shouldn't run around and get into bad company and go astray.

> She's worse off. She dogs herself. She goes from marriage to common law to prostitution. She is constantly slipping. No other man wants them. They are not educated and have nothing to offer but love and not much of that.

> I think she's worse off because if she's a young woman she has to have sex and if she don't have a husband she goes from one man to another. She misses the care that her husband gives her and also the rest because she has to work hard because he is not there to give it to her. Women make it so bad on themselves. They go from one man to another, and this just runs them down.

> She is worse off cause I know. Without a husband she has no

one to depend on, help raise the children, talk to her, take her out. She misses the companionship, the economic support, having a father for the kids. With the husband he is in charge. Without it the woman is in charge of the house and the kids.

Better off:

She's better off. I don't want another man over my children.

She'll be better off. She might run into the same thing. She'll miss his bringing in the money. You need money to support children. About all she can do is go on welfare or get her a job.

She'll be better off. She won't have to feed him. When a husband doesn't do for you, you have to go on your own. She can get more out of him now; he have to help me or he don't come in. If you're married, he do what he wants. There are times when she is by herself and gets lonesome and wants her husband.

I think she's better off. It's something wrong with all the men. She be better off if she got a job and worked herself. She misses his company; most of the time she's lonesome.

She's better off. He wasn't doing nothing for her. She can get something better for and by *herself*. Find something out there. She misses sleeping with him.

It's a 50-50 basis. Some women will better themselves if they don't (remarry) and others will worsen themselves. She misses the companionship. She gets tired of being alone all the time. They have to do the best they can, sneak out the back. You have to do this when you have children.

It is apparent that the issue of remarriage is highly problematic for these women. They cite the need for financial support, masculine authority with the children, and love and companionship; yet many of them feel that the chances of getting this kind of support from another husband are as poor as they turned out to be in their first marriage, and a woman may be better off trying to provide support and authority on her own, despite the tremendous difficulties of doing so.

But what is most striking in their comments is the belief that if the woman tries to make it on her own, she will find her life singularly ungratifying because of the lack of love and companionship that comes from even an imperfect marital relationship. Despite the great poverty of the women in Pruitt-Igoe, despite the hand-to-mouth existence they have to fight for, it is the lack of an intimate relationship that causes them the most suffering. Their emphasis on companionship may come in part because while the kind of material support they desire is more than their potential husbands can provide, they believe that the gift of love and companionship is within the capacity of any well-intentioned man. For all the difficulties of their previous marriages, most wives experienced some gratification in their relationship with their husbands and it is this that they miss most. More than three-quarters of these women responded to the question about what a separated woman will miss most by mentioning companionship, or love, or sex, while fewer than one-third mentioned economic support and security.

The human problems with which separated women are confronted are regarded as not really amenable to a satisfactory solution. Half the separated women who were asked what a woman can do about what she misses either said they did not know or that there was nothing she could do. If the problems that accompany separation are defined economically, then the solution is straight-forward—going on welfare or getting jobs—but this does nothing about the problem of companionship. Women will recommend stoicism, but they know it is small comfort, and they consider an existence without some kind of meaningful companionship too much to ask of themselves or of their sisters. Taking a boyfriend is the only feasible solution, but it is regarded as a palliative rather than a resolution of the problem. Taking boyfriends also exposes the woman to considerable moral danger in her own eyes and in the eyes of her children and others who may be significant to her.

Boyfriends

Despite their uneasiness, our data suggest that the majority of single and separated women from time to time accept boyfriends and come to think of their relationships with these men as to some extent mitigating the loneliness, and sometimes also the financial strain, of heading a household alone. The minimal definition of the role of "boyfriend" seems to be that of a man who sees the woman with some regularity and with the shared expectation that the relationship will provide companionship and a sexual relationship, if not love.

Contrary to the popular notion that when lower-class Negro families break up the husbands continue to maintain sexual relationships with their wives, ex-husbands seldom seem to fulfill the role of boyfriend. In general, when a relationship is maintained between the family and the ex-husband-father it is through the children, with the husband and wife keeping at arm's length. Indeed, women often deal with their ex-husbands only through their children, giving older children directions about what and how they are to communicate with their father. When ex-husbands contribute regularly to the household, they may occasionally demand the right to have sexual relations with their former wives, but such a relationship is fraught with tension and generally the wife submits rather than participates willingly. It is understood that the situation may change so that the couple may live together again, but this is defined almost as a new relationship and the husband may engage in a new courtship of his wife, seeking to persuade her that he loves her, that he will prove a steady provider, that she and the children will be better off if he is allowed to come home. For the most part, however, the relationship with the ex-husband is distant and the children see him only occasionally. Although the father may pride himself on his continuing ties with his children, the irregular and unpredictable times at which they see him is likely to make these occasions stand out as special (and ambivalent) for the children and their mother.

If the woman wants companionship and less ambivalence in a relationship with a man, she must turn to a boyfriend proper, that is, to a man to whom she has not been married and who is not the father of any of her children. Perhaps the majority of separated women at one time or another take a boyfriend, and very often if they stay unmarried for several years will have two or more boyfriends during that time. Such relationships are often begun in a casual way. In response to loneliness and to vary the housework-dominated character of her life, the woman may decide to visit taverns with a girlfriend, or to spend time outside, on the project grounds, or she may meet an eligible man in the course of visiting relatives and friends in their homes.

As a relationship develops, the man and woman both come to define it by specifying that he is her boyfriend. The nature of these relationships varies a great deal, but two dimensions seem to account for the major variations observed in our field work.[11] First, the extent may vary to which the boyfriend's involvement is defined as essentially and only with the woman rather than with the children as well; the boyfriend can be defined as the woman's *companion* or as a *quasi-father*. Second, the extent may vary to which the boyfriend contributes to or takes from the material assets of the family. In some cases the man makes direct and regular money contributions, and in other cases he makes regular purchases of particular goods such as groceries or irregular major purchases such as furniture or clothes for the woman. It is understood that in return for these contributions he is entitled not only to the companionship and sexual favors of the woman but also to have her prepare some of his meals, perhaps do his laundry, and so on. The reverse flow of assets is also observed, in which the woman gives money to the man, or buys him expensive clothes, or perhaps even makes the down payment on a car. In the first case the boyfriend can be considered *supportive;* in the latter case (in the parlance of the ghetto) the boyfriend takes on the role of *pimp.*

With these two dimensions, there might theoretically be four types of boyfriend: one who is supportive and orients himself mainly to the woman (*the supportive companion*); one who takes materially from the woman and orients himself only to her (*the pimp*); one who contributes to the family materially and orients himself to some extent to all members of the family (*the quasi-father*); and one who derives material benefits from the relationship but also develops involvement with the children as well as the

11. The following section is adapted from Schulz's more extended discussion of boyfriend relationships; see Schulz (1969).

woman (*the quasi-father pimp*). The latter type has not actually been observed. Some women are willing to buy companionship for themselves, but they do not seem to be interested in buying fatherly relations for their children. The pimp relationship seems exclusively based on sexual gratification and generally includes a good deal of possessiveness toward the pimp, but he is not regarded as a particularly desirable person to have around the children.

Based on an intensive study of a small group of families in the project, Schulz has described the nature of the relationships existing for the supportive companion, the quasi-father, and the pimp. His data suggests that although the pimp has received a good deal of attention, in fact the other kinds of boyfriends seem to predominate. The more reciprocal and less exploitative kinds of relationships have been noted in the literature but have not been as fully elaborated, perhaps because they are less dramatic. However, Hylan Lewis, in his study of a small town in North Carolina, observes that "gifts and some degree of support from the male are taken for granted and freely discussed. There is some informal ranking of men on the basis of regularity and amount of gifts and support." [12]

Probably the most desirable kind of boyfriend from the woman's point of view is the quasi-father. This relationship seems to persist for longer periods of time than others. It also seems to be more conducive to a resolution of the conflicts the woman may feel about her need for personal companionship, her sense of responsibility to her children, and her desire to maximize feelings of respectability even in a relationship which she herself regards as undesirably irregular. Schulz observes that:

> The distinguishing marks of the quasi-father are: 1) he supports the family regularly over long periods of time (eleven years is the longest known though this was interrupted by a short marriage; five years is the longest consecutive time known at present). Often he will go with his woman to the store and buy her week's food. 2) His concern extends to her children more directly as well. He will give them allowances or spending money; attempt more or less successfully to discipline them; and will take them out to the park or the movies or to other places for entertainment. 3) He frequently visits the family during the week and may (but usually not) reside with them in the project. The relationship is ordinarily conducted not clandestinely, but in full knowledge of kin on both sides, particularly the parents if they reside in the same city with the couple. In return for this he receives: 1) his meals (some or all if residing with the family); 2) washing and ironing; 3) sexual satisfaction; 4) *familial companionship*. In short, he seems to be bargaining for more than just a woman in seeking intimacy in the context of a family. To illustrate let us take the example of Jay and Ethyl.
>
> Ethyl Perry (33) went with Jay (24) for over five years. During that time he took her out, bought her the majority of her furniture, and

12. Lewis (1961), p. 84.

supplied her with $15 to $20 per week, usually by buying her week's food. In addition, his family contributed several pieces of furniture and occasionally invited Ethyl over for meals. None of her six children are his. Ethyl described Jay as a "nice person . . . kind hearted" and by this she meant ". . . he believes in survival for me and my family, me and my kids. He don't mind sharing with my youngsters. If I ask him for a helping hand, he don't seem to mind that. The only part of it is that I dislike his drinking."

Jay's concern for Ethyl's children was expressed in various ways. Dovie, Ethyl's 15-year-old daughter, saw Jay as being bossy. "He be all right sometimes but he drinks and that's the reason I don't like him. . . . He tries to boss people. Like if my boyfriends come over here he be saying I can't have no company." But Mary, her 18-year-old daughter, revealed that Jay gave her a small washing machine for her babies' diapers. She said, "My mother's boyfriend bought it. . . . It was about three days after my baby was born."

Jay's concern was expressed in other ways as well. He took the children to the movies, to the park, gave them a small allowance as spending money each week when he bought the groceries and once, when Ethyl was sick, he took care of the youngest two for nearly a month while she was in the hospital. During the years that they were going together Jay visited the family several times a week most frequently spending the weekend with them. He continually asked Ethyl to marry him though Ethyl felt he was only half serious. I asked Jay why he bothered to take care of Ethyl and he replied, "That's a personal question. . . . Well, first of all I help her because I love her and we're going to get married sometime, but not just now because we can't afford it." . . . Ethyl broke up with Jay and never seriously considered marriage while going with him. . . .

Marriage may or may not be a result of a quasi-father relationship, but it does provide the context in which a woman with children is likely to make up her mind one way or another about a man. It is interesting to remember here that three of the five women (in Schulz's study) still living with their husbands began their relationship "commonlaw." Only one of the quasi-fathers at present lives with his woman.[13]

The supportive companion relationship is less complex. Here the man "keeps a woman;" he is interested in a steady heterosexual relationship, but he does not want to assume paternal obligations. Schulz describes this kind of relationship as follows:

> In this community such a relationship is likely to occur between an older man (late twenties, early thirties) and a younger woman (early twenties, teens) who has had children "outside of wedlock" . . .
>
> The boyfriend provides a regular "weekend away" at his apartment or other suitable place where they can be together away from the

13. Schulz (1969), p. 137–139.

children. He takes her out, provides her with spending money and a good time. Should she conceive a child, he is least likely of all types to want to assume support of the child. Responsibility is what he is trying to avoid.

The example of Madeline (sixteen) and Jerry (twenty-three) is a case in point. The knew each other about a year during 1959–1960. Madeline had already had two children by two other men. Jerry came by for dinner occasionally, but usually he made the weekend scene at a motel apartment he rented for the occasion. When Friday came round, he would give Madeline money which she often turned into dresses, or other items to enhance her appearance. Madeline says, "Jerry's not like a lot of men that you find. A lot of men, if they do something for you they feel they own you." Jerry gave her "$15 or $20, sometimes more" each week and had keys to a two room kitchenette for the weekend. Madeline says, "We were always together (on the weekend). Where I went he usually went, where he went I went. We'd go to the apartment and everything. But lots of times we would go and just watch TV or sit and talk or have a drink or something. Then we would go—especially in the summer time— we'd go there because they had air conditioning."[14]

The boyfriend as pimp represents both a subcultural hero for some young men and an occasional reality. Here the man who "pimps" a woman extracts support from her in return for his professions of love and his demonstrated ability to satisfy her sexually. The traditional meaning of the term is still known, denoting a man who derives his livelihood from the earnings of prostitutes whom he "runs," but the term is applied more broadly to any man who gets money from a woman, however she earns it. The ideal women for a man to "pimp off of" is a woman in her thirties or forties who has a well paying and steady job as a nurse, small business proprietor, or the like. However, few men are so lucky, and most pimps are reduced to winning small rewards from clerical or domestic workers or from welfare mothers. Established or aspiring pimps look forward to the tenth of the month, "Mother's Day," when the welfare checks arrive and a lonely recipient may be in the mood to reward an attentive young man with a few dollars. If such a relationship can be regularized, then the young man has established himself as her pimp. Schulz describes the relationship as follows:

Pimping seems to be the younger man's approach to the dilemma of poverty, low status in the larger culture, and unemployment. In the language of the street, a "cat" is usually a pimp. . . . The role of the pimp, then, is most characteristically that of a young man seeking an older woman who may have a comfortable income and feels that her powers of persuasion are fading. Sam explains the willingness of a woman to "pimp a man" under the rubric of "she loves him." Love,

14. Schulz (1969), p. 142.

for Sam, implies a willingness to do anything for a person who is loved including "bringing them their slippers, lighting their cigarettes . . . man, if a woman loves you, you got it made, there ain't nothing you have to do . . . you don't have to lift your little finger."

This conception of love is in keeping with a general tendency to demand evidence of concern even to the point here of exploitation in the small matters of everyday life. One man explains the problems of the city life in terms of a declining emphasis upon concrete and traditional expressions of love. . . . The pimp takes advantage of this need to concretize relationships. He constantly demands that his woman demonstrate her affection by providing him with a high standard of living (by ghetto standards) while he demonstrates his by his capacity as a lover. The final insult of the pimp—and the fear of any woman keeping one—is that he will take her money and spend it on other women, demonstrating that despite her care for him, he cares not a whit for her. The pimp is, in some sense, the urban counterpart of the relationships between rural woman and the wandering men who moved from lumber camp to lumber camp living off the women they could find in each. Here the exchange, however, was rarely money, but rather more an exchange of intimacies.[15]

Supportive Fathers

Any of these three types of relationships can, and often does, result in the woman becoming pregnant and the man becoming the biological father of one of her children. If that happens, the issue of whether the woman should marry her boyfriend comes into sharper focus. As with pre-marital pregnancies, the result may be the termination of the relationship as one or both partners come to feel that they cannot continue as before but that marriage would be unwise. However, the man may continue in his role as boyfriend, functioning as the quasi-father in much the same way as before except that he is now the biological father of one or more of the children, and this is recognized and understood by all the members of the family.

Perhaps more commonly, once the decision is made the boyfriend may assume somewhat the same role as that of an ex-husband, in that now he relates to the family more through his own children than through the woman. A boyfriend relationship is dependent on an implicit voluntary commitment to the family unit, and when that voluntary quality is subverted by the acknowledged responsibility of paternity, the relationship tends to be upset. The relationship with the woman may become more attenuated and intermittent; the man may direct his attention more to occasional contact with the children and think of himself less as the woman's regular boyfriend, much as the ex-husband alters his role after separation. The limited quality of the boyfriend relationship, whether that of supportive companion or quasi-father, contributes to the relationship's

15. Schulz (1969), p. 84–85.

stability, but only so long as pregnancy does not take place. Nevertheless, some relationships of the type Schulz calls the "supportive biological father" do persist for quite a long time:

> Here the concern of the man—and largely that of the woman also—is to support the children whom they have brought into the world without seriously considering marriage to one another. In some instances the man or woman may well be married to someone else. The man's support may be voluntary . . . or it may be as the result of a voluntarily signed acknowledgment that the children are his.
>
> In the case of Leona Wards (50) and Larry (49), Leona was married once and had four children by her first husband. His "cutting out" and drinking led to a separation and Leona took up with Larry who gave her three children, in ages now from 18 to 13, before he married another woman a couple of years ago. He played the role of supportive biological father before he married. They had been going together for nearly 16 years though only Leona was true to the relationship. She has never remarried and claims that even now she has no boyfriend because they are too much trouble at her age although she admits that she would enjoy a companion in her declining years.
>
> Larry has taken the children on long trips like the one to Arizona in 1963, he has bought them clothes, especially at Christmas time, and has paid regularly the amount of $15 to $20 a week for their support since 1954. At that time he acknowledged that the children are his and the court fixed the amount for their support. . . .
>
> While it is true that Larry is legally obligated to care for his children, it is noteworthy that he claimed them as his in the first place and that he supports them in gifts over and above his legal obligations. His inability to believe that Leona was true to him, plus her reluctance to have a stepfather over her husband's children, at least one of whom has not yet left home, contributed to the factors other than economic that mitigated against their marriage—but did not prevent them from courting for 16 years.[16]

These various extra-marital relationships suggest several important generalizations. Exploitative attitudes by men and women toward each other seem to be particularly characteristic of the younger ages. Boyfriend relationships in later years have a much more subtle character and can be understood as efforts to approximate, insofar as circumstances and realistic expectations allow, a conventional conjugal relationship. The good boyfriend relationship is clearly modeled on conventional marital relationships, and on superficial observation of a quasi-father relationship it would be hard to tell that the couple was not indeed married.

The desire of men to establish quasi-father relationships (and among men past their twenties such relationships with women friends seem most common) suggests that they are as strongly motivated toward companion-

16. Schulz (1969), p. 139–141.

ship as the women. Indeed, the men often pay handsomely for the privilege of such a relationship, contributing regularly a high proportion of
their income to the families of their women friends. It is poignantly obvious that they are buying the closest approximation to a family life that
they can afford. From the woman's point of view, it is equally obvious
that such a relationship is often the best approximation to a stable marriage she feels she can make at that particular time. She respects the man
for the contributions he can make to her and her family's well being; she
reciprocates by caring for him, by being affectionate toward him, and by
encouraging her children to like and respect if not love him.

Both parties may be reluctant to subject this kind of gratifying if not
ideal relationship to the stresses that the greater responsibility of marriage
would place on it. For his part, the man is still able to engage in behavior
that might be considered undesirable in marriage, such as drinking too
much or spending a great deal of time away from the family (even maintaining a separate abode). For her part, the woman is not forced to set
standards for his behavior that he obviously will not be able to meet, and
in many cases she is able to preserve welfare support, a stable if small
income that would have to be foregone if the relationship were legitimated. In many ways, the existence of quasi-father relationships is the
strongest possible testimony to the fact that these lower-class Negro men
and women do not reject the conventional ideal of marriage. Being unable
to support marriage, they work out relationships that approximate it within
the limits of the instrumental and expressive demands they can support.

8.
Clara Johnson and Her Family

In the fall of 1963, nine persons lived in the Johnson household: Mrs. Clara Johnson (50 years old), her seven children, and her granddaughter. Her daughter, Mary Lou (18), had given birth to Jane just a month before Boone Hammond started visiting with the family. Mary Lou was not married.

The other children were Esther (16), Bob (15), Richard (13), Elizabeth (12), Barbara (11), and then Muriel (10). Mary Lou had been born to Clara and Albert Grady during the time they were married. All of the other children had been fathered by Robert Johnson, her common law husband of some dozen years. Robert Johnson had died five years before our research started. Although he had not always lived with his family, Mrs. Johnson felt strongly enough about her relationship with him that she had dropped her married name and taken his name.

When Hammond first met the Johnsons in their large tenth-floor apartment, he learned that Mrs. Johnson had lived in St. Louis for over 25 years: "I'm an old citizen." She had moved from Mississippi to join her older brother after her parents had died. She had moved into the project after her common law husband's death because the house they had lived in was being torn down in a "slum clearance" program.

In their first interview, as they talked about the project, Hammond learned of some of the problems Mrs. Johnson had.

> There's so much trouble in the laundry room having your clothes taken that you just have to stay there with them all the time. I've had overalls, sheets, and pillow cases stolen. You can't hang nothing up there without them being taken. If you hang them up in the morning and go back to get them in the evening, they'll be gone. I have had clothes taken two or three times.

> You know, mister, it's hard to bring up children without any father. I had to bring up these children myself without the help of a father.

One-month-old Jane was brought out for Hammond to see, and as he played with the baby Mrs. Johnson observed:

> You look like you like babies.

I love babies, especially when they're this age. I have five of my own.

> Are you married?

Yes, very much so.

> That's a shame because I have some lovely daughters here that need a man. Even the baby stops crying when she is held by a man. These girls have done pretty good though. My oldest daughter is 18 and she just had her first baby. It's hard for a girl to wait that long without having one around here. There was a girl in the next building who is 13 and has a baby. Do you know, I was 32 before I had these children. They don't wait that long today. I think I did a pretty good job, don't you?

I Always Try to Do My Part

After the brief initial interview, Mrs. Johnson had to take Esther to the hospital for some surgical work. She asked Hammond to help her sort out various papers that were necessary to get a clinic card and in the process Hammond learned that she paid $51 per month rent for her four-bedroom apartment and that her ADC payment was $202 per month, the sole regular income for the family. Hammond drove them to the hospital and said he would be visiting them again.

On his next visit, Hammond observed that a couple of the children were at home. Mrs. Johnson indicated that sometimes the children would stay home from school and went on to say, "All of my children are in school and they're all in special classes." She had mentioned this in the previous interview, and was under the impression that being in a "special" class meant that somehow they were doing very well and were being treated "specially" because of this. In fact, as one of the other children observed, they were in special classes because they were regarded as slow; although Mrs. Johnson heard this, she seemed to ignore it. Each time she mentioned the children's special classes Hammond observed that she seemed to light up with pleasure at the idea.

In these first interviews it was apparent that Mrs. Johnson wanted very much to present an impression of herself as a constructive and cooperative project citizen. Thus, when Hammond brought up the subject of what might be done to make things better in the project, she commented,

> You know I always try to do my part. For instance, I always sweep outside my door and down the steps. I even sweep

down to the next landing where the lady sweeps up her dirt too. The people in this building know that I do my part in trying to keep the building clean. There have been times when I have started all the way up here and cleaned the steps all the way down to the bottom with all my kids helping me. Last year I did such a fine job that all the people in the building said they were going to get together and buy me a nice present at Christmas time because I helped them to keep the stairways so clean. Of course, they never did really give me anything though. Me and my family always try to do our part. Other people in this building help too. The lady across the hallway cleans the steps when it's her turn.

I just sit up here in the apartment and take care of my kids and try to make this home as comfortable as possible. Try to take care of ten people. It can be a pretty hard job by itself. It's especially hard in a place like this where people don't care about each other and the children are so bad. People don't raise their children like they did when I was coming up down in Mississippi. When I was a girl, you didn't see a lot of little girls walking around pregnant like you do now, because the girls didn't get out to do the kinds of things that they do in these apartments. There is a little girl down the hall now who is 13 years old and has a baby. Now you know, that's a shame. I raised my daughter all the way up to the age of 18 before she had a baby. I think that's doing pretty well.

When I was comin' along, you didn't see boys and girls slipping around the way that they do today, because it wasn't possible for them to do it. When a boy and a girl got together they did it like this: the boy came over to the girl's house and was invited in so that he could say 'hello' to the mother and then he was invited to sit down in the living room. If he had anything to say to the girl he said it right there before her mother and father who were in the same room or in a room nearby. If it was summertime they might be out on a porch in a swing, but mama would go out every now and then to see that everything was going along okay. There wasn't any chance for any foolishness to take place.

When Sunday came, and all during the week, too, we went to church. Now the preacher preached against all kinds of sin, and especially the kind these kids are doing nowadays, slippin' around havin' children. He would point people out in church right along with mother and dad; there wasn't any of this staying behind or sending the kids out to church and not goin' yourself and half the time the children not getting there. The parents took the children right along with them, and came back home with mama.

You didn't see kids talking back to their parents the way these kids of mine talk back to me and you didn't see kids hanging around the streets at all times of the night. They didn't need all those policemen and social workers and things to take care of people's kids for them because mama and dad they took care of their own kids and if they got out of line they would spank them so hard with a switch that they wouldn't want to do it again.

But times aren't like they were in the old days and we have to try to raise our children the best that we can now. I have to try to do what I think is best for my kids and everybody else has to try to do what is best for theirs. It's hard to raise a kid in a place like this, but where else can you go? A person with a family as big as mine cannot get one of those Jews to rent him a house in any other part of the city, because we have too many kids. If you do find one it's not worth having, so this is really the best place for a person with a large family to live. I have been here for nine years (sic). I try to raise my children the best that I can, mister. I stay up here in the apartment all the time—Clara don't go nowhere, wash, iron, mend clothes and fix the food for them to eat and pray to the Lord that I'm doin' everything okay, that's all that I can do.

Because of her daughter's recent pregnancy, Mrs. Johnson had an immediate personal reason for engaging in what was a common comparison on the part of older southern-reared people in the project. Very often they contrasted what they think of as the more controlled and "respectable" southern small town and rural social environment in which they grew up to what they see as the disorganized and seductive environment in which their children are growing up. In the process, of course, they tend to idealize the southern setting, but the statistics on illegitimacy rates and marital instability in the urban north compared to the rural south suggest that there is a kernel of reality in what they are saying.

When Hammond visited the home a week later he came late in the afternoon and observed the members of the family as they had their evening meal. As they came home from school they went to the cupboard to get a dish for eating, served their food from the pots on the stove, and sat down to eat, one at a time as each came in. The meal consisted of mustard greens from one pot and cornbread from a pan. Each child took the cornbread and broke it into little pieces on top of the mustard greens and mixed them together very thoroughly, eating it without utensils. Mary Lou, who was the last to eat, took a small mixing bowl which she made about three-quarters full with greens, then cut a large piece of cornbread and crushed it on the top of the greens. Then she mixed it together with her hands, squeezing the juices into the bread, and took a large onion which she diced and sprinkled on top of the food. On top of this she spread ketchup. When all was mixed together she sat down in the living room, eating the food with her fingers.

Mrs. Johnson had a great deal of difficulty controlling her children. The apartment was always very noisy when more than a couple of them were around, and she relied heavily on blows to make the children obey. Thus when 12-year-old Barbara started to follow her older brother as he was going to the store, Mrs. Johnson told her to change her clothes first. The child insisted on leaving. Finally her mother said, "'You come back here or I'm going to get my belt. You just stay right there until I come back." She went to one of the bedrooms and came back with a large belt and made two or three swings at Barbara, who went into the bedroom and crawled beneath the bed and started to cry. Mrs. Johnson observed, "I'm sorry, Mr. Hammond, but sometimes I have to get after these children. Barbara sort of pushes me a little hard and she always runs under the bed when I get ready to spank her. She's always done that, ever since she's been a little girl. But she's just one of my kids, and I really love her."

Hammond also observed that the boys smoked. When 14-year-old Richard asked him for a cigarette, Hammond said that he could give him one only if it was all right with his mother. She said, "That's all right, he smokes and so do the rest of them. I used to try to stop them from smoking, but they just kept it up anyhow and they were smoking in the halls and in the streets. They were begging cigarettes from everybody, so I thought if they were going to smoke I would just go ahead and buy them cigarettes myself when I could." She turned to the children, "You kids worry people to death about cigarettes. (To Hammond) If they're going to smoke, they should be able to buy their own, because I can't do it always."

People Just Won't Let You Be

Mrs. Johnson seemed to spend a great deal of time working out her rights with the various bureaucracies in which she was enmeshed and defending herself against their efforts to keep money from her. She told how the Housing Authority had increased her rent by $1.50 a month when Mary Lou's baby was born, but the welfare office refused to raise her allotment even though there was one more member of the household. In addition, they confused her considerably by suggesting that perhaps they would take Mary Lou off ADC and put the baby on. She was also much involved with the social workers in the school system. The school had expelled Richard the previous spring because he was not doing well and was a trouble maker, and he had not yet been allowed back in. She was to go for a conference at the Board of Education, and we learned later that Richard was finally readmitted.

While Hammond and Mrs. Johnson were discussing these problems, one of the daughters returned to say that the lady downstairs had called the police to report that one of the Johnson boys beat up a child outside the apartment building. Mrs. Johnson commented that she was not one "to get shook up" about things like this, because the police were always coming to her house and telling her how bad her children were. She thought it was too bad that parents had to always call the police and not talk to her first. She tried to get along with all the parents in the building, and whenever she observed trouble with other children, she would always talk to their parents and not the police. Hammond asked her if she thought the police would really come.

> Oh yes, they'll be over here in a minute. They're always over here about me, about my children. You know when my kids were small they used to come home every day crying and runnin' in from the courtyard with somebody chasin' them in here. The kids were always beating my children up. Now that my children have grown up and are able to take care of themselves, the people say that my children are beating their children up. It's not that they're beating the other children up, it's just that they have gotten big enough to protect themselves now. My kids used to come in here with their clothes all torn off of 'em, where a kid had beat them so bad below and sent them upstairs naked. They used to run them out of their brand new shoes, the kids would come in barefooted. I never said a thing about it, but I tell my kids now not to come in this house telling me that somebody has beaten them up, because if they come in here telling me that somebody has beated them up then I'll tell them that if somebody beat you up then I'm going to beat you up myself. That way the child gets a double beatin'. So now, instead of havin' somebody beat them up out in the streets, my children beat the other kids up first, so the police say that my kids are bad.
>
> I don't like to see a lot of trouble around here, I try to help everybody to get along fine, but you know people just won't let you be. I very seldom ever go downstairs except to go to the store or to the clinic, but they are always talking about how bad Clara is and Clara don't do anything but sit here in this apartment all day long.

The Housing Authority records confirmed Mrs. Johnson's statement that the family was no stranger to the police. There were numerous complaints about the boys—breaking windows, "playing ball in the vicinity of a building," fighting. There was no record of complaints against the girls, although Mary Lou had been warned after her baby was born that if she had any more children out of wedlock she would be asked to move.

In addition, there were several complaints against Mrs. Johnson herself for "peace disturbance" and one for "abandoning her children." The latter complaint was ironic because it arose after Mrs. Johnson had to be taken to the hospital because of a serious "blackout." There were a number of complaints against her for drunkenness, cursing, screaming, and slamming doors. A couple of years before she had been cut on the wrist by an unknown assailant and a year before that she had gotten into a fight with a man who came to her apartment wanting to drink with her. Both had been arrested and charged with assault and peace disturbance. At that time the project police had noted that the apartment was unkept and in deplorable condition, that Mrs. Johnson was frequently under the influence of alcohol, and that when the police sought to do something about-her various diffi-culties the children always interfered, using loose and vulgar language. In the first year of her tenancy the Housing Authority had begun an evic-tion process but it had been cancelled. Although the Authority must ob-viously have been tempted to act against her on later occasions, she was never evicted, perhaps because, as she later told Hammond, she had never been in arrears in her rent.

Mrs. Johnson was herself disturbed by her past drunkenness and ill-nesses, and she seemed to be making real efforts to extricate herself from the difficulties she kept getting into. During the year in which Hammond visited the family he never observed Mrs. Johnson to be drunk (although she told him she still liked her wine), suggesting that she had brought her behavior under control. However, the effect of her past behavior on her ability to sustain her authority with her children was not so easily undone.

They Want to Get My Money

Hammond next visited the Johnsons a few weeks before Christmas and the apartment was full. Not only were all the children present but Mrs. Johnson's steady boyfriend, "Mule," was there and an insurance man seek-ing to collect two months back payment on a policy Mrs. Johnson held. Hammond was introduced to Mule for the first time, although he had seen him once before, when he had called in Mrs. Johnson's absence. Mule had eyed him suspiciously then, but was much friendlier now; apparently Mrs. Johnson had explained that he was not a competing boyfriend but a uni-versity student who was interested in life in the project. Mule did not live in the project, but he was a frequent visitor to the Johnson household and from time to time made contributions by buying groceries and wine.

Mrs. Johnson told the insurance man she could not pay him until Christ-mas because she was very pressed for money, because the ADC allowance had not been increased after baby Jane was added to the household. The insurance man did not press her, saying that he would be back after Christmas. This was the day when the ADC checks arrived and Mrs. John-son was adding up her bills for the month. She apparently owed over $120 for groceries and $51 for rent, leaving her less than $30 for all other ex-penditures for the coming month. She told Hammond that she had already been to the Salvation Army and the Lutheran Community House to place orders for baskets of food for Christmas dinner. She had done this the year before and had gotten a Christmas meal in this way.

Also present were two men visiting Mary Lou. They seemed to be in their early twenties and were sitting around very comfortably, as if they were used to visiting the apartment, although in fact Mrs. Johnson said she did not know who they were.

As the children came home from school for lunch, they were all very noisy, wanting to know from their mother whether the check had arrived yet. The children kept yelling at her, saying that they wanted new "brogues" (shoes) for Christmas. They knew that the shoes they wanted cost $4.50 a pair and kept telling her she could afford this. When she explained that she would not have enough money to buy shoes for everyone, that some children would have to wait until after Christmas, the children were upset and began to scream at her, to fuss and fight and chase each other around the house. In turn, Mrs. Johnson screamed at them, telling them that she could not help it, that it was just the way things were and they would have to accept it. Despite this, the children were fighting with each other to try to get the key to the mailbox so that they could go down to get the check. They did not seem to understand their mother's insistence that almost all the money was already committed to paying bills. Instead, they asked Hammond if he would take them to the shoe store on Franklin Avenue once they got the check.

Finally Mrs. Johnson quieted the children down and started them eating their lunch. As they returned to school, they were still all talking about the check and about the new shoes they hoped to get. Hammond was puzzled by their unanimous desire for new shoes; no other articles of clothing were mentioned, nor was there mention of anything else they might like for Christmas. After the children left, Mule explained that he was able to visit that day because it was too cold for him to drive the junkyard truck as he usually did.

Mrs. Johnson took Hammond aside and whispered that she did not know the two young men who had come to visit Mary Lou and she thought Mary Lou had promised these men money. She was afraid that when she cashed her check Mary Lou would give some of her money to the boys, that the boys were waiting for her check to come and for her to cash it. She did not want to cash her check as long as the boys were around; she did not think she could trust Mary Lou not to give them money.

While this was going on, the young men were eyeing Hammond and Mrs. Johnson suspiciously. Hammond felt they sensed that Mrs. Johnson was aware of what they wanted and was consulting him about it. Mary Lou, however, did not seem at all concerned, but was instead basking in the attention the boys were paying her. She spent her time walking around the living room, flirting with the boys. Then she tried to get the key to the mailbox so she could get the check, but her mother refused, saying that she was in no hurry to cash it. Mrs. Johnson finally gave in and gave her the key. Mary Lou left and came back shortly, telling everyone to look out the window. When they did, they observed two young men taking a check away from an elderly lady who appeared to be about 70 years old. One boy snatched the check and threw it to the other after the lady had taken it from the mailbox. The boys ran across the grounds with two project policemen in pursuit.

When this episode was over, Mrs. Johnson asked Hammond to come back into the bedroom to talk to her. She again expressed her discomfort at having the young men in her house, saying they had been sitting there for several hours and she did not know much about either of them except she thought that one of them was the father of Mary Lou's baby, though he did not contribute anything to the support of the child and never talked about or showed interest in her. The incident they had seen out the window was making her even more nervous about the young men, so she asked Hammond for advice. They agreed it would be best not to cash the check and to try to get the men out of the apartment, but in the end she decided that she would simply try to out-sit them, hoping they would leave before Hammond. Mrs. Johnson said it would do no good to try to persuade Mary Lou to get the men to leave, that she could not be trusted with money because she had become so wild since the birth of the baby that her mother could no longer control her. Mary Lou always had a man around the apartment and there was nothing Mrs. Johnson could do about it.

At this point Mule came into the bedroom, announcing that he didn't trust the two young men. As the three of them relaxed in the bedroom, Mrs. Johnson contrasted Mule with the young men in the living room. Mule had never asked her for money in the seven years she had know him; instead, he helped her out whenever he was able. He gave her money sometimes, and he had taken care of the children when she went to the hospital.

All of them observed how cold it was in this top floor bedroom. The wind came through the warped metal casement windows and the radiator put out very little heat. Mrs. Johnson said that when it really got cold she had to keep the oven on. This part of the apartment was so cold that the paint on the ceiling was buckling because of moisture freezing in the roof. Although she had complained several times to the Housing Authority, they had done nothing about it.

There was a bottle of wine on the chest of drawers in the bedroom and Mule took a drink from it. Mrs. Johnson was very angry about this, saying that he showed no respect for her, drinking in her bedroom and in front of Hammond. Though Hammond demurred, she was still angry, saying that, after all, it was her wine and that he did not ask her if he might drink. She did not like his drinking in front of the company; she herself would not drink in front of company or her children. Mule told her to go to hell, saying that she was trying to be "uppity."

Finally the argument subsided and Hammond and Mrs. Johnson returned to the living room, where she kept up a steady flow of hints to the young men to leave because she had to go to the store to shop. Finally they started to leave. Hammond had to leave at this time, too, so he rode down in the elevator with the two young men. They asked Hammond for money and he told them he didn't have any to give them. The men were persistent in their requests, but Hammond was also persistent in his refusals. In the elevator the young men stood very close to Hammond, cornering him in an apparent effort to intimidate him into giving them a dime, but they did not go further than intimidation. In the end, Hammond gave one of them a ride toward the West End and heaved a sigh of relief, as, presumably, did Mrs. Johnson.

She Was Hit with an Ugly Stick

When Hammond visited the Johnsons after the New Year, he found that the three youngest girls had received new shoes for Christmas but there had been no presents for any of the other children. The rest of the children were to get their new shoes when the next ADC check came. Despite the great uproar they had caused the previous month, they did not seem resentful, but were looking forward to the new check and to receiving their shoes then. On this visit, Hammond observed that when they ate their supper the family was using the drinking glasses he had given them as a Christmas present and in addition they had somewhere found forks with which to eat. The children tended not to sit down to eat a meal, but rather they ate a small amount of food and then returned 15 or 20 minutes later for another small amount, continuing this until they were full; this pattern of serial eating seemed well established in the family. Although there was not an organized family meal and people ate out of all kinds of dishes including ice cube trays, Mrs. Johnson always prepared a large amount of food and no child ever complained that he did not have enough to eat.

During most of Hammond's visits there had been two or three boys in the apartment spending time with Mary Lou or Esther; this time there were two teenage boys paying court to Esther. Mrs. Johnson never seemed to know who the boys were; in many cases they seemed to be total strangers. Yet the boys never seemed to behave as strangers but made themselves completely at home, walking freely through the apartment. From time to time they would disappear into one of the bedrooms with Mary Lou or Esther. Mrs. Johnson simply ignored them. On this particular occasion the boys went into the bedrooms with Esther several times for 20 minutes or half an hour.

Though Mrs. Johnson seemed to make no effort to control her daughters' behavior, she talked over and over again of her wish that her daughters would get married as soon as possible. She seemed to feel very strongly about this, and Hammond thought she would be happy to see them marry any male who came along. She felt that she had labored long and hard to "bring them up" to their present ages and that it was now time for them to get out of the house and to help her by making contributions to the family exchequer. She spun out this point of view in great detail in front of the children in such a way that Hammond got the impression she was lecturing the children through him. She saw herself as a "widow woman" who had given up many of the enjoyments of life to make sure that her children were provided for. She said that she lived for the day when she could sit back and have her children take care of her, yet she doubted that this would ever happen because the children did not seem to care anything at all for her; they looked out only for themselves.

Each time Hammond came, baby Jane was brought out for him to hold; Mrs. Johnson seemed very proud of the child and very attached to it. Although the Johnson family was rather dark in complexion, the baby was very light and had curly brown hair; she was always neat and clean, and everyone in the apartment seemed to do their share in taking care of her except her mother, who ignored her most of the time. The children and Mrs. Johnson were attentive to the baby's needs, immediately changing her diapers whenever she was wet, washing them and hanging them out to dry. Mary Lou, in contrast, seemed to spend most of her time in the streets and with her boyfriends, depending on the others to take care of the baby. Mrs. Johnson saw Hammond as a special kind of person because he was interested in the baby, in contrast to the young men who came to visit her daughters, none of whom ever seemed to notice the baby.

Mrs. Johnson complained again and again about the change in Mary Lou's behavior since Jane was born. Before, Mary Lou hardly ventured outside of the house; now she was never at home. Mrs. Johnson could not understand what had happened to Mary Lou; she acted "like a wild woman" and would come home just long enough to eat and then grab her coat again. When she heard these things, Mary Lou would only laugh and offer nothing in her defense.

Hammond was puzzled by the attraction Mary Lou seemed to have for the young men, because he found her fat, sloppy, unkempt, wholly unattractive. Despite this she seemed cocky and self-assured. She did not seem aware of the monetary interest the men took in her, behaving in a very coquettish fashion around them. Hammond thought it would be considered in the jargon of the streets, that "she had been hit with an ugly stick." Occasionally she took off for several days, supposedly to visit cousins of her own age in East St. Louis. There she would sample the high life by going out with her girl friends.

They Can Never Say I Don't Feed My Family

On a subsequent visit Hammond wanted to complete the information on a form the researchers tried to fill out for each family being studied. He was surprised to discover considerable resistance to giving him what seemed like straightforward information. Apparently any discussion of the fact that most of her children were not by her legal husband, Mr. Grady, made Mrs. Johnson very defensive. Thus Hammond started the marital history by asking if she was married first to Mr. Grady.

> That's my lawfully married husband. The other is just common law. He was just common law. Is that what you all want to find out—about my rep? Just like these folks over there (at the welfare office). They know these children is not my law-

> fully married husband's. Now see, there's a lot of women living here that have got children and have *never* been married. If you went over there to that office, they would tell you Mr. Johnson is not that woman's lawfully married husband. Just her children's father. My lawfully married husband is not these kids' father.

Hammond explained that all he was trying to find out was what the children's last names were and whether one of them was named Grady. Finally Mrs. Johnson explained that Mary Lou's last name was Grady but that all the other children were named Johnson. But she kept coming back to her concern:

> I'm not mad, but I just want to let you know that I have been a married woman, you see, me and my husband separated and he got a woman and went his way and I got me a man and went mine.

As she described her long history with the welfare department, it was obvious that the many discussions of the children's fathers and of her marital status had made her sensitive. She referred again and again to the fact that she had to put Mr. Johnson in jail for "one year and one day" for not supporting the children and that she had been getting welfare assistance ever since. In her mind it was clear that Mary Lou's name was Grady and all the other children were named Johnson and it didn't matter what the welfare department said.

> So they don't worry me about the Gradys and they don't worry me about the Johnsons. What little they gives me I thank them for it. Like I told them, I thank them for getting me a place to lay down to sleep, a few biscuits and cornbread and my kitchen, and I don't have to be out there trying to get knocked down and beat up and everything, but I think I earn what little I am getting. I think I earn that. Honest. I pitched the battle with the whole seven, and now with the whole seven I fought it up to here and now here come the grandbaby and I'm still fighting it. See, I'm still doing it. And when he put up a year and one day in the workhouse, the judge said Robert Johnson's children will be put back on the child aid. See now, they was put on since the day that he was sentenced. They sent me out a grocery list to eat on until the next month.
> Now I'll tell you, a whole lot of them get cut off (welfare) because in place of taking care of home they get their check and they say, 'Come on, girl, we're going to ball all night'. Now you ain't never come in my home and caught me out of here a day since you've been coming here. I is in here tending to my home. If I wouldn't be up here, I would be down there in that hall. And as far as taking a drink of wine, you know you can easy pick up 60¢. I ask you for 60¢ or 35¢ and go and get a fifth of wine. But I can't ask you for enough food to feed these

kids on, or ne'er a sheet, or ne'er a pillow case, or ne'er a blanket to go on the bed, or ne'er a mattress, or linoleum to go on the floor. I have people coming to me and saying, 'Mrs. Johnson is throwing her check away,' but I have ne'er thrown ne'er a check away and I have fitted it up to this point.

I'm not able to work. I suffer with high blood pressure and fainting, and you know, anytime you suffer with high blood pressure you suffer with heart too, and nerves too. Nerves, see, I got bad nerves. It's times here when I suffer from nerves. I have to walk. I have to get up from here and I have to walk all night long. But if I be quiet, you know, no disturbing or anything, well I can do pretty good. At times, wherever you are, if this spell hits you, you know if it hits you you just fall out. I feel them coming and whenever I feel these spells coming I just take it easy.

A couple of months later, Hammond arrived to discover the two Johnson boys in the gallery on the elevator floor one floor below the apartment. They were pushing baby Jane in her stroller to amuse her. Neither had gone to school that day because they did not feel like it. When Hammond entered the apartment he was struck by how very clean it was, because the apartment was usually rather dirty and the furniture pushed around at odd angles. This time the apartment was spotless and the furniture had been neatly arranged.

Mule was there, and at first Hammond was uneasy because Mrs. Johnson had told him on an earlier visit that she had broken up with Mule. Nothing was said about this, however; Mule was friendly and acted as if nothing had happened; so Hammond took his cue from him.

There was also a salesman in the apartment who had come to collect payment from Mrs. Johnson. She told him that she did not have any money, and after discovering that Hammond could only lend her 15¢ and that Mule did not have any money, said he would have to come back another time. Mule told her that she needed money to buy tomato paste for the spaghetti to be made, and she was concerned that they did not have money for wine. She asked the salesman if he could loan them some money but he said that he did not have any either. The salesman seemed quite at home in the apartment and not at all concerned that he was not going to be paid. After a few minutes he left.

Mule was preparing lunch, as he did from time to time. In addition to the money he occasionally contributed to the household, he helped out in other ways. Once, for example, he had painted the apartment with paint supplied by the Housing Authority. Today Mule was barbecuing pork neck bones in the oven and preparing spaghetti. Richard was sent to the store for tomato paste; while he was gone, Mule cooked chopped bacon, green peppers, and onions to add to the paste. Then he completed the spaghetti and tended to his pork neck bones. In the meantime, Mrs. Johnson made biscuits, observing that "they can say a lot of things about me, but they can never say I don't feed my family."

Hammond asked Mule where he had been and said that he had missed him. Esther chimed in to say that, "Mule and mama had a fight and Mule left for some other woman." Mule denied this, saying that he had just not been around for a while.

Esther, who obviously had been dying to tell the story to Hammond, chimed in,

> Mama whipped the hell out of Mule right here in this house on account of that other woman he said he had. And I saw him downstairs talking to her and he came upstairs and told mama, and mama went downstairs and told that woman not to be shaking her fat ass in front of her man or she would snatch that dress right off her. Then old Mule ran upstairs and that woman ran away. But Mule is jealous, too. He told a man that used to come to see mama sometimes to stay away from his girl-friend and stay out of her house or else he would cut his throat. They done got good now though, cause I heard them bed springs rocking all night long last night. Ain't that right, mama?

Mrs. Johnson told Esther to hush, then looked at Mule. They both laughed.

Tell It All Like It Is

Hammond and Mrs. Johnson had an opportunity to talk quietly one evening while all the children were outside playing. She reminisced about her early years in St. Louis and about where she worked before marrying Mr. Grady, who was 65 years old when they married. As always, she was deeply concerned about the family's income, spending a great deal of time trying to persuade the welfare office to increase the allotment to take account of the addition of baby Jane but getting nowhere. As part of her maneuvers, she and Mary Lou had sought to get the prosecuting attorney to bring action against the man Mary Lou said was Jane's father, but he had denied this and the strategy had failed. She was looking forward to being old enough to get her husband's social security, but that was a long time in the future.

She still hoped that somehow her children would get jobs and support her, although she had given up on Mary Lou. She was pleased that Esther had graduated from elementary school and would be going to high school next year, and she wished that Mary Lou had graduated. Richard, how-ever, had failed the eighth grade and would have to go back and take another test. If he failed again, she said, they would put him out of school. Then when he was 16 perhaps he could get a job and that would be of some help. Hammond asked her how important she thought it was to finish school.

> Aw, I think it's real nice. You know, for him to finish up. And anyways, you know after they finish they go and finish out of

these high schools and they try to get them in colleges or
something. I do want to see all of my kids get an education,
cause you see I didn't have a chance. You know, like these
children, see, they got all the chance in the world. And I didn't,
because, you see, after my father died my mother had to put
me in a home. Mama had children just like I had mine. And
I had to be out there in the white folks' kitchens for a long
time. Don't be no jobs then like it is now.

That summer both Mary Lou and Esther became pregnant. Hammond
was not visiting the family often at this time, but he learned about the
pregnancies and that Mary Lou had moved back into the apartment from
the room she had been sharing with her boyfriend. The following March
Hammond arrived late one afternoon to visit and to bring some clothes,
blankets, bottles, and diapers which he knew Mrs. Johnson could use for
the expected babies. He discovered that Mary Lou already had a boy who
was then about two or three weeks old.

When he arrived he found the family in an uproar. There was much
yelling and screaming between the mother, the two eldest daughters, and
Richard. Although such screaming was not unusual in the Johnson household, Hammond sensed that the tension was greater than he had come to
expect. Mary Lou was sitting in a chair against the window crying, tears
flowing down her face, dressed as if she had been out on a visit. Esther
was also very neatly dressed. All the other children were there, and there
was also a girl sitting on the couch with the younger Johnson girls. Mrs.
Johnson was standing behind the table near the kitchen sink with a mean
look on her face, swollen with anger. She told Hammond that she could
not even leave the house without someone in her family causing trouble
and having the police brought in. It was a dirty shame that two people,
brother and sister in the same family, could not even get along together
for an hour while she was gone. It made it look bad for her to have the
police called to her house for "a bunch of bull shit," especially when she
was not there. She was "mad enough to bite nails in half." The younger
girls were sitting attentively on the couch, not saying anything, but once
in a while coming out with a sneer or a mild laugh. Mary Lou continued
to cry. Esther was also obviously angry, glaring at Richard. Richard was
standing against a wardrobe, looking nonchalantly around the room with
his coat and hat on, as if he were ready to depart at any moment.

Mrs. Johnson said that what had happened that day was uncalled for.
Esther said, "Well that black motherfucker started it," pointing to Richard.
She told her mother that she had been left in charge and "that mother-
fucker did not have anything to do with the shit; if he had kept his damned
ass out of it no shit would have started. If I could have got hold of a knife
I would have cut his motherfucking throat."

Esther said, "He is a little ugly looking black bastard and no brother
of mine," and Mary Lou joined in: "The motherfucker ain't no brother of

mine either." This was the first time Hammond had heard any of the children cursing in the presence of their mother, but Mrs. Johnson stood passively by and did not try to curtail the cursing. Instead, she turned to Hammond and said, "You know, Boone, it is a shame to go away and then come back home to a mess like this." She said that she and Mary Lou had gone to the hospital so that Mary Lou could get a check-up. She said, "You know, she just had that baby and the doctor told her before that she wasn't to have any more because they had to take it out the other way (Caesarean section) and if she had any more it would hurt her or might not come out alive. But since she went ahead and had it anyhow we had to keep going back and getting these check-ups for her. So while we was gone all this shit took place."

She said that when she left the house, Richard and Esther were home and she told Esther to look after Jane and the new baby while she was gone. While she was gone for about two hours a fight developed between Esther and Richard. It seemed that the babies were asleep and Richard, wanting to hold the new baby, picked him up while he was asleep. Esther then came into the room and told Richard to lay the baby down because the baby was asleep and her mother had left her in charge. Richard told her to "kiss his ass;" he was not going to lay the baby down; he was not doing any harm by holding it. After further argument Esther hit him. Richard said that he ignored this first assault, but Esther, now enraged, hit him again. Richard laid the baby back in its bed and took a swing at Esther, knocking her onto the couch. The two continued to fight until Esther saw that she was getting the worst of it, when she ran down the stairs to another apartment and called the police. The police came (they sent two cars), but at first they were not able to gain entry to the apartment because Richard had barricaded the door with an ironing board and several other pieces of furniture. He was not able to hold them off for long, however. The police forced their way into the apartment and began to pound Richard on the head with their night sticks. He resisted but they subdued him and left the apartment without arresting him.

Mrs. Johnson asked, "What do you think of this, Boone, when brothers and sisters can't get along together and have to have the police called in to handle them?" Hammond said he thought that it was a pretty bad situation when brother and sisters could not get along, that he was very disappointed with both Esther and Richard. Richard hung his head in shame, but Esther responded that "none of this mess would have started if it hadn't been for that motherfucker" (pointing to Richard). He said, "I didn't do nothin' but pick up the baby." She said, "You know mama left me in charge and I don't know what you was doin' in here foolin' with the baby anyhow. The baby was asleep and you came in here fuckin' with it and wakin' it up. You should have kept your black ass hands off the baby. I told you to leave it alone and put it down. If I could have got hold of a knife I would have cut your motherfuckin' throat. I'm still gonna try to cut your goddam ass." She said that she had tried to get to the butcher knife in the drawer under the sink so that she could cut Richard with it, but he had blocked her.

Mary Lou had been sitting quietly nodding her head in affirmation of Esther's statements. Then she said, "Mama is always taking up for those goddam boys and makes it hard on us girls. The best thing that she could do is to put those motherfuckers out of this house and then everything would be all right. They ought to get their black asses out or I'm gonna get mine out."

Hammond then put his foot in it. He tried to explain that it was the mother's responsibility to take care of all of the children until they became of legal age, 21 for boys and 18 for girls. Because he had known the family for a year and a half and had built a close relationship with them, his words were taken seriously. Mary Lou, still crying, said, "You say mama should take care of the boys until they're 21 and put the girls' asses out when they're 18 so you say mama has to let the boys lay around so long as they want to until they become men and then they can lay around after that if they wanted to but the girls have to go. I know what you're saying, you're slick. You're telling mama to put us out and let the boys stay." Hammond demurred but Mary Lou was not to be stopped, "I'm hip to your game, I know what you're saying. Don't nobody have to put me out of this house. I'll leave this motherfuckin' house myself and find someplace else to stay. I'll get me an apartment of my own and move out of this damn hole. You think they're gonna take my babies away from me —ain't nobody gonna take my babies away from me.

"These boys ain't shit. They're a bunch of lazy bastards and they let their mama take a whole bunch of shit off of them and she always takes up for them and puts us girls down. Those boys can get by with anything but we can't. Bob is not even my brother, we don't even have the same name and I wouldn't claim that motherfucker." Esther chimed in, "That ugly motherfucker's not my brother. Look at him, he looks like something out of the goddam jungle." She stamped her foot and pounded the window sill. "I wouldn't have nothin' to do with him and I want him to get his black ass out of this house." Mary Lou came back to her theme: "Mama ain't doin' shit for me and neither are Bob and Richard and I'll leave this motherfuckin' house quick and get my own apartment. I'll move back with my boyfriend."

Hammond, now drawn fully into the argument, asked Mary Lou how she could move out because she had two babies and no husband. Mary Lou became enraged again, saying, "I don't need no goddam husband. My boyfriend'll take care of my babies anyway. I can move back with him any time I want to and out of this motherfuckin' house. I just didn't want to live with him now but he'd take me back if I wanted. He brings the baby things sometimes." Mrs. Johnson disagreed, saying that ever since the baby had been there the boyfriend had not done anything for him or given anything toward his care: "Everything that baby eats and wears comes out of my (ADC) check." Mary Lou said, "It doesn't come out of your check. The baby has a check of his own." Mary Lou, by then very angry at Hammond, told him that she could take care of herself if she moved out: "Don't you worry your black ass about it. I'll get the money from someplace." Then her mother said, "I don't know where you'll get it because so far you haven't been able to get ahold of any money yet. I'm not gonna have those babies out in the street. They're gonna stay here even if you do move out. I'll not have it, not knowing who's taking care of them."

Mary Lou moved to attack her mother, "I don't know what you're raising all the hell about. You had all those kids and didn't have no husband. They don't even know who their daddies are." Mrs. Johnson became very excited: "I did have a husband when I had you, a lawfully married husband by the name of Grady, and when I had all the rest of you I was living in common law with Robert Johnson. I'd been living with him until the day I had him arrested for nonsupport of the children. All the children have the same father except for you, Mary Lou, and your father was Mr. Grady." Mary Lou retorted, "Well, he didn't do shit for us and neither did you." Mrs. Johnson said, "I took care of all you kids and raised all of you and raised you to the age of womanhood and besides I took care of your baby too. You can get out if you want to but your kids aren't going anywhere."

Barbara began to chuckle. Esther said to her, "What are you laughing about, you little bitch? In another year you'll be pregnant, too, running around here fuckin' everything with a dick on it. I don't know what in hell you're laughin' at."

Hammond said something about the problem of girls becoming pregnant but the fathers of children not supporting them, and Esther retorted, "The motherfucker that made me pregnant is going to take care of my baby or I'll get me a butcher knife and slice his fuckin' stomach open. That son-of-a-bitch had better not walk down the street and let me see him or I'll cut his throat. I know he's going to take care of my baby because we're going to court next week." Mary Lou said she was going to take her boyfriend to court, too.

Mrs. Johnson then said, "Since you're getting so smart, Esther, I'm going to go on and tell it all like it is. Your boyfriend's mother called me and told me not to bring my black ass or my black ass daughter over to her house to try to make her son marry you. She said her son wasn't going to marry anybody until he was 21 and she didn't even want to see or hear me. I'm not going near that woman's house. Besides, they told me at the welfare office that if you don't go back to school after you have the baby they're gonna send you away. Since you're talking so big I'm just going to tell it all like it is."

Bob began to laugh. Esther turned on him. "What in hell are you laughin' about? You're a no good motherfucker and you couldn't make no babies. You been out fuckin' everything walkin' and still don't have no babies to show for it. That's true of Richard too. Neither one of you are men cause you don't have no babies at all. You started all this shit this afternoon about babies. (Addressing the group) If the motherfucker wants a baby let him go and fuck and get him a baby like I went out and fucked and got mine. I went out and fucked until I got me a baby." Hammond said that perhaps her brothers used contraceptives because they did not want to father children. "Those black motherfuckers don't know shit. They just ain't man enough to make babies."

Seeing that he was only making matters worse, Hammond started to leave. Mrs. Johnson summed up by saying, "You see, Boone, how hard it is for me to bring up a family. Here I thought I had the girls all straightened out and both of them come up pregnant at the same time, and then they sit around and talk to me like I'm some kind of dog and not their mother. I just don't know how a poor old woman can make it. If it weren't for the Lord to help me through I guess I'd just keel over and die."

About two months after the argument, Bob and Esther fought again and Esther gave him a cut with a butcher knife that required 21 stitches. The police came this time, too, but no charges were filed, although Esther was told that if she ever did anything like that again she would be sent to the girl's training school.

She's Got Her Mother's Fighting Blood in Her

When Hammond visited the family a month later, he learned that Esther had a healthy baby girl the week before. While he held the baby, Hammond was told that Richard was on his way to court. He was dressed in new and neat clothes for this appearance. His mother explained that because he was out of school and in trouble fairly often the court had considered sending him to the boy's training school, but had decided that if he would get a job, contribute part of his earnings to his mother, and stay out of trouble, he could stay home. If he did not do so, he would be sent to the training school as soon as there was an opening there. Richard had fund a job working on a coal truck and earned $3 a day; he gave his mother $2 and kept the other dollar for himself. Mrs. Johnson seemed proud that he was working and contributing to the family. He was the first one to do so.

Hammond noticed that Mrs. Johnson's face was scratched and that she had a black eye. He asked what had happened, and she said that Esther had gotten mad at her and beat her up. She said that Esther had beat her "good." She said that she had tried to fight her off but she had reached an age now that she could no longer cope with Esther in a physical battle She was laughing about the affair and said that her daughter was a fighter just like she used to be. She said that Esther did not take any "shit" off anybody, not even her mother. She had called the police, and when they came Esther cursed them out and fought them too. She said Esther fought them for a half hour before they were able to subdue her and take her to jail. Mrs. Johnson said that while Esther was in jail she raised so much hell that they didn't know what to do down there. She stayed there for three or four hours and when they let her go she cursed them out again. When she got home Esther almost started another fight and she almost had to call the police again. Mrs. Johnson seemed proud of the fact that Esther was able to fight and that she cursed and fought the policemen. She said she used to act the same way when she was younger—Esther had her mother's fighting blood in her and probably would not be afraid of anybody. Esther said that she was not afraid of any motherfucker and would fight man, woman, or dog at any time. She was laughing and smiling while she said this and her mother was looking at her with pride, also smiling, enjoying what her daughter was saying.

Mrs. Johnson left for the grocery store with Mary Lou and Bob. Hammond asked Esther why she had fought her mother. She said that her mother began "talking a lot of old silly shit to me, telling me what to do and not to do and I didn't want to hear it." She said that her mother made her mad and she began to fight. It seemed that Esther wanted to move out of the apartment and take the baby with her. Her mother told her she could go but the baby was going to stay because, as she had said on an earlier occasion, she did not want her grandchildren out in the street running around with her daughters. She said she wanted them at home with her where she knew they would be well attended. Esther said she wanted to take her daughter with her and she did not want her daughter to stay at home with her mother.

Hammond asked Esther where she intended to move, and she said she was going to move out west (in St. Louis) with her boyfriend. He asked if it was the same boy who had fathered her baby and she said no, "I haven't seen that motherfucker for months. He didn't come over to see me in the hospital. He didn't even send word to me." She said that at the same time he had made her pregnant, he had also made another girl pregnant and that the other "bitch" was running around the project telling everybody that the same boy had fathered her baby. Esther said, "If I catch that other bitch I'll whip her black ass." She had heard that the other girl was in the project visiting and she had been trying to get out so she could catch her; as soon as she caught her she was going to jump on her and "stomp all the shit out of her." She said the bitch had no business running around bragging about who the father of her baby was. If she saw the baby's father she was going to get a butcher knife and slice his throat; she said that she had tried to do it before.

A week later Esther moved in with a girlfriend. She moved alone, however, because her mother would not allow her to take the baby with her. Hammond asked Mrs. Johnson when she expected Esther back and was told that Esther could stay away as long as she wanted but that she was not going to take the baby with her; that the only way she could get the baby was to get married or to come back home and stay.

Two months later Hammond returned with a large box of baby clothes for the new babies and a few things for the older children. He found Mrs. Johnson, Esther, and Bob in Esther's bedroom, playing with the baby. As he walked in, Hammond noticed that Mary Lou's baby boy was on the floor near the window in the living room, lying asleep on a small blanket, but he did not see Mary Lou. He told Mrs. Johnson that he had some more clothes for her in his car and asked if Bob could go down and bring them up. Bob went to get the clothes and they moved to the kitchen area. When they got there, Mary Lou was sitting on the table, half crying and half mad. Her mother asked what the matter was, but she would not answer. She kept looking down at the table, then over to her mother, then over to Esther, giving Hammond an occasional glance, and then back down at the table again. No one seemed to know what the trouble was.

Mary Lou finally told her mother that she had heard her, Esther, and Bob back in the bedroom talking. She said they were talking about her and would not allow her to come back into the bedroom with them. Mrs. Johnson denied this, saying they would have loved to have her back there with them. She said they were just back there laughing and playing with the baby and she felt that she just did not want to come back. Esther tried to reassure her that they had not been talking about her at all. Mary Lou said, "Yes, you have. I know that you bastards have been back there talking about me again." Mrs. Johnson said that she did not know why Mary Lou felt that way; she always talked like they were plotting against her but nobody around the house ever felt that way about her. She said this was just something that Mary Lou was always carrying around in her mind.

Bob reappeared with the box of clothes. Mrs. Johnson then sat down beside the kitchen table and told Bob to bring the box over to her. She began taking the clothes out of the box, commenting on how large a box it was and how many clothes must be in it. She continued to take the clothes out and her eyes began to light up as she saw what it contained. Some of the clothes, she said, would be fine for Esther's baby because they were boy's clothes. Still other articles of clothing would fit some of her other daughters, and there were some of Hammond's old clothes that would fit her sons.

As she pulled the clothes out Esther would say, "I want that, Mama." and Mrs. Johnson would hand it to her. She did this until she had a small stack of clothes in front of her. All of this time Mary Lou was looking down at the table and seemed very angry. She did not ask for any of the clothes. Mrs. Johnson told Mary Lou that she wished she would stop acting that way, nobody was mad at her and nobody had been talking about her and she wished she would join them in sharing the fine clothes Hammond had brought. After receiving a pile of clothes Mary Lou began to smile and talk a little.

It took Mrs. Johnson about half an hour to go through the pile of clothing and sort it all out. When she reached the end she clapped her hands and jumped up, saying, "Thank the Lord for having Boone and his family look out for poor old Mrs. Johnson." She told Hammond to come back that night because she was going to buy something to drink. She said tonight was the night she was to get paid for babysitting. Hammond asked whose baby she was sitting with and was told that Esther's boyfriend paid her $22 a week for sitting with Esther's baby and fixing his meals every evening. She explained that Esther had a new boyfriend who worked at a restaurant downtown; they were going to be married in about a month and Esther was getting ready to move out of the house next week. She called the boy her son-in-law. This man, however, was not the man who fathered Esther's baby, he was a half-brother of one of the boys who lived in the next building and who ran around with Bob. Mrs. Johnson said he and Esther had already picked out a house and the furniture they wanted, and they were going to live "out west." From the way she talked, however, it was clear that they planned to move into the apartment for a while before they married.

Again Mary Lou's head dropped and she began to cry quietly. Mrs. Johnson seemed quite unaware of Mary Lou's envy of her sister. She was so happy to think that someone wanted to marry one of her daughters, that one of them would be out of the house with someone else taking care of them, that she did not seem to think about Mary Lou's reaction.

Esther brought Hammond some pictures showing her boyfriend, Bob, and herself, from which Hammond judged the boy to be about 23. She said they had been taken several weeks earlier when they had gone out to an amusement park. She said that they had all had a ball; before they left they had been drinking vodka, and Richard had so much to drink they had to carry him up the stairs and put him in a chair in the living room, where he fell out. The others had continued on to the carnival where they drank more vodka and orange juice and all got really high. Her boyfriend had spent $53; they had so much to eat and drink that they could hardly hold it all. Bob had gotten so drunk that on the way back he kept getting out of the bus seat, trying to give it to women saying, "Here, baby, you can have this seat." He had been acting "silly and crazy" all the way back. She then went to the back room and got the dress, shoes, and stockings she had been wearing that night. She said her boyfriend had bought all the clothes for her right before they had gone out.

Mrs. Johnson told Esther to go back and bring her own new dress to show Hammond. She said that her new boyfriend had bought this dress for her, and he also had a car. They had been out the past weekend, she had had a ball and had gotten "running drunk." She had not gotten home until 4:30 in the morning and then she was so drunk that her kids had to help her into the bedroom. Esther verified this and said she had to undress her mother and take all her clothes off and hang them up. Mrs. Johnson was smiling, obviously happy about all this, she was proud to let Hammond know she had a new boyfriend, especially one with an automobile. He asked what had happed to Mule and she replied that they still saw each other but that his brother had been sick and he had been away helping to take care of him.

Before Hammond left, Bob brought up a fairly new racing bicycle that he said he had stolen while coming back from downtown. He said it was just sitting there so he brought it home with him; his mother did not seem to disapprove. He also told Hammond quietly that his younger sisters had gone downtown with some other girls in the next building and had stolen a bag full of jewelry that they were hiding at another girl's house. He said later on they would bring the bag home and tell their mother somebody had given it to them. He was going to go down and steal another bicycle because he did not really like this one, he wanted one of those new stingray bicycles with the little wheels, large seat and high handlebars, but he could not find them around the project because only the white boys had them. He was going to go out to Forest Park to get one; he would take one of his friends out with him on the handlebars of his bicycle, steal the new bicycle and have his friend bring his old bike back while he rode the new one.

As Hammond was leaving, Esther asked if she could go with him to the research project apartment to get some rubber bands. The boys left with them and as they walked over they were joined by a young man, Joe, and several younger boys. On the way up to the apartment, Joe asked Esther if she would give him some of that "pussy" and she told him to go to hell. When they got to the apartment he asked her again to give him some "pussy" and pulled her into the back room and closed the door. After a few seconds she opened the door and came out laughing. She told him to leave her alone, that she was not going to give him "shit." She said goodbye, but Joe persuaded her to come back again. Hammond told her to leave, but each time she went out the door she came back again. Instead of rejecting Joe, she acted as if she were thrilled by his attention and kept coming back for more. Her brothers told her to go on into the back room with Joe, that he would "put a dick in her." She said that he would not do "shit" to her but she kept hanging around and he kept "feeling her up." Hammond resolved the situation momentarily by taking them all downstairs.

9.
Parents and
Their Children

The Elusiveness of Family Solidarity

One of the striking things about Clara Johnson is her "down home" quality, despite the fact that she has lived in St. Louis since the 1930's. She came there as an adult, and apparently twenty-five years of living there have not significantly changed her way of looking at the world, except perhaps to add to it a general sense of dismay at how different things are from the way they were in the small Mississippi town in which she grew up. She seems hardly urbanized, even compared to many of her age peers who have been in the city for a shorter length of time. Perhaps it is that she has only dull normal intelligence; or perhaps it is easier to cleave to her small town ideals than to confront all the unpleasantness around her. In any case, to herself she is simply "poor old Mrs. Johnson," who grew up working in the white folks' kitchen and is now a "widow woman." In her mind, "Clara don't do anything but sit here in this apartment all day long and do her very best to take care of her children."

But Clara Johnson had mastered one urban skill, although she was perhaps not as creative with it as some other people in the project. She had learned how to operate in the complex of public and private welfare agencies on which she had to depend for food, shelter, and clothing for her family. Despite the many troubles she and her children had gotten into, she apparently managed to maintain good relations with the welfare office and the Housing Authority and to make use of settlement houses and the public hospitals and clinics when necessary. She never knew exactly where she stood with these agencies because their rules and regulations kept confusing her; equally, it may be that they never knew where they stood with her because her capacity to confuse was great as she talked about her family's situation. Nevertheless, she did manage to make the bureaucracies produce the basic resources she needed for herself and

211

212 BEHIND GHETTO WALLS

her family and to ward off their incursions on her family's autonomy. She was never evicted, despite all the complaints against the family; her son never did go to the training school; and for all their experience on the edge of the law, none of the children spent time in jail.

"Poor old Mrs. Johnson" wanted to maintain that in the eyes of the community she was—barring misunderstandings—a respectable woman working very hard to raise her children respectably. From time to time her protestations of respectable manners seemed quite ludicrous, as when she upbraided Mule for drinking wine in her bedroom in front of Hammond. But Mule called her pretended respectability by a name that deflated it—she was being "uppity." There is a self- and other-deluding character about these protestations of respectability. Mrs. Johnson takes on the "phantom role" of a poor but respectable widow woman, but the pretense is thin, honored by none of her children and only superficially by Mrs. Johnson herself.

Until recently she had been a heavy drinker and involved in violent behavior toward her neighbors and her boyfriends. By her own standards her behavior seemed to have gotten out of hand, and by the time Hammond came to know her she was making real efforts to bring it under control, perhaps because of fear for her health. In any case, her "disreputable" behavior seemed to have strong repercussions on her children. As she continually complained, none of them seemed to respect her. Her daughters in particular were vociferous in demeaning her status as a mother, in minimizing her authority over them; they seemed to have settled on "shamelessness" rather than "respectability" as the basis of their behavior. Mary Lou was not particularly clear about what she was doing and why she was doing it, but Esther was quite explicit, not to say profane, in disavowing any responsibility to live up to the moral standards which her mother used as weapons against the children.

As a mother, Mrs. Johnson performed only one function with consistency and determination. She fed, clothed, and sheltered her children. Despite all the apparent disorganization and the lackadaisical quality of her home life, she was tenacious in assuring that they kept their apartment, never failing to pay the rent on time so that the Housing Authority was reluctant to evict them no matter what they did. Similarly, with occasional help from one of the girls or from Mule, she prepared meals for them that never failed to fill their stomachs. Despite the tremendous strain of supporting nine people—later 11 with the two new babies—on $202 a month, the children had clothes that may have seemed inappropriate but were always in good condition.

Despite the violence and aggression of which Mrs. Johnson was capable, and despite the determination she showed in meeting the basic tasks required of a mother, she seemed deeply passive toward her world. She was almost incapable of disciplining her children in any routine fashion. She responded to the dangers her children brought into the house passively:

she simply outwaited the two boys she suspected of wanting her welfare check; she never objected to the rude and inattentive boys her daughters brought home, she never objected to the frequent appearance of the police to restore order in her children's relations with each other and with their neighbors. Only when there were grave threats to the family as a collectivity did she respond with vigor and assertiveness. Then she would behave violently if things were out of hand, or use the "poor old Mrs. Johnson" approach to the agencies that were supposed to provide assistance.

As a result, there was among the Johnsons little feeling of family solidarity. The children and their mother were accustomed to living together and took it for granted that they would do so, but they did not regard themselves in any pervasive way as a solidary unit separate from the outside world. Instead, the home territory was readily invaded by anyone who established a relationship with one of the family, and the children were ready to derogate and demean other family members, to tell Richard that "he is no brother of mine" or to tell their mother that she was no better than they because all but one of her children were illegitimate.

Little of the activity in which the members individually engaged was converted into a shared sense of family membership. For example, in another family with many of the same difficulties, each escapade was likely to be converted into a story to tell the other family members and which allowed all of them to enjoy a sense of shared life. Only rarely was there anything of this quality in Hammond's experience with the Johnsons.

The older children seemed to have a consistently harsh view of their world. Within this context, they were inclined to feel sorry for themselves from time to time, and to feel justified in taking an exploitative attitude toward others. All the children were heavily engaged in the street world of the project and of the ghetto that surrounds it.

Mary Lou seemed in many ways very naive. She was very much like her mother in her passivity, and like her mother, she could easily strike an outside observer as being not very bright. Even so, she managed to surround herself with boys, and in her nonverbal way pursued an active heterosexual street career. Bob, more than any of the other children, kept his own council, and Hammond learned very little about him and his life during the two years that he knew the family—only enough to know that he participated actively in the petty, juvenile lawbreaking which was common in the project.

Esther and Richard were the liveliest members of the family and as a result easier to get to know. Esther's potentiality for violence grew during the two years that Hammond visited the family. She seemed determined to take from the world whatever she could get her hands on, and she felt deeply the wish to destroy anyone who got in her way, whether it be her mother, her boyfriend, the "other girl," or her brothers. Perhaps as she neared the end of her adolescence she realized that she was not going to get a much better break than her mother, so she was tempted to use violence in a desperate effort to get what she wanted (a husband, a home of her own, some modicum of affluence), or at least to get even with those who frustrated her.

Richard was in many ways the most complex of the older children. For all his violence and petty thievery, he had a strong streak of tenderness which stood out as unusual in a boy his age. He enjoyed the babies, liked to hold them and care for them. He was fond of the dog and puppies that Mary Lou had when she lived for a brief time with a boyfriend. His peers apparently had to push him into much of the heterosexual activity in which he engaged. They seemed to know that he drew back from exploitative relations with girls and so they would urge him on and try to set up situations of sexual adventure for him.

Overall, what is unique about this family is the ubiquity of violence in its members' relationships with each other and with the outside world. Otherwise, what went on among the Johnsons could readily be matched with other families in the project. The mother's and daughters' preoccupation with the transition from adolescence to womanhood, signalled by their pregnancies, and their ways of handling the fact of illegitimacy are common in the project. The grandmothers often become the protectors of the babies, and their mothers often embark on a new career of vigorous participation in street life. Mrs. Johnson forcefully affirms the commonly held view that the baby must have a stable and secure home, and his grandmother must step in and keep the baby, if his mother is not willing to provide a stable relationship.

Considering how frequently the daughters overrode their mother's objections to their behavior, ridiculing rather than obeying her, it seems remarkable that there was no doubt in anyone's mind that Mrs. Johnson's insistence on keeping the babies if their mothers moved out would be observed. Perhaps for all their bravado the daughters were acknowledging that they stood little chance of providing a home even as stable as their mother's. In any case, they knew themselves to be more concerned with establishing gratifying relations with the men in their lives than with mothering their children. Indeed, in a sense they were not neglecting their responsibilities to their babies because they knew they would be loved and cared for by their mother and by their younger siblings.

The fight between Esther and Richard about who was to care for Mary Lou's baby while his mother was out of the house and the family argument that ensued after the police had ended the fight brought into focus many of the issues around which Johnson family life revolved. The psycho-social underpinnings of life are often laid bare in serious quarrels, and in their argument the fact was highlighted that it is only by the barest margin that Mrs. Johnson could hold her family together. It became apparent during the argument that the children had learned that they do not constitute a legitimate, unquestioned family group. For all her pretense, the mother cannot really maintain that the children are all legitimately entitled to be together, to carry a name and identity in common.

The argument represented a vicious unmasking of individual pretenses to being competent individuals. The efforts of the two girls to present themselves as masters of their own fate were unmasked by the mother, and the girls unmasked the pretensions of the mother and of their brothers. When the 13-year-old daughter expressed some amusement they turned on her, telling her that it would not be long before she too became pregnant. Each member of the family in turn was told that he can expect to be no more than a victim of his world, but also that this is somehow and inevitably his own fault.

Masculinity was consistently demeaned in this argument. Bob has no right to play with his niece; the boys are not really masculine because at 15 and 16 they have yet to father children; their own father was a no-good who failed to do anything for the family. These notions probably came originally from the mother, who enjoyed telling the story of having her common law husband imprisoned for nonsupport, but her tales came back to haunt her as her daughters accused her of being no better than they in her ability to find support and nurturance from a man. In contrast, the girls came off somewhat better than the boys, although they had to accept the label of stupidity because they had failed by inconveniently becoming pregnant in the first place. At least they had children and therefore some meaningful connection with life. They had participated in something important and dramatic while the boys, despite their sexual activity, "can't get no babies."

Legitimacy

The households of Pruitt-Igoe have on the average a larger number of children than most American families. There are four minors in the average project household; one quarter have fewer than three, while 42 per cent of the households have three, four, or five, and a third have six or more minors. The average woman in Pruitt-Igoe has given birth to five or six children by the time she completes her child-bearing years. (In addition, about a quarter of the women have had at least one miscarriage.) We are talking, then, about large families.[1]

In Pruitt-Igoe, and in the white and Negro lower class generally the birth of children is unplanned. In 1966, about 45 per cent of the births in the project and in the nearly private housing were illegitimate.[2] There were no differences in the incidence of illegitimate births or in the characteristics of illegitimate mothers between these two areas. The housing project by itself does not seem strongly to influence illegitimacy.

The proportion of illegitimate children varies markedly by birth order. Seventy-three per cent of the first-born children in the project were illegitimate in 1966, compared to 50 per cent of the second-born and 25 per cent of the third and subsequent births. Fifty-three per cent of all illegiti-

1. These figures are based on a project census conducted in 1964 by the Missouri Department of Welfare and on our 1965 questionnaire survey.
2. Base on St. Louis Vital Statistics Records analyzed by Ladner (1968).

mate births were first births. However, people in Pruitt-Igoe reflect a general pattern of having a higher proportion of illegitimate births at higher birth orders than the white population.[3] In Pruitt-Igoe almost one third of the illegitimate births are third or higher order children. These births are not so often to women who have never married, but to women whose marriages have been terminated.

The proportion of illegitimate children living in the project during our study is probably somewhat lower than the 45 per cent of 1966 births because a significant proportion, though not a majority, were born when their mothers were still residing in rural southern areas where illegitimacy rates are not as high. But it remains probable that over half the families in the project have at least one "outsider," the term often used to designate illegitimate children.

The unplanned nature of birth is also indicated in the direct testimony of mothers in our 1965 sample. They were asked whether at the time of each pregnancy they "wanted a child very much," "wanted one, but not very much," "didn't care," "didn't want a child" or "very much didn't want a child." Forty per cent of all pregnancies were characterized as "not wanted" and half of these were very much not wanted. In an additional 12 per cent of the cases, the mothers said they did not care much one way or the other. Only 36 per cent of the children were "wanted very much."

Variation by birth order is again quite marked. The second child is clearly the most wanted. The first child is either very much wanted or not wanted at all, and after the second child the proportion of wanted children declines sharply and the proportion of unwanted increase (See Table 9–1). However, less than half the women said they very much wanted a child when they got pregnant even with the second child. The large families in

Table 9–1

Proportion Wanting Child, By Birth Order

	Wanted Very Much	Wanted, but Not Very Much	Didn't Care	Didn't Want	Very Much Didn't Want	Don't Know	No. of Births in Sample
			per cent				
First child	42	10	9	16	22	1	165
Second child	47	11	14	15	12	1	145
Third child	41	14	13	16	13	1	124
Fourth child	33	17	16	20	13	1	105
Fifth through eighth child	27	14	11	28	20	–	226
Ninth and higher order	–	2	6	37	55	–	52

3. See Kingsley Davis (1965).

the project are seldom the result of positive choice; only one third of the women who had four children very much wanted a fourth child.[4]

These proportions of wanted children probably over-represent the degree of positive motivation because of the general tendency to cast a halo retroactively over events that must in any case be accepted. Once birth is a fact most women find meaning and gratification in their children, even though if their pregnancies required positive decisions the number of births would have been sharply reduced—in all likelihood by at least half.[5]

The circumstances which enter into the legitimacy of a child's birth become an important though often implicit aspect of his social identity. They are not matters of indifference to the adults who must care for and recognize him, and during the process of socialization they cease to be matters of indifference to him.

In families which contain varying mixtures of illegitimate and legitimate children, each child's legitimacy affects the meaning he has for his parents and his siblings. In addition, many families contain the children of several different fathers, whether legitimate or not. Each child carries as part of his social identity a designation as a particular man's son or daughter, even though he may not carry that man's name if he is illegitimate. These elements of personal biography are usually taken for granted within the family and openly discussed when they are relevant to family life, with the result that most children early learn their own genealogy and that of their siblings. In some families, however, efforts are made to conceal genealogical information, so that when the child later learns "the truth" it may come as a shock to him and cause some social disorientation until he absorbs his "correct" identity and learns the meanings it will have for him.

These events are handled in different ways by different families, and the particular constellation of "outsiders" and children of different fathers varies from one family to another and through time within each family. It is therefore difficult to generalize about the effects of the frequent departures from the conventional standard which even in the ghetto remains a family composed of two biological parents who rear only their own children to majority. However, it is clear that at the very least deviance from the cultural ideal raises issues and ambiguities which are frequently disturbing to parents and children. Where deviations exist, they provoke an underlying sense of vulnerability and discreditability subtly affecting the child's ability to build and maintain a sense of common family membership and solidarity.

4. On the basis of a national sample, Whelpton, Campbell and Patterson (1966) found that a higher proportion of Negroes experience excess fertility than comparable whites. On the one hand, Negroes have less access to and knowledge of contraception, and on the other hand, they actually want fewer children than comparable whites. See Whelpton *et al.* (1966), p. 363 ff.

5. Whelpton *et al.* (1966) suggest that Negroes who have not graduated from high school want an average of about three children (p. 350).

Early Childhood

Whatever the events that produce the child, he is usually treated with warmth and loving attention, despite his instrumental care being perhaps insufficient or erratic by pediatric standards. Seldom is there not at least one person in the household who enjoys handling and caring for the baby and who tends to him in an interested and enthusiastic way. Most often, of course, this is the mother, but it may be a grandmother whose older daughter is working or whose young daughter has given birth to an illegitimate child. In the latter case, as in the Johnson family, it is not at all uncommon for the girl to turn the baby over to her mother while she pursues an active career in her adolescent peer group. Often in larger families quite a number of people attend to the baby's needs: older sisters, the mother, and sometimes the grandmother as well. In this situation the baby may be the subject of constant attention, being passed from hand to hand or later toddling from person to person and always receiving amused interest. Consequently large babies and toddlers generally seem secure in their homes; they explore them freely and take gratification in the physical manipulation of objects and in interaction with the people there.

The relationship of the men (if any) in the household with babies and toddlers seems to have little pattern. Some men are interested in babies and participate in the handling and interacting with them; other men are indifferent to younger children and usually ignore them. The latter pattern seems to be more generally expected, and it is cause for some comment if a man does show interest in babies. He is thought to be an unusually good man if he demonstrates his interest in any consistent way.

Lower-class Negro women do not show the deep psychological involvement with infants and young children that is characteristic of higher social classes. They rarely manifest the anxious attention to children, the sense of awesome responsibility along with the pleasure, that is characteristic of many working-class women. Nor do they have the sense of the instrumental, almost occupational, challenge of rearing children properly that is characteristic of the middle class. Among lower-class Negro women, taking care of babies is regarded as a routine activity which is not at all problematic. There is no great concern with the child's development, little anxiety about the appearance, crawling, talking, walking, and other signs of growth and maturation. These things come as they come, with little more than passing comment on the part of the mothers and others who care for the children.

As the child matures, he is socialized mainly in terms of standards of obedience and simple sociability: he is expected to "fit in" the household routine as best he can and as soon as possible. Even here, however, the objective is more one of reducing the amount of trouble the child makes for others than of "testing him" to see how well he is developing and how socialized he is becoming. There is only mild pressure toward obedience through the toddler stage, and there is wide tolerance for messiness and "babyish" behavior.

Children enter into household affairs at a very early age. Homes in Pruitt-Igoe are "adult centered," in the sense which Herbert Gans has used the term;[6] the important matters are those of adult concern, and there is little effort to base household activities on the children and their needs. At the same time there is relatively little effort made to insulate children from adult activities and events. They are generally allowed to observe whatever is going on within the home, and their presence is simply ignored when important adult activities are taking place. If they intrude to such an extent that their behavior distracts adults, they are likely to be disciplined harshly, but if they are reasonably quiet there is little effort to segregate them from the adults. Children soon become knowledgable about the adult world, first as it impinges on the household and later as they hang around outside with a parent or older sibling.

The world that the children are allowed to observe is highly stimulating and often anxiety-producing, especially in frequency of violent behavior, arguments, fights, police activities, and the like. The children's sophistication bothers their mothers greatly, but they generally feel there is little they can do to insulate their children's awareness, particularly of their own family's deviance from the norms in which they are instructed at home and elsewhere. Their awareness becomes a weapon in children's efforts to establish early independence from parental standards and discipline.

Adult interest in and interaction with children declines rather sharply as they move toward the school years. Children of four, five, and over seem to be regarded as much less interesting than babies and toddlers, and adults and older siblings are more likely to ignore them, to push them into the background of family activities. Such a development is hastened if new babies join the family. Often children at this age seem a little lost, not knowing quite how to relate to others or how to get the attention and opportunities for gratifying interaction they would like to have. However, they generally retain an outgoing orientation toward their environment and are quickly responsive to the opportunities it provides for interesting activities and relationships. They are remarkably friendly, even with strangers.

At this age children begin to learn the lesson of "go for yourself." During the immediate preschool and early school years, it begins to become clear that they must work out their own strategies for eliciting the kinds of responses they want from others in their environment. As children in Pruitt-Igoe begin to learn this lesson, they are likely to impress an observer as remarkably mature compared to their middle- or working-class age peers.

6. Gans (1962), p. 54 ff.

They have a sense of social assertiveness and a tenuous self-confidence that can be engaging despite its insistence.

The adults generally take a kind of amused pride in the apparent maturity of these youngsters. The children learn that they can gain attention by their ability to perform in expressive adult ways, by using the special ghetto language, by trying seriously to learn the current dances, by imitating adults' "hip" and "cool." The development of these abilities is often aided by their older siblings, who in relaxed moments may act as instructors and audience for their performances. Both the needs and opportunities of their situation place a premium on the development of expressive skills, to overcome the growing disinterest which significant others manifest toward them.

If the child is able to elicit the kind of response he desires by the development of these techniques, he may for some years continue to feel himself at home in his world of adults. If he cannot elicit such responses, he tends to turn his attention very strongly to his peers and to begin to build with them a society that restores the sense of meaningfulness and status he has begun to lose within his family. If he cannot elicit gratifying responses either within the family or from his peers, he tends to become withdrawn and may appear to be dull or retarded, non-verbal and introverted.

This process, involving the outcome of the crisis when the baby becomes "just another child," may account in considerable part for the large number of Pruitt-Igoe children who are handicapped. Problems with speech, apparently autistic behavior, lassitude that suggests retarded development —all seem much more common in Pruitt-Igoe than in working- or middle-class communities. To some extent this symptomatology may be organically based, and is exacerbated by poor medical care and the generally greater tolerance which the people of Pruitt-Igoe show for handicaps and disabilities of all kinds. But there is reason to believe that a great deal of the "retardation" that impresses the casual observer, that is frequently commented upon by teachers and school officials, may be more directly a product of the social processes by which some children become "losers" very early in life, withdrawing from interaction of all kinds because they are unable to elicit gratification either within their family or with their peers.

It is important to understand that in our data withdrawal and apparent retardation represent only one very small subgroup among the children whom we observed. It is a striking subgroup, both because it seems larger than in other kinds of communities and because it stands out sharply in contrast to the lively and outgoing majority of children in the project. Theories of "cultural deprivation" and of the "non-verbal" character of lower-class Negro children have gained much currency, but any theory which seeks to account for the eventual poor school performance of lower-class Negro children must account for and be based on an understanding of the assertive and outgoing majority.[7]

School Years

Mothers in Pruitt-Igoe introduce children into the instrumental organization of the family at early ages, to help with the heavy demands of homemaking. Girls in particular may take on significant responsibilities— caring for babies, cleaning the house, cooking. As such patterns of responsibility become established, they help to solidify the relationship between girls and their mothers. Although girls may resent the limitation on their freedom dictated by these responsibilities, they are not often very heavy (and certainly not when contrasted with the responsibilities their mothers probably had as girls in the rural south).[8] The girl's instrumental role within the household is an important part of her growing sense of identity as a woman-to-be. As her ability to function effectively increases, the recognition her mother gives her in this identity becomes more and more important to her.

Boys live in a more anxious and ambiguous situation. There is less for them to do; they may undertake chores such as going to the store or occasionally cleaning up, but in general they are not expected to take so much responsibility as girls. It is not considered fitting that they do woman's work, and their mothers generally regard males as basically irresponsible. As a result, their sense of solidarity with their mothers is not strong, and they do not acquire the girls' feeling that a recognized and valued identity is coming into being.

Mothers generally seem to prefer their girls, in the sense that they have closer and more taken-for-granted relationships with them. They may enjoy their sons and take pleasure in their exploits or their hopes, but there is greater distance in their relationships with them and more of a sense of unreality about starting them on the road to valued adult roles. Even the central concern that mothers have about their girls, that they will become prematurely pregnant, serves to solidify their relationship and to reinforce the girl's identity as a woman in process of becoming. After all, whatever the unhappy normative meanings of illegitimacy, pregnancy signifies the valued role of motherhood. Thus, there is in the relationship of mothers and daughters a deep sense of the two as units in the stream of motherhood. The older the girl becomes the more apparent is this sisterly quality in their relationship.

These experiences play an important part in developing among girls a greater self-confidence and sense of having a valid place in the world than

7. For impressive evidence of the superficiality of the presumed nonverbal disabilities of ghetto children see Hamblin, Buckholdt, Buschell, Ellis and Ferritor (1969) and Buckholdt (1969).

8. Schulz (1969) discusses in some detail the memories of southern women in Pruitt-Igoe concerning these responsibilities.

among boys. Here is the beginning of a long sequence of development that leaves adult women feeling more in control of their intimate social world than men, that leaves men feeling more vulnerable in that intimate world. The experiences that give boys a comparable sense of validity and potency are largely those of the peer group, toward whose activities their mothers take a jaundiced view. School accomplishment, as an alternative, is hard to obtain and difficult to communicate to mothers. Boys find themselves in a situation where what gives them a sense of valid identity is not deeply meaningful to their mothers, so there is a disjunction between how they are recognized outside and within the home. This disjunction causes uncertainty in their thinking about themselves.

Whether a child is legitimate is also a factor in the developing mother-child relationship. It is not merely that mothers may prefer legitimate children or that legitimate children may feel more secure in their family membership, although both of these meanings generally occur at an overt level. In addition, the closeness of the mother's relationship with the child seems often to vary covertly with the particular meanings the mother attaches to the child and the circumstances of his birth. Sometimes, for example, mothers develop a particularly close relationship with an illegitimate child, especially a girl, communicating to the child in subtle ways a feeling of commonality between them. The mother and child are tied in a special way by the contingencies of non-normative birth, and as the illegitimate girl grows up her mother may communicate to her a feeling that like sisters they share the same fate. The mother may transmit to the child not only a demand that she live up to particular moral standards, which may be enforced much more strictly for her other children, but also a simple understanding that they are of like kind. The girl may feel hurt as it becomes apparent that her mother regards her to some extent as stigmatized, but at the same time feels comfort and closeness in her relationship with her mother, a feeling that becomes a source of security in adversities and that facilitates her rejection of childishness.

There are, of course, other possible influences of illegitimate status on the psychosocial role of a child. For example, the child may be subject to greater rejection than his legitimate brothers; this is particularly true for boys and particularly if the marriage remains intact. Thus the matter is much more complex at the covert level than is apparent in the mild stigma attached to the status of "outsider."

The Outside World and Parental Controls

The problem of control becomes paramount as children enter the school years. Pruitt-Igoeans' deep pessimism about human nature, their bedrock conviction that most people will do ill when it is in their interest, that doing ill is more natural than doing good, interacts with the normal contingencies of life that make doing good very difficult. Parents feel that luck more than anything else determines whether their children grow up conforming to their ideas of goodness. They hope that their children will have luck, but in time they become increasingly desperate and then increasingly hopeless.

Parents use three principal techniques to control the child and to discourage unconstructive behavior. (Mothers are more deeply involved in control activities. Even when a father is present in the home, he tends to stand somewhat aloof from child discipline, except in situations of particularly destructive or disrespectful behavior.) These techniques are: (1) efforts to isolate the child from opportunities to become involved in trouble by keeping him at home; (2) physical punishment for irritating or frightening behavior, particularly that which occurs within the home itself; and (3) cautionary horror stories about the dangers in the outside world and what can happen to the child if he becomes involved in it.

Isolating the child from the outside world is a technique most appropriate for young children. Most mothers in Pruitt-Igoe try to keep their children within the apartment as much as possible, or allow them to venture outside only when a responsible member of the family can watch over them. One often gets the impression that mothers try to hold them virtual prisoners within the house, so great is their fear for their physical and moral safety outside.

However, mothers know they cannot succeed with this strategy as the children grow up. Children get a taste of freedom as they walk to and from school and they increasingly demand the right to come and go as their peers do. To the extent that mothers try to maintain isolation, they undermine their own legitimacy because of the palpable "unreasonableness" of this effort. From the point of view of the child, the outside world is interesting and rewarding and he downgrades the dangers it might represent. Only parents who remain energetically vigilant can isolate their children through adolescence. Teenage girls, for example, may not be allowed to spend time outside the home (except for school) unless they are accompanied by a responsible adult. But few mothers can maintain sufficient authority to carry out such strict discipline more than intermittently.

Lower- and working-class families in general make greater use of physical punishment than do middle-class families, and Pruitt-Igoeans conform to this pattern. But physical punishment is not an everyday affair and seems to be used mostly when the child becomes older, more as an expression of parental exasperation or desperation than as a calculated technique of control. In general, Pruitt-Igoe children do not seem to be greatly intimidated by the threat of punishment and respond to it primarily by trying to conceal those activities they think may sufficiently anger a parent to trigger a beating.

When parents have given up trying to isolate their children, they resort to detailing cautionary horror stories in an attempt to reason with the child and influence him to control his own participation in the dangerous outside world. Stories about "what can happen" seem to be an important way of sensitizing the Pruitt-Igoe child to the negative potentialities of his environment. However, because these stories are usually presented in overly dramatic terms, they provide poor guides for behavior; if the child were to draw the intended deductions from them, he would voluntarily isolate himself from participation in his peer group. Of course, he is not at all inclined to do this because he finds participation gratifying.

These horror stories often deepen the child's conviction that the avoidance of trouble is a hopeless endeavor and encourage him to tolerate and manipulate the negative possibilities of his world rather than to avoid them. The child's perspective may develop in a direction radically different from his parents'; the adults see the world as unremittingly dangerous, while the children perceive it as offering many opportunities that make courting of danger worthwhile, especially because danger is unavoidable. The child absorbs the conventional standards reflected in the stories, and can talk eloquently about how "bad" is the world in which he operates. But while he learns caution and circumspection, he mainly learns that he must run risks and must engage in behavior which he knows is not "right" if he is to become a fully committed person in the peer-group world that is the only one available to him.

As their children grow older, parents increasingly limit their efforts to exercise control over their behavior. Sometimes they seem to do this voluntarily, sometimes grudgingly, but they have no choice; as their children mature, they become increasingly autonomous, increasingly skilled in manipulating the available cultural materials to put themselves on a more equal footing with the parents. As Pruitt-Igoe parents withdraw from close monitoring of a child's behavior, they cannot realistically be very sanguine in their evaluation of what the child is likely to do with his autonomy, and they must withdraw more rapidly and more completely as the child grows up because they have less and less to offer the child for his adherence to the standards they wish to enforce. In the end, the parents' fear is generally realized that the child will get out into the larger world before he is ready to resist its destructive potential. As this happens, parents tend to reduce sharply their surveillance of their children's activities to protect themselves from the punishing information that might come their way if they paid more careful attention.

Many Pruitt-Igoe parents feel a covert hostility toward their children, which arises from many sources—their feelings about how the children came into the world, their sense of inadequacy to meet the child's demands for support and protection, and often their resentment about having been saddled with responsibilities for children too early in their lives. These feelings may be quite threatening to the mothers. As Schulz observes, on the basis of his intensive studies of ten Pruitt-Igoe families:

> Contrary to what one might assume from the evidence of large families and husky, smiling women, it is not uncommon for project

women to feel themselves "overrun with children." Their tendency to feel this way varies with their birth order. Those born first and consequently forced early to assume the responsibility of raising "her" (their mother's) children feel the strongest resentment. At nine they were caring for her babies, feeding them and changing their diapers. At 13 they were "given the children" as their major responsibility. They express a deep-seated anger and resentment against these children who deprived them of their girlhood and a strong ambivalence over their own children who came along later in life and restrict the freedom of their womanhood. They give evidence of experiencing both an intense feeling of guilt over this hatred, and a strong desire to identify with their daughters and thus regain their girlhood vicariously.

This ever-present guilt causes some lower-class mothers to seek compensation in indulging their children and letting them have their way. But the hatred is not thereby dissipated. It remains always in the background and sometimes—particularly in the case of firstborn daughters who have become mothers—it breaks through their apparently easy-going and indulgent natures in uncontrollable anger. This anger is so close to the surface in the case of some mothers that they are afraid to discipline their children for fear that they will go too far and seriously hurt them.[9]

The prevalent sense of impotence about rearing children as parents wish tends to undercut, day by day and year by year, their efforts to teach their children how to operate in the Pruitt-Igoe world—to avoid its troubles and to acquire the kinds of skills and moral biography that might allow them to escape it. Both the effort to teach the children and the failure of the teaching have consequences for the child's identity as he grows up. The parents try to teach the child what life is supposed to be like and how he is supposed to live it. In doing so they communicate an image of conventional American family and community life, but always in the context of the quite different life actually experienced by both parents and child. At the same time and in specific adaptation to their own world, they try to teach the child to be rationally self-protective, to avoid trouble, to cope with peers and officials in such a way that they will not suffer.

Parents communicate to the child that if only he does right he may be safe, but in fact, he discovers that when he does right he is *not* safe, and very often he does not want to do right because the things that are wrong are more interesting and stimulating. Similarly, the parents' efforts fail to teach the children to be well behaved in school. Typically, good behavior does not make the child's teachers interested in him or rewarding toward him, and he is left to cope with a school situation that offers him little but demands much in the way of self-control.[10]

The parents' efforts to instill in the child a basic image of the good working-class child—lively, happy, well behaved, carefully respectful in

9. Schulz (1969), p. 175–176.
10. See Rist (1970) and Talbert (1969).

dealing with authorities—in the end get the child nowhere. The authorities do not respect him; his peers do not reward him for "respectable" behavior; the conventional image offered him by parents acquires in Pruitt-Igoe a greater aura of unreality than for other children. There results in the child a particular kind of consciousness which his parents also have, a consciousness than maintains to some extent and on some occasions that everything is "all right," that one is a fully moral person in an adequately moral world, but at the same time that is permeated with a sense of impotence, an awareness that oneself, one's parents, and everyone else fall significantly short of being a good person. The resulting overt stance often involves an apparent sense of conventional self-assurance, under which there is a deep sense of being unable to control what is going on, of being unable to go through life without being damaged and shamed by its events.

Shame and Guilt

The observer is struck by how large shame looms in the control mechanisms and the feelings about self of adults and children in Pruitt-Igoe. Shaming is a common control technique in the project. Children are shamed for not doing the right thing, but they are also shamed by parents and peers for not being tough enough to cope with their problems. Finally, they may be shamed for unsuccessfully claiming to be what they are not, as in the frequent use of the phrase, "I know you shamed," in situations where the individual arrogates to himself desirable attributes which are patently false. As the child grows up he increasingly acquires an awareness that nothing he can do will protect him from danger and attack, whether from his parents for failure to meet their standards, or from his peers for failure to meet their contradictory and manipulative orientations, or from caretakers (e.g. school teachers and police) who always seem to want from him something other than what he is doing.

The black child's experience in the slums of the 1960's recapitulates the black man's experience in the New World, which has been most centrally shaming in stripping him of his power to make autonomous decisions in his own culture and society and preventing him from reconstructing a new society in which he was other than a slave or servant. This historical experience gives the child hated models of shamed and impotent identity, and also some models of desperate escape from that identity. In his socialization he is forced continually to undergo experiences of being shamed, shamed by his own body which is hungry or hurts from the beatings he receives, shamed by those he loves who seem to want from him things he cannot possibly produce (and he cannot know they are simply not producible given his resources), and shamed by the caretakers of the community who are supposed to help him learn how to escape. His experience convinces him that he is too weak to meet the varying and conflicting demands made upon him by those who have the power to reward him with the things he values.

Alvin W. Gouldner has observed that most discussions of normative behavior tend to be based on the assumption of guilt as the deviator's response to norm violation, but that shame as much as guilt may be the
source of moral anxiety. In his discussion of Greek culture, he observed
that the ancient Greeks were particularly vulnerable to a sense of shame
because of their view that norms were most importantly matters of
achievement and competence rather than matters of good and evil. Deviance tended to generate shame rather than guilt, because it was perceived
as a deficiency, a failure rather than as the transgression of a norm that
represented an absolute good.[11] This view is roughly consonant with that
of Talcott Parsons, who sees guilt as arising from the perception that one
is undeserving in terms of the standards of the internalized father and
therefore is experienced as internalized "disesteem," while shame arises
when one perceives that his response is not in accord with the attitudes
of the internalized mother, and is therefore experienced as internalized
"depreciation." In Parson's view the punishment represented by guilt is
the highly abstract awareness of being denied esteem, while the punishment represented by shame is the more concrete sense of a termination of
nurturance from significant others.[12] In these terms, shame represents
weakness because it signals the inability of the individual (by virtue of his
deviant behavior) to elicit the rewards from others that he desires. Guilt,
however, involves a strictly intrapsychic transaction between an internalized representative of the abstract principles to which one is expected to
conform and the ego as perceiver of behavior.

Defined in this way, it becomes apparent that guilt is a luxury available
only to those who have solved their problems of self-maintenance in the
external world so well that they can afford to focus their attention on an
internal dialogue with their super-ego. Psycho-dynamically, it seems probable that guilt as an effective inhibitor of deviance can arise only in situations in which individuals have the opportunity to develop (in fantasy if
not in reality) an orderly, predictable and loving relationship with their
parents, and to regard the parents as themselves capable of living up to
the norms which they proffer. Shame is a universal intrapsychic experience, however; whether the relationship to the parent is orderly and loving the individual is confronted with the withdrawal of nurturance when
he fails to conform to the norms proffered by those around him.

Our data suggest that in Pruitt-Igoe shame is by far more common than
guilt in response to norm violation. This is implicit in the findings dis-

11. Gouldner (1965) observes, "Shame, by contrast, is that form of anxiety occuring
when a person perceives himself as having failed at some effort of achievement in a
manner visible to others whose approval he desires. Shame is the anxiety of being
found wanting by others who, either in fact or fantasy, are thought to know of this
failure. It is an anxiety about reputation, about the image of the self held by others.
The overriding concern here is anxiety about the opinion of others; and this norm is
used, not simply as a a brute fact of social life, but as a proper principle for the guidance of one's own behavior" (p. 84).
12. Parsons (1955), p. 89–90.

cussed in Chapter 3, in which again and again the emphasis is on the effect of deviance on an individual's status within the group rather than on the violation of absolute standards. A girl experiences shame at becoming premaritally pregnant or acquiring a reputation for promiscuity because these demonstrate her inability to negotiate successfully a transformation from childhood to respectable adulthood. It is "what she has done to herself" rather than to an absolute moral system that seems most salient.

One solution to the problem of shame is the development of a reactive display of self-confidence and self-assertiveness. The child is instructed in this public stance by his peers and often by his parents. Pride then becomes the defense against an underlying sense of shame. The child in Pruitt-Igoe may learn two kinds of pride and which will dominate depends on his particular experiences. The first, less common, is pride in being able to adhere to standards of respectability, and therefore holding oneself above the unrespectable elements in the community. This pride comes more easily to older women than to children because church-oriented respectability does not offer children very much, but a few families (like the Madisons) manage to build their lives around respectable peer-group activities. This kind of adaptation points toward the possibility of social mobility, but prideful identities based on respectability are extremely vulnerable to pressures from the surrounding world and heavily dependent on a sense of progress toward conventional status. Without manifest progress, a person is vulnerable to the shaming activities of his less respectable peers; he is "some kind of fool" for denying himself the gratifications of the street world to no good purpose.

The more common kind of pride in the ghetto has at its base "knowing no shame;" it is the pride that comes from wholehearted participation in the unconventional opportunities provided by the ghetto world and from learning to be a skilled practitioner of the arts of "cool" and "working game." Here the individual, based on a tough and pragmatic assessment of what his world is like, comes to have pride in himself because he is able to survive and to take the gratifications he wants. But he must maintain his pride in the midst of a hostile world. Not only do conventional pressures conspire to undercut his claim to autonomy and to shame him by converting his maneuvers into moral and practical failures, but also those who are playing the same game seek to shore up their own pride by manipulating him, by extorting gratifications from him without giving commensurate return. As the child grows, he can find his own family a distinctly unsympathetic refuge from his attempts at the role of "cool cat" either because of a moralizing response, or because the family undercuts his pretentions by telling him he is still a baby, still too weak to make out successfully in the tough outside world.

Pride is, therefore, a tenuous accomplishment in the ghetto whichever strategy is chosen, and the individual himself learns that fact intimately.

His pride becomes prickly and over-insistent, exposing him to even greater risks of being "cut down to size." It is only the most skilled individuals who learn how to modulate their assertion of respectable or manipulative pride to ward off the many possibilities of shame.[13] Girls have an inevitable edge over boys because they can retreat to the pride of motherhood, even though to have that opportunity they may have to undergo the degradation of being victim to their own "bad" behavior.

An underlying sense of impotence that accurately reflects the nature of their lives is probably the central dynamic involved in the orientation toward immediate gratification of lower-class people, an orientation that is much noted in research and is strikingly apparent in Pruitt-Igoe. The traditional statement of this point of view is that lower-class people are not able to defer to long-term goals and are responsive only to the possibilities of immediate gratification. This manner of stating the situation implies that a failure to defer gratification is irrational and self-indulgent.[14]

In fact, however, people in a lower-class community such as Pruitt-Igoe cannot choose between immediate and deferred gratifications; the only gratifications available must be taken when they occur or must be foregone entirely. The child growing up in Pruitt-Igoe learns that the available gratifications are cheap, plentiful, and do not require much planning or time for development. The child can get small change from his parents or even from strangers to buy candy or soft drinks, but he does not receive an allowance which he is expected to save so he can buy the latest $15 toy, nor can his parents budget for expensive presents at birthdays or Christmas. The windfalls that occur from time to time, for instance, when a proud father returns with full pockets and hands out five-dollar bills, occur out of the blue; they cannot be planned for. The child learns to spend his windfalls at once, and for things that can be consumed in common with others. If he tries to hoard, he will be subject to pressure from his siblings and peers to share his goods or to give them up entirely.

Pruitt-Igoeans are socialized to enjoy and to give enjoyment immediately, because their relationships cannot be counted upon to be stable enough to encourage deferring gratification in the hope of a long-term and more secure flow of interpersonal rewards. The individual learns that he may be able to count on people to give him something right now, but even with the best of intentions they are not likely to reward any forebearance by producing gratification for him in the future. Similarly, he learns that what he can do for others he should do at once, because he does not sufficiently control his own life to count on being able to meet the needs of a good friend at some future time. Spontaneity comes to be valued over other styles of interpersonal relations not so much for its own sake as be-

13. For a discussion of violence as a last resort strategy to maintain status and ward off shame see Short and Strodtbeck (1965), pp. 127–140.

14. For a critique of the deferred gratification argument concerning the middle and lower class, see Miller, Riessman and Seagull (1965), pp. 285 ff.

cause the only choice is between spontaneous mutually gratifying activity and moodiness, withdrawal, or anger at any given future time. People learn to endow relationships of the moment with attributes that are conventionally attached to more stable relationships. Thus, one's "running buddy" or "main man" is not necessarily a friend of long standing with whom one can expect to be close next year; more likely, he is a friend with whom the contingencies of the moment establish a special compatibility. At the root of the orientation toward immediate gratification, then, is a sense of unpredictability and of impotence, a feeling that one cannot control the future as one might wish.

The sense of impotence and the nearness of shame account for still another quality of the experiences of those who grow up in a world like Pruitt-Igoe: a preference for activity over reflection. The maintenance of pride requires that one not examine too closely his situation in the world, that one immerse oneself in the activities of each moment. Both children and adults in the project shy away from any consistent thoughtfulness about themselves and their lives, particularly when alone or in situations of intimate interaction. Reflection about one's life, one's past experiences and what is likely to happen in the future, is likely to flood one with the re-experience of negative events and the anticipation of future problems. As one woman said, to think makes her feel depressed.

The accomplishment of a viable adaptation to a depriving and difficult world is so tenuous in Pruitt-Igoe that the individual learns to avoid any assessment of what he has become and where he is going.[15] He has enough trouble resisting the negative effects of anger, depression, and nervousness without magnifying them through the cultivation of thoughtful introspection. Parents are likely to resist self-examination in their children because they know that confrontation with the facts of their existence is likely to be more punishing than rewarding. The child may think about the future, but he generally tends more to fantasy than to planning and anticipatory socialization to conventional models. His fantasy is compensatory rather than anticipatory, in the sense that the child dreams about things he knows he probably cannot have, and sharply demarcates his fantasy life from his day-to-day experience in school, and the streets, and at home. Even his interest in fantasy tends to decline as he learns that the future offers little more than the present. Instead, the child's attention is fixed ever more completely on the possibilities for gratification that come from peer group participation, because there, at least, his experience teaches him he can find what he seeks even though the cost looms large.

The Breakdown of Parental Control

The child is insulated minimally from adult activities, within the household and on the streets, and he finds what he observes always fascinating,

15. The negative view of thinking is also a characteristic of white lower class persons. See Rainwater, Coleman and Handel (1959), pp. 58 ff.

sometimes gratifying, and often very frightening. The underlying sense of intimidation and fear that lower-class children have about their world is apparent in their fantasies of aggression, hostility, and destruction and their ever-present sense of being potential victims. However, they learn as they grow older that there are ways to avoid being merely a passive victim and that if they learn the rules of the street they can find gratification in those initially frightening activities.

The child's knowledge of the adult world becomes strategically important to him in seeking to negotiate his independence from his parents (and his older siblings, if they have authority over him). All that the child sees becomes grist for his mill in handling his relationships with other people. The child often observes parents and always observes adults engaging in behavior he has been taught should be disapproved—fighting, sexual irregularities, drinking to the point of lack of self-control. This, combined with the horror stories his parents tell him about such behavior, serves to teach him a world view in which his community is a place where respectable standards are generally ignored, a place where the supposed costs of deviant behavior are often not paid.

Children keep careful books on their parents. They note any deviance from respectability which they observe, and to add to the dossier they maintain any gossip that comes their way, for example in family arguments at which they are interested bystanders. Younger children simply absorb this knowledge without making use of it in their overt behavior, but older children (particularly adolescents) begin to use their knowledge to discredit their parents and to weaken their authority. This kind of negotiation between parents and children is, of course, common to all families; children are careful observers and harsh judges of their parents because evidence of their deviance from the standards which they seek to enforce is one of the child's few weapons in resisting parental authority. In a community such as Pruitt-Igoe children often acquire a much more discrediting dossier on their parents than in more conventional communities, not only because the parents more often deviate from conventional standards but also because the social ecology of the family's activities is such that it is more difficult for the parents to conceal their deviance from their children.

Not only do children use the knowledge they have acquired, but the parents also perceive themselves to be discreditable, and they will often avoid discrediting confrontations by not enforcing their standards upon the children. They feel vulnerable in their efforts to exercise authority, vulnerable to being shamed by their children, and this situation allows the children to arrogate to themselves quite early the right to set their own standards. Just as peers are careful about judging each other's behavior and concentrate primarily on the appropriateness of the other's actions toward themselves rather than on the morality of the other's behavior outside the peer relationship, parents come increasingly to adopt a standard of quasi-equality in exercise of authority toward their children.

Fights between parents provide a particularly striking example of this dynamic. Both vicious verbal disputes and fights in which the husband beats his wife and the wife reacts aggressively to defend herself are common. In all cases in our field observations the children sided with the mother. This partisanship was mostly verbal, involving words of support for her and condemnation of the father, but on some occasions children actively went to the mother's aid. The father who engages in such behavior finds his moral authority over his children almost totally undermined, and he can assert his authority only in physical ways. Schulz observed in his intensive study of five families with male heads that the father's authority within the family was strongly related to the extent to which he appeared to adhere to respectable standards. Where he deviated from these standards, by fighting with the mother, or drinking, or philandering, his ability to influence his children was markedly reduced.[16]

Even though the children sided with their mother when she was attacked, she lost authority in their eyes because of her vulnerability. After all, she had demonstrated by her very inability to control the marital relationship that she herself could not live by the standards she offered her children. If she reacts to marital difficulties by heavy drinking or by taking a boyfriend, this too enters the children's calculations of whether they will obey her.

The Adaptivity of Parent-Child Patterns

As the conjugal organization of Pruitt-Igoe families represents an effort to adapt to the exigencies of the world in which Pruitt-Igoe men and women live, the characteristics of parent-child relationships develop as they seek to adapt to the requirements of relating to their children in that kind of world, teaching them to function in it, and protecting their own self-esteem as best they can. The system of parent-child relationships is strongly influenced by the children's own assertion of autonomy as they, too, try to adapt to the Pruitt-Igoe world. As the relationship between husbands and wives can be characterized as relatively loose, there is looseness in the parent-child relationship. Parents cannot protect their children from the troublemaking influences of the outside world nor from trouble between spouses within the family, and they cannot provide the resources that would allow children to regard themselves as "ordinary Amercan kids." Further, in adapting to the stresses of their own adult roles, parents often engage in behavior which they have taught their children is immoral or unrespectable, and the children acquire knowledge of this behavior in the ordinary course of growing up.

Because parents cannot protect their children and because they often engage in behavior that undercuts their efforts to enforce respectable standards, they tend to lose legitimacy in the eyes of their children. The perception that parents are not so competent as they present themselves is

16. Schulz (1969), pp. 180 ff.

initially frightening and disturbing, because it increases the children's sense of vulnerability and their fear that they will not be properly nurtured. However, as they grow up their fear becomes less salient, because they learn to operate autonomously to maximize their own security. But their concern with what they see as parental failings continues because of the implications of these shortcomings for their own identities. The child comes to understand that as he grows up he is likely to be no better than his parents in his ability to protect himself from the troublesome world or to avoid behavior that falls short of the requirements for living "the good life."

The reduced legitimacy of parents is alternately concealed and unmasked within the family, depending on the events of the moment. Mothers are conservative in their orientation, wanting family relationships and activities to proceed quietly and without conflict, seeking to avoid circumstances in which their authority will be challenged and the children's low regard for them manifested. Therefore, mothers often ignore behavior of which they disapprove and gloss over children's deficiences rather than confront them.

As a result of the strains to which they are subject, most families in Pruitt-Igoe develop a structure of internal family relationships that is quite open to penetration by the outside world. The boundary between the family and the outside is not so strongly maintained as in other social classes. The family is held together by a set of expressive and instrumental functions parents perform for their children, and to some extent children for their parents. But the boundaries of the unit are readily broken by any member who feels he needs to bring in outsiders or take the resources of the family away for his own use. This is perhaps the strongest difference between lower-class and stable working-class family organization.

This structure is highly adaptive to the street world, because it allows family members to participate freely in the outside world (as they must to develop a sense of meaningful identity) and at the same time preserves a strong sense of affiliation through the mother-child tie. To avoid the disruption that would result from the conflicts within the family that inevitably ensue from the pressures of the ghetto, it is necessary that the members implicitly agree that each person can do as he will, including behavior that threatens other members of the family, so long as he does not permanently challenge the reality of family ties. Children will (resentfully) tolerate a succession of boyfriends because they know that their mother's needs cannot be met within the family; similarly, mothers will tolerate the presence of strangers in the household, "friends" of their children, even where they are frightened by them.

This kind of family organization facilitates the use of street resources, but it limits the ability of the family to resist the incursions of street life and thereby sustains the vulnerability of its members to the outside world. From one perspective, Pruitt-Igoe families fail to protect their members from the street, and this is a common complaint of family members about each other. From another perspective, however, this kind of family organization toughens its members for operating in the outside world by gradually attenuating the child's hopes; he learns that he cannot look to the family as a barrier against pain and frustration, although from time to time he may find within the family a temporary refuge. He is toughened also by learning within the family (by direct experience and by having interpreted and validated there his outside experiences) a world view which tells him that unless he is very lucky his life will not be very different from that of the older people around him. He might as well go about the business of learning to cope with life as it is rather than life as he would wish it to be.

10.
Alice Walker Becomes a Woman

When David Schulz first met Alice Walker, she was a 15-year-old high school student solidly integrated into the Pruitt-Igoe peer-group society. When he ceased field work with the family two-and-a-half years later, she was a married woman, the mother of two children, and intermittently separated from her 20-year-old husband. Schulz conducted intensive field work with the Walker family and with the young man who became Alice's husband.

Alice herself was conceived during Mrs. Walker's first relationship with a boy, when she was 14. Her boyfriend had left her in rural Alabama without knowing she was pregnant. She married Mr. Walker, before Alice was born; he had willingly accepted the fact that his first child would be an outsider. Mr. and Mrs. Walker had four more children: Eleanor, 14; Jane, 12; Carrie, 10; and Mary, 5.

Mrs. Walker found her marriage satisfying for the first few years, but after the birth of several children her husband started running around and drinking and began to fight with her. Eventually she left him to come to the city where she stayed with relatives, and finally she decided to make the separation permanent. The family had lived in St. Louis for only five years when they moved into Pruitt-Igoe, and had lived in the project only a few months when Schulz started working with them.

As he got to know the family he learned that Mrs. Walker, whose disposition was impressively sunny compared to most women in the project, had a steady boyfriend who contributed regularly to the family exchequer and who spent a good deal of time in the apartment. The Walker family was, therefore, somewhat better off than most families in the project. Although Mrs. Walker's ADC payments were only slightly over $100 a month, she supplemented this by earning about $75 from part-time work and her boyfriend's contributions amounting to as much as $80 a month. This income, of about $250 a month for a household of only six persons, was managed frugally and carefully by Mrs. Walker and produced a home considerably better furnished and cared for than the average Pruitt-Igoe household.

Within the limits of what is possible in a community such as Pruitt-Igoe, the Walker family was able to make for itself a life that was reasonably satisfying for its members. The conflicts that became apparent during the course of field work were handled without the violence or entrenched hostility between family members that were observed in other families with many of the same problems. For considerable periods of time things seemed to go well for the family, although eventually most of the members came to feel the oppressive impact of the dangers and deprivations of the ghetto.

During the summer of 1964 Schulz began regularly to interview Alice Walker about how she spent her time. The adolescent social world was in full summer swing and Alice, although she had lived in the project only a short time, was an enthusiastic participant.

The Kids Up in the Projects

> I really like the people here, kids mostly. When I first moved up here, really I didn't want to move up here myself. I had made so many friends down where I lived and I would miss them and I didn't want to move up here at first, and I just stayed in the house all the time and my sister, she's 12, and my other sister, she's 10, and my baby sister, she's 6, and my brother 14, they always go outside and say I got a sister upstairs and all that stuff and you know the kids around here, they want to meet me so my sister brought two of them up here one day and so they talked me into going downstairs; they gave a hop downstairs.

What's a hop?

> Well that's a dance, you know, a dance, a get-together, a teenager dance, and there was seven kids and we all talk and they was showing me how to dance up here and I was showing them how I dance, you know, I showed them how we danced where I lived before and we all got together and danced.

How many people come to these normally?

> Well, approximately it would be about, let me see, well all the kids in this building plus the kids over at Pruitt, it would be about 50 kids at least. Well, you see somebody, like you're downstairs, says 'We're going to dance' so they start playing music they just come. Most of the kids in this building are already downstairs and we just start dancin' and we start passing chairs around, we pass them back and forth and they be going to get some of their friends to come over and have a good time.

What are you going to do when you get finished with school?

I plan on being a secretary. I don't know, I always wanted to be a secretary. My auntie was a secretary and I see her typin' all the time, so when I went to high school I signed up for typin' and I take typin' and a little shorthand this year, and a little typin' this year. When I was in the 9th grade I took a little shorthand.

At Schultz' request, Alice kept detailed records of her activities for several days. These records indicated clearly how absorbed she was in the activities of her peer group. She had three or four close friends from her old neighborhood (which was not very far away) with whom she spent a great deal of time and who together attracted boys for various kinds of joint activities.

One Sunday the girls went to church; they sampled different churches in the neighborhood just to find out what went on in them, without having any particular religious impulse. They spent three-and-a-half hours in a park, playing ball, telling jokes, singing, talking, sleeping, and drinking. Then they went to a double feature with the same group of boys with whom they picnicked in the park. After that they went for a ride and the boys bought them hamburgers. They arrived home at midnight.

On Monday Alice spent her time with a different group of adolescents, all project residents. In the morning she went to the store for her mother, then she visited an aunt for two-and-a-half hours and watched T.V. She spent the afternoon at home with her friends cooking dinner for the family and after dinner played ball outside the building with some of the same friends. Then she visited a friend's house for a long time, playing cards and listening to records. Then the party moved to her boyfriend's house where they talked and danced till 10:00, when she went home.

On the following two days she followed much the same routine: helping an aunt wash clothes, watching T.V., going out to buy ice cream, cleaning her boyfriend's house, always with several boys and girls. A great deal of her time was spent with three close friends. The oldest, Susan, was just 18; the second, Norma, was 16; and the third, Dolores, was looking forward to her 15th birthday that summer. Schulz observed that among the activities listed frequently in Alice's records was talking with these three girls, so he asked what they talked about.

Well, we was talking about me, Norma was at least, about how much fun we used to have going to school and how we miss school. We talked some about how this seems to be the dullest summer we had and Dolores she said "I'm kept busy," you know she have a little child; and Susan, well she kept busy too because she got a job, and Norma said, "Well I'm busy but those kids worry me." You know, talking all that stuff and I was telling them about my boyfriend I had since I moved in the projects and they was talking about how bad work was and all that stuff and girls talking. Normal talking about, you know, (laughs) she was saying that her and her boyfriend, you know, well you don't know, do you?

No, I don't know.

Well anyway she said her and her boyfriend had a sexual intercourse and she was afraid she was pregnant and I asked if she came on her period for that month and she said no and I said uh-uh and we started rolling. Well anyway she not pregnant though she just, well, she went to the doctor and the doctor said well there's nothing wrong with her and she said she don't know what's wrong with her. Now she doesn't think she's pregnant. You know, we was talking about stuff like that. Dolores ask her how had she been feeling cause she know she been, she had a child, she have had a baby and I guess she know how things are, I don't.

How did she get this child?

Well, (laughs) she was going with this boy named, what's his name? Joe, yeah, she was going with him. She never had a sexual intercourse with a boy before, before she met him and so he talked her into it and well I don't know, I don't guess they neither one of them knew what they were doing exactly but you know. Everybody thought Dolores was the angel of the crowd and they said Norma be the first one to have a child, then me, then Susan, and Dolores wasn't going to have one, but she was the first one to come up with a child and everybody was . . . Well anyway she have the cutest little girl now, just ooh she's so cute, sometimes I want one but I say I think I'd wait, (laughs) really though.

How does Dolores get along with the child?

Well it's all right cause I mean these people lives next door, she live in the project and the people live next door to her, they keep the baby all the time and I don't know, well, she do all right with the baby but they keeps the baby all the time. Dolores can't never get a chance to keep the baby much, she got a little job baby-sitting, cause her mother keep her a lot and Dolores gets a chance to go places with us, and this boy, the father, he's got a job working down at the store and that help too and I don't think she got on, uh, I don't think she got on to Child Aid yet. She said she was going to try but I don't think she, her mother, want her to, but it's so much trouble and all that, so she just say she can make out cause she make $35.00 a week and the boy he making pretty good too and they do pretty good.

Does he help her?

Oh yes, he do buy the baby food, and well she don't drink much milk any more but he use to buy the baby's milk, clothes, and diapers and all that stuff but now the baby getting pretty big, the baby's about nine months or ten months. I know for Easter he went down and bought all the whole outfit, you know, the Easter outfit, and they was looking cute but Dolores don't go with him anymore. She like him but you know, but she was going with another boy.

I don't know who she going with now cause we don't see each other like we use to and they don't like the projects no way. They're afraid to come up here and Susan and Norma and Dolores, well anyway they afraid somebody might try to jump on them. Well they not afraid to fight 'em but they just don't like the projects, you know, because the projects have some kind of reputation for fightin'. I don't know what it is but I didn't want to move myself but it was for the benefit of me and my mother's family. And so I was going to live with Norma but I started thinking that my mother she probably feel bad over it because thinking I wouldn't want to live with her but that wasn't true. But I didn't want to move out, I almost cried, I didn't want to leave that place. I don't know why but I just seem like I felt lost but I met the kids up in the projects. Everything seems to be all right and then me and Alfred started talking, you know.

She Can Have a Whole Lots of Men Up Tight

How do you feel about having relations with boys?

Well myself I'm afraid, my grandparents ever since I was little and I live about 12 or 13 years with them and, you know, I promised them, made them a promise that if I came up here, you know, they thought that I was going to—which I do a little bad things that I didn't use to do when I was with my grandparents. I promised them that I wasn't going to get pregnant at least until I finished school, and so the only way I have a sexual relationship with a boy that both of us use some kind of protection. I told Alfred that I didn't want to get pregnant and he said that he didn't want me to get pregnant either, because he wasn't ready to be no father and I told him I wasn't ready to be no mother. See Alfred uses these, you know, what you called those things, rubbers or something. I use some kind of pills (suppositories). They small pills but you have to use them five minutes before you have an intercourse with a boy and I use that and afterwards I take a douche to clean myself out so make sure that nothing passes by. (laughs)

Where do you buy these pills?

I don't know cause I don't buy them, my mother gives them to me. She said she understands how girls are these days and they going to do things like that because that's life. I have a very understanding mother. She don't want me to come up having a baby and I don't want to have one myself. She also told me how to do after I finish.

Where do you have relations with boys?

Well, with Alfred I be at home. We be in our room, we be in my room rather, we be talking and telling jokes and everything and be some other kids up there too and they all be talking and laughing and everything. They ask me can they do that in my house and I say no, I'm not running a whore house here and so they leave. I don't know where they go but mostly boys take the girl up in the middle of the projects and I told Alfred that he would never get me in the middle of the projects. I meant to say, you know, on the stairs, and I told him that he would never get me up there and neither the washroom or the storage room, nowhere else. I said before I do that I'll be at my own house but usually a boy takes a girl to a hotel but I don't know, somehow I don't like the idea of going to a hotel with a boy. I never liked that cause even my friends, Norma and Susan and all them, they always go to a hotel with a boy and everything but myself I don't like it.

Do you have some understanding with your mother regarding this?

Well once when she thought I was pregnant and she told me that if I was she wasn't going to try to get rid of it and that I was just going to go head on and have it. Next time try to be more careful and, you know, she said she understands, but I have held out better than she was because she had me after she was 15. She told me when I start to, you know, and made me feel kinda of bad (laughs), you know. I was about to cry and everything and I said, 'Mama why don't you take me to the hospital and see if I'm pregnant because I really don't think I'm pregnant.'

How long have you been making love with boys?

Well about, let me see, when I first started I was 14, I think it was, I wasn't quite 14 I was just coming—I think it was about this time of the year when I was 13. It was an older boy anyway, 19, and I had a crush on him and I thought I would do anything to get him. So that's my first mistake I ever made. You know, I was down there dancing and I was talking to him and everything and I should have known better than to tell him that I would do anything, all you have to do is just ask (laughs). So he asked (laughs) and I did, you know, but I know better now, I don't start no stuff, I don't get strung out over no boy.

A boy he tries any kind of method just to get you to make love to him and don't care, you know. He may say a whole lots of ole stuff about he love you and which he might be telling you the truth sometimes but a girl have to look out sometime where she can read through the lines and she know better. Like when I came up here the boy I was going with, I wasn't quite hep to boys up here but boys here are a whole lot different from what they are down South. See, he told me that he liked me and that he'd never have anybody else to love, you know, like he liked me. Let me see, I was still 14, I came up here in June '62 and anyway see I had met nobody hardly up here then and, my uncle, he's 19 and he had tried to tell me. He told me not to be strung out over no boy 'cause here if they know that they got you strung out, if they know they can get you they'll say 'Man I got that up tight, I can get that when I want to.' He tried to tell me a whole lots of stuff, you know, every time he tell me I wouldn't never pay him any attention 'cause I don't know, I like this boy and I didn't know how this boy was. Now if a boy tell me that I'm crazy about you, everytime I kiss you you make something go through me, I say yeah, I know just what goes through you (laughs) and say stuff like that you make them mad, they'll stop jivin' you and carryin' on and they won't get mad when they know that you not going to fall for that stuff so quick.

Do you plan to get married?

Yeah, yeah I plan to but myself, I was wanting to finish school and I want to become a secretary. I want to get me a job and go to trade school and try out some typing stuff like that and I want to get me a job being a secretary. Then if I want to get married I'll do that, I had said I was going to wait and try to be about at least 20 or 24, something like that. For one thing I don't want to get tied down with kids. I like kids; I love them but yet and still I want to have fun, I don't know, I want to have fun while I'm young I guess. I shouldn't feel that way, you know. If I wait until I get 20 or 30 and marry, then have a child, when I get 40 the child will just be getting 10 or something like that. When I'm 20 or 30 or something like that then I'd be 40 and I'd be too old to even take care of my kids. That thought came to mind but another thing is that, what if I go ahead on and get married when I'm 19 or 18 and have a child maybe two or three just while I'm hitting 21 and my husband might leave me like most of them usually do or might not want to marry me, I mean I be already married but have kids and he might not want to take care of the kids or something like that. He might not want to get into a home. What I want to do when I marry, I want to get into a home of my own, have my own back yard and front yard and stuff like that. If I can find some boy who's going to give me a home of my own and going to treat me nice and not going to beat me and not . . . You know, take me out sometimes on a few dates and sometimes and keeping plenty of food in the house and something to drink and stuff like that and if we do have a child I might want to go some night, he might too and we'd get a babysitter to keep the child if we have one during that time. We could agree to all business and make sure everything work out that way, what I mean it's all right.

What kind of reputation do you have among your girlfriends? You said earlier they thought you were second in line to get pregnant.

Well see, me, we all likes to go. We likes to ride and you know drink a little stuff like that. Norma's mother and Susan's mother they keep stuff to drink and they allow us to drink just as long as they know who's drinking and they don't allow us to drink too much and stuff like that. You see they know if they allow us to drink then when we go out with the boys and they buy us but we know how to control ourselves. In other words we don't drink too much so we get drunk. Boys think when girls get a few drinks in them they can take advantage of them but it's not that way with us. We know how to socialize and then we might buy a fifth full of bourbon or something like that. Usually we get vodka or gin, the vodka we drink with orange soda and gin we usually have a Seven-Up or something like that. If we be somewhere where's some ice cubes we get them but if we don't we just drink it like that.

Everybody says Norma wasn't any good and I'm next and then Susan and Dolores but really it's not nothing to do with that. See, a boy might say, "Hey girl let me talk to you." Norma might be the first one to say "Go ahead on and talk," something like that. So might be someone else in the car with, might be one more boy in the car with him or just might be one boy and so he say "Hey I want to talk to you" and I say "Well there so many yous up here, if you want to talk to me my name is Alice," you know, a whole lots of stuff like that. What I mean, me, Norma and Dolores and Susan, we likes to flirt (laughs). I guess if it was Dolores, she would say "Go ahead on boy," something like that. Everybody when they see us coming they say, "Here comes the four cousins." We just have some kind of reputation but didn't nobody know what it was.

How many boys have you had relations with?

Uh, well, uh, three boys and it was the first boy and then it was a boy named . . . What was his name? That was Harry of course and Alfred and it was another boy. It's four. That's the only four boys I have.

How many times with these boys?

Well one time with each except Alfred. I think it was about three times with him. The last time was the next to the last Friday in June. I always keep up with them, what I mean I know—I don't know exactly the dates but I keep up with the month and day in case I do get pregnant I know because I can go back and see, I always mark it on the calender and it's full of marks.

It was something going on that night and I think we had had a hop under the building, it was something like that and my mother was going to a party somewhere and she told Alfred to stay up there until she gets back and, you know, with me until she get back. I think it was raining or something that night because I was scared, I'm scared of lightning and thundering and she told him to stay up there with me until she get back and he wanted to too. And so he had been drinking and I was mad and he was going to insist on me having an intercourse with him, so I just went on just to keep from having an argument with him cause he made me mad. I think we had been somewhere dancing or was it up my house? I know that evening my mother had asked Alfred to stay, she had told him, "I'm going to a party tonight, Alice. Now, you going to be scared to be here by yourself?" My little sister is gone down South and my baby sister is over by auntie's house and my brother was spending the night with his friend so I was there by myself and she said "Alfred you going to stay here until I get back. Stay with Alice until I get back" and he said, "Yes ma'am I'll stay with her," and I said, "Didn't anybody ask you" (laughs).

We went somewhere about 10:00, naw, it was about 9:00. Oh yeah, his sisters and they boyfriends and some more girls come up to my house and brought some records up there and see I haven't got any of the latest records. We was playing records and dancing and carrying on and the boys left, it was about 9:00 I believe it was and they left and when they came back they was feeling mellow. So Alfred was sitting looking silly and everybody was dancing and carrying on and everybody started leaving so and then wasn't nobody there but me and Alfred and I was sitting there looking at Alfred standing there looking at the ceiling and I was sitting there looking crazy too (laughs). So talking 'bout, "You know I'm feeling good don't you" and I say, "I don't know how you feeling, I ain't got your feeling," you know stuff like that and so he came over there and sit on the couch beside me and so he said, "I want you to do it for me tonight." I said, "You want me to do what for you tonight?" You know I don't know why but I like to hear a boy, see how they going to—I hate to hear a boy say, "I'm want you to do that," I want if they going to say it come on out and say it to me. So I made him mad and he said, "Okay you acting smart ain't you" and I said, "I'm not acting smart."

He start to fuckin' and carrying on and everything. That's the silliest thing I ever did.

How do other boys bring the subject up?

Well one boyfriend brought me home one night and I told him I had a nice time today and hope we could get together again and he said he did too and he was tryin' to ask me for a chance or something like that and I told him, "Now you know me and you are just friends," and so he said, "Okay, I hope you change your mind, good night." And he kissed me good night and so he said, "You want me to go up on the elevator with you?" and I said, "Will you please, I'm afraid." So he went up on the elevator with me and waited until I got in my house and left. When we say asking for a chance we mean trying to go steady with us, you know, but I told him I already had a boyfriend and he said, "Ain't no harm in having two" and I said, "I know that," but I said I don't want to have no two I just want one and I want friends just like that and he said, "Well we'll keep on the friendly basis as long as you want to."

Tell me more about "cat." Just tell me first of all, what is a "cat"?

Well it could be a girl or a boy and they wants to be cool, wants to be hip, jive, you know, a jive person. They think they hip and don't know nothin' and a cat is almost like the same thing. They wants to be cool and try to pimp off of—if it's a boy he try to pimp off a girl. He going to lovey dove up on her and if she got some money or even if she keep money, if she got a job he going lovey dove up on her. He going kiss her and mess around with her and I mean she might be the ugliest thing in town but he going do that just to get her money. He going mess around with her, you know, other boys don't do that so she's going to think that he really love her so he gonna get her money and gonna forget her. They don't wants to work. They too lazy to work to get any money and they know you got some money and they going if they can they gonna use their power to get the money from you.

Power?

What I mean all they tricks like telling the girl that she got Cleopatra eyes and all that old stuff and you sweeter than a cherry so sweet, you know, and all that old stuff and whole lots of stuff and you know, just pimp up.

Give me an example of being "cool."

Usually a cat gonna be running with another cat and so they going to be walking and they gonna be talking loud and want some attention and somebody might say, "Ah look at that old cool cat, think he cool but you ain't cool," and stuff like that and so he gonna come there and talking about, "Jack, why don't you tell me who is cool if I ain't cool," all that old stuff, you know, he wants to be more than anybody else, I guess something like that. I don't know what it is that they wants to be but it something like that. I likes 'em. They a lots of fun to be with but they kind of get on my nerves calling you "Jack" and "Jim." A girl can't be no cat too much. A girl she wants to be a cat she wants to have all the boys up tight and running behind her and she think that you can have any boy you want and she gonna try to take your main squeeze from you, that's what she gonna try to do and usually she do it, how I don't know.

What do you call a "player" contrasted to a "cat"?

It's almost the same but see, a cat, he don't be like a player. A player got him more than one but a cat just got him one up tight and iffen he get tired of that one, he go get him another up tight but a player he gonna mess around and get him five or six of 'em. He gonna mess around with this one and that one and they don't be interested in neither one of 'em but he gonna have all of them up tight and so like he might say, "I can get that when I want to." And he means he can have sexual relationship with this girl anytime he want to, he might say that, which he probably could, you know, a player. But a cat, he might not—a cat ain't going to say that he's just gone, say, "Jack, you know, man, this broad, well she crazy 'bout me," and stuff like that, but a player gone to say, "I can get that when I want to, I got it up tight." And then he might say, "Man if you want that, you can get that too if you want it." You know, stuff like that.

What can a women be?

Well, a woman, she can be a player better than most mens can be a player 'cause a woman can (giggle) she can have a whole lots of mens up tight which all these men gonna be giving her money and she might and she probably ain't gonna be giving up nothing herself but a little love and not sexual, you know, and, uh . . .

Tell me more about you and Alfred being together.

Well like I said he had been drinking a little and he was feeling good and usually when they feel that way they wants to do that too. Anyway he kept on asking me and kissing me and telling me everything that he wanted to do that and all that stuff. And I was saying, "Do what?" and he said, "Ah you know," and then he say, "I want to make love to you." And so I said, "you go ahead and make love" just like that but what I was meaning was go ahead and kiss me and talk all those sweet words that he wanted to, but anyway I finally went on and gave in and I went on in my room and I undressed and I put another—I put one of those big old kinda or a some kind of a towel my mother had and I laid that on my bed so I wouldn't mess my bed up. Anyway I was laying there and I told him I wasn't going to lay in there all night and stay awake so he comes on in and myself I'm ashamed to look at a boy and I'm ashamed for one to look at me so I was trying to hide, you know, I was balled up in a knot with my eyes closed, didn't want to look at him and he was wanting to know whether should he take off all his clothes or not and I said, "You do what you want to do." But anyway he took off his pants and his shirt and he kept on his tracks (shorts) and he had already put his protection on, his rubber, and so anyway he came on and the next thing he finally found the hole and anyway then he went in.

Does he find it himself or do you help him?

No, that's one thing I never do, if they can't find it, they don't need it (laughs). That's why he was kinda of mad, he wanted me to help him find it and I said, "I ain't doing nothing, you find it if you want to, if you don't you can get up." Anyway he found it and he started rolling, I was just laying still and then he said, "You got one of the most" something—it was funny to me, he tickled me, he said something about finding my hole, he said something 'bout "I believe you hole is just like you, it be always trying to waste time," (laughs) something like that he said, "to open up," or something he said, I started laughing.

Anyway we went on and went for about 45 minutes I think it was and the reason he got up was because he felt that, you know, he wanted to go in the bathroom and get it out after he finished so I guess he thought I was going again so he just—I fooled him though cause when he got up I got up too and put on my gown and a house coat and so I went on. When he came out of the bathroom he was fixing to go back in my room and I said, "Well you go on and sit in the living room 'til I get through." So he said uh, "Well, uh." I said, "That's all for to-night," (laughs) just like that and he said, "Okay," so he kissed me and he went on in there and put on some records and I just was thinking everything and feeling good too and I was in there and I took me a douche and I washed myself up and everything and I put on me some clean underclothes and put on me another skirt and blouse and I went in there and set down and he said, "You know your mother told me to stay up here until she gets back," and I said, "You don't have to worry, I ain't going to send you home," and he said "I just thought maybe." I said, "If you want to go you can go head on, you done got what you want so go on," just like that and so he said, "See, you always end up making yourself mad."

Which I always do anyways and I just sit there—we just sit there and look at each other I guess, and he said, "Come on, I like this record," Jerry Butler was singing, "I Need to Belong to Someone," and we was dancing off that and talking 'bout (giggle) he tickled me talking 'bout, "You got—you got those dreamy Cleopatra eyes." And I say, "Oh yes, I just know I have!" (laughs) You know, that's the way I said it. So anyway he said, "And look at you." And it was something else he said he tickled me, I made him mad 'cause I was agreeing to him and he didn't believe—he know, he knew that I didn't believe him, that's reason he saying it. He said, "You better than any girl I ever had," you know what I mean, sexually like, and I said, "Yeah, I just know I am" (sarcastically). I was dancing and he had me real tight up like this and he said, "You don't believe nothing I say," and then he hit me, I said, "Okay, now look you go right now, I'm tired of you, let's go." He didn't hurt me, he just done like that, just lightly. I got mad, I already was mad 'cause I was mad at myself and him and I don't know why I was mad at myself and him. I know why. I didn't really want to do anything that night.

Did you enjoy making love?

Well I enjoy making love when I wants to. When we be sitting alone and we be talking and we don't be heavy, I mean he be talking nice and I be believing him when he be saying those things about, you know, like he don't be talking a whole lots of jive about my Cleopatra eyes, all that stuff. I remember once he said, "Out of all the girls I've had and I've had some pretty girls, like that," and he said, "I had to pick the ugliest one." I likes to hear something like that, you know a whole lot of stuff, I say, "Yeah" and he said, "Wonder why I say things like that about you, you always sound as though you believe me." And I said, "I don't know," like that (giggle). Anyway he be talking around and he don't be exactly asking me to do that but he just be making me feel good and making me excited, you know. He know, I guess he know I get weak in my knees and so we be dancing and I just get weak in my knees. I can't stand up or something and I be trying to dance and be falling all over and everything (giggle). Then he'll finally ask me so then that's when I'm just not good but otherwise I like it. I enjoy making love when we go about 15 minutes and we take a break. He be right on top of me and we be both rolling and he be kissing me right round my neck and everything and saying things and be talking about he love me and stuff like that and I be saying I love you too and all that stuff and be asking him do he really mean that or is it just because he's right on top of me and saying those things. And then we usually take a break and go again.

Do you have an orgasm when you make love?

Yes. It's kinda long with me. Before I make love I feel weak and after I make love I feel weak. I feel good or something but I feel kind of weak and I don't want to talk, I don't want to say nothing but just to lay in his arms and have him holding me and listen to what ever we play on the hi-fi or radio or anything, and so that's the way we usually do. Anyway after we finish cleaning up and everything and then he might tease me about some of the things I be saying and he was talking 'bout I was in there moaning and groaning like you in a trance or something and stuff like that, you know, I be kind of laughing at him and anyway I feel kinda good myself.

I try to go for about three more weeks before I do it again. When Alfred and I first met, he went with me for about almost four weeks before I gave in because if you give in to a boy right away he going to think you ain't no good and anybody can do that to you but you just hold yourself as long as you can and then that's what I try to do so that's why sometimes I get mad at myself because I say I could have held back longer than what I did. That's why I'm going to start holding my temper and stop going and doing that which I know ain't helping me none 'bout losing my temper in that way (giggle).

Do you talk with your mother about sex?

Yes.

How do you talk to her?

We be in there talking sometimes on one subject and end up talking on another. I mean once when I was sitting down and I was telling her about this boy that I was crazy about and all that stuff and she told me she remember once when she was crazy about a boy and she did, she was really talking about my father, and she did something for him that she really didn't regret but she said, "You see the results." And I be asking her, "What?" and she be saying, "You." Then she say, "Well I know that you say teenagers don't do that but as long as they using some kind of protection to protect themselves from having or if they think that they capable of getting married or capable of taking care of the child they can go head on and have the child," and things like that cause she said, "I know teenagers these days are going to do things like that," and she'll say, "Like most of these kids 'round here now always pregnant and just 14 years old," and stuff like that and she'll say, "You done held yourself up this long, I hope you can hold yourself up longer," and all that stuff.

She be telling me all about some of the things she done had and some of the things she could have did and she say, "That's why I want to see you at least get through high school and if you want to, go to college or trade school and get you a good job," and she'll say, "I'm not trying to run your life for you but this is what I always wanted to see." She say, "I know you always wanted to be a secretary," and she say, "if you really want to be enough just don't let nothing stop you from being it." And so that's why I be knowing that she be wanting to tell me that she didn't want me to come up having a baby and stuff like that. She be telling me about her boyfriend and she was telling me about him and she told me she thought she was pregnant and I said, "You better not be pregnant." And I said, "I don't want no more little ugly sisters and brothers. I tell all of them, I'm telling all of 'em, I telling everybody." So I told my sisters and we say, "Okay, you have another little baby and we going to kill it for you," and she say "All right now."

And then she'll tell me bout she have sexual relationship with him, she just like me and well, I'm just like her rather, and she say they was out and having a little fun and they was drinking and he said, "I'm just about ready to go to bed," and mother said, "I am too so you can take me home so I can go to bed," (laughs) and so that's the way I'm always be going. She say, "Yeah, I'll go out all right and have a little fun with you but I don't want to have that kind of fun." Then I say, "I don't blame you," (laughs) like that and so and she say to him, "You all right but that's all you think about." I don't know why but I always like to know the man who she going out with, I don't know why, I don't think I know more than she do. When she went out with this one man he kinda of looked kinda of like he was kinda of a guy who is real nice around your children and everything but when he get you out by yourself he might be kind of rough and that's exactly what the kind of man he was. Mother told me he got a little heavy and was driving reckless and everything and she was afraid and she was ready to come home and he didn't want to bring her home but anyway he finally brought her home and I usually sit up when my mother goes out on a date—when she goes out with a man and everything, I sit up and wait for her until she come home.

She say she going to start thinking about settling down. I say, "I know, if you mean we going to take care of you you don't have to settle down. I say now you can't be getting married no more and all that stuff." I don't know, don't none of us want her to marry again. We say we can take care of you and take you to our house or if you want to live by yourself and have a boyfriend but you don't need to get married no more. I don't know why we don't want it—not because we afraid we going to have some more little sisters and brothers which it wouldn't make us much difference but it would be 'bout time for her to stop even thinking 'bout having any more kids. And I always have wanted to take care of my mother when I got grown or something 'cause I wanted to pay her for the things she had done for me which I know I never can repay her but you know, do something for her.

A couple of weeks later Schulz interviewed Alice about her feelings toward her family and about her aspirations for herself.

I love my family. My mother, she is very understanding, and my sisters, they okay, too, at times, you know how sisters are, having little falling out and fights and things, but altogether we all right, including my brother, which we don't get along too good, but really I love my whole family. For one thing, I think my mother she make it the way it is because she is so full of life and we all tease her and joke her and she tease and jokes us and we just one big happy family and it's all right too. Sometimes, you know, how most families have little falling outs, but . . .

What do you usually have falling outs over?

Well for one thing it really be mostly my fault, since I am the oldest I think I should boss everybody in the house and they not going to give it to me, so I ask them nicely to give it to them but it is up to me to take it so they get mad at me and start talking about my father and I start talking about their father and sometimes we end up fighting between me and my brother. He gets mad cause I might hit one of his sisters and sometimes I get mad because he hit one of my sisters.

Whose sister is whose?

Well, really now we all sisters and brothers. I'm just the only one has a different father, we all have the same mother, so therefore we all sisters and brothers.

Do you feel this?

Yes I do. To tell you the truth, I don't know, I think if I had to live with my family, my mother and sisters and brother and their father, if I had to live with them, I think we all wouldn't be like we are now, you know, saying, 'you not my sister' sometimes when we angry with each other. If I had to live with them and was raised up together, I don't think things would be as they are now, I mean they okay but sometimes . . .

Who brings it up the most?

My other sister. She's quick tempered, she easily gets angry and you can be teasing with her about the way she get angry and she get a knife at one of us and we get angry, don't like for nobody to pull a knife out on us anyway, and we get angry and end up fighting and talking about each other's dad or something like that.

How about your younger sister?

I think I like her better than . . . yeah, most families do have a pet, I think she's my pet. For one thing she's always saying to me, "Alice, you so nice," and stuff like that, and she's real sweet, since she is the baby she don't want nobody else to be petted more than she is. If she sees somebody else be getting petted more than she is she going to get angry, start crying and sucking her thumb. That's about all I can say about her. My other sister, oh she's a hot mama. You know she's fast, she going to do things that she sees.

What kind of person are you, Alice?

Oh, I'm wonderful (laughs). Seriously, though, I guess I'm just about like my other sister. I want things to go my way too, and if they don't go my way I'm going to try to make it go my way and most of the time they don't usually end up that way. I'm not easy to get angry as one of my sisters are and my brother. I can hold my temper a little longer but I can't hold it too long, cause if somebody just keep on aggravating me, I'm going to get angry right away. I think, you know, I'm okay (laughs).

What kind of things do you like?

Well for one thing I like to listen to music and I like dancing and I like baseball, I like to watch it, which I don't know too much about it. I like to go to school, games like basketball and football and things like that, and I like getting together with a crowd, somebody who is interesting to talk to, you know, know a lot of jokes. I like to be around people who is lots of fun. I don't like to go to no place where everybody grin at each other and look at each other and they ain't got nothing to say but maybe think up a little corny joke and say it and everybody try to laugh it off which isn't really funny. I like to go where everybody is laughing and talking and dancing and drinking and eating and just having lots of fun themselves, and one thing, this might be strange, but I like housekeeping when I can do it the way I want to do it, like for instance after I finish eating dinner, my mother says wash the dishes. I don't wash the dishes right then, I want to sit down and relax and let my food digest, but mother say wash the dishes after dinner, so I don't want to wash the dishes, what I like to do I like to sit down and relax, clean the table off and stack the dishes in the sink and then about 30 minutes later I get up and wash the dishes. Once I had to write an essay on—well, I didn't have to write one on this subject, but I did. I made up a subject about when my mother was away on a trip I had to take care of the house and I got a B on it. I like to houseclean and cook and things, I would like to cook and stuff like that, and when I was in the eighth grade I used to help in the school cafeteria, cooking.

If you had whatever you'd like, how would you like your life to turn out?

Oh well, I think I would like to be a secretary about three years, I guess I would be about 23 then, about 23 or 24, something like that, and then I would start looking for somebody to marry. Well I wouldn't look for nobody to marry but, you know, course I would be going out on dates, but if somebody be interested in me I might be—I always have hopes that I could get out and get me a home of my own and a car and then a husband. Then I want to help my baby sister through college if she want to go. I always have said when I finish school I am going to be a secretary and when I be a secretary I am going to help my sisters through school and my baby sister through college.

Do you think there's much chance of your being a secretary?

Well I think so. I don't exactly know. I want to be it so badly that I might not turn out to be a good secretary because I want to be a secretary so badly. When most people want something so badly they usually end up not turning out right, but I think if I just try and do my assignments and try to remember things, all about what is supposed to be done and things like that, I think I can make it.

I Wanna Marry and I Don't Wanna Marry

You talked about envying Dolores for having a baby last time we talked. Would you like to have a child yourself?

I want to have a child, but I want to have one the right way. I want to have a child when I get about 19 or 20. I know I want a child but I don't wanna have it. I wanna have it. I wanna have it. I don't know what it is I want. I wanna have it but if I have it right away now, I don't know whose it would be. I mean, that would hurt my parents and my grandmother.

What does a child mean to you?

I don't know, why I just love children. I always have liked kids, you know, I'm always playing with kids, giving them money and all that stuff. But one of my own I think I feel like I have something to really love, someone who really needs me and needs understanding and needs love and all that if I have a child of my own. Like most of these girls they get babies and let anybody keep 'em, not my child, 'cause I want to have everything that I can afford to give her and all that stuff. I don't know why, I always have been like that.

That's what I told Pete last night. I said, "I'm quittin' school and get me a night job." He said, "I ain't gonna let you quit school." I said it just to see what he was gonna say. See, he graduated hisself. I said, "I'm quittin' school." He said, "I'm not gonna let you quit school since you ain't got but about two more years and when you finish high school I'm gonna buy you a ring and we will get married." I said, "Do you really believe so?" He said, "I want it to be that way." I said, "I want it to be that way, too. I wished I was already finished school."

Would you want to be married when you have a child or not? Do you want the child more than marriage?

I don't think so. I mean I want marriage too but I don't wanna marry too early. I wanna marry and I don't wanna marry. I don't know whether I wanna marry too young or not because I wanna see more than what else is in life beside just marriage. I wanna get around and see can I meet somebody else. I might meet somebody else later on while I'm married and then your marriage won't work out, you see. As mama says, shop around, see do you really wanna marry this guy, if you wanna live your whole life with him and all that stuff. Before I wanna take those vows I wanna be sure of myself.

In what way?

That I can be a good wife to my husband and a good mother to my daughter, I mean to my children, to my child and that we can have love and understanding. Have a good home, you know, and we understand each other and what my husband say sometime won't always so right and I don't want—you know, like no married couple not gonna be happy unless they have a few disagreements. I want it to be that we don't have no disagreements. I want it to be so that we can straighten 'em out without a whole lot of separation and divorce and stuff like that.

How are you and Alfred getting along now?

Aw, I can't stand that boy. He think he heavy. He think he real real cool. I can't stand him. I mean his mother gets on me, every time me and Alfred break up she think she got to put us back together or somethin' like that. Which she did every time we broke up.

And I started runnin' around with all the girls in the building 'cause don't none of 'em really mean as much to me as Norma do. Me and Norma is almost like sisters, I think, and don't none of 'em mean as much as Norma, 'cause I can tell

Norma anything and Norma tell me all her troubles and I tell her mine and all these girls in the project is just two-faced. One set of girls they all stick together, they run together. There's about two or three that don't run with them, I used to be with this big crowd. I kinda cut them loose 'cause they was kinda jive.

Alfred's family, they gonna have to start somethin'. See, she don't like this girl called Joanna, she don't like her but her and Joanna's mother are good friends. When me and Alfred was goin' together I used to go down her house a lot and then when Alfred come up my house all them would come from down his house so I used to go down there. I stopped goin' down there so much and Alfred stopped comin' up to my house and I was kinda glad and I stopped goin' down his house. And they come talkin' about, "Yeah, you done got with Joanna now and you don't think about nobody else." I said, "Naw, I think about y'all." "Yeah that's all you do is think about us. You don't even come down to see us." I said, "I come down there." I said, "I can't come down there every day. I have to stay at home and help mother clean up," and all that stuff. "Yeah, I ain't seen you. Everytime I see you, you up to Joanna's." I said, "I help her iron up some clothes when she was getting ready to leave. I ain't never helped her clean up her house." Which I used to help Alfred's mother and his family help them clean up they house and all that stuff. But and then he gonna have nerve enough to tell me.

I said, "Well, Alfred, me and you through now ain't we?" I thought he was going to say yeah but he said, "Naw, I still like you but see you still messin', you goin' around with Joanna." "I thought you was likin' Joanna," I said. "Yeah, uh huh, I know you did." He come talkin' about he thought I was goin' with Joanna. He made me so mad. I said, "Yeah, I was likin' her real good. We gettin' real strong now." He said, "Aw girl, you know I was just playin'." I said, "Well don't play with me like that. I don't play like that."

He said, "I get mad cause I see you with Pat all the time." I said, "You ain't got no reason to get mad cause you see me with Pat," just like that. See, Pat remember that time when Alfred slapped me and pushed me down on the curb. I don't know how it got back to Pat cause I didn't tell nobody. His sister must have told somebody, if it had done get around to Pat. Pat told him if he ever put his hands on me again he was gonna slap him and so he said, "Man, she my woman I can do what I want to." Pat said, "Naw you won't either. You won't do nothin' to her, not long as I'm around."

By the middle of August Alice had a new boyfriend.

His name is William Allen Jefferson, everybody call him Bill. My mother, she don't exactly approve of it 'cause he's 22 years old and he's been married, I mean he have two kids. He have one kid by his ex-wife and he have a child by another girl. And I don't know why I like him so but I do. My mother she don't exactly approve of it but I don't know, I just can't help it, I just have to see him. I don't know why I feel this way about it but I do feel much different than I used to do about a boy, 'cause I never felt this way about any boy exactly, you know. I thought I felt the same way about Pete but it's somethin' about him I don't like so much. I don't know exactly what it is but it just makes me feel so good sometimes.

Bill and I have known each other about three months and we used to just be friends, you know. We just be messin' around and talkin' and I used to try to get him in with one of my friends. He used to like her and he used to come up and get me all the time and say, 'Come on, let's go over to her house,' and every time we go over there she wouldn't never be at home so everybody seen us walkin' together. That's the time when Alfred accused me of goin' with him, but I wasn't going with him at the time. And me and Alfred broke up because of him and he knew that that was the reason and he told me that he didn't want to cause us to break up and I told him that he wasn't the cause of us breakin' up and then he tried to explain to Alfred that me and him used to be together all the time was because I was tryin' to get him in with one of my friends. And Alfred didn't want to take it that way and so finally he started believin' it about Bill and so we went back together.

And, so anyway, me and Bill started playin', you know, messin' around. He'd be, "Come here, girl," and I say, "You come to me," and all that old stuff, and so, "If I have to come to you, I'm twistin' your arm off." And so he'd get hold to my arm and he'd be just twistin' my hand. And so, you know, it's just a lots of fun so then one night we went to this party and I was dancin' with him and he asked me did I think it was possible for me and him to get together. And I said, "Well, I don't know. You know I'm still goin' with Alfred. I don't think so. I don't think there'd be a possible chance, 'cause you supposed to be goin' with my friend." "I never will get too far with her." And so we said we'll see what happens.

So me and Alfred wasn't on good terms then no how so I said, "I'll give Alfred about another week and if he still act the same way, then it's over with." He said, "Okay, but I don't want to be the cause of it. I don't know why people always want to blame me for something which I never be doin'." He said, "I was young when I got married." He kept on a lots of stuff about when he got married and he wasn't exactly forced into it but he got this girl pregnant and he was in the army and this girl's mother went to his commander or somethin' and told him to let him home on leave so he could marry her daughter 'cause she's pregnant by him so he came home and married the girl. He said they was all right but he'd bring home all his money, his pay check and give it to her. Then he wouldn't take nothin' out but his carfare back and forth to work.

And so he was talkin' all that old stuff about how they broke up and all that, and then he told me about how people always pick on him and I could see that much for myself, 'cause the other day Alfred and another boy and somebody else was in the middle gamblin' and Alfred's father caught Bill. He wasn't exactly gamblin' then but he was stoopin' down so that made Alfred's father think he was. So his mother called down to Bill's house and told Bill's mother that "Bill been up in the middle gamblin' with my boy," and she said, "Well, Bill is right here," and so she said, "Well, tell him to come up here." And so he went up there and I went up there with him 'cause we was goin' out and so she talkin' about, "If I ever catch you gamblin' with my son again I'm gone have you put in jail." And he just looked at her. I knew he felt kind of bad. I did too. And then she said, "I ought to have you put in jail anyway for goin' with her." I just, I swear I could have fainted, I could have choked her to death she made me so mad. And so Bill said, "Well, I wasn't out in the middle with your boy or nobody else gamblin." He said, "I was upstairs tryin' to fix me somethin' to eat." He said, "I haven't been downstairs none today. I been downstairs once and I came right back up, I got back in the bed 'cause I been waitin' for a phone call about this job." You know, he was talkin' just as nice, just as slow. I know he was tryin' to keep from gettin' mad for one thing. I know how he is, he's high tempered, you know. And so she said, "Well, I'm just tellin' you. I don't want you to be runnin' around with these boys no more. If I catch you with them again, I'm gonna call the police. I'm gonna call the guard on you," she said.

Have you had relations with Bill yet?

No.

Has he ever asked you?

No.

How does this make you feel?

When I first started talkin' to him I thought all he wanted was to have sexual intercourses with me and after one week, I asked him, I say, I told him, "I thought the only reason you was goin' with me was because you . . ." "Yeah, I know, you thought I wanted to do that but I got two babies now and it seems like every time I touch a girl I get a baby. That's not really true but I want you to finish school and I wants to get a good job and if we still feel the same way about each other like we do now because besides my two babies you is the only thing I really care about now." And so I asked him, "Do you really mean that?" He said, "If I didn't mean it I wouldn't have said it."

He makes me so mad sometimes. My mother say he's married. See she think that just because he been married that he after the same thing I thought he was after. And so she knew he didn't have no job at the time but he got one now. He got it yesterday and he went to work yesterday for the first time. And she thought that because he didn't have no job maybe he was just messin' around with me tryin' to . . . if I had a little money I was gonna give him all my money. Now how she got all this information I do not know. She knew how old he was before I did, I knew he was 20 or somethin' but I didn't know exactly how old. I think that Alfred's mother told her all this stuff, she one little nosey child, I mean woman. But I still go up there. She have lots of food to eat and ice cream and cake and stuff, she can cook real good, she makes some good ice cream. I just go up there and eat and tell her, 'Aw, you know I love you,' and all that stuff. "Naw, you don't want me no more, I'm not your mother-in-law no more." I said, "What you talkin' about, me and Alfred still . . . he still like me. Maybe we can get together," and all that old stuff. "Gone in there and get you some ice cream and cake." See I just fool her 'cause she don't know no better.

Well how do you and Alfred stand now?

We still friends, that's about all. That's about all. I mean I have no feelings for him like I used to. I don't know what he have toward me but I don't dig it any more. I can't go with him no more.

Schulz did not see the family again until late in the fall when he learned that Alice was still going with her most recent boyfriend, Bill. Schulz asked what had gone on in her life during the intervening three months.

Not much, really. Of course you know that me and Bill are going steady and me and him have had a couple of fights. This girl was giving her husband a birthday party and my mother and her friends was all invited. And anyway, he had been drinking some that night and we all was over to my house dancing and playing cards. Alfred came up there and his sister was bringing cans of beer up there from the party giving it to us. We was all sitting down at the table playing cards. You know Bill still thinks I go with Alfred. I told him I didn't 'cause I love him. I was standing behind Alfred bending over him looking at his cards like this and I was picking out of his hand throwing down cards 'cause he didn't know how to play this game—they were playing whiz—and I was showing him how to play. I didn't think it was no harm, I was just showing him how to play. So he called me and he said, "Come here, Alice," and I went outside to see what he wanted and he got mad and said "I'm fixin' to go." I said, "Why? We're gonna play next." And so he said, "So you can be alone with your man," like that. I said, 'Oh, you're gonna leave me so I can be alone with my man, how is that possible?" He said, "Don't get funny." I said, "I'm not getting funny. I just get tired of you telling me that I still go with him and I know I don't. If you want to leave me you go right ahead on," and he slapped me. Just because I said that he slapped me. I said, "I don't know why you did that but I know you won't do it no more."

Then I went back in the house. He came back in and he grabbed me by my arm and pulled me back outside. I said, "Don't try to pull me back outside, I'm not coming back out there." I was scared because I know if he had gotten me out there he would try to hurt me. And he said, "Alice, come on. I ain't gonna do nothin' to you." See, he had been drinking and when he be drinking he do all kinds of crazy things. I have kind of gotten him out of that drinking now since we've been goin' together, he don't drink now as much as he used to. He was really loaded that night. He said, "Alice, come on. I want to talk to you." I said, "We can talk right here." We were standing behind the door, you know, there's a closet there. He said, "Look, don't be gettin' smart with me." I hadn't did nothing or said nothing. Then Alfred said, "Come on, Alice, show me the rest of the game." Then Bill said, "She ain't gonna show you nothin' and everybody started laughin' because I had been showin' him all through the game and then all of a sudden he got mad. Everybody was laughin' and talking and carrying on and Alfred won the first game because I was showing him what to play. Alfred said, "Oh, that's my baby. See, she's showing me how to play." You know, just saying stuff like that and Bill got mad.

We're planning to get married. My mother, she kind of figures something is going on. I didn't tell her because he ain't talked to her yet. He's supposed to go back to the army. He's been once but they sent him a letter asking did he want to come back so he said he was going back and take me with him when he go. I told him that he was going to have to talk to my mother cause I doubt if she's going to let me go just like that, so that's what we talked about last night. I want to go because I don't want him to leave me here, I mean, I know if he leave me here I won't be here when he get back. I know if he go he's going to have to stay. I think they're gonna send him right on overseas and he'll have to stay over there 18 months. Then when he do come home, that's a year and six months, you know, that's a long time. Somebody will tell him, "Man, your woman been goin' out with men." It wouldn't mean nothin' to me, I would just be going out to have some kind of company or something, but he don't like that stuff so it would be best for him to take me with him to keep an eye on me 'cause I know him, he's just the type to try to kill somebody (laughs). He might try to kill me.

When he gets angry most of the time he don't know what he be doing. That's the way he did me that night. I don't know why he got so mad. He got me by my neck and he tried to choke me and I kept scratching him, scratching him on his arm and he got mad. I know he didn't like nobody to scratch him but I don't like nobody to get me by my neck either. He told me, "Girl, I'm gonna hurt you if you keep on messin' around these other niggers." I said, "I ain't messin' around with nobody." Then he said, "Hey girl, stop lying to me." And so Alfred and his brother tried to stop him, so he got mad at them and wanted to fight them. See, that's the way he do.

When somebody try to stop him from doing something and he's already angry he just acts like he goes crazy. I don't know what's wrong with him. But now he's not that violent. We broke up for about three weeks after that (laughs). We had started back to school. He was seeing me every once in a while. I wasn't talking that much to him but I'd see him on Saturday and speak to him and keep on going. He'd keep on going too. We both wanted to stop and talk to each other and so one day I wasn't feeling good. He came upstairs and he told my sister to tell me to come to the door. She told him, "She's sick, she can't come to the door." Then he said, "Tell her she don't have to come to the door if she don't wanna come." And I had to get off that bed to go see what he wanted. He didn't want nothin'. He said, "I just wanted to see you. I hadn't seen you today." I closed the door in his face, he made me so mad. I thought he was going to apologize. I went to the hospital the next week, then I didn't see him that first week I came home. I was just talking about him. I said I didn't never want to see him no more.

How are you and Bill getting along sexually?

Well I told him I didn't want to, you know, I'll say, "Well I want to wait." Well really out of the four months we've been going together we had sexual relationship I'd say about four times, I think it's four times. Really when he first started going with me we didn't even talk about the subject. That's why I started liking him, cause, you know, out of all the other boys I knew that's the first thing that comes up. We can go together about two days and the next day they will be talkin' about "when you gonna do that for me?" and all of that bull stuff. Anyway, me and him went together for a whole month and he didn't ask me nothin' like that. Then we started talking. I asked him why he didn't ask me. I was wondering because everybody was talkin' about he ain't no good and he's gonna try to do this and that but he was different with me. I was wondering and I asked him. He said, "Well, everybody's been talkin' about I've been just going with you to do what I want to do with you but I want to prove to you that it's not all of that," so I just said, "Oh." He asked me if I wanted him to and I said, "No." I told him that I was just wondering. I said, "I'm very flattered." He said, "Well, you don't mind doing nothin' like that, do you?" I said, "No" and so he said, "I was about to get around to asking you."

He tickled me the way he asked me. He was kissing me one day and he said, "Oh, Alice, you're so soft," and it tickled me. I always get tickled when somebody says something like that to me. I said "I am?" just like that. You know, I always be teasing him. So then he said, "Yeah." He was talking so serious that I knew what he was getting around to then. I said, "Oh, Bill, baby you're so strong" (laughs). He said, "Aw, girl, you're full of bullshit!" just like that, you know. Then I started kissing him again. Then he said, "Oh, Alice, I just can't take it no longer." I said, "What you can't take?" He said, "I just can't take it, I just can't take it." I said, "What can't you take, Bill?" He said, "I need you, I need you." I said, "You do?" He acted like he was about to cry or something talking about I need you, I need you. I said, "Oh baby!" and he got mad.

Anyway we was over at his sister's house and I was sitting there watching television and it was a story on I like to watch and every once in a while he would just hold me and carrying on, I don't know what he was trying to do. Anyway, he tickled me. I was just watching television and I wasn't paying no attention to him. All of a sudden he got up and got mad. He said, "I'm fixin' to go, I'm leaving." I said, "Why?" He said, "You ain't paying me no attention, you see what I'm trying to do." I said, "What are you trying to do?" He said, "You know what I'm trying to do." He wouldn't say it for nothing, he just kept saying, "You know what I'm trying to do." We were babysitting for his sister and so all of the kids were asleep. He said, "You know good and well them kids ain't gonna wake up." I said, "Wait until the story goes off," and he got mad. Anyway, he sat up there and waited too. When the story went off he started kissing me and it got so I couldn't take it no more myself. I really like the way he do it 'cause he just thrills me so. He'll start kissing me first and then he will start, I don't know, doing something. He will be breathing—he don't be breathing hard but he would be breathing around my neck and then run his hand up and down my spine. I kept saying, "You be calm now." He kept on doing that and then he kissed me on my neck and I just laid on back then. And so he said, "I don't think I'm gonna do it." I got mad. I said, "That's O.K., that's O.K. Go on, I don't wanna do nothing no way." That's one thing between me and him, when we do something—I mean when we start doing something we always be teasing each other, and I don't know, we have so much fun together. Anyway, we ended up doing something that night anyway, in the bed he sleeps in. He was living with his sister at the time.

His mother told me that while he was overseas he was sending $120 a month home. When he came home his wife didn't have no money and he was wondering what she did with all his money but that didn't bother him too much but when he got home his wife wouldn't let him touch her and she was just acting altogether different. So he was wondering what was wrong and one night he came home and caught his wife in the bed with another woman and he said he tried to kill both of 'em. I guess that's one of the reasons he like he is—fussy. I guess he always think about that. He thinks I'm going to do the same thing. I try to tell him that I'm not. Anyway he . . . I don't know . . . He tells me all the time, 'If I ever catch you doin' that I'm going to kill you. I let her go but I'm going to kill you' and all that stuff. Anyway, I think he just be talking to scare me.

I don't know if he's leaving (for the army) next week or next month. I want to go and I don't want to go in a way. If he has to leave next week then I know I couldn't go because it will be too soon for me to try to get ready or to try to get married. My mother wouldn't be ready for me to go—which I wouldn't want to go myself until we got married. He doesn't know what he's going to do, he doesn't know if he's going to go back or not but see it's kind of hard for him to get a job.

He had a pretty good job before he got in this big old mess trying to help out his sister and got busted. Some fellows were meddling with his sister and she didn't want to be bothered. She was in a tavern and he went in looking for somebody, at least that's what he told me. He might have been in there with another woman for all I know (laughs) but that's what he told me. This fellow started slapping his sister and she slapped him back and he was fixing to stick a knife in her. He went up to them and said, "Wait a minute, what's going on?" He was standing up there talking to him, at least that's what they told me, I didn't know anything about it until he was in the hospital. See it was three on him before his brothers came. At first he was asking his sister why she slapped him. She said he was bothering her and she told him to stop meddling her. Then he asked her if she knew him and she said, "Naw, I don't know nothing about the nigger." And then this stud looked at him and said, "What you got to do with it anyway?" He said, "Be quiet, I ain't talking' to you yet now," just like that. Then the nigger pushed him and hit him and busted his lip, so he hit him pretty hard because he wasn't expecting all of that and he knocked two of his teeth out in the front. You know he's pretty strong and he can fight pretty good—ain't nobody going to beat him. Then he hit him and he hit him, this is the way he was telling me. He was fixing to stomp him and then this boy's brother came in and got him by the arm.

I guess that's how Bill broke his wrist. You know when he was in the army he learned a lot of stuff so I guess he used one of his tricks, I don't know what he did but anyway he did something. Another boy came in, it already was hurting him and he was trying to take on all three of them and he sprained his back. I said, "You're pitiful, child." It wasn't funny. It scared me at first because I thought he was dead. They were saying, "He's gone now," and that just frightened me, I was just crying that morning and I was a nervous wreck. When I went out there to see him I couldn't see him until 12:00. I was mad. I got out to the hospital at 10:00. He couldn't go to work and I don't know what he did but whatever it was he had to use two hands. He called and told them about it. About a week before that he had been sick and the doctor out there had sent him home and he was just about ready to go back to work and then this happened.

Then Alice told in great detail about continuing to see all her other boyfriends at parties or on dates, and of her narrow scrapes in trying to conceal these activities from Bill. The conversation turned to Alice's 13-year-old sister.

She's got lots of boys following behind her too. She's kind of sneaky with hers. My mother told her about that too. She said, "Alice comes on out with hers but you're sneaking around with yours." She said, "I ain't doin' nothing," I let her go with me sometimes and when a boy starts talking to her I say, "Wait a minute, you're not talking to my sister. Let me know what you're saying back there." He was back there trying to kiss her and all that stuff. I said, "No, don't by trying to kiss her." She don't really like to talk about him. I hope she don't turn out to be one of those old things, you know, a bulldagger. I don't think she will. She likes this one boy, at least I think she do. When she goes out with me she acts like she's so afraid of boys but when she's around these other girls she don't do what they do 'cause I know a lot of them do what I wouldn't do. This one girl, I won't call her name, but I know she let my cousin and Alfred and a lot of more boys get her because I know she gave it to my brother. I was laughin at the nigger. I said, "Uh huh, I guess you can pick your girls right now won't you." He was so mad at me.

She's just shy and she just ain't used to boys. I was that way when I started out. You see how I am now, don't you. Maybe she's ashamed of me. Maybe she doesn't want to do anything around me since I'm her oldest sister. Maybe she is shy.

If It Didn't Happen to Me It'd Happen to Somebody Else

During the rest of the fall Schulz spent most of his time with other members of Alice's family and did not learn until the end of December that Alice was pregnant. In an interview he asked Mrs. Walker,

What kind of problems do the kids share with you?

They don't have too very many problems, sickness, somethin' hurt 'em, or they hurt themselves, somethin' like that—when they get in a fight with somebody or have a discussion or somethin' like that, or if they get a skinned nose or somethin' like that maybe. And I don't know why, I afraid Alice she have more problems than the other ones. She sickly. I don't know whether she ever tole you this or not but she has to drop out of school in December, (laughs) well, cause she got pregnant. This guy, Bill, did you see him here? That is the biggest problem I've ever had. I work with it the best way I can. She's wants to getting married but I haven't decided. I don' like him a lot—I don' hate him, but you know, he's a lots older than she is. If they'd of listened to me, I told them, I talked to her and him, I said, 'Now listen, things like this could happen,' but after she told me, it didn't surprise me too much, it just hurt so bad. I got over the hurt part. I sit down and talked to him about it.

She came out of the house one day, she was going back to school and I was going out to the cleaners to pick up laundry and she said, "Well, I'm not going to school, I'm going to tell you something." I started getting dressed. I said, "Well you better go on, you're going to be late for school." I said, "What you tell me?" She kept her eye on the paper, she was scared to tell me. I asked her, "Come on, tell—I have to go." And she just said, "I'm pregnant—I think I'm going—I'm pregnant." And I just sit right down (low laugh). I says, "I'm just knocked off my feet." I said, "What!" I didn't say nothing, I didn't say nothing for about three days and I sit down and talk to her about it.

How long has she been pregnant?

I guess about four months.

Why did she have to drop out of school, I don't understand.

She's so sickly, you know, and she has this accident and she had to stay out of school lots. I don' know what to do but to keep her home. I don' want to make up her mind for her, I just don' know what to do from morning to night. I help her all I can. I would rather have her go back to school.

How is it that she got pregnant? I thought she was very careful.

That's what I thought too. She knew all about sex 'cause I sit down and explained it to her often and I don't know how it happened.

What would happen if Alice decided not to get married? Would you take care of the child?

I don' know, it would be pretty hard in my position. I would do all I could for her. I don' know, I guess I would have to. I'd do the best I can for her. I would like to if she didn't get married.

Although Schulz visited the family several times over the next three months, Alice always managed an excuse when he suggested that they sit down for a long talk. Finally, by the end of March when she was big with child, Alice was ready to talk. She started by indicating that Bill had gone back into the army expecting to come back for a wedding before too long. Schulz asked when she first knew she was pregnant.

Let me see, in January I guess. I had been knowing it but that's when I went to the clinic and found out for sure. I was kind of disappointed and I know I hurt my mother quite a lot but it's happening every day so if it didn't happen to me it'd happen to somebody else. I don't know how I feel about it really. First I was scared 'cause I didn't know what mother would do when she found out that I was still seeing that man (Bill), 'cause I didn't know what he was going to do 'cause I knew he already was married and hadn't gotten a divorce yet but he had been talking about getting one and I was still seeing him.

What did he have to say?

He was happy about it and he said, "I know you want to marry me now, don't you." I asked him did he still want to marry me and he said, "Yeah." He said that's what he wanted, to have a child by me, and I said, "Yeah" (laughs). He started trying his best to get a job, so he went back to the army and he said you can get a divorce easier when you're in the army but I don't know nothing about that though. He told me he had put in for one on his letter and so I don't know.

Will his wife grant him a divorce?

Well she should but he has grounds to get one. For one thing she left him anyway, that's what he told me, and from what I know of her she was a freak. She go with women or women go with her. She has said that she would give him a divorce because to her (laughs) he was just another guy in her life and didn't mean anything to her no more so he asked her would it be all right. She told him 'Yeah' and so I guess she is gonna go on and give him one.

How is that you got pregnant?

It sort of surprise me too. I don't know what happened. He wasn't like everybody else, he was more mature than anybody else I had been with. Really I fell in love with him, that's what happened, and the rest of 'em—I don't know, I don't think I really was in love with 'em.

You didn't care whether you got pregnant?

Yeah, 'cause everybody was telling me this and that way to do and what not to do and all that old stuff. My mother she was right though, but I don't like nobody to tell me what to do (laughs) and I guess that is what it was. But he was so much different from all the rest of the guys, he never would have a sexual intercourse with me unless he asked was it all right and did I mind, you know.

I didn't even know I was pregnant until a couple of months ago. I knew it but I couldn't tell anybody.

What finally got you to the point where you felt that you could tell someone?

I had told this girlfriend. She told me that she was pregnant like that and so I said, "You is?" and so she said, "Yeah" and she told me her father had took her to the hospital and all that stuff and I don't know, how she got real sick. And so I said, "What if I get sick," she said, "What's wrong with you," and I told her, "I believe I am too" (laughs). And so she said you better tell somebody so you can start taking them pills, there's some pills you supposed to take so you won't get so much pain or something. And anyway I told some other girlfriend too.

I knew my mother kinda suspected something, kept on watching me and all that stuff, so I said, "Mother, I guess I got something to tell you" (laughs). She said, "What you talking about?" and I said, "I'll tell you in a few minutes," just like that and I didn't feel like going to school that morning, that's what it was. I said, "I think I'm pregnant," and she said, "What you mean you think you pregnant?" I said, "I don't know but I think I am though," and she said, "Yeah, it happened," and she said, "Bill the father?" and I said, "Who else?" At first she couldn't stand him but she like him pretty good now, I think. I think they kinda hitting it off pretty good and Bill told his mother and then Alfred's mother got hold to it and she got in it and talking about it and all that stuff and then everybody got to talking. They just talking about, you waited till you had two more years to go to school (laughs), talking a lot of stuff like that and it made sense though, it made me feel kinda bad, you know. But afterwards everybody started talking about, you take care of yourself and you do this and don't do too much hard work and all that old stuff and so I said they might as well talk like that 'cause I got it now (laughter). Nobody bawled me out, mother, she didn't bawl me out but I know she was hurt.

Bill he got mad because people blamed him and told me if I wanna I should just stay with my family and live with the baby 'cause he wasn't gonna put up with that mess no more and he got mad and so I said, "I don't care 'cause I can have my baby and keep it myself" (laughs). You know, I got mad and started crying (laughs) and he got mad, I thought he was going to beat me up. He left after that (laughs). I was so mad at him and so I told him, "Don't ever come up here no more," and so we broke up for about two weeks I guess and he kept on standing up there asking can he come up and so I never did tell him nuthin' and then I started sending for him and he didn't even come.

And so one day I seen him downstairs and we started talking. I was going to the store and he walked up to the store with me and when we came back he said, "Can I come in?" and I was trying to play hard (laughs). I said, "You can come in if you wanna," and so my mother said, "What's wrong with y'all, you ain't been coming up." He said, "Naw, Alice told me not to come up here no more," and I looked at him and said, "Naw, he just told me he got mad 'cause everybody was talking about he was not to blame for it," and I said, "He the only somebody could be the blame," like that, I was mad, you know. And mother said, "Listen at her talking like that. Don't pay any attention now that's just the way pregnant people act." I looked at her—she made me mad too and then I went into the room and started crying.

Schulz did not visit the family again until June, and by then the baby had been born. He talked first with Mrs. Walker, who explained how the fatherhood of Alice's baby had finally been assigned not to Bill but to Alfred.

How are Alice and Bill doing these days?

About this baby idea, she told Alfred she was pregnant first and she didn't tell me until December. He told his oldest sister. He didn't tell his mother either. So I guess after he didn't say nothing and after she started seeing Bill she told him she was pregnant and I guess he went along with it. Anyway when I asked her who was the baby's father she said it was Alfred.

Now she says it's Alfred's child?

Yeah, he knew all the time it were but he never did tell me or his mother. And so I don't know what's going to happen with Bill but a lot could happen because they're not married.

Does Bill know about this?

No.

He thinks it's his child?

I guess he do. I asked Alice why she tell him. I was going to because I didn't know, he was mature enough he should make sure hisself. 'Cause I told him I didn't want him to see her when he asked me. She told me first and I told her naw, he was too old. He's more matured than she were.

So how are Alice and Alfred getting along these days?

They get along fine. He comes and keeps the baby during the day, comes and sit up with her at night, him and her and the baby watch T.V.

Who's caring for the child these days?

Well his mother and myself. My brother he helps for the baby too.

Does Alice take care of it?

Yeah, she bathes it and everything, washes the clothes.

On the same day Schulz talked with Alice as she did her laundry in the fourth floor laundry room.

He's now Alfred's child?

Yes. That's the way it was all the time, but see didn't nobody know but me and I was going with Bill and I was pregnant with Alfred's baby and I wasn't about to tell him that I was pregnant with somebody else's baby. Since didn't nobody know I was going to let things work out the best way they could. And when everybody found out the baby was Alfred's, you know when the baby was born everybody could see the baby didn't look like Bill, so I just went on and put it like that and that's the way it was.

Have you told Bill about it?

Naw. He's supposed to be home this month. I'm scared. He haven't wrote since I told him about the baby was born. I don't know what was wrong. I don't know, he be mostly in the field all the time. He don't have time to write. Mother wrote and told him . . . she wrote him a letter and I don't know what she told him on her letter. He might have got mad on that.

What do you think's likely to happen when Bill comes home?

Well if he don't know I'm going to tell him when he come home about everything. I don't know what he going to do. I think I was afraid to tell him. For one thing he wanted so much for me to have a baby by him I just couldn't see myself telling him that I was pregnant by somebody else and he was going with me and I was going with him and everything and we were talking about marriage, I was kind of afraid to tell him that I'm pregnant by somebody else. So since wasn't nobody else going to say nothing about it since didn't nobody else know nothing about it I just let it stay like it were. So after the baby came everybody can see that it didn't look nothing like him.

Alfred's mother came into the laundry room and Schulz asked her how she felt about the baby.

Oh I wouldn't take nothing for him. I want her to go back to school though and finish school 'cause she's almost finished. I'd take care of the baby.

When she left he asked Alice if Bill had gotten his divorce or not.

Naw, he just wrote and told me he got a divorce but I don't think he got one myself, 'cause if he had got a divorce I would have known about that 'cause his wife is a hell cat. She would have really been blown up and she probably would have took some kind of action 'cause she don't like me noway and she kind of thought I was pregnant by Bill and she would have brought all that stuff up. It would have been a whole lot of mess so I don't think he got no divorce 'cause she's acting too friendly with his mother.

Do you want to get married?

Well I wanted to. I don't know what I want really, not right now. I want to. I want to have a name for my baby, you know. I know I'm not marrying Bill cause I'm scared of him. I can't marry nobody I'm scared of. I don't think I was aware of it but when a person keep on doing things over and over again you start thinking about it. When you're separated for a person you have time to think about it and that's what I've been thinking. I didn't have time to do anything until the baby came and now . . . I don't know.

Have All the Fun You Want Just as Long as You Support Me

After the baby was born Alice moved into the apartment of Alfred's parents, but when Schulz visited the apartment several months later he discovered that Alice had moved back with her mother after a falling out with Alfred. However, they continued to see each other and were tentatively discussing getting a blood test so that they could get married. By this time she was pregnant again, although we do not know whether either of them was aware of the fact at the time.

On this visit Schulz found Alice, Alfred, and their baby in the Walker apartment. Alfred was discussing with Alice the possibility of going for blood tests; he suggested that his sister wouldn't mind sitting with the baby, and Alice got up and gave her the baby. She seemed to have made up her mind to go, but Alfred kept insulting her and hitting her in the face playfully. Alice responded only by telling him not to do that. Alice sat down, and Alfred sat on the couch. He was miffed and asked from time to time why they couldn't go, but Alice kept replying that she couldn't go because the baby would not stay with his sister. They bantered with each other to relieve the tension, and Alfred said, "She really is a pretty good girl who would do most anything I asked." Alice said, "That's all right as long as you keep paying me." Alfred denied that he was supporting her in any way. Alice said, "Oh yes, you give me half your money." Alfred said, "I've only given you five or ten dollars at the most." Alice insisted that he was contributing regularly and she didn't care what he did as long as he continued to support her.

Alfred's sister observed that the license bureau was going to close and they'd better hurry up. Alfred responded, "We ain't going." Alice laughed and repeated, "We ain't going," but she seemed sad. Alfred was breathing heavily and was quite gloomy. He finally asked Schulz to take him out to the West End where he had earlier said he had girl friends. Alice apparently knew about this because she responded, "I don't care what you do, go ahead, go out there and have all the fun you want just as long as you support me, as long as I get your money, because I do love money."

Shortly after this Alfred joined the Job Corps and went to camp in California. A month later he came back on a short pass. His mother, Mrs. Walker, and Alice had arranged a large wedding, and so the two were finally married. He did not return to the Job Corps; instead they set up housekeeping in his parents' apartment. As part of the wedding celebration Alfred had gone off with a number of his friends and gotten high on alcohol and marijuana. Alice had spent the time chatting with her girlfriends and examining the wedding presents. She commented that their wedding night had hardly been traditional.

> I was sleepy (laughs). So was Alfred, he was drunk and I was tired and everything, too tired to think about doing anything like making love (laughs). It tickled me.
>
> Is he different as a married man then he was when he was single?
>
> Sort of, in a way. For one thing now I can tell that he cares for me more than before and I know one thing, he's much more jealous than what he used to be. Like last night I asked him, I say, "Two girlfriends are going somewhere Friday night"(laughs), I said, "Aw, boy." Then he started talking all that stuff. I didn't feel like fussing with him so I said, "That's

all right." I really didn't have nothing to wear, I didn't iron nothing to wear. He don't act like he used to. He used to say things that hurt my feelings all the time which he really didn't mean them, 'cause he would apologize. He helps me. Sometimes I don't even want his help because he be in my way. He helps with the cleaning up the house that I have to do, he helps with the baby more than he used to do.

I think he'll make it pretty good when we get a house by ourself but now, we have little disagreements. I run to his mother and he run to her and asks what she says to get her opinion on it. If she agree with him I get mad but she mostly agree with me though, so he get mad. He says, "I'll be glad when I get a house by myself then I don't have to take that, I'll have my own say" (laughs). I think we're much better now. Every time he gets ready to go somewhere he tells me he's going and he'll tell me he'll be back at a certain time. He don't never be back on time but it's just the idea of him telling me. Sometimes he'll be over a hour late. He'll tell me he's going but he ain't going to never say "Is it all right?" but I don't mind. Sometimes I be glad to get him out of the house.

Do you think you'd like to spend the rest of your life with him?

I really don't know (laughs). For now I like him but after we had had a argument I might tell you "Naw" (laughs), but really I think I would. If we do have little disagreements he always be the one to make up. So as long as he'll be like that it's all right with me. I guess I would like to spend the rest of my life with him, I guess, I really don't know.

Later Schulz asked Alfred how he felt about marriage.

I had a whole lot of feeling about marriage, it was good and it was bad, you know. But still I say some parts of marriage are good and some are bad. When I was young I said I never would get married in my life. That meant it was bad. Then when I got a little older I thought marriage was all right, that means it's got its good points and it's got its bad points. Then I got a little more older and I said, "Oh well." I started messing around with a whole lot of girls. Now I like marriage. I liked Alice but I really didn't have too much intention of getting married to her until my mother and her mother and my father got to talking. I wanted to marry Alice and all that. Me and my mother got to talking. She said, "You're going to marry her?" I said, "Yeah, I'm going to marry her." I was just saying that to lead them all on to it and trying to get out of it. So I promised her a long time ago that if I ever got her pregnant again I would marry her, but I didn't know it was going to be this quick. She's pregnant three months now, this month. Then she said, "I'm pregnant." I said, "How come you didn't stop

yourself from getting pregnant?" She said, "Because I wanted
to marry you and you can't get out of it now." I tried to get out
of the wedding and my sister and my mother kept throwing it
up in my face so I went on ahead and married her. I liked her
a lot too. She probably thinks I like her more than I ever liked
her in my life but I'm doing that because we're married. It
wouldn't make sense to walk around the house mad at each
other every day so I'm using a different attitude toward her.

Do you feel that you'll be married to Alice all your life?

I don't know. Financially, I ain't got no kind of money, I'm
speaking on my terms. If I got a good job and got to make a
whole lot of money and she messed up a whole lot of money,
I'm not saying she's messing up money now but if she ever did,
I guess I would get a divorce, but as far as now, I can't say. I
know from now until I'm 21 years old I will. I will probably
be able to afford a divorce if I wanted one but until I'm 19 or
18 or something like that I can't get no divorce.

In the next few months Alfred and Alice got their own apartment in a
nearby building and furnished it nicely with furniture their parents managed to get for them. The second child was born and Alice settled into the
routine of mother and homemaker. Within a few months, however, they
separated. Alice moved back into her mother's apartment, providing babysitter service while her mother worked.

How did you happen to separate?

Well he just told me to get out. It's hard to tell what happened
exactly. After he jumped on me I just picked up my clothes
and left. I guess he was kind of feeling bad that day. We went
down to his mother's apartment early in the morning and he
was talking about a neighbor having had so many cars and
was thinking maybe he ought to have a car so he could putter
under the hood awhile. I told him that he didn't know anything about what was going on under the hood of a car. His
mother said he didn't know anything about what was going
on under the hood of a car, inside the car or outside the car.
Then she and I and his sisters all started to laugh at him. I
guess that sort of got him sort of mad, I don't know. Later on
that evening his mother brought me some shoes but Alfred
had bought me some shoes too. At any rate he got mad and
when she left he jumped on me and beat me up side of the
head and I had a couple of bruises around my eye and it was
kind of black and blue and he told me to get out so I left and
came back and picked up my clothes the next day.

Well, are you just have a squabble or are you all through?

Well I called my dad in Chicago and I'm supposed to leave

for Chicago any day now. As far as I'm concerned we're finished.

In fact, however, the separation lasted for only a couple of weeks, and
then Alice moved back into the apartment with Alfred.

When Schulz next talked to Alice she seemed to have settled into the
role of Pruitt-Igoe homemaker. Though she was now only 18 years old,
she had many of the same problems and concerns as older women in the
project who were maintaining tenuous marriages and mothering several
babies.

I understand that marriage changes a little bit when you have
a second child.

Yeah, in a way. It ain't that much different to me because it
seems like my first child, really, as far as taking care of it. I
didn't have that much to do with him, I always had somebody
to clean him and bathe him and all that stuff so I didn't have
to do too much with him, but it's different with her. It's not
that I don't have nobody to do for her but it's just the idea that
I'm in my own house now and I'll be here by myself if Alfred's
not around. I have to do it myself and it's just become a natural thing to me now, it's a routine thing. I get up and feed her
breakfast and clean her and stuff. Actually it just seems like a
first child to me. I really have the responsibilities of a mother.

How are you and Alfred getting along?

We're doing all right I guess, I mean we're doing fine.

How did you make up after the separation?

I don't know, let's see . . . Well actually he kept on telling me
about he was starving and all that stuff. I just, I don't know,
his father was kind of wanting it. See his mother and father,
they wanted us to make it out and do the best we could with
it and so did my mother. Everybody was talking about don't
be doing this and you shouldn't do that and all that stuff and
I just . . . And he had gotten the job and he told me he was
going to start working and keeping his job, not doing like he's
been doing, you know, get a job and keep it two or three weeks
and then quit and all that stuff. Anyway, he was talking all
that stuff. It wasn't no sense in me staying down there burden-
ing my mother with my problems so I just came on back up
here and we worked it out pretty good.
  The only problem is that I want to get out and get me a job
myself. I don't know what to say for him. One minute you
think everything's going all right . . . I guess some of it is my
fault too. It's not . . . Most of the time it's not *our* money or
our house, it's always *his* house and *his* money and *his* this and
that and if I say it's mine it ain't mine. I put up with it but I get

kind of sick of that stuff. That's why I've been looking for a job but I ain't been too successful with that. Maybe if I get a job I can kind of help with some of the bills and pay some of the rent, maybe then he wouldn't say all of it is his. I don't know, maybe he just do that for orneryness.

.What does he earn now?

I think it's a $87 a week or something like that, I mean that's what he brings home. We buy $20 worth of groceries and we pay $5 a week on that hi-fi and I take out $10 for my coat. I mean this is just some things, we do a whole lot of different things with it. We buy clothes and the bills and the rent, you know, stuff like that. It's just whatever that's supposed to be done and so much for entertainment.

What do you spend for entertainment?

Well actually it's no more than about $10 a week because he takes his father out to the taverns or some place and he buys beer for his mother, you know how much beer she drinks, it takes about that much. Sometimes it's not that much because we have about $15 or something left over on a Monday and just spend it up doing nothing with it, you know, buying things for the baby or for the boy.

So he brings home a check on Friday and during the course of the weekend you pay for the food and pay your bills and entertainment and so on and by Monday you have $10 or $15 left?

Some Mondays. Some weeks he buys something for himself, like this weekend he bought him a cashmere coat, well he didn't pay the price for it, he got it out of the pawn shop. He paid $46 for it. I sent in $5 on my coat and we bought the $20 worth of groceries and that was that. You know I got my five and he had about ten or something, I don't know how much he had left, but I had about five dollars left out his money I had taken to do the things I was supposed to do.

He don't never say nothing about his money. He might spend up all of his money and then ask me for two or three dollars. I tell him I'm not going to give it to him because, you know, he wants to go over to the pool room and shoot some pool. I tell him I'm not going to give it to him and he might get mad and start talking about, "It's my money" and all that stuff. I just got mad and go on and give it all to him. So he don't never spend it all though, that's one thing about it, he'll just go and spend what he wants to and bring the rest of it back. If I don't take it he'll just lay it down.

One thing I hate is that he always gets mad and don't want to take me no place and I be kind of wondering sometimes is he just being so honest and everything with me while I'm at home to make me think everything is all right and he's going out with his father and you know . . . You know how women think anyway. I don't like to go to no tavern myself. I guess when I was 15 or 16 or 17 I was always in a tavern drinking and carrying on. Anyway I don't like that no more, I guess it's because I did it so much, but he likes going to taverns and I don't. I mean I don't mind going but he don't never want to take me. I went out with mother and her boyfriend about two weeks ago to a party. It was all right but it wasn't . . . the party wasn't nothing. It was people and everything. I met a nice young man there and we sat there and talked and carried on. It wasn't no fun. The music they was playing was for old folks and I just couldn't stand that. I just prefer staying home and watching television or listening to the hi-fi or something than going with somebody old and not my age. I like to go to the show and maybe go to a party. I might want to go out some place quiet. I don't like to go to no tavern with all these folks talking loud and all that stuff. The music is loud and you can't hear yourself talk and all that. But he likes it and I guess his father likes it because they always go out together. Anyway, it's all right. I can sit here and watch television and enjoy myself.

11.

The Peer Group and Adolescent Socialization

The adolescent experiences of Alice Walker are characteristic of one aspect of socialization into the Pruitt-Igoe world. The events, contingencies, and predicaments of private life in Pruitt-Igoe do not come as a surprise to the young adult as he finds himself involved in them. As Alice moved through middle and late adolescence, she began to see more and more clearly the shape her life would probably take. She approached her world with a tough cheerfulness that is both engaging and sad, engaging because one must admire the realism which lies behind her determination to find what pleasure she could in the frantic pace of adolescent peer life, sad because she had hoped for more; as tough as she seems, she could not protect herself from the disappointments built into her milieu. Following Alice through two-and-one-half years of growth to eighteen-year-old maturity, it comes as no surprise that she concludes, "It's all right. I can sit here and watch television and enjoy myself." And she waits, knowing it will not be long before the final break with her husband and soon she will be on her own, like her mother.

All of the negative potentialities of the Pruitt-Igoe world and most of the strategies by which one seeks to contain them are familiar to the young adult. The only thing that is likely to surprise the individual as he goes through adult life is the strength of his own feelings about the things that happen to him. Socialization into the ghetto world may function effectively to acquaint the individual with the important contingencies of his world, to give him a perspective that makes what happens understandable and manageable; but socialization is less effective in preventing feelings of sadness and rage, desperation and hopelessness.

Anticipation

Long before adolescence, children in Pruitt-Igoe begin to form an understanding of the adult world, to adopt the typical attitudes toward it that they see others take and to try out the various possible adult identities revealed to them.

Their interest in the more grown-up world is greatly heightened, in the immediate pre-adolescent period, from eight to twelve. Children then begin to devote more and more of their play, discussions, and observation to perfecting a consistent understanding of the adult world and their own potentialities for participation in it.

Imitation of grown-up behavior is commonly observed in the project. It is facilitated by the openness of adult and adolescent behavior, and by the ease and speed of communication among the children themselves. The pre-adolescent peer group exchanges much information about what they see, in their own homes and outside, and they do so freely and with great élan. Adolescent activity is perhaps more open to their observation than adult behavior because much of it takes place outside, in hallways, stairwells, galleries, laundry rooms, and on the project grounds. But each child also observes what goes on in his own home and in the homes of his own and his parents' friends.

Spatial and age segregation reduce the ability of pre-adolescents in the middle and working classes to maintain surveillance of grown-up activities; these separations are not so marked in the ghetto community. Adults of higher status tend to go out of the home more for their recreation, to conduct more of their adult activities after the children are asleep, and to conceal more adult matters from their children. All of these techniques combine to "protect" children from the observation of matters that are beyond their years. Similarly, children in these classes keep their quasi-adult activities secret from their parents. The same concealment is attempted in Pruitt-Igoe, but it is not so readily achieved, and anyway adults there are more likely to ignore children whom they see engaged in smoking, gambling, and other adult-like behavior. Pruitt-Igoeans think of pre-adolescence as a period of intense imitation of adults, a conception not shared by middle- and working-class adults, who are more likely to consider their children "innocent" of such knowledge and activity.

Pre-adolescents are traditionally regarded as asexual, both as a moral imperative and, in most of the working and middle classes, as a fact. Pruitt-Igoe parents agree that pre-adolescents should be sexually innocent, but they know that in fact they are not. The precocity of their children is a matter of great concern, which may be expressed either in moralistic and conventional terms or in a more cynical way. One mother said:

> These kids grow up fast in this project. The five and six year old heifers (girls) know as much about screwing as I do. My six-year-old boy has already punched (had intercourse with) two or three of these fast chicks, and I'm teaching my four year old boy how to be a lady-killer too. I can't hide the facts of life from them because they see them every day on any stairway, hall, or elevator in the project.

Pruitt-Igoeans regard the sexual interests and activities of pre-adolescents as natural, if lamentable. Some parents and older siblings (particularly males) are proud of the sexual activity of the pre-adolescent boys in the family, predicting with pleasure that they will grow up to be accomplished ladies' men. The middle-class tendency to regard "premature" sexual proclivities as somehow aberrant is not apparent in this community. The child's heterosexual interests are regarded as essentially of a piece from infancy on.

Sexual behavior is among the favorite topics of conversation of adolescents and adults.[1] Children are often present during such conversations, and they early learn the words, concepts, implications, and meanings of sexual terms. Even without direct exposure to sexual behavior they can appear to be remarkably sophisticated.

One of the ways this knowledge develops is through learning to "joan," to master the traditional stories or "toasts" of Negro folklore.[2] Field workers were able to engage pre-adolescents in discussions of "joaning" and "the dozens" and joke-telling readily, once the children learned that they would not be punished for their openness. Even though adults are aware of the sexual sophistication of their children, they are ambivalent about its expression; they may be disapproving and punishing when it is "inappropriately" expressed, and yet they may express amusement and pride when a child demonstrates ability as a performer of sexually loaded folklore. The child therefore may feel secure about displaying his ability only among his peers, or among adolescents who feel less responsibility to disapprove than the adults.

In one discussion involving several pre-adolescent girls, a six year old, Jane, displayed considerable knowledge of traditional "joaning" techniques and toasts. She started off with simple phrases from the traditional rhymes:

> You're gonna joan, you're gonna joan too fast,
> Your Mamma got a pussy like an elephant ass.
> You're gonna joan, you're gonna joan too fast.
> Your Mamma got a boody like a elephant ass.

The field worker had considerable difficulty getting Jane to explain the meaning of terms like *pussy* but this was due more to the child's caginess than her lack of knowledge of sexual anatomy.

Telling toasts is a competitive situation. In this discussion, the oldest girl present, who was 12, teased Jane for her pretended bashfulness. Jane responded with the following attack, a move in the game of the dozens:

1. The role of talk, observation and imitative play in Pruitt-Igoe pre-adolescent sexual learning has been analyzed by Ladner and Hammond (1967). The following discussion is adapted from their work.
2. See Abrahams (1970) for an extensive analysis of jokes, toasts and the dozens from a Philadelphia ghetto neighborhood.

> I was walking through the jungle
> With my dick in my hand
> I was the baddest mother fucker
> In the jungle land.
> I looked up in the tree
> And what did I see?
> Your little black mama
> Trying to piss on me.
> I picked up a rock
> And hit her in the cock
> And knocked that bitch
> A half a block
>
> I hate to talk about your Mama
> She's a sweet old soul.
> She got a rap-pa-tap-pa tap dick
> And a pussy hole.
> Listen Mother fucker
> You a two-timing bitch
> You got a ring around your pussy
> Make an old man rich.

Her friend responded in like manner:

> Your mama don't wear no drawers
> She wash'm in alcohol
> She put 'em on a clothesline
> The sun refused to shine
> She put 'm in a garbage can
> They scared old garbage man
> She put 'em on the railroad track
> The train went back and back.
> She put 'em in the midnight train
> They scared old Jesse James.

The first element and the most pervasive early influence in the sexual socialization of pre-adolescents is learning sexual talk. The development of sexual talk and conceptualizations is necessary for knowledge of actual sexual behavior to be interpreted and for the child to learn the meanings of sexuality in this culture. But together with exposure to sexual verbalization goes the frequent observation of sexual activities. Many pre-adolescents can tell stories about watching sexual behavior within the household (involving the mother and her husband or boyfriend) and elsewhere. Pre-adolescent children often make a kind of game out of trying to observe adolescent sex in the halls and stairwells, and in any case there is a fair probability of stumbling upon such activity as they wander through their buildings.

Two pre-adolescent boys told of following one of their older brothers when he took his girlfriend to the family's apartment:

> They went up to Dirk's house. They were in the bed, in the bed. He got on her and started rolling. They were in there for a long time. They took off their clothes and cuddled up in bed. Me and Dirk was peeking in there.

Similarly, two eight-year-old boys described happening upon an event involving a 13-year-old boy and a 14-year-old girl:

> He had a man-size penis and he was down there hurting her 'cause she say "Let me up." He told her to shut up and slapped her. She was crying. He put his hand over her mouth. Then we slammed the door and he stopped because of the noise. Then she came out. She could barely walk. Then he came out all smiling.

Learning through talk and observation provide pre-adolescents with fully developed conceptions of sexual behavior and of its desirability.

This learning has the predictable consequence that the children move early and easily from passive observation and conversation to active participation. The children have learned that adolescents form boy-girl relationships so they play at those particularly in the latter part of pre-adolescence, and they formalize their activity by thinking of themselves as having play girlfriends or boyfriends. In Ladner's systematic interviews of 30 girls (15 of whom lived in the project and 15 in the neighborhood outside), she discovered that 29 of the girls recalled having play boyfriends in their younger years.[3] The age at which they had their first play boyfriend ranged from four years to 13, with an average age of eight. These dyadic relationships grow naturally out of the larger peer groups of the children, in which boys and girls tend to play together much of the time.

Pre-adolescent pairing off is not highly formalized nor is it expected that these relationships will last for long, but they seem to be important in giving the children an early sense of participation in the grown-up world. The relationships are primarily social and are modeled after the "going steady" pattern of the older children. Thus, in Ladner's study the pre-adolescent girls reported activities with their boyfriends such as smoking, bike-riding, hitting each other playfully; the boys bought sweets for the girls or protected them from others; they shared their possessions and played games.

Evolving naturally from the play relationships, but not necessarily confined to them, is the actual engagement in activities defined as sexual. Boys and girls in the project attach significance to the play kiss. This kind of kissing is defined as unserious and is usually confined to a smack on the cheek or a brief brushing of the lips. In Ladner's sample, 27 of the

3. Ladner (1968).

30 girls remembered having a play kiss, and the majority said this first kiss had come from one of their early play boyfriends. At this stage the children sometimes organize games such as "Catch a Girl, Kiss a Girl," or "Spin the Bottle," or "Play House," or they play at weddings and being married.

Fairly often this play eventuates in playing at sexual intercourse. The boy will ask the girl if she will "do it" with him. Children describe play intercourse as imitative of what they have learned about relationships between adolescent boys and girls. When a field worker asked a group of girls who ranged in age from 7 to 12 how boys broach the subject of play intercourse, she received the following description:

> *First Girl:* (They say) come on, baby.
> *Second Girl:* Some boys say, "It's about time we do more than kissing. It's time for us to get serious. Down to goods."
> *Third Girl:* Sometimes they tell us to come somewhere and look around and they want to do something to us. And then they just tell us to come on in the room and we go ahead. Especially when we be riding on their backs and necks. They say, "What are you all going to give us?" Then they make up a plan and then we get on their necks and they carry us in the washroom.
> *Field Worker:* What does he do first?
> *First Girl:* He tells us to lay down.
> *Second Girl:* Or he'll tell you to stand up against the wall.
> *Field Worker:* Which is the best way to do it?
> *First Girl:* Laying down.

It is difficult to determine from such descriptions how closely the behavior approximates sexual intercourse. When a field worker broached this subject with the same group by asking what the boy does when they are "doing it," she got the following response:

> *First Girl:* He will pull his thing out of his pants and try to put it in you.
> *Field Worker:* What do you mean by putting it in you?
> *First Girl:* He will put it between your legs.
> *Field Worker:* Does he put it inside you?
> *First Girl:* No, some girls say their boyfriends do, but he just put it up there.
> *Field Worker:* What do you mean by just putting it up there?
> *First Girl:* You know, he just put it between your legs, 'cause it will hurt, they say, if you let him put it up in you.

The girls are obviously ambivalent about playing at sex with boys, just as they will later be ambivalent about actually engaging in coitus. However, they are committed anticipatorily to the role of sexual partners as part of their developing conception of themselves as women. When one seven-year-old girl was asked about her attitude toward play intercourse, she responded:

> **I don't mind boys doing it to me, but I ain't too crazy about it because it gives me heartburn.**

And an eight year old commented:

> **I don't like any of these boys around here because they "do it" with you and then they "do it" with somebody else and they act like yourself ain't yourself.**

This sophisticated comment proved to be an echo of an attitude the girl had learned from an older sister, who complained about the lack of respect that boys show girls after they persuade them to engage in coitus.

As they move into puberty, then, most adolescents in Pruitt-Igoe know in broad outline the sexual roles that are available to them in their community, and they have participated in a process of extensive anticipatory socialization in those roles.

Though the girls (and to some extent the boys) may hope for romantic love relationships in the future, both have become fully cognizant of the competitive, manipulative, and exploitive perspectives which dominate sexual relations in the community. They are aware that the sensible person is constantly on guard against being taken advantage of and that he must know how to "go for himself" if he is to defend himself against the dangers inherent in participating in his adolescent peer group. But all of this is known uncertainly and imperfectly; anticipation is not the same as realization, and for all their seeming sophistication and knowledgeability, adolescents begin their teen-age period with trepidation as well as fascination. They are beginning to be "hip to the game," but in the jargon of the streets they are not yet "ready." The task of early adolescence to which they turn their attention with great energy is to find those experiences as a result of which they finally *are* "ready."

Participation

When people in the ghetto refer to someone as "ready," they mean that he is thoroughly at home in the ghetto world, that he knows the street and how to operate in it, how to appreciate what is to be appreciated there, how to defend himself against its dangers, and how to win the rewards that are available there. This is one goal of participation in adolescent peer groups. The adolescent wants to become an accomplished operator in the streets to feel at home and as secure as possible in his world.

Young teenagers often give the impression of diving into the adolescent scene with a great deal of enthusiasm and attentiveness. However, part of what must be learned through participation in the adolescent peer group is not only to participate in it but also how to exercise care so that one does not lose more than he gains by his participation. Young adolescents are often regarded as over-enthusiastic and over-anxious in their participation, and often they pay a high price before they learn the less obvious lesson of how to protect themselves.

The peer groups of adolescent boys and girls in Pruitt-Igoe are loose, and the membership of cliques is constantly shifting. The school is the center for the peer group at its widest extension. There are neighborhood groups and smaller cliques of running buddies or close girlfriends, but all of these orient themselves to the school. It is the one place where the larger community of adolescents collect, and where peer relationships form which then may break off and sustain themselves as separate cliques. Both elementary school (in St. Louis lasting through the eighth grade) and high school become centers of action for the peer group. So important is the school that even after adolescents drop out, they may hang around hoping to get back into the action. Older adolescents drop out of school when they feel they are no longer dependent on the peer group at its widest extent, but the tenuousness of smaller-scale relationships often prove this to be a mistake, and the adolescent may re-enter school or merely hang around during the hours when the action occurs—before school starts, after it ends, and during recesses and lunch periods.

This important function of the school should be an educational asset in that it offers a reason for staying in school. Unfortunately, the disjunction between the instrumentally-oriented classroom activities and the expressive peer-group activities is so great that adolescents often feel pushed out of school even when they do not want to leave. Much of the student-inspired ferment in inner-city high schools seems directed toward reducing this disjunction, as in the demands that smoking be allowed or in pressures for the school to remain a community center for adolescents, even for those who no longer attend classes. The disjunction seems stronger for boys for whom there is often a real conflict between achievement in the peer group and achievement within the school. There is a less sharp disjunction for girls so long as they do not become pregnant. When girls talk about their daily lives they are much more likely to introduce the instrumental aspects of schooling, to talk about learning typing, shorthand, bookkeeping to get a good white-collar job when they graduate. Although boys often have occupational aspirations, their day-to-day conversation does not so often reflect perception of the school and school learning as personally instrumental; they know that to have a good job one must graduate from high school, but they seem to find the curriculum less relevant to their aspirations than do the girls.

The intimate peer groups of both boys and girls tend to be fairly small; most adolescents have only three or four friends with whom they spend much time. Girls seldom congregate in groups larger than this except at parties; boys are more likely to do so. There were no large gangs in the project at the time our study was going on, and indeed, large named gangs like those described in Chicago and New York are not common in St. Louis. Boys sometimes spoke of gangs, but they seemed to be using the term to refer to the looseknit network of their peer group because they had learned to regard it as appropriate for adolescent social organization. The central unit of the peer group seemed to be that of "running buddies," two or three or four boys who spent a great deal of time together, and the groups called "gangs" did not seem to be more than aggregations of running buddies who knew each other and whose cliques overlapped. These so-called gangs did not serve their "members" even for protection; protective solidarity was accomplished only by running buddies defending each other. The Pruitt-Igoe gangs were named after a particular leader, generally a boy whom the others admired for his expressive skill and bad reputation, and were not given the romantic and more abstract cognomens used elsewhere.

Some of our field workers wasted quite a bit of time trying to make contact with the gangs described in this way until they discovered that they did not in fact exist, that there was no enduring form of organization of peers intermediate between the small unit of close friends and the larger collectivity of all the boys in the project. Thus, the adolescent boy in Pruitt-Igoe is not confronted with highly organized social space, involving turf belonging to particular gangs, or age-graded membership groups through which he can progress as he grows up.[4] Instead, he is very much on his own in forming friendships with particular boys and engaging with them in their activities. These close friends will tend to change throughout his adolescent career because there is little premium attached to friendships that persist through time.

Although long-lasting ties are not general, the boy feels a strong sense of masculine and age-graded solidarity, so that he is at home with others of his age even when he does not know them well. He is not confronted with questions of loyalty to particular sub-groups within the larger adolescent society; his social world is not highly structured and bounded, but is made up of networks of buddies which overlap continuously to the edge of his social life space. However, some principles of affiliation are emphasized within this generally unstructured aggregate. Boys will generally find their running buddies among peers who live near them in the project or with whom they have ties of kinship. These are not conscious principles supported by a cultural rationale, but simply the result of frequency of contact and a generalized feeling that the more you know about a person, the more reliable he may prove to be as a buddy.

The principal activity of the peer group relationship of both boys and girls is talk. Talk goes on primarily within groups of the same sex but also in augmented mixed groups. The subjects are varied, but telling of personal experiences and retelling experiences shared by the group are the staples of conversation. Girls talk with each other a great deal about their boyfriends. Boys talk less about their girlfriends and more about various

4. For a sharply contrasting situation in an ethnically mixed lower class area, see Suttles (1968).

kinds of exploits. All of this same-sex peer talk constitutes an exchange of masculine or feminine testimony.[5] By talking a boy shows that he is becoming a more mature male within his culture and a girl shows that she is becoming a more mature female. The testimony exchanged confers this kind of identity on the speaker and vicariously upon his listeners. The competitive interaction in talk which involves testing and often derogating responses by the audience shapes the performance of the actor towards the group's conception of a more mature person of his sex. When the individual fails to give a convincing performance the response of his audience impels him to test new modes of adulthood; when he proves convincing all members of the group are strengthened in their assumption of adult behavior.

All of this talk and the activities which provide the raw material for it codify a particular kind of existence taken for granted by the adolescent ghetto resident. As children grow up they come increasingly to understand the nature of their world; now they can begin the serious work of effecting an adaptation to it in competitive cooperation with their peers. The children have learned foremost they must depend on themselves for what they get, on their own ability to manipulate the meager opportunities that come their way. Central among these opportunities is attracting collaborators among their peers. They learn that to attract collaborators they must manipulate inter-personal relationships to give the appearance of having more to offer than in fact they have, and they learn to watch for opportunities to take what they need without more than passing attention to the niceties of conventional morality.

Boys and young men, who are provided fewer social resources than girls, are most assiduous in developing techniques for manipulation. The principal manipulative technique is skill in social interaction, with heavy emphasis on talk and the gestures and actions that augment communication. The linguistic styles of ghetto youth for actualizing different strategies of interaction are highly structured, although the structure is more often implicit than explicit. *Rapping, shucking, jiving, running it down, griping, copping a plea, signifying, sounding*—all of these terms specify particular techniques for manipulating the interaction to get what one wants.[6]

The logical development of the ethic of "go for yourself" is a highly exploitive attitude toward all potential resources. In this form the ethic appears as "Do unto others before they do unto you," a sentiment sufficiently generalized that bumper stickers proclaiming it have been prepared. The world is defined as one in which there are not enough good

5. For a discussion of the mutual exchange of testimony in building family solidarity and individual social identities, see Hess and Handel (1959).

6. See Hammond (1967), Kochman (1968), and Kochman (1969) for discussions of the interpersonal functions of black idiomatic speech.

things to go around. Therefore, for the individual to get what he wants, someone else has to give it up or forego it.[7]

The strategies of the ghetto are those appropriate to a zero-sum game, with two important qualifications. The competitive self-enhancement that comes from "rapping" and "running it down" seems to be simply one form of zero-sum game; to the extent that an individual enhances his status in the group by his excellence in these personally expressive styles, the status of the others is lowered relative to his. However, because the ethic of interaction requires that people be allowed to take turns at rapping, and because if they do it well their accomplishments are recognized by others in the group, the result of a session of conversation can be the enhancement of the self-esteem of all members of the group because they have all performed well at the game.[8] There remains in implicit group performances the notion that others—not members of the group—would have been too "lame" to do as well. Only in the most tenuous way, although increasingly in recent years, has this group pride been based on a belief that all "members" of the black world have distinctive abilities that set them apart from and above white society. At this widest extent the concept of "soul" serves to make blacks winners in a zero-sum game with whites.

A second qualification of the zero-sum game hypothesis applies principally to boys. Sexual conquest as a source of personal achievement is plentiful; there is perhaps more than enough to go around. One's score in the heterosexual game involves the frequency of intercourse and the number of different women with whom one has had or can have intercourse. So long as men are not possessive about their women (and the women cooperate), it is possible for all to be winners in this game. Everyone can have plenty of "trim" as long as he has mastered the technique of "whipping the game on the foxes." The tenacity with which males support a system of heterosexual relations that violates the standards of sexual loyalty most of them support in the abstract is perhaps due to their desire to preserve one of the few resources for self enhancement that is plentiful in their environment.

The availability of this resource is enhanced by a relatively low awareness of age segregation in heterosexual relations. It is considered appropriate for males to put the make on women in a wide age range, from the early teens through at least the middle thirties. Younger women are considered valuable because of their greater sexual attractiveness and older women because of their greater access to money and other goods. Older men are, of course, free to compete with the youngsters for women and girls, but older men, starting perhaps in the middle twenties, tend to withdraw from active participation in this competition. They tend to settle on

7. Foster (1965).
8. Gans (1962) describes a similar pattern of informal social interaction in the peer group society of Boston West End Italians.

one or two women with whom they establish close relationships; because of this withdrawal the subjective sense of the availability of sexual resources for younger males remains high.

When a male player in this game shifts his emphasis from the number of women that are "strung out" over him to establishing a relationship in which one woman is sexually loyal to him, he reinstates the zero-sum situation, because he removes a resource from the common pool and at the same time makes himself vulnerable to the threat of other participants rapping to his girl. The stance of a participant toward exclusivity in sexual relations appears almost as if it were consciously calculated. One can observe the self-protectiveness, the hedging of bets, that participants relinquish when they decide to emphasize sexual loyalty on the part of their girls.

For the adolescent boy, the peer group is a school in which he can acquire the skills of dramatic self presentation, in which he can perfect an expressive style of interaction and modes of calculation based on the gains likely to come from the exercise of expressive skill. His peer group holds out to him the goal of becoming an accomplished performer on various ghetto sets in order to win rewards of goods and status.[9] His peer group suggests to him that expressiveness can be a lifelong career; it validates a world view in which security and affluence will probably come not from conventional performance in schools and on the job but from learning how to hustle. The ideal—to which he must respond, though he may do so with ambivalence—is the complete hustler, who gets what he wants by working on people's minds, who can produce rewards with a minimum of effort and a maximum of style. The complete gamester can calculate a game for every need, whether for money, status, protection from danger, or sex. He may be a "pimp," specializing in having a number of women support him, or he may work the street more broadly, "running games" on friends and strangers of both sexes.

The complete hustler is, of course, a cultural myth, realized by few men and fewer boys for even a short period of time and by still fewer as a career. The lesser role available to the ordinary practitioner of the street art is simply that of being "cool," of knowing one's way around the streets. The man who is cool is quick to pick up the few and unpredictable rewards that come his way and sustains a tenuous sense of dignity by squeezing what he can from his own and his friends' successes and from rapping with them. Because of the looseness of the peer group structure, his effort to sustain himself in the eyes of peers is facilitated by frequent changes in the membership of his group; the failures of his past are lost in the social biography possessed by his current "running buddies."

Because "go for yourself" leads to "do unto others," each participant in the peer-group society expects others to be similarly motivated to "do unto him." Equally important with running a game for gain is the ability

9. See Horton (1967) for a discussion of sets as focused gatherings of ghetto peers.

to defend oneself against manipulation, exploitation, and aggression by others. There is in the peer group a premium on defense, although this skill seems to take longer to perfect. The very activities that are likely to produce rewards are also likely to expose one to danger, because the zero-sum situation stimulates persons to react violently when they learn they have lost. To be cool means to learn how to minimize dangers and to cope effectively with the inevitable attacks that will be directed against the successful practitioner of the street arts.

Most boys in the ghetto understand that they may have to defend themselves against physical attack and that they need weapons to do so; carrying guns and knives is primarily regarded as a defensive measure. But weapons are recognized as presenting another kind of danger because one may use the weapon in anger and thus make unnecessary trouble for oneself. These themes of defense and violence appeared clearly in a discussion with a 13- and 17-year-old boy. The 17 year old (Alex) commented that one should not try to take a friend's girl unless he told him first. He said:

> You mustn't go up to the girl and tell her, "Look, baby, I want to snow you," or something like that, because if she'd let you then he might come around and see the girl the next day and she say, "Well, I go with such and such a fellow." He gonna get mad then. He take care of you and her.
>
> *Fieldworker:* So if he does ask her and he finds out that you had talked to her until she wouldn't have any further use for him, then what would happen?
>
> *Alex:* Well first he'll try to snow back to her and he'll try to talk enough talk so he can get her back. Well most likely the average boy will snow until he can't snow no more, till he get mad, then he might smack her around a little bit. Then he'll go to get the boy and smack him a little bit or put the gang on him or something—but I wouldn't try to get the girl back.
>
> *Fieldworker:* If he can't whip the guy that had snowed on this girl and he can't convince the girl that she should be with him instead of the guy that stole her, then what happens?
>
> *Alex:* He'll go outside and go and get the gang to whoop him over, and he might just get mad enough to go and get a rifle or a gun and take care of him hisself.
>
> *Other boy:* That would be nonsense, killing somebody for something like that, cause there are many other girls. The less you carry a weapon . . . if you don't carry a weapon you'll find out you can solve more problems by talking, but if you have a weapon in your pocket and somebody gets too smart, the first thing you're gonna do is go for your weapon.
>
> *Field worker:* Would you say that most of the guys in your group carry something?
>
> *Alex:* No, me myself I usually leave my gun in the house. Some of them have knives and guns, mostly everybody I know

> have a gun and a knife. Maybe some of them keep the knife in their pocket and leave the gun at home. The gun is more trouble than the knife. Some of them might not carry knives. Most of them don't carry anything. I went and got my gun a couple of times but by the time I get it in their face I change my mind and feel sorry for him because he don't have no gun. They don't have no gun, they don't have no nothing, just mouth. I go on back home.
>
> *Field worker:* What do you think you would have occasion to use a gun or knife for?
>
> *Alex:* Like if somebody hurt somebody I might . . . like somebody who mean a whole lot to me and somebody hurt them. Then I would go home and get my gun. If he attempted to kill me, swing at me with a knife or gun or almost bust my head with a brick or something (then I might do it). So far as hitting me with his fists, that don't mean nothing 'cause I think I'm big enough to fight anybody out there.

The individual's problem in defending himself is that however rational he tries to be about not over-reacting to failure in the zero-sum game, there is always the danger that others will prove irrational, either by pushing their advantage too far or by over-reacting themselves, by failing to avoid "trouble" when they could. Alex rendered this general judgment on his peer group when he commented on the field worker's intention to write a book about adolescent boys in the project.

> If you write a book it should be called "The Hoodlums."
>
> Why?
>
> Because they is nothing but bums living around here. I hate to say it but I'm a bum myself.
>
> Why are they bums?
>
> Because they don't know what to do but stay in trouble.
>
> What makes them bums?
>
> Because to live around bums, you have to be a bum. Wherever you live you have to have friends, and if you have friends you want to be around them, and if your friends steal—you know money is kind of tempting and if they get money you is going to want some of that money and they is not going to give you any if you is not any help. As you grow up you learn little things and as you learn them you think you can get away with everything. And when you get caught it don't mean much so as you go along getting caught it don't mean anything to you and you keep stealing as you go along.

Alex knew from personal experience the difficulty of defending himself without exacerbating his troubles. He had spent six months in a boys' training center for "assault with intent to kill." He explained the event like this:

> Well, we were in the show and he was with his girl and there was a lot of crowd around, you know, just around. And I asked his girl for a piece of candy and he jumps up and smacks me in the face with a cap. Well, I could whip him. By me whipping him I take the cap and hit him in the face. He grabbed me around the throat again so I pushed him against the wall again and I hit about three or four times and he said, "Now I'm going to kill you," and he stuck his hand in his pocket. Well I went in mine and I was just a little faster than he was and I cut his throat.

In the masculine peer group, the individual learns not to count on more than short-range solidarity with his peers. The strategies of individualistic manipulation, exploitation, and aggression are such that friends may quickly turn into enemies, and therefore it behooves the sensible person not to reveal himself fully even to those on whom he counts for cooperation in pursuing his goals. Boys and young men live in a particularly anomic world. They are never certain that their apparent solidarity with their friends is real because they know that professions of friendship and loyalty can be part of a game and that the claims they would like to believe they can make on their friends may not be honored. They may try to exempt a few relationships from these general rules, but as they acquire experience they learn not to count very heavily on loyalties within the peer group.

Girls' peer groups are not nearly so anomic in character. The girls seem to develop more of a sense of comfortable solidarity and affiliation among themselves. Although membership in their intimate circles will change from time to time, the intensity of competition within the group is not nearly so great and girls do not show the constant concern about being exploited by those who are supposed to be their friends. There is, of course, the ever present danger that another girl will steal your boyfriend, but because girls are less aggressive in heterosexual relationships than boys are expected to be, the threat is more manageable. Girls share their possessions somewhat more freely than boys, with less concern that they will not get them back.

It may be the greater security of girls in their peer groups occurs because they are less dependent on them than the boys. Girls are able to develop closer and more successful relationships with the women in their families and less stress is put on their peer-group relationships because they do not have to fulfill their needs exclusively within them.

There is a clear-cut model for the boy who pursues the goal of respectability. He stands aside from the excitement of the street and ignores the possibilities of interesting adult activities like drinking, heterosexual relations, and stealing. Instead, he devotes himself to school accomplishments, to becoming a leader of organized activities in school and church; he may have a part-time job, and he spends his remaining time at home. This is, of course, the classic pattern of the slum child who is aiming toward escape. Few boys in Pruitt-Igoe approximate this model, and those who do are highly distinctive among their peers. One 15-year-old boy presents a clear conception of what is necessary to avoid the "bad" life of adolescence in the project. He was a high school sophomore who was doing his best to get ahead. He commented:

> *Joe:* A project like this isn't so bad; it's just that the boys don't have anything to do. They sit around and they ain't got nothing to do so they just get into trouble, like "Let's beat up this old man," and "Let's rob this old lady," "Let's get the meat man." So the fun boat and these community centers around help because before they started putting up centers and swimming pools and things the project was just a little bit bad. If we just had a little bit more and the project police cleaned out some of the bad boys it would get a little bit better as a place to live in. (If there were more to do) they wouldn't have any time to do anything bad.
>
> And it's up to the parents too because you know, a lot of them don't care too much about the kids. They just have them, and you know, don't think about them. The kids go around half hungry and they take it out on others. They try to get them to sleep and they hollar at him and they argue at him and they go outside and somebody, a friend, could try and be nice to him but they take it out on him. You know, you kind of keyed up and you kind of a little bit on the cross side. You go around somebody and say something just kind of you know riled up. You get mad and want to hit him. They go on and hit him, they think that's just easing off their troubles, that makes them feel like, act like, it took a burden off their backs.
>
> And I think these mothers should sit down and talk to their girls about this intercourse or rather sexual communications between boys and girls. The way these boys are committing intercourse with these girls, just leave 'em, and the girls they aren't taking care of themselves, so how are they going to take care of some baby. Girls aren't even 14, not even age of consent, and they going around and committing all these things with these boys in washrooms and in the middle (stairwells)—stuff like that. I try. I use protection of some kind that helps a little bit against some disease. But sometimes people have protection and if the girl isn't clean, doesn't clean her body and stuff like that, well, that little piece of rubber don't help one bit.

Field worker: What are some of the things you like about living here and some of the things you don't like?

Joe: I have a lot of fun. Sometimes I go down to DeSoto and
watch the boxing matches and some of my friends are boxing
down there. I like to go there and do that. Sometimes I go
swimming. I can't swim, I just go down there wading. Some
of my friends tried to teach me. You have pretty good fun
around here if you keep out of trouble. And most of the time
trouble comes through you, you just have to try to avoid it. I
play softball, football, sit on the grass and everything.

Field worker: What are some of the things you don't like:

Joe: Certain people that live down here. I would like to criticize the project police, and I don't like certain people down
here that try to be bad. You go to the store and they gonna
ask you to lend them a nickel. You say you ain't got no nickel,
they wanta search you. You say you got a nickel, they still
wanta search. And people don't like to be searched and that
leads up to a fight and most of them be with gangs. When
they be by themselves they ain't nothing. They is like a pack
of wolves. They ain't nothing when they by themselves. . . .
The most thing I don't like about down here, you can't even
fight clean. Like you fight somebody, you don't know
whether he gonna take out a gun, a pair of wrenches. Shoot
. . . don't even want to fight nobody fair around here. Best
thing to do is wait 'til he turns his back and best man for
hisself. . . . And see the way I try to play it is, don't hang
with them, just get to know 'em, you know. You see 'em, say
hi and bye. You know, know everybody so you can go when
you want, but don't hang with them or nothing.

Joe tried to make sense out of his world, to understand why so few of
his peers seemed interested in pursuing the respectable course he had
chosen. The only model that was available to him for explanation was
highly moralistic. He tried to formulate his views of "project life" in an
essay for one of his classes in school, and also for the fieldworker.

Project Life

My name is Joe Jefferson, my 15th birthday just passed, I am a
sophomore in Vashon High School and quite naturally I live in the
Pruitt project. The place is a good community but it's just the occupants and outsiders who have given the projects such a bad reputation. Something should be done about this, but what? Should we
send more force in by hiring more policemen? Or do just the opposite way, by this I mean set up more "Boy Scout organizations" or
build more recreational centers, start more "boys clubs" and set up
more guidance programs, these things help this project become a

better place to live. I am going to tell about the project in which I live.

Utilities and Conveniences

Occupants of this Pruitt project are pretty darn blessed because they don't have to pay gas and light, they just have to make one payment for everything, and this payment is cheap also. And as for conveniences occupants have them all. They have installed stoves, refrigerators, radiators, cabinets, and closets too. There are also incinerators too for them to burn their trash and garbage and they even have elevators but they are out of order most of the time or stuck between the floors of these 11 story buildings. There use to be telephone booths in the lobby also they had cigarette machines with all these conveniences there should be no trouble at all.

The People

The people of this project are mixed of various kinds. There are the nice and kind, and then there are the mean and brutal, there all kinds of people down here winos included. Also dope addicts and these so-called cats think they are bad and can't be whipped. Mostly all of them hang in gangs and carry knives all the time. And the sissies so they are called by the cats, because they don't like to fight or do not drink or smoke, but they are the smart ones, they live longer. There are also many crazy people down here too, watch out for them. These are just a few of many kinds of people.

Gang Fighting

Gang fighting is nothing unusual in the Pruitt Project. Don't think that gang fighting is just in the Pruitt but (it is) in the Igoe, Vaughn, Village, and Peabody also. Gang fighters are usually composed of cats as you could have guessed, because when two groups of boys meet, each group thinking they are the baddest and coolest. You get a real gang fight. How can this be stop? Don't ask me. There are at least ten big gangs alone here in the Pruitt, such as Big Boy's gang, Harry's gang, Curly's gang, the Blue Dragons, The Black Cats, the Red Devils, The Playgirls, The Pruitt Petticoats and about three more gangs. See what I mean.

Conditions

The conditions down here are pitiful. People act as they were some kind of creatures or animals. Some dogs have enough sense to use the sandbox but some of these people go around urinating and letting their bowels go on the steps, in the halls, washrooms and even the elevator. Children write all over with chalk, crayon and even paint. They mess the walks all up. If you could see this place you'd think it was a prison because they had (to) bar the lights, windows and even vacant first floor apartments to keep those things from being destroyed. We have incinerators. Where do they throw their trash? All over the halls. What do you think should be done?

Sexual Relations

Intercourse is very common in all the project but it is used more in the Pruitt home more often. Why? This I don't know either. Maybe it's because most of the whores and prostitutes live in this vicinity than any other project, or maybe most of the girls in the community don't ever care. But this I do know, most Pruitt home girls are stupid about sex and prevention of pregnancy or childbirth. A lot of boys are the same and some of them are just too evil and mean to go to the drugstore and get a rubber. And they aren't that high. All they have to do is let their whiskey or wine go a day or two and buy some protection. They're only three for 60¢.

Education

There is no use for anyone of school age being out of school because there are plenty of schools for everyone. There are enough teachers in this district but some people just don't even want to go to school. In St. Louis they pay some high school drop-outs money to go to school. For people in the Pruitt district they go to these schools mostly: Pruitt, Carr Lane and Branch, Blewitt, Jefferson and some go to Divell. For Catholics there is St. Bridgets', St. Leo's, St. Nicholas, and Providence. There is no excuse for no one to be out of school.

Employment

Occupants in the Pruitt homes district have very few jobs because most of the women just sit up on their butts getting welfare checks better known as "Mother's Day checks," on the tenth of every month. Some women and men try to get out and work and support their families. Jobs for youths are not too easy to find but if you really want a job you can get one. There are a lot of jobs for youths and adults also. Employment is pretty darn close to us too, because you can go down on Sixth to the Missouri Employment Agency.

Apparently Joe was unable to stand aside from the action of the project without moralistically condemning all those who participated in it. His route to respectability makes him sound like a junior Uncle Tom. Perhaps only a sense of revulsion bolstered by moralistic self-congratulation is adequate for resisting his temptations—and even Joe does not resist them all; he cannot pass up the sexual opportunities available to him, compromising instead by making an effort to protect himself against disease and unwanted fatherhood.

Other boys who are less intent on a respectable course also develop a caution about the dangers of enthusiastic participation in peer group activities and use as their guideline an effort to "stay out of trouble." They may participate with friends, some of whose activities they disapprove, but they try to remain uncommitted so that they can remove themselves from situations in which they are likely to become involved in fights, to become drunk and uncontrolled, or impregnate a girl.

Most boys are not able to forego the attractions of the peer group. They commit themselves rather fully to its activities and engage in behavior they know to be dangerous—stealing, carrying weapons, putting the make on any girl they can. Many develop a simpler criterion for avoiding the destructive possibilities of participation: they try to stay out of jail. They come to take for granted normal dangers of their participation such as being picked up by the police and getting in trouble with project officials and other adults, but they try to avoid situations in which they are likely to be charged and sentenced for a crime. The prospect of jail is intimidating, and they have some understanding that conviction is a major turning point which forecloses later opportunities for a conventional good life.

Sexual Socialization in Adolescence

As boys and girls become participants in the adolescent peer group and visible to adults as sexually mature, their expectations and experiences encourage sexual activity "for real" as opposed to childish play. Adolescent development toward sexual maturity can be marked off by a series of "firsts." Girls in Pruitt-Igoe and the private neighborhood nearby recognize three firsts: the first "real" kiss, the first "real" boy friend and the first "real" experience of coitus.[10]

The first real kiss seems to stand out as the turning point demarcating their passage from childhood into adolescence. A real kiss is one that involves mouth and tongue contact, deep kissing as opposed to superficial lip kissing. In contrast to play kissing, it represents a social situation which both parties take to be seriously sexual, although not necessarily leading to sexual intercourse. In Ladner's sample the girls reported having their first real kiss (defined by them as "when I knew what I was doing") at an average age of 13, with a range from 9 to 15. All but three of the 30 girls reported having at least one "real" kiss by the time they reached 15. The boy with whom they shared this kiss was not necessarily their first real boyfriend but he was usually a friend whom they knew fairly well.

The kisses developed out of the adolescent peer-group activity which regularly brings boys and girls together, which provides boys with an opportunity to talk to girls, to express their appreciation of the girls' charm and attractiveness and to measure their success in talking by their ability to win a kiss. From this kind of socializing which takes place informally on the project grounds, in the school yards, and often in the apartments of the participants, the girls and boys have ample opportunity to get to know each other, to dance, to rap, to begin to think seriously about each other. The next turning point develops from this interaction—the first "real" boyfriend or girlfriend. Girls make important distinctions between the real boyfriend of adolescence and the play boyfriend of pre-adolescence, again in terms of the seriousness and potential consequences of the relationship. The real relationship involves a clear understanding that courting is going

10. Ladner (1968).

on, although it may not have any immediate consequences for either party. It is generally informally public in that peers are aware of the existence of the relationship and siblings and parents may be informed. In Ladner's sample, the mean age for the first real boyfriend was 14, with a relatively narrow range of 12 to 16. Only four (three of whom were under 15) of the 30 girls had not had a real boyfriend by the time of the interview.

The relationship with the first real boyfriend, or any later boyfriend for that matter, tends not to be particularly long-lived; most of these relationships probably last for less than three months. Even so, they are highly significant to the girls and generally to the boys. Neither partner ceases all interaction with persons of the opposite sex, but interaction with other boys or girls takes on a different quality, because now there are implicit questions of loyalty and belonging to consider.

It is probable that for boys the first real girlfriend is less important than a girl's first real boyfriend because boys are expected to be more promiscuous. If they are seriously modeling themselves on the ideals of the street, they try to maintain more than one girlfriend at a time, and they consider themselves free to seek sexual relationships with older women. The girls are likely to be more romantic about their first boyfriends. They will maintain friendly relationships with other boys only so that they do not isolate themselves from the peer group, knowing that they cannot count on the permanence of their boyfriend relationships.

Pruitt-Igoe adolescents will go on to other relationships defined in essentially the same manner. It is important to understand that this pattern of sequential, close, heterosexual relationships does not constitute a system of adolescent dating, which rarely occurs in this community. Instead there are two kinds of heterosexual interaction, one involving groups of boys and girls who spend time together and may pair off preliminary to the establishment of more durable relationships, and the other involving the clear public acknowledgment that such a relationship exists. There is some disagreement among the adolescents and their parents as to what "dating" means; the consensus tends to be that it is not desirable. Some take the position that dating is a euphemism for promiscuity; others maintain dating would be preferable to long-lasting relationships because boys and girls would not become over-involved with each other emotionally, but that it is not feasible. One 18 year old summarized the dominant view as follows:

> You might have one boy that you go with, that's all right. It's just like that. You just have one boyfriend because Negroes don't do that dating stuff. Because these boys, they say you're his woman, and if you go running around with a whole lot of boys all the people around you are going to say you're a tramp and you're just running around. Your boyfriend is going to get mad and quit you or hit you or do something to you. That's the same way with girls too. When a lot of boys be coming up

to your house (my mother says), "What are all these boys doing coming up here?" and all that kind of stuff, so I just have one.

Discussions of dating and its infeasibility make clear some assumptions underlying the dating pattern which bear most heavily on the role of the girl, but apply somewhat to the boy. The concept of dating is based on the assumption of an autonomous female who has the right to maintain limited social heterosexual relations with a number of boys. She must be a moral person who can be trusted to limit her level of heterosexual involvement with dates in a "respectable" way, so that her multiple relationships are not promiscuous. Neither of these assumptions would be acknowledged as valid or desirable by most of the people in the community. Parents and boys will not acknowledge the right of a woman to involve herself with several men at the same time, nor will they trust her to limit the level of her involvement to avoid promiscuity. In the view of Pruitt-Igoeans, males and females are not constituted to tolerate the sexual limitations that a dating system imposes.

Boyfriend and girlfriend relationships are not sexually elaborate before coitus; there is no established pattern of heavy petting in this society. Before intercourse most of the time boys and girls spend together is spent with others; when they are alone, their sexual activity tends to be confined to a few "real" kisses and perhaps light petting, and they spend most of their time talking, playing games, or watching television. Heavy petting in the manner of middle-class adolescents—involving genital contact, semi-nakedness, or manipulation to the point of orgasm—is not considered as an alternative to coitus. Instead, sexual interaction is either limited or progresses with relatively few preliminaries to intercourse. Heavy petting as it is practiced in the middle class involves the same assumption which makes dating possible: the idea of an autonomous girl who has the right to distribute her favors and who can limit her involvement with any particular boy to preserve the possibility of socially accepted relationships with a number of boys. The middle-class pattern is also based on the assumption that boys will "go as far as they can" but will not use force to push sexual intimacy beyond the level the girl will accept, that they will acknowledge the girl's right to set finely graded limits on the degree of intimacy. Again, such assumptions simply do not accord with ghetto conceptions of what boys and girls (or men and women) are like.

From these "real" relationships, then, there develops rapidly a new turning point in the sexual career. There is a fairly clear understanding that following the establishment of a relationship, the boy will ask to be "given a chance;" he will suggest sexual intercourse and the girl will recognize such a request as legitimate. The girl expects to be allowed to make the choice; she expects the boy to try to make a positive choice seem attractive and desirable; and further, she expects eventually to let him have a chance. Having a chance means that the boy can openly talk about and suggest sexual intercourse without implying that the girl is promiscuous. If the girl refuses to give the boy "a chance," she may do so in such a way to suggest that he may broach the subject again at a later time, or she may indicate that she is not at all willing to consider the possibility of coitus as a normal development in their relationship.

Despite the pride boys take in sexual conquest and despite their assertions about the ready availability of girls as sexual objects, they often seem remarkably patient in their relationships with girls, and they rarely terminate such relationships automatically when intercourse is refused. However, if the girl is not willing to give the boy a chance by the second or third time he asks, their relationship does degenerate, sometimes by mutual agreement and sometimes by the boy's decision to move on to greener fields.

The first real sexual intercourse, the first time a boy or girl "does it," represents the final turning point in the development of a heterosexual career. Eventually the majority of girls give their boyfriends "a chance." In Ladner's sample, the median age of first sexual intercourse was 15 years, with a range of 13 to 18. In our 1965 questionnaire survey the median age of first sexual intercourse for 150 adult women was 16 years. (Many of these women had been reared in the rural South, where they were not as fully exposed to the sexual pressures of a ghetto peer-group society, but even so the age difference for first intercourse is not great.) Adults in the project tend to exaggerate the "immorality" of teenagers, perceiving a much greater gap than in fact exists between their own "traditional" adolescence and that common in the project. For example, all our data suggest that first intercourse occurs on the average at age 15, whereas the average age guessed by adults in the project was 14; similarly, people in the project guessed that the average age of first pregnancy was 14 years, while Ladner's analysis of birth records in Pruitt-Igoe suggests a median age of 16.5. Although the girls in the project tend to validate the pessimistic expectations of adults about their sexual behavior, they show more resistence than the adults give them credit for.

The Development of Sex Role Conceptions

The peer group provides the principal stage on which sexual identities are fashioned and tested.

Ladner indicates how the peer group affects the manner in which girls develop conceptions of their femininity:

> The conceptions of emerging womanhood the girl held were strongly conditioned by her relationships with her male companions. If boys teased her about having small breasts, hips or legs, she might begin to feel inferior about these traits and develop the negative self-conception that she had not quite measured up to required standards.
>
> Peer group interaction was the source of much discussion about appropriate normative behavior related to emerging womanhood. It is

typical in peer groups for girls to experiment with such valued items in their identity kits as lipstick, hosiery, tight sweaters and skirts. Experimentation involving non-material things was carried out in a similar manner. Perhaps the most vital function of the peer group in this regard was its role as a clearinghouse for ideas and as a judge or evaluator for sifting various ideas as to the best or most appropriate form of behavior in specified situations. Girls relied heavily upon their peers for counsel and advice, and they also reciprocated with the same. A strong value was placed on having sincere friends who could be depended on to share secrets, offer sound advice, and offer companionship when needed. Close friends were expected to fulfill the above obligations constantly. Failure to do so aroused feelings of distrust, sorrow and a strong tendency to categorize the insincere friend with other individuals whom she had, for whatever reason, come to regard as unconcerned with her welfare. . . .

In the peer group there was considerable discussion of conceptions and misconceptions of subjects related to womanhood such as menstruation, kissing and sexual intercourse, boyfriends, and so forth. Almost every facet of a girl's sexual ideas were verbally tested with her peers. They shared information and advice on onset of menstruation, first sex encounter, pregnancy, abortion and contraception. Moreover, the discussion of ideas generated the appropriate and acceptable norms governing these areas of behavior. There was much disagreement within the peer group over what the regulative norms should be. That is, rarely did the girls arrive at a set of beliefs and attitudes that formed their sexual identity without first engaging in intensive discussion with peers about relevant facts and issues. They also gave much self appraisal to the same.[11]

A central theme in the concerns expressed and acted out by girls within their peer group and in their relationships with boys is the testing of their femininity. This appears most clearly, as with adolescent girls of other classes, in their preoccupation with making themselves physically attractive. The transition to adult femininity is made in this respect by different girls at different ages. In Ladner's sample, the girls varied considerably in the maturity of their dress, some seeming to conceive of themselves as pretty little girls and others reaching out for much more adult fashions.

The emphasis on clothes, of course, brings the girl directly against the financial situation of her family. Thus, the few girls in Ladner's study who came from more prosperous homes had more fashionable clothes and hair styles than the girls from families in which there was little money available for this kind of display. The girls who were involved in stealing stole almost exclusively to dress well rather than to resell their acquisitions.

Attractive dress and personal grooming, though a relatively universal preoccupation of girls in the project, is not immediately or consistently apparent to the observer. In several cases field workers characterized girls

11. Ladner (1968), p. 88–90.

in families they were studying as sloppy and unkempt, only to discover with surprise that on certain occasions (such as the flowering of a romance) the girls would dress in high fashion. Similarly, a field worker observed a 14-year-old girl who dressed in a wide range of styles, appearing most often in little-girl or tomboy clothes (jeans, ragged shirt, outsized shoes) only to appear on other occasions elegantly coiffed and in an adult cocktail dress. Mastery of the adult mannerisms and style of interaction that goes with this kind of dress also came often as a surprise to the field workers. A wide range of age-specific styles of presentation is available to these adolescents, perhaps reflecting the generally low degree of age segregation characteristic of this community. In the middle class, this kind of alteration between girlish and womanish ways is familiar in the late teens but is regarded as abnormal in the early teens.

With immersion in the peer group and dependence on it for standards of behavior and resources comes a progressive attenuation of parental ties and control during adolescence. The attenuation is perhaps less for boys, who generally are not close to their parents and whose adult activities do not compete as much with their status as children in the family. The important feminine activities—taking on sexual roles and eventually motherhood—make plain to the family that the girls are moving toward greater and greater equality with their mothers. The assertion of independence of parental control is consequently more clear-cut for girls. Anxiety about premature involvement in sexual relations and pregnancy makes parents more vigilant about their activities, and this conflicts with their desire to participate in a peer-group society that always involves exactly what their parents fear; hence, the issue cannot be ignored or concealed as it can for boys. The girls often complain about the strictness of their parents and they make use of peer group solidarity and the apparent "innocence" of spending time with their girlfriends as ways of attenuating parental control. Ladner observes:

> The girls who considered themselves more mature and deserving of their freedom often accused their parents of not wanting them to grow up. A conversation with five girls (two in the sample and their peers) illustrates this sentiment:
>
> Respondent: Another problem with some of the parents is you can't reason with them. They think you're getting smart if you try to reason something out with them and get an understanding. Like if your mother tell you you can't go out one night and you ask her why, they'll say, "What are you talking about why?" They start getting mad and fussing and everything. *They don't want you to grow up.* (Emphasis mine). I'm 18 but my mother still treats me like I'm 11.
>
> Interviewer: Why do you think your parents don't want you to grow up?
>
> R: I guess they feel as though they're losing their family. Like my mother, one day she'll tell me to do around the house and everything so I don't know what's wrong with her.

Liberation from parental control means that the girl is able to do more than come and go as she chooses. It means that she has the freedom to make other important decisions about her life: decisions about whether she should stay in school, take a job, get married, have children, try to become successful, and other significant occurrences which must eventually be dealt with. Liberation for the girl also means being able to make a wrong or ill-fated decision. They felt that they should be free to decide whether or not they wanted to become involved with a male who was held in ill repute in the community, to decide if they wanted to have sexual relations without being told by parents that they could. They frequently complained that their parents refused to allow them to exercise their own judgment in these affairs.[12]

The model for feminine participation in the peer-group society is the attractive, self-confident, autonomous young lady who knows her way around the streets, who is able to withstand the efforts of her parents to treat her as a child, and who modulates her relationships with boys so that she keeps them interested while remaining free to determine the extent of her sexual involvement with them. She learns how to fend off the boys who rap to her while keeping them interested, how to play one boy against another to make herself more desirable. She explores more deeply meaningful relationships with a real boyfriend, while being careful not to let him take her for granted.

However, in the background there is another feminine role model which she views with increasing seriousness, although she tends also to be ambivalent about it. She knows that she cannot always be a swinger, no matter how attractive that possibility seems. She knows that eventually she must settle down to be the strong woman who rears a family, and that the solidarity with her girlfriends which is so much taken up with questions of dress, girlish gossip, and boys will eventually become the solidarity of women who must provide the backbone for the community. From his TAT analysis of the girls in Ladner's sample, Levy observes:

There is a general absorption with what kind of woman to be. This usually means deciding what kinds of interpersonal relationships one can have. An outstanding figure in the TAT stories is the hard working woman. She takes care of the home, tries to keep up the house and instructs the children. Most of the girls feel they are of an age where they do not have too much to learn from such a woman but can start to be like her in their own knowledgeability about the realities of the world. This womanly role is seen as a source of warmth and security, a pleasant expression of kinship and feminine continuity from one's grandmother to one's child. For some there is this refuge, a good feeling of family life going on at home, singing, eating, laughing.[13]

12. Ladner (1968), p. 99–100.
13. Levy (1968), p. 233–234.

Ladner observes:

> All of the girls with the exception of one expressed a desire to even-
> tually marry and have a small family (usually two children) . . . The
> idea of a stable marriage, on the one hand, was appealing because
> of the potential security it offered. The desire to have a stable and
> secure marriage where the husband fulfills the function of stable
> provider often gave the only strong hope for the necessities of life—
> which parents had not been able to afford—even if it is only a wish
> for the future. . . .
>
> Yet, there is another angle from which this model of ideal woman-
> hood can be viewed. The hard working woman who is a good mar-
> riage partner and mother and who also fills in as a backbone of the
> family when circumstances force her to do so was viewed with
> ambivalence. Although this is viewed as a positive model, it has cer-
> tain features that prevented the girls from viewing it in an entirely
> positive manner. Under close examination, one finds that they had
> a concern that their lives not become drab and unexciting. They
> wanted to worry about the responsibilities of wife and mother. There
> was a strong feeling that one should not have to surrender her free-
> dom completely.
>
> Moreover, the stable and hard working woman model is not always
> rewarding. Frequently this type of woman has been abandoned by
> her jobless husband, and has sometimes had a series of unfortunate
> relationships with men. . . .
>
> Sometimes making the strong commitment to the role of the proper
> woman ended in disillusionment and despair—disillusionment be-
> cause things did not turn out as they were expected to, and despair
> because the end product of one's hard work to fulfill this role was
> met with unfortunate circumstances that were difficult to over-
> come.[14]

Although most of the meaningfulness of this role is established by observing older women, particularly the women of their own families, by the
time the girls reach the mid-teens they are exposed to the womanly role
as it begins to be practiced by their peers. Every girl knows one or two
others who are pregnant or who have babies, and at least part of the
energy of these girls has to be directed toward equipping themselves as
responsible women. Just as mutual testimony about the fun aspects of
sexual maturity reinforces the image of the attractive girl, so now the
mutual testimony (in friendship groups of girls who have and have not
had babies) works over the more traditional model of womanhood, which
begins to seem less and less distant.

When boys and girls begin to have sexual relationships their conceptions of themselves are radically altered; they regard themselves as grown
up in a way they have not previously been able to do. There is little need

14. Ladner (1968), p. 93–95.

for boys to conceal the fact that they are no longer virgins, at least within their peer group, and so they tend to be open about their sexual experiences. Even for the girls, however, participation in sexual relations does not long stay secret. There is much to be gained from publicity within their intimate group about this added evidence of maturity, particularly when it is acquired in the context of an apparently solid relationship with a boyfriend.

Even at the price of uncertain moral status, girls typically have a sense of desirable maturity once they have passed this signpost in development. There is an effort to manage the situation, to neutralize the dangers of immorality, of promiscuity and pregnancy, by emphasizing sexual intercourse as appropriate mainly in the context of affectionate relations with a boyfriend. Girls expect to be careful about their choice of sexual partners so that each particular relationship can be justified as meaningful and not a case of immoral promiscuity. In their relationships with particular boys they also may try to ensure their respectability by reducing the frequency of intercourse to an occasional accommodation of the boyfriend rather than a regular and taken-for-granted activity.

Only rarely in our field data do adolescent girls indicate an autonomous interest in coitus, even when they have engaged in intercourse with more than one boyfriend. In Ladner's sample, only half the girls who had had sexual intercourse indicated that they derived any particular enjoyment from it, and only two of the 15 girls said they had orgasm during intercourse and enjoyed specific sexual gratification. In short, these girls seem to have a basically passive attitude toward coitus, and it means more to them for their developing identities than for the pleasures of the act itself.

It is probable that the Pruitt-Igoe girls have sexual relationships primarily because they are pressured by their boyfriends and because if they do not eventually cooperate they have to accept a definition of themselves as immature. In this they share more than may be apparent with middle-class girls, who often maintain that they engage in necking and petting because it is expected rather than because they actually enjoy the behavior. However, one has the impression that middle-class girls more rapidly find heavy petting pleasurable and learn to look forward to its repetition, perhaps because it represents a compromise between the potential moral costs of sexual relations and the cost in perpetuated childhood status of not engaging in any kind of sexual activity. The lower-class girl is presented with an all-or-nothing situation in which to have the status of maturity she must run greater moral risks.

There is also more ambivalence among the boys about having sexual relations with a girlfriend (in contrast to a girl who can be regarded as promiscuous or an easy mark) than is superficially apparent. The boys often feel uneasy about the responsibility they take on when the relationship proceeds to this point. Although the street code legitimates intercourse with any girl on whom one can "whip enough game" the boys are not so committed to the street ideology that they are utterly unaware of responsibility. From both sides the relationship tends to be ambivalent, with a good deal of covert strain and hostility in it, and one of the reasons for the rapid turnover in boy and girlfriends is that as the relationship goes on, this hostility is liable to come to the fore. The girls tend to be angry with their boyfriends after intercourse which seems temporarily to decrease their intimacy with each other. Both parties to the relationship which has within it a sense of exclusiveness are likely to become more jealous at the same time that the peer group encourages them to pay attention to other potential partners. A combination of jealousy about their partner's "talking to" other boys and girls, and of underlying anger and anxiety plays an important part in the attenuation and eventual dissolution of these relationships.

Careful analysis of the ways in which girls regard their boyfriends and of their behavior and verbalization in connection with sexual intercourse suggests that their participation in sexual relationships is implicitly part of an exchange system: becoming a sexual partner is a way of repaying the boyfriend for certain rewards and of insuring the continuation of those rewards. Even before sexual relations the boy confers a good on his girlfriend by asking her to let him "do it." Because he phrases his request in a culturally specified way that tells her how attractive and exciting she is to him, he confers on her the status of attractive mature female, denying that she is just a child or so ugly that no one would be interested in her. For his request to be rewarding it must be made respectfully. If he presses his attentions on her roughly or in an offhand manner, he is suggesting that she is a "pig" who may be sexually used but is not sexually valued.

When the girl decides that she will "give it to him," she does so in payment for other rewards that she has received or can receive if she cooperates in this way. One of these is "being in love." The girl wants to be grown up enough to be really in love, and one way of signifying this is to participate in a sexual relationship, which solidifies her claim that she is a mature young lady. It confers this status not only to herself, but to her public by virtue of the fact that the boy has acknowledged that he "belongs to" her in this particularly serious way. Her sexual favors also represent payment for a varied collection of material rewards which the boyfriend may have provided: automobile rides and going to exciting and interesting places (movies, hamburger stands, or whatever). As Ladner has noted, the exchange of sexual services for what to middle-class eyes seem paltry material rewards is understandable in the context of the extreme socioeconomic deprivation of the group.

One might also wonder why the sexual favor that is so grudgingly given, so tightly rationed, with so little opportunity for development into a fully satisfying sexual act should be so assiduously pursued by the boys. The answer, of course, lies more in the social meanings attached to having a girl who will "let him do it" than in the sexual act itself. The effect is primarily on the boy's self concept and on his status within the group, reflecting his masculine maturity in his ability to attract girls and persuade them to have coitus with him. When boys and men speak of sexual relations as particularly gratifying, rather than as scores in the street game, they are usually talking about sexual partners who are older and more experienced than the teenage girls.

The validation of masculine and feminine ego and social identities is both current and prospective. The establishment of a steady relationship which includes sexual intercourse provides a basis for dreams about future ties in stable marriages. It is not so much that the adolescent partners think about marrying each other some day as that their establishment of this kind of intimate relationship makes married future seem much closer. For boys this is perhaps one of the less salient meanings of their relationships, although it is not inconsequential. For girls, however, a steady boyfriend relationship, and the acceptance of their responsibility to have intercourse with their boyfriend, makes their dreams of future marriage more real.

Girls at this stage begin to think in realistic terms about marrying and settling down and having children. They hope for stable providers with whom they can achieve a good life and at the same time continue to have a little fun. Part of their readiness to give up their boyfriends as the relationships begin to go sour comes from the fact that they are quite hardheaded in assessing the ability of a boyfriend to provide them with this kind of life, and they almost always find the boy wanting. Unless the boy clearly is going to finish high school and gives strong evidence of being work-oriented, the girl is doubtful about her ability to make it with him. If she becomes pregnant they may go through with a marriage "to give the baby a name," but they do so for the most part with their eyes open, knowing that their chances for a permanent relationship are slim.

In fact, participating in the established system of boyfriend relationships tends to destroy the possibility of achieving the dream of a good life. The girl selects boyfriends who seem interesting, fun, accomplished in rapping, and these boys are not likely to be among those who will achieve the occupational success necessary to be good providers. Knowledge of this fact contributes to the dissolution of the relationships, but a succession of such relationships, with their attendant dangers of premarital pregnancy, makes the girl less attractive as a respectable partner.

By the time the girl reaches the end of her teens, she is liable to have gone through a series of experiences during which the dream of a good life crumbles and remains only in the form of a hope against hope, a wish that luck might come her way and that somehow she can extricate herself from the vicious circle of ghetto heterosexual relations. Her experience is liable to leave her feeling that the only thing a man can be counted on to provide is an expressive relationship centered on sex and good times, and that she will have to depend on herself to accomplish the instrumental tasks of acquiring income to support herself and her children.

The effects of the transition from virginal to sexually experienced status are quite marked, and most girls who make the decision to let the boy "do it" come quickly to regard themselves as mature and knowledgeable. Because sexual intercourse may begin as early as 13, quite young girls often behave socially as more mature than older girls and are so regarded by those around them. In Ladner's sample, the greater maturity of the non-virgins was apparent both in the field data and in the TAT protocols. Inexperienced girls turned often to their more experienced peers for advice and information, and the latter became the experts on courtship problems, on the considerations that go into the decision to give a boy a chance, and on the possibilities of having a baby and what one might do about it.

The greater maturity of the non-virgins was also manifest in their attitude toward their boyfriends. They tended to make more demands on them and to hold them to standards of seriousness and responsibility that seldom occurred to the virgins. The non-virgins had a less casual and less fun-oriented attitude and began to model their relationships on marriage, or on the relationships of adult women with their steady boyfriends. It is likely that the increasing seriousness of the obligations the girls suggest to their boyfriends has much to do with the anger and rejection the boyfriends often begin to manifest toward their girls shortly after they begin to have sexual relations with them.

The virgins, in contrast, tended to romanticize their relationships with boys, both their current boyfriends and those they dream of for the future. They were more likely to describe their boyfriends in terms of handsomeness and superficial social characteristics, such as a "nice smile." They were also more likely to be attracted to "nice boys" and to those who engaged in "clean fun" rather than in street activities. The boys cater to these desires on the part of inexperienced girls by concealing their commitment to street values, by presenting themselves as "nicer" than in fact they want to be. Thus we often find girls saying that only after they had engaged in sexual relations with their boyfriends did they learn of his involvement with the police, with a "rough crowd," with other girls.

The younger virgins are likely to speak in moralistic terms about girls whom they know have sexual relations with their boyfriends, but they eventually become more sophisticated and pragmatic in their attitudes and begin to talk about avoiding sex because it is liable to bring problems rather than because it is immoral. During this time they may begin to take a harder look at their boyfriends, to be less romantic about them, and perhaps to break off relationships with boys who press them for sexual opportunities. The virgin's experience over time, however, tends to con-

vince her that she is fighting a losing battle, that unless she is willing to
forego a steady boyfriend relationship, she will eventually have to give in.
Thus 15-year-old Judith observed of her relationships with boys:

> I haven't had sex with any boy yet, I don't know why. When
> boys ask me I tell them to wait until next week and when next
> week comes I don't never see them. I try to hide from them.
> They don't find me because most of the boys live in my moth-
> er's building (she lived with her grandmother) or, you know,
> I know them so I tell them to come over there and when they
> come I don't be over there. When I do see them they ask me
> what happened. I tell them I'm sick, I've got a disease or some-
> thing. I try to get out of it. . . . When the boy I'm going with
> now asks me to do that I might do it. . . . I might be 16 by then
> and I might do it with him . . . because I like him a lot.

What is particularly striking about Judith's description of her situation is
her implicit assumption that she has no right to her virginity. She is reduced to delaying tactics, and to selecting the boy with whom she will
have intercourse rather than whether she will have it at all.

Because the virgins are confronted with what they know to be a major
decision about their moral careers, they tend to be anxious, cautious, and
fearful in their attitudes toward the adolescent world, despite their great
interest in participating in its activities and in putting their childish years
behind them. As time goes on, girls who remain virgins tend to feel more
and more isolated within the peer group, as the girls around them are
increasingly involved in sexually mature relationships, and especially as
more and more of their girlfriends have babies. Though they may feel that
these events represent moral misfortune for their peers, the day-to-day
reality they perceive is that these girls are significantly and meaningfully
involved in life, while they are sitting on the sidelines. Unless a girl finds
strong support in her family and much gratification there, and unless she
is doing well in school and has a real chance to graduate and succeed in a
white-collar occupation, she begins to feel increasingly that she has little
to lose by following her sisters' example and seeking the gratifications that
come from being fully in the swim of boy-girl relationships.

The non-virgins tend to be more autonomous from their families than
the virgins and are more critical of parental control. In part this is a result
of their participation in sexual relations, whereby they come to regard
themselves as grown up; in part they have broken away from what they
perceive as restrictive parental control precisely to become involved in
sexual relations. Girls who have engaged in sex sometimes communicate
this fact to their mothers to signify that they will no longer accept controls
that might be appropriate for children.

From his analysis of the TAT data, Levy concluded:

> In sum the non-virgins differ from the virgins as being more mature,
> more actively rebellious and more determined to act out unwilling-

ness to listen to mother; more bent on gaining satisfactions that are highly pleasurable, that signify real womanhood, autonomy and a break-through to something better in life; and because they seek the comfort and closeness sexual relations bring, or promise.[15]

In contrast, the virgins are more dependent on their families, and although they complain about parental restrictions, are more willing to acknowledge them as valid. The few girls who remain virgins into their late teens usually have a close relationship with their families. As their ties with their peer groups are attenuated, by virtue of their abstinence from its sexually mature activities, they rely increasingly on participation in family activities to compensate. In many ways, these girls exhibit family relationships more characteristic of the stable working and middle class. They direct themselves toward a feminine maturity that is like the more responsible, less exciting, sex-segregated working-class model.

Virgins often characterize their families as very strict, and with good reason; their mothers may not allow them to be out alone except with someone considered to be a "responsible adult." The strictness, however unpleasant it may seem, is accepted by these older girls as an expression of the family's concern for them, rather than as an exercise of arbitrariness. Such a strategy for preserving virginity is, however, constantly vulnerable to the impact of the streets. The older virgin is lonely; she feels left out of the world of her age mates; she wants eventually to marry, and therefore she wants to find a boyfriend who will "respect" her. Thus she continues to be exposed to the pressures of her boyfriend to give him a chance, and despite the family's partial success in isolating her from peer group pressures, she may eventually submit.

In summary, an examination of the considerations that go into a girl's decision to participate in sexual relations suggests that few girls in the ghetto are strongly motivated to begin sexual relations in early or middle adolescence, but their commitment to peer group activities and to the pursuit of maturity inevitably involves most of them in sexual activity despite their own feelings about the costs involved. The girl has two strategies available to retain her virginity, and both involve costs. The first, universally employed at least for a time, is to establish a real boyfriend relationship but try to avoid its development to the point of intercourse. Because boys constantly press for this privilege in response to the pressures of their own peer group, the girl is very likely to lose her boyfriend if she refuses to have intercourse with him. If she were willing to have a succession of frustrated boyfriends or accept the possibility that she have none, she could avoid sexual intercourse but this would deprive her of the gratification of feeling she is mature because she is "in love," and paradoxically it might also expose her to the risk of being defined as promiscuous, because if she goes from boy to boy she will be suspected

15. Levy (1968), p. 232–233.

of having sexual relations with all rather than none. She has few resources to make a claim to "respectability" credible; on the few occasions when boys talk about girls who are known as "respectable" they refer to those who are succeeding in school and who plan on white-collar careers.

In an alternative strategy, a girl may cleave to her family, spending much more time with them than most girls want to spend, and accept parental restrictions and controls without rebellion. But this, of course, is very difficult for an adolescent to do, unless family relationships are particularly gratifying and the family can provide her with more resources than is general in the ghetto.

The pressure from boys for sexual privileges is a result of their commitment to the values of the street culture and of the fact that the costs of engaging in sexual relations with girls do not seem great. Participation does not require them to forego other kinds of opportunities, and they know that the girls' families cannot effectively control their behavior. Adolescent boys in the ghetto have come to feel that they are not likely to have work careers that will produce more than small and intermittent incomes; even if they feel some responsibility to support their children, it will not prove costly because they will not have much income from which that support could come. Similarly, they are not concerned with dropping out of school to support their children, because they have given up hope of going far in school and they know that they cannot expect stable and well paying employment whether they stay in school or drop out.

In short, the probability of winning the rewards that might have to be foregone as a result of becoming sexually involved are regarded as so low that the risks that ensue from being held responsible for sexual behavior are minimal. This basic socioeconomic fact of life leaves the way free for the elaboration of a street code that justifies and makes attractive attitudes toward heterosexual relationships which, in turn, reinforce the difficulty of reducing the frequency of unwanted premarital pregnancies and of becoming self supporting before starting a family. Instead, the focus of the adolescent peer society is on the availability of sexual partners and the establishment of love relationships as a measure of maturity. Boys are encouraged to exploit love relationships for increased prestige and material rewards. Girls are encouraged to establish such relationships as a mark of their maturity and, by maintaining contact with the streets, to protect themselves against the disloyalty of their boyfriends. Their behavior encourages the dissolution of their love relationships, because of the heightened suspicion and jealousy that each partner has of the other.

Because each partner brings few resources to the relationship, because each is encouraged to exploit it for social and material gains, each by his very attempts to make it steady and satisfying tends to contribute to its dissolution. The peer society which is organized around street activities provides insurance against these all-too-apparent risks, by providing for the ready substitution of boy and girlfriends once their relationships break under the weight of the demands both partners bring to them.

Transition

The transition from adolescence to adulthood is clearly and tangibly marked for the girl by her pregnancy and the birth of her first child or by marriage, whichever occurs first. Marriages tend not to occur before 18, unless the girl is pregnant or has had a child, and the early transitions therefore are those signaled by pregnancy. Pregnancy in mid-adolescence is common in the project (over half of the girls in the project have their first pregnancy before the age of eighteen) so this particular manner of making the transition is familiar and taken for granted.

The transition for boys from adolescence to adulthood is not so clearly marked. Becoming an acknowledged father confers something like adult status, but with more reservations than for the girl, because the boy cannot assume the role of head of family that is essential to acceptable father-hood. Dropping out of school is often a way of saying that "I am now a man," but part of the problem of adolescent boys in establishing a secure social identity is that they do not have available the unchallengeable grounds for claiming adult status of the girl who has borne a child. One of the reasons boys put up little resistance to marrying girls whom they have made pregnant may be that it is a way they can achieve formal recognition of their adulthood.

Pregnancy is a salient problem for girls, and they discuss the possibility frequently in their peer groups. They acknowledge its inevitability once they begin sexual relations with boyfriends; they merely hope they will be lucky, that they will not become pregnant or at least that pregnancy will be delayed while they continue their participation in adolescent sexual relationships. Their basic understanding is well reflected in the comments of 15-year-old Anna, when the interviewer asked her about the possibility of becoming pregnant:

> Well I take a chance. If you get pregnant you're pregnant and there's nothing you can do about it. I feel that if a person wants to have sex before they get married then go ahead because you can marry a boy and that's all you worried about then. I don't have anything against girls who get pregnant before they're married as long as they's got a way to support their baby without going out on the corner and picking up everybody they meet—as long as the boy is going to help support it.

Because girls take for granted that pregnancy is the likely outcome of sexual relationships with their boyfriends, it is surprising that they refer to becoming pregnant as a "mistake." They seem to be implying that engaging in coitus is itself a mistake and that pregnancy makes that mistake evident. Girls often argue that every girl is entitled to one mistake and therefore that the first pre-marital pregnancy should not be condemned; it is excusable. They are most concerned to limit themselves to one mistake, which they seem to regard as a kind of average for their group, as behavior that will not greatly disadvantage them. They tend to condemn girls who have more than one pre-marital pregnancy, and who are thereby exposed to the risk of earning a reputation as promiscuous, immoral, "a no good tramp." In one group discussion, five 15- to 18-year-old girls sought to bring into some kind of coherence their conflicting understandings that pre-marital pregnancy was not in accord with their norms and that it was nonetheless very common indeed. In response to the interviewer's question, "Would any of you be ashamed to have a baby without being married?" they said:

> *Respondent 1:* I wouldn't.
> *Respondent 2:* I wouldn't.
> *Respondent 3:* I wouldn't.
> *Respondent 4:* I wasn't ashamed.
> *Respondent 5:* It's really no reason to feel shame because there are a lot of people walking around here unmarried and you'll just be one more in the crowd. You shouldn't feel inferior or anything because there are a lot of people in your class.
> *Respondent:* And then too if it wasn't any more and you're the only one and there wasn't any crowd I don't think that's anything to feel ashamed of. Everyone has needs that they have to satisfy. I don't really think it's a big sin. Everybody makes mistakes.
> *Respondent:* I think if I was the only one or one of a few then I would be shamed. Now girls don't be ashamed and you just expect a girl to get pregnant now because so many girls do, but before 1960 it was something for everybody around the corner to talk about and everything. Now somebody will say so-and-so is pregnant and everybody will say "oh" and go on about their business.
> *Interviewer:* Do the babies who are born illegitimate get stigmatized?
> *Respondent:* The other little children are illegitimate, too, most of them, so they don't laugh at each other and say those kinds of things.
> *Respondent:* That doesn't matter, they don't care whether you have one parent or two parents. It just doesn't matter as much as it did when my mother was coming up when everybody had a father and their father's name. Children are more mature than our parents were.
> *Respondent:* The only time this question would arise is when people have arguments and start calling each other names. They do it a lot of time. But they don't mean it because they're probably illegitimate themselves. They'll call you

that if you've got two daddies and mothers. They say that anyway so you can't tell the ones who are illegitimate from the ones who have parents.

This discussion makes clear that the threat of shame, although real, can be countered by the assertion that so many girls have illegitimate children.

It is important to note that pregnancy is a girl's mistake, not a boy's. The father may be unhappy that his girlfriend is pregnant, he may be concerned about marriage and other demands she may make on him and about the effect of her pregnancy on his relationship with her, but he does not feel that he has done anything wrong; he does not see himself as at fault. Only the few boys who cultivate a respectable style feel that they have a responsibility to guard against pregnancy.

The "one mistake" logic makes it possible for girls who become pregnant to continue to maintain, although with reduced optimism, their fantasies about achieving a "good life." Becoming mothers will make it more and more difficult for their belief that their earlier aspirations for a good marriage or a chance to work at an interesting and respectable job will come to pass, but for a while at least their insistence on having made only one mistake allows tham to feel that their aspirations have not been entirely foreclosed. Thus pregnant girls will continue to talk about going back to school, getting jobs as secretaries, entering nurse's training. It is only after the baby has been born and some time has passed that they give up their dreams and settle into the role of unmarried mother or wife and mother in a tenuous marital relationship.

Pregnancy places considerable stress on the relationship of the pregnant girl and her boyfriend.

Girls feel they have a right to insist that the boys acknowledge their special obligations, by virtue of their relationship and its apparent result. They will probably also experience anger and hurt in their attitudes toward their sexual partners. It is often only too apparent to the girl that the boy does not feel he shares in the mistake, although he may continue to profess his love and offer somehow to fulfill his obligations. The girl often seems simultaneously to withdraw her affection and interest from the boy and to expect him to be more attentive and loyal than in the past. She may refuse to see him or become hostile and abusive when she does, but at the same time she feels that he should continue to consider himself her boyfriend and should not move on to another girl (a development she might have accepted during earlier periods of strain on their relationship).

The boy has to contend with his own stresses. Before his girlfriend's pregnancy he has been little concerned with the attitudes of her parents toward him, but now he must worry lest they apply pressure to him for marriage or support for the child. Similarly, he must become increasingly concerned about how his parents will react and whether they will side with him in his desire not to be pushed into marriage should his girlfriend and her parents try to tie him down. At the same time, he feels pride at having demonstrated his sexual maturity by impregnating the girl, and he may enjoy the good-natured kidding of his buddies about this. Even that pleasure, however, can be marred by doubt as to whether he is in fact the father, and if there is any reason to suspect that his girlfriend was seeing another boy without his knowing about it, his peers may equally enjoy kidding him about this possibility. His solution may be to avoid the girl, using as a pretext her anger and rejection of him and his conviction that the pregnancy is after all her fault. He may stop coming around to her house, and he may take up with another girlfriend as a way of making public that her pregnancy is not to serve as an excuse for extending his relationship with her. However, he may decide—either on his own or as a result of pressure from the girl, her parents, and his parents—that marriage or cohabitation is reasonable, that it is a fitting expression of his love for the girl. In any case, the period after the pregnancy has become socially acknowledged is tense, and the relationship can no longer be what it was. It must either become closer and formally acknowledged or it must be broken.

Girls tend to conceal their pregnancy for some time; indeed, they often do not acknowledge the pregnancy to themselves until they can no longer avoid doing so. They seem generally to tell their girlfriends they are pregnant before they tell their mothers, and mothers may be unaware of the pregnancy for as long as four or five months. By the time the pregnancy becomes central in everyone's attitude toward the girl, she is already a noticeably pregnant woman. As pregnancy progresses, girls often find the inevitable limitation of their activities and their confinement frustrating, and this undoubtedly contributes to their anger toward their boyfriends. They are suddenly put in a very different position from that which they have come to expect as carefree adolescent girls.

An effort is always made to establish social fatherhood, most often before but sometimes after the birth of the child. Everyone involved—the girl, her parents, boys who might be candidates, and the girl's peers—is concerned to attach the child socially to a particular man as its father. In most cases this is not difficult; the girl has had intercourse within the relevant time only with one boyfriend. Even where there has been a shift of boyfriends, however, efforts are made to settle on one boy as the father (as in the case of Alice Walker). In Pruitt-Igoe the attribution of social fatherhood is a collaborative endeavor. Fatherhood must be ratified by the girl, by her parents, by the boy, and by his parents to be fully established, and this ratification takes place before an audience composed of others who know them, both at the adolescent peer level and in the informal social network of the parents. Because in Pruitt-Igoe both the girl and her boyfriend are likely to be residents of the project, this activity takes place in much the same way as in a small town. In less clearly demarcated neighborhoods, and particularly where the boy and the girl come from different neighborhoods and their parents are unknown to each other, the social attribution of fatherhood results from more formal kinds of negotiation.

In either case, fatherhood will generally be acknowledged first through a commitment to contribute to the support of the child and later by actual contributions, which may be so small as not to constitute support in any real sense but which represent a symbolic acknowledgement of fatherhood and kinship. The father has an abstract responsibilty to support his child, but it is understood that he probably cannot because he is a teenager, unskilled, without a job, and his family may be too poor to help. It falls to the girl and her parents to provide sustenance, shelter, and clothing for the child. However, the symbolic contributions of the father and his family are of considerable social importance in locating the child within a kinship network; they also prove that while the child may be legally illegitimate and not bear the father's name, his mother and father have not sunk so low as to bring him into the world without a male who will recognize him as his offspring.

Symbolic contributions are negotiated between the families and the boy and girl themselves. It seems important to everyone concerned that whatever agreement is made be lived up to, at least for a short time. The father may agree to buy milk and makings for the child's formula, or to provide baby clothes or furniture, or to make small money payments. The particular goods exchanged do not seem to be of great importance, although the more valuable they are, the better. What is important is that the father or his family make at least a few "payments" after the baby is born to fix firmly, even if only symbolically, the fact of his paternity. The girl and her parents know that legally it is possible to hold the father responsible for full support of the child. However, from their point of view this would in most cases be pointless, because the father cannot in fact support the child any better than ADC or the family's own resources.

Out of pregnancy, the birth of a child, and the establishment of social paternity comes the full transition of a girl to adult status. To the extent that a boy participates in the ceremonial acceptances of his fatherhood, his adult status is also more firmly fixed; short of marriage, however, he is not subject to the same kind of abrupt transition as the girl. Her transition is the subject of both a great deal of comment by those who know her and her own self-observation. It is widely acknowledged that she has ceased to be a teenager, even if she is still only 15 years old. She has performed the central defining act of mature womanhood; she has brought another life into the world. Mothers in Ladner's study were quick to say that daughters had become grown when they had babies, that they had "done as much as I have done" by giving birth. There remain only the entailed tasks of rearing the child, and it is taken for granted that she will carry them out.

For a while, some girls may use their new status to act with fewer parental restrictions the role of young women on the town. Just as the girls become more assertive toward their parents once they have engaged in sexual intercourse, they now move to a new level of assertiveness, stating by their actions as well as words that their parents can no longer determine their actions. They expect to talk with adults as adults, especially within the family where their grown-upness is most clearly apparent from the presence of the new baby. Because an adult woman may do what she wants and because the girl has felt restricted during pregnancy, she may go out more than she has ever done, finding new boyfriends and seeking the high life of bars and dancing places. Her mother finds it understandable that she is expected to care for the baby during this time. After all, she knows how to do it, and she may in fact enjoy the simpler and less problematic pleasures of mothering a baby rather than a troublesome child or adolescent.

Girls who make use of their adulthood in this way often seem irresponsible and the observer may be surprised by how few sanctions are brought against mothers who run out on their babies in this way. However, observation of households in which this situation exists suggests that the mother need not regard herself as irresponsible because she has put the baby in the care of a woman whom she knows can care for it and has good reason to love it. It may well be that this kind of arrangement is functional for a time, because the mother has many reasons for hostility toward her baby, and the distance she can achieve from it makes it easier to reduce her ambivalence toward the child.

If pre-marital pregnancy results in marriage, the woman can embark fully on her adult career. If it does not, to regard herself as an adult and respectable woman within the limits allowed by "our life" she must at some point make a serious effort to establish a conventional and stable marriage. The effort may be a hopeless gesture; she may marry the man who has impregnated her only to separate from him within a few months, with a feeling that at least they have tried to do things right. It may be a more hopeful act, in which the couple try to move toward a good life, no matter how inauspicious their adolescent experience has been. In either case, the transition of marriage is made by almost all lower class Negro women, in their efforts to achieve adulthood and respectability.

When a boy and a girl begin a real relationship, when that relationship progresses to the point of sexual relations, they know they are moving toward marriage and the establishment of a family. Whether their relationship will continue to this point, whether pregnancy or marriage will come first, whether marriage will follow if pregnancy comes—these remain uncertain and problematic, but the direction of the relationship is not. From a relatively early age lower-class Negro adolescents are involved in relationships that are implicitly those of mature courtship, however childish and playful they may seem to the outsider; the actual event of marriage, therefore, may seem anti-climatic and the choice of mate almost fortuitous, for all that the boy and girl may feel they are in love with each other. Their experiences during courtship are built on the conceptions they have of themselves and their life chances, and the more pessimistic their assesment about their chances, the less important the particular choice of mate seems to them.

This is not to deny that these young men and women have strong human feelings for each other, but these feelings are readily generated out of their interaction rather than the result of the search of middle-class youth for "the one man" or "the one woman for me." As for lower-class whites, courtship that is directly focused on engagement and marriage tends to be short compared to middle-class experience. It must be short because of the generalized assumption in the lower class that relationships with others are of necessity impermanent and brittle.

12.

The Salad Days of John Martin

As Boone Hammond walked through the project on the hot summer evenings of 1964, he often observed groups of people standing and sitting around in the breezeways under the buildings. One particular group attracted his attention because the same four or five adults seemed always to occupy the center of attention. They were members of a family who lived in a first floor apartment. Sometimes they brought out a hi-fi console and played records, organizing an impromptu dance; at other times there was no music, only conversation. The focus of attention was John Martin, an 18-year old who had recently been discharged from the army—honorably, he claimed. Another participant was John's older brother, Arthur, who was married and lived outside the project but was apparently a frequent visitor. His wife had just given birth to their sixth child and he had brought his other children to stay with his mother while his wife was in the hospital.

One evening Hammond observed that the conversational center of the group seemed to be shared by five persons: John, his mother (who appeared to be in her late sixties), Arthur, and two young women, Josephine and Margaret, who seemed to know the family very well, but were not part of it. Josephine was in her mid-twenties and lived in the same building; she was married and had several children. Margaret was perhaps in her early twenties. A group of some 20 other adults and children were listening to the conversation among these five. The listeners ranged from six or seven years of age into the sixties. All seemed to be following closely what was said and done by the five major participants.

Hammond approached the group because he was interested in collecting views about the Democratic primary election held the previous week, in which a popular Negro state legislator had won the position of ward committeeman from one of the few remaining white political functionaries in the area. He started the interview with his tape recorder running because he had discovered that people in these informal outdoor groups were not put off by having their conversations taped. As the conversation went on for the next three and a half hours, the subjects discussed became increasingly personal, but no one seemed to mind the fact that it was being recorded; whether it was being recorded or not, they were performing for a rather large audience.

Mrs. Martin responded to Hammond's statement of interest in the primary by saying that she hadn't voted; as he started the tape recorder she explained why.

Mother: I didn't vote because I have a son and a daughter— one is 18 years old and the other is 21 and both of them is out of a job.

Hammond: Did they both graduate from high school?

Mother: One of 'em graduated from high school and other one quit in the 12th grade and both of them is lookin' for work and neither one of them haven't found any. That's why I didn't vote because I figured that they would say what they would do when they got in and they will do the same thing that they doin' now. Everybody, almost all the youngsters, is out of work. A lot of the candidates promise to do what they say they're gonna do and then when they get in they still do the same thing they did before they got in and that's the reason why I didn't vote.

Josephine: Man, I wouldn't vote for nobody.

Mother: Tell him the reason why you didn't vote.

Josephine: For what? I'm goin' on 30 years old and I ain't got a job yet. Man, what are you talkin' about, why didn't I vote? Yeah, I graduated and gonna graduate again. No, I'm not 30, but I ain't votin' for nobody. Vote for what! Them phonies sittin' up there behind them desks. You talkin' about vote!

Hammond: Well, you can vote them phonies out and vote some new ones in their place.

Josephine: Naw, they're all the same. When you get through with 'em they're all the same. No, really, I don't wanna talk and I don't wanna vote. All of them's the same, baby.

John: Mostly everything today—even the service—I found is ran by politics. I mean politics is the world today really, and the man that's got something can put anyone in somewhere and govern him, yeah, with his money instead of him going and running for the ticket. He can get somebody and put 'em in and back 'em himself. That's all it is is politics today.

You see, as far as since I've been out—let's see, I've been out of the military about a week now—and even in there if your old man's got something to do with politics you ain't got no sweat. But if you're just a nobody in there trying to be somebody, then you've got it kind of hard. You have a lot to cope with.

Hammond: All right, from the knowledge you have about the committeeman and committeewoman, what do they do? Do you have any idea at all of what they do?

John: As they go from those little pamphlets that they hand out they be talking about jobs, better education, better support in the neighborhood, and all this stuff. And yet as you look back and see prior to the elections this is the same talk. All right you elect this man and he goes so far and what happens? Look at the area, it's self-explanatory. It's self-explanatory itself, you can look around and see. Just look. You can look and see what they're actually doing.

Margaret: Well, if we can start votin' for the man that will get Tucker (then Mayor of St. Louis) out, I'll vote then. I don't know about all of these committeemans and stuff. The only thing I know is I just want Tucker out of there, that's all. He's prejudiced and he won't hardly do anything in our neighborhood. That is, he'll tear down and build new projects, that's the only thing that I seen him did.

John: It's like, callin' no name, a chemical company that I went to get a job at, a friend of mine he went over there and got a job too. When he first applied for the job the man told him he wasn't taking any application. His brother grew up with the company and he got him on over there with pull, see. So I went over there an' I was lookin' at the bulletin board and it had on there a job and it had several jobs and the cheapest paying job was $2.14 an hour, but yet and still when I went and talked to the man he said "no openings." The job that I was applying for was a receiver and checker. It started off at $2.90 and I was a specialist in that field, see I have approximately 32 college hours in that, that is, the equivalent of 32 college hours, but it's just the way the things are arranged. See, no pull no job.

I say the way the world is going pretty soon there are going to be a lot of Negroes out of jobs and a lot of whites because it's mostly politics. I mean the way it's runnin', it seems to be the way it's gonna be in the future.

Hammond: Why do you think that is?

Mother: This modern machinery they got to take the place of men and jobs.

John: But look, most of the Negroes here in a world of automation, most of the Negroes don't have money to go to school and learn it. All right, when I first went into the service I went to school for exactly ten weeks and was awarded six college hours. I went to Fort Benning and I was an inventory management specialist. I learned the manual and mechanized systems of punching cards and all the different computers. All right, I couldn't get a job out here doing that. It's just a waste. They say the only way that the Negro can get what they want in the world today is to go into the service and be taught this field but when you get back out into civilian life and you can't get a job in this field. It's always something that they gonna say. It's somethin' holdin' 'em back. See it's two career fields that I could go into and that's receiving intake or document control.

Margaret: It doesn't do any good to learn anyhow because when you come out you can't do anything with it.

John: That's right, you can't cash in on it.

Josephine: But it don' mean nothin'.

Mother: Naw, it don't mean nothin' if you can't do nothin' with it.

John: My NCOIC (non-commissioned officer in charge) once told me, he said that the best way to do—he was from the northern part of the country—"Martin," he say, "you a Negro and the best thing that you can do is to get in there and make a career out of the army because out on the outside it's gonna be hard and you ain't gonna be able to get a job."

In the army they do teach you everything you need to know. They teach you what they call a lesson plan. You set it in this key punch which is a rotating wheel and it's a pattern and you can only type so many forms and there is a format from which to type. But you can't learn everything in school and that's one way that the white man has actually got the Negro. They teach you one thing in school and yet and still they don't give you time to practice and if you do practice you don't know nothin' except gettin' your lesson. I mean, but see the way I always did, I always thought a little bit ahead of them. I had some Negro friends that had a higher rank than I did and I always got with them and tried to advance myself, but everyone can't do that, everyone is not able.

This is what I can't understand though. Say you have 50 guys and you send 40 white guys to IBM school and then you send ten Negroes to keep the congressmen down— really, that's what you do. They have to keep these fields integrated because the army will preach they're not prejudiced, but the base I was on I can say myself I really do feel that, and most of the Negroes feel that it was prejudice and it was because the big brass was prejudice and they stuck together see. It was a colored guy walkin' around there with 16 years time and was a corporal. He knew more about the organization than some of the NCO's they had walking around there, but he had no rank, he had no say-so, and that's what I can't understand, any time a man has 16 years time in the service under one field he should rank more than a corporal. You look at it that way—the man is four years from his time.

Mother: Because he was colored, that's what.

John: And he threw a congressional investigation on the base and you know what they did? Sent him over to this head shrinker and the NCOIC went in first and talked to him for about half an hour, then they sent him in and the psychiatrist told him that he was going to send him up to the hospital. They didn't even talk to him, just told him they was gonna send him up to a hospital. Told him he didn't have a choice, that if he didn't go they were going to put him out on a 3916 so he went up there. I guess he went up there and messed the psychiatrist's mind up when he found out wasn't nothin' wrong with him, but the psychiatrist reported that the man was a day drinker, see, just to get him out, see. That was just a coverup for the congressional investigation, see. There's a whole lot to it. I mean it's team work. And that's one thing I can fault the Negroes about, they don't stick to-gether like they really should but yet and still they sit back and talk about the white man this and the white man that.

Josephine: By the time you go and get all of us together, all of our kind together, all of us poor folks together, and go and get one of our kind in somewhere, then they just snob-bish and just like them white people they don't do nothin' for you. So see, so now why should we beat our brains out trying to get them somewhere and when they get some-where they don't even know us. They wouldn't even speak to us if they saw us somewhere.

Mother: That's the reason why I didn't go over there and vote.

John: It's a lot of Negroes today, when they get those positions —well on the base I was on, when they get 'em in the rank they do think twice before they look to they soul brothers because they know if they went out the way—on our base it wasn't too many Negroes, see, where I worked at—and they know if they went out all the way trying to help this guy, even though he's right, even though he's right, if you try to help him and it's not enough of you to do something you would come out on the losing end, see. They knew all the time what was going on and when you see a man, your fellow brother getting messed up so many times—so many of 'em get messed up comin' and goin' on 3916 and this and that, get busted—well, you're not gonna try to fall on the bad side of the white man. No fool would do that.

Mother: Ain't nobody in the world going to say nothin' to me and I don't say nothin' back to them. I don't care how white or how colored he is.

Margaret: Well I think our men should go out and do some-thing but there are some that can't.

John: Just like for today, you know where you find most of your educated people at? Right down there on 17th and 14th and 20th and Franklin with a wine bottle right in their back pocket.

Josephine: Well no wonder, they go nuts. They go out and get all this education and they can't get a job.

John: They can't get no job, they don't have nothin' else to turn to, all they can do is sit around and drink that good wine and wait until they get 65 so they can draw that pension. But yet and still when the white man drives through he say, "Look at 'em, look what they do."

Arthur: Now wait, now don't you talk too fast. You had an opportunity, you didn't take it.

John: What opportunity?

Arthur: To get a high school education. Now let me tell you something about wine heads, now don't you tell me nothing about wine heads.

John: Those are your smartest people. If you take a written survey or just go around and talk to them . . .

Arthur: You know why?

John: No, why?

Arthur: You just can't explain it in a conversation.

John: Anything can be explained in a conversation, or attempt to be.

Arthur: But I can explain a few words but you wouldn't understand what I'm talkin' about. Look, them same people that you see down there, what you call bums, in your language what you call bums, they ain't no bums. They got more up here, but they just don't take advantage of it.

John: That's what I been trying to say.

Josephine: And then there are a lot of them who study for one thing and get a college degree and they won't take anything else and if they can't get a job in what they study for then they just fall all apart and that's what happens to them. Anything else would make them feel like a failure.

Arthur: It's just like you, John, you can't get a job now.

John: But I'm qualified.

Arthur: Yeah, you qualified, but you ain't got no job.

John: Why qualify the Negro if you ain't gonna give him the position for what he got and when he come to you you turn him down? Answer that for me.

Arthur: Yeah, you qualified but ain't gonna get it. All right then, now see that's what I'm saying, but don't put it on no wine heads.

Hammond: What John is saying is that their failure to achieve their goal, to get what they've been trying to get, is what drives them to drinking wine, not the wine causing them not to do what they started out to do. It's the other way around.

Arthur: Look here man, you drink a little whiskey yourself.

Hammond: That's right.

Arthur: But you don't go to that extent though, I know what

you mean. But here's what he said though, he said it's colored folks down there because they're wine heads.

John: No, I didn't say that.

Arthur: Didn't he say that? You can't call nobody no wine head,
man.

John: I didn't say that, I said that those are your most educated
people.

Arthur: Don't say that no more, John, don't talk about no wine
heads no more, don't say that no more.

John: (Emphatically) I will say it. I will say it.

Arthur: You ain't even old enough to vote yet, John. You
talkin' too much out your mouth.

Mother: They ain't nothin' but wine heads. If they drinks I
don't care if it ain't nothin' but soda and they become a
fiend to it, then they is just as bad as they were drinking
whiskey or wine.

As the conversation shifted to the topic of winos and alcoholism Arthur
became very excited. He reacted as if the topic presented him with a
direct confrontation. At the time he was slightly under the influence of
alcohol, and it later turned out he had a serious drinking problem.

John: You're wrong, you wrong. You've got a narrow outlook
about this thing.

Arthur: I ain't got no narrow outlook, I ain't no wronger than
you are.

John: You right, you're right. But look who's going to be here
to rule the day you're gone? I'm gonna be here longer than
you are.

Arthur: I don't know, not necessarily.

John: It's the younger generation that's going to rule this place.

Arthur: I don't think that you'll be here no longer than me.

John: Well I do, as far as life expansion is.

Arthur: Have you had any experience? No. I'm just talking
about the way you use your words, the way you use your
language, that's what I'm talkin' about. If you want to talk
about something, look at all them Hoosiers down there, all
them red necks, white folks in jail. Ain't nothin' but red
necks down there.

John: Right.

Arthur: All right. Now he gonna talk about all of us, all of our
colored folks . . .

John: No, I didn't say that. I didn't call no names.

Mother: He didn't call no names.

Josephine: He didn't call anybody's name or talk about anybody colored.

John: We was talkin' about getting a job and I was referring
back to the Negroes, the Negroes right now. The Negro, it's

opening up for him a little bit right now, but the time I was referring to the wine heads—what made them become alcoholics was because they couldn't even get an opening.

Josephine: Or they lost their families, you know, because they couldn't get a job and stuff.

John: I'll say this, let me say this—why give a man something when you're going to take it right back from him? That's what I was referring to.

Arthur: Referring to?

John: (To Hammond) You understand what I mean, don't you?

Arthur: All right, let me tell you something then. Now look you was in the service, wasn't you?

John: Yeah, I was in the service.

Arthur: Uh huh. You was the underdog in a way of speaking? But the white boy wasn't. All right then, you know what I was told once when I first got there? We was issued our town passes. We was under this man. He kept all the colored boys. There was six of us. He told us, he told us, "Say, you don't need to go downtown; it ain't nothin' down there." And we went downtown and we made it our business to wear our class A's, and we got down there and there was Miss Anns, Miss White Girl, and they went for heads, they went for colored boys, and the CO found out that a friend of mine, he was actually having friendly conversation with a white girl. He's from the north, he's not prejudice you know, he don't have to cope with this everyday stuff that they do down south. See, it's no racial discrimination up north; it's some, but it's not much you know. Anyhow, the boy was put on a 30 day restriction and also had his town pass taken just for speaking to her.

Josephine: Why they were prejudice!

John: That's what I'm tell you, the base was prejudice. This boy had two years of service, he had two weeks to go, he was getting shipped to France and anyhow he went downtown and saw this white girl. He was riding in a car and he turned around and waved at her. It got back to the base. This white girl told her mother and it got back to the base that this colored boy hollered out of the car and waved at her and she didn't like that. The boy got a 3916.

Hammond: Which was what?

John: I tell you, it stated military life and conduct unbecoming an enlisted man. How can this man be unadaptable to military life with two years of service just for waving at someone?

Margaret: That's what I don't understand about you colored men.

Arthur: What? You ain't got no wind.

John: Let me tell you somethin', that's the way it is in the

service whenever the white man want to get under you, he
don't use this (shaking his fist), he don't use his fist, when he
wants to get under you he used his mind.

Arthur: You can't make it. You can't make it, see, because in
the service they against the Negro anyway.

Josephine: You can't make it out here. These white men, you
just "yes sir" to them and take all kind of stuff off these
white men. You scared to talk to the white women and they
say anything they want to your colored women.

John: That's what I mean. See, I been a lot of "Boy" since I
been in the service, I done been a lot of "Boys." It's "Boy"
this and "Boy" that and "Boy, do this" and "Boy, do that."

Mother: It ain't a lot of stuff, it's a lot of shit. Well, see, I don't
say "Yes, Ma'am" to nobody unless I want to say it.

Arthur: Right here in St. Louis—see, it ain't too much freedom
here but it's better than down there, down south. When I
go down there the company don't mess with me. I go down
there and I do my work and I don't get up on none of my
co-worker, you know.

John: You know why they don't mess with you? They need you.
You hold something, you hold a prize possession. You're a
prize possession down there. The work that you turn out a
day is equal to two of their guys and then still they won't
turn out that. In other words, you're a skilled worker down
there and they ain't gonna let you go, see?

Arthur: But ain't no big deal on it.

John: I know it.

Arthur: But I'm talkin' about as far as prejudice.

John: You're getting underpaid for it too.

Arthur: I been down there, me and John, and we talked to Al
—wanting to have some colored folks down there.

John: I know it. I went down there and when I went into that
office to apply for a job, I didn't see nothin' but white girls.
He had his whole administrative staff, secretaries, the whole
office, the whole administrative personnel workers was
white.

Josephine: Are the Negroes in the background? They in the
back workin' like a dog.

Arthur: And they prejudice down there, you know as far as
that's concerned. You know they don't want to hire no
colored women down there. They hire colored mens, but
they don't want to hire no colored womens. See, what is
wrong there? Well, he done whupped it down to me and
told me like it is. He said, "See, we ain't got nothin' but
white girls workin' here because if I hire some colored girls
here they will all leave me. You can understand that, can't
you?" But we trying to get a union in there now and we're
supposed to go out to the Chase Hotel Saturday night and I
got some guests that is supposed to go out there with me.

You dig tryin' to put that union through down there?

Hammond: I understand, then you'll have some strength behind you.

Arthur: Sho nuff.

Margaret: Is they gonna raise these women on welfare, these committeemen? Is they gonna give these girls any more money?

Hammond: I don't know. Did you talk to them?

Margaret: No, I don't know nothin' about them.

John: But with my skill my brother tried to get me a job down there, but I can't see myself working for $1.25 an hour like my brother say. With the skill that I got—see I'm a specialist in both fields that I'm in and I would like to get paid as a specialist—but, see, if it's nothin' but sweeping the floor as long as I'm a specialist in the field that I'm in I should know more about sweeping the floor than anybody else. It's nothing to sweeping the floor, but I should know little tricks and trade 'bout it. I should know more about upkeeping a floor or something. It's more than just knowing how to do it, and I think that by me taking a job down there at $1.25 an hour with no raise plus if they haven't got a union, I'll be taking an underpaid job. I'm worth more than that.

Arthur: Then why come you don't go down to McDonald like I told you to?

John: Well, at the present, see . . .

Arthur: Naw, it ain't no present, you just don't wanna do nothin'! You don't want nothin', John! What I'm trying to say is you got to crawl before you can walk.

John: Naw, naw, what I'm trying to tell 'em is this. I'm not saying that I don't want to work, but see what it is, I have 32 days after I'm out of the service to take the test. I'm studying. I want to be down at the post office, be a postal clerk, and I'm reading and I'm studying up on this so when I go down there and attempt to take the test, I won't make no fool out of myself. You can't go rush into this. You've go to prepare yourself for everything you do.

Mother: You tryin' to work harder to keep from getting a job than you are tryin to get one.

Arthur: You know what he wants? You say you've got to crawl before you can walk but he don't want to work, he want a brand new car. He want me to buy him a brand new car but yet he don't want to work.

Margaret: But once you get stuck on one of these old jobs, one of these little left hand jobs, you be there the rest of your life.

Mother: He a damn liar. He'll be waiting a hell of a long time if he think I'm gonna buy him a car. He'll be walkin' on those two rubber heels for a hell of a long time.

John: McDonald, all right, what can I do when I get there?

Receiving and checking? You've got to know something out to McDonalds before you can get in.

Arthur: You know what he told me? He said if I go over to McDonald I work six months and get laid off. I told him you ain't got nobody but yourself, bank your money while you're makin' that money.

Hammond: He's tellin' you right.

Arthur: That's what I told him.

John: Well I tell you, I like to party a lot too.

Arthur: Well you can party, but look, you don't get something for nothing. You've got to work for what you want. Look how I come up.

John: But look how long that's been.

Arthur: So what? I was still workin'. The thing wrong with you is you don't want to sacrific nothin'.

John: You don't have to sacrifice when you got it up here (pointing to his head). The white man don't sacrifice.

Arthur: The thing that's wrong with him is that he's been petted all his life.

Mother: You're a damn liar, he ain't been petted. In 1944 my mother worked for $14 a week.

John: Mama, that was a long time ago and at that time you could get by with $14 a week.

Mother: Since you know so damn much why don't you go out and get you a job paying three or four dollars an hour.

John: I have tried. I have went to the best places.

Arthur: Well, don't you come back down there no more where I'm workin' if they got a job open and you don't want it cause it's too small pay.

Josephine: Well what you makin' now?

Mother: He ain't got a damn thing now.

John: I have bills to pay but since I'm not working the people I owe bills to can't get on me now because I'm not working, right? But look here, once I start working anywhere the first thing the white man's gonna say is I hired this Negro and what did he do? He get garnishees on his job and this and this and that, right?

Arthur: That don't make no difference, you ain't makin' shit now and if you get a job you can start payin' some of them off.

John: Now it don't make no sense. If the man fire you for a letter of indebtedness, it's gonna be hard to get a job somewhere else if the man let you go.

Arthur: Naw, it ain't gonna be hard to get nothin'. When you were born, was you walkin'?

John: (laughing) I ain't never crawled. My mama carried me till I was able to walk.

Mother: You're a damn liar I ain't never carried your black ass around.

John: The only time that I'll crawl is when I get to be 175 years old.

Mother: You're a damn lie, you black bastard; you're gonna get your black ass out of here and get some money so you can pay this $122 phone bill or you gonna get your ass out of this house.

John: I tell you, if I don't ever get a job, I'm going to go on and pimp, that's what I'm going to do.

Mother: Naw, they need to go on and send your damn ass to the crazy house.

Arthur: Naw, they ain't got to go do that. I tell you what. One of them women get out there and smother that pussy in your face, you'll cut it loose. (The whole crowd broke up laughing.)

Josephine: You gonna look funny, mother fucker, down on your knees eatin' pussy.

John: Well I'm gonna tell you, I went to the psychiatrist's office one morning. I was in my class A's clean as I could be and I went in and the man, I started talkin' to him. You know what he did? He laid down on the cot and gave me the pencil and paper and he started tellin' me that when he was a little baby he fell down the steps and this and that. (Everybody said he was out of his mind.) But all jokes aside though, I'm not gonna settle for anything less, I want the best.

Hammond: I'm sure you do and all the rest of us want the same thing, but the point is that you can't start off with the best all of the time. Sometimes you've got to start at the bottom and work up.

John: I don't want to work for 90¢ an hour five days a week.

Arthur: Ain't no 90¢ an hour, it's at least $1.25 starting off down there where I work.

John: All right, $1.25 an hour.

Hammond: All right, that's $10 a day, $50 a week.

John: All right, they're gonna take out right? I have no dependents, they're gonna take out right?

Hammond: Yes, but at $50 a week they're not gonna take that much out.

John: But they're gonna take out enough because look . . .

Arthur: Naw, they ain't gonna take out over $6.

John: They are gonna take out because look here I've got bills here, bills there, bills . . .

Josephine: How are you taking care of your bills now, John? How are you paying them now?

John: What? Well, I haven't gotten a letter—I've gotten one letter, a bill for $21 and some odd cents.

Josephine: What you gonna do when you get two or three letters?

Mother: I ain't gonna put out nary a damn thing. They can come here and get every damn thing he got.

Arthur: You know what I'm trying to show him now, he said his credit ain't established where he's goin' now. If she (referring to the mother) lay down and die now, if I lay down and die one day, and he get up in age and he won't find a woman to take care of him. . . .

John: If she lay down and die, if you lay down and die? What could I gain by you laying down and dying?

Arthur: If we lay down and die you couldn't get no credit at all. You couldn't get credit the first. Right now I wouldn't co-sign for a dime for you.

John: See there! See there! And you my flesh and blood, but you wouldn't do that. See there! See there! Don't you know that if you were to die today or tomorrow I would help you out (laughing).

Arthur: You know why I wouldn't co-sign for a dime for you? Cause you're lazy, John. That's what's the matter with you, you're lazy.

Margaret: What's wrong with these men today, anyhow? They lazy, they don't wanna work. They get families, marry these girls and get families and things and then they want to lay around.

John: (laughing) You know why? Because they know if they try to get a job they couldn't get one.

Margaret: I don't understand why it should be that way. I don't think it's actually that way, but most of the men are just like that.

Mother: But you know what? If I had knowed it was gonna be like this I woulda done somethin' to try to keep your black ass in the army and if it don't get no better I'm gonna try to get you back in there now. If he don't get a job that's what's gonna happen.

John: You can't do that, I'm too smart.

Arthur: The only thing wrong with John is that he is lazy and he don't want to work. When I was his age I used to shine shoes to try to make some money. At that time I didn't have no car and I used to get on the bus and ride it to way down on Carr Street and then I had to get a transfer on the way. Then I'd walk way back up on Jefferson and Franklin and start shining shoes and be up there until 9:00. Then I would close the joint up. Then I would walk over to the Y and pick up my little girl, you know.

John: I don't want to go through all of those changes, see. He was crawling (laughing), he did enough crawling for me and him both. That's what I'm trying to say, see? That's gone. Now he done did enough crawling for both of us.

Mother: Look, you ain't been on your own for a long time.

John: I know I ain't on my own and I don't intend to get on my own.

Mother: You a damn lie.

John: And I'm not gonna get on my own until I get ready.

Mother: Well, you just sit up here until you get naked, ragged, and hungry, and then I bet you'll get your black ass out of here and get some work.

John: Yeah, if that happens, yeah, I'll go to work. But as long as I don't have to, I'm not gonna budge out of this house.

Arthur: See?

John: Sure, if you don't have to, why do it? That's like they say "Why do Negroes get out here and steal so much?" 'Cause they haven't got no job. If they had a job they wouldn't steal 'cause they don't have to. All right, why don't I work? 'Cause I don't have to, but when I have to, I am.

Mother: I'm going to see that this bastard get a job if I have to go down there with him.

(Arthur reached into his pocket and pulled out a roll of money which looked to be about $70 or $80 and told John that he had better get out and work so that he could have something like this in his pocket also.)

John: Well, look, you flashin' now but you know what? This time next week you'll be crying.

Arthur: Crying? For what?

John: You got a wife and kids.

Arthur: When this is gone I can go get me some money. My credit is so good that I can go anytime and get me some money. I don't have to worry about it and when I get some I wouldn't give you a dime. I wouldn't buy you nothin'.

John: That's why you bald headed now, running around worryin' about how you gonna pay them Jews.

Arthur: You'll be bald headed before I am. You know what's going to happen to him? He's going to be flat on his back in one of them wooden boxes, that's what's going to happen to him.

John: But, see, if you earn money a young girl ain't gonna do nothin' but go on and get all your money. She gonna mess your head up and get all your money.

Josephine: She ain't gonna do nothin'.

John: Because look, when a man starts working and earning an honest dollar instead of going to his woman and getting it, he gonna realize the value of a dollar.

Hammond: Well why can't you do both of them since you're bent on going that route?

John: Huh? Well, I'm not going that route. I can, but they won't give me no job so I just have to stick to the one (getting money from the women) (laughing). I tried to teach my brother but see, he's married.

Hammond: What are you going to do when the babes play out.

Josephine: The same thing that he's doing now.

Hammond: What's that?

Josephine: Not shit.

330 BEHIND GHETTO WALLS

John: Look here, God created woman.

Josephine: God created woman to be free.

John: It's only two things I like. I want me a 1965 Cadillac and some dead presidents (money) in my pocket.

Josephine: And do you know how he is going to get it? He gonna be a pimp. And he gonna have to be a freak cause all them pimps is freakish and you know what he gonna have to do? He gonna have to be doin' a whole lot of this. (She opened her mouth and made a licking motion with her tongue.) He's going to have to eat pussy a while. And you talking about a job? You gonna have to have a job if you gonna be a pimp cause you gonna have to get your prostitutes out of jail.

John: They got theyselves in there didn't they? Well they can just get theyselves out.

Josephine: You gonna get 'em out.

John: Naw I ain't either. So I lose one so what?

Josephine: What you talkin' about lose one? You ain't got shit now. You ain't got none to begin.

John: You know what, if they get in jail you know what I'll do? I'll fire 'em right then.

Josephine: What you talkin' about fire, you ain't gonna fire nobody. You ain't got 'em in the first place, when you think you got 'em another man's got 'em all the time. Ain't no woman's got just one man. It don't go that way. You don't know what you talkin' about, John.

Mother: That punk don't know shit.

Arthur: I told you he wasn't ready, he don't know what he's doin'. He's a fool. If I had a babe out on the corner and she got in jail, I'd have to get her out because that's my bread and butter.

John: I don't really want to go that route. I tell you what I want to do . . .

Arthur: You ain't ready, John. You been in the service and traveled around, I thought that when you came back out you would be into something but you ain't ready. I keep tellin' you you don't know nothin', you ain't shit, you don't know what's goin' on. He don't know where it is.

John: I tell you what, I tell you what I wanna do. I'm working on a big investment right now which I haven't invested a dime out of my pocket right now because I don't have a dime to invest. This little old registered nurse, you understand, she really goes for me, and I haven't seen her but once, but just by my conversation with her on the phone. I heard her bankbook was longer than the Jefferson bus that runs out there. She's driving a 1964 Chevrolet, black and white. And all I want is me a job and let her keep me going. That's all I need.

Arthur: Well, if she's got all of that then you don't need to work.

John: Well see, this broad she's older than I am. It makes me feel that I should be out working, too. I just can't see taking her dry, taking her money. Look, mama want me to work but I can't see myself taking money from one woman and giving it to another (laughing). I can't see myself getting money from one woman and then giving it over to another. No stuff, that's just the way that it is. She's older than me, much older than me. I said, "Look, baby, I ain't got no money, and I'm expensive and I like to have women give me nice things, clothes and money, to show me that they appreciate me."

Arthur: Well I tell you, the type of clothes that you wanna wear that money will be used up in a little or no time at all.

John: So what, she's making more. She can get plenty more where that came from.

Arthur: That little $100 a week that she's making ain't shit. She give you the money and you ain't gonna do nothin' but go downtown and buy some old cheap-ass clothes. I can go down to Wilkinsons right now and buy me a $250 suit and a pair of Bannister shoes at the same time.

John: Let me tell you how it was before I went to Uncle Sam. I had rags from way back. I had nothin' but the best. I gave all my rags away cause I din't think that I was coming back and all that I didn't give away I lost in a crap game. I'm gonna tell it like it is rather than tell it like it 'twas. Oh I was clean, and me working part time after school but I wasn't making enough money to wear the kind of clothes that I was wearing at the time. My womens was helpin' me.

Mother: You a damn lie.

John: Who?

Mother: You. Your auntie bought them for you

John: Who? Who bought them Bannisters that I got for Easter? Who bought them Bannisters that I had for my Easter present? Them black ones? Who paid $37.67 for 'em? Go on and tell it, who was it?

Arthur: You didn't.

John: I know I didn't. Go and tell him who paid $185 for that grey sharkskin that I had? Who did it?

Arthur: Your woman didn't. Aunt Emma did because I saw her paying the bills on it.

John: That's what you thought.

Arthur: I ain't thought nothin', I seen her payin' it.

Mother: She sure did. I can show you right now where she helped pay for that suit.

John: And my Bannisters?

Mother: No, she didn't bought them. Geraldine bought them for you.

John: (laughing loudly, clapping his hands and jumping up and down) All right then!

Arthur: You might be laughing but that wasn't your woman no way.

John: She wasn't? Well, who's was she then?

Arthur: I don't know but she wasn't yours. You ain't nothin' but a fool if that's what you think.

John: All you got to do is get you a old woman. My plan used to be from 25 to 35, now it's from 55 to 65. All over 70 I'm going to kiss on the nose.

Margaret: You mean kiss on the pussy.

Josephine: John, why don't you stop all of that dreaming.

John: Huh? Let me tell you one thing. All you got to do when you get an old woman is just hug her, just make some sweet times and after that she don't want no more (laughing). Watch out, dear Fannie Lou! Just give them hugs and kisses when they want 'em, just give 'em to 'em.

Arthur: You can't work nothin' out, man, cause you don't know how to do nothin'. One of them old women get a hold of you she'll drain you, she'll drain you to death, she'll wear you out cause you don't know how to do nothin'. They'll put you in a world of trouble cause you ain't nothin' but a ignorant scobe.

John: No, they won't do that to me. I'll make out a schedule. This is Maybelle, she's 65. This is her day, one day a month. This is Bessie, two weeks later, she's got one day too. This is . . .

Arthur: You got to work three hours with them old women, and you'll be so tired and you still got to keep it like that.

(Arthur placed his hand at his crotch, and with the other hand he raised his index finger indicating an erect penis. The crowd let out a roar of laughter.)

Hammond: I hear you.

Arthur: You've got to work about three hours but after ten minutes you will look like this.

(Arthur held up a curved finger indicating a limp penis, and the crowd broke out in an even louder roar of laughter.)

Arthur: You can't keep on no hard, John, for more than ten minutes because you don't know what to do, you ain't ready. After ten minutes your dick would be soft as cotton.

John: Then I would wait until morning to work out.

Josephine: John, you ain't doin' nothin' but dreamin', baby.

John: I'm not dreamin!

Mother: One of these old women will wear your black ass out.

John: I'm not dreaming, but I've got to get me a young woman to keep myself going. But like I say it's only a joke. I'm not really going to do any pimping but if I am going to pimp I'm not going to wear myself out on all them women. But like I say I can't see my woman out working for eight hours a day and give me the money, then I give it to her (his mother).

Mother: You're a damn lie. If you get some money, you gonna give me some. (The crowd began laughing again.)

John: I would get out and get me a job and give my mother my share and have my woman give the money back to me. That way I'm not taking the money out of one woman's pocket and giving it to another.

Mother: He'd better git his ass out of here and try to do something to take care of this telephone bill.

John: I'm gonna take care of it. You know how I'm gonna take care of it? I'm going out on the west coast.

Mother: I thought when he come out of the army he's be done learned something.

Arthur: I thought that he would learn something too, I thought that he would learn something when he got out of the service but that scobe don't know nothin' about life. You don't know nothin' about life, scobe.

Josephine: John, the dream pimp.

John: Dream pimp? I'm not gonna be no pimp, I'm not gonna be no pimp. All jokes aside, I'm not gonna be no pimp. But I tell you one thing, I am gonna get me a good woman who's got something so when I get in trouble I can fall back on her. Like this girl over here (pointing to Josephine) I wouldn't go with her for her money.

Margaret: That's right, you'd have to give some to her.

Josephine: All you want, John, is for some girl to cock her leg open so that you can fall in there and fuck any time you want to and then get up and say thank you. Don't no nigger fuck me unless he got $10 or $12 to give me before he starts. I don't come that easy.

Arthur: If you not gonna go with a woman for her money, what have you got to give her?

John: Self.

Arthur: What?

John: Self.

Arthur: Shit, like that girl over there, if you go with her and don't give her any money then I know there's something going on. If you're not giving any of that money up then I know you're down there eating some of that maidenhead.

Josephine: Yes, I'll let him do that all day long, but I ain't letting no nigger fuck me just cause I wanna fuck because I don't ever wanna fuck that bad. And if the feeling hits me I can go upstairs and jack off this pearl tongue (clitoris) all day long and the longer that I pull on it the better it feels. If I don't feel like going all the way up there I can just cross my legs real tight like this and start shaking my leg back and forth like this and bust my nuts ten time while I'm sitting here talking to you and you'd never know a thing about it. I don't need no nigger to put a black ass dick in me.

Margaret: Me either. I'll go upstairs to the bathroom and jack off in a minute.

Josephine: And anyhow, John, I've got so much pussy down here that if you got in it I wouldn't even know you were there. You couldn't even tickle these sides.

Hammond: You know what they say about those little women.

John: Yeah, I know what they say, big girl, big cock.

Hammond: Little girl, all cock.

Josephine: I don't know about the rest of 'em but that's true with me. You'd have to have one all the way down to here (pointing to her knee) before I could even feel it, and then it had to be this big around. Ain't none of you all got enough dick here for me. That boy over there (Arthur) his dick is short and fat. That boy there (Hammond) his dick is long but it's not round enough. And John, your dick is just too short, period. There's nothing that you could do for me and if you could I wouldn't let you no how. You too damn young and ignorant. Now that boy walkin' along there, he is tall and thin. Now he's got a great big dick, that's just the kind that I need.

Hammond: You can't be serious, girl. There's no way in the world for you to tell the size of a man's penis just by looking at him.

Josephine: Shit, nigger, as many niggers as I have fucked I can look at a man right away and tell what size dick he's got.

Hammond: You would have to give that a test over a large number of men.

Josephine: I have.

Hammond: Oh, I see.

John: Let me tell you something. I'm going to keep a lot of broads, you can believe that, and I ain't going to eat no maidenhead either. I'll whip a broad's head if she don't come across with some of that ass fast enough. Yes sir.

Arthur: But you ain't gonna be no pimp.

John: No, I ain't gonna be no pimp.

Arthur: Well there ain't no pimps no more that don't do that.

John: Well I ain't gonna do that and I ain't gonna be no pimp neither. It's like I said, I want a broad that's good to me and that's got a job and can help me out and when I get in trouble she can come along and get me out of a strain, you understand. And as long as I got my job I'm not losing anything, because the pimps lose. They happy for a month and then they sad the next month.

Arthur: What you want is a woman who'll go out and work eight hours a day and at the end of the week bring all the money to you.

John: I don't want no woman like that, I wouldn't want a woman like that.

Arthur: And she be out there hussling and if she didn't bring no money home then you'd want to whip her ass.

John: I don't want no woman like that. I don't want no woman like that.

Arthur: I tell you, you ain't ready, boy, you don't know nothin' about life.

John: All jokes aside about the pimp, but I want to have me a girl, but she has got to have something.

Josephine: Don't worry about them girls.

Mother: They ain't worryin' about your black ass.

Josephine: Don't think you gonna lay down that money in your pocket and then fuck and then when you get up don't give the girl nothin', that ain't gonna work.

Arthur: What she's tellin' you is right, John. I thought that when you went into the service you'd learn something but you ain't learned shit.

John: What that scobe (Arthur) is talking I don't wanna hear. He's talking that old talk that every time you lay down you've got to have some money in your pocket, but I ain't that way. I feel this way about it, (singing) "I have had my fun if I never get no more . . ." (to Josephine) Hey, baby, if your old man come in with $10 ain't he gonna be able to get what you got?

Josephine: No he ain't.

John: Well you ain't gonna be my woman then.

Josephine: Ain't nobody gonna fuck me for nothin'. If you lay down with me, you got to come up with some bread and that's all there is to that, John. You can't do that here.

John: I know I can't do that, that's why I'm looking for somebody that's got somethin' so that I can do it.

Josephine: You misunderstand me. If a man gives me somethin' then maybe later on he comes back and I give him something, but the way you talkin' about, if you give me ten you're gonna want back 20 and that ain't gonna work.

John: That's the only way I play it. Look here if I give a woman a quarter I want 50¢ back.

Josephine: See there.

John: That way I'm gonna be twice as good as she is.

Josephine: See there.

John: (Laughing) That's the way it is baby.

Josephine: You just ain't right, John.

John: If I give a girl a quarter today, tomorrow I want 50¢ back—that's just life. Preservation, self-preservation, self-preservation is the first law of nature, right? No, but seriously, I just sit down there and blow (talk) with them and tell them what I'm going to do. I tell them that I'm going to be a pimp, but I'm really not. I come down with my slides (beat-up old shoes) on. They say what you doin'? I say I'm pimpin', baby. I ain't going' nowhere, I sleep all day long . . .

Josephine: And ain't got a dime.

John: And I ain't got a dime wondering where my next half meal is going to come from.

> *Arthur:* You ought to stop all that stuff, John. You walkin'
> around here just like you is now talkin' that shit all day
> long, wishin' you had a suit on and a tie and Bannister
> shoes but you gonna be just like you is now if you don't
> get your ass out of here and get you a job one of these days.
> *Hammond:* He's telling you right, John, you should look out
> for yourself and try to look out for home.
> *John:* (Laughing and breaking up) I am trying to look out for
> myself.
> *Arthur:* Man, you ought to stop that lyin'. You the onlyest nig-
> ger I seen in the service that's been out longer than you
> been in: you just a God damn lie. This nigger come home
> every time he had a opportunity all during the week, every
> week-end, trying to find some pussy. Shit, he stayed at home
> more than he did in the service.
> *Josephine:* When he first came home out of the army he came
> in here talkin' about buying a piece of pussy. I told him,
> "Man, you at home now, you don't have to do that. It's
> somebody around here gonna give you some."

For the next year Hammond saw John Martin fairly often and got to
know several of his friends, particularly his main running buddy, Albert.
Albert was a high school senior who was doing well in his school work
and who subsequently went on to college. They spent a great deal of time
together, competed for the same girls, and experimented with various
ways of living the high life.

The following winter Hammond arranged with John to maintain a
diary, indicating what he had done each day, where, and with whom.
John started on this task with great enthusiasm and accumulated approximately ten days of "daily activity sheets." However, he made the mistake
of leaving them at a girl friend's house, and when she got angry with him
she would not give them back. Hammond had lent him a tape recorder
so that he could fill out his daily activity records by dictating tapes. Having lost the records, John sought to reconstruct from memory his activities
during the last ten days of January.

> Friday morning I went up to this girl named Jane's house.
> That's where we all get together and buy drinks. This is for
> the kids that don't go to school, they all buy drinks and play
> records, just live it up, you know, do anything you want to do,
> until about 4:00. So I didn't stay, I went up to the school to
> play around with the girls, walked the halls, then I came home
> that Friday night and got plastered, drunk, and as I recall
> nothing happened.
>   That Saturday I went over to this girl named Sarah's house.
> She live in Igoe. I been trying to make this broad, you know,
> use my game on her, but the broad is a little bit too fast in one
> way because her mother is coaching her. And if I can work

out an angle where I could snow her mother instead of her—at the same time I'll be snowing her—but I'll have to snow her mother to get my game over on her. But I can't recall anything that happened real serious last weekend.

That Monday nothing happened, just goofed around, went over to see Sarah a couple of times. We talked and talked and talked. I called her on the phone a couple of times. Then Thursday, when the school kids was out of school (a holiday), I went down to this girl Mary's house, the broad I'm supposed to be going with. She cooked breakfast for me. After we got through eating breakfast, around 11:00, we watched TV, at least she did, but I didn't want to look at those programs. She threw her thigh, her left thigh across my lap, and her arms around me and was watching television, and I could see these pretty beige thighs. She tempted me and I told her if she wanted to continue to watch television that she would have to refrain from her motivations. Anyway she pulled me to her and kissed me, and I automatically laid on her and started the circle motion. I took her upstairs and we got in the bed and I took off my pants, just going to get in the bed and play with her you know. Before I got in the bed I saw the broad didn't have nothing on so I got back out of bed and pulled my clothes off and got naked. We was both nude, onliest thing she had on was a housecoat. So we lay up in the bed and fucked until about quarter to twelve and we got up and we washed up and I went to the store and came back and she prepared lunch. I came home and I called her and then I went right over to Sarah's house about 8:30 that evening.

That Saturday nothing happened. This week, Monday—or was it Sunday—Sunday, yeah, I indulged in a little relationship, sexual relationship, with this girl upstairs on the fifth floor, her name is Virginia. It was only an act for money. The broad gave me $5.00, then she turned around that evening and gave me $10, and so I went back over to see Sarah because that little broad has actually got me going, and I sat there and I bullshitted around with them for a while and I came back home.

At this time tonight it is now 3:35 in the morning. Well tonight, earlier tonight, or earlier this morning I should say, around 2:00 a.m. me and Virginia we started again and I went back up there around 12:05. I sat there and I bullshitted around over there. My aim was to go there and get some money because the $5 that I had had, I had goofed it up with Sarah, not spending it on her but just spending it around freely to get the broad's attention in some way. This time I went back up to Virginia's house and it was 2:00 when we started with our relationship. She was laying on the couch, I knew that if I kept messing with her I would get her in a position where she would want to screw, I was laying on the couch and she asked me could she lay down with me. I told her she could if she wanted to so she laid there and I commenced to rub her thighs, then she rolled over face to face and I took my hand, I rubbed her cheeks, I was for hours rubbing these big yellow cheeks, she was moaning and telling me to stop and about that time she had about six inches of tongue down my mouth moaning and she was getting flusterated and she told me, she say, "Are you going to fuck me tonight?" I say, "No" and she say, "Well, why you make me suffer in this way?" And at the same time my dick was getting hard, and she grabbed my dick and she just squeezed that motherfucker and she told me, she say, "Please, I need it," and then at this time we went into the back room .

I didn't want to get on the bed because I didn't want to make any noise to wake up her mother so we got on the floor, she put a pillow down to rest her head on and we got on the floor, she put one leg on the chest of drawers in her room and the other one on the end of the bed and I fell between her thighs and we fucked and we fucked and we fucked. We fucked in so many positions it wasn't even funny. To me it was just a job. And I went on and we fucked and we fucked and the broad was coming so frequently, so fast, anyway the broad was coming like water running over a dam, and at this time I changed position by putting the calf of her leg upon my shoulder and I buried my dick as far in her cunt as I could get it and my balls were slapping her ass, making a sloshy sound.

When I got through with the broad I got up and she say, "When can I get this again?" I said, "Never." See, I have to play this role for one simple reason. If the broad expect to get this all the time, and finds out that I'm enjoying it just as much as she is, then she wouldn't be pouring to me like she is, she wouldn't give me like she was. Anyway I told the broad I was getting ready to go. I had to get up in the morning and take this tape recorder back, so the broad said she would leave her key down to my house tomorrow morning when she leave for school and that if I wanted anything in the house I could go up and get it. So I told the broad that I wanted a soda. The broad gave me a cold soda, I came on downstairs and now I'm drinking some soda and some Seagram's VO and I'm high as I want to be. Well, I might have left something out, but if I did it wasn't nothing too much of importance, just everyday routine.

A few days later John continued to dictate, this time with Hammond present.

Today the first place I went to was down to my sister's house, I got there around 2:00 and I left there around 8:00 that evening. I watched the kids while she went to the hospital.

While I was there I got on the phone and I was talking to this broad Mary, that's Albert's girl he's trying to rap to. But the way she's going about it she likes to talk to me more than she do him. I don't know what's going on, but I tried to shoot her down. He's tried to go with the girl and she digging him and me too, see, because I went with the broad before he did.

She called me and we started bullshitting and she kept asking me when I was going to come out. I said that I wasn't coming out, cause it was too far. See, she has this record of mine and she keeps reminding me that she's got it, you know, and hoping that I'll come out and get it.

We were talking about sex mainly. I was asking her if she had had any relationships with boys before and she stated that she had and I was wondering how long it was since she had this relationship. I was just beating around the bush to see if the broad was really screwing, see, which she is but she hasn't been screwed in quite a while and I believe this is what the broad wants to do. Albert, he kind of prolong his processing of a broad. With me, I'm pretty fast, either I get it or I don't, no hard feelings behind it, because either way you go, either she is going to screw or she ain't.

She wants to screw him to tell the truth. I know this by her conversation. I asked her, if it got bad outside and Albert was out there, where would he stay, and she say he would stay at her house, see. I say, "Where would he sleep, on the couch?" She say, "No, with me." And I asked her was she serious and she said, "Yeah." She stay with her mother, but probably what it would have been, he'd of probably stayed on the couch and she'd of probably snuck down there.

Did you have any other phone calls while you were there?

Yeah, Virginia called me and asked me did I need any more money. She asked me how much money I had and I told her that I had some change. She said, "Oh well, I got $4.75 I will give you when you come home." But I never did get it because I didn't go up there.

How old is Virginia?

She's 16. She got kicked out of school, her mother take her back. She gets smart with the teachers, man. She go to school when she get ready, man. When she get there she got a lot of lip, you know. I believe that the broad is trying to case me, she likes to be here with me in the day time, you know, she likes being around me. I don't know if the girl is a fuck fanatic or what, man, but she likes to screw. She told me one time if she could just touch me she would nut all over herself. Yeah, and that has been true.

How did you first meet her?

I was with a whole lot of friends. I dug her coming upstairs one night. I had on this jersey, this red jersey, it was black and had red going down the front of it, and I said, "Say, baby, what's your name?" and she kept going up the steps. So I call her and I say, "Next time you come by knock on my door when you come back" and she said, "Okay," so she knocked but I wasn't there because I was just messing around with her, you know, just ball a game down to her. And we got together on a BST—in other words the Bull Shit Trip, see—and ever since then it's been mellow.

I mean the broad was messing with this bull dagger, one of her friends was a bull dagger. I believe I was high one night and I think I saw this broad kiss her man, I'm not for sure. I asked her did she kiss her, she say, "No," she say, "Alice tried to kiss me." Yeah, she said she tried but she wouldn't let her. She say Alice had been trying to get her to go along with her program and she can't see it that way. She say no girl can't do nothing for her and she said what was taking her so long about going with me was Alice. Alice was telling her things against me, and I noticed by when I got up there Alice would hate for me to come up around her, you know.

How old is Alice?

About 16. Virginia was telling me that Alice was doing it to this broad, their friend, Alice's running partner. A friend of mine was going with this girl and he never fucked her, her and Alice was good partners and Alice was spending the night with this girl and she would do exactly everything Alice would say. And Virginia say that her and Alice snuck in her house some time, kissing, you know, and carrying on. And I came in at the right time, I guess. It takes a while before you meet the guys. The guys like to wait around and observe you for a while, and I think that by me moving fast and moved in on her, this stopped the process of Alice and her, you know.

And I ran my game down to her. One night I knew I could do something to her. This is what really made her have confidence in me—I told her I wouldn't do anything to her the first night that I met her anyway, which I would of, but the broad had been drinking plus she had told me she was on the rag, man. That's the onliest thing that stopped me, but I didn't let her know that. I said, "I wouldn't do nothing to you anyway because you is under the influence of alcohol and I don't want you saying I took advantage of you" I say, "Because I think a whole lot of you," you know, just my bullshit game. She fell for it and next thing I know I have my way with her.

Three or four days later we was on the couch one night and her mother was in the back room asleep and I jammed on the couch and man her cunt was tight, man, it was real tight. She had been fucked before but she hadn't been fucked in quite some time. Her mother was in the back room with the door shut asleep.

What do you think would have happened if her mother had found you?

Well, I always look at it this way, when I found out how old her mother's boy friend was I didn't really give a damn, man. He's about 17, 18, he's younger than I am.

Do you think her mother knows that you are trimming her?

Yeah, I have stayed up there all night and fell asleep, her mother has awakened me and told me to go lay in her bed, that she's going to work. I lay in her mother's bed, her mother cover me up and then she go on to work around about 8:00 that Saturday morning. Her mother act like she dug me from the git go. When I told her my age, she looked at me and I wondered why. I thought she was thinking I was too old for her daughter. And she is so nice to me, she would buy me beer and always want me to come up there and sit and bullshit, and then I have to start playing a kiddish game—you know, acting like I wasn't mature enough for my age—to get her mother off my back.

Because I could just see what would happen, because her mother got in the way or I would have to jam her too. I'm going to tell you, I'd of jammed that broad because she is the one that's got all the financial situation covered. I would of jammed her instead of the other cat. She going out buying him nice clothes and things she would have been buying me. She bought the cat a $75 watch for a birthday present or Christmas present and he been fucking with her ever since.

At first Virginia enjoyed fucking but she didn't act as other girls did, she didn't carry on them moans and groans until after I had fucked her about five or six times. I don't know if she was trying told her feelings back or what but that's when she really started getting into the act of it. I used to fuck her every day, sometimes twice and three times a day, but I seen myself wearing myself out fucking this broad every day and sometimes two and three times a day. She wanted to have it all the time.

Some people say that you can fuck for 15 minutes and you through but I remember the time my dick would get real hard so it just hurt. Now it don't do that any more, it just be throbbing and hurting, it doesn't do that any more, it just get hard you know. I just go and get that pussy, man. This is my aim towards any woman. I don't have to get my motherfucking nut. I want to please her, man I *have* to please her, see. And I get on this broad, man, I might just fuck around with her and fuck her and I will feel my nut coming and I will stop and just squeeze, you know, just till it go back down. In other words when I'm fucking her, I ain't got my mind on fucking at all and I don't get no feeling whatsoever. I don't have my mind on it, and then when I really put my mind on it and my mind is in her mood and how she moving and the movements of her body, see, then I go and get my nut.

After I get my first nut, oh man, it takes me forever to get my second. It takes me forever and the broad is in for a naturally good fucking, I ain't bullshitting. I just stay there just as long as she wants to. If you make a broad feel good the first time you do something for her, they know what they in for when they see you. They can look at you—like you look at a broad who looks real good, and you didn't even fuck this broad before and being around her your dick can get hard just thinking about the times you've had, and you say, "Well that broad sure enough going to throw a good fuck if I can get her to fuck me." And that's the way she probably thinks, see, it's no different. Just like we sit here and we try to scheme on a broad to get that pussy, she's scheming to get what she can out of us. She wants to fuck just as much as we do, but a broad has a certain extent of pride where she won't come out and ask you for it like you would, see. But she would beat around the bush and let you know that she want to fuck and if you can't take it from there, you lost.

 I can make her so hot and leave her alone till where she will just come out and ask me. At one time she wouldn't, cause she would let me fuck around with her to the point to where I was going to get it—you know, I tell her to take her clothes off—but now, see, since I'm working my game on her I got her where I want her. I could play that I don't want that pussy. If she found out I was enjoying it then she wouldn't be beholden to me. So this is what I got to look out after and as long as I can get her to beg me for this dick and make her suffer . . . I believe that when a broad wants to fuck bad, the longer you prolong it and the more you make her suffer, when she get it she appreciate it more.

She told my mother one time I fucked her, man. I didn't know about it. She told my mother that I could actually really fuck, you know. She told my mother this! She actually told my mother this, and she told my mother that I could fuck real good! My mother, I don't know if she was shocked or what. She'd sit around the house and say, "Whew." She'd grab her cunt and start, "I'm hot, I wish John would come home so he could give me some of that good dick." It got so comical to my mother, you know, till she must have enjoyed this because it was something odd. No other girl had done this, see, and carried on the way she did. My mother said that she had a white liver, now what that is I don't know. My mother say usually when people got white livers they like to fuck a lot, you know, and the person that they marry don't live too long, she say, because she be too much for them. She say, "If a man has a white liver and likes to fuck a lot if he married a girl he would kill her eventually." Now how much of this is true, I don't know. I hope like hell I ain't got no white liver because I *love* to do it.

You see to me there's no color scheme, a broad is a broad. The only thing a white broad got different on me, on my kind of girls, and that's the majority of the whites talk proper. If they don't talk proper they from down South and they got a southern accent. That's the only difference. Now as far as making love to a white broad I haven't experienced that and I don't think they can love as good as our girls can, see. I mean, I believe Negroes, everything he does he bes the best at it. He was among the best. I think the Negroes inherited this from our forefathers, we had to inherit it because the Negroes have to be better than the white man, twice or maybe three times as good as the white to get a job equal to him or get in sports equal to him, so therefore a Negro has got the advantage in equalization over the white man in most everything he do. I mean a white man can go out and he can train for maybe six or seven years and a Negro get out there and say I'm gonna whip him, a boxer, for instance, or some kind of sports.

Now like me, it'll hurt me to my heart if a broad tell me I didn't screw her right because this is something I believe, this is something I believe. I believe in this. I mean to some guys sex is a serious thing to play with.

But as I recall as I was coming up and I was fucking this broad she was 18 and I was only 15. I had just learned how to get my nuts off, you know, and I was on the broad and I started humping and I got my nut and got up, you know. So the first time she didn't say too much about it. The second time I got ready to get up and the broad took her knife—she actually had a knife the second time I got up—and she said, "You motherfucker you, you move I'll kill you." And that's way the about women, that's what learned me about women. And my cousins used to tell me they said, "You know too much," like somebody said when you were coming up, "You know too much for your own age." Plus when you on a woman you don't work out for yourself, you gotta please them too and I wasn't self-conscious of that.

Do you think the average Negro man thinks that way?

Naw, because if it was there wouldn't be so much of this wrong doing, man. Somebody ain't kicking them covers right, Jack. You got to look at it that way. He's not kicking those covers 'cause if he was there wasn't no way in the world his wife would go out and have somebody else. Especially in the teenagers coming up now, they have to get the pussy and they have to rush and they be mad as a motherfucker if they don't get they nut. They fucking in the hallways, they get down there, they fuck and fuck and fuck, they get they nut and they through. They little dick get soft and they through, you see what I mean? And the girl might have got no satisfaction, not satisfied at all.

You know I've really got self-conceited on this I've sort of formed a complex about this, I'm conceited man. This broad, a friend of mine's sister, I was fucking her and sneaking and doing it, you know so he wouldn't find out. And she went with exactly three guys and you know they wasn't getting that pussy, I was the one that was fucking her. She wouldn't give it to them. She's pregnant now, I got her out of my hooks when I went to the service. But she was going with my brother-in-law and I took her from him and he was going with her for about four months and I was fucking her the four months he was going with her. The only thing he had going in his corner was that he might dress nice and he was in the letterman's club in school, shit like this.

But I don't give a damn, you can be a brute, Boone, you can be a brute. You can be a wino right off the corner and if that wino can satisfy that college girl and a professor cannot satisfy this girl whatsoever, who do you think she's gonna fall to when it comes to making her feel good? Who do you think she gonna fall to?

To the wino.

Right, because she's getting the satisfaction, she's getting satisfied out of this, right?

About this time John took a regular job at which he worked steadily, turning over a good portion of his earnings to his mother. He no longer had all day to sow his wild oats, but he still had evenings and the weekends. For two or three months he and Albert had been experimenting with marijuana. They liked the way it made them feel, either by itself or in combination with alcohol, and John appreciated the fact that it made him slower to reach orgasm when he was with his girlfriends.

One Friday evening late in March Hammond joined them about 9:30 for a night out. Earlier in the evening John and Albert had started smoking grass and drinking. A third young man, Malcolm, was with them. Malcom was not as close to John and Albert as they were to each other, but they knew him quite well. He had dropped out of school and was working steadily in a service station. Unlike John, Malcolm was generally very quiet and not interested in the pimping style that John was cultivating. As we will see, however, he was not quite the "hayseed" that his dress and demeanor at first suggested.

The evening started, as it often did when Hammond met with John and his friends, with a trip to a carry-out Chinese food restaurant near the project where they could buy large quantities of fried rice with pork or shrimp for a small amount of money. If they were more flush, they would buy egg foo yung or other Chineses dishes. John insisted that they stop at a liquor store first; he collected money from each of the other men to get together enough for a half pint of scotch. John was high on marijuana and alcohol and delayed the group at the liquor store and in the restaurant. He mixed up the money he had collected, had a hard time finding enough to pay the bill in the restaurant, and kept accusing the others of holding out on him. He had made a scene in the restaurant, arguing with the waitress and taking up a great deal of her time, but because he was so obviously high rather than mean, no one took offense at his behavior.

Back at the apartment John and Albert complained while they ate about how they had wasted the evening because they had not gotten any of their broads. After they talked about girls for a while, Albert decided to call Sally, his regular girlfriend. In the course of their conversation, Sally told Albert that she thought she was pregnant because her period was two weeks late. She told him to get ready, because she thought he was going to be a father. He replied over and over again, "Uh huh, uh huh, uh huh, I don't want to hear that shit." He told her that she had been pregnant before and she knew how to get rid of a baby and she had better start planning to do it because he was not ready to get married. He wanted to go to college. He was not going to marry her and then leave her behind for somebody else to be fucking, he said. At this point, John started sounding on Albert, saying "That pussy's everybody's now," that anyone could have have Sally now and for the next nine months no one would have to take blame but Albert. Albert seemed upset, but John was not daunted. He tried to persuade Sally to send Mary, one of his girlfriends, who was staying with Sally, to the apartment. In the end, Albert hung up without either girl promising to join them.

John continued to tease Albert about becoming a daddy, and Albert continued to maintain that Sally would not have the baby. Then John and Malcolm both started telling Albert that the baby might not be his anyway, but Albert maintained that he was the only one who had intercourse with her in the past month. Albert finally told Hammond that he was "crazy about that girl" and that if she would not have an abortion he would probably marry her, though he hated to think about that possibility.

The marijuana and the scotch were taking their effect and finally John went to sleep. Albert and Malcolm continued to talk about girls and Albert began to describe his sexual history, mentioning by name about ten girls with whom he had had intercourse. This led to a discussion of venereal disease, and Albert said he had gonorrhea three times in the past two years. He had become quite expert at diagnosing the symptoms and at obtaining treatment. Malcolm was not as experienced but had "the claps" once. Albert felt that he was lucky because he had never had syphilis, a disease he considered to be much more dangerous.

Malcolm said he had gotten "crabs" (lice) from a girl once and Albert remembered that one of John's cousins also had them. It was assumed that one got crabs from intercourse with a girl who had them, and Malcolm pointed out that one of the reasons he knew his father was promiscuous was because he often bought a blue ointment that is used to treat crabs. This conversation went on until about 1:00 a.m. when John began to wake up.

At this point Albert happened to notice Hammond's tape recorder and suggested that they set it up and do some "joaning" on it. Albert put the recorder in the middle of the floor and he, Malcolm and Hammond arranged their chairs around it next to the couch where John was still resting. The contest started with each person contributing bits and pieces from various "toasts" but then rapidly moved to a fairly organized game of "the dozens." Both Albert and John prided themselves on their ability to tell jokes, joan, and play the dozens. It was unclear whether they knew that Malcolm was also an accomplished performer. Perhaps Albert thought they could show him up, but they discovered that he was not at all "lame" at the game.

Performance in this game is as much a matter of gestures, intonations, voice change, and rhythm as it is of words. It is not possible in print to do more than indicate very roughly and in pale colors the quality of the game. All through the performance there was uproarious laughter by the speakers and their audience. Occasionally the performance was interrupted until they could get control of themselves and start again. As the tape was started, Malcolm sang a few lines.

> *Malcolm:*
> Down in New Orleans where everything is fine,
> All of them cats just drinking that wine.
> Drinking that mess till broad daylight . . .
> *Albert:*
> Motherfucker in that old tree.
> Walking through the jungle with my dick in my hand,
> I'm the baddest motherfucker in the jungle land.
> *Malcolm:*
> Well the doctor told Shine,
> 'I'm gonna cut your dick off your ass,'
> And Shine said,
> 'Doctor, is that all you gonna do?'
> The doctor said,
> 'Hell no, your nuts go too.'
> *Albert:*
> Well I fucked your mama in a barrel of flour.
> She shit tea cakes for a half an hour.

Malcolm:

> I fucked your mama between two splinters.
> I hung my dick and it stayed all winter.

These lines were said in very strict cadence; when one speaker finished, the other picked up the cadence without missing a beat. Thus the verbal form is that of a competition but there is also implicit cooperation so that the beat is maintained as each participant takes the floor.

Malcolm:

> I remember in the old days I didn't have no dick,
> I fucked your mama with a walkin' stick.

Albert:

> I member in the old days I didn't have no dick,
> I fucked your mama with a walkin' stick.
> She had 99 babies and a kangaroo;
> Now tell me, motherfucker, who is you?
> I took your mammie to Niagra Falls,
> Wouldn't nothin' fuck her but a broke dick dog.

John:

> (Waking up enough to participate)
> I saw your mammie run across the field.
> I shot her in the ass with a chesterfield.

Albert:

> Well I fucked your mama on a dime
> Couldn't nobody get nothin' but me and
>   Frankenstein.
> I fucked your mama on a red hot heater
> I missed her cock and scorched my peter.

Malcolm:

> I fucked your mama in a pot of rice.
> The baby jumped out shootin' dice.
> One shot seven and one shot eleven,
> Ain't nare one of them black motherfuckers
>   goin' to heaven.

John:

> I saw your mama on Tenth and Grand
> Sellin' her pussy to a peanut man.
> I saw your mammie on Tenth and Garr
> Sellin' her pussy to a man named Star.

Here, as everyone laughed, Albert put out his hand to shake with Malcolm in mutual congratulation saying, "Give me one and I'll owe you four." By this he meant "Give me one finger and I'll owe you four fingers"; they shook hands by crooking their index fingers together.

Malcolm:
> I member in old days when times was rough
> Your mama sellin' pussy for a dip of snuff.

John:
> (adlibbing)
> I member back in abdab tacka
> Your mama sellin' pussy for a little tobacca.

Albert:
> (laughing)
> Give me two and I'll owe you three.

Malcolm:
> Fucked your mama behind the shack
> Couldn't nobody get none but me and my rat.

John:
> Fucked your mama on a red hot heater
> Missed her pussy and scorched my peter.

Malcolm:
> The Mississippi River is wide and muddy.
> Your mama's cock is deep and bloody.

Albert: (slapping his leg.) Goddam, I got to play that one back
I got to play that one again, I got to play that one back.

Malcolm:
> I seen your mama in the white folks' yard
> Greasing her pussy with some coal lard.

Albert:
> I saw your mammie layin' in the grass
> Eatin' shit out a dead man's ass.

John:
> I saw your mama sittin' on a track
> Eatin' shit out a dead man's sack.

Albert:
> (Picking up from John.)
> Along came a train and said choo choo
> You ain't gettin' none of this do do.

He said your mama's . . . He said the Mississippi river is
deep and muddy, your mama's cock is what?

Malcolm:
> Deep and bloody.

Albert:
> Give me two and I owe you three
> Give me two and I owe you three.

(After a lull.) What you doin'? Come on, let's get goin', put
somethin' on there.

Malcolm:
    I fucked your mama behind the log.
    Couldn't nobody get none but me and my dog.
Albert:
    I fucked your mammie in the tub
    Couldn't get none but me and flub-a-dub.
    I fucked your mammie in the alley.
    Couldn't nobody get none but me and dilly dally.

Come on John, you gotta help me. This motherfucker is too much. Get on him, too. He's hard on me. He's hard on us.

John:
    I fucked your mammie on the stool
    She ended up hollering' saying loop-de-loo.
Albert (to Malcolm):
    Give me one, I got to owe you four.
John:
    I fucked your mama on a bowl of salad.
    Your ass jumped out lookin' like salad.
Malcolm:
    I fucked your mama on top of the moon.
    She had four thousand babies and three baboons.
Albert (adlibbing):
    I fucked your mama on a pillow
    She had six babies and one gorilla.
John (adlibbing):
    I fucked your mama on a chain.
    She had four babies and one tangarang.

This cracked John up; he rolled back and forth on the couch kicking his legs in the air, thoroughly enjoying his skill.

Albert: No, not tangarang. You mean orangutang.
John: No, I mean tangarang. This motherfucker (Malcolm) beyond the orangatang.

    Oh there,
    He walks like a natural man
    He talks like a natural man
    But he's a brute.

With this John got up from the couch, directing his comments explicitly to Malcolm. Malcolm in turn rose from his chair and walked over to John. They stood in the middle of the floor, toe to toe, with their faces about six inches apart. Then they began exchanging verses very directly aimed at each other. They were not angry, however; they were smiling and enjoying themselves. Hammond felt that their enjoyment and good feeling would persist only so long as they managed to make immediate rejoinders to each other; should one's ability to keep up the game flag, he would become irritated and much less good-humored.

Malcolm:
> Fuck your big fat black mama
> With her hair stickin' straight up on her head.

John:
> Ho there he looks like a natural man
> He talks like a natural man
> But he's a brute.

Malcolm:
> And your mama's a gorilla.
> Your mama is named Magilla the gorilla.

John:
> I found him
> The chief of the heart of the Mongo
> Up in the tree
> Playing with his little brother
> Tossing coconuts
> From the deep heart of the congo
> He walks like a knock kneed ape.
> He talks like a knock kneed ape.

Malcolm:
> You smell like a mosquitoed elephant.

John:
> Boy, your breath smell like wootan, pootan, panacoop.

Malcolm:
> Your breath smells like nine yards of bugger-bear farts.

John:
> Your breath smells like git back.

Malcolm:
> Your breath smells like this, that, the other,
> Frog shit and peanut butter.

Albert: (Screaming at the top of his voice) I got to hear that again. I got to hear that again. I got to hear that again. I got to play that again. John you gonna have to run with me. I got to cut him loose. Too much. I got to cut him loose. He said your breath smelled like this, that and the other. What did you say? Cat shit and peanut butter.

Malcolm:
> Your breath smell like dumb blood.

John (adlibbing again):
>Your breath smell like this, that and do,
>You ought to smell his mammie's breath too.

Malcolm:
>Your breath smells like old grass
>Coolin' the breeze from a monkey's ass.
>Your breath smells like air breaks from a gorilla's ass.

At this time the game was at its highest point. As each man screamed his lines at the other he used a wide range of facial gestures and movements of his arms, hands, and legs. John in particular acted with great élan. When he felt he had scored he jumped up and down and stomped his feet one after the other. Malcolm was cooler and confined his movements to less elaborate facial gestures and hand movements. John also used a wide range of speech styles to heighten his performance; sometimes he screamed and sometimes he talked very softly; sometimes he was laughing as he contributed a verse and at other times he was in very serious and composed much in the manner of a Baptist preacher at his most serious, using a deep and sonorous voice and speaking very slowly.

Albert: John's getting beat.
Malcolm: Your breath smells like chan.
John: Hey, hey, you ugly boy . . .
Malcolm:
>You ugly. You're a ugly motherfucker.
>You so ugly that you could look up a
>   camel's ass
>And scare the humps out of his back.

Albert (addressing Malcolm and teaming up with John):
>You're a ugly motherfucker and you still
>ugly.
>You bumpy faced bastard you.

Malcolm:
>Nigger, under his arms so funky
>He smell like a vulture flapping his
>   wings.

Albert: You bumpy faced bastard.
John: Hey, hey, hey you. Hey, Malcolm.
Malcolm: Who me?
John: Yeah. I'm trying to figure out what you is.
Malcolm:
>I know what I am.
>Just try to find out what you is.
>You look like a motherfuckin' mis-treated
>   chicken neck.

Albert: He got you, John. He got you. Oohwee, a mistreated chicken neck.

John: You a goddam lie, you know what?

Albert (pressing the issue): He said you look like a motherfuckin' chicken neck, a mistreated chicken neck.

Malcolm: That mother fucker's neck look like spider webs.

Albert (rubbing it in): Man, he got you, he talkin' about you bad.

John: I can't joan with this motherfucker. He's too much.

Malcolm:
Look like Frankenstein's first cousin
Dr. Hyde's sister's uncle's son.

John:
Well let me talk about your cripple,
Knock teeth, knock kneeded, no teeth,
Crippled ass auntie's bowlegged daddie's sister's brother.

Malcolm:
What about your bubble eyed, boobooed
Grandsister's brother's first cousin's son.

John:
What about your pie faced auntie
In Bigfoot, Georgia, next door to Smallfoot.

Malcolm:
Motherfucker's feet . . .

John (with preacher's voice):
You know what?
I remember you.
We used to be down on 17th and Franklin.
We were standing at the bakery and you'd
be down under us.

Malcolm: Uh-huh I can remember when you used to suck dicks and I didn't.

John: Yeah?

Malcolm: Uh-huh

John: You don't know what you was missin'.

Malcolm: You possom eyed motherfucker you.

John: You know what? You look like three baboons.

Albert: What'd you tell him John? He don't know what he missin'!

John:
Cause I sucked your mammie's dick
So how in the hell you got here?
That's the reason why I'm trying to figure
out
Who you is.

Malcolm: Motherfucker look like a scared dog.

Albert (laughing): He ran out. He ran out then.

John: Look here, boy. (voice dropping) Let me look at that shirt you got on.

Malcolm: Look at this one you got on.

John (grabbing Malcolm's shirt): You know what this is?

Malcolm: Damn right, a good lookin' shirt.

John: No, this is a Seemore shirt.

Malcolm: Yeah, see more skin than you do shirt.

John:
> No, uh-uh, uh-uh. Your mama done seen this
> More times than she done see you.

Malcolm:
> Don't be callin' me no motherfucker,
> You don't see my shoes under your mama's
>> bed.

John:
> You know what? You know what? That's all right.
> What did you do the time that you came there
> And caught my dick in your mama's mouth?

Malcolm:
> You say your dick in my mama's mouth?
> Ain't that what you said?

John:
> What did you do? What did you do when you found that?
> When you came in and I had my dick in your
>> mama's mouth?
> What did you do then?
> What did your mama say to you when you came
>> in there?

Malcolm: You say . . .

John: What did you do when you caught me in your mama's bedroom?

Malcolm: You ain't never been in my mama's bedroom.

John: You's a goddam lie.

Malcolm: Black, skinny bonefaced motherfucker.

John:
> Boy you know what? You look like
> You got a bad case of diemonia.
> Turn and mona.
> By exposing yourself you just got racked.
> Yes, I'm boody struck and wants to fuck,
> Got grindin' you on my mind.

Malcolm:
> You look like a motherfucker raggedy ranger.

John:

Bend over and I'll stick you with this strainger.

(getting very serious)
You know what?

Albert: Malcolm done quit it. Malcolm done played out.

Malcolm: Naw, I'm just waitin. I'm gitting myself together and I'm gonna whip 'em all on you at once.

John:

That's what you better do.
Your mama looking like dehydrated balls.

Malcolm:

Your mama lookin like . . .

John:

And your dilapidated moldy daddy,
That motherfucker so old
Till when he choke dust come out of his
ass.

Malcolm:

Your daddy worked in a motherfuckin coal
yard so long
Till when he fart coal dust come out of
his ass.

John:

That's all right, your daddy's the onlyest
man that I ever seen
Could run through a coal mine and leave
a white streak on him.

Malcolm:

Your mammie look like she been raised
In a barrel of butcher knives.

Albert: God damn! Ooohwee! God damn!

Malcolm: Your mama look like a cat named Frankenstein.

John: You know what . . .

Albert: Swimmin' in a barrel of butcher knives. God damn!

Malcolm: And smell like a barrel of dicks.

Albert: In a barrel of butcher knives. God damn!

John:

But you know what?
Of all the animals I'd rather be a monkey
And jump on your big fat juicy mammie
And do the old fashion fuck.
Of all the animals I'd rather be a mosquitoe
And jump on your mammie and lose my peter.
Of all the things I'd rather be some water
And jump on your mammie and fuck her like I oughtta.

Albert:

> Of all the animals in the world . . .

Malcolm:

> I'd rather be a rooster
> And jump on your mammie
> And fuck her like I useta.

Albert:

> Yeah, yeah. And you motherfucker
> Talking a big barrel nose bad motherfucker.

Malcolm:

> You damn right.
> You a bad motherfucker from jungle land.

John:

> I fucked your mammie with peter pan.

Malcolm:

> I'm the baddest motherfucker in the
>   jungle land
> Wear keen toed shoes split tailed coat,
> I fucked your mammie
> Right there in the front doo.

Albert (laughing): Wear keen-toed shoes and split tailed coat
I fucked your mammie in the front doo.

Malcolm: Now play that over, let's hear it.

John: Uh uh. I ain't through with you yet. You rudabaker-faced motherfucker.

Malcolm: You motherfucker you look like—

John: Look like a turnament nest done delapidated.

Malcolm: Your nose look like a broke dick.

John: Boy you know what?

Malcolm: Got moscocious done dinocious at the head.

Albert: Moscocious?

John: Bondinocious.

Malcolm: About the head.

John: Your mammie sufferin' with a bad case of halitocious.

Malcolm: Your mammie sufferin' with ixdididacious, defondiracious.

Albert (laughing and screaming): This motherfucker can't read or write and got more vocabulary.

Malcolm: I use them big words on 'em like esdesmosdociousdey.

Albert: His mother got a bad case of what?

Malcolm: Bondiscocious. And in short, this motherfucker got a stroke at the nose.

Albert: In other words, bondinocious is a stroke at the nose?

Malcolm: Right.

By this time the participants had exhausted themselves so Albert turned off the tape recorder and carefully put it away, and they all went home.

In the next several months Hammond saw John and Albert from time to time, spending evenings with them much like the one just described, and hearing John's stories of his complicated relationships with all his girlfriends. As time went on, his girlfriends seemed to become increasingly irritated as his game of playing one against another began to catch up with him. However, he was still very much involved with Virginia and Mary. Mary did not live in the project, but the two girls communicated with each other by phone, Mary telling Virginia "all kinds of bad things" about John.

In June, John and Albert had an experience that impressed them greatly. They told the story to Hammond as follows: they were walking down the street near the project one Wednesday night. A white man had pulled up alongside in his car and asked if they would like to go with him to Gaslight Square (the main white night-life area of St. Louis). He explained that he was from Des Moines, that he worked in an electronics firm, and that he was in St. Louis to pick up some supplies needed at his factory. They decided to go with him and for several hours visited clubs in the Gaslight Square area. They all found these clubs rather dull, although it was the first time that John or Albert had been there. They suggested they go on to a Negro club that played jazz records on week nights. The boys thoroughly enjoyed themselves and so, apparently, did the white visitor. They were much impressed by the fact that he was a college graduate and an executive in a firm and that even so he enjoyed spending time with them and treated them as his equals. Albert, who was very interested in mathematics, enjoyed talking with him about math and was especially pleased to learn that he could hold his own until the discussion turned to some of the more complicated points of quadratic equations. They were pleased by the fact that the man understood their jargon but did not try to imitate it, knowing that if he did so he would sound "lame." The man said he had $20 to spend for the evening; John had $50 in his pocket, but the man would not let them buy anything, and he was able to insist on this without seeming condescending.

The boys had not been to this club before, but they knew it to be a middle-class Negro night club with some white clientele, and they were pleased that they could lead the visitor to a place he enjoyed more than the white clubs of Gaslight Square. The man said that he did not like Gaslight Square because the people acted too fancy there, and that he found their club more comfortable. They were surprised that the man seemed simply to want company; they expected a homosexual advance to be made at some point in the evening, but none came. Indeed, there was no indication that the man wanted anything other than what he said he wanted, a pleasant evening on the town with some companions.

Hammond was impressed that neither John nor Albert tried to take advantage of the man by drinking up his money. They wanted to reciprocate and pay for their share of the drinks, but the man would not hear of it. Hammond was so used to the pleasure they took in manipulating others that this behavior stood out in sharp contrast to their usual attitudes. It became apparent that the reward of being treated as equals was far more significant than anything they might have gained by exploiting their host for his money. The event was particularly significant for Albert because he had just graduated from high school and was thinking seriously about going to college.

With the wide swath that John cut through the girls in the project and the surrounding neighborhood, it is surprising that he managed to avoid trouble with jealous boyfriends and husbands. His girlfriends were often angry with him because his attentions were distributed freely, but none of them seemed inclined to attack him. Instead, they seemed to accept him pretty much as he presented himself; as one of his more mature girl-friends phrased it, "That boy is just fuck crazy." None of the violence that is risked by acting the role of a "player" seemed to touch him. On one occasion in June, however, Hammond was present when John and Albert came very close to trouble. The evening started in the usual way, with the purchase of a large box of fried rice and pork at the Chinese carry-out restaurant. Then they bought three quarts of malt liquor and started toward one of the housing projects on the north side of the city to visit one of John's girlfriends.

When they arrived, John said, "Come on, everybody, let's get out and go on up to the babe's apartment." But Albert was uneasy and replied, "Naw, you go on up and check things out; then come back and we'll go up with you." Albert, ever sensitive to John's game, added, "I'm hip to your game. You don't know whether that broad has got a stud up there or not and you want us to go up there and back your play in case she's got somebody there. You've brought me down here three times now, gaming me about this broad's sister that I've never seen yet. Besides that, John, I'll be truthful with you—your broad is really digging me, I just didn't want to tell you."

Having been put down in this way, after more argument John went up to the girl's apartment alone. He returned after quite a long time with another young man. John seemed tense and the other man seemed angry. The man looked closely at Albert and Hammond, then back at John, and said, "There's some shit in the game and I intend to find out what it is. My old lady's watch and ring are missing and I know John, I don't think he would take it. But I don't know about this other motherfucker, his partner [looking at Albert]."

It developed that the man was the estranged husband of the girl John had come to see. He was very angry because a watch and ring he had given his wife had disappeared from the apartment on Thursday, two days earlier. He obviously suspected that either John or Albert had taken them. Finally they convinced the man that they had not been at the apartment the previous Thursday, though they had been there on Wednesday and Friday, and that therefore they could not possibly have taken the watch and ring. At this point the man scratched his head and began to change the focus of his suspicion. He said, "Well wait a minute, man, my old lady might be trying to put me in a motherfucking trick. That whore might have pawned the motherfucking shit or give it to some other nigger and now she's afraid to tell me. I've been checking her story and it's got all kinds of motherfucking holes in it now. If you weren't down here Thursday, then I know it's some shit in the game. Let's go on up and question that whore."

He and John started up to the apartment, and at John's urging, Hammond and Albert accompanied them. The man questioned John and Albert closely about when they had been at the apartment, when they had arrived and left, and whether they had seen the watch and ring while they were there. He was assembling evidence to determine exactly how his wife had put him in a trick bag. He finally decided, "I think the whore is fucking around with some other dude and either she done pawned the motherfucking watch and ring or either she done give it to this dude and she's afraid to tell me now. I went with the whore for three years and then I was married to her for three years and I can tell when the whore is lying to me and when she ain't. The bitch looks like she's lying to me now. I just wanted to get it all together before I go in. Now let's go inside."

When they entered the apartment Hammond was surprised by how nicely it was furnished. There was not a great deal of furniture, but it was new and pleasantly arranged and the apartment was immaculate. The wife turned out to be about 19 years old. She came into the living room carrying an eight- or nine-month-old baby in her arms. She was obviously frightened of her husband and as he questioned her angrily she began to cry.

He challenged her with the fact that she said John and Albert had visited her on Thursday and they said they had not been there. She said, "Well, I forgot what day it was. They've been down here damn near every day this week and maybe I did get mixed up." He insisted, "I think you're lying to me, bitch. You might be done pawned that motherfuckin' shit. These cats told me they didn't take it and I believe them. You've been fucking around with some other dude and I think you're afraid to tell it. I ought to whip your motherfuckin ass right now." With this he hit her on the side of her head and she fell off the chair. As she got up she started to leave the room but he dragged her back, saying, "Where you going, whore? I didn't tell you to leave. Bring your black ass back in here." John, Albert, and Hammond looked at each other and wished they were somewhere else. Each sat very quietly in the living room drinking from their quart of beer and trying to think of a way to get out before the man turned his anger to them.

The man continued his indictment of his wife. "Whore, you've been lying to me all night long. First you told me that these guys were here

Thursday, then they say they wasn't. Now you talking about you don't know what day it was. What in the fuck you want to lie for? If you pawned the shit, tell me and I'll get it out. If you gave it to some other dude, tell me that too so I can get it from him, but either way let me know what's going on before I have to stomp your ass. You told me when these dudes came here Friday you wouldn't even let them in the door and that was about 6:00, you said you told them to go someplace else because you had to go out, but the dudes told me you let them in the house and they stayed here until 9:30.

With this John and Albert realized that the man had tricked them into an unnecessary admission that they had spent time with his wife on Friday evening. When John realized this he started shifting uneasily in his chair. At this point the man got up and took a butcher knife from his pants. He walked into the kitchen and laid the knife down on the kitchen table. The woman left the room to go to the bedroom, then she came back and the man came out of the kitchen and sat down.

He continued to say that he would do anything for his woman, rob, steal, or kill. He had been in jail and while there had decided that he would come back and make a home with her. He said, "A lot of dudes say they don't care what their wife does as long as she doesn't bring it up in their faces, but I don't feel that way about it. I don't want her to be doing a motherfucking thing if I'm supposed to be married to her. I've been out on the streets and I've learned a lot of things out there but I'm about ready now to come on back and settle down. But with the way my old lady is acting I don't know whether or not I can make it." He said that he did not mind coming to the apartment and seeing a couple of dudes like John and Albert sitting there, talking friendly with his wife, but he didn't want them to be sitting up there trying to work game on him in his own house.

Hammond thought he was trying to do two things at once. He wanted them to know that it would be dangerous for them to continue seeing his wife, and yet, he was trying to convince himself not to take drastic action toward them or her. He told his wife, "You have a good asswhipping coming as soon as these people go." A few minutes later Hammond decided that the tension had subsided enough for them to leave safely, so he told John and Albert that he had to be going. They said their good-byes and got down the stairs and into their car as quickly as they could. As they left, John commented, "I'll never go back down there again!"

But otherwise he was undaunted. As they drove up to their building in Pruitt-Igoe, John spied Margaret walking in front of one of the buildings and said, "Look, there's Margaret. Let's call her over to the car and pull a train on her." Hammond observed, "Not in my car. If you want to pull a train on her, you'll have to do it someplace else." By this time John was used to Hammond's steadfast refusal to participate with him in his pursuit of girls, so he and Albert got out and took Margaret upstairs to one of the laundry room floors. Hammond assumed they tried to persuade her to have intercourse with them, but they stood near the gallery window and Hammond could observe that they were making very little progress, despite the fact that John, at least, had had relations with Margaret before. Because it was then almost 1:00 a.m., Hammond drove home.

13.

Negro Lower-Class Identity and Culture

The traditional end to a story about a young man sowing his wild oats is that after a while he begins to settle down. One of the most sharply etched tragedies of the ghetto is that young men with the intelligence and vigorous reach of John Martin have so few opportunities to realize a valued self-identity through constructive engagement with the world, either in school or at work. John, however, was able to progress over the next few years through a series of jobs to a responsible position in one of the agencies concerned with social and economic welfare in the city. In this job he was able to use his intelligence and his quickness in a constructive way.

During his salad days John achieved the status of a small-time cultural hero in his community. He never made it big, like the "pimp" who ends up with a large wardrobe of expensive clothes and a shiny Cadillac "hog." He probably did not want to; the underlying seriousness of his stance toward the world would have kept him from finding these objects rewarding. However, he moved through his world with great élan and achieved one ideal of the young men in his group, having a number of simultaneous girlfriends all of whom admired and to some extent depended upon him. He moved from girl to girl, from binge to binge, always maintaining a good-humored cool and managing to conceal—except in his frank sessions with Albert and Hammond—the extent to which he deeply distrusted his world and was always on his guard.

An appropriate ending to the story would require that eventually he fall in love with a girl and then be confronted with a desperate struggle to overcome his own deeply ingrained belief that human relationships are little more than one person trying to game the other. In the case of Thomas Coolidge the kind of misery that this kind of situation brings was apparent, but perhaps John will be as lucky in avoiding that danger as he was in avoiding the violence often associated with free-wheeling sexual adventurism.

The Poor Are Different from You and Me

As long as there have been poor people there have been commentators on their lot. Since the Industrial Revolution this commentary has been important in political dialogue concerning the causes and cures of poverty and in social welfare policy generally. As David Matza has shown, there has been a succession of fashions in the concepts applied to understanding "the disreputable poor," and these fashions have been consequential for the ways the larger society has dealt with poor people.[1] Another stream of social commentary has accompanied the arrival and persistence of Africans in the New World. Because almost all of them have until very recently been poor, conceptions of the poor and of the black have had a natural kinship. The enterprising historian can match almost every statement made about the European-American poor with a comparable statement about the Afro-Americans.

In the 1930's these two streams of social observation began to come together in the work of social scientists concerned with social stratification in the United States. Out of their work has grown the most influential concept of the past two decades for trying to make sense out of the situation of the American poor in general and the Negro American poor in particular. This is the concept of the lower-class subculture.[2]

Some 25 years ago, when social scientists of remarkably diverse persuasions were undertaking the final burial of biological determinism, Allison Davis sought to show that "just as the members of the higher skilled working class and of management act in response to their culture, their system of social and economic rewards, so do the underprivileged workers act in accord with their culture." Davis sought to demonstrate that social rather than biological factors accounted for:

> . . . the habits of shiftlessness, irresponsibility, lack of ambition, absenteeism, and of quitting the job, which management usually regards as a result of the "innate" perversity of underprivileged white and Negro workers . . . are in fact *normal responses* that the worker has learned from his physical and social environment. These habits constitute a system of behavior and attitudes which are realistic and

1. Matza (1966). The concept of a lower class (lower-lower class) and its culture was developed most systematically in the work of W. Lloyd Warner and his co-workers; see Warner (1962), Davis (1948), Davis, Gardner, and Gardner (1941).

2. More recent work detailing black and white lower class cultural patterns includes Miller (1958), Gans (1962), Rodman (1963), Clark (1965), Lewis (1955), Hollingshead and Redlich (1958), and Cohen and Hodges (1963). Somewhat independently, Oscar Lewis began in the late 1950's to develop his concept of the "culture of poverty". The patterns Lewis describes characterize, he believes, only a segment of the group that Warner and his followers have analyzed under the rubric of lower-lower class. Lewis uses the concept to apply only to the most deprived, poorest, and most disorganized segments of the lower-lower class; see Lewis (1959), Lewis (1961), Lewis (1968).

rational in that environment in which the individual of the slums has lived and in which he has been trained.[3]

While terms like *normal, realistic,* and *rational* may seem overly sanguine, Davis' classic analysis of lower class job behavior and motivation still has the ring of validity. Davis was concerned with the contending possibilities of expressive and instrumental role systems as these facilitated day-to-day adaptation to the exigencies of the lower-class situation. He observed that "the most powerful of all the forces that keep (the underprivileged worker) in his present way of life and work are the pleasures that he actually can attain by following his underprivileged culture." Davis saw these "pleasures" as selectively emphasized by the lower class in the absence of the more conventional rewards available to higher status groups.

The concept of the lower-class subculture has been one of the mainstays of professional attempts to comprehend the life, the motivations, and the problems of the least well off portion of the population. However, it has been interpreted in two different ways in the sociological and anthropological literature of the past 30 years dealing with the distinctiveness of lower-class norms and values from those of the larger, "conventional" society. The now classic views, fathered most directly by Allison Davis and further developed by Walter Miller, holds that there is a distinctive culture that characterizes those who are brought up in the lower class world:

> Now a child cannot learn his mores, social drives, and values—his basic culture—from books. He can learn a particular culture and a particular moral system only from those people who know this behavior and who exhibit it in frequent association with the learner. If a child associates intimately with no one but slum adults and children, he will learn only slum culture. Thus the pivotal meaning of social classes to the student of behavior is that they limit and pattern the learning environment; they structure the social maze in which the child learns his habits and meanings.

> In the slum, as elsewhere, the human group evolves solutions to the basic problems of group life. . . . Because the slum individual usually is responding to a different physical, economic and cultural reality from that in which the middle class individual is trained, the slum individual's habits and values also must be different if they are to be realistic. The behavior which we regard as "delinquent" or "shiftless" or "unmotivated" in slum groups is usually a perfectly realistic, adaptive, and—in slum life—respectable response to reality.[4]

By the time some ten years later that Walter Miller applied these views to the understanding of gang delinquency, the assertion of a distinctive lower-class culture was even more sharply drawn:

3. Davis (1946).
4. Davis (1948), p. 10–11.

There is a substantial segment of present day American society whose way of life, values, and characteristic patterns of behavior are the product of a distinctive cultural system which may be termed "lower class." Evidence indicates that this cultural system is becoming increasingly distinctive, and that the size of the group which shares this tradition is increasing. . . . The standards of lower class culture cannot be seen merely as a reverse function of middle class culture—as middle class standards "turned upside down": lower class culture is a distinctive tradition, many centuries old with an integrity of its own.[5]

In apparent opposition are the views of such general theorists as Parsons and Merton, who seem to maintain that American society possesses a single system of values which is "morally integrated," shared by most actors in the society "in the sense that they approve the same basic normative patterns of conduct."[6] This contrary view was developed by Merton in his well-known essay on social structure and anomie:

Our egalitarian ideology denies by implication the existence of non-competing individuals and groups in the pursuit of pecuniary success. Instead, the same body of success symbols is held to apply for them all. Goals are held to transcend class lines, not be bounded by them, yet the actual social organization is such that there exist class differentials in accessability of the goals. . . . "Poverty" is not an isolated variable which operates in precisely the same fashion wherever found: it is only one in a complex of identifiably interdependent social and cultural variables. . . . When poverty and associated disadvantages in competing for the cultural values approved for all members of the society are linked with a cultural emphasis on pecuniary success as the dominant goal, high rates of criminal behavior are the normal outcome. . . . When we consider the full configuration—poverty, limited opportunity and the assignment of cultural goals—there appears some basis for explaining the higher correlation between poverty and crime in our society than in others where rigidified class structure is coupled with *differential class symbols of success.*[7]

One can construct out of the writings of Davis and Miller on the one hand and Parsons and Merton on the other a counterpart of the classic exchange between F. Scott Fitzgerald and Ernest Hemingway. Fitzgerald said, "The rich are different from you and me." Hemingway retorted, "Yes, they have more money." The advocate of a distinctive lower-class culture will argue the counterpart of Fitzgerald's notion: "The poor are different from you and me." The advocate of the universality of societal values will reply, "Yes, they have less money."

5. Miller (1958).
6. Parsons (1954), p. 72.
7. Merton (1957), p. 146–147.

It is an interesting and important issue, but its status in the sociological literature is curious. Neither of the sets of scholars whose views are presented above deal with the conceptual problems of maintaining that there does or does not exist a distinctive lower-class culture.[8] Davis and Miller use the concept of lower-class culture as a preface to their presentation of field research concerning lower-class behavior, and Merton uses his ideas about the dominance of a common "success goal" in American society to illustrate his more general theory concerning social structure and anomie. The relatively offhand way in which the competition between these two concepts developed has meant that the dialectic between them has never been fully explored or adequately tested against empirical research.

The unthinking application of each of these paradigms to lower-class behavior by subsequent commentators has sometimes made lower-class persons appear as "conceptual boobs," to use an expression coined by Harold Garfinkel.[9] Both Davis and Merton are in fact seeking to come to terms with the adaptiveness of lower-class behavior, but their focus is different. Merton seeks to highlight the stratification system and the general social and cultural situation of the lower class by using the concept of anomie: he seeks to show that lower-class behavior can be regarded as arising from an effort to adapt to a disjunction between universal American goals and the lack of access lower class people have to these goals. His approach is macrosociological. Davis' approach, however, involves microscopic examination of the exigencies of day-to-day life of lower class people. He seeks to show how they construct their adaptations to the lack of opportunities in their environment and how they selectively emphasize the opportunities that are available to them, primarily opportunities for "bodily pleasures" of various kinds.

As these views have permeated sociological and psychological research on the lower class, the central role of creative adaptation has receded. Perhaps the most successful attempt to deal with these issues is in Hyman Rodman's concept of the "lower class value stretch," an adaptive mechanism by which "the lower class person without abandoning the general values of the society, develops an alternative set of values . . . (so that lower

8. Both Merton and Davis, whose differing approaches to lower-class behavior were worked out at about the same time, present a polemic against biological determinism. For Davis, lower-class culture demonstrated the primacy of environment over heredity, of nuture over nature, in explaining the behavior of its members. Merton's views concerning anomie (the disjunction of culturally prescribed goals and institutionalized means for their achievement) attacked the view that lays responsibility for the faulty operation of social structures to the failure of social control over man's imperious biological drives. The biologies they were against, however, were slightly different. Davis polemicized against race or class biological inferiority, Merton against Freud's biological drives. Davis, a psychoanalytically-oriented learning theorist, preserved a common human biology as an important element in his theories, while Merton sought to eschew biology, or at least to hold its effects constant.

9. Garfinkel (1967).

class people) have a wider range of values than others within the society. They share the general values of the society . . . but in addition they have stretched these values or developed alternative values, which help them to adjust to their deprived circumstances."[10] Rodman's formulation avoids the pitfall of implying that lower-class persons are ignorant of or indifferent to conventional norms and values, or that they persist in maintaining allegiance to conventional norms despite their inability to achieve success in their terms.

Merton's application of the concept of anomie to American social structure and his emphasis on the relationship between opportunity to accomplish in terms of culturally induced goals and the person's position in the social stratification system provides a useful starting point for relating the structural position of the lower class to the subculture developed as adaptation to that position. Much work in the Mertonian tradition and by investigators such as Cloward and Ohlin, Srole, and Mizruchi clearly establishes that a sense of anomie occurs more frequently at lower levels of the stratification system than at higher levels.[11]

In explicating his concept of anomie, Durkheim observed that "no living being can be happy or even exist unless his needs are sufficiently proportioned to his means." Man's biological nature does not limit his needs as effectively as does the biology of other animals. For a man to be happy, then, "a regulative force must play the same role for moral needs which the organism plays for physical needs. . . . Society alone can estimate the reward to be prospectively offered to every class of human functionary in the name of common interest."[12] Durkheim sees anomie as a particular kind of human suffering which arises when man's activities lack moral regulation. In a non-anomic society, men restrict their desires by acknowledging particular moral regulative mechanisms as just.

Merton's contribution in reformulating the concept of anomie is to note specifically that the needs Durkheim postulated are "culturally induced, deep motivations" which, though they may be related to the biological drives of man, are not determined solely by these drives. He describes the anomic situation as one in which men want something their culture tells them is legitimate to want, but do not have legitimate means to satisfy their desires and, therefore, seek other means which the culture regards as illegitimate. The particular situation of which Merton writes is one in which society first seduces some of its members into wanting something and then denies them the means for obtaining the recommended reward.[13] Durkheim's formulation was more general because it dealt with needs however they come about and was similarly abstract in its statement of the kind of regulation of these needs necessary to avoid the anomic

10. Rodman (1963).
11. Cloward and Ohlin (1960); Mizruchi (1964); Srole (1956a and 1956b).
12. Durkheim (1951), p. 246.
13. Merton (1957), p. 131–139.

situation. Durkheim's view was remarkably similar to that of Freud in *Civilization and Its Discontents*. Although Freud was more interested in man's resentment at the necessity of limiting his needs, he phrased his understanding of this necessity in much the same way as Durkheim.[14]

The needs that trigger men's actions must be learned; man comes into the world with certain drives but does not come programmed to channel those drives toward specific goals. As Melford Spiro has observed, "The combination of man's mammalian drives (hunger, sex, etc.) and his plastic hominoid constitution (paucity of instincts) requires that means of drive-reduction be learned." Further, "the combination of man's organic needs (protection against weather, predatory beasts, etc.) and his hominoid constitution (generalized and fetalized) requires learned means of protection and adaptation. Human social life demands that forms of social interaction, methods of social cooperation, techniques of conflict resolution, and the like be learned."[15] The variability of human cultures indicates that there are many possible ways in which the relatively small drive equipment the human being brings into the world can be channeled to facilitate biological, psychological and social adaptation. Observation of human culture also tells us that societies are not always successful in apportioning the needs they stimulate to the means they allocate to individuals for satisfying these needs.

The need structure imbedded in the personalities of the members of society is the result of interaction of their biological constitution with the experiences their society has permitted them. The means structure for the satisfaction of these needs involves most directly the role systems the society makes available to its members. Men's needs generally are satisfied in the process of performance of roles. The relationship between the needs of individuals and their performance of roles is complex indeed, as Sprio has demonstrated. It involves both conscious and unconscious needs directly and indirectly related to particular role charters, and intended and unintended, recognized and unrecognized, functions for both the person and the society.[16] In any society there is available a complex set of possibilities for the satisfaction and regulation of culturally-conditioned needs in the performance of socially necessary roles.

In most societies there will be one institutional framework that is the major focus for the generation, satisfaction and regulation of needs. In many non-industrial societies kinship and other related institutions such as age grades have this function; the most important things about a man are bound up in his kinship and age grade statuses and roles which define the larger part of who he is socially and why he has the right to exist. He

---

14. "The element of civilization enters on the scene with the first attempt to regulate these social relations. If the attempt were not made, the relationships would be subject to the arbitrary will of the individual" (Freud, 1961).

15. Spiro (1961), p. 95; also Rappaport (1960), and Hartmann (1958).

16. Spiro (1961), p. 108–116.

realizes his sense of what is coming to him, as he does what is desirable, and what is possible from his position in this structure. In our kind of society the major focuses are the nuclear family and the economy. The interpenetration of statuses, roles and expectations between these two institutional systems is great. Men are guided to earn rewards through participation in the occupational order and to translate the income and prestige they receive from their participation into rewards from their families and friends.[17] Women may derive their major sense of place in society from their performance of the complex of roles organized around the household and nuclear family, but because the maintenance of their households requires income and is sustained by the prestige attached to their husbands, they too are centrally committed to the economy. Their principal function is to translate the income received by their husbands into need satisfactions for all of the members of their household.

The sociological and psychological literature is replete with discussions of the identity problems inherent in the efforts of individuals to succeed in one or the other of these structures. Merton's analysis of the dynamics of anomie in American society takes off from a consideration of the importance of success as the major "culturally-induced, deep motivation" inculcated by that society. He notes that the limitless quality of the goal of success qualifies it as the anomie-producing agent specified in Durkheim's analysis. He then outlines several adaptations to the American situation in which there is a dissociation between the culturally-prescribed aspirations for success and the socially structured avenues for realizing those aspirations (that is, the limitation of access to both the learning structures and the performance structures which might make such goals feasible).

Our effort to understand the differing behavior of social classes is furthered by substituting a two-valued model for Merton's single-value "success" model of anomie. The first can be called *career success*. This is essentially what Merton is talking about, but he gives success an unnecessarily restricted connotation by insisting on money as the central goal: "Money has become consecrated as a value in itself over and above its expenditure for articles of consumption or its use for the enhancement of power." This does not fit the facts of American occupational or consumer behavior at any class level. It is more reasonable to argue that money is merely a symbol that helps individuals determine whether a person has become a big man. The central goal in striving for career success is to elicit the responses from others that validate one's identity as important, powerful, prestigious, rich, significant. While it is true, as Merton argues, that the institutions of communication in American society (mass media, education, and so forth) tend heavily to reinforce the success goal, evi-

17. "A man's work is one of the most important parts of his social identity, of his self; indeed, of his fate in the one life he has to live, for there is something almost irrevocable about choice of occupation as there is about choice of a mate" (Hughes, 1958).

dence also exists to suggest that matched against these pressures are other pressures within the same institutions which serve to legitimate "lesser" goals at each status level along the way from total failure to whatever the pinnacle of success might be.[18]

The second complex of culturally defined goals, which is opposed to the goal of career success, might be called the goals of the good American life. Whereas the career success goals point in the direction of becoming a big man, the goals of the good American life point instead in the direction of becoming a happy man. This goal complex is clearly suggested in two of Merton's adaptations to anomie—ritualism and retreatism, most particularly the former—but Merton sees these as responses to the dominance of the success goal rather than existing somewhat in their own right. It would seem more reasonable to view the goals of the good American life as having a considerable history and evolving in a rather apparent line from what appear to be the central goals of peasant life.[19]

Whereas the careerist seeks to be a big man, the adherent to this opposed goal-complex seeks rather to be a good provider. The orientation is to consumption rather than production; to the security of ascription rather than the open-ended, onward and upward, quality of career success.

These two goal systems are in contention both in the minds of certain individuals and between groups of adherents. It is probable that prosperity in the country generally tends to reduce the number of persons who concentrate sharply on the one-value success model. A poor middle class finds it difficult to see any solution to their need for a valid identity other than that of striving somehow to get to the top of the heap. A prosperous middle class or working class is better able to envision a satisfying life anchored in consumption, "living well with the Joneses" rather than keeping up with or surpassing them.[20]

18. Berger (1966).

19. For descriptions of this life style, see Rainwater, Coleman and Handel (1959), Handel and Rainwater (1964), Rainwater and Handel (1964), S. M. Miller and F. Riessman (1961), Gans (1962), and Ryan (1963). As Harold L. Wilensky (1960) and Marc Fried (1965) have noted, the concept of career is not applicable to most blue collar workers, for whom there is little of the orderly, step-by-step, upward movement implicit in that concept. The distinction between career goals and provider goals is essentially that between a particular kind of social status and a particular standard of living conceived in material terms. The consequences of two such orientations in terms of political issues related to the situation of Negro Americans is well presented by Wilson (1960), in his discussion of "status ends" and "welfare ends" as sometimes contradictory goals which confound Negro leadership and the exercise of political and community power.

20. This retreat from striving after excellence (which is a substitute for money) tends to horrify intellectuals, because it represents a retreat from the masculine identity they seek. Men like C. Wright Mills seem to have a great deal more admiration for the acquisitive businessmen of the old middle class than for the contented, prosperous consumers of the new middle class. Mills (1951) commented: "There is a curious contradiction about the ethos of success in America today. On the one hand, there are still compulsions to struggle, to 'amount to something', on the other hand, there is a poverty of desire, a souring of the image of success."

These contending goal complexes represent different kinds of aspiration, and in our culture the careerist outranks the man who simply wants himself and his family to live well. But the defenses against any claim of blanket superiority for careerist goals are strong in both the middle class and the stable working class. While to most Americans democracy and equalitarianism mean that everyone should have a chance to achieve as high a status as he is willing to work for, it is equally clear that for most Americans democracy means also the right not to play the game and still keep one's self-respect.[21] There are two ways, then, in which an American can seek a life in which his needs are proportioned to his means. He can orient himself toward success in a career sense, toward money and higher position in whatever hierarchy is appropriate to his occupational role, or toward success in terms of the good American life, by trying to be a good provider for himself and his family according to his own consumer-oriented standards.

Lower-class people are amply exposed to both of these cultural ideals. They know that some people make it big by the jobs they have and the money they are able to accumulate, that others do not make it so big but manage to live comfortably in homes in pleasant neighborhoods, surrounded by an increasing measure of material comfort. Most-lower class people at some time entertain aspirations in one or both of these directions, and it makes no sense to talk of a lower-class culture so divorced from that of the larger society that the validity of these goals is denied. However, many lower-class people come to the conclusion that neither of these ways of life are possible for them.[22] The personal experiences that lead to this conclusion are a product of the structural position in which lower-class people generally and lower-class Negroes most particularly find themselves. The particular position of lower-class Negroes historically and contemporaneously has set in motion certain adaptive processes which result in a kind of community life that further lessens their possible achievement of either of these conventional ideals.

The two primary forces that create and maintain the lower-class Negro community are economic marginality and racial oppression. Lower-class Negroes are economically marginal because they cannot find a rewarding place in the economic structure of the city (or the countryside, for that matter). They are not able to find stable employment at the going wages for valued employees; instead, they are confined to low-wage work and to

21. For a discussion of the multiple meanings of egalitarianism in American society, see Warner (1962), particularly p. 129–131, and Lipset (1963), particularly chapters 6 and 7.

22. See Cohen (1955) and Warner, Havighurst and Loeb (1944) for a discussion of middle class-lower class confrontations in the school system, and Miller and Harrison (1964) for a description of the "now" and "if" worlds of lower-class high school dropouts. David Matza (1964) touches on the same dual orientation in his introduction of the concept of "drift" between behavior consonant with the subculture of delinquency and that consonant with the orientations of the larger society.

jobs where intermittent employment is the rule. This means that lower-class Negro families are markedly deprived compared to others in the society in their ability to make use of the goods and services that constitute the going standard of American life. Poverty in American society is a phenomenon of relative rather than absolute deprivation. It is not so much that these families do not have the resources for a minimum standard of subsistence; their standard of living would be envied by the stable working and lower-middle class in many parts of the world. Men can exist happily and healthily on much less than the American poor have available, but only if their level of living does not mark them as different from and socially inferior to the great majority of their society.

Racial oppression exacerbates the relative deprivation of lower-class Negroes in almost every aspect of their lives. Not only does it further entrench their economic marginality, but it also obliges them to pay higher prices for consumer goods through the maintenance of exploitative separate markets and to suffer the disadvantage of the inferior public services that are available to them, ranging from less effective sanitation to inferior schools.

Economic marginality and racial oppression combine in the city to produce effects directly on individual lower-class Negro citizens and their families and on the community structure of the ghetto, and the ghetto structure affects the lives of individuals and their families. The community structure of the lower-class Negro ghetto is weak and disorganized in its ability to provide constructive support and social control over its members. The combination of economic marginality and a weak and unprotective local community structure confronts individuals in the ghetto with two hard facts of life. The first stems from the effect of low income and is magnified for Negroes by the special market constraints operated on them: families in this lower-class world are not able to find enough money to live an acceptable standard American life. They learn instead that the best they can expect is despised housing, an inferior diet, and few of the available pleasures. This inability to be like everyone else robs the lower-class Negro of a sense of personal meaningfulness and efficacy which is the accustomed and expected patrimony of the ordinary individual in the simpler, more "primitive" tribes in the "underdeveloped" parts of the world.

Lower-class people are constrained to live among others who are equally marginal in economic terms, and in the community that grows up in this situation, a premium is placed on the exploitation and manipulation of peers. The individual's daily experience teaches him that his peers are dangerous, difficult, and out to exploit him or hurt him in petty or significant ways. He learns also that those who are socially superior to him take the attitude that he is of little consequence and, therefore, that he can be forced to accept inferior service and protection from the formal institutions of the community. To some extent the individual can isolate himself in the ghetto from a constant awareness of relative deprivation, but he cannot isolate himself from the problems of ghetto life; he is continually confronted with a world full of dangers—not just the physical dangers of the ghetto world, but also the interpersonal and moral dangers of his exploitative milieu.

Lower-class whites and Negroes have reacted to their historical situation and to their own experience in resourceful ways that are designed to achieve a way of living from day to day and year to year. They are not simply passive targets of the destructive forces which act upon them; they react adaptively, making use of the human resources available to work out their strategies for survival. These strategies often cause considerable surprise and outrage among those better off in the society. But lower-class adaptations also have self-limiting qualities which serve to perpetuate some of the destructive elements in their situation and to frustrate individuals who try to enter more advantaged social strata.

A close look at lower-class life must impress the observer with the human creativity that goes into the effort to survive. Two particular aspects of these adaptations are important to our analysis. Lower-class styles of life are heavily oriented to defense against the many dangers presented by this world. Techniques of relating to other people are markedly defensive; individuals manipulate and exploit others where possible and at the same time try to ward off manipulation and exploitation by others. This contributes a pervasive tone of guardedness and mistrustfulness to interpersonal relations within the community. Defensiveness also permeates the self-system of lower-class people, encouraging them not to care too much about anything because it may be taken away at any moment, hopes are more often frustrated than realized, and one never knows how much to count on other people.

A second important characteristic of lower-class adaptations is an emphasis on "stripped down" ways of organizing social roles and relationships. Because of the restricted and uncertain resource base of the group, lower-class people learn to organize their relationships with others in a simpler and less elaborate way than more affluent people. This stripped down form of institutionalizing group activity ranges from the prevalence of female-headed households to the lower development of formal organizations in the lower-class slum or ghetto.

Similarly, informal social relations seldom acquire the stability and permanence they are likely to enjoy in stable working-class neighborhoods. Individual social integration is achieved through constantly shifting alliances rather than through a durable social network, such as in stable working-class communities, or through the still more formal bureaucratic statuses that characterize the middle-class individual.

It is impossible for lower-class Negroes to achieve a conventional way of life that provides them with a sense of regulation and harmony between their needs and the possibilities for their satisfaction. As a consequence, their personal lives are subjected to great stress. They are required to relate to each other in the light of their knowledge that they and their peers share in their ostracism from a culturally valid American life. The group, through historical time, and the individual in his own lifetime must discover ways of adapting to the stress which comes from the fact that the larger society does not (refuses to, is unable to) guide them toward a status which allows the regulation of needs and satisfactions.

The study of lower-class subculture, lower-class styles of life, lower-class personalities is, then, the study of the ways individuals and a class of people adapt to their disinheritances from their society. In their view, no valued and meaningful place is made for them, and they are denied the fundamental human equality that comes from having a functioning place in a society. Instead, they must find ways of living with the knowledge that they are embarrassments in their own world.[23]

The Search for a Valid Identity

Recent conceptualizations of self processes seem rather remote from the ordered and open world implicit in the thought of early social psychologists and philosophers such as George Herbert Mead.[24] Social life inevitably moves along, but a varied chorus of social scientists suggest that its movement and direction are problematic. Whether one attends to the brooding presence of existentialist thought in the social sciences, to the vision of sociopathic society Erving Goffman offers us, to the study of the fate of personality in concentration camps and the application of the insights of these studies to Negro personality under American slavery, or to reading about what happens to a seemingly self-assured individual when he is deprived of all environmental stimuli, he is impressed by the constant struggle of individuals to maintain a sense of self and identity.[25]

The world of the lower class, the poor, the slum dweller, is certainly one in which social and cultural processes do much to challenge identity and little to sustain it. Individuals are constantly exposed to evidence of their own irrelevance, and they experience much less guidance toward self-validation than do typical middle-class persons. The identity problems of lower-class persons make the soul-searching of middle-class adolescents and adults seem like a kind of conspicuous consumption of psychic riches.

Despite many differences in details there is a broad convergence in much of contemporary research on the lower class, whether in relation to education, juvenile delinquency, other deviant behavior, life styles, or a more abstract concern with anomie and alienation. This convergence

23. See Beck (1966).
24. Glaser and Strauss (1964).
25. Henry (1965), Bettelheim (1960), Cohen (1953), Elkins (1959), Robertson (1961).

focuses on the lower-class person as caught in a conflict among his own needs, the orientations offered by the example of the life around him, and the orientations offered by the representatives of the larger society with whom he has contact. The main conceptual task in extending our understanding of the lower-class world is that of specifying the relationships among these three variables.

The need for a valid identity is fundamental; everyone needs to "be somebody." The great variation in the kinds of person one can become, even within the same society, suggests that the particular somebody one becomes is not nearly so important as that it be a somebody who is recognized in some sense a valid expression of the human condition. Gregory Stone has observed that almost all of the investigators who have used the concept of identity

> . . . imply that identity establishes *what* and *where* the person is in social terms. When one has identity he is *situated*—that is, cast in the shape of a social object by the acknowledgment of his participation or membership in social relations. One's identity is established when others *place* him as a social object by assigning him the same words of identity that he appropriates for himself or *announces*. It is in the coincidence of placements and announcements that identity becomes a meaning of the self.

It is exactly this coincidence of placements and announcements to which the term *valid identity* refers here.

For Erik Erikson the achievement of identity comes about when "the young adult gains an assured sense of inner continuity and social sameness which bridges what he *was* as a child and what he is *about to become* and also reconciles his *conception of himself* and his *community's recognition of him*." Erikson sees identity as "self-realization coupled with a mutual recognition."[27] Society is a system in which roles and identities are allocated to its members.

Each identity is a particular configuration of the role positions in which the individual has been recruited and which he has achieved and also a distinctive sense of uniqueness and connectedness which he has distilled from his experiences.

The maintenance of a valid identity is a life-long task, beginning in infancy and continuing until death. Internal or social pressures at any time can cause a crisis in which the individual is forced to call into

26. Stone (1962). For other discussions of the symbolic interaction approach to the question of identity, see Strauss (1959), particularly the discussion of "status forcing" (pp. 76–84) and "transformations of identity" (pp. 89–131), and Goffman (1963), particularly the distinctions among social identity, personal identity, and ego identity (p. 23, 56–57, and 105–109).

27. Erikson (1959), pp. 110–114.

question the validity of the person he thought himself to be. As Erikson has noted, adolescence and young adulthood (however these may be chronologically defined in different cultures) brings the tasks of identity formation to sharpest focus because it is during this time that the person must begin to relate the statuses he held by virtue of his age, sex, and kinship position to those he will fill in his mature life.

A valid identity is one in which the individual finds congruence between who he feels he is, who he announces himself to be, and where he feels his society places him. Individuals are led to announce a particular identity when they feel it is congruent with their needs, and the society influences these needs by its willingness to validate such announcements by a congruent placement. As individuals seek to build identities valid in terms of their own needs, they use the resources—the values, norms, and social techniques—which their culture makes available to them. Each individual tries on identities that emerge from the cultural material available to him and tests them by making appropriate announcements. If these announcements meet with success, he will maintain his identity until it is no longer validated by others or no longer congruent with his inner promptings.[28]

One of the deepest anxieties human beings can experience is that which comes from the loss of a sense of identity.[29] Such a loss comes about either when there is a disjunction between the self being announced and the needs pressing for gratification or when the announced identity is not validated by others.[30] In either case, the identity becomes invalid for the

28. I am indebted to Alvin W. Gouldner for noting a possible "consensual" error in the above formulation. That is, others do not confirm the individual's announcements automatically, their placements are a function of their own motivations or strategies in the situation. Placements of announced identities are hard won in processes of interaction in which both announcer and placer have stakes in the outcome which affect the other's willingness to confirm an identity. One kind of power in an interpersonal situation involves an individual's ability to significantly affect the identity processes of another by choosing to confirm or disconfirm the latter's announced identity.

29. See Goodenough (1963), particularly his discussion of "identity and personal worth". "Human beings are anchored to reality and purpose by a firm sense of who they are. There are few human conditions more frightening than amnesia, where the individual, cut off from such a sense, drifts aimlessly, his actions without meaning or purpose to himself. When an amnesia victim goes to some authority in his plight, it is to get help in finding out *who* he is. And it is always striking to see how zealously other people set to work to hook him back onto the identity from which he has come loose. Whatever his problems may be, there seems to be no way to get at them until he recommits himself to a particular identity in a world of other identities, and until he becomes a specific person again" (p. 176).

30. The subjective experience of a disjunction between announced self and pressing needs is well know psychiatrically as "depersonalization," a situation in which the individual says to himself, "I am no longer Me," or "My body does not seem to be part of Me"; see the discussion by Federn (1955), p. 241–260, and Fenichel (1951), p. 354–358. In depersonalization the repressed needs seeking expression in behavior call into question the validity of the self-announced (conscious) identity. On a more superficial level, identity processes are sufficiently complex to allow this very fact to be built into announced identity, as when the individual regards himself and is regarded by others as a "bored" or "blasé" type.

individual, once he recognizes the state of affairs. For a time he may not do so, resisting recognition with intrapsychic mechanisms in defense against internal invalidation or by self-delusion about social invalidation.[31]

Once an identity is recognized as invalid, the anxiety which descends upon the individual pushes him toward seeking another valid identity. In a tightly organized society where the individual has relatively few choices of the kind of valid identity he can build up through his life, he has the security of knowing the expectable payoffs for assuming various identities and thus has a sense that his efforts to gratify his needs are justly regulated. However, in a society in which there are many roles and relatively open access to them, the individual is in a more uncertain situation because he is exposed to a greater possibility that the identity he announces will not be validated either by the larger world or by his own needs (this latter because his needs have themselves been influenced by the more varied social system).

Anomic situations may not arise or at least may not persist in such an open society, so long as there exists a set of roles to which the individual is guided providing him with a valid identity. In Merton's terms, as long as the individual has a social place in which he can find satisfaction from the achievement of his own (culturally-induced) goals and also derive satisfaction directly from the institutional modes of striving to attain his goals, anomie will not result.[32] But anomie may occur if the individual is not able to maintain a valid identity. This may happen either because in acting out the roles in which he is placed by society he experiences such frustrations that he cannot accept the identity as valid or because his efforts to achieve a valid identity in terms of the cultural models the society recommends do not result in placement.[33]

In the anomic situation the individual finds that his efforts to achieve a valid identity along the lines supported by the larger society are in vain.

31. The idea of "self-delusion about social invalidation" seriously oversimplifies the matter for the purpose of brevity. What is important phenomenologically, of course, is whether the individual perceives social response as validating or invalidating his announced identity. Nevertheless, the evolving consequences of an interaction process are such that there will generally be some correspondence between the announcer's perception and the "real" behavior on the part of the others with whom he interacts. The extent of this correspondence is problematic in any given situation, and probably varies, as Marc J. Swartz has noted in a private communication, according to the kinds of "objective" verification accompanying different roles: "That is, the verification the person receives in one role or complex of roles gets to him in a more undeniable way because it comes with a palpable sign. When you get a high salary, or are initiated into an age grade, or something else 'objective,' it may be that you get a firmer and more useful confirmation of your identity than if you participate in a role whose consequences are not so palpable and undeniable."

32. For an example of the importance of cathexis of institutionally canalized modes in successful role performance, see Henry (1949).

33. The sense of estrangement and alienation that stems from the first possibility is described by Erich Fromm in this way: the individual "has become estranged from his own life forces, from the wealth of his own potentialities, and is in touch with himself only in the indirect way of life frozen in . . . idols" (1961).

His identity is questioned either by intrapsychic pressures or by the society. But because a tenable life requires a sense of valid identity the individual has no other choice than to try again. If his efforts are outside the range of what is deemed culturally appropriate, he will be marked as deviant, but if he manages to formulate an identity and find a group that validates it, even deviant life becomes tenable. This is the situation in which the lower-class person finds himself.

If a valid identity does not lie in the direction of a viable economic role (either directly or in the purely instrumental terms of allowing a man to be a good provider or a woman to be a good housekeeper and mother) then one must seek in other ways to construct a self which provides some measure of gratification of needs and earns some measure of recognition of oneself as a social being.

Behavior considered to be deviant, either by members of their own groups or by others can be regarded as an effort to attain valid identity, to gratify the prompting of internal need and to elicit recognition from those around them.[34] Deviance from conventional cultural norms is an organized effort to achieve valid identity in a situation in which this has not been possible within the limits of the norms. When individuals persist in deviant behavior it is because they find in it a tenable identity, one that is validated internally and by a group of significant others. The shifting from one kind of deviant behavior to another sometimes exhibited by individuals who embark on deviant careers comes about as they learn in each new "kick" that there is no valid identity for them there.[35]

The Expressive Style of Adaptation

In previous chapters we have discussed depressive, violent and respectable styles of adaptation to the stresses of lower class life, and have described expressive adaptations as constructive efforts of young lower-class Negroes to fashion a gratifying way of being. Many of the varied kinds of behavior in which the adolescents and young adults of the ghetto

34. The process of finding a valid identity through deviant behavior is not unitary. Thus some individuals fall into such identities by seeming accident, that is, by a process of differential association which gradually leads to their being inculcated into a deviant subculture and to their learning the deviant "needs" central to the deviant identity. In other cases, deviants start out with deviant needs and seek communities in which these needs will be recognized as constituting the core of a deviant identity. In the first case the "square" becomes a "cat" from the outside in; in the second case he ends up in the same place by a process which completes his identity from the inside out. The first possibility has been the focus of theoretical development by sociologists such as Edwin H. Sutherland (*The Sutherland Papers*, Albert Cohen, Alfred Lindesmith, and Karl Schussler [eds.], 1956) and Howard Becker (1963). The second possibility has been developed predominantly by psychologists and psychiatrists, for example, Friedlander (1947) and McClosky and Schaar (1965). It is unfortunately true that each school holds at arms' length the alternate possibility.
35. See the juvenile delinquency literature previously cited and also Yablonsky (1962). Similar movements from one kind of deviancy to another are apparent in case studies by Hughes (1958) and Greenwald (1958). See also the excellent theoretical paper by Cohen (1965).

engage suggest that an expressive life-style is characteristic of lower-class people. This style involves the preoccupations Herbert Gans has dubbed the "action-seeking" way of life and Harold Finestone describes as the "cats-and-kicks" syndrome.[36] The literature on juvenile delinquency (particularly that which derives from participant observation techniques) contains rich and varied examples of this orientation to action, and the community studies of lower-class life and our field data from Pruitt-Igoe all suggest that many deviations from conventional styles are variations on this theme.

The cultivation of a particular kind of dramatic self is both a goal for individuals in a lower-class setting and is functional in putting together a valid identity. In the expressive life style instrumental orientations to living are consistently downgraded, recognized mainly in terms of the bare necessity of keeping body and soul together from day to day, while self-expression is emphasized, elaborated, and held out as possessing intrinsic merit.

At the broadest level, all of the highly stylized activities described in Chapter 11 and illustrated in the profile chapters seem to be non-utilitarian. Their primary purpose does not seem that of furthering the acquisition of goods and services, nor the satisfaction of purely biological needs. The expressive style can be used to gain income or sex, but these are not the main goals of the style. All of these activities represent different versions of a single adaptation in lower-class Negro society, which has as its primary goal the maintenance of reciprocity between members on the basis of a symbolic exchange of selves, an entertainment of each by the other. As Jules Henry has noted, persons living in a hopeless world may develop for their survival mechanisms to focus their energy on modes of action that continually tell them they are alive.[37] The expressive style is a way of accomplishing this, and also a way of building and maintaining connectedness with others in the context of an overall structure of relationships that provides few traditional and solid axes of affiliation, duties, and expectations.

Given the characteristics of the society system that brought Negroes to the New World and in which they have survived, the development of the self-as-currency is highly adaptive. Slaves did not have access to material objects that could be used to symbolize their connectedness, nor were they allowed to develop a system of roles that could bind them in social space and give them a sense of continuity through time. Rather, owners sought to make their slaves dependent upon themselves and allowed only a minimum of structure to develop within the slave community.[38] While Negroes have increased in autonomy since the Civil War, white society has continued to break down and disrupt the construction of either communal or bureaucratic systems of social relations among Negroes and between

36. Gans (1962), Finestone (1964).
37. Henry (1965).
38. Elkins (1959), Stampp (1956), Tannenbaum (1963), Herskovits and Melville (1928).

them and whites.[39] The community to which Negroes must adapt is one in which there is a low expectation of reward based on ascribed status (familial, sexual) or for conventionally achieved status. In their world, one learns that one has to "go for yourself," relying on the response of others to measure success. If one is successful in creating a dramatic self, a kind of security has been gained because that self can neither be taken away nor spent (at least in the short run). If one is successful in establishing relationships of symbolic reciprocity with others similarly seeking to maximize a dramatic self, then the self is constantly replenished.

This elaboration of an expressive self plays a central dynamic role in most forms of lower-class deviant behavior. It is directly relevant as a motivating force for alcohol and drug involvement of all kinds. The culture encourages individuals to seek idiosyncratic and nonrational experiences, such as fighting as a self-maximizing mode of relating to the world (in some juvenile gangs a reputation may be acquired either by "burning" another or being "burned"), or sexual activity as a way of presenting the self as unique and powerful. In all of these activities two things are going on at the same time: the individual is experiencing a heightened sense of himself as a total being and he is accumulating an attractive social identity.

This particular kind of self is symbolized in the concept of "soul." The admirable person is one who has much soul (and in one song, soul is equivalent to body; the singer indicates he has 170 pounds of soul). Although it is customary to think of the individual as having many selves which are independently activated in different role relationships, it is difficult to get away from the idea that behind the various selves there somehow lies an individual's particular identity which is more of a whole and involves less psychic division of labor. In the Negro lower-class there has been little to encourage the adaptations that multiply selves in role-specific activities. Instead, heavy emphasis has developed on the self as an all-purpose object, on holistic notions such as "soul," "heart," and "rep."

The central or core self is implicit in Goffman's discussions of role distance; he is at great pains to show that individuals always try to discourage others from confusing them with their particular roles. Goffman suggests that the individual seeks to protect his other selves from denial in any given interaction. He quotes Sapir's comment that "the endless resdiscovery of the self in a series of petty truancies from the official socialized self becomes a mild obsession of the normal individual in any society in which the individual has ceased to be a measure of the society itself."[40]

In lower-class Negro society there are, instead, wholesale truancies from an official socialized self which can not come into being, although in some circumstances it is necessary for individuals to maintain that they do

39. Whitten (1969).
40. Goffman (1961), p. 146–147, 151.

indeed possess such a self. The holes and tatters in that self suggest *phantom roles* and *phantom self*, a notion developed by Alvin W. Gouldner and Jules Henry to conceptualize the fact that respondents in the Pruitt-Igoe study often arrogated to themselves role and self attributes on which their claims were very tenuous. For example, a man speaks of himself as a bellboy, but his "job" consists only of awaiting a call when the hotel that occasionally employs him needs extra help; a mother speaks of herself as carrying out maternal activities (bathing children, preparing meals) when in fact she does them infrequently. In this way particularly are conventional phantom roles incorporated into the identities of lower-class Negroes; they serve to bridge the gap between desire and reality, to expand the self in a situation where the self-expanding possibilities of actual activity are scarce and intermittent.

Clearly some individuals realize the subculture ideal of a dramatic identity more effectively than others; some are better at rapping, some are better singers, some are better drinkers or fighters or preachers or better at experiencing religious ecstasy ("getting happy") than others. The individual who does better at these things receives more fully the rewards his subculture has to give him; the person with soul becomes a leader, whether in the church or the tavern or the street, the laundry room or the bedroom. People offer him recognition and he provides them with opportunity for vicarious experience, for learning, and for a reaffirmation of the particular world view which lies behind this cultural ideal.

But it is easy to present an overly romantic view of this cultural pattern; it can wear itself out quickly. An adaptation to a particular situation need not be a perfect adaptation. The combination of rewards to be derived from the performer role sustain this cultural pattern even though it very seldom pays off in the way those who strive to fill the role may want.

The dramatic self is, in one or another of its forms, the valid identity to be achieved within the expressive style of life. It is a self markedly at variance with the official socialized self legitimated by the dominant sections of American society. Only when the dramatic self is turned into an occupational role, as among Negro musicians and athletes, does it earn credit in the middle class. Otherwise the behavior that comes to be highly valued by the lower-class person seems to the middle class simply an expression of the "shiftlessness," "irresponsibility," "lack of ambition," and "untrustworthiness" of people who are of no account, who do not have valid identities.

The range of behavior of this kind observed in Pruitt-Igoe and in other investigations fit rather neatly into Talcott Parsons' category of "the immanent quality-perfection ideal" as one type of social value orientation.[41] The particular version of this ideal that seems best to characterize the expressive life style can be described in Parsons' pattern variable scheme

41. Parsons and Shils (1952), p. 43 ff; Parsons (1951).

as "ascriptive, particularistic, self-oriented, diffused, and affective."[42] In the development of the dramatic self, the whole emphasis is on *qualities*, on what a person *is* by virtue of his actions rather than on what he *does*. The Negro language of the dramatic self is replete with terms for these desirable qualities—"rep," "soul," "being saved," "being happy."[43] The goal of this expressive system is the cultivation of self given to others for their gratification. Used as currency in the establishment of social relationships, such investment earns dividends for its further enhancement. The institutional settings for its development are the street, the church, and the family; the activities central to its cultivation are those of membership.

In contrast, work is an activity in the instrumental system, a system that involves the learning structures of the school and the performance structures of the workplace. These institutional settings place heavy emphasis on instrumental behavior and allow little play for self-expression. The activity central to the instrumental system is not membership but individual production, not exchanging selves but making and doing something.

In the course of development of the lower-class individual, he is gratified most often by action involving affectivity, particularism, self-orientation, ascription, and diffuseness. At the same time his experiences characterized by the opposite pattern variables are frustrating, punishing, or at the very least, not gratifying. In the schools (which are oriented toward

42. The immanent quality-perfection ideal involves "a valuation on the harmonious and acceptive adaptation to the given situation, making the most of it as an expressive opportunity." It involves "valuation of general affective action in relation to ascriptively designated particular persons or groups (e.g., generalized gratification expectation in connection with individuals or groups having certain qualities and having a particularistic relation to ego.)" In terms of the types of ego's goal striving toward classes of objects, Parsons characterizes this particular social value orientation as follows: (1) in goal striving in relation to ego's own body there is "acceptance of opportunities of any gratification as they occur or as need emerges. No attachment to specific objects or modes of gratification." (2) In terms of alter's personality there is "acceptance of any alter as a satisfactory partner for enjoyment of any gratification as needs arise and as opportunities occur. No joint exercise with alter to achieve hitherto unrealized goals." (3) With respect to the physical environment there is "acceptance of available opportunities for any kind of gratification as they occur and as need arises. Efforts to ward off losses taken only with respect to most immediately enjoyed gratification opportunities but in view of wide substitutibility of gratification objects."

43. Parsons notes of the value components of role expectations of the ascriptive-particularistic orientation that "there is the orientation of action to an expectation of conforming with a standard governing the conduct of actors possessing certain qualities assessed in the light of their particular relation to the actor. There is an orientation toward an expectation of diffuse affective expression toward an object on the basis of qualities in a particularistic relation to actor." This extremely abstract statement catches much that is central to the activity of "sounding" (i.e., dialogue of mutual insult) which many observers have spoken of as the central interaction pattern of lower class boys and young adults. In sounding there is a dialogue of ascription; ego ascribes certain negative qualities to alter and certain positive ones to himself. It is through this process as much as by performance that the individual's status within the group is established and maintained and at the same time constantly challenged.

affective neutrality, a seeming universalism, heavy emphasis on collectivity, achievements, and specificity) he finds himself generally out of step
on the first day and falling further and further behind as time goes on.[44]
The lower-class child learns early that he is not likely to achieve a sense
of valid identity along these lines and turns instead toward the prevalent
expressive orientations that promise gratification now.

At adolescence and later, in company with like-minded peers, the lower-
class boy sets out to *be* someone through the technique of developing the
dramatic self and exposing himself to experts at the technique. By the
time he moves into the labor market he finds that he has few of the skills
that market requires and a good deal of doubt about the possibility of
gaining self-validation in an occupational role. His estrangement from
the role model of "job holder" leads him sometimes to exaggerate the
ease with which he could get a good job if given a chance, and at other
times to express his conviction that the instrumentally-oriented occupational world will never give him a chance to have and hold a job.

In response to all this, many lower-class men assign a low priority
to work stability in the way they live their lives.[45] As Davis points out in
his article on the underprivileged worker, they engage in behavior that
inevitably leads to being dismissed, or they quit their jobs because "no
one's gonna give me a hard time, who do they think I am?" Similarly, they
stretch out the time between jobs by failing to seek work energetically,
falling back on their kin or girlfriends for money. In the meantime, they
still have something important to do: they continue to seek and sustain
valid identities before an audience of their peers. Lower-class boys, therefore, show relative disinterest in the kind of available instrumental activity
for which they are prepared and a strong preference for getting along in
ways that do not require one to be a steady worker and good provider.

Girls find themselves constrained to function instrumentally much earlier
in their lives than they would wish. They find these constraints frustrating
because they lack the resources to fulfill their roles in ways that will earn
them social rewards. As they age, they find expressive opportunities declining and feel increasing frustration in their instrumental concerns, and
they tend to adapt in self-constricting depressive ways.

Men and boys do not hold to expressive styles without ambivalence,
but they do regard expressive achievement as expectable, understandable,
and even gratifying alternatives one may legitimately choose in a situation in which it is not possible to be someone by working toward an
"official socialized self" as good provider or career man. We have considered those forces in the world of lower-class individuals that encourage

44. See Equality of Educational Opportunity (1966).
45. Schwartz and Henderson (1964); see also Gursslin and Roach (1964) for a discussion of psychological characteristics which interfere with lower class workers' performance of skilled work.

the search for a valid identity in an expressive style of life, to the detriment of the instrumental tasks of learning and earning an income. But the situation is not so simple. Lower-class individuals do seek accomplishment in instrumental areas and may from time to time try to establish validated images of themselves by pursuing goals related to work and job stability. Even the individual who seems very much enmeshed in an expressive way of life may "suddenly" devote himself assiduously to a job, limit his involvement in expressive activities in the interest of keeping that job, and direct the money he earns toward the goal of a stable life. How can this happen?

Presumably if an individual begins to shift the focus of his energies away from the cultivation of a dramatic self, it must be because this activity is not meeting his needs. A constant source of frustration to most lower-class individuals is their awareness that despite the surface validity of the self they present, their behavior is not consistent with some of the standards of the larger society which they have internalized, often in spite of themselves. They are made aware of their deviance not only by ubiquitous middle-class representatives but by others in their own world, who for selfish or moral reasons call into question the validity of their identity by suggesting that it is not in line with normative standards. Seeking to become a valid person in a more conventional way remains attractive even though the probability of success may be low.

In addition, cultivation of the expressive style of life is accompanied by its own frustrations. The rewards of expressive behavior may be meager, and the aggressive competition for status may constantly call into question the individual's status as a successful practitioner, resulting in considerable anxiety. This heightened anxiety will generally intensify an individual's efforts to compete successfully, but if it becomes too great he may say to himself, "What am I doing anyway? Why don't I try to get a job and settle down?"

So for a variety of reasons, lower-class individuals may from time to time seek valid identities in instrumental role performance. Such a man either seeks and gets a job or begins to pay more than minimum attention to the one he has. His primary motivation may still be directed toward expressive goals—for example, more money will enable him to have fancier clothes or go to more expensive bars and nightclubs or buy a better car. However, continued success at work will increase his subjective estimate of the probability of achieving a valid identity in an instrumental role. Few lower-class men direct their aspirations toward career success, but the goals involved in "the good American life" have been internalized long ago and seem increasingly feasible as their employment is more stable and their income increases.

Especially when a man becomes the head of a family (with the entailed tasks of being a good provider, father, and husband), he will feel constrained to moderate the goals of the dramatic self. Women tend to be more verbal and more energetic than their men in their affirmation of the values of "the good American life." Once they are mothers there is less to be gained by women in an expressive direction, and they tend to be more preoccupied with achieving a decent and stable material standard. They are ready to reward and to punish the men in their household, depending on how well they succeed as providers. Dramatic changes occur within the short span of a day or two in the authority which an unemployed versus employed father can have in his household. The father gets a job and his wife and children are willing to listen to him and do what he says. The father loses his job and the wife becomes much stricter in her evaluation of his demeanor. In one case, a woman had her husband kicked out of their apartment because he scratched her furniture, was unemployed, and could not pay for its repair.[46]

This kind of encouragement of stability, of the pursuit of material well-being, is not so powerful in the lower class as in the working and middle classes because generally it is only a man's own family who reinforce such behavior. His peers are likely to criticize the fact that he no longer seems loyal to the group or to respond positively only to the expressive investment of his income in flashy objects and "living it up." But these kinds of expenditures threaten his family and lower his status within it, and the criticism of his peers further encourages unpredictability at work (absenteeism and hang-overs) which increases the likelihood that he will lose his job and his income.

When an individual can hold a steady job and thereby increase his subjective estimate that he can "be someone" as a worker and provider instead of just as a dramatic self-object, he begins to moderate behavior that is detrimental to the pursuit of this new goal. If he keeps his job long enough and gets enough money from it to be validated in the role of good provider, he is much more likely to organize his life consistently around the pursuit of a more stable life style.[47]

Negative Identities

The dramatic self as a tenable identity in the lower-class Negro world is a difficult achievement. It is wrought against a background of constant assaults on the individual, constant frustration of his efforts to become meaningful and rewarding. It is not surprising that identities based on expressive styles of adaptation are often subverted by negative interpretations of whom one has become. The use within one's family and community of models of respectability means that the individual is constantly

46. The effects of employment and unemployment on the family status of men have been well documented over the past thirty years; see Bakke (1940), Komarovsky (1940), Koos (1946), Dyer (1964), and Yancey (1967).

47. Davis (1946) observed this phenomenon in the striking changes of behavior of men who found steady work for the first time during World War II (p. 100 ff.).

vulnerable to the conversion of his positive social identity as an expressive achiever into a negative identity as immoral, or incompetent, or a failure. Parents' attitudes to their children's participation in the street world can play a significant role in heightening the child's ambivalence about the achievement of a valid identity through expressiveness.

It is in the family that the child learns the most primitive categories of existence and experience, that he develops his most deeply held beliefs about the world and about himself.[48] From the child's point of view, the household *is* the world; everything he meets as he moves out of it and into the larger world is interpreted in terms of his particular experience within the home. The painful experience of a child in the Negro slum culture is therefore interpreted as in some sense a reflection on this family world. The impact of victimization is transmitted through the family, and the child cannot be expected to have enough sophistication to see exactly where the villains are. From the child's point of view, if he is hungry it is his parents' fault; if he experiences frustration in the streets or in school it is his parents' fault; if the world seems incomprehensible to him it is his parents' fault; if people are aggressive or destructive toward each other it is his parents' fault. If a subculture could exist in which there were comfort and security within the family and the individual experienced frustration only when he moved into the larger society, the family might not there be held to blame. The effect of the caste system in which the Negro American lives, however, is to bring home all of the victimization processes, and to bring them home in such a way that it is often very difficult even for adults to see the connection between the pain they feel at the moment and the structured patterns of the caste system.

In most societies, as children grow up and are formed by their elders into suitable members of the society they gain a sense of competence to master the behavioral environment their world presents. In Negro slum culture, growing up involves instead an ever-increasing appreciation of one's shortcomings, of the impossibility of finding a self-sufficient and gratifying way of living.[49] It is in the family first and most devastatingly that one learns these lessons. As the child's sense of frustration builds, he too can strike out and unmask the pretensions of others. The result is a peculiar strength and a pervasive weakness. The strength involves an ability to tolerate and defend one's self against degrading aggressions from others and not to give up completely. The weakness involves a re-

48. Parsons concludes his discussion of child socialization, the development of an "internalized family system," and internalized role differentiation, by observing: "The internalization of the family collectivity as an object and its values should not be lost sight of. This is crucial with respect to . . . the assumption of representative roles outside the family on behalf of it. Here it is the child's family membership which is decisive; thus, he is acting in a role in terms of its values for 'such as he'" (Parsons and Bales, 1955, p. 113).

49. See the discussion of Negro self-identity and self-esteem in Pettigrew (1964), Kardiner and Ovesey (1962) and Grier and Cobbs (1968).

luctance to embark hopefully on any course of action that might make things better, and particularly any action that involves cooperation with and trusting attitudes toward others. Family members become potential enemies to each other, as the frequency of bringing in the police to settle family quarrels shows all too dramatically.

Parents' conceptions of children make them constantly alert to evidence that their child is as bad as everyone else. This reflects basic views in lower-class culture that human nature is essentially bad, destructive, immoral. If a mother can keep her child insulated from the outside world, she thinks she may protect him not so much from the world as from himself; once he is let out, badness will come to the fore because that is his nature. In the child's identity development he is constantly exposed to labeling by his parents as a bad or potentially bad person. Because he does not experience his world as gratifying, it is easy for him to conclude that this lack of gratification is due to the fact that something is wrong in him, and this can readily be assimilated to the definitions of himself as a bad person that are offered him by those with whom he lives. In this way the Negro slum child learns his culture's conception of being in the world, a conception that emphasizes inherent evil in a chaotic, hostile, destructive world.

These same processes operate in white lower-class groups, of course, but added for the Negro is the reality of his blackness, and some of the effects of this reality can be traced in the pejorative terms used in the Negro slum culture. Three distinctive appellations are common in making negative references to oneself and others: *black ass, nigger,* and *motherfucker. Black-assed* generally has negative connotations, but *nigger* and *motherfucker* can be either negative or positive, depending upon the context. These terms together symbolize the core of a primitive level of identity which Negroes in this lower-class culture incorporate into their self-concept to some degree and which they may cope with in a variety of ways.

In the urban North the initial development of racial identity in these terms has very little to do directly with relationships with whites. A child experiences identity placement in the context of the family and in the neighborhood peer group, and he seldom hears these terms used by whites. Ghettoization masks the ultimate enemy so that an understanding of the fact of victimization by a caste system comes late; it is laid over conceptions of self and of other Negroes derived from intimate, and, to the child, often traumatic experience within the ghetto community. In the ghetto school his Negro teachers may overtly or by implication reinforce his community's negative conception of what it means to be black. Thus he has little opportunity to develop a more realistic image of himself and other Negroes as being damaged by whites and not by themselves. In such a situation, an intelligent man like Thomas Coolidge (Chapter 2) can say with all sincerity that he does not feel most Negroes are ready for integration; only under intense personal threat coupled with exposure to an anti-white ideology did he begin to see through the direct evidence of his daily experience.[50]

Living in the heart of a ghetto, then, *black* comes to mean not only deprivation and frustration but also membership in a community of persons who think poorly of each other, who attack and manipulate each other, who give each other small comfort in a desperate world. Black comes to stand for an identity as no better than these destructive others. The individual feels that he must embrace an unattractive self to function at all.

Some families manage to avoid the destructive implications of *black-assed* and maintain solidarity against assaults from the world around them, and there it may be possible for children to grow up with a sense of Negro and personal identity that allows them to socialize themselves in an anticipatory way for participation in the larger society. Such a broader sense of identity, however, will remain brittle so long as the individual is vulnerable to attack both from the white community as "just a nigger" and within the Negro community as "just a nigger like everybody else." The destructive unmasking of essential identity as black is least likely to occur within families where the parents have a sense of security. With security, they have less need to protect themselves by disavowing responsibility for their children's behavior and denying them their patrimony as products of a particular family rather than an immoral nature and an evil community.

The elements of identity bound up in the label *motherfucker* are less clear, though they may overlap in meaning with *black-assed* because of the sexual connotations of *assed*. We know that *motherfucker* can be applied to both boys and girls, men and women. The contexts in which the term is used suggest a compounding of meanings—the sacredness of family relations, profane sexual laxity, and the exploitative and aggressive wresting from others of what they would not give freely.[51]

The term acquires its particular social significance in the lower class Negro world as a commentary on, an observation about, the disjunction between the monogamous and circumspect *ideal* about with whom and under what circumstances women should have sexual relations, and the

50. It was in the case of Mr. Coolidge (Chapter 2), also, that we observed one of the few times in all our field work when black was used with prideful as well as negative connotations. It was after our field work had been completed that black pride, black consciousness, and the like, became a keynote of the public presentation of Negroes to each other and to the white audience. One would expect that given the rise of black consciousness the positive and negative meanings of blackness will co-exist for some time to come. It is unlikely that the negative identity elements attached to blackness will disappear until such time as the regular experience of impotence connected with being black also disappears.

51. See discussions of the dozens by Dollard (1939) and Abrahams (1962).

fact of widespread sexual involvement between men and women who are not married to each other and whose "illicit" relationships are taken for granted.

Motherfucker is a way of describing this aspect of family and sexual life in the Negro slum culture; it says, in essence, "in our world, every man is a motherfucker and every woman is a motherfucked." The term functions to legitimate sexually exploitative activity on the part of both men and women because it says, "That's the way it is, let's not kid each other." By juxtaposing the semi-sacred idea of motherhood with the idea of a woman who is available to males other than her spouse, and by suggesting the relationship of older women to younger men it also supports the systematic de-emphasis on age homogeneity of sexual partners that is apparent in lower-class Negro life.

At a more personal and less structural level, the term serves as a wry commentary on (and facilitator for) the manipulation and exploitation of women for nonsexual rewards, and more generally of one person by others regardless of sex. The term uses a sexual metaphor to suggest more broadly a quality of interpersonal relations. In the most taboo sense, a *motherfucker* would be a son who had sexual relations with his mother, that is, a man who achieved a gratification that was proscribed for him. Even more broadly, of course, the sexual involvements of men and women, particularly of mothers and their boyfriends, are ones that can be resented when they take the mother's attention and nurturance from her children.

Whether the literal motherfucker is a son or a boyfriend, he is deriving gratification at the expense of others who depend on the woman for the gratification of their more legitimate needs. This definition of the word, which may appear overly literal, actually corresponds to the situation of many lower-class Negro men and women who find that to satisfy their needs they must manipulate and exploit others in ways that are not regarded as legitimate, and yet that they themselves are the victims of such manipulation and exploitation by others. The commentary embedded in the term tells its users and its hearers that their world is one in which manipulation, seduction, and exploitation are the way it is; that people are more likely to get what they want by taking it than by waiting for what they are legitimately entitled to receive. For this reason, *motherfucker* can be used in an admiring, an abusive, or a derogating way—admiring if the emphasis is on the apparent potency of the one referred to, abusive if the emphasis is on the immorality of his exploitation of others, derogating if the emphasis is on his inability to get what he needs in legitimate ways.

At the emotional level, one must take into account the hostile and aggressive connotations of this old Anglo-Saxon word, *fuck*, which overlie its denotation of sexual intercourse. In the harsh jargon of the lower class and their middle-class imitators, someone who is "fucked" gives up goods for no commensurate return; something is taken from him; he is misused.

In this sense the term applies to business or political dealings as well as to the bedroom. The fucker is a robber, as reflected in the meanings of *rape*. Indeed, the generalization of *to fuck* to nonsexual matters such as business and political dealings applies equally and in exactly the same way to the verb *to rape*. One can substitute the word *rape* in any sentence which uses *fuck* in connection with such dealings without changing the meaning in any essential way. At the emotional level, the term *motherfucker* suggests the hostile, aggressive quality of much of interpersonal relations in Negro lower-class society, as well as the facts of interpersonal manipulation and exploitation.

With these various meanings bound up in the term *motherfucker*, it signifies for the Negro lower-class user an image of himself and of others as persons who get what they want by manipulation and seduction because they are not rightfully entitled to what they seek and therefore it cannot or will not be freely given to them. The term also involves the notion that the individual is not strong enough or adult enough to achieve his goal in a legitimate way, but is rather like a child, dependent on others who tolerate his childish maneuvers, or dependent on others to actually be as vulnerable as he so that he can exercise over them the tyranny which children exercise over families that are not in complete command of their own needs and wishes.

The Negro Lower-Class Subculture

An examination of the problems of constructing a valid identity in the lower-class Negro world highlights the adaptiveness of lower-class subcultural characteristics. These characteristics are the result of the exercise of human rationality by a people who have lived for several hundred years in a situation of oppression and deprivation. Family behavior proves to be a particularly sensitive indicator of the extent to which lower-class subcultural adaptations combine a commitment to conventional norms (as Merton and his followers stress) and a daily struggle to cope with the situations that arise when the effort to live up to these norms fails (as Davis and his students stress). The essential elements of Pruitt-Igoe views about marriage, sexual behavior, and procreation can be summarized as follows. These views are expressed both as general philosophical statements about the world and in responses to day-to-day living.

> Lifelong marriage is the only really desirable way of living. A person with the proper social and cultural characteristics (respectability, education, job) should be able to contract and maintain such a marriage, provided he can find a partner with similar characteristics.

> Children should be born only in marriage relationships; to procreate outside marriage is to fall short of the way things ought to be.

Any kind of sexual relationships outside marriage is dangerous, although it is attractive. A double standard applies in the realm of ideals, at least, in that sex outside of marriage is more dangerous for women then for men.

There is little ambiguity about these norms concerning sex and procreation as they apply to how good people would behave in a good world. Sexual and procreative events outside of the context of marriage are not normative and they are held to involve costs.

But reality makes it extremely difficult to live up to these norms. The individual's chances to succeed in the outside world are low, and the pressures from his peer group toward deviance are great. For all but exceptional individuals, deviance from the sexual and procreative norms is very likely. Resistance is weakened when one does not possess attributes and abilities that allow him to make out in more conventional ways when one does not manage to get enough education, hold a job, etc.

Therefore deviance from the norms must be tolerated and it is possible to live a life that departs significantly from the way one thinks life ought to be lived without ceasing to exist, without feeling totally degraded, without giving up all self-esteem.

Once one learns that such a life is tolerable it is possible for individuals to engage in "rebellion" a la Merton. One may call into question both the cultural goals and the institutionalized means for achieving them, and seek to put in their place contrary goals and means that bring action and norms more closely in line and thus reduce cognitive dissonance. However, it is important to remember that rebellion is not revolution, that the pull of the old norms is great, and that very few lower class individuals end up defining their own interests as lying ideally in the support of the deviant norms rather than the conventional ones.

With respect to the central importance of marriage, the compromise solution most frequently adopted in the Negro lower class is to marry fairly quickly, particularly in response to the pressures of pregnancy or extensive sexual activity that begins to look promiscuous, and to hope against hope that the marriage will work out and last so that one may achieve conventional status. Therefore, lower class Negro Americans tend to marry fairly early rather than to go through a series of mating unions (including domiciliary ones) and crown their sexual careers with marriage as in the Caribbean. The corollary of this difference, however, is that among urban lower class Negroes in the United States first marriages often break up (indeed, a majority probably do) whereas in the Caribbean legal marriage tends to be more stable.

Expectations concerning widespread sexual activity continue throughout life to pose a constant threat to the stability of relationships in which people try to "do right," to maintain stable relationships. The Negro lower class conforms to Bernard Farber's model of permanent availability of all men and women as mates. Men are seen as the main carriers of this tradition, but women are also active participants. Although there is much evidence of the double standard as representing a more ideal state of affairs than equality in sexual relations, it is believed that women are almost as likely to be "disloyal" to their mates (either marital or non-marital) as are men. There is evidence, however, that to a considerable extent the sexual freedom that women claim is reactive to a conception of men as so likely to transgress that a woman is a "fool" for being single-minded in her loyalty.

We can conclude this recapitulation of the Pruitt-Igoe data by saying that it seems that lower class Negroes in America and lower class Negroes in the Caribbean share very similar problems in connection with bringing their behavior into line with norms concerning sexual and procreative activities and that their cultural adaptation to these problems seems remarkably similar. In both areas the norms support legal marriage and legitimate birth as the only really proper way to establish families. In both areas women are more dedicated to these norms than men although both sexes recognize their legitimacy.[52]

The result of the impersonal socio-economic forces and the interpersonal forces of the community which militate against living up to these norms is that a set of more or less institutionalized alternatives to conventional

52. The issue of normative and deviant mating and family behavior in Caribbean areas is a complex one about which social scientists continue to be in contention. Nevertheless, it seems reasonable to conclude from the published materials that in most parts of the Caribbean many of the same normative issues concern the lower class Afro-Americans that we have seen are of concern to Negroes in the United States, and that the structural stresses which produce these concerns are analytically similar despite the many cultural, social, demographic and economic dissimilarities in the two areas. See Blake (1961), Goode (1960), Goode (1966), Henriques (1953), Otterbein (1965), Rodman (1966), M.G. Smith (1962), R.T. Smith (1963), Solien de Gonzalez (1961), Stycos (1964) and Whitten (1969). Raymond T. Smith offers a conclusion concerning family norms in the West Indies that is similar to the one outlined above for Pruitt-Igoe:

> The fact is, of course, that lower class West Indian Negroes hold contradictory views about what is desirable or possible for them . . . The problem is to uncover the source of (the) patterned deviance from societal values.

> There is a fundamental dissonance between the accepted ideals of these societies and the objective possibility of their realization by the majority of people. This is not due simply to a failure to master instrumental norms; it has to do with the mode of integration of colonial or ex-colonial societies around the acceptance of white superiority while at the same time political power was deployed for the maintenance of a fixed pattern of social and economic relations. (Smith, 1963, p. 44).

behavior have developed historically for adapting to the actual pressures under which men and women live in the ghetto, but these adaptations are not basically satisfactory to those who make use of them. These is much pain, frustration, and tension built into these ways of living, and people are vulnerable to the awareness that they have fallen short of full moral status, to attributions of this kind made both by themselves and by others.

Evocative definitions of culture usually define the concept as referring to "a way of life" or "a design for living." Culture is social heredity, transmitted from one generation to another and shared by the collectivity. Culture is a system of symbols which orders experience and guides behavior.

The term *subculture* suggests that within a collectivity possessing a culture there are groups displaying variations in designs for living that are presumed to have significant consequences. Because the social scientist discovers culture or subculture by abstraction from the behavior of persons in a group, the decision to define particular subcultures is to a certain extent arbitrary. This arbitrariness is reduced only by demonstrating that the variations one believes to exist are sufficiently consequential to be of use in understanding behavior within the larger collectivity.

Culture as social herdity, as a transmitted symbol system, has two main dimensions. It involves *existential* predications about the world and *evaluations* of what is good, not so good, or bad about that which is said to exist. Culture involves an "is" component and an "ought" component. These components are lumped together in the inventory of elements traditionally said to comprise culture—knowledge, belief, technology, values, and norms. As Clyde Kluckhohn observed, the existential propositions in a culture always carry implicit in them evaluative overtones, and equally important the evaluative elements of culture (values and norms) always carry implicit in them entailed existential concomitants.[53]

If one accepts the definition of *subculture* as referring to a distinctive pattern of existential and evaluative elements, a pattern that distinguishes a particular group in a larger collectivity, and is consequential for the way their behavior differs from that of other groups in the collectivity, there is no doubt that the concept of lower class subculture is useful. All who have studied lower-class people, whether under the influence of the Mertonian emphasis on general cultural norms (Cloward and Ohlin) or under the influence of strong proponents of class subculture (Davis and Miller), have produced findings concerning lower-class behavior and belief that suggest a distinctive pattern. This pattern is made up of some elements shared with the larger culture and others that are peculiar to the smaller group and it is the configuration of both that is distinctive to the lower class.

There is relatively little disagreement about the distinctiveness of the existential perspectives of lower-class people. All investigators present

53. Kluckhohn (1951).

compatible findings, to the general effect that in the lower-class view the world is a hostile and relatively chaotic place in which one must be always on guard and careful about trusting others, in which the reward for effort expended is always problematic, in which good intentions net very little.

The evaluative aspects of lower-class culture are more complex, and disagreement about them among observers results basically from the lack of realism of separating the normative from the existential. Every norm predicates several existential conditions which come most clearly to the surface when people seek to justify their deviance from norms. At such times people say they will live up to the norms of their group *if they possibly can,* and it becomes apparent that conforming to norms requires social logistic support. People often blind themselves to this requirement when they evaluate other people's behavior, but those who are similar in lacking resources generally develop some understanding and tolerance for each other's deviances from conventionality.

Norms with their existential concomitants can be regarded as a group's rules for playing a particular game that represents one kind of adaptation to its environment. Individuals in the group negotiate with significant others to be allowed to play the normative game—to get into it and for the resources that will allow them to play it. If the individual is not allowed to enter the game (for example, Negro slaves under slavery), or if he cannot obtain the resources to play the game successfully and thus experiences constant failure, he withdraws. In his pursuit of a valid identity he will then try to find another game to play, either one that already exists or one that he invents. Merton's well-known notion of adaptations to anomie suggests several kinds of attempts to create new games out of the wreckage of failure.

But what if there are many people who cannot play the normative game, who are in constant communication with each other with generational continuity among them? In that case, the stage is set for the invention and diffusion of a wide variety of substitute games. In the case of New World Negroes, these substitute games were worked out long ago, subject to modification by each generation depending on the situation (urban or rural, employed or unemployed) in which they find themselves. Each generation learned the substitute games (in the family and in peer groups) at the same time that it learned the normative rules. The adaptations of each generation conditioned the possibilities of subsequent generations for adapting to the requirements of the normative games.

Nevertheless, it is clear that in the American context each generation of Negroes has had a strong desire to perform successfully in terms of the norms of the larger society and has made efforts in this direction. The inadequacies of the opportunity structure have doomed most Negroes to failure in terms of their own desires, and therefore have facilitated the adoption of the readily available alternatives. In this way one might say that the social ontogeny of each generation recapitulates the social phylogeny of Negroes in the New World because the basic socio-economic marginality of the group has not changed in a direction favorable to successful achievement in terms of conventional norms.[54]

If a group becomes *totally* isolated from the dominant group whose games they cannot play, they will establish normative games of their own, but if they continue to some extent under the influence of the dominant group, their substitute games cannot acquire full normative character. Instead, the games may become pseudo-normative—the players assert to each other that their game has moral justification, but careful observation of actual behavior belies their statement. David Matza has described the manner in which this process operates for juvenile delinquents, who develop ideologies that seem to legitimate delinquent activity as normative, but in which as a matter of fact the delinquents themselves do not really believe.[55]

The force of the normative game of the larger society, reinforced in countless ways by all its institutions and ideologies, makes it very difficult to have a competing game with a normative *cachet*. Though competing games may be tolerated because the larger society is unwilling or unable to provide everyone with the resources to play its normative game, efforts to declare the competing games normative are inevitably frustrated.

Given this power of conventional society, members of the lower class are likely to be socialized to recognize the normative status of conventional games even though they eventually discover that their own best course, given the world as it is and as they see it, lies with substitute games. As Goffman observes:

> The stigmatized individual tends to hold the same beliefs about identity that we do. . . . The standards he has incorporated from the wider society equip him to be intimately alive to what others see as his failing, inevitably causing him, if only for moments, to agree that he does indeed fall short of what he really ought to be. Shame becomes a central possibility, arising from the individual's perception of one of his own attributes as being a defiling thing to possess, and one he can readily see himself as not possessing.[56]

The substitute games developed in the lower-class world have as perhaps their most important function the insulation of the individual from a full and sharp awareness of these facts, and from the shame that goes with this awareness, but careful observation reveals that the stigmatizing standards are nevertheless internalized and have their effects.

54. Norman F. Whitten has begun a systematic exploration of the role of socio-economic marginality in producing similarities among the adaptations of New World Negroes in a wide variety of seemingly different ecological and cultural settings. His preliminary analysis is reported in Whitten (1969). Another approach to the creativity of lower class Negro adaptations is represented by the work of Robert Coles (1967).

55. Matza (1964).

56. Goffman (1963).

The substitute game involves an appropriate structure of rules, but these rules have a purely operative character. It is difficult for the players to institutionalize the rules as normative except in a way that acknowledges them as substitutes. For example, there are rules about how to retain self-esteem even though one is the mother of illegitimate children. One girl commented that her mother reacted in this way to her pregnancy: "She cried, she was hurt. And she told me that because I made one mistake, don't wallow."

So conventional society inculcates its norms even in those persons who are not able to achieve successfully in terms of them, and prevents contrary views from acquiring full normative status. By what processes is this done? How is it possible to persuade lower-class people to accept norms that are punishing and to accept the label of deviant, the status of a stigmatized person?

All individuals in the group will to some extent and under some circumstances assert the validity of conventional norms and the invalidity of substitutes. (Even in Jamaica where non-legal unions are in the majority, 20 per cent of all first unions, and a somewhat higher proportion of the first domiciliary unions, involve legal marriage.)[57] There are too many "squares" around who can interfere with efforts to negate the conventions. These individuals counter the existential challenge to the norms by demonstrating that it is possible to live up to them even with few resources. In addition, they acquire a vested interest in derogating and demeaning those around them who do not live up to the norms. To the extent that they have power and prestige in the informal social networks of the lower-class community, they are able to act against an overthrow of the norms. The sliding scale of leniency in evaluating deviation for "me," "you," and "the other fellow" means that even individuals who are themselves involved in playing unconventional games will on occasion, particularly when angry and in a mood to degrade the status of others, assert the validity of the norm.

The aging process also assists in sustaining the validity of conventional norms. In a lower-class community the older people become, the more conventional their views become, and the less deviant their behavior is likely to be. In their contest with younger persons for the right to define what is and should be and to control the social and economic resources of the group, older adults acquire a vested interest in the conventional norms as part of their armament against the young who are challenging them. Just as there is conflict between men and women, there is also conflict between young and old. Women and older persons may have to accept a great deal of deviant behavior, but they may feel that it lessens their own chances of a secure and respectable life and therefore may stand in explicit opposition to deviance.

57. Stycos and Back (1964).

These conflicts at the interpersonal level are given expression in the indigenous lower class institutions that are organized around the support of conventional norms or carry such support with them. The church is particularly important in this respect; most of the content of church sermons is solidly in support of conventional norms (despite the conflicting message of ecstatic music and behavior during church services).

Finally, almost all of the externally-based institutions with which lower-class people come into contact are ranged in support of conventional norms: schools, stores, work places, public agencies. These institutions sometimes punish them directly for not living up to conventional standards, and their functionaries constantly demean and derogate the status of lower-class people, responding especially to indications that they are not "respectable" in behavior and attitudes. Major support for conventional norms comes from this kind of day-to-day contact with conventional functionaries. What comes across most clearly to the lower-class person in these settings is that he would be much better off if he were able to live in a conventional way because other people would not "bug" him so much.

The result of these processes is the development and maintenance of a lower-class subculture which is distinctive yet never free of conventional culture and its norms. Lower class subculture acquires limited functional autonomy from conventional culture, just as the social life of the lower class has a kind of autonomy from that of the rest of society. As Gouldner has observed, the phenomenon of functional autonomy in social systems arises in situations where full integration cannot be achieved with the resources available in the system. A compromise solution is for sub-units of the system to pull apart, to survive on their own since they cannot survive together.[58]

This functional autonomy of lower class subculture is in the interest of both the larger and the smaller society. Lower-class people require breathing room free from the oppressive application of conventional norms. Persons in conventional society are freed from the necessity of confronting the fact that their norms are constantly disregarded and that the mechanisms that are supposed to insure their observance do not operate effectively.[59]

Lower-class subculture can be regarded as the historical creation of persons who are disinherited by their society but who retain limited functional autonomy for their group. In this situation, they develop existential perspectives on social reality (including the norms and practices of the larger society) which allow them to stay alive and sane, to hope for a reasonably gratifying life and that somehow they may be able to find admittance to the larger society for themselves or their children. Such a subculture is the repository of a set of techniques for survival in the world of the

58. Gouldner (1959).
59. See Beck (1966) for a discussion of the embarrassments which the existence of a lower class segment of the society creates for the conventional ideology of a society.

disinherited, and in time these techniques take on the character of substitute games with their own rules guiding behavior. But these rules cannot
provide a lasting challenge to the validity of the larger society's norms
governing interpersonal relations and the basic social statuses involved in
heterosexual relations, marriage, and parent-child relations.

Discussions of lower-class culture in isolation from the social and economic setting to which that culture is an adaptation will generally prove
to be misleading—and with respect to policy, pernicious. The dynamic,
adaptative quality of any culture must be at the center of attention if
social process and social change are to be understood. Planned social
change intended to solve the problem of American poverty requires
simultaneously an appreciation of lower-class culture and a systematic
understanding of the day-to-day social situations which that culture reflects—and for which it provides the tools for folk understanding, evaluation and adaptation.

In Pruitt-Igoe the lower-class world is defined by two tough facts of life
as it is experienced from day to day and from birth to death: deprivation
and exclusion. The lower class is deprived because it is excluded from
the ordinary course of American working- and middle-class life, and it is
excluded because it is deprived of the resources necessary to function in
the institutions of the mainstream of that life. The lower-class Negro is
doubly deprived and doubly excluded. The basic deprivation is, of course,
low income, but from this deprivation flows the sense so characteristic of
lower-class people that they do not have the price of participation in the
many different kinds of rewards that ordinary society offers. They live in
a society that is structured to make life livable for average people, and they
quickly learn that people with incomes significantly below average cannot
move around freely and confidently in such a society. The ways of living
which lower-class people work out are adaptations to this disjunction
between the demands society makes for average functioning and the
less than adequate resources they are able to command in their own lives.

14.
Toward Equality

During the past decade social scientists have been called on more than ever before to address themselves to problems of directed social change in the United States. A wide range of social scientists have accepted the fact that their work should be relevant to contemporary society and to the needs of American society in the future. Yet the question remains, "In what way should the social sciences be relevant?" Should that relevance be of an engineering kind, helping to design more efficient programs within the narrow specifications worked out by policy makers who set the goals? Or can social science be directly relevant to the setting of the goals themselves?

We can draw a distinction between policy and applied research in connection with poverty programs that has been developed by Irving Louis Horowitz more generally in examining the relevance of social science to contemporary affairs.[1] Governmental programs increasingly require research aimed at the strategies that should be pursued to further the Constitution's goal "to form a more perfect union, establish justice, insure domestic tranquility, to provide for the common defense, to promote the general welfare . . . " Although governmental policy is seldom seriously discussed at this level, administrators are giving more careful attention to the formulation of particular goals and programs; this is the significance of "program planning budget systems," "long range policy planning," systematically developed social indicators, presidential reports on the social state of the union, and so forth. All of these are different ways of bringing under rational scrutiny the purpose to which American government is directed rather than simply the means by which it is pursuing vaguely defined and taken-for-granted purposes.

There is long continuum from the most abstract statements of purpose, such as promoting the general welfare, to the most detailed questions of

1. Horowitz (1967).

398

social engineering, such as the optimum size for a Head Start class. In between there are many challenging questions to which social science can address itself, moving from the somewhat broader issue of whether there should be a Head Start program to the still more general utility of educational programs as a strategy in combating poverty to the broadest question of whether it is poverty as such that is a problem or whether the "poverty problem" is not really one of income inequality.

The social sciences have contributions to make at each level of this problematic continuum. Today a great deal of research is supported by the various government agencies which have responsibilities for problems of poverty, disadvantage, and discrimination, but most of it is directed at applied rather than policy questions; such research is based on the assumption that a given policy is desirable and that research is meant to evaluate only the effectiveness of particular programs in the service of that policy.

It is unfortunate that there has been so little demand for research and analysis oriented to social policy at higher levels of generality. Indeed, the nation has had to rely on individuals who independently stand back and try to put the central policy issues before the public or whose basic research into lower-class behavior by its very vividness calls particular operational strategies into question.[2] In this way certain "academic" issues in social science have begun to have an importance for policy at the broadest rather than at the programmatic level. The juxtaposition of the findings of these social scientists and our knowledge of government operations often seems to call into question the wisdom of many of the procedures being followed.

From Public Housing Problems to Income Inequality

Our Pruitt-Igoe work provides an example of the shifting relationships between policy and applied questions and research findings. The study was designed as research into community life in a large public housing area. The original sponsors clearly hoped that out of the study would come specific guidelines for dealing with a host of problems in that particular housing project and in public housing more generally. But we found ourselves systematically pushed to questions at even higher levels of policy as our research developed and we sought to relate our findings to what was being done in social welfare services and the war on poverty more generally.

In the beginning, we were concerned with what our findings suggested about how public housing might operate more successfully. After a while that question seemed to become less relevant and we became concerned with the relative effectiveness of a range of strategies—housing, social welfare services, remedial and special educational programs,

2. Gans (1968), Moynihan (1969), Miller and Riessman (1969) and Schorr (1968).

job training programs—to cope with the problems of poverty. As time went on we began to shift again, to the more general question of whether poverty itself is a meaningful concept when defined in terms of some absolute standard, and whether the phenomena of poverty—the social pathology that everyone seems to have in mind when he worries about this problem—will persist so long as one segment of the population receives income considerably below the median for the nation as a whole. We eventually arrived at the question of the relationship of income inequality to the general welfare.

Each of these shifts in level came about in an effort to determine what lower-class culture is and how it is related to government programs intended to remedy poverty. We asked ourselves about each issue of policy, "Given what we understand of the situation of the lower class, can this strategy succeed?" In each case—improved public housing procedures or concerted social services or the war on poverty's varied bag of tricks or doing away with minimum subsistence poverty altogether—we found little reason to believe that the strategy would succeed in diminishing the strength of the subculture of exclusion and alienation from society or in reducing markedly the incidence of what is viewed as the social pathology of the slums.

How one answers questions about lower-class culture will influence the policies one considers likely to solve the problem of poverty. There are fateful implications involved in whether there is a distinctive social heredity, a "way of life," transmitted from one generation of lower-class persons to another, and how such a culture is transmitted. The broadest issue is whether those who take their lead from Parsons, Merton, Cloward and Ohlin are right in saying that lower-class persons simply do not have the means to behave like others in society and they would immediately do so had they the means, or those who follow Davis, Miller, and Lewis are right in saying that lower-class persons have a distinct and coherent way of life that would interfere with rapid change should the means become available to behave in accordance with conventional norms.

If one takes an extreme view that everyone in America shares a common culture, one is led to emphasize job training, improved elementary and high school education, community action to provide means of achieving power, and so on. This is the spirit in which the war on poverty was initiated, its goal was not directly to provide resources to destroy poverty but to provide opportunities for people to achieve their own escape from it.[3] However, if one believes there is a distinctive lower-class cultural heritage, one would predict that such programs would have little effect on poverty because of persistent life styles that would render them unattractive or meaningless.

3. See Moynihan (1969); Sundquist (1968); and the various papers in Sundquist (1969).

What then should be done if this is the case? One view is that the transmission of lower-class culture from one generation to another must be interrupted in favor of transmitting cultural elements that will enable lower-class people to function in stable working or middle-class ways. A popular version of this policy is simply to remove lower-class children from their homes and to provide in American *kibbutzim* an environment in which conventional culture is transmitted and lower-class culture is not available. Less drastic versions involve special educational programs to remedy cultural disadvantage, preschool programs such as Head Start, adult education to bring about cultural change through instruction in consumer education and prevocational training in etiquette, dress, speech, and the like.

But from the point of view of modern culture theory, there is one great difficulty with such strategies. Culture is generally defined as an adaptation to the social and ecological situation in which groups of people find themselves, and anthropologists are fascinated with uncovering the many ways in which it is shaped by the environmental requirements of tribal and peasant peoples in all parts of the world and of those who dwell in urban industrial societies.[4] But if culture is an adaptation to life situations, and if it is transmitted as the accumulated knowledge of the group about how to behave in those situations, and if that knowledge is systematically reinforced by the experiences of individuals as they grow up and go about their daily lives, then one can predict that any effort to change culture directly by outside educational intervention is doomed to failure. People have no incentive to change their culture, indeed they would suffer if they tried, unless there is some significant change in their situation.

Any realistic assessment of the likelihood of a payoff from any of these strategies, whether requiring change in opportunities or in culture, requires a consideration of middle-class culture as well as that of lower-class people. As Herbert Gans has recently pointed out, a proper definition of the "culture of poverty" ought to include those characteristics—cultural and institutional—of conventional society which serve to sustain and militate against any change in lower class behavior,[5] and which are part of the environment to which lower-class people adapt by developing their own subculture. Central to the caretaker culture is the apparent inability of public institutions to change in ways that allow them to serve lower-class populations without also demeaning them, or to obligate the tremendous resources that would be necessary to carry out culture change or opportunity programs that might prove effective. The central characteristic of the middle class, the caretaker, component of the culture of poverty is the almost total unwillingness of conventional society to admit its

4. Bennett (1964).
5. Gans (1969).

complicity in the suffering and exclusion which lower-class people experience.

This line of analysis leads to the view that if lower-class people are to be enabled to participate successfully in conventional society, *the social and ecological situation to which lower class people adapt must be changed*. This requires understanding of what it is about this situation that makes lower-class cultural adaptations occur and persist. These adaptations are not to absolute deprivation, not to a living standard that is below some arbitrary minimum, but rather to relative deprivation —to being so far from the average American living standard that one does feel part of his own society. Policy that is consistent with such understanding will therefore have to be addressed to relative deprivation, to inequality rather than poverty as such.

The Essential Issue: Poverty as Low Income

A person is poor when he does not have enough money. The nation has a poverty problem because too many families and too many individuals do not have enough money. What is "enough money?" To answer in terms of an income sufficient to live at some subsistence level defined as adequate has been the major error of the traditional approach to American poverty. Very few American families and individuals have so little income that they cannot meet their *minimal* needs. Only in the worst backwaters of our society does lack of income prevent people from having food, clothing, shelter, and other goods superior to those which have sustained human beings from the beginning of time.[6]

The problem of poverty is a problem of relative deprivation. A family is poor when it does not have enough money to live in the conventional style of the average American, when its low income does not allow it to buy the products and services that *Americans* need. These needs are social needs; they are needs for the housing, furniture, clothes, food, and services we all regard as reasonable and expected for the American family.

Those who live below the going standard of American affluence form a kind of underclass. They sense their own exclusion from conventional society but they are not isolated from knowing about it, about how Americans are expected to live and that they cannot achieve such a life. Even were they willing to ignore this knowledge, the rest of society constantly forces it upon them in many subtle ways, from the school teacher who talks to her ghetto class about the Thanksgiving turkey to the clerk in the ghetto store who communicates to his customers his sense that they are different from ordinary people (otherwise they would not be in his store.)

6. Such backwaters do exist, however, as the nation discovers anew every few years. See Coles (1969).

It is obvious from this diagnosis that the problem of American poverty can be solved only be redressing the relative deprivation of those at the bottom of the income distribution. We might say, for example, that there will be no poverty in the United States when those now in the lowest third of the income distribution have their incomes raised to a point close to the median income for the nation as a whole. (Average income would of course go up under these circumstances, but median income—that amount at which half the families are below and half above—need not change at all.)

It is unfortunate that in the voluminous discussion of poverty during this decade, the nub of the problem—low income—has tended to be overlooked. The popularization of phrases like the "culture of poverty," as well as the wishfulness of the affluent and the hard-pressed professionals and politicians, have encouraged the belief that there is something more to poverty than just low income. As a result, there has been a great deal of emphasis on the social and personal pathologies that accompany poverty. Such pathologies are indeed inevitable concomitants of poverty, but this knowledge is no justification for shifting the focus of attention from the cause of the situation—low income—to its effects.[7]

The culture of poverty is made up of ways of adapting to the circumstances of daily life that make that life tolerable. At the same time, these very ways of life interfere with the efforts of the poor to escape from their situation. For this reason, lower-class culture places an important constraint on poverty policies, but it is not a defining characteristic of poverty, nor a proper central focus of intervention strategies. The special ways of adapting by the poor suggest only that effective poverty strategies have to change their income situation before requiring changes in their behavior and their attitudes. The major reason for the failure of most anti-poverty programs so far is that they require the poor to change their behavior before they have gained the resources that would change their situation.

The political challenge is to design programs that maximize the number of people who can obtain enough money to live in the same way that ordinary Americans live. That is the sole appropriate test of a successful poverty policy—not how it changes the poor's work habits, nor how much community power it seems to give them, nor how it improves their communication with the power structure, nor how it increases the test scores of school children—but that poor men and women now have enough money to buy a reasonable approximation of the standard package of goods and services that the average American regards as his right.

When the issue is phrased in this way, some critics suggest that such a goal is simply a way of saying that the poor have to become conven-

7. Elsewhere I have discussed the various diagnoses of poverty, including those that emphasize pathology, that are intended to neutralize society's anxiety and discomfort caused by the existence of this group. Rainwater (1967).

tional Americans, and that because there are a lot of things wrong with conventional Americans, the elimination of income poverty is an unworthy goal, a half-measure; conventional society must be changed first. This view involves a false stereotype of the average American as a kind of assembly line product, each individual like every other individual; in fact Americans at any level of income live in a great variety of ways. Some sink everything they have into a house while others use their money for clothes and vacations or tithe fully to their churches. Some live close to home, conforming to puritan standards; others live active social lives by going to movies, parties, and corner taverns. We tend to ignore this variety because each of these patterns of behavior is a way of living the average American life accepted as "conventional" and tolerated as such. With money in their pockets, the poor would have many models of average American life to choose from, not just one. In fact, they might invent other models of their own—and no one could then deny them the right to do so, because by earning a conventional income they would acquire the right to live their own lives without opprobrium.

Equalizing Income

The little we know about what Americans think about poverty, deprivation, and discrimination suggests that most Americans want a society in which there is no class of people below "the average man" in terms of prestige, income, or other advantages. So much do Americans cleave to this ideal of averageness that 80 per cent of them call themselves middle or working class (rather than upper or lower) and very few will admit to being in the lower class. Although a denial of reality, this behavior suggests that for Americans the good society is one in which each man and woman can earn the right to approximate the average standard of living. While they do not like the idea that average resources should be handed to anyone on a silver platter, they believe that a successful American society would be one in which each person does earn such a standard of living because of the opportunity and security that are available to him.

Today's political challenge is to govern the society so that these ideals are realized but to realize them they must first be consciously faced. The ideal that no family should fall far below the median standard has not been fully articulated in modern times; to the extent that the issue has been dealt with at all, it has been in terms of minimum rather than median standards of living. The various standards that have received widespread attention since the beginning of the war on poverty represent compromise with the American ideal, which beleagured politicians and welfare workers have accepted and established because they have so little hope that anything more can done.[8] Liberals, particularly as they are incorporated into the political and welfare establishment, find it hard

8. For a historical review of poverty standards, see Ornati (1966) and the papers by Smelinski, Fuchs and Miller in U.S. Chamber of Commerce (1965).

to imagine programs that go beyond slight improvements in present welfare measures. The new radicals seem equally wedded to ungenerous conceptions of what American society might be, because they confirm their pessimistic view of the world and their cataclysmic preference for some kind of revolution.

The emphasis on minimum standards, on "poverty lines," which influences so much of their thinking today, is subject to a very real embarrassment. As the nation becomes more affluent, the poverty line seems to creep up. The "subsistence package" seems to require more in the way of goods and services in each successive decade. Most definitions of minimum standards revolve around inadequate diets and are supposed to reflect a line that separates life and death, or at least sickness and health. Such a standard is concerned with man as an animal and with keeping him alive; even so, it seems to creep up perceptibly with each decade.[9] Why should this be so? I believe it is because the inventors of these standards do not really believe that an animal standard is meaningful, because they do believe that to survive as a *person*, individuals and families must approximate the average standard. Would it not be better to explore and try to find rational ways of achieving a truly human standard?

I believe it is unlikely that the nation can eradicate poverty unless it can engineer a radical shift upward in the income of those who now fall in the lower half of the income distribution. The notion of income equity requires a floor for family incomes, with no family falling below that floor, and thereby itself is little different from the strategies of guaranteed minimum income that have been much in the news of late. However, in the strategy proposed here the floor is set not in absolute terms but relative to the median family income for the nation. Such a standard is dynamic, in that it takes account of the upward movement of median incomes as GNP increases.

We are concerned here with changes in the shape of the income distribution not with the absolute amount of the minimum that is accepted as the standard. This is because any absolute amount (even one that rises along with cost-of-living increases) will tend to lag behind the more rapidly rising median family income. Except for a small proportion of families whose income is below subsistence level, the real poverty problem is one of relative deprivation. If this problem is solved, the problem of that much smaller proportion of the population for whom absolute deprivation can be said to exist is automatically solved.

Income redistribution should be pursued in terms of raising the income of heads of families, not of the family as a whole. An equitable society should not require its families to achieve median income by

9. For example, Ornati's analysis suggests that standards of "minimum subsistence" for a family on welfare or poverty-line budgets, phrased in constant 1960 dollars, have increased from $1,386 in 1905 to $1,765 in 1940 to $2,662 in 1960. Ornati (1966), p. 149, 150.

forcing wives and children to enter the labor market. Americans want a society in which a decent standard of living can be achieved by heads of families and whether the wives and children also work should be optional.

Family size should also be considered a matter of personal option. With birth control services widely available, the number of children a couple has may be regarded as a kind of consumer choice—some people prefer to spend their money on additional children, others prefer to have fewer children and spend their money in other ways. When the target of policy is a minimum subsistence income the size of family becomes an important variable, but when the target is achieving a median income family size becomes less of an issue.

The goal, then, is to change the shape of the income distribution. Data showing income by head of household are not available, so let us take an example using the probable 1970 urban family income distribution. Median family income was about $10,000. About one-third of the population was in income classes $2,000 or more below the median, and similar proportions were that far above median, leaving about one-third of the families in a broad middle income band of $8,000 to $12,000. When we propose to eliminate relative deprivation by having no family with income below the median, it is often objected that this is a statistical impossibility. It is, of course, true by definition that if more than 50 per cent of the population is at the lowest point in a statistical distribution, the median is also the lowest value. But income distributions are usually measured by classes, so that our standard simply proposes that the income floor be in that income class which also contains the median. An income distribution in which the minimum income of heads of households was no more than $1,000 away from the median would substantially eliminate relative deprivation. Using the 1970 family income distribution as an example, a minimum of $9,000 would meet this goal; the income class $9,000 to 9,999 would have contained slightly more than 50 per cent of all families.

The goal described here involves an approach that equalizes income from the bottom up. Such a goal could probably be attained in a few decades without making inroads into current income of above-median families by distributing a large part of the annual increases in national income to the lowest income groups, thus mitigating the problems of direct confrontation involved in the older model of "soaking the rich to give to the poor." With proper planning, it should be possible to achieve such a redistribution without provoking great opposition from higher-income groups, particularly because many economists believe that greater income equalization would result in much larger increases in gross national product and therefore in national income than are now envisioned.

The Failure of Traditional Strategies

One could argue that the goal of redistributing income to do away with relative proverty has been implicit in traditional social policies in the sense that these are ostensibly directed toward helping people find opportunities, "get on their feet," so that they can earn average status. Therefore, no basically different strategies are needed, it is only necessary to pour more resources into traditional social work, income maintenance, educational and community action programs, and perhaps make some technical improvements in how the programs are organized and put into practice. My reading of the evidence suggests that this is not the case. Before arguing for a basically different anti-poverty strategy, for a strategy of resources equalization rather than services and opportunities, let us consider why it is that traditional anti-poverty programs have proved so puny in their effect. Our discussion here is necessarily only a brief summary of much work by other investigators on these programs, but it is necessary to at least note the experience with these traditional strategies to show why different kinds of strategies must be considered.

Federal, state, and local governments have instituted a bewildering array of programs to cope with pieces of the poverty problem. These programs are designed either to assist the poor or to control them (as with the police and those parts of the court system concerned with wage garnishment, rent delinquencies, and so forth). Added to these government programs are the thousands of small and large volunteer efforts across the country which seek to do something for the poor, ranging from providing them with "Culture" to providing emergency relief. Despite all this activity, it is becoming increasingly obvious that little progress is being made toward reducing the incidence of relative poverty and of social problems related to poverty.

One such problem—crime—has recently come to the center of the political stage. "Crime in the streets" has come to signify all the fears that whites have of Negroes. What people have in mind in public discussion of this issue is characteristically the slum-generated variety of petty crimes against property and personal assault. Yet it is a fact that most of these crimes are committed by lower-class persons against lower-class victims of the same race.

When this issue is coupled with white concern about riots, as usually is the case in public dialogue, it comes dangerously close to providing a basis for strongly repressive action toward the poor. Indeed, perhaps the most significant consequence of the issue is in its value for the police and similar agencies of control in bolstering the legitimacy of their demands on the public treasury. Public attitudes emphasizing "law and order" sustain the competitive claims of these agencies against the "do-gooding" elements in the public bureaucracy.

Federal programs emphasize a service strategy rather than an income or resource equalization strategy for reducing poverty. Most federal programs have tried to provide one or another kind of service which it is presumed will help individuals find and take advantage of opportunities to move out of poverty, or to change themselves so that they are ready to take advantage of opportunities. The alternative strategy, which would provide the poor with the resources (principally income) to alter directly their situation of poverty and in their own time and way to change their lower class adaptations, has not been an important feature of federal activity. Although social security has been an important resource against poverty in old age for many Americans, its redistributive impact is small. The other large federal income program, AFDC, has grown to its present size without strong public support, and has become an embarrassment to policy makers. Its recipients have been constant targets of services interventions which are often made the price of continued support.

Most federal programs developed logically out of the basic social work orientation of the early twentieth century. It was assumed that the job of those who wish to help is to provide charity and emergency assistance to "unfortunate" individuals. There has been little effort to face the fact that American poverty is generated by the same social and economic system that produces affluence and security for the majority of the population. Until government strategy addresses this fact and the issue of the ways in which the "normal" operation of the socio-economic system generates conditions which perpetuate the existence at the bottom of the society of a group of persons who do not have the advantage of an income close to the median, we can expect little progress in eliminating poverty-related problems.[10]

The major service strategies embodied in federal programs have been the following:

Welfare Services

These represent the generalization of traditional social work activity, in which the poor are to be helped by getting them to change their habits (by family counseling, probation work, the inculcation of better housekeeping and consumer skills) or by providing them with things that they need but cannot buy (medical and legal services, food stamps). Indeed, a large part of welfare "service" has ended as the provision of expert counsel on how the poor person must guide himself through the maze of the social welfare services themselves. As a result, social workers spend a large portion of their time "referring" clients from one service to another. A more Kafkaesque situation would be hard to imagine.

Housing Programs

Federal programs show a line of development—from slum clearance to public housing to urban renewal to urban rehabilitation to model cities— ostensibly designed to provide better homes for those who cannot afford decent housing on the private market. These federally subsidized services have succeeded in moving many poor people from one place to another, but they have provided very few with good housing and have had almost no impact on the poverty problem as such.

10. For discussions of the development of modern welfare policy as it relates to poverty as currently defined, see Moynihan (1969), Marris and Rein (1967) and Gladwin (1967).

The original logic of federal housing was that by removing people from the slums and providing them with decent housing, their other difficulties would begin to disappear and they would be better able to take advantage of opportunities to improve themselves. In fact it has developed that "decent housing" does not really make for any major changes in the life situation of the poor. In addition, whatever changes might occur come to naught because there are not sufficient opportunities available in other areas, particularly in employment. As a result, in many cities public housing has simply become a more visible kind of slum, and by its very existence as a *public* program highlights the failure of the federal response to poverty.

Other federal programs—particularly slum clearance and urban renewal—have proved to be irrelevant to the problems of the poor; indeed these programs instead of serving are another imposition on them because the poor are typically displaced from their own homes to make way for new homes too expensive for them. The model cities program offers little promise of significantly altering the defects of previous programs in the housing area because it merely extends to larger geographical areas programs that themselves failed to reduce poverty.

Educational Programs

In recent years growing awareness that employment is essential if poverty is to be reduced has led to great emphasis on various kinds of educational programs. For example, job training programs have been developed to equip young adults for available employment. These programs—from the Job Corps to vocational rehabilitation and youth opportunity centers—have had very little effect. It has proved exceedingly difficult to persuade the trainees to stay in the program, and problems of low motivation and lack of persistence have been characteristic, manifested in high drop-out rates and low levels of achievement. The facts of the labor market have confirmed the suspicion expressed by the trainees; many of the training programs have proved irrelevant to employment opportunities because much of the training has been for nonexistent jobs and employers have been reluctant to hire the trainees despite all the high-level exhortation for private industry to "meet its responsibilities."

Other programs to remedy "educational disadvantage" have been instituted within the regular school system, the most widely publicized being Head Start. These programs have similarly shown little success in raising the achievement level of slum children. The problem seems to be two-fold. First, the schools must work against heavy negative influence of the environment in which the child lives. If that environment convinces him that there is no hope of getting anywhere in life, it is difficult for him to respond otherwise in school. Equally important, and despite the success of some small-scale programs, it has proved impossible for administrators and teachers to maintain a consistently constructive approach to motivating the students from kindergarten through high school. Whatever effectiveness an individual Head Start or grade school teacher may have in breaking through the hopelessness manifested by the children is vitiated because many other teachers who are less concerned are liable to emphasize order and decorum rather than helping the children to learn. When the slum world represented in the children confronts the middle-class world in the teacher, the result seems to be a school system that becomes inimical to consistent achievement by the students. It is doubtful that even massive infusions of money will improve the relationship of deprived and excluded children and the less than saintly human beings whom one can expect to man the slum schools.

The Community Action Programs

The various programs established by the Office of Economic Opportunity have had a considerable impact on the local political situation of many cities, but there is little evidence that they have had any major effect on poverty. They have undoubtedly increased the political sophistication of some poor people, provided jobs for many middle-class people and a few poor people, and heightened our awareness of the poverty problem; but there is little about these programs that would reduce the number of people who are poor. In fact, they have had primarily the effect of emphasizing the special status of the poor, and catering to it. Thus, the special services for the poor that have developed in the community action programs themselves are based on an assumption of the continued existence of the poor. Only if the poor will always be with us can the neighborhood law firm or the community health clinic be accepted as constructive. However, if one takes seriously the initial goals of the war on poverty—that poverty should be eliminated and not alleviated or institutionalized—then the sense of failure and frustration which those in community action feel no less than observers can be understood.

Barriers to Effective Service Programs

Social science research has identified several problems which seem to characterize all federal programs that rely on a service strategy. The most intensive research has been on federal housing and urban development, but parallel findings are available for most other programs in the federal welfare effort.[11]

Local Politics

The effectiveness of federal programs is severely hampered by the very nature of local government in the United States. These programs are intended to attack problems that require planning and action for the needs of large metropolitan areas, but the fragmented and overlapping structure

11. These problems have been analyzed most cogently by Roger Montgomery (1967), and the following is an adaptation and expansion of his discussion. See also Gans (1968).

of local government, which administers the programs, makes their implimentation generally difficult and sometimes impossible.

These difficulties are most apparent in housing and urban development where the governing authority of a metropolitan area is divided among a central city, a variety of suburbs, and perhaps also a county board controlling unincorporated districts. There is no way to effectuate far-reaching change in housing patterns and quality in the area as a whole; there is little public housing in the suburbs because the suburbs do not set up public housing authorities. Similarly, federal educational programs must work through the several school boards in a metropolitan area, and it has so far been impossible to respond in any systematic way to the educational needs of a metropolitan area as a whole.

Further, political science research shows us that most local governments are at best slow to solve the problems of their areas. To some extent this results from the low level of resources available to them, to some extent from their lack of political sophistication, but in any case, they have seldom done more than sit passively while problems in their area went from bad to worse. Therefore, the demands made by federal programs for local governments to exercise initiative, to make rational choices, to view their problems from other than short-term political perspectives, are unrealistic. These difficulties are even greater where—as in the central cities —the incidence of poverty is high. Widespread poverty and slums place great strain on municipal administration and services and the lack of adequate resources (social, political, economic) to meet them at the local level reinforces a tendency to evade and cover up these problems rather than confront them.

These difficulties are made more severe still by the complex network of administrative entities superimposed on an already fragmented collection of local governmental units. In addition to cities, suburban villages, townships, and counties, there are (as agencies of one government, or separately constituted units) city plan commissions, boards of education, federally-supported agencies and corporations. The separate but overlapping responsibilities of the parts of this network result in a multiplication of the number of places where veto power can be exercised over particular objects. As a result, the design of programs at the local level is tailored more to the needs and demands of local agencies than to what may have been intended at the federal level or to the requirements of effective problem solution.

Problem of Definition

Almost all federal programs, partly because of over-elaborate conceptualization and partly out of a history of legislative compromise, are burdened by difficulties of defining what can be done and who is eligible for benefits. The more complex the rules involved in a particular program, the more likely the agency is to become bogged down in whether the rules permit it to undertake a particular project. These circumstances also lead the program to be diverted by punitive hunts for "chiselers," for people and organizations deriving illegitimate benefits, even when they are insignificant among the larger number that might be served.

Bureaucratic Standards

In housing as well as other areas, those who are supposed to be served are subject to the norms of professionals. Low-income people do not decide what kind of housing they are to have; instead, this is decided by middle-class architects, agency bureaucrats, and city councils. Similarly an agency may decide upon the services the low-income person needs: he needs child welfare services but not a television set, welfare mothers do not need telephones, low-income families need an expensive education but low welfare payments. Most Americans set their own priorities because they buy most of their goods and services in the private market, but the elaboration of federal welfare programs leaves the low-income person with his priorities set by others. It accomplishes little to try to improve this situation by community involvement in decision making; from the low income family's point of view, it is a small improvement to have these priorities set by one's neighbors rather than outside bureaucrats. It would be much more desirable for the people involved to set these priorities themselves.

Monitoring Problems

It has proved exceedingly difficult for the federal government to keep track of what is done with the money appropriated for service programs and to assess the impact of those programs. The statistics routinely collected by administering agencies tend to be related to the work load of the bureaucracy rather than to the consequences of spending money. Indeed, many agencies seem actively to avoid collecting information that would allow an impersonal evaluation of the effect of their programs involved. This is to be expected where evaluation is difficult at best and negative results would endanger the administering bureaucracy itself.

Where the effects desired are quite simple—like social security where all that is required is to get the checks to the recipients—the monitoring problem is equally simple. However, where a program seeks very complex effects, such as "changing the morale of a neighborhood," the monitoring problem becomes nearly impossible. The more complex the specification of a problem the greater the temptation for the bureaucrats involved to persuade the legislature and the public of their value by empty but glowing generalities. Eventually, however, such a public relations strategy is self-defeating, because promising more results than are delivered leads to general disillusionment with yet another "promising program."

Workload Problems

Because of over-elaboration of procedures, rules, and eligibility requirements, each agency tends to be so weighed down with the intermediate process between appropriation and result that results are either long-delayed or never materialize. This is especially apparent in housing and urban development, because of extremely complex processes of planning and approval. Another result of unproductive workload is to make services to the poor unnecessarily expensive. It often costs more to build low-income housing under urban renewal regulations than it does to build middle-income housing under more routinized FHA regulations. In the end, the federal treasury absorbs not only the cost subsidizing the poor person's inability to pay middle-income rent but also the cost of the elaborated workload of the urban renewal agencies and of the developer.

The Enterprise Effect

Service agencies almost invariably become devoted to protecting and advancing their interests as enterprises in ways that may become unconnected with the problems that called them into existence. Urban renewal programs which began with the goal of eliminating slums and providing decent housing become large scale builders, stimulating the development of new stadiums, high-rise and high-income apartment houses, and so forth. Because local service agencies report to federal counterpart agencies through a complex set of channels, they become isolated from the presumed recipients of their services and from other local agencies with whom they share responsibility. On a national level, this enterprise effect leads to such disgraceful performances as the Public Housing Administration's lobby against the rent supplement program, or the battles among federal agencies about which of them should absorb the programs developed experimentally by OEO.

Another manifestation of the enterprise effect is seen in a shifting focus about who is being served. Where programs for the poor require the services of private interest there is a strong tendency for the responsible agency to shift the focus of its service from the poor to these other parties. For example, housing and urban development officials have been more zealous in serving builders than in serving those who were supposed to benefit from the buildings. While great energy was invested in acquiring and clearing land, the problem of relocation was shoved into the background until it became a national scandal. Similarly, the state employment services have oriented themselves more strongly toward the needs of the employers than those of job seekers. Health programs were readily directed more toward the desires and needs of physicians and hospitals than toward those of patients. Again, the more complex the interorganizational relationships demanded by the programs, the more likely are these shifts to take place.

Thus, the principal generalization which emerges from a wide range of research on housing and urban development and on other service institutions is, as Roger Montgomery observes, that *the elaborate array of special purpose institutions created to supply goods and services to the poor simply has not worked.*

These problems have been recognized over the past few years by an increasing number of policy makers, and there has naturally been an effort to remedy them. Unfortunately, this effort, particularly by officials of the federal agencies involved, has taken the form of tinkering with the organizational machinery rather than developing strategies to obviate the necessity for institutional elaboration. Instead of recognizing that these problems almost inevitably result from the development of service programs with highly specific aims, there has been an effort to develop some kind of organizational device to remedy them. We have seen a progressive generalization of categorical approaches, from uncoordinated single programs through concerted service programs to community action programs to model cities programs. In each of these steps there was an effort to "coordinate" federal activities over a progressively wider geographical and agency range, yet the results were as disappointing as before. It is as if a failure to "concert" social services in a small area (like Pruitt-Igoe) led to a belief that one might be successful in coordinating them at the larger and more complex level of community action, and finally at the ambitious level of a model cities area. In each case, the increased demand for planning and coordination required new bureaucratic operations at local and federal levels. The result was only to exacerbate the problems outlined above.

It is easy to imagine that when model cities fails as a strategy we will have programs that move on to "model metropolitan areas," "model states," and "model regions."

Stigmatization of the Poor

An additional and overriding difficulty with all service programs for the poor is that they are for the poor and for no one else. This creates political difficulties because of the opposition of the non-poor to spending their "tax dollars" in this way; but even more important, it inevitably reinforces the stigma of poverty. One who makes use of these services by that very act labels himself as socially inferior. No matter how hard social workers and other protectors of the poor try to conceal the invidiousness of the label, it remains visible to the poor themselves and to the larger society. The more elaborate the service framework becomes, the more the poor person is locked into his stigmatized status.

This is not merely an abstract issue; it is brought home to the poor person by the very attitudes typical of the caretakers who man the service institutions. These attitudes are most blatant in the old line agencies such as the schools, the police, the sanitation services, the welfare department, and the like. Even in such newer and therefore still malleable agencies as the community action programs, the caretaker is always tempted to hold himself out as a more worthy person than those he serves. The housing project manager who berates those at a tenant meeting for not listening to him because after all he has given up his evening at home to help them, the community action official who speaks of the goal of "his" program as teaching poor people good habits of life communicate in their behavior and attitudes a demeaning and derogating stance to the poor. No amount of radical punitiveness toward caretakers is likely to diminish this tension in cross-class relationships. Indeed, were militants themselves to man the service institutions they would probably develop over time the same derogating attitudes toward their charges, though their rhetoric might be different.

The obverse of the stigmatizing effect of service programs is what has been called *the credentials effect*,[12] which is characteristic of any program that raises the average level of achievement in the society without at the same time equalizing achievement at the lowest levels. The effect is most dramatic with respect to education, but the concept probably has parallels in other institutions.

As the educational level of the population has risen, employers have consistently raised the educational requirements for jobs. Where a grade school education might have sufficed for a particular factory job in the past, personnel managers are now inclined to require a high school education, and there are many jobs for which a college education is now required that two decades ago would have been filled by high school graduates. Employers justify these requirements on the basis of the increased complexity of jobs, but there is little evidence to support their claims. Employers believe that education is somehow an index of the quality of the worker, and they have raised their requirements to insure the highest possible quality of their work force, without determining whether such requirements have any relationship to job performance.

This credentials effect will exist as long as there are more workers in the labor force than there are jobs. Service programs that provide job training may even heighten the credentials effect, as long as there is a slack labor market. Those unskilled poor who did not receive training would be disadvantaged in seeking jobs that they can now fill, if standards were raised to take account of the increased supply of trained persons. (Such an effect, of course, would only be apparent at a much higher level of job training than now exists.)

The Collectivity versus the Individual

A final problem which has been particularly apparent in housing and urban development programs and is now appearing in various community action programs is a confusion of a human collectivity or of a geographical area with its individual members. An early manifestation of the problem was in the slum clearance program, where the emphasis was on clearing the slums rather than on solving the problems of the people who lived in them. Later, in urban renewal and now in model cities programs, the

12. Miller (1968).

administrators have tended to concern themselves with making the city look nice, believing that thereby problems are somehow solved. It is perhaps natural for mayors and other local officials to be concerned with the appearance of things because the visible aspects of the community are the most available for judging whether anything has been changed.

Community action programs seem similarly to evoke a conception of "the community" as an almost physical object, much like "the city." Much of the rhetoric of community action and of the new militants, black and white, suggests an ideological exaltation of "The Neighborhood" or "The Blacks," in place of the varied needs and aspirations of the individuals who make up those collectivities. In some ways our over-sophistication about the dynamics of city life—about the rise of successive ethnic groups in the 19th Century, or the interdependence of interest groups in a social system—tends to distract us from the more ordinary and less dramatic goals of individual families, who are concerned not so much for "community self-determination" as they are for their own self-determination. It is seldom recognized that families which are economically weak are just as vulnerable to exploitation and mistreatment at the hands of a supposedly self-governed neighborhood as they are at the hands of City Hall. It is only the poor who are fully subject to the rules set by community leadership, because it is only the poor who do not have the option of moving elsewhere if they do not like the decisions their self-governing community makes.

Standards for Policy

If we combine the diagnosis of poverty the prescriptions for the elimination of relative deprivation, and the analysis of the failure of traditional strategies, we can begin to specify the standards that must be met by an effective poverty policy. To achieve the goal of an income distribution in which no family would have an income significantly below the median, to solve the problem of poverty, that is, by insuring that families have enough money not to be poor, the following policy guides seem most central.

A rational policy must link the productive potential of the poor with the needs of the country as a whole. Our society is not yet so fully automated that it does not need the labor of all of its able-bodied members to realize its promise fully. Indeed, the cybernetic society of enforced leisure will not be with us for several decades, and perhaps it will never arrive. The productive potential of the poor must be utilized for economic and political reasons, and because the poor can become fully participating members of the society only through having an opportunity for useful employment.

From a political point of view, the society as a whole, and particularly the working and lower middle class must be offered good reason for committing significant resources to the elimination of poverty. To date, the reasons offered have been primarily moral or negative and these alone will not suffice. Morality is unpersuasive, and the negative reasons—to avoid riots, crime in the streets, the blight of slums, lower-class control of the cities—have limitations built into them. After all, there are other policies available for coping with those problems—notably punitive and repressive measures which are appealing to the working and middle classes no matter how much social scientists may argue that they are self-defeating. In addition, these negative reasons for eliminating poverty are self-limiting, encouraging the state to do just enough to alleviate the desperation of the poor so they will stop causing trouble for the rest of society. But "just enough" is not enough, because it will not produce a lasting change in the social structure so that poverty is not regenerated.

Use of the productive potential of the poor emphasizes what *all* citizens gain from eliminating poverty and supports programs that do not perpetuate the emergency character of most legislation and administration in this area. Specifically, this standard finds "last resort" employment policies wanting, because they provide "make-work" jobs rather than work that is actually needed by the society.

The productivity of the poor can be considered in terms both of current and eventual productive potential. Currently a large proportion (but by no means all) of the poor can function only at the unskilled or semi-skilled level. Our economy has developed in a way to reduce employment opportunities at this level. One of the first goals of a rational poverty policy, therefore, must be to increase employment opportunities for those with low levels of skill.

However, one can expect those who are presently poor eventually to function at higher skill levels. For individuals who have already completed their schooling, this skill upgrading can best be accomplished by on-the-job training that accompanies steady employment. More important, the children of the current poor, if their families have adequate incomes, will learn more from even the schools that currently exist. By moving toward the elimination of poverty among the adult poor, one will be making the greatest possible contribution to eliminating poverty in the next generation because the children will be able to move into higher skill levels than their parents.

A rational policy must protect against the destructiveness of poverty for those families in which employment income is not adequate. There must be programs which insure that no family lives any significant portion of its life together in poverty. Employing the productive potential of the poor will go a long way toward providing such protection. In addition, however, other techniques will have to be developed to protect families and individuals against the destructiveness of poverty where they cannot earn the required income. We require a proper recognition of the social costs of allowing families to exist in poverty, and techniques that obviate the necessity of their doing so without at the same time reducing the incentive to work.

A rational policy must operate to enhance personal freedom. The best way to preserve freedom of choice is to enhance family resources for participation in mainstream institutions. As we have seen, the services offered by the present special programs for the poor in several ways limit the freedom of their recipients. Community power programs, for example, increase the freedom of those (usually a minority) who participate in them, but they limit the potential freedom of all the members of the community who are affected (sometimes adversely) by their decisions. Similarly, all programs that tie benefits to location limit individual freedom. For example, programs that provide funds for housing in ghetto areas but confer no benefits on those who wish to live outside these areas arbitrarily and unnecessarily limit the freedom of the recipients; however well intentioned a model cities program may be, individual freedom is limited by virtue of the fact that one is entitled to benefits from it only so long as he remains in the area.

Programs that try to force change in the individual's attitudes and way of life before he has enough income to determine changes for himself obviously interfere with his freedom. Glaring examples of this interference abound in programs for the "culturally disadvantaged," under the guise of teaching work habits, or job interview skills, or the like. Why should lower-class Negroes have to be taught to speak "properly" to qualify for jobs if there is really a productive contribution they can make to society? Whatever its importance in social ranking, the Brooklyn accent or the speech of white Southerners has not been an important barrier for hundreds of thousands of Americans, yet these accents in their full glory are no less difficult for a small-town midwesterner to understand than a lower-class Negro accent for a middle-class white person.

Just as institutional tinkering has proved irresistible to high level planners, "person tinkering" seems irresistible to those who wish to help the poor, and a rational policy will eschew this kind of misuse of programs. This is not meant as a justification for the way of life of the poor, nor an argument that it has an intrinsic merit that is to be preserved at all costs. The burden of proof of what change in the individual is necessary rests on society and not on the individual. Because the individual has every motivation to change in whatever ways are necessary to gain the rewards he wants, the choice of how to change and how much to change is better left to him.

A rational policy must allow for the time it will take to transform society into one that is free of poverty. Even with the best possible policies, vigorously pursued and properly funded, it will take at least a generation for the poor to acquire the kind of experiences they need if they are to sustain themselves through employment to produce equality of results as well as abstract equality of opportunity in our society. Such a transformation will occur during a time in which the affluence of all levels of society is increasing. Median family income goes up a few dollars almost every year, even allowing for inflation, and there is an increasing dollar gap between the poor and the average man. (That gap has increased over 50 per cent in the past two decades.) The task is to close that gap rapidly at the same time that the median is increasing.[13]

Implementing Rational Policy

Once policy makers have a clear understanding of the basic causes of poverty and the changes in the socio-economic system that are essential to eliminate poverty, it becomes possible to design programs in a more rational way. Descriptions of the history of current programs indicate that they were thrown together on a crash basis, that they reflect a collection of ideas already developed by various government agencies in pursuit of their established objectives, and that no systematic thought was given to the nature of poverty before the programs were legislated.[14] The result was little more than an upgrading of previous social welfare, training, and coordinating approaches.

Employment for the Poor as the Keystone

Employment of the poor at decent wages requires full employment in the total economy and this means that much of the strategy for a war on poverty must be formulated, under presidential leadership, by such agencies as the Council of Economic Advisers, the Treasury Department, and the Federal Reserve Board rather than by welfare-oriented agencies like the Department of Health, Education, and Welfare, the Department of Labor, and the Office of Economic Opportunity. But our experience during recent years and analysis of the skills of men at poverty levels suggest that aggregate demand strategies to create tight full employment will be necessary but not sufficient to bring about the changes desired. The federal government will have to develop major programs designed to increase governmental and private demand for low skilled workers.

In the past two decades, government spending has been heavily weighed toward creating demand for relatively skilled workers. The increasing sophistication of the goods and services used by the defense establishment and programs such as the exploration of space and the development of supersonic aircraft have been major elements in creating this demand. America's fascination with science, technology, and education has been reflected in a consistent bias on the part of administrations and Congress toward projects requiring high technology and professional manpower; the more mundane goods and services that might be provided

13. Increasing affluence also has social consequences. More and more young people are going to college, and with increasing diffusion of high culture and sophisticated attitudes through the mass media, there is an increasing social gap between the low income person and the average American. If this gap is not redressed, there will be a constant danger that the credentials effect will set the poor back in their efforts to achieve equality at any time that the labor market slackens.

14. Moynihan (1969); Sundquist (1968); Sundquist (1969).

by lower-skilled individuals have gotten short shrift. An administration with a rational poverty policy would systematically assess programs to determine the contribution each would make toward reducing unemployment and raising wages at the lower-skilled levels. In a very real way, the cost of the space program or the supersonic transport is not just the money to be paid out as part of those programs. Added to this cost should be the cost of the opportunities foregone for creating employment and investing in human capital at lower skill levels. That cost can be measured by the degree to which spending the money on programs that would have employed lower skilled people would have reduced welfare costs, police cost, costs of riot damage, and so forth.

In short, an administration dedicated to eliminating poverty would search out among the many worthwhile activities that the government might support particularly those activities which could be accomplished with a relatively high proportion of low skilled labor.

New Forms of Income Maintenance

A national income maintenance program would have two central features: individuals would be universally and automatically eligible when their incomes fell below a certain level, and the benefits conferred would be high enough to eliminate poverty as it is now officially defined. Such a guaranteed annual income is not likely to have wide popular support so long as at least a significant minority of the poor are poor by virtue of the fact that they do not work; thus employment programs should have priority over income maintenance programs in the timing of new attacks on relative poverty. (This does not ignore the possibility that a subsistence level negative income tax or family allowance program might be funded without major employment programs, but what we know of poverty suggests that such programs would have minimal impact, particularly on the worst off portions of the poor.) However, employment programs by themselves have distant time horizons for eliminating poverty, and significant segments of the poor would not be affected by them in the beginning. It is likely that by the time the nation is persuaded that most able-bodied persons who can work are working, it would be possible to institute a major income maintenance program. Such a program would probably have to combine the universal eligibility features of a family allowance and the technically superior financial features of a negative income tax, with its sliding scales of rates on earned income; despite all of the argument between the advocates of these measures; such a combination is not technically difficult.[15]

The popular appeal of such programs would be enhanced by the hostility and frustration that is now evoked by the AFDC program, which

15. See particularly Green (1967); for other discussions of family allowance and guaranteed incomes, see Schorr (1968), Vadakin (1968), Tobin (1964), and Lampman (1959).

would be replaced. The new programs could be administered in relatively simple and straightforward ways by agencies such as the Internal Revenue Service and the Social Security Administration, which are not tainted with the failure of the public welfare agencies. A negative income tax or family allowance program could free state funds now heavily committed to public welfare, increasing the appeal of the new programs at the state level. With welfare activities substantially reduced, the states would have funds to devote to urban and educational programs without bankrupting themselves.

Linking the Poor to Society's Needs

Some government programs will directly generate more employment for the poor; others will do so indirectly, by increasing the purchasing power of the poor, some of which feeds back in the form of increased employment opportunities. This section presents some examples of programs intended to have a primary employment effect, which meet our criterion of providing opportunity for the poor and at the same time serve the pressing needs of the whole society.

Pollution

Pollution problems are becoming more obvious and more urgent, and there is danger that the nation will try to solve these problems with its complex technology rather than making adequate use of low technologies to provide a base on which high technology can make its maximum contribution. Roger Starr and James Carlson outline this problem with respect to water pollution in the cities.[16] They note that a major contribution to the pollution of city water is made by inadequate sewer systems, which fail to collect and direct to treatment all the sewerage and all the run-off from rain. They suggest that new construction and replacement of ineffective sewer systems in the nation's cities would require an expenditure of some $30 billion, generate about a million man years of work at low skill levels and provide direct wage payments to low skilled workers of over $2.5 billion. This number of jobs would provide a year's employment for three-fourths of all males in the nation who are currently unemployed for five weeks or more. Starr and Carlson refer to government funding possibilities which make a permanent contribution to the quality of life of the total society and at the same time provide employment for the poor as the *strategy of cross-commitment*. It is just such a strategy that we have in mind when we suggest linking the poor's productivity to society's needs.

Urban Sanitation and Beautification

Barry Commoner has argued that rat control programs which emphasize the development of poisons, rat birth control, and so forth represent

16. Roger Starr and James Carlson (1967).

a high technology solution for a problem to which low technology is more applicable. He suggests that intensive programs of refuse collection and sanitation might well have a greater effect on the control of rats without increasing the danger of chemical pollution and poisoning.

Cities that are dirty and messy, and therefore provide good homes for rats, are also dreary and run-down. In most such cities there are many abandoned and condemned buildings, whose owners cannot be made to tear them down at their own expense while the city does not have money to tear them down. Like rat control, government-funded clean-up programs could make a significant contribution to the city as a more habitable place. Such programs would probably have a finite time limit; if sufficiently funded presumably there will come a point when all the abandoned buildings would be torn down, the abandoned cars dragged away, and the decades of accumulation of refuse and rubble cleaned out. However, after several years of such work it might well be possible for city sanitation departments to keep cities from running down again.

Special Purpose Facilities

A variety of useful services can be provided by relatively unskilled labor without heavy commitments to capital expenditures. For example, if buildings are torn down "pocket parks" could be developed in their place. Some abandoned city buildings (e.g. fire stations) might be turned into recreation centers or birth control clinics which could be staffed by residents of the area.

All of these special programs should be regarded as temporary and provision should be made for them to be self-liquidating as their clients' incomes increase.

Public Services by Nonprofessionals

The largest government services—the schools, the hospitals and clinics, the police departments, social work agencies—have all been highly professionalized, and there has been a constant strain toward increasing the educational level of those who work in them. Much division of labor and "deskilling" could be instituted in these service agencies to provide beginning jobs at the unskilled level. A school that uses teachers' assistants not only conserves the professional manpower that is in short supply but also humanizes the school room situation and provides more individual attention for the students. Parallel examples can be found in hospitals and clinics, in police departments and in social welfare agencies. The concepts involved in the development of these deskilling programs have been well outlined by Arthur Pearl and Frank Riessman in their work on "new careers for the poor."[17]

Not only is this new careers approach useful in providing income to the poor but it in fact increases the productivity of the governmental agency

17. Pearl and Riessman (1965).

by introducing a more rational division of labor. The combination of such a division of labor with organized on-the-job training programs allows the poor to move up to higher skilled jobs within the institution as they acquire more experience.

Conclusion

The past few years have seen the end of the New Deal era in American public policy, an era in which our society has gone far toward assuring most Americans a life of unparalleled affluence and domestic security.

We now begin a new era in American political history. With intelligent political leadership, the nation can move toward assuring affluence and security to those who have so far not benefitted from the achievement of the New Deal's goals. Without good sense and constructive leadership, we can look forward only to a society in which affluence and security are progressively limited by the poverty, insecurity, and exploitation of the poor. The nation may survive, but it will be a distinctly uglier, meaner, more repressed, and more frightening place to live.

If a start is to be made toward eliminating poverty, the first requirement is to reject the myth that the increasing affluence of the nation will automatically give everyone—including those now at the lowest levels of income—larger and larger slices of the pie. From 1947 to the present, 20 per cent of American families have each been earning less than half the median family income. Each year the absolute dollar gap between them and the rest of the nation increases.

Domestically, there has been no contradiction so stark—and perhaps so fateful—as that between our dramatic success in increasing the prosperity of the "poor but honest" stable working class and failure to provide for those at the lowest level relative to other Americans. Even after allowing for inflation, the urban working class has nearly doubled its income in the past 20 years; its members can afford to look back, across an almost incredible and ever-increasing gap, at how much worse off their parents were. But for the American underclass the widening gap across which they stare is *up*. They too have seen somewhat more money, but not much, and with each decade a larger chasm appears between what they must accept and the comforts and necessities the class above them has come to take for granted.

To make the contrast even sharper, a reverse situation has developed in the political conditions of the two classes. The development of political consciousness and effectiveness in the working class, that great hope of liberals and radicals of the depression years, must now be considered a failure. The working class is assuming an increasingly conservative and hostile stance toward doing what will be necessary to help those below them rise more rapidly. However, the political ferment of the various groups that make up the American underclass has set in motion processes that promise possible political success—the bare beginnings of a mobilization toward the basic changes necessary if America is no longer to have poor people.

Social scientists have been slow to provide detailed knowledge of what has become apparent as the central fact about the American underclass— that it is created by, and its existence is maintained by, the operation of what is in other ways the most successful economic system known to man. It is not so much that this good system has excluded the underclass as that the manner of its operation produces and reproduces such a class. Social scientists have a great deal to tell us about the life styles of various class groupings and how they must learn how to survive, but the larger societal mechanisms that produce the underclass have been largely ignored. Economists have found this subject much less exciting that "the big picture" of the aggregate economy. Sociologists have found it much easier to go to the people of the underclass to find out how they survive, as we have done in this book, than to find out why they must survive in those ways.

Social scientists have failed to recognize that to understand modern industrial society they must know what resources are necessary for a person to behave in ways that allow him to be a full member of that society. It has become increasingly clear that the relative deprivation of the underclass is at the heart of their marginality and their alienation. No matter how much their incomes rise, their misery and its attending problems will continue so long as there exists in the society this group of people whose level of living is far below that of the average Americans.

The recognition that it would require a basic change in how income is distributed to do away with the shame of an underclass has forced "sensible people" to despair that anything could be done; they could not conceive that society might be willing to pay the cost. Instead, intellectuals converted the existence of inequality into an issue they could use as a club in their battles with their competitors in the elite. Radicals and conservatives, liberals and moderates—all have developed versions of what the underclass means and needs that fit into their general ideological stances, but that bear little resemblance to the real situation.

There is reason now to hope that social scientists are in a better position to develop proposals that could have some impact on the problem, but it is the political hope for translating these proposals into policy that remains in question. The challenge of the next decade will be primarily political. Can support be mobilized for the changes that must be made—a mobilization that will require more realism than we have had in underclass politics in recent years? Can the middle and working class's deep political insecurity, which persists despite its affluence, be effectively circumvented or used to good political purpose?

In any case, we hope that one result of social science efforts will be for "thinking people" to stop deluding themselves about the underclass. It is a product of an economic system so designed that it generates a destructive amount of income inequality, and we must face the fact that the only solution of the underclass problem is to change that inequality-producing system. The underclass must reach economic equality with "average" Americans so that in the end others do not decide what they can and cannot have but they can make those decisions for themselves as "average" Americans do.

Bibliography

Abrahams, Roger D. "Playing the Dozens," in *Journal of American Folklore*, 75:209–220, (July, 1962).

————. *Deep Down in the Jungle*. Hatboro, Pa.: Folklore Associates, 1964. (Revised edition, Chicago: Aldine Publishing Company, 1970.)

Architectural Forum: The Magazine of Building. "Slum Surgery in St. Louis," Vol. 94, (April, 1951).

Bailey, Thomas Pearce. *Race Orthodoxy in the South and Other Aspects of the Negro Question*. New York: The Neale Publishing Company, 1914.

Bakke, E. Wright. *Citizens Without Work*. New Haven: Yale University Press, 1940.

Baldwin, James. *Nobody Knows My Name*. New York: The Dell Press, 1961.

Banfield, Edward C. *The Moral Basis of a Backward Society*. New York: Free Press, 1958.

Banfield, Edward C. and Martin Myerson. *Politics, Planning and the Public Interest*. New York: Free Press, 1955.

Batchelder, Alan B. "Decline in the Relative Income of Negro Men," in *Quarterly Journal of Economics*, 78:525–548, (November, 1964).

Beck, Bernard. "Welfare as a Moral Category," in *Social Problems*, XIV:258–277, No. 3, (Winter, 1966).

Becker, Gary S. *Economics of Discrimination*. Chicago: The University of Chicago Press, 1957.

Becker, Howard S. *Outsiders: Studies in the Sociology of Deviance*. New York: Free Press, 1968.

Bell, Norman W. and Ezra F. Vogel. *A Modern Introduction to the Family*. New York: Free Press, 1960.

Bell, Robert R. *Premarital Sex in a Changing Society*. Englewood Cliffs, N.J.: Prentice-Hall, 1966.

Bellush, Jewel and Murray Hausknecht (eds.). *Urban Renewal: People, Politics and Planning*. Garden City, N.Y.: Anchor Books, 1967.

Bennett, John W. "The Significance of the Concept of Adaptation for Contemporary Socio-Cultural Anthropology." Paper presented at Eighth Institutional Congress of Anthropological and Ethnological Sciences, Tokyo, 1968.

Bennett, Lerone. "Negro Mood," in *The Negro Mood and Other Essays*. Chicago: Johnson Publishing Company, 1964.

Berger, Bennett M. *Working Class Suburb: A Study of Auto Workers in Suburbia*. Berkeley: University of California Press, 1960.

————. "Suburbs, Subcultures and Styles of Life: Problems of Cultural Pluralism in American Life," in *Planning for a Nation of Cities*, Sam J. Warner (ed.), Cambridge: M.I.T. Press, 1966.

Berger, Peter L. and Thomas Luckmann. *The Social Construction of Reality*. Garden City, N.Y.: Doubleday, 1966.

Bernard, Jessie. *Marriage and Family Among Negroes*. Englewood Cliffs, N.J. Prentice-Hall, 1966.

————. "Marital Stability and Patterns of Status Variables," in *Journal of Marriage and the Family*, XXVIII:437 (November, 1966).

Bernstein, Basil. "Public Language: Some Sociological Implications of a Linguistic Form," in *British Journal of Sociology*, XI:271–276, (September, 1960).

Bettelheim, Bruno. *The Informed Heart*. New York: Free Press, 1960.

Blake, Judith. *Family Structure in Jamaica*. New York: Free Press, 1961.

Blau, Peter M. and Otis D. Duncan. *The American Occupational Structure*. New York: Wiley, 1967.

Blauner, Robert. *Alienation and Freedom: The Factory Worker and His Industry*. Chicago: The University of Chicago Press, 1964.

————. "Negro Culture: Myth or Reality?" Paper presented at the Southern Sociological Society meetings, Atlanta, Georgia, 1968.

Bledsoe, Albert Taylor. *An Essay on Liberty and Slavery*. Philadelphia: J. P. Lippincott and Company, 1856.

Bogue, Donald J., Bhaskar Misra and D. Dandedar. "A New Estimate of the Negro Population and Negro Vital Rates in the United States, 1930–1960," in *Demography*, Vol. 1, No. 1, 1964.

Bordua, David J. "Delinquent Subcultures: Sociological Interpretations of Gang Delinquency," in *The Annals of the American Academy of Political and Social Sciences*, 228:120–136, 1961.

Bott, Elizabeth. *Family and Social Network*. London: Tavistock Publications, 1957.

Boyer, Ruth M. "The Matrifocal Family Among the Mescalero: Additional Data," in *American Anthropologist*, LXVI:593–602, No. 3, (June, 1964).

Bremner, Robert H. *From the Depths: The Discovery of Poverty in the U.S.* New York: New York University Press, 1956.

Broderick, Carlfred B. "Social Heterosexual Development Among Urban Negroes and Whites," in *Journal of Marriage and the Family*, 27:200–212 (May, 1965).

————. "Sexual Behavior Among Pre-Adolescents," in *Journal of Social Issues*, XXII:6–22, No. 2, (April, 1966).

Brotz, Howard. *The Black Jews of Harlem*. New York: Free Press, 1964.

Brown, Claude. *Manchild in the Promised Land*. New York: New American Library, Inc., 1966.

Buckholdt, David. "The Language Exchange: Therapy for Language Failure Among the Disadvantaged." Thesis, 1969, Washington University, St. Louis, Missouri.

Caplovitz, David. *Poor Pay More*. New York: Free Press, 1963.

Cash, W. J. *Mind of the South*. New York: Alfred A. Knopf, Inc., 1960.

Cayton, Horace R. and St. Clair Drake. *Black Metropolis*. New York: Harper & Row, 1962.

Chilman, Catherine Street. "A Comparative Study of Measured Personality Needs and Self-Perceived Problems of Ninth and Tenth Grade Students." Doctoral Dissertation, Syracuse University, 1959, pp. 258–259.

Chinoy, Eli. *Automobile Workers and the American Dream*. New York: Random House, 1955.

Clark, Kenneth. *Dark Ghetto*. New York: Harper & Row, 1965.

Clark, Kenneth and Talcott Parsons (eds.). *The Negro American.* Boston: Houghton Mifflin Company, 1966.

Cloward, Richard A. and Lloyd E. Ohlin. *Delinquency and Opportunity: A Theory of Delinquent Gangs.* New York: Free Press, 1960.

Cohen, Albert K. *Delinquent Boys.* New York: MacMillan, 1955.

————. "The Sociology of the Deviant Act," in *American Sociological Review,* Vol. XXX, No. 1, (February, 1965).

————. "Social Disorganization and Deviant Behavior," in *Sociology Today,* Robert Merton *et al.* (eds.). New York: Harper and Row, 1965.

Cohen, Albert K., Alfred Lindesmith, Karl Schuessler (eds.). *The Sutherland Papers.* Bloomington: Indiana University Press, 1956.

Cohen, Albert K. and Harold M. Hodges. "Characteristics of the Lower Blue-Collar Class," in *Social Problems,* X:303–334, No. 4, (Spring, 1963).

Cohen, Elie A. *Human Behavior in the Concentration Camp.* New York: W. W. Norton Company, 1953.

Coleman, James Samuel. *Equality of Educational Opportunity.* Washington: U.S. Department of Health, Education and Welfare, U.S. Government Printing Office, 1966.

Coles, Robert. *Children of Crisis: A Study of Courage and Fear.* Boston: Little, Brown & Company, 1967.

————. *Still Hungry in America.* Cleveland: World Publishing Company, 1969.

Coser, Lewis. "The Sociology of Poverty," in *Social Problems,* XIII:140–148, No. 2, (Fall, 1965).

Dansereau, H. Kirk. "Work and the Teenage Blue-Collarite," in *Blue-Collar World,* A. B. Shostak and W. Gomberg (eds.). New York: Prentice-Hall, 1964.

Davis, Allison. "The Motivation of the Underprivileged Worker," in *Industry and Society,* W. F. Whyte (ed.). New York: McGraw-Hill Book Company, 1946.

————. *Social Class Influences Upon Learning.* Cambridge: Harvard University Press, 1948.

Davis, Allison and John Dollard. *Children of Bondage: The Personality Development of Negro Youth in the Urban South.* Washington, D.C.: American Council on Education, 1940.

Davis, Allison, Burleigh B. Gardner and Mary R. Gardner. *Deep South.* Chicago: The University of Chicago Press, 1941.

Davis, Allison and R. Havighurst. *Father of the Man.* Boston: Houghton Mifflin Company, 1947.

Davis, David Brion. *The Problem of Slavery in Western Culture.* Ithaca N.Y. Cornell University Press, 1966.

Davis, Kingsley. "Some Demographic Aspects of Poverty in the U.S.," in *Poverty in America,* Margaret S. Gordon (ed.). San Francisco: Chandler Publishing Company, 1965.

De Jesus, C. M. *Child of the Dark.* New York: E. P. Dutton, 1962.

Demerath, Nicholas J. "St. Louis Public Housing Study Sets Off Community Development to Meet Social Needs," in *Journal of Housing,* XIX, October, 1962.

Dollard, John. *Caste and Class in a Southern Town.* New Haven: Yale University Press, 1937.

————. "The Dozens: The Dialect of Insult," in *American Image,* 1:3–24, 1939.

Drake, St. Clair. "The Social and Economic Status of the Negro in the United States," in *Daedalus,* Fall, 1965, p. 772.

DuBois, William E. *The Souls of Black Folk*. Greenwich, Conn.: Fawcett Publications, 1965.

Duhl, Leonard J. (ed.). *The Urban Condition*. New York: Basic Books, 1963.

Durkheim, Emile. *Suicide*. John A. Spaulding and George Simpson, translators, New York: Free Press, 1951.

Dyer, William G. "Family Reactions to the Father's Job," in *Blue-Collar World*, A. B. Shostak and W. Gomberg (eds.). New York: Prentice-Hall, 1964.

Eckstein, Otto. *Studies in the Economics of Income Maintenance*. Washington: Brookings Institute, 1967.

Elkins, Stanley. *Slavery*. New York: Grosset & Dunlap, Inc., 1959.

Elliot, E. N. (ed.). *Cotton is King, and Pro-Slavery Arguments*. Augusta, Ga.: Pritchard, Abbott and Loomis, 1860.

Ellison, Ralph. *Shadow and Act*. New York: Random House, 1964.

Erikson, Erik H. *Childhood and Society*. New York: W. W. Norton, 1950.

————. *Identity and the Life Cycle*. New York: International Universities Press, 1959.

Erikson, Kai T. "Notes on the Sociology of Deviance," in *Social Problems*, 9:307–314, 1962.

Essien-Udom, E. U. *Black Nationalism: A Search for Identity in America*. Chicago: The University of Chicago Press, 1962.

Farber, Bernard. *Family: Organization and Interaction*. San Francisco: Chandler Publishing Company, 1964.

Federn, Paul. *Ego Psychology and the Psychoses*. New York: Basic Books, Inc., 1955.

Fenichel, Otto. "On the Psychology of Boredom," in *Organization and Pathology of Thought*, David Rappaport (ed.). New York: Columbia University Press, 1951.

Ferman, Louis A., Joyce L. Kornbluh and Alan Haber (eds.). *Poverty in America*. Ann Arbor: University of Michigan Press, 1965.

Ferman, Louis A., Joyce L. Kornbluh and J. A. Miller (eds.) *Negroes and Jobs*. Ann Arbor: University of Michigan Press, 1968.

Fiedler, Leslie. *Waiting for the End*. New York: Stein and Day, 1964.

Finestone, Harold. "Cats, Kicks and Color," in *The Other Side*, Harold Becker (ed.). New York: Free Press, 1964.

Firth, Raymond (ed.). *Two Studies of Kinship in London*. London: University of London, Athlone Press, 1956.

Fisher, Ann *et al.* "The Occurence of the Extended Family at the Origin of the Family of Procreation: A Developmental Approach to Negro Family Structure." Paper presented to the American Anthropological Association, Denver, November, 1965.

Fisher, Robert, M. *Twenty Years of Public Housing*. New York: Harper Publishers, 1959.

Fitzhugh, George. *Sociology for the South or the Failure of Free Society*. New York: B. Franklin, 1865.

Fleisher, Belton M. *The Economics of Delinquency*. Chicago: Quadrangle Books, 1966.

Foster, G. M. "Peasant Society and the Image of the Limited Good," in *American Anthropologist*, Vol. 67, 1965.

Franklin, John and Isidore Starr. *Negro in Twentieth Century America*. New York: Vintage Books, 1967.

Frazier, E. Franklin. *Negro Youth at the Crossways*. Washington, D.C.: American Council on Education, 1940.

————. *Black Bourgeoisie*. New York: Collier Books, 1962.

_____. *The Negro Family in the United States*. Chicago: The University of Chicago Press, 1966.

Freud, Sigmund. *Civilization and Its Discontents*. Standard Edition, Vol. XXI, London: Hogarth Press, 1961.

Fried, Marc. "Grieving for a Lost Home," in *The Urban Condition*, Leonard J. Duhl (ed.). New York: Basic Books, 1963.

_____. "Transitional Functions of Working Class Communities," in *Mobility and Mental Health*, Mildred Kantor (ed.). Springfield, Ill.: C. C. Thomas, 1965.

_____. "The Role of Work in a Mobile Society," in *Planning for a Nation of Cities*, Sam B. Warner, Jr. (ed.). Cambridge: M.I.T. Press, 1966.

Fried, Marc and Peggy Gleicher. "Some Sources of Residential Satisfaction in an Urban Slum," in *Urban Renewal: People, Politics and Planning*, Jewel Bellush and Murray Hausknecht (eds.). New York: Anchor Books, 1967.

Frieden, Bernard J. and Robert Morris (eds.). *Urban Planning and Social Policy*. New York: Basic Books, 1968.

Friedlander, Kate. *The Psycho-Analytical Approach to Juvenile Delinquency*. New York: International Universities Press, 1947.

Fromm, Erich. *Marx's Concept of Man*. New York: Frederick Ungar Publishing Company, 1961.

Fuchs, Victor. "Toward a Theory of Poverty," in *The Concept of Poverty*, Washington, D.C.: Task Force on Economic Growth and Opportunity, Chamber of Commerce of the United States, 1965.

_____. "Redefining Poverty," in *The Public Interest*, No. 8, (Summer, 1967), pp. 88–95.

Gans, Herbert. *The Urban Villagers*. New York: Free Press, 1962.

_____. "Effect of the Move from the City to Suburb," in *The Urban Condition*, Leonard J. Duhl (ed.). New York: Basic Books, 1963.

_____. *Levittowners*. New York: Pantheon Books, 1967.

_____. *People and Plans: Essays on Urban Problems and Solutions*. New York: Basic Books, 1968.

_____. "Class in the Study of Poverty: An Approach to Anti-Poverty Research," in *On Understanding Poverty: Perspective from the Social Sciences*, Daniel P. Moynihan (ed.). New York: Basic Books, 1969.

Garfinkel, Harold. *Studies in Ethomethodology*. Englewood Cliffs, N.J.: Prentice-Hall, 1967.

Gebhard, Paul H. *Pregnancy, Birth and Abortion*. New York: Harper and Brothers, 1958.

Gladwin, Thomas. *Poverty U.S.A.* Boston: Little, Brown & Co., 1967.

Glaser, Barney and Anselm Strauss. "Awareness Contexts and Social Interaction," in *American Sociological Review*, Vol. 29, No. 5, 1964.

_____. *The Discovery of Grounded Theory*. Chicago: Aldine Publishing Company, 1967.

Glazer, Nathan. "Introduction," in *The Negro Family in the United States*, E. F. Frazier (ed.). Chicago: The University of Chicago Press, 1966.

Glazer, Nathan and Daniel P. Moynihan. *Beyond the Melting Pot*. Cambridge: M.I.T. Press, 1963.

Glenn, Norval D. "Negro-White Differences in Reported Attitudes and Behavior," in *Sociology and Social Research*, 50:199, (January, 1966).

Glick, Paul C. *American Families*. New York: J. Wiley, 1957.

Goffman, Erving. *The Presentation of Self in Everyday Life*. Edinburgh: University of Edinburgh, Social Sciences Research Center, 1958.

_____. *Encounters*. Indianapolis: Bobbs-Merrill Company, 1961.

————. *Stigma: Notes on the Management of Spoiled Identity.* Englewood Cliffs, N.J.: Prentice-Hall, 1963.

Goode, William J. "Economic Factors and Marital Stability," in *American Sociological Review,* 16:803, (December, 1951).

————. "Illegitimacy in the Caribbean Social Structure," in *American Sociological Review,* XXV:21–30, No. 1, (February, 1960).

————. "Note on Problems in Theory and Method: The New World," in *American Anthropologist,* Vol. 68, No. 2, Part 1, (April, 1966).

Goodenough, Ward Hunt. *Cooperation in Change.* New York: Russell Sage Foundation, 1963.

Gordon, Margaret (ed.). *Poverty in America.* San Francisco: Chandler Publishing Company, 1965.

Gouldner, Alvin W. "Reciprocity and Autonomy in Functional Theory," in *Symposium on Sociological Theory,* Llewellyn Gross (ed.). Evanston, Ill.: Row, Peterson, 1959.

————. "The Norm of Reciprocity: A Preliminary Statement," in *American Sociological Review,* 25:161–178, (April, 1960).

————. *Enter Plato.* New York: Basic Books, 1965.

Goveia, Elsa. *Slave Society in The British Leeward Islands at the End of the Eighteenth Century.* New Haven: Yale University Press, 1965.

Green, Arnold W. "The Cult of Personality and Sexual Relations," in *Psychiatry,* 4:343–348, 1941.

Green, Christopher. *Negative Taxes and the Poverty Problem.* Washington, D. C.: The Brookings Institution, 1967.

Greenwald, Harold. *The Call Girl.* New York: Ballantine Books, 1958.

Grier, William H. and Price M. Cobbs. *Black Rage.* New York: Basic Books, 1968.

Guild, June. *Black Laws of Virginia.* Richmond, Va.: Whittet and Shepperson, 1936.

Gursslin, Orville R. and Jack Roach. "Some Issues in Training the Employed," in *Social Problems,* 12:68–77, No. 1, (Summer, 1964).

Hagood, Margaret J. *Mothers of the South.* Chapel Hill: University of North Carolina Press, 1939.

Halliday, J. L. *Psychosocial Medicine: The Study of the Sick Society.* New York: Norton, 1948.

Hamblin, Robert, *et al.* "Changing the Game From 'Get the Teacher' to 'Learn'," in *Trans-action,* January, 1969.

Hammond, Boone. "The Contest System: A Survival Technique," St. Louis: Washington University Masters Essay in Sociology, 1965, (mimeographed).

————. "Jargon: The Language of the Ghetto." Ph.D. Colloquium, Department of Sociology and Anthropology, Washington University, St. Louis, 1967.

Handel, Gerald and Lee Rainwater. "Persistence and Change in Working Class Life Style," in *Blue-Collar World,* A. B. Shostak and W. Gomberg (eds.). New York: Prentice-Hall, 1964.

Hannerz, Ulf. *Soulside: Inquiries into Ghetto Culture and Community.* New York: Columbia University Press, 1969.

Harrington, Michael. *The Other America.* New York: MacMillan Company, 1962.

Hartmann, Heinz. *Ego Psychology and the Problem of Adaptation.* London: Image Publishing Company, 1958.

Harwood, Edwin S., "Work and Community Among Urban Newcomers: A Study of the Social and Economic Adaptation of Southern Migrants in Chicago." Unpublished doctoral dissertation, University of Chicago, 1966.

Henriques, Fernando. *Family and Colour in Jamaica*. London: McGibbon and Kee, 1953.

Henry, Jules. "White People's Time, Colored People's Time," in *Transaction*, 2:31–34, No. 3, (March, 1965).

Henry, William E. "The Psychodynamics of the Executive Role," in *American Journal of Sociology*, Vol. 54, No. 4, 1949.

Herskovits, Melville J. *The Myth of the Negro Past*. New York, London: Harper and Brothers, 1941.

Hess, Robert D. and Gerald Handel. *Family Worlds*. Chicago: The University of Chicago Press, 1959.

Hess, Robert D. and Roberta M. Bear. *Early Education*. Chicago: Aldine Publishing Company, 1968.

Himes, Joseph S. "Negro Teenage Culture," in *Annals of the American Academy of Political and Social Science*, 338:92, (November, 1961).

Hippler, Arthur E. *Hunter's Point: A Northern U.S. Urban Negro Community*. Forthcoming.

Hollingshead, A. B. *Elmtown's Youth*. New York: J. Wiley, 1948.

Hollingshead, A. B. and Frederick Redlich. *Social Class and Mental Illness: A Community Study*. New York: J. Wiley, 1958.

Hollingshead, A. B. and L. H. Rogler. "Attitudes Toward Slums and Private Housing in Puerto Rico," in *The Urban Condition*, Leonard J. Duhl (ed.). New York: Basic Books, 1963.

Horowitz, Irving Louis. "Social Science and Public Policy: An Examination of the Political Foundations of Modern Research," in *International Quarterly*, Vol. II, No. 1, (March, 1967).

Horton, John, "Time and Cool People," in *Trans-action*, 4:5–12, (April, 1967).

Hughes, Everett C. *Men and Their Work*. New York: Free Press, 1958.

Inkeles, Alex. "Industrial Man: The Relation of Status to Experience, Perception and Value," in *The American Journal of Sociology*, LXVI:1–31, (July, 1960).

Jacobs, Jane. *The Death and Life of Great American Cities*. New York: Random House, 1961.

Jeffers, Camille. *Living Poor*. Ann Arbor: Ann Arbor Publishers, 1967.

Johnson, C. *Shadow of the Plantation*. Chicago: The University of Chicago Press, 1934.

————. *Growing Up in the Black Belt*. Washington, D.C.: American Council on Education, 1941.

Jones, LeRoi. *Blues People*. New York: W. Morrow, 1963.

Kahl, Joseph. *The American Class Structure*. New York: Rinehart and Company, 1957.

Kain, John F. "Housing, Segregation, Negro Employment and Metropolitan Decentralization," in *Quarterly Journal of Economics*, February, 1968.

Kaplan, Bert. *Studying Personality Cross-Culturally*. Evanston, Ill.: Row-Peterson, 1961.

Kardiner, Abram and Lionel Ovesey. *The Mark of Oppression*. New York: Meridian Books, 1962.

Karon, Bertram P. *The Negro Personality*. New York: Springer Publishing Company, 1958.

Keil, Charles. *Urban Blues*. Chicago: The University of Chicago Press, 1966.

Kephart, William M. "Occupational Level and Marital Disruption," in *American Sociological Review*, 19:459, (August, 1955).

Kinsey, Alfred C. *Sexual Behavior in the Human Male*. Philadelphia: W. B. Saunders, 1948.

————. *Sexual Behavior in the Human Female*. Philadelphia: W. B. Saunders, 1953.

Klein, Herbert S. *Slavery in the Americas: A Comparative Study of Cuba and Virginia*. Chicago: The University of Chicago Press, 1967.

Kluckhohn, Clyde. "Values and Value Orientations in the Theory of Action," in *Toward a General Theory of Action*, Talcott Parsons and Edward A. Shils (eds.). Cambridge: Harvard University Press, 1951.

Kochman, Thomas. "The Kinetic Element in Black Idiom." Unpublished paper read at American Anthropological Association Meeting, Seattle, Washington, November 21–24, 1968.

————. " 'Rapping' in the Black Ghetto," in *Trans-action*, Vol. 6, No. 4, February, 1969).

Komarovsky, Mirra. *The Unemployed Man and His Family*. New York: Dryden Press, 1940.

————. *Blue Collar Marriage*. New York: Random House, 1964.

Koos, Earl. *Families in Trouble*. New York: King's Crown Press, 1946.

Kriesberg, Louis. "The Relationship Between Socio-Economic Rank and Behavior," in *Social Problems*, 10:334–353, No. 4, (Spring, 1963).

Kriesberg, Louis. *Mothers in Poverty: A Study of Fatherless Families*. Chicago: Aldine Publishing Company, 1970.

Kunstadter, Peter. "A Survey of the Consanguine or Matrifocal Family," in *American Anthropologist*, 65:56–66, No. 1, (February, 1963).

Ladner, Joyce. "On Becoming a Woman in the Ghetto: Modes of Adaptation." Unpublished dissertation presented to the Graduate School of Arts and Sciences Washington University, St. Louis, June 1968.

Ladner, Joyce and Boone Hammond. "Socialization into Sexual Behavior." Paper presented at Society for the Study of Social Problems Meetings. San Francisco, 1967.

Lampman, Robert. "The Low Income Population and Economic Growth." Study Paper No. 12. Washington, D.C.: United States Congress Joint Economic Committee, 1959.

Landy, David. *Tropical Childhood*. Chapel Hill: University of North Carolina Press, 1959.

Leggett, John C. *Class, Race and Labor*. New York: Oxford University Press, 1968.

Lemert, Edwin M. *Human Deviance, Social Problems and Social Control*. New York: Prentice-Hall, 1967.

Lerman, Paul. "Argot, Symbolic Deviance and Subculture Delinquency," in *American Sociological Review*, April, 1967.

Levy, Sidney, "Twenty-Nine Negro Lower-Class Adolescent Girls: Thematic Apperception Technique Analysis," in "On Becoming a Woman in the Ghetto: Modes of Adaptation," Joyce Ladner. Unpublished Dissertation Washington University, St. Louis, 1967.

Lewis, Hylan. *Blackways of Kent*. Chapel Hill: University of North Carolina Press, 1955.

————. "The Family: Resources for Change," in *The Moynihan Report and the Politics of Controversy*, Lee Rainwater and William Yancey (eds.). Cambridge: M.I.T. Press. 1967.

Lewis, Oscar, "An Anthropological Approach to Family Studies," in *American Journal of Sociology*, 55:460–475, (March, 1950).

————. *Life in a Mexican Village: Tepoztlan Restudied*. Urbana: University of Illinois Press, 1951.

————. *Five Families*. New York: Basic Books, 1959.

————. *Children of Sanchez*. New York: Random House, 1961.

————. *La Vida, A Puerto Rican Family in the Culture of Poverty: San Juan and New York*. New York: Random House, 1966.

————. *A Study of Slum Culture: Backgrounds for La Vida*. New York: Basic Books, 1968.

Liebow, Elliot. *Tally's Corner*. Boston: Little, Brown and Company, 1967.

Lincoln, C. Eric. *Black Muslims in America*. Boston: Beacon Press, 1961.

Lipset, Seymour M. *The First New Nation*. New York: Basic Books, 1963.

Lomax, Louis E. *The Negro Revolt*. New York: Signet Books 1963.

Lopreato, Joseph. *Peasants No More: Social Class and Social Change in Southern Italy,* San Francisco: Chandler Publishing Company, 1967.

Lyford, Joseph. *The Airtight Cage*. New York: Harper and Row, 1966.

Mailer, Norman. *The White Negro*. San Francisco: City Light Books, 1957.

Marris, Peter and Martin Rein. *Dilemmas of Social Reform*. New York: Atherton Press, 1967.

Matza, David. *Delinquency and Drift*. New York: J. Wiley, 1964.

————. "The Disreputable Poor," in *Class, Status and Power,* Reinhard Bendix and Seymour Lipset (eds.). New York: The Free Press, 1966.

May, Edgar. *The Wasted Americans*. New York: Harper and Row, 1964.

McClosky, Herbert and Schaar, John. "Psychological Dimensions of Anomy," in *American Sociological Review,* (February, 1965), 14 ff.

Merton, Robert K. *Social Theory and Social Structure*. New York: Free Press, 1957.

Meyerson, Martin, Barbara Terrett and W. Wheaton. *Housing, People and Cities*. New York: McGraw-Hill, 1962.

Miller, Herman P. "Trends in the Income of Families and Persons in the United States, 1947–1960." Washington, D.C.: United States Department of Commerce, Bureau of the Census, 1960.

————. "Changes in the Number and Composition of the Poor," in *Poverty in America,* Margaret S. Gordon (ed.). San Francisco: Chandler Publishing Company, 1965.

————. *Poverty American Style*. Belmont, Calif.: Wadsworth Publishing Company, 1966.

————. *Income Distribution in the United States*. Washington, D.C.: U.S. Department of Commerce, Government Printing Office, 1966.

————. "The Credential Society," in *Trans-action,* December, 1967.

(November, 1963), p. 18–20.

————. "The American Lower Classes: A Typological Approach," in *Blue-Collar World,* A. B. Shostak and W. Gomberg (eds.). New York: Prentice-Hall, 1964.

————. "The Credential Society," editorial in *Trans-action,* December, 1967.

Miller, S. M. and Frank Riessman. "The Working Class Subculture: A New View," in *Social Problems,* Volume 9, 1961.

Miller, S. M. and Ira Harrison, "Types of Dropouts: 'The Unemployables'," in *Blue-Collar World,* A. B. Shostak and W. Gomberg (eds.). New York: Prentice-Hall, 1964.

Miller, S. M., Frank Riessman and Arthur A. Seagull. "Poverty and Self-Indulgence: A Critique of the Non-Deferred Gratification Pattern," in

Poverty in America, Louis A. Ferman, Joyce L. Kornbluh and Alan Haber (eds.). Ann Arbor: University of Michigan Press, 1965.

Miller, Walter B. "Lower Class Culture as a Generating Milieu of Gang Delinquency," in *Journal of Social Issues,* 14:5–19, No. 3, (1958).

―――――. "The Corner Gang Boys Get Married," in *Trans-action,* 1:10–12, No. 1, (November, 1963).

Miller, Warner. *The Cool World.* New York: Fawcett World Library, 1959.

Mills, C. Wright. *White Collar.* New York: Oxford University Press, 1951.

Minsky, Hyman P. "The Role of Employment Policy," in *Poverty in America,* Margaret S. Gordon (ed.). San Francisco: Chandler Publishing Company, 1965.

Mizruchi, Ephraim. *Success and Opportunity.* New York: Free Press, 1964.

Montgomery, Roger. "Comment on Fear and the House-as-Haven in the Lower Class," in *Journal of American Institute of Planners,* Vol. XXXII, No. 1, (January, 1966).

―――――. "Notes on Instant Urban Renewal," in *Trans-action,* 9:9–12, No. 4, (September, 1967).

Moore, William. "A Portrait: The Culturally Disadvantaged Pre-School Negro Child." Unpublished Doctoral Dissertation. St. Louis: St. Louis University, 1964.

Morgan, James N., *et al. Income and Welfare in the United States.* New York: McGraw-Hill, 1962.

Moynihan, Daniel P. *The Negro Family: The Case for National Action.* Washington, D.C.: Office of Policy Planning and Research, U.S. Department of Labor, 1965a.

―――――. "Employment, Income, and the Ordeal of the Negro Family," in *Daedalus,* No. 4, 1965b, p. 94.

―――――. "A Family Policy for the Nation," in *America,* 113:280–283, (September, 1965c).

―――――. *Maximum Feasible Misunderstanding.* New York: Free Press, 1969.

Myrdal, G. *An American Dilemma.* New York: Harper and Brothers, 1944.

―――――. *Beyond the Welfare State.* New Haven: Yale University Press, 1960.

―――――. *Challenge to Affluence.* New York: Pantheon Books, 1963.

Neugarten, Bernice. *Personality in Middle and Late Life.* New York: Atherton Press, 1964.

Ornati, Oscar. *Poverty Amid Affluence.* New York: Twentieth Century Fund, 1966.

Osofsky, Gilbert. *Burden of Race.* New York: Harper and Row, 1967.

Otterbein, Keith F. "Caribbean Family Organization: A Comparative Analysis," in *American Anthropologist,* Vol. 67, No. 1, (February, 1965).

Paneth, M. *Branch Street.* London: G. Allen and Unwin, 1944.

Parker, Seymour and Robert Kleiner. *Mental Illness in the Urban Negro Community.* New York: Free Press, 1966, p. 253.

Parsons, Talcott. *The Social System.* New York: Free Press, 1951.

―――――. "An Analytic Approach to the Theory of Social Stratification," in *Essays in Sociological Theory,* Talcott Parsons (ed.). New York: Free Press, 1954.

Parsons, Talcott and Edward Shils. *Toward A General Theory of Action.* New York: Harper and Row, 1952.

Parsons, Talcott and Robert Bales. *Family Socialization and Interaction Process.* New York: Free Press, 1955.

Passow, A. H. *Education in Depressed Areas.* New York: Bureau of Publications, Teacher's College, Columbia University, 1969.

Pearl, Arthur and Frank Riessman. *New Careers For the Poor*. New York: Free Press, 1965.

Peattie, Lisa R. *The View From the Barrio*. Ann Arbor: University of Michigan Press, 1968.

Pettigrew, Thomas. *A Profile of the Negro American*. Princeton: Van Nostrand Inc., 1964.

Powdermaker, H. *After Freedom, A Cultural Study in the Deep South*. New York: Viking Press, 1939.

Rainwater, Lee. *And the Poor Get Children*. Chicago: Quadrangle Books, 1960.

————. "Marital Sexuality in Four Cultures of Poverty," in *Journal of Marriage and the Family*, 26:457–466, No. 4, (November, 1964).

————. *Family Design: Marital Sexuality, Family Size and Contraception*. Chicago: Aldine, 1965.

————. "Marital Stability and Patterns of Status Variables: A Comment," in *Journal of Marriage and the Family*, 28:442–445, (November, 1966).

————. "Crucible of Identity: The Negro Lower-Class Family," in *Daedalus*, 95:172, 216, No. 1, (Winter, 1966).

Rainwater, Lee, Richard Coleman and Gerald Handel. *Workingman's Wife: Her Personality, World and Life Style*. New York: Oceana Publications, 1959.

Rainwater, Lee and Gerald Handel. "Changing Family Roles in the Working Class," in *Blue-Collar World*, A. B. Shostak and W. Gomberg (eds.). New York: Prentice-Hall, 1964.

Rainwater, Lee and Marc Swartz. "Urban Working Class Identity and World View." Unpublished Report. Chicago: Social Research, Inc., 1965.

Rainwater, Lee and William Yancey. *The Moynihan Report and the Politics of Controversy*. Cambridge: M.I.T. Press, 1967.

Rappaport, David. *The Structure of Psychoanalytic Theory*. New York: International Universities Press, 1960.

Reise, Hertha. *Heal the Hurt Child*. Chicago: The University of Chicago Press, 1962.

Reiss, Ira L. *Premarital Sexual Standards in America*. New York: Free Press, 1960.

————. *The Social Context of Premarital Sexual Permissiveness*. New York: Holt, Rinehart and Winston, 1967.

Riessman, Frank. *The Culturally Deprived Child*. New York: Harper, 1962.

Rist, Ray C., Jr. "The Socialization of the Ghetto Child into the Urban School System." Unpublished Dissertation presented to the Graduate School of Arts and Sciences, Washington University, June, 1970.

Robertson, Malcolm H. "Theoretical Implications of Sensory Deprivation," in *Psychological Review*, 11:33–42, 1961.

Rodman, Hyman. "The Lower Class Value Stretch," in *Social Forces*, 42:205, No. 2, (December, 1963).

————. "Illegitimacy in the Caribbean Social Structure: A Reconsideration," in *American Sociological Review*, 31:673–683, (October, 1966).

Rohrer, John and Munro Edmonson. *The Eighth Generation Grows Up: Cultures and Personalities of the New Orleans Negroes*. New York: Harper and Row, 1960.

Rosenblatt, Daniel and Edward Suchman, "The Underutilization of Medical Care Services by Blue-Collarites," in *Blue-Collar World*, A. B. Shostak and W. Gomberg (eds.). New York: Prentice-Hall, 1964.

Rosengren, William R. "Social Class And Becoming Ill," in *Blue-Collar World*, A. B. Shostak and W. Gomberg (eds.). New York: Prentice-Hall, 1964.

Rossi, Peter H. and Zahava D. Blum. "Class, Status and Poverty," in *On Understanding Poverty*, Daniel P. Moynihan (ed.). New York: Basic Books, 1969.

Rubin, Morton. *Plantation County*. Chapel Hill: University of North Carolina Press, 1951.

Ryan, Edward J. "Personal Identity in an Urban Slum," in *The Urban Condition*, Leonard J. Duhl (ed.). New York: Basic Books, 1963.

Sapir, Edward. *Culture, Language and Personality*. Berkeley and Los Angeles: University of California Press, 1964.

Schorr, Alvin. *Slums and Social Insecurity*. Washington, D.C.: Government Printing Office, 1963.

————. *Poor Kids*. New York: Basic Books, 1966.

————. *Explorations in Social Policy*. New York: Basic Books, 1968.

Schulz, David A. "The Role of the Boyfriend in Lower-Class Negro Life." Paper presented to the Midwestern Sociological Society, 1967.

————. *Coming Up Black*. New York: Prentice-Hall, 1969.

Schwartz, Michael and George Henderson. "The Culture of Unemployment: Some Notes on Negro Children," in *Blue-Collar World*, A. B. Shostak and W. Gomberg (eds.). New York: Prentice-Hall, 1964.

Scitovsky, Tibor. *Papers on Welfare and Growth*. Stanford: Stanford University Press, 1964.

Sexton, Patricia. *Education and Income*. New York: Viking Press, 1961.

Shannon, A. H. *Racial Integrity and Other Features of the Negro Problem*. Nashville: Publishing House of the M. E. Church, South, 1907.

Sheppard, Harold L. and Herbert Striner. *Civil Rights, Employment, and the Social Status of American Negroes*. Kalamazoo, Mich.: W. E. UpJohn Institute for Employment Research, 1966.

Short, James and Fred Strodtbeck. *Group Process and Gang Delinquency*. Chicago: The University of Chicago Press, 1965.

Shostak, A. B. and W. Gomberg (eds.). *Blue-Collar World*. New York: Prentice-Hall, 1964.

Simmel, George. "The Poor," in *Social Problems*, XIII:118–140, No. 2, (Fall, 1965).

Slater, Eliot and Moya Woodside. *Patterns of Marriage*. London: Cassell and Company, 1951.

Smith, M. G. *West Indian Family Structure*. Seattle: University of Washington Press, 1962.

Smith, Raymond. *The Negro Family in British Guiana*. London: Routledge and Kegan Paul, 1956.

————. "Culture and Social Structure in the Caribbean," in *Comparative Studies in Society and History*, 6:24–26, (October, 1963).

Solien de Gonzalez, Nancie. "Family Organization in Five Types of Migratory Wage Labor," in *American Anthropologist*, Vol. 63, No. 6, (December, 1961).

Spear, Allan H. *Black Chicago: The Making of a Negro Ghetto, 1890–1900*. Chicago: The University of Chicago Press, 1967.

Spiegel, John. "The Resolution of Role Conflict Within the Family," in *A Modern Introduction to the Family*. Norman Bell and Ezra Vogel (eds.). New York: Free Press, 1960, p. 375–377

Spinley, B. *Deprived and the Privileged*. London: Routledge and Kegan Paul, 1953.

Spiro, Melford. "Social Systems, Personality and Functional Analysis," in *Studying Personality Cross Culturally*, Bert Kaplan, (ed.). Evanston, Ill.: Row Peterson, 1961.

Srole, Leo. "Social Integration and Certain Corollaries: An Exploratory Study," in *American Sociological Review*, 21:709–716, 1956a.

————. "Anomie, Authoritarianism and Prejudice," in *American Journal of Sociology*, 62:63–67, (July, 1956b).

Stampp, Kenneth. *The Peculiar Institution.* New York: Alfred A. Knopf, 1956.
————. *Era of Reconstruction.* New York: Alfred A Knopf, 1966.
Starr, Roger and James Carlson. "Pollution and Poverty: The Strategy of Cross-Commitment," in *The Public Interest,* Winter, 1968, p. 104–131.
Stone, Gregory. "Appearance and the Self," in *Human Behavior and Social Processes,* Arnold Rose (ed.). Boston: Houghton-Mifflin, 1962, p. 86–118.
Strauss, Anselm L. *Mirrors and Masks: The Search for Identity.* New York: Free Press, 1959.
Stromberg, Jerry. "A Preliminary Report on Housing And Community Experiences of Project Residents." Occasional Paper Number One. (mimeographed). St. Louis: Washington University, Social Science Institute, 1966a.
————. "Perspectives on Pathology, Socialization, Religion and World View of (Project) Residents." Occasional Paper Number Five. St. Louis: Washington University, Social Science Institute, (mimeographed). 1966b.
————. "Private Problems in Public Housing: A Further Report on the Pruitt-Igoe Housing Project," Occasional Paper Number Thirty-Nine, St. Louis: Washington University, Social Science Institute, (mimeographed). 1968.
Stromberg, Jerry *et. al.* "A Comparison of Pruitt-Igoe Residents and Their Non-Public Housing Neighbors." Occasional Paper Number Ten (mimeographed). St. Louis: Washington University, Social Science Institute, 1967.
Stycos, J. Mayone. *Family and Fertility in Puerto Rico.* New York: Columbia University Press, 1955.
Stycos, J. Mayone and Kurt Back. *The Control of Human Fertility in Jamaica.* Ithaca: Cornell University Press, 1964.
Sundquist, James. *Politics and Policy: The Eisenhower, Kennedy and Johnson Years.* Washington: Brookings Institute, 1968.
————. (ed.) *On Fighting Poverty: Perspectives From Experience.* New York: Basic Books, 1969.
Sutherland, Robert. *Color, Class and Personality.* Washington, D.C.: American Council on Education, 1942.
Suttles, Gerald D. *The Social Order of the Slum: Ethnicity and Territory in the Inner City.* Chicago: University of Chicago Press, 1968.
Taeuber, Karl and Alma F. Taeuber. *Negroes in Cities.* Chicago: Alpine, 1965.
Talbert, Carol S. "Black-American Children in Contemporary Education; Separating the Real From the Ideal." Unpublished Master's Thesis, Anthropology Department, St. Louis: Washington University, 1969.
Tannenbaum, Frank. *Slave and Citizen: Negro in America.* New York: Random House: 1963.
Thernstrom, Stephan. *Poverty and Progress: Social Mobility in a 19th Century City.* Cambridge: Harvard University Press, 1964.
————. "Poverty in Historical Perspective," in *On Understanding Poverty: Perspective From the Social Sciences,* Daniel P. Moynihan (ed.). New York: Basic Books, 1969.
Tobin, James, "The Case for an Income Guarantee," in *The Public Interest,* No. 4, (Summer, 1964).
————. "On Improving the Economic Status of the Negro," in *Daedalus,* Fall, 1965.
Udry, J. Richard. "Marital Instability by Race, Sex, Education, and Occupation Using 1960 Census Data," in *American Journal of Sociology,* 72:203–209, (September, 1966).
U.S. Chamber of Commerce. *The Concept of Poverty.* Washington, D.C.: Task Force on Economic Growth and Opportunity.
Vadakin, James C. *Children, Poverty and Family Allowances.* New York: Basic Books, 1968.

Valentine, Charles. *Culture and Poverty*. Chicago: The University of Chicago Press, 1968.

Wade, Richard. *Slavery in the Cities, The South 1820–1860*. New York: Oxford University Press, 1964.

Warner, Sam, Jr. *Planning for a Nation of Cities*. Cambridge: M.I.T. Press, 1966.

Warner, W. Lloyd. *Color and Human Nature*. Washington, D.C.: American Council on Education, 1941.

————. *Democracy in Jonesville: A Study in Quality and Inequality*. New York: Harper, 1949.

————. *American Life: Dream and Reality*. Chicago: The University of Chicago Press, 1962.

Warner, W. Lloyd, *et al. Who Shall be Educated? The Challenge of Unequal Opportunities*. New York: Harper, 1944.

Whelpton, Pascal, A. Campbell and J. Patterson. *Fertility and Family Planning in The United States*. Princeton, N.J.: Princeton University Press, 1966.

Whitten, Norman. *Class, Kinship and Power in an Ecuadorian Town*. Stanford: Stanford University Press, 1965.

————. "Adaptation and Adaptability as Processes of Microevolutionary Change in New World Negro Communities." Paper presented at the Annual Meeting of the American Anthropological Association, 1967.

————. "Introduction," in *Afro-American Anthropology*, Norman Whitten (ed.). New York: Free Press, November, 1969.

Whyte, William F. "A Slum Sex Code," in *American Journal of Sociology*, 49:24–31, No. 1, (July, 1943).

————. *Street Corner Society: The Social Structure of an Italian Slum*. Chicago: The University of Chicago Press, 1943.

Wiener, Jack. "Mental Health Highlights," in *American Journal of Orthopsychiatry*, XXXIX:530 ff., No. 3, (April, 1969).

Wilensky, Harold L. "Work, Careers and Social Integration," in *International Social Science Journal*, 12, 1960.

Wilner, Daniel. *The Housing Environment and Family Life*. Baltimore: The Johns Hopkins University Press, 1962.

Wilson, James Q. *Negro Politics*. New York: Free Press, 1960.

Wiltse, Kermit. "Orthopsychiatric Programs for Socially Deprived Groups," in *American Journal of Orthopsychiatry*, 33:806–813, No. 5, (October, 1963).

Wynn, Margaret. *Fatherless Families*. London: M. Joseph, 1964.

Yablonsky, Lewis. *The Violent Gang*. New York: Macmillan, 1962.

Yancey, William. "The Culture of Poverty: Not So Much Parsimony." Unpublished manuscript. St. Louis: Washington University, Social Science Institute, 1964.

————. "Intervention Research: A Strategy of Social Inquiry." Dissertation presented to the Graduate School of Arts and Sciences, St. Louis: Washington University, 1967.

Young, Leontine. *Out of Wedlock*. New York: McGraw-Hill, 1954.

Young, Michael and Peter Willmott. *Family and Kinship in East London*. Baltimore: Penguin Books, 1962.

Index